THE HISTORY
OF THE UNITED STATES

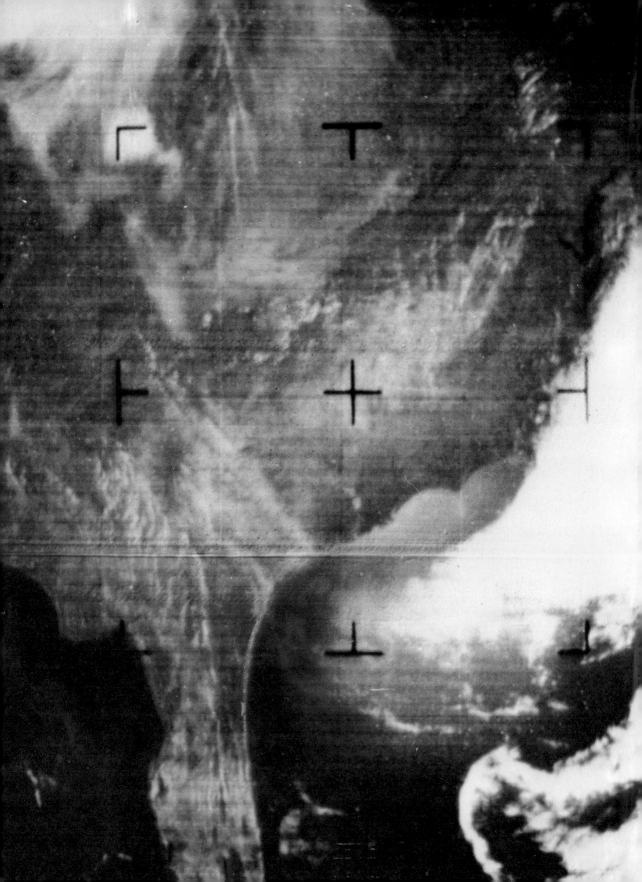

THE

HISTORY

OF THE

UNITED

STATES

Oscar Handlin

CHARLES WARREN PROFESSOR OF HISTORY, HARVARD UNIVERSITY

VOLUME TWO

Holt, Rinehart and Winston

NEW YORK • CHICAGO • SAN FRANCISCO • ATLANTA
DALLAS • MONTREAL • TORONTO • LONDON

Frontispiece: The Eastern Seaboard, Chesapeake Bay, Great Lakes, Gulf of Mexico, and Florida Peninsula, May 15, 1966, as seen by Nimbus II, U.S. Weather Satellite developed by NASA's Goddard Space Flight Center (NASA).

Part opening photographs: VI. Glass Works, Wheeling, West Virginia; lithograph from *Illustrated Atlas of the Upper Ohio River Valley,* 1877 (Library of Congress). VII. Theodore Roosevelt, *ca.* 1908 (Brown Brothers). VIII. Clemenceau (left), Wilson, and Lloyd George leaving Versailles after the signing of the Peace Treaty, June 28, 1919 (The Granger Collection). IX. The D-Day invasion of Normandy (Robert Capa, Magnum). X. The atomic cloud during the "Baker Day" blast at Bikini, July 1946 (Brown Brothers).

Design: John King
Cartography: Joseph Stonehill

PREFACE

The perspective of both the writer and the reader of history changes somewhat with the approach to contemporary events. The periods of time covered in the narrative become progressively shorter because the details seem more important the nearer they are and also because it becomes more difficult to sort out the long-term trends. It is only as time makes the consequences clear, that the significance of incidents and persons emerges.

Furthermore, the closer the student stands to events, the less complete is the record. We know a good deal about the diplomacy of the Spanish-American War, but somewhat less about that of World War I and still less of World War II. About Korea and Vietnam, despite the outpouring of books on the subjects, information is fragmentary.

Yet while remaining conscious of the limits of his information, the historian is responsible for the same critical interpretation of the recent as of the remote past. The fact that he stands relatively close to the events in his story complicates the problem of understanding them but also lends a special urgency to his effort to discern the forces that have a direct bearing upon his own life and upon his own society.

Cambridge, Massachusetts   O. H.
September 1967

CONTENTS

Part VIII. THE QUEST FOR AN OLD ORDER, 1912–1929

MAPS

INDUSTRIALIZATION

1850–1890

VI

THE DEVELOPMENT
OF MODERN
INDUSTRY

51

While the Civil War and Reconstruction absorbed the outward attention of the people of the United States, other forces profoundly transformed the country. Even when the newspaper headlines still dealt with battles and debates over the fate of the freedmen, the interior pages carried news of industrial and commercial developments that were fully as significant.

In the forty years after 1850, the United States ceased to be primarily an agricultural nation producing raw materials for the more advanced economies of Europe; it became one of the world's great manufacturing powers. That change and the associated increase in population, wealth, and productivity altered the country's social and political order and in time drew it into a new role in world affairs.

The Civil War did not cause industrialization but the conflict, which came while the process was already under way, stimulated the complex transition from the early cotton mills of Lowell to the great steel plants of Gary and Homestead. Enormous sums of capital, whole armies of labor, and great skill in organization were necessary to economic development.

Economic Growth

DESPITE THE DAMAGE DONE by the war and by the disorders of Reconstruction, the American economy continued to grow after 1865. The gross national product more than doubled between 1865 and 1890; and in the 1880s alone the national wealth mounted from about 25 to about 46 billion dollars.

A good part of the rise was due to the increase in population. There were more hands at work. The number of Americans just about doubled in the three decades between 1860 and 1890. The high rates of natural increase and of immigration both continued. Economic and social change in the Old World still displaced millions of peasants, whom the steamships now brought across the Atlantic in greater numbers than ever. Fully 2,000,000 German, 1,500,000 Irish, and 1,300,000 English newcomers reached the United States between 1861 and 1890. The dislocations in Europe that left families without land and workers without jobs now extended into the north, and some 850,000 persons arrived from Scandinavia. Smaller contingents began coming also from eastern and southern Europe. In addition, about 1,000,000 Canadians crossed the border during this period. These newcomers contributed to the man power that spread American settlement, filled much of the remaining empty space of the continent, and rapidly expanded the output of commodities. And they with their earnings added to the vast internal market that consumed the products the country produced.

Manufacturing

Increasingly, the productive system was based on manufacturing. The development under way since early in the century continued. The first factories, which had depended on water

Edward C. Kirkland, *Industry Comes of Age* (New York, 1961) is a good survey of business development between 1860 and 1897.

Population of the United States

(in thousands)

	Native White	Foreign-born	Nonwhite	Total
1850	17,382	2,240	3,639	23,261
1860	22,896	4,096	4,521	31,513
1870	29,443	5,493	4,969	39,905
1880	36,950	6,559	6,753	50,262
1890	46,089	9,121	7,846	63,056

Immigration to the United States

(in thousands)

Decade	Number of Immigrants
1861–1870	2,323
1871–1880	2,814
1881–1890	5,292

power, on rural labor, and on the ready demand for cotton textiles and other consumer goods, became anachronistic after 1850. Industry then spread into the cities, began to harness machines to steam, and enlisted a permanent labor force composed of immigrants. It also learned to diffuse its products to nationwide markets.

The Effects of the Civil War Americans were thus well prepared to meet the challenge of war and to take advantage of the opportunities of peace. Ironmasters and clothing makers felt the immediate stimulus of orders and high profits; costs did not count when it came to supplying the men at arms with boots or uniforms or guns. Inflation further encouraged the venturesome, as rising prices eased the problem of repaying the sums borrowed for expansion.

The whole environment was congenial to business. The triumph of the North over the South was the victory, too, of the system of free labor over the slave plantation. In both sections the outcome generated confidence in manufacturing as the economic order of the future; and the political power of the Republican party, committed to high tariffs, seemed to guarantee the gains of those who invested in that future. In this stimulating setting, an advancing technology

War and the Spirit of Enterprise

When in New York the other day, I found that party of English capitalists were delighted with their visit with you, and seemed especially polite to me on that account. . . . But for my political employment I could have received from them very lucrative employment in the prosecution of their vast railroad schemes. Even as it is, if they, within six months, show their ability to execute their plans, I will identify myself much more with them. The truth is, the close of the war with our resources unimpaired gives an elevation, a scope to the ideas of leading capitalists, far higher than anything ever undertaken in this country before. They talk of millions as confidently as formerly of thousands. No doubt the contraction that must soon come will explode merely visionary schemes, but many vast undertakings will be executed. Among them will be the Pacific R. R. and extensive iron works, like some in England. Our manufactures are yet in their infancy, but soon I expect to see, under the stimulus of a great demand and the protection of our tariff, locomotive and machine shops worthy of the name.

—John to his brother, William T. Sherman, November 10, 1865. R. S. Thorndike, ed., *The Sherman Letters* (New York: Charles Scribner's Sons, 1894), p. 258.

GUSTAVUS SWIFT was born in 1839 on a Cape Cod farm in Massachusetts. One of twelve children, he had little opportunity for schooling and at fourteen went to work for his brother, the village butcher. By the time he was twenty he was taking cattle to Boston each week and peddling meat in the vicinity of his home town. In 1872 a partnership with James A. Hathaway permitted him to expand his business enterprises.

Swift discerned that it was inefficient to transport live cattle and slaughter them close to market; it would be far cheaper to butcher the animals close to the source and ship only the meat. He moved west, first to Albany, then to Buffalo, and finally to Chicago. There in 1875 he took the risk of sending carloads of dressed beef to Boston under refrigeration.

It was difficult, however, to persuade local butchers that the product carried such a long distance was safe. Swift had to set up his own sales organization throughout the country, and he arranged with the Grand Trunk Railway for expeditious transportation, building refrigerated cars at his own expense. By 1885 his affairs had prospered to such an extent that he could incorporate his business and turn his attention to the export market. Within a few years he was distributing American meat in England, Japan, China, the Philippines, Singapore, and Honolulu. When he died in 1903, production and distribution of this basic staple had been thoroughly modernized.

made numerous innovations available to enterprising men. The results became apparent in the transformation of old industries and the creation of new ones.

Consumer Industry The manufacture of cotton goods followed a pattern already well established, but on a larger scale. The 5¼ million spindles of 1860 had become 14¼ in 1890, and the number of bales consumed mounted from 845,000 to 2,500,000. After 1865, the woolen and the boot and shoe industries, too, adapted to large-scale factory production. The handicraftsman steadily lost ground to the machine as output soared.

Bold enterprisers on the lookout for opportunity helped transform the fabrication of other consumer goods. Chicago had already seized the lead over Cincinnati as a meat-packing center

Advertisement for a New Labor-saving Device. Lithograph, 1869. (Library of Congress)

when Gustavus Swift devised the means of shipping the products of his plant over long distances in refrigerated cars. Sales soared thereafter as his competitors imitated him. In Minneapolis, Charles A. Pillsbury took a chance on a new process for milling spring wheat; in 1883 he was able to build the largest mill in the world. Other great companies produced the sewing, washing, and reaping machines that now came into use in thousands of homes and farms. Scores of lesser plants turned out the watches and hats, the tobacco, furniture, and soap, Americans used in steadily mounting quantities.

Heavy Industry The multiplying factories generated demands of their own. The need for buildings and equipment and for the railroads that were to move the stream of goods created a market for machinery, for engines, and for rails that absorbed the output of the rising, and changing, iron and steel industry.

The manufacture of iron had a long history in the United States. Already in 1850, hundreds of furnaces, forges, and rolling mills were in production in many parts of the country. Typically, these were small enterprises, employing from 16 to 50 hands; the largest used 130. They depended upon charcoal, and therefore consumed large quantities of wood, a fact that limited their size and often led to their placement close to the forests, where fuel costs were lowest.

Louis F. Swift, *The Yankee of the Yards* (Chicago, 1927) is a laudatory but informative biography of Swift.
Allan Nevins, *Abram S. Hewitt* (New York, 1935) contains a good account of the early iron industry.

5000 OVENS. CAPACITY 8750 TONS DAILY.

Process of Manufacturing Coke at the Works of the

H.C. FRICK COKE COMPANY,

CONNELLSVILLE COKE REGION PENNA

POST OFFICE. PITTSBURGH PA.

Mining Coal.

Watering and Drawing Coke.

Manufacturing Coke, Connellsville, Pennsylvania. Lithograph by National Bureau of Engraving. (Library of Congress)

In the decade before the Civil War, the iron-masters learned to use the more economical anthracite coal as fuel; by 1865, only 25 percent of the output still depended upon charcoal. In the years that followed, coke—distilled from coal —provided a still more efficient substitute. No longer tied to the forests, the ironmakers expanded their operations, located their furnaces near the cities where transportation facilities were best, and clustered at the locations where coal and iron ore were most accessible. They were then in a position to profit from an invention that profoundly influenced the economy.

Steel   In 1856 William Kelly in America and Henry Bessemer in England had discovered how to purify molten iron by means of blasts of cold air, the essential first step in the cheap production of steel. Furnaces using the process were not then feasible except on a larger scale than was common in the United States at the time. Not

until 1865 or 1866 was the first American Bessemer plant built. In 1867 the country produced fewer than 20,000 long tons of steel. Growth thereafter was phenomenal, particularly when the even more efficient open-hearth process came into use in the 1870s. By 1890 the American output amounted to 4,277,000 tons, and was greater than that of Britain.

The scale of operations changed radically. In the 1870s a Bessemer converter handled 5 tons of metal at once. Andrew Carnegie's Lucy furnace, which went into production in 1872, was 75 feet high and 20 feet across; that year it processed 13,000 tons, and its capacity increased steadily. In 1890, the average furnace in the United States was turning out 25,000 tons annually, and the largest over 100,000 tons. Ingenious plant superintendents like Captain William R. Jones or Alexander L. Holley untiringly devised new procedures to increase efficiency.

6

The rapid increase in total capacity and in the size of each unit threw production out of phase with demand and created violent fluctuations in price and output. In December 1881, for instance, steel rails sold for $60 a ton, a year later for $39. The risks of a wrong estimate were as great as the rewards of a correct one. The entrepreneurs hoped, by control of each stage of fabrication from the raw ore to the finished product, to keep the supply of materials steady and assure a market for the output. Integrated mills did not attain all these objectives, but they permitted rational planning and could afford the services of trained engineering personnel and the prompt introduction of cost-saving innovations. By 1890, the process of drawing together the massive units of fabrication was well under way. As a result the metal in various degrees of malleability and in a multitude of forms was available to the makers of rails and machines, of agricultural utensils and building materials, and of a multitude of other products.

American industry was then supplying a growing part of the needs of the home market. Imports of iron and steel had remained important until 1883; then they declined and the United States came to be an exporter. Meanwhile, from the early 1870s on, prices of iron and steel fell steadily.

There was dramatic growth in the manufacture of glass and a significant beginning in aluminum, which shared some of the characteristics of steel. They too depended upon technological innovations and upon the ability to draw men and capital together in large enterprises. The United States possessed not only the basic raw materials but also the waiting markets, the abundant labor, and the entrepreneurial skill needed to raise the level of production. The availability of basic materials in turn stimulated every other form of construction and manufacturing.

Mineral Resources

Industrial expansion meshed with the development of expanding mineral resources. The

Steelmaking by the Bessemer Process, Pittsburgh. The converters at work. Wood engraving after Charles Graham, *Harper's Weekly,* April 10, 1886. (Library of Congress)

Oil Wells, West Virginia, *ca.* 1880. (Culver Pictures)

older sources in Pennsylvania continued to yield iron ore until the end of the century. But new fields in the Lake Superior region began to add to the supply in the 1870s; and in the 1880s rich deposits between Chattanooga, Tennessee, and Birmingham, Alabama, were tapped. The steelmakers could expand without concern about the adequacy of supplies.

Fuel for processing the ore and for the other needs of industry was abundant and cheap. The economy no longer depended upon the anthracite coal of eastern Pennsylvania. After 1870 a vast bituminous field that stretched from Lake Erie to northern Alabama put seemingly endless sources of energy at the disposal of Americans. Substantial stores of petroleum had by then also become available, although its main uses were still as kerosene for illumination and as a lubri-

cant. The successful drilling of the first commercial oil well near Titusville, Pennsylvania, in 1859 led to the exploitation of extensive deposits in that state and in West Virginia. In 1885, the Lima field in northern Ohio and Indiana added to the flow. The 1880s also witnessed a start in generating electricity for light and power. There was energy enough for all the needs of the nation.

When Americans considered these finds, they were tempted to believe that nature, if not Providence, had singled them out for blessing. Rich mines of copper, silver, and gold rested beneath their mountains. Abundant stands of timber in Wisconsin, the Pacific Northwest, and the Southern uplands supplied their requirements for lumber. An unending series of new

Paul H. Giddens, *The Birth of the Oil Industry* (New York, 1938) is the standard account.

8

discoveries compensated for the depletion of old sources. Here was all that was needed for a modern industrial economy.

Industrial Reorganization

It was not quite that simple. The land was richly endowed. But coal and iron were inert until men put them to use, and to the Indians petroleum was only a peculiar noisome medicine. To take those materials out of the earth and transform them into rails and engines and buildings demanded distinctive skills and habits organized in a complex network of productive relationships.

The Engineers Operation of the great plants that darkened the skies of Pittsburgh and other cities required a high level of technical training. Men like Captain Jones had learned from experience, coming up from the ranks of labor in small machine shops and foundries. But in the new factories the mass of laborers worked at unskilled tasks that gave them little opportunity to understand the process of production, and even ingenious tinkerers could not readily master the great new machines. It took an educated expert to keep abreast of developments in competing industrial countries—France, Germany, and England—as well as in the United States.

The Rensselaer Polytechnic Institute, founded in 1824, stood practically alone before the Civil War in offering such instruction. A few mechanics' schools like Cooper Union (1858), West Point, and the scientific departments of some colleges also made an effort in that direction. But industry required far more trained personnel than these pioneers could produce. The Massachusetts Institute of Technology, opened in 1865, devoted itself primarily to pure and applied science and furthered the education of engineers. Others followed. Their graduates organized societies of mining, mechanical, and civil engineers, began to publish journals, and acquired professional status.

Planned Production The informed superintendent labored to organize the factory so that he could manage the complex steps of production efficiently. Knowledge of how best to employ a new machine in the plant was often as important as its invention. Alexander L. Holley, for instance, was able to place each Bessemer converter so that it could easily be serviced and yet stood between the blast furnaces and the rolling mills; it could thus receive the heated pig iron directly from the former and pass the still hot ingots straight to the latter. The rewards for careful planning of the various elements in the continuous process of production were enormous. Improvisation would no longer do.

The position of the human beings in the plant changed subtly. The Homestead Steel Plant, 10 miles outside of Pittsburgh, by 1890 employed almost four thousand hands. This was exceptional, but by that year it was not unusual to find five hundred names on a factory payroll. The workers no longer moved informally under the oversight of the owner. They handled expensive machinery, labored in large groups, and performed tasks that were but parts of a whole. Their performance, like that of the machines, had to be accounted for by rational control and organization. A uniform discipline brought the hundreds of men, women, and children to their appointed places at the appointed times. A rigid calculation of costs determined what their wages would be and what hours they would labor. A hierarchy of foremen, department overseers, and first hands passed commands from the superintendent to the laborer in a totally impersonal relationship. Subjection to this regime was central to the grievances of many workingmen in these years.

Finance The mammoth scale of the new enterprises created a novel relationship between the firm and its capital. The Trenton Iron Works, formed in 1847 to buy Peter Cooper's iron mill in a big deal for its era, started with $300,000 invested by a handful of men. By 1860, the number of stockholders who held shares in the company, then valued at $1,000,000, was still less

Making Steel

The Jones mixer, a huge iron chest lined with refractory bricks, and capable of holding fifty to two hundred and fifty tons of liquid pig metal . . . is hung on trunnions, so that it may be swung to and fro like a cradle; for here the contents of many ladles are mixed to equalize the variations of both chemical composition and temperature. . . . One by one the ladles are emptied into the mixer, the liquid flowing clean and creamy, with fairy lights dancing over its surface. Whenever a few drops spill to the ground they rebound in thousands of tiny points of fire, exploding with the noise of a miniature fusillade. A boy of thirteen or fourteen, his imp-like face black with soot, stands near the flaming funnel of the mixer, shouting shrill directions to his fellow demon, who . . . reverses the five-ton ladles with the ease of a society woman emptying her cup of tea. At night the scene is indescribably wild and beautiful. The flashing fireworks, the terrific gusts of heat, the gaping, glowing mouth of the giant chest, the quivering light from the liquid iron, the roar of a near-by converter, the weird figure of the child and the pipings of his shrill voice, the smoke and fumes and confusion, combine to produce an effect on the mind that no words can translate.

—J. H. Bridge, *History of the Carnegie Steel Company* (New York: Aldine Book Company, 1903), pp. 143, 144.

Casting the 24-ton Anchor for the Brooklyn Bridge, South Brooklyn Steam Engine Works, 1873. (The Bettmann Archive)

than a hundred. Typically, enterprises in the next decade were operated by small groups through such closely held corporations and through partnerships that plowed their profits back into the business as it expanded. Entry into many industries was relatively easy; a small oil refinery cost $10,000; as late as 1879, the average glassware plant employed a capital of less than $100,000.

But as the factories grew and the size of the investment increased, aggressive entrepreneurs began to seek additional capital through the sale of securities to members of the public unconnected with the enterprise. By 1870, the process of financing the railroads had already shown that substantial resources were available in the hands of people and institutions willing to invest them in return for speculative profits and dividends. Manufacturing corporations soon learned to spread their securities among large numbers of holders. In 1890, even the greatest firms were still identified with individuals like Andrew Carnegie, John D. Rockefeller, or Henry Clay Frick who owned and managed them. But an ever broader public was becoming involved in these industries as stockholders.

The Problem of Order As enterprises large and small jostled for position in a rapidly changing situation, the nature of the competition among them changed. True, expanding demands created attractive opportunities, but prices generally fell after 1865 and created imposing risks. A newly invented machine or process, or a lucky discovery of minerals, could decisively alter the conditions of doing business, particularly since new companies easily mushroomed. The opportunities for getting rich were enormous, but so were the chances of being wiped out.

Free and open competition remained the professed ideal, adhered to with especial vigor by relative newcomers still trying to establish themselves. But the large established enterprises sought to stabilize their position and minimize the hazards. Refiners and millers, for instance, paid high prices when crude oil or wheat was in limited supply, but then might find the market for kerosene or flour glutted when new wells or bumper harvests came in. Such entrepreneurs were eager for a more orderly business pattern.

Overexpansion, 1888

A new common enemy has sprung up, which threatens our property with virtual confiscation. . . . Large output, quick sales, keen competition, and small profits are characteristics of all modern trade. We have the advantage in our business of always being in fashion; the world requires so much bread every day, a quantity which can be ascertained with almost mathematical accuracy. . . . But our ambition has overreached our discretion and judgment. We have all participated in the general steeple-chase for pre-eminence; the thousand-barrel mill of our competitor had to be put in the shade by a two-thousand-barrel mill of our own construction; the commercial triumph of former seasons had to be surpassed by still more dazzling figures. As our glory increased our profits became smaller, until now the question is not how to surpass the record, but how to maintain our position and how to secure what we have in our possession. . . . In the general scramble we have gradually lost sight of the inexorable laws of supply and demand. We have been guilty of drifting away from sound trade regulations until our business has not only ceased to be profitable but carries with it undue commercial hazard.

—Speech of the Vice-President of the National Millers' Association. D. A. Wells, *Recent Economic Changes* (New York: Appleton-Century-Crofts, 1889), pp. 79 ff.

ANDREW CARNEGIE was born on November 25, 1835, in the Scottish village of Dunfermline. In 1848, the Carnegies sold whatever they had, borrowed £20 for the passage to America, and tearfully left their home. They settled in Allegheny, Pennsylvania, where Andrew worked as a bobbin boy in a cotton factory, adding his weekly $1.25 to the family income.

There followed years of hard labor by day and study by night. The ambitious lad, moving from position to position, became private secretary to T. A. Scott, a division superintendent of the Pennsylvania Railroad, and rose to an executive post when Scott became president. During the Civil War, Carnegie helped organize the transportation and telegraph systems of the Union armies.

He saw that the current method of building railroads would soon be obsolete; rickety wooden bridges and trestles were already falling apart. Grasping the opportunity, Carnegie organized the Keystone Bridge Company to specialize in the construction of iron spans. To assure himself of supplies, he ventured into the manufacture of iron and steel and in two decades made himself master of the first vertically integrated industrial empire in the United States. In 1885, when he was fifty years old, he controlled the mines that produced the raw materials, the ships and railroads that carried them, and the fabricating plants that worked them into finished products.

Pondering the meaning of his migration and of his success, Carnegie concluded that the vast riches accumulated through free enterprise were both an evil and a danger, unless periodically redistributed. Every man had the obligation to devote as much time to disposing of his fortune as to assembling it. The man who died rich, died disgraced. Carnegie spent the years between 1900 and his death in 1919 responding to his own challenge. He gave away more than $350,000,000, and by his will most of the residue went to public purposes.

Carnegie hoped to increase the capacity of the individual to help himself by mastering his environment. Education, he believed, developed men's powers without lessening their self-reliance. Libraries, research, schools, and institutions for the achievement of peace were therefore the chief objects of his beneficence. His example was the most important single stimulus that made the possessors of other great fortunes aware of their responsibilities.

Charles A. Pillsbury therefore invested in grain elevators to protect his supplies and in the Minneapolis, Saulte Sainte Marie & Atlantic Railway to control his freight rates. The outstanding practitioner of such vertical integration was Andrew Carnegie. Bridge building led him to steelmaking, which drew him into coke production and then into railroad building and the ownership of coal and ore deposits. But this course required exceptional amounts of capital, and most producers preferred to put their profits into expansion of the activity with which they were most familiar.

E. C. Kirkland's introduction to Andrew Carnegie, *The Gospel of Wealth* (Cambridge, Mass., 1962) is an excellent analysis of the steelmaster, and the essays by Carnegie that follow throw light on the ideas of the time.

The alternative form of combination—horizontal—was more attractive but more difficult to achieve, for it depended on the willingness of all the makers of a given article to unite or to agree to limit competition. The cost of transportation was often a critical variable. The railroads too had an interest not only in protecting their business against competitors but also in an orderly flow of goods so that they could plan their traffic efficiently. To that end, they were willing to give large shippers rebates; and those who enjoyed such discounts had a marked advantage over their rivals.

Pools and Combinations When the practice of rebates spread widely, it reduced the profits of the carriers and more nearly equalized competitive conditions. The producers then had to adopt other means to attain the order they sought. Some joined pools, or voluntary agreements, to divide the market among themselves. John D. Rockefeller and a group of other Midwestern refiners thus hoped to use the South Improvement Company to allot quotas to its participants and to assign agreed-on percentages to the railroads which served them. In return, Rockefeller and his allies expected a rebate on every barrel of oil transported, whether by members or nonmembers. Refiners who refused to cooperate therefore indirectly subsidized those who did. During its brief existence, the Company thus controlled competition. In 1885, the producers of steel rails voluntarily curtailed production; and in 1887 they set up a pool to limit the output of each mill, so that prices would be stabilized by removal of the incentive for competition.

These arrangements did not remain harmonious long. Amicable understandings were effective when markets expanded and each plant operated at close to capacity. When demand slackened, however, each entrepreneur forgot the gentlemen's agreement. No sanctions then restrained him from pursuit of his own interest.

The merger of competing firms was an alternative to the pool. In 1870, John D. Rockefeller and his associates formed the Standard Oil Company of Ohio, which bought up a cluster of oil refineries in Cleveland and its vicinity. In the 1880s the Edison General Electric Company united a number of small producers.

But the law and popular opinion set limits to such combinations. Even the informal pools were tainted with illegality and subject to public disapproval. For more than a century, Americans had been hostile to monopoly; the East India Company's tea and Jackson's war on the Bank of the United States came readily to mind. Businessmen were therefore reluctant to form such organizations as in Europe produced the mammoth cartels. In most states, the common law in fact forbade any combinations in restraint of trade; and the pools were vulnerable to prosecution as conspiracies.

The Trust In 1882, Rockefeller's attorney, S. T. C. Dodd, proposed a way out. The stockholders of the Standard Oil Company of Ohio, in return for trust certificates, assigned all the property of the corporation to a board of nine trustees, which managed the enterprise free from public scrutiny and without legal restrictions. In the next few years the same nine men by the same process acquired control of almost all the important oil refineries in the country, each of which continued its own operations under the general direction of the trustees. Other ingenious entrepreneurs, too, experimented with the device to achieve the control they could not attain through open combination.

By 1890, however, there was still no solution to the problems of competition and order acceptable to producers, consumers, and the public. In oil, steel, and electrical equipment, a few large firms had acquired a preponderant position, but even they were not free of challenges from outsiders. In most branches of industry, rivalry was keen enough to focus considerable energy on the problems of marketing. Transportation, communications, and advertising came to be increasingly prominent in the calculations of businessmen.

▼

The growth in industry in the forty years after 1850 had far-reaching implications for the whole nation. The change in the scale and in the form of production vitally affected every sector of the economy and every section of the country. The farmer and the shopkeeper as well as the laborer and the businessman all had to adjust to it.

Furthermore, the legal, political, and social institutions developed in an earlier era now felt the pressure to accommodate a totally new way of life. Americans had created a massive mechanism for producing the material goods they needed. They had to learn to live with it.

Paperbacks for Further Reading

Thomas C. Cochran and William Miller, *The Age of Enterprise* (Harper Torchbooks) is a general social history of industrial America. Louis M. Hacker, *The Triumph of American Capitalism* (McGraw-Hill Paperback Series) contains an optimistic account of this period. There is a brief analysis of the population movements of the 1880s in Maldwyn A. Jones, *American Immigration* (Chicago History of American Civilization Series). H. Wayne Morgan has edited a broad reappraisal in *The Gilded Age* (Syracuse University Press). Andrew Carnegie, *The Gospel of Wealth* (E. C. Kirkland, ed.; Harvard University Press) is an interesting contemporary statement. Ralph Andreano, ed., *The Economic Impact of the American Civil War* (Schenkman Publishing Co.) is a useful collection of conflicting views.

NATIONAL COMMUNICATIONS

52

The immense expansion of settlement and of manufacturing between 1850 and 1890 was closely connected with the development of a national transportation system. Growth of the means of communication facilitated the advance to the frontier, lowered the costs of agricultural and industrial products, and created a great national market stimulating to the economy. Conversely, the spread of population and the rise in the output of the farms and factories generated opportunities for entrepreneurs willing to promote ventures that would reach the distant areas.

The results were substantial. The railroad not only extended across the continent but also penetrated to every part of the vast country. It contributed significantly to the integrated pattern of communication the United States enjoyed in 1890. The cost was more difficult to estimate. The process of construction was wasteful and generated practices from which the whole society suffered, then and later.

Promontory, Utah, May 10, 1869. In a ceremony marking the completion of the first transcontinental railroad, gold spikes were driven into the last tie. The engines of the Union Pacific and Central Pacific then touched noses, amid cheers and picture-taking. Photograph taken from the cab of the Union Pacific engine. (Union Pacific Railroad Museum Collection)

Railroad Building

THE RAILROADS BUILT before 1850 were profitable enough to create visions of the conquest of the continent by the iron horse. Speeding across the plains or trundling up the hillsides, the locomotives stirred the dreams of every onlooker. There was something romantic in the very concept of the conquest of space by the man-made machine. In many localities the burgeoning manufacturer could make out, in his mind's eye, an endless line of freight cars loaded with his products; the farmer saw his grain

hauled to distant purchasers; land speculators were sure that the cars would come back crammed with settlers; and promoters and investors were confident that the value of securities would sky-rocket.

Now and again the railroad boom was interrupted by periodic panics and depressions, but this did not halt the general expansion of the network. The miles of track multiplied fivefold in the two decades after 1850 and tripled in the twenty years after 1870.

The Transcontinentals In a great burst of construction, four bands of iron thrust westward

What the Engines Said
(Opening of the
Pacific Railroad)

What was it the Engines said,
Pilots touching, — head to head
Facing on the single track,
Half a world behind each back?
This is what the Engines said,
Unreported and unread.

With a prefatory screech,
In a florid Western speech,
Said the Engine from the WEST:
"I am from Sierra's crest;
And if altitude's a test,
Why, I reckon, it's confessed
That I've done my level best."

Said the Engine from the EAST:
"They who work best talk the least.
S'pose you whistle down your brakes;
What you've done is no great shakes, —
Pretty fair, — but let our meeting
Be a different kind of greeting.
Let these folks with champagne stuffing,
Not their Engines, do the *puffing*.

"Listen! Where Atlantic beats
Shores of snow and summer heats;
Where the Indian autumn skies
Paint the woods with wampum dyes, —
I have chased the flying sun,
Seeing all he looked upon,
Blessing all that he has blessed,

Nursing in my iron breast
All his vivifying heat,
All his clouds about my crest;
And before my flying feet
Every shadow must retreat."

Said the Western Engine, "Phew!"
And a long, low whistle blew.
"Come, now, really that's the oddest
Talk for one so very modest.
You brag of your East! *You* do?
Why, *I* bring the East to *you!*
All the Orient, all Cathay,
Find through me the shortest way;
And the sun you follow here
Rises in my hemisphere.
Really, — if one must be rude, —
Length, my friend, ain't longitude."

Said the Union: "Don't reflect, or
I'll run over some Director."
Said the Central: "I'm Pacific;
But, when riled, I'm quite terrific.
Yet to-day we shall not quarrel,
Just to show these folks this moral,
How two Engines — in their vision —
Once have met without collision."

That is what the Engines said,
Unreported and unread;
Spoken slightly through the nose,
With a whistle at the close.

—*Bret Harte's Writings, Poems* (Boston: Houghton Mifflin Company, 1902), pp. 304–305.

from the Mississippi to the ocean's edge. The projected railroad to the Pacific had early become a political question; there had been a good deal of maneuvering in the 1850s over its location. In 1862 the proponents of a middle route won out. The Federal government encouraged the plans of the Union Pacific to move westward from Omaha and of Collis P. Huntington's Central Pacific to build eastward from Sacramento. Actual construction began in 1865, and after four laborious years the two lines met in Utah.

Rival promoters, however, secured charters for other transcontinentals. The Northern Pacific laid out a project to reach from Chicago and Milwaukee to Portland and Seattle; the Southern Pacific planned to run from Los Angeles to El Paso and then eastward; and the Santa Fe had

Robert E. Riegel, *Story of the Western Railroads* (New York, 1926) is a good general narrative.

Oscar Lewis, *The Big Four* (New York, 1938) is a stimulating biography of Huntington and his partners, the builders of the Central Pacific.

COLLIS P. HUNTINGTON was a driving force in the development of the Central Pacific Railroad. A powerful man, 6 feet tall, who carried his 200 pounds with ease, he made a deep impression in personal encounters and cynically sprinkled his letters with profanity. He used what means were necessary to have his way.

Born in 1821 in rural Connecticut, Huntington went to work at the age of fourteen and through peddling earned the capital he needed to set up shop in Oneonta, New York. The gold rush brought him to California in 1849, but one look at the diggings persuaded him that he would do better selling supplies to miners than wielding a pick. In Sacramento, he prospered to such an extent that he could join Mark Hopkins, Leland Stanford, and Charles Crocker in organizing the Central Pacific to build across the Sierra Nevadas.

Huntington was the Eastern contact of the Big Four. In Washington, he lobbied to protect the road's land grants and to defeat a rival Texas and Pacific route. In New York, he bought supplies, raised capital, and managed the securities of his various firms. After 1870 he focused his interests primarily on railroads.

The construction profits were tremendous but came largely in the form of stock, so Huntington had to strive for efficient operation to safeguard his gains. Skillful manipulation of various construction and operating units, most of them leased to the Southern Pacific Railroad, which was organized in 1884, enabled him to protect his interests. His fortune therefore grew rapidly. Meanwhile he bought into the Chesapeake and Ohio Railroad and the Pacific Mail Steamship Company. When he died in 1900, a Fifth Avenue mansion and a princely son-in-law testified to his imperial position.

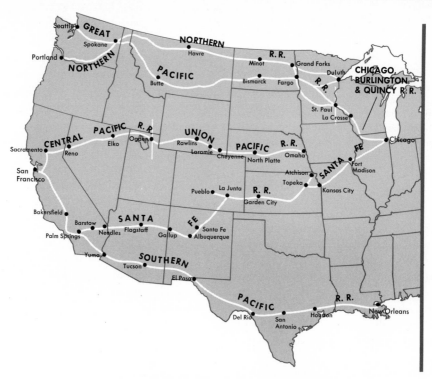

THE TRANSCONTINENTALS, 1850–1890

18

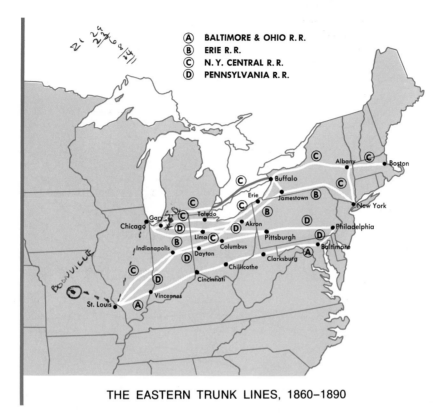

THE EASTERN TRUNK LINES, 1860–1890

its terminus in San Diego. Although these railroads were not fully in operation until the 1880s, still another competitor appeared on the scene in 1890 when James J. Hill combined a number of smaller corporations to form the Great Northern, which ran from St. Paul to the west coast. In addition, the Santa Fe and the Chicago, Burlington, and Quincy developed extensive routes in the trans-Mississippi interior.

Integration The elaboration of the railroad network in the older regions of the country was less dramatic but fully as important. Four great east-west systems linked the Atlantic seaports with the Mississippi Valley. By the 1870s, the New York Central, the Erie, the Pennsylvania, and the Baltimore and Ohio had consolidated the earlier smaller roads between their termini and were developing connections with lines running to the far west. In addition, thousands of miles of track fed traffic to the trunk lines. The

process was slower in the South although there was a flurry of construction in that region in the 1880s.

The efficiency of these roads depended on their ability to move large quantities of heavy freight over long distances. Since each had been built by its own promoter, there was no uniformity in locomotives or rolling stock or even in the types of coupling; in 1861, seven track widths were common, ranging from 4 feet, 3 inches to 6 feet. In the next three decades there was a gradual standardization at 4 feet, 8½ inches. It was then possible to move the cars of one line over the tracks of another and thus avoid the cost of transshipping the cargo. Increasingly too, common operational practices furthered cooperation, and fast freight and express companies expedited the movement of goods.

Edward Hungerford, *Men and Iron* (New York, 1938) is an account of the New York Central.

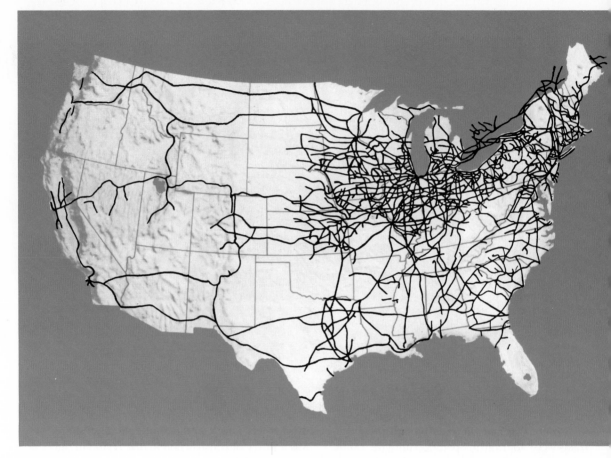

RAILROAD MILEAGE IN 1890

Physical improvements also helped. Iron and steel bridges, capable of bearing greater loads, replaced earlier primitive wooden spans, and many rivers were crossed for the first time in the 1870s. Invention of the air brake by George Westinghouse in 1869, the appearance of automatic block signals and of steel instead of iron rails, and better techniques for laying the roadbeds permitted the railroads to use heavier equipment at greater speed and safety, and at lower cost. The Pullman car added a touch of luxury to travel by rail.

As a result, the volume of freight and the number of passengers soared. Conceivably, the canals and waterways still in use might have borne more of the traffic, and additional waterways might have been built in the absence of railroads. Roads might also have been spared the neglect from which they suffered in the decades between 1860 and 1890. But even making allowances for these hypothetical alternatives, the railroads created a net saving in transportation costs; and since in actuality it was the iron horse that fired the imagination of society, the economy expanded its facilities for communication through extension of the rail network.

Bridge on the Pittsburgh & Western, About 1880. The Howe truss was a common type of wooden bridge. (The Smithsonian Institution)

The Luxuries of Travel, 1871

When night comes on the passengers prepare to try to get some sleep. In the sleeping cars the armchairs are rapidly transformed into beds, separated from one another by boards. Each window allows for two beds, one on top of the other, unless the traveler has taken a section; that is, the whole space of one window. Under the shelter of the heavy curtain men and women put on their night things, in the interests of cleanliness pin a handkerchief over the pillow provided by the authorities, lie down on or scramble up to their beds, and strive to sleep, in spite of the noise, the shaking, the dust, the stifling atmosphere, and the nauseous smell of this most infernal dormitory.

—Baron von Hübner, *Promenade autour du monde* (Paris, 1873), vol. I, p. 57.

Railroads in the United States, 1850–1890

Year	Mileage	Stocks and Bonds Issued* (thousands)	Passenger Miles (millions)
1850	9,021	318	
1860	30,626	1,149	
1870	52,922	2,476	
1880	93,262	5,402	7,000†
1890	166,703	10,122	12,522

* Includes electric railroads.
† Estimate.

The Role of Government

Railroad Financing The costs of expanding the railroads were tremendous. The amount of capital invested in them doubled in each decade after 1860 and in 1890 stood at well over ten billion dollars (at a time when the total national debt was about one billion). To accumulate funds of this magnitude, promoters tapped a variety of sources.

They counted on a long tradition of government assistance for internal improvements. In 1850, a Federal land grant had aided the construction of the Illinois Central Railroad; that became a precedent for similar benefactions to the transcontinentals after 1862. Generally, in return for undertaking to complete their roads in ten or twelve years, the corporations received a specified number of sections along their rights of way. Some states, like Maine and Texas, also used their domains to stimulate construction; others were willing to lend their credit to guarantee the bonds of the railroads. And many a city or town, persuaded that the coming of the rails would turn it into a metropolis, was willing to make donations or loans or, more usually, to subscribe to securities.

The value of the grants was difficult to assess. The broad bands of land marked out on the map looked more substantial than they were, for sections reserved to the government were interspersed with those given away. Furthermore, few railroads were able to meet the conditions the law imposed on them; and their agents in the Federal and state capitals had to cajole or bribe legislators to secure extensions and prevent forfeitures. The subsidies were of some assistance, but far less than appeared on paper. By 1881, for instance, Federal law had set aside almost 180 million acres for this purpose; but only 33 million had actually been patented, and less than half of that had been sold for a total of $71,000,000, divided among a score of competing corporations.

As important as the amount actually contributed by government was the psychological stimulus such support gave to private investment. Every new road was a speculation; it was some reassurance to those who took the risk to know that the government stood behind the venture. Later people thus persuaded would learn to their grief that a state could readily default on its obligations. For the moment, however, its involvement was a token of added security.

Private Capital   The bulk of investment was private, and some roads like Hill's Great Northern never enjoyed government aid. Sales of stock rarely brought in more than the cash for organization and surveys. By the time gangs went out to work on the roadbeds, bond issues were necessary, floated among the public at large if possible. Some promoters managed to persuade banks to make loans against the bonds as security; others operated through intermediary construction companies, which raised their own capital on the strength of lucrative building contracts. About one fifth of the capital came from Europeans, notably English, Dutch, and German investors; the balance, from the savings of Americans.

The returns were uneven. In the 1870s and 1880s the general trend of both interest and dividend payments was downward, and some ventures never rewarded those who had faith in them. Since the process was speculative, securities found an ample market in prosperous times but no takers in periods of financial stress. As a result, roads were overbuilt at high cost during booms, and bore the heavy charges for debt when the economy contracted. All too often, too, the dishonesty of promoters and speculators and excessive payments to construction companies controlled by insiders added to the handicaps under which the railroads labored.

Competition   Above all, the railroad pattern followed no coherent plan but operated by competitive trial and error, with the key decisions frequently made by speculative promoters. New York was connected with Washington by two routes, with Chicago by four, and with Boston by three. Competition was wastefully keen and gave rise to unfair tactics, as there were few recognized standards by which to establish pricing policies. A road that had to bid against a rival for through traffic usually had a monopoly of the business between intermediate points; it was therefore tempted to charge more for the short haul than for the long haul. Aggressive companies tried to seduce shippers by rebates and sought favors from politicians by the liberal use of passes. Such practices created an incentive for pooling arrangements in which competing roads divided the market in order to be able to keep rates high.

Consequently, the transition from popular approval to popular dislike was quick and easy. The citizens who had eagerly persuaded the railroad to pass through their town, within a few years were aggrieved; interest on the bonds was unpaid, and the returns from the sale of corn and wheat were being lost in transportation costs.

Some railroad men were themselves unhappy about excessive competition and tried to establish means of self-regulation. In 1875, twenty-two southern roads, and a few years later, groups of eastern and western lines set up associations to govern their rates. But such control was subject to evasion and evoked the protests of users.

Regulation Proposals that the government itself operate the railroads gained little support. Competition seemed preferable as a means of furthering efficiency and lowering costs. The proper function of government therefore was regulation. In 1844 New Hampshire had created a railroad commission to supervise the railroads within its borders. After the Civil War other states followed the precedent. Massachusetts in 1869 established one pattern; its commission was primarily advisory, with publicity its chief sanction. But Illinois, a year later, went further; the agency set up in accord with the constitution enacted that year could actually fix rates and operating conditions: In the case of *Munn* v. *Illinois* in 1877 the Supreme Court upheld the constitutionality of such controls.

Commissions set up under state laws, however, were ineffective. Some were bureaucratic and inefficient and, in any case, transportation increasingly passed across state lines and thus escaped local supervision. In the Wabash case of 1886 the Supreme Court ruled that only Congress, acting under the Commerce Clause, could control the interstate movement of passengers and goods. That decision made national action imperative; and by then both shippers and railroad men favored a Federal solution that would spare them the burdens of dealing with numerous, sometimes conflicting, state commissions.

The Interstate Commerce Act of 1887 emphasized the desirability of competition by forbidding rebates, discrimination between long and short hauls, and pooling arrangements. It also created a commission of five members which could investigate abuses but which had to seek redress through the courts. The new agency's powers were thus limited to begin with; and the judiciary would soon circumscribe them further. The desire for order had brought the rail-

The Power to Regulate, 1877

Looking, then, to the common law, from whence came the right which the Constitution protects, we find that when private property is "affected with a public interest, it ceases to be *juris privati* only." This was said by Lord Chief Justice Hale more than two hundred years ago . . . . Property does become clothed with a public interest when used in a manner to make it of public consequence, and affect the community at large. When, therefore, one devotes his property to a use in which the public has an interest, he, in effect, grants to the public an interest in that use, and must submit to be controlled by the public for the common good, to the extent of the interest he has thus created. He may withdraw his grant by discontinuing the use; but, so long as he maintains the use, he must submit to the control.

—*Munn* v. *Illinois* 94, United States, pp. 124–126.

roads and their users to the point where they acknowledged the utility of regulation. But Americans still had faith in expansive free competition.

The Communications Network

Shipping and other forms of communication were distinctly subsidiary; whether they thrived or not depended on whether the railway still left them a function. Although the volume of foreign trade continued to mount, the percentage borne by American carriers declined after 1860; the tonnage of vessels under the flag of the United States fell precipitously. Foreign competition was severe, and Americans found alternative modes of investing their capital more attractive. Traffic on the inland waterways in this period expanded somewhat; but canal and coastal shipping was clearly outdistanced by the railway. By contrast, the telegraph network expanded rapidly; and Alexander Graham Bell's invention, the telephone (1876), came into widespread use in the 1880s. Meanwhile, Cyrus Field's cable had opened communication across the Atlantic in 1866.

Until the 1880s the demand for improved transportation within the growing cities re-

Gross Tonnage of United States Merchant Vessels, 1850–1890

(in thousands)

Year	Total	Engaged in Foreign Trade	Internal, and Coastal and Fishing
1850	3535	1,440	1,798
1860	5354	2,379	2,645
1870	4247	1,449	2,638
1880	4068	1,314	2,638
1890	4424	928	3,409

Alan Trachtenberg, *Brooklyn Bridge* (New York, 1965) is an exceptionally thoughtful treatment of the bridge and its meaning.

mained unsatisfied. The Brooklyn Bridge, completed in 1883 after fifteen years of effort and at a cost of $10,000,000, was an engineering triumph. A few places like Washington and Buffalo had adequately paved streets, but Chicago was more typical of the country at large; in 1890 two thirds of Chicago's roads were unsurfaced. In the 1880s the horsecar was still the mainstay of American rapid transit. New York, Kansas City, and Brooklyn experimented with elevated railways, but as long as steam locomotives supplied the traction, the expense was heavy and the inconvenience considerable. Some municipalities tried out cable cars conveyed by grappling through a slotted trench to an endless moving steel cable. Urban transportation was not convenient, swift, or cheap until after 1888, when service began in Richmond, Virginia, on Frank J. Sprague's line of cars which drew electricity from an overhead trolley wire supplied from a power station. In the next two years fifty cities adopted the new system.

Distribution

Effective communications depended not only on the physical existence of the rails and wires that carried people, things, and messages but also on a dependable set of relationships among dispatchers and receivers. Before 1860 such connections had been largely personal. The merchant or manufacturer acted through agents he could trust. The ship's captain or supercargo disposed of the commodities after he reached port; or goods were consigned to factors, who made the sale on behalf of the owner.

From Producer to Consumer Agricultural products were conveyed from the farmer to the processor or consumer by modifications of this system. The perishable crops went to commission merchants, who sold them at prices established by the variations of local supply and demand. The market for the great staples was more orderly. Brokers in the important towns bought up the cotton or wheat, paying a price

New York Central Elevator, New York. Enormous quantities of grain were brought in from the West. Wood engraving, *Frank Leslie's Illustrated Newspaper,* November 10, 1877. (Library of Congress)

determined by the fluctuations of central commodity exchanges.

A much more elaborate pattern developed for manufactured articles. At the chief regional distribution points, wholesalers bought stocks of goods and divided them into job lots—smaller quantities to stock the retailer's shelves. The wholesalers or jobbers spread through the country, thereby linking the manufacturer with every crossroad shop. The wholesaler also supplied three to six months' credit to his customers and thus eased the capital requirements of trade. A corps of traveling salesmen made the rounds of

neighborhood stores or passed from village to village, carrying in their sample cases the products of distant factories.

Retail Trade A multitude of retail shopkeepers were the building blocks of the distribution system. They carried on the ultimate transactions with the consumer, who paid for the products of industry. Thousands of general stores in rural districts carried a variety of products; in the cities, more specialized enterprises handled food, dry goods (textiles), and hardware. Retailing extended to the ambitious an opportunity to enter trade with only a slight

New York Dry Goods District, 1880s. The caption describes it as "The largest in the world, covering a space of 135 acres, containing 4,500 firms, employing $800,000,000 capital." Photolithograph by J. J. Fogerty, 1886. (Library of Congress)

investment. The shopkeeper who knew his customers could offer them a year's credit, and acted as intermediary by selecting the products that satisfied their tastes from among the outpouring of goods at the factory.

Measured by its ability to distribute the products of industry, this elaborate system was effective. But it required the services of thousands of people, and this added heavy costs to the price paid by the final purchasers. There was scope therefore for the ingenuity of entrepreneurs whose efforts to economize began to rationalize and order the patterns of distribution.

In the 1860s, for instance, George F. Gilman, who was selling coffee and tea in New York City, linked a number of outlets in a chain. By 1870, the eleven stores of his Great Atlantic and Pacific Tea Company enabled him to bypass middlemen and save on the costs of credit and distribution. In 1879, F. W. Woolworth started to sell a variety of five- and ten-cent items in his shop in Lancaster, Pennsylvania. In the next decades, he too developed a chain in Eastern cities.

Improved transportation, which permitted a reduction of postal rates, and the introduction

GEORGE F. GILMAN was a hide and leather dealer in New York City when he began, in 1860, to dabble in tea. He was then thirty-four, and had no doubt learned something about importing from his father, a shipowner in Maine. Gilman kept scheming for a way to make it big. His skill was in advertising. He devised a club plan through which he sold directly to groups, presumably at lower cost, and retained the middlemen's charges himself. At the same time, he continued to add units to his chain of retail stores. By 1871 his Great Atlantic and Pacific Tea Company had outlets scattered from Saxtons River, Vermont, to Baton Rouge, Louisiana, and was also doing a mail order business.

Gilman's was a one-man operation. His central policy was to concentrate on the high-volume distribution of a few items such as tea, using any means available — the mails, across-the-counter sales, and itinerant peddlers. He kept few records and made important decisions himself. In the 1870s his business had grown too large for him, and he was becoming impatient with the details. He had personal troubles, too, stemming from a dispute with his brothers over their inheritance.

In 1878, he entered into a partnership with George Huntington Hartford, who had worked in the St. Louis branch of Gilman's leather company. Hartford took over, systematized the enterprise, expanded the number of stores, and added a full range of grocery items. By the end of the century, the A & P was firmly established on a national basis.

It was characteristic that when Gilman died in 1901 he left — along with a young widow who lived in his house and claimed to be his adopted daughter — his affairs in a tangle. There was neither a will nor a written partnership agreement with Hartford. By then, the methods of the old-fashioned trader were anachronistic. But Gilman's energy had launched retailing upon a modern course.

of rural free delivery created opportunities for innovation in supplying the rural markets of the nation. In 1872, Aaron Montgomery Ward's mail order business brought tempting catalogues to thousands of farm households; shortly it was joined in this by Sears, Roebuck & Company, and the sales of both firms grew steadily.

The growth of cities created still other merchandising opportunities. Enterprising dry goods dealers took to adding new lines of goods to their stores — crockery, kitchen utensils, furniture, clothing. Increasingly, family purchases were being made by women, who might be tempted by various items when they came to buy muslin or woolens at Macy's or Wanamaker's. At the central point of the streetcar network, the department store offered shoppers a variety of goods at a fixed price, and the chance of a bargain drew growing numbers to its doors.

Meanwhile, some manufacturers began to develop sales organizations of their own. In the hope of controlling the market for its products, the Standard Oil Company dealt with retailers through its own subsidiaries rather than through wholesalers who also handled the kerosene of its competitors. The mistrust of Western beef in the East forced Gustavus Swift to go directly to the butchers. The need for servicing a complicated mechanism led the Singer Sewing

Boris Emmet and J. E. Jeuck, *Catalogues and Counters* (Chicago, 1950) is a good history of Sears, Roebuck.

Advertisement for a Cure-all. Lithograph, 1867. (Library of Congress)

Machine Company to establish its own outlets. In any industry, however, it took great effort, skill, and capital to locate representatives in every corner of the country.

Changes in the techniques of advertising aided the manufacturer. Newspapers were still the primary medium, but after the Civil War department stores introduced display ads that gradually pre-empted the prime space formerly given over to many notices a few lines long.

Agencies appeared which were capable of inserting the producer's description of his wares in hundreds of newspapers at once, and magazines with national circulation now opened their pages to such material. By 1890 billboards filled the blank spaces along roads and streets. National advertising took the power of choice out of the hands of the retailer, for his customers now ceased to ask for soap or cocoa and demanded Pears' or Baker's.

Boston, 1870. Photographed from a balloon by J. W. Black. (American Museum of Photography)

Urban Growth

The city was the focal point for much of this activity. Although it now housed a good deal of manufacturing, it remained primarily a transportation, distribution, and management center. As its varied functions expanded, its population swelled and spilled far beyond the narrow limits of mid-century. In 1890, almost 30 percent of the people were residents of places with 8000 or more inhabitants. In 1870, twenty-five cities boasted of populations of 50,000 or more; in 1890, fifty-eight could do so. Fewer than 5,000,000 people lived in such communities at the earlier date; almost 12,000,000 did so at the later, and by then three cities had gone above the million mark.

This growth magnified the unsolved urban problems inherited from the period before the Civil War. The physical difficulties of building

Urban Growth, 1850–1890

Year	Population of the United States (millions)	Cities of 8,000 or More		Cities of 25,000 or More		Great Cities of 1890*	
		Number	Population (thousands)	Number	Population (thousands)	Number	Population* (thousands)
1850	23	85	2,897	76	783	24	2,085
1860	31	141	5,072	87	1,264	28	3,350
1870	38	226	8,071	92	1,914	28	4,861
1880	50	286	11,318	96	2,710	28	6,694
1890	62	448	18,284	96	4,291	28	9,697

* With a population of 100,000 or more in 1890.

houses for the additional residents, supplying them with water and light, removing the wastes they created, and enabling them to ride to their jobs were imposing enough. More complex still were the difficulties of establishing order through democratic government, providing protection against fire and violence, and satisfying the social and cultural needs of the assembled multitudes. The efforts to meet these needs were painful. This was the price Americans paid for creation of the massive switching points in the national distribution system needed by an industrial economy.

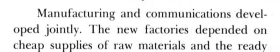

Manufacturing and communications developed jointly. The new factories depended on cheap supplies of raw materials and the ready dispersal of their products throughout the country. The new railroads depended on a rising volume of traffic and on reasonably priced equipment. The distribution network passing through the cities connected them. The whole phenomenal growth required a fluid supply of capital which encouraged the risk taking involved in expansion.

Paperbacks for Further Reading

John F. Stover, *American Railroads* (Chicago History of American Civilization Series) is a concise general account with a clear treatment of this period. Alfred D. Chandler, Jr., ed., *Railroads: the Nation's First Big Business* (Harcourt, Brace & World) contains a useful collection of primary materials.

FINANCING AMERICAN CAPITALISM

53

The transformation of the American economy called for substantial investments of capital. The expansion of industry and the construction of a national communications network depended upon the capacity to accumulate, from a variety of sources, the funds needed for construction.

This was a problem also in other societies that made the transition to industrialization at the same time and later. In many countries it proved necessary to use force to diminish consumption and thus compel people to make savings available for investment. The American system of government blocked the adoption of that expedient; saving and investment remained voluntary, induced by distinctive social and political conditions. New institutions developed which directed the flow of resources into the economy. The process, however, raised a profound question. Was a system of law and government that rested on the personal ownership of property appropriate to the impersonal corporation, which controlled wealth of a magnitude inconceivable to the founders of the Republic?

THE WAY TO GROW POOR. ✳ THE WAY TO GROW RICH.

Exhortation to be thrifty. Lithograph by Currier & Ives, 1875 (Library of Congress)

The Social Setting

TO THE SUCCESSFUL ENTREPRENEUR of the second half of the nineteenth century the process by which he accumulated capital seemed simple. His ability earned profits which he prudently refrained from spending and instead put back into his business. Thence expansion! Those who failed were either the less able or the less prudent. The proper concern of the industrialist was to keep his profits rising and his costs falling. So ran the commonly accepted belief.

There was enough evidence in the careers of Rockefeller, Carnegie, and Swift to lend credibility to this argument, which conformed with the older Puritan idea that Providence rewarded the virtuous. A good deal of the popular litera-

ture of the 1870s and 1880s expounded the maxim that, with luck, pluck would win out.

The Costs of Free Enterprise It was not so apparent at the time, however, that special conditions in the social environment permitted managers to keep costs low and thus assemble the surplus for reinvestment. Taxes were minuscule; and since they were assessed mainly on property, fell most heavily on landowners. The levy on incomes imposed in the North during the Civil War disappeared in 1871, and businessmen suffered little from the burden of supporting either state or Federal government.

Business escaped costs for which other societies might have held it responsible. The factory owner who laid off his laborers bore no charge for their support; if they became dependent,

32

Looking Out for Oneself, 1884

It seemed to him, then, that those fellows had put it up on him pretty steep, but he owned to himself that they had a sure thing, and that they were right in believing they could raise the same sum elsehwere; it would take all of it, he admitted, to make their paint pay on the scale they had the right to expect. At their age, he would not have done differently; but when he emerged, old, sore, and sleep-broken, from the sleeping car in the Albany depot at Boston, he wished with a pathetic self-pity that they knew how a man felt at his age. A year ago, six months ago, he would have laughed at the notion that it would be hard to raise the money. But he thought ruefully of that immense stock of paint on hand, which was now a drug in the market, of his losses by Rogers and by the failures of other men, of the fire that had licked up so many thousands in a few hours; he thought with bitterness of the tens of thousands that he had gambled away in stocks, and of the commissions that the brokers had pocketed whether he won or lost. . . .

Lapham stood in the isolation to which adversity so often seems to bring men. When its test was applied, practically or theoretically, to all those who had seemed his friends, there was none who bore it; and he thought with bitter self-contempt of the people whom he had befriended in their time of need. He said to himself that he had been a fool for that; and he scorned himself for certain acts of scrupulosity by which he had lost money in the past. Seeing the moral forces all arrayed against him, Lapham said that he would like to have the chance offered him to get even with them again; he thought he should know how to look out for himself.

—William Dean Howells, *Rise of Silas Lapham* (Boston: Houghton Mifflin Company, 1912), pp. 449, 450–451.

he could contribute to the charity that fed them, but he did not have to. Yet he knew that hands would be available to tend his machines when he needed them. The mill owners could take water from the streams and pour back waste as they wished without charge; it was not their concern if the smoke from their chimneys befouled a whole valley.

Nor did the costs of the failures fall on the shoulders of the successful. The competitive trial and error that diverted passengers and freight from the canal and river boats injured their owners but created no obligation for the railroads that captured the traffic. A new route or a new invention ruined some to make wealth for others. Each individual pursued his own welfare, seeking only to outdistance his rival; that was the law of economics and of life.

The Role of Government It was considered desirable to hold government action to a minimum, not merely to lower expenditures and taxes but also to prevent interference with the victory of the fittest. In practice, an imperfect world still needed some political action. In the United States, for instance, infant industries required protection against the cheap labor of Europe; each particular interest struggled for higher rates on its products and lower rates on the raw materials it needed, but the general level crept steadily upward after 1872. By the 1880s, there was a grudging recognition that fair competition depended upon the acceptance of general rules, which only the government could impose and enforce. The limited powers granted the Interstate Commerce Commission were nevertheless not to constrain the entrepreneur in his proper pursuit of profit.

Indeed, the legitimate function of government was to protect that quest without interfering with it. Property was the saved earnings of labor, and therefore a natural right. Consequently, it was the duty of the now uniformed and disciplined police forces to defend property not only from thieves but also from unruly agitators and workingmen. Otherwise the incentive to produce would disappear.

It was also the obligation of the state to secure the individual against more subtle threats to property. Any impairment of the right to form contracts freely and to have them enforced was dangerous, whether it emanated from a private conspiracy or from governmental meddling. Each person could ply what trade he wished, buy and sell, hire and take employment, as an act of his own will and with total assurance that the courts would uphold any agreement he made. There was a growing awareness, too, that the judges would strike down any limitation on that liberty. In the Wabash case (1886), they had explained that the Fourteenth Amendment's guarantee of due process was substantive; it forbade not only arbitrary procedures but any state action that diminished man's right to property.

This social and political environment was congenial to enterprise. It set a premium on work, saving, and investment; that is, it encouraged the accumulation of the capital, for which there were many demands in the economy.

Fiscal Policy

Capital Requirements Before 1860, the experience of the railroads had already shown that some enterprises could not develop through the ploughing back of profits by individuals but needed larger sums than any single entrepreneur commanded. Numerous investors had assembled the required funds. As needs grew and as industry learned to use the same methods, the states eased the legal restrictions on incorporation and the ranks of the participants broadened.

Promoters not only competed with one another but also had to make investment attractive to people who might use ready cash in other ways. Repeated injunctions to frugality urged people not to spend in consumption what they might save; even the advertising of the period

Sidney Fine, *Laissez Faire and the General-Welfare State* (Ann Arbor, Mich., 1956) contains a solid account of the conflict in American economic thought after 1865.

stressed the economy as well as the desirability of a product. The spendthrift not only wasted his substance but kept it from productive use.

The expanding requirements of individual enterprises likewise demanded financial resources; businessmen could usually employ in their own operations the money they were asked to invest in stocks or bonds. What flowed into one channel was diverted from another.

International commerce, as earlier, also influenced the domestic supply of currency. Exports usually offset only partially the rising volume of American imports. Cotton continued to find plenty of buyers in England, France, and Germany. In the 1880s, however, foodstuffs met increasing competition in Europe from Hungary, the Ukraine, and Australia, and the sale abroad of some American processed and manufactured goods did not compensate for the contracting market for agriculture. The result was a persistent deficit in the balance of payments. Europeans investing in the United States made up for some of the outflow of gold, but the overall pattern of trade was not such as to create substantial surpluses in the hands of Americans.

Capital thus was not spontaneously generated. It was laboriously assembled, by a mechanism and for incentives that grew increasingly powerful after 1860.

The Money Question Since early in the nineteenth century many Americans had believed that an easier money supply would encourage investment and raise prices. It was unnecessary to accept the accidental limits set by the amount of gold or silver available; the government could manage the currency by authorizing emissions of paper. This argument attracted speculators and other debtors, as well as farmers. Resistance to it came from people who mistrusted any tampering with the economic mechanism, which they were convinced automatically adjusted the supply of money to the demand. In the contest between the two views after 1865, the deflationary position generally won out.

Actually, the circulating medium, after first

BALANCE OF INTERNATIONAL PAYMENTS, 1866–1890
Total United States goods and services, in millions of dollars

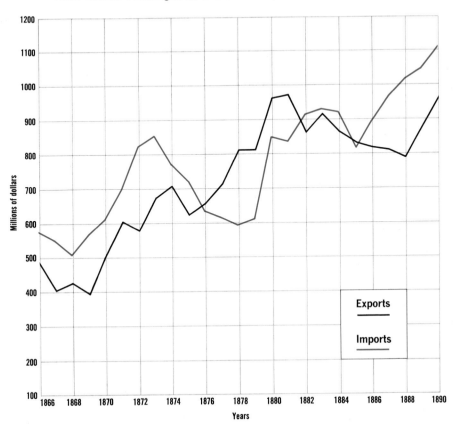

Exports

Imports

Morality and Money, 1866

Every change in the value of the dollar is an evil. But it is less injurious to national wealth when the creditor is benefited at the expense of the debtor, than in the opposite case, because, as a general rule, the creditor class are disposed to save their money, and the debtor class to spend it; and when the debtor pays more than he justly owes he is compelled to be more frugal, while the creditor receives a greater reward for his frugality, and is therefore encouraged to be more frugal. Frugality being the foundation of all national wealth and strength, the habits which conduce to wealth and strength are encouraged by an appreciation of the currency.

—Simon Newcomb "Our Financial Future," *North American Review*, CII (January, 1866), pp. 110–111.

Commercial Banks in the United States, 1850–1890

Year	Number	Assets (millions)	Notes Issued (millions)	Deposits (millions)	Loans (millions)	Investments (millions)
1850	824	$ 532	$131	$ 146	$ 364	$ 21
1860	1,562	1,000	207	310	692	70
1870	1,937	1,781	336	775	864	470
1880	3,355	3,399	318	2,222	1,662	904
1890	8,201	6,358	126	4,576	3,854	1,173

contracting, expanded although not as fast as the demands upon it. The stock of currency held by the public between the Civil War and 1879 ranged between $500,000,000 and $550,000,000 and was gradually diminishing. In the next decade it multiplied, from $624,000,000 in 1880 to $888,-000,000 in 1890. Included in these totals were both specie and paper, but the various components fared differently in these years.

The supply of gold coin declined steadily from 1862 to 1875, then recovered somewhat. In the ten years after 1880 it tripled as a result of the activities of Western mines. Silver, on the other hand, became so rare that the United States had practically ceased to coin it by 1853. A law in 1873 provided for the minting of silver only in coins of less than a dollar. Ironically, discoveries immediately thereafter increased the amount extracted to such a degree that the Bland-Allison Act of 1878 ordered the minting of from $2,000,000 to $4,000,000 a month; by 1890 about $375,000,000 had been added to the currency in all denominations.

Several kinds of paper served as legal tender, but the supply was much less flexible than the proponents of inflation desired. Gold and silver certificates were simply equivalent substitutes for the metal, so the amount depended on the quantity of specie available. During the war, the Union had also issued about $450,000,000 in greenbacks, notes backed only by the government's willingness to receive them for all obligations except customs dues. The greenbacks were not redeemable for specie and consequently were far less valuable than gold; in 1865, $100 in greenbacks was worth only $65 in gold. This recourse to the printing press had been an act

of desperation justified by the war emergency; with peace it was assumed that the greenbacks would be withdrawn. The amount in circulation remained stable until 1875, when a law directed the Treasury to redeem some and to exchange the remainder at par with gold after 1879. In the 1880s, about $350,000,000 worth remained outstanding.

The supply of notes issued by banks was also limited. The Federal law of 1864 had taxed the paper of the state banks out of existence, and the national banks could issue only an amount up to 90 percent of their holdings of Federal bonds. Since the national debt declined from just under $3,000,000,000 in 1865 to well under $2,000,000,000 in 1890, the quantity of such paper was actually diminishing. Other ways of meeting expanding business needs had developed by then.

Credit and Savings   With the currency thus restrained, most transactions involved some form of credit and most savings were held in account books rather than in cash. Banks acquired a new importance; they practically lost their former note-issuing function but became the instruments for managing the credit of the economy. The number of commercial banks doubled between 1860 and 1880 and then doubled again in the next decade. Their assets tripled in the first interval and nearly doubled in the second. The amounts deposited in commercial banks rose steadily from between $700,000,000 and $800,-000,000 before 1870 to $3,000,000,000 in 1890.

Irwin Unger, *The Greenback Era* (Princeton, N. J., 1964) analyzes the political forces that influenced fiscal policy between 1865 and 1879.

FRIGHTFUL LOSS OF LIFE.

Among the Killed and Injured in this Terrible Fire are Several Members of the United States Mutual Accident Association, whose Claims will Receive Prompt Settlement.

MORAL—INSURE IN THE UNITED STATES MUTUAL ACCIDENT ASSOCIATION, 409 BROADWAY, NEW YORK.

$5,000 Accident Insurance
AND
$25 Weekly Indemnity
At a cost of about **$11** per annum.

Membership Fee - - - $4.00.

$10,000 Accident Insurance and **$50** Weekly Indemnity at corresponding rates.

More than 1,500 Claims have been Paid.

ALL VALID CLAIMS PAID AT SIGHT.

More than **10,000** Leading Business Men Insured in this Association.

Write for Circular and Application Blank. European permits.

CHAS. B. PEET, President.

(Of Rogers, Peet & Co.)

JAS. R. PITCHER, Secretary.

RECENT LOSSES PAID:

EVANS G. WILEY, of Urbana, O............$5,000.00	CHARLES S. BOYD, of Philadelphia, Pa......$5,000.00
REAMER F. COPELAND, of Waukesha, Wis.. 5,000.00	BRACKET H. BADGER, of Fond du Lac, Wis. 5,000.00
HARRIS I. FELLOWS, of Albany, N.Y...... 5,000.00	CHAS. J. KING, of Littleton, N.H........... 5,000.00
JOSEPH M. GOODHUE, of St. Louis, Mo..... 5,000.00	DAVID C. BALLANTINE, of Lincoln, Neb.... 5,000.00
JAMES H. SLEDGE, of La Grange, Ga....... 5,000.00	P. J. O'BRIEN, New York, N.Y.............. 5,000.00

Insurance Company Advertisement, *ca.* 1883, Showing the Burning of Newhall House, Milwaukee. (Culver Pictures)

Their ability to make loans and investments increased correspondingly.

Meanwhile other financial institutions were gaining strength. Savings banks, first established before the Civil War to encourage thrift among workingmen, became common, and deposits in them climbed from under $400,000,000 before 1870 to $1,300,000,000 in 1890. The reserves of life insurance companies also increased and had to be judiciously safeguarded, as the catastrophic experience of the depression of 1873 showed.

Life Insurance in the United States, 1850–1890

Year	Number of Companies	Insurance in Force (millions)
1850	48	97
1860	43	173
1870	129	2,006
1880	59	1,522
1890	60	3,522

Opportunity came to **JAY COOKE** in 1861, when he formed his own banking house. He was born in 1821 in Ohio and went to work as a shop clerk at the age of fourteen. He held jobs in St. Louis and Philadelphia and gradually learned something about banking, but when he was forty there was little to distinguish him from many other men in trade.

The election of the Republicans made the difference. Lincoln appointed as Secretary of the Treasury Governor Salmon Chase of Ohio, an intimate friend of Jay's younger brother Henry, who was a newspaper editor in Columbus. This gave Cooke a tie to the new administration, and when the war created a heavy demand for cash, Chase came to him. Cooke arranged with an association of New York banks to advance $50,000,000 to the government, the amount to be repaid from the sale of the seven-thirties (bonds bearing interest of 7.30 percent).

Success encouraged Cooke in 1862 to act as distributor for a new loan of fully $500,000,000 at 6 percent. In little more than a year he had the whole amount sub-scribed. By then his network of correspondents was so effective that he remained fiscal agent of the Department of the Treasury even after Chase resigned. In six months in 1865 Cooke distributed $600,000,000 in new seven-thirties.

Once the war was over, Cooke decided to use his organization as the basis for a general banking business, and he opened branches in New York and London. He intended to capitalize on the railroad boom and turned to financing the Northern Pacific, but the methods that had proved adequate earlier were now ineffective. Cooke had to compete with other investment interests, and he lacked the contacts to secure the necessary funds. The road had only reached the Missouri River when his money gave out. On September 18, 1873, Jay Cooke & Company closed its doors and a panic ensued.

Cooke lived until 1905 and regained some of his fortune through mining investments in Utah. But he did not participate in the great development of investment banking in the last quarter of the nineteenth century.

Investment Banking

Bankers of another sort were more concerned with major investment than with day-to-day commercial transactions. Jay Cooke & Company, Drexel, Morgan & Company, and Kuhn, Loeb & Company engaged in activities that were an outgrowth of the business of the great international merchants of an earlier day. The banking house J. & W. Seligman & Company had actually begun with dry goods. Like their predecessors, these firms were private and emphasized family connections and personal judgment. Ties with a foreign house were important. John Pierpont Morgan began his career with George Peabody & Company of London; August Belmont was an agent of the Rothschilds. Sometimes such men still handled commodities, but they had acquired capital and skills they could now put to more profitable uses.

In the past the overseas merchant had always had to know the price of gold and the cost of bills of exchange. Frequently he had made loans to princes. His successors now did the same; they traded in money and purchased the bonds of governments. However, they found new opportunities in the securities of railroads. For instance, when William H. Vanderbilt decided to sell his 250,000 shares of New York Central stock for $30,000,000 he asked John Pierpont

Henrietta M. Larson, *Jay Cooke, Private Banker* (Cambridge, Mass., 1936) is a scholarly account.

Frederick L. Allen, *The Great Pierpont Morgan* (New York, 1949) is a well-written, sympathetic biography.

JOHN PIERPONT MORGAN had a background different from that of Jay Cooke. This helps explain the success of the one and the failure of the other. Morgan, born in 1837, the son of a Yankee banker whose interests centered in London, received much of his education in Europe and settled in the United States only shortly before the Civil War. In 1860 he became the New York agent for his father's firm, and a decade later he formed the banking house of Drexel, Morgan & Company, influential connections in London and Paris being his chief asset.

In 1873, Cooke's weakness gave Morgan the opportunity to break into the extensive refunding operations of the Federal government, a field that he soon dominated. His interests spread to railroads in 1879, just when a new boom began. His ability to sell substantial amounts of securities to English investors gave him the leverage in the 1880s to reorganize the Philadelphia and Reading, the Chesapeake and Ohio, and various other railroads.

Imperious, confident, tough, he had power and knew how to use it. The concerns of lesser men did not trouble him. He made a plan and carried it through. The disorderly character of American economic growth annoyed him. He preferred to have the railroads and factories operate by calculable rules, just as he wished to see firm values in another of his zealous pursuits, art. The desire for order and stability became his passion.

After 1890, Morgan dealt as an equal with Presidents Grover Cleveland and Theodore Roosevelt in settling national monetary and labor problems. In this same period he extended to industry the principles he had already applied to railroads, organizing the United States Steel Corporation and other large integrated corporations. He was striving then to fit the productive system into one big efficient business. He died in 1913, just as the world he had helped shape was about to disintegrate.

Morgan to make the arrangements for him. So, too, Jay Cooke undertook to float the securities of the Northern Pacific.

The investment banker assumed such obligations not only because he had vast resources of his own but also because he could pass the securities on to the financial institutions with surpluses. His prestige and reputation for sound financial judgment made his offerings attractive. Corporate bonds formed less than 1 percent of the assets of a sample of life insurance companies in 1860; in 1890, the amount had risen to 22 percent. In the same period the investments of commercial banks, too, mounted rapidly. The investment banker's connections permitted him to find markets for stocks and bonds also in Europe.

By 1890, financial power had given the investment banker a key position in the economy. Naturally he took an interest in the corporations whose securities he sold to his customers; as a matter of course, he became a director of commercial banks, life insurance companies, and railroads. Interlocking roles such as these added to his resources and his strength.

His operations centered in New York City, which had become the financial capital of the nation. In 1870, Philadelphia and Boston were still potent rivals; in 1890, the great port on the Hudson stood alone. Substantial advantages brought it supremacy. It had the preponderance of transatlantic trade and therefore handled the related fiscal transactions. Moreover its cosmopolitan society made it more receptive to outsiders than other Eastern cities. Above all, the process by which corporate securities passed into the hands of individual Americans revolved about the exchanges of New York. On Wall Street, great fortunes could be won or lost.

Security Markets

Business-minded Americans were already acquainted with the methods of buying and selling stocks and bonds before 1860, but the number of persons involved was limited and investments were usually in local enterprises. The Civil War spread the habit of investing among professional people, farmers, small entrepreneurs, and clerks. The financial needs of the Union touched off vast bond drives; Jay Cooke, banker for the Federal government, at one time employed 2500 salesmen to dispose of the bonds. Purchases were patriotic and men of modest means learned to give their savings this form. They would be willing customers for railroad, and later for industrial, securities.

Speculation   The exchanges had long maintained a market within which stocks and bonds could always be traded, but the telegraph made that market national. The brokers who held seats on the New York exchanges could act on behalf of customers anywhere in the country, and they developed a country-wide network of correspondents.

The investors were not primarily concerned with interest or dividends; the average yield of corporate securities was low and was declining. The lure to purchasers was a rapid and dramatic appreciation of capital values. They were speculating on a rise that would bring them a fortune. Cash was therefore not necessary; one could pay down as little as 10 percent, borrowing the rest until the price rose enough to liquidate the debt. In a decline, alas, the 10 percent was lost.

After the Civil War, gambling was illegal in almost all states. Nevertheless every large city had its numbers games, its keno parlors, and an abundance of other establishments where the venturesome could take a chance. Speculation in stocks offered respectable citizens an opportunity to win by taking a risk without the odium of breaking the law, indeed with the virtuous assur-

ance that they were thriftily helping develop the country's transportation, mining, and industry. There were losers as well as winners, but the outcome was presumed to result from shrewd calculation rather than from the accidental turn of a card.

That there were abuses in the system was well known. Bucket shops never executed the orders of their customers. If the price went down, they simply pocketed the sum invested; if the price rose, they cheerfully credited the victim's balance until his fortune turned. When their obligations became too heavy, they simply absconded. The law was not often able to catch up with them.

How to Lose $100,000, ca. 1880

My friend Northrop said, with surprise: "Can't see how a man can make and then lose a hundred thousand dollars."

Here's the solution: . . . The man who never before had a hundred dollars, a man who begins to feel poor when he gets the first $50,000, a man who constantly and wilfully and determinedly persists in getting over his head in the confusing waters of speculation, who belittles the size of his pile, as he associates with millionaires, joins in their schemes and buys their stock; the shoddy man, who looks 'wise as a forest of owls,' and believing he is great because he has been lucky; he who gives bad advice and refuses good; he who has an expense account, that, like the impending avalanche, will snowslide him to poverty; he it is who loses a hundred thousand dollars. Not one in a thousand of these fellows ever make it back. Their time is now occupied in thinking of their past greatness, and they drift along Time's rapid stream until they whirl into the vortex of despair.

—James Wardner, *Jim Wardner of Wardner, Idaho* (New York: Anglo-American Publishing Co., 1900), pp. 64–65.

Yields and Values of Common Stock, 1871–1890

| Year | Yield (percent) | | Index of Prices |
	Industrials	Railroads	1941–43 = 10
1871	4.80	5.48	4.69
1880	6.85	4.64	5.21
1890	5.07	3.54	5.27

There were perfectly legal, if perhaps not precisely honest, ways to profit by manipulating supply and demand. The exchanges dealt not only in present but also in future deliveries. The bears sold short securities they did not yet own and tried to depress the price; the bulls bought and tried to raise the level. Ownership was less important than the gain from the fluctuations. Various groups pooled their resources to be able to change the price by throwing large blocks of securities on the market or by making concerted heavy purchases. The ultimate goal was a corner, control of the whole available supply, which permitted the speculator to set the price he wished for the stocks due him. It helped in such maneuvers to have influence within the corporations whose stocks were traded. Daniel Drew, as treasurer of the Erie Railroad, could print as many shares as he wished when he sought to lower the price. It was useful, too, to own a newspaper, as Jay Gould did, so that strategic rumors could be planted to sway the gullible. It was even more advantageous to own a few judges and legislators, to be sure that the limits of the law remained flexible.

Those who lost heavily on Wall Street howled in protest, but they kept coming back for another try, as did the patrons of the keno parlors. Daniel Drew, Jay Gould, and Jim Fisk were scoundrels, but many an American felt a scarcely concealed admiration for their escapades and dreamed of emulating them. Making a fortune their way was easier than by frugality, punctuality, and hard work. The number of investors grew, although the number who succeeded may not have.

The Depression of 1873 Occasionally there were panics. On the Black Friday in September 1869 when Jim Fisk's effort to corner the gold market failed, hundreds of unwary speculators plunged to their ruin although the responsible culprit escaped unharmed. Lesser incidents frequently dragged down the unwise or the unlucky.

A panic could deepen into depression when the effects spread through the whole economy. In September 1873, Jay Cooke's firm failed,

The Railroad Barons, 1871

The . . . men at the head of vast combinations of private wealth . . . controlling the rapidly developed railroad interests . . . have declared war, negotiated peace, reduced courts, legislatures, and sovereign States to an unqualified obedience to their will, disturbed trade, agitated the currency, imposed taxes, and, boldly setting both law and public opinion at defiance, have freely exercised many other attributes of sovereignty. . . . Single men have controlled hundreds of miles of railway, thousands of men, tens of millions of revenue, and hundreds of millions of capital. The strength implied in all this they wielded in practical independence of the control both of governments and of individuals; much as petty German despots might have governed their little principalities a century or two ago. Thus by degrees almost the whole of the system of internal communication through the northern half of the United States has practically been partitioned out among a few individuals, and, as proximity, or competition on certain debatable grounds, — the Belgiums of the system, — brought the interests represented by these men into conflict, the series of struggles have ensued replete with dramatic episodes.

—Charles Francis Adams, "An Erie Raid," *North American Review*, CXII (April, 1871), p. 242.

having become overextended in the effort to build the Northern Pacific. Depositors began to make demands on other banks, which had to call in their short-term loans. Failures multiplied; confidence dwindled; security prices dropped. With money unavailable, the fall crop movements were paralyzed and foreign ex-

Julius Grodinsky, *Jay Gould* (Philadelphia, 1957) is an objective study of the business career of a speculator.

Jay Gould's Private Bowling Alley. Colored lithograph, 1882, by Frederick Burr Opper, from *Puck,* a weekly published in New York. (The Granger Collection)

James Fisk (1834–1872). Photographed in 1870. (The Granger Collection)

change was blocked. People began to hoard cash, so credit contracted further. Factories cut their production, and railroad and building construction halted. Unemployment grew and consumer purchasing power declined. For six years the country knew the meaning of depression.

Recovery came in 1879 and despite minor setbacks lasted until 1890, but the events of 1873 revealed the vulnerability of the new economic system. The depression was world-wide; indeed some of Cooke's difficulty originated in his inability to sell in Europe the bonds he had expected to sell there. In the United States and elsewhere, the panic and its aftermath showed the extent to which economic expansion had become dependent upon speculative capital. Growth did not come through coordinated calculations but through the conglomerate decisions of thousands of individual investors. That was the source of its strength and of its weakness.

Wealth

At the time, people applied to the economic system a test that raised a question which was difficult to answer. The economy produced a wonderful outpouring of goods. Who shared the wealth?

There was no precise answer, only a gross impression. The great benefits flowed not to the men in the mills or the mines, not to the farmers and shopkeepers, not even to the ordinary manufacturers, but to relatively few individuals who occupied strategic positions in the control of capital.

Before the Civil War $100,000 was a substantial fortune; only twenty-five New Yorkers and nine Philadelphians each possessed a million dollars. Stephen Girard's $6,000,000 estate (1831) was altogether unusual. After 1870, the scale changed radically. By 1890, the Vanderbilts were worth $300,000,000, the Astors $250,000,000, and Andrew Carnegie, Marshall Field, and Jay Gould had all gone well above the $100,000,000 mark. There were then 3000 ordinary millionaires, a hundred of whom enjoyed annual incomes—untaxed—of more than a million dollars. Had these vast accumulations been earned by exercise of the traditional virtues?

Americans regarded these amazing figures with admiration, envy, and mistrust. They were glad to have the convenient transportation and the cheap goods the railroad and the factory made possible, but when they contrasted the lot of the fortunate with that of the other citizens of the Republic, they were bound to wonder about the effect on society of such enormous disparities among its members.

Estimated Distribution of Wealth, 1889

	Number of Families	Average Wealth per Family
Rich	235,310	$186,567
Middle	1,200,000	6,250
Workers and farmers	11,565,000	968

Source: "Owners of the United States," *The Forum*, VIII (November, 1889), p. 269.

Construction of the manufacturing and communications plant basic to an advanced industrial economy called for the investment of large sums of capital. In the United States, individual entrepreneurs operating through a private mechanism for managing capital and credit took the risks and the rewards.

The process worked. The factories appeared. Trains with freight and passengers moved across the continent. The nation grew in population, wealth, and power. But it paid a price for the rails and machines; and it quickly discovered that fundamental political and social adjustments to the new conditions necessarily followed.

Paperbacks for Further Reading

Richard Hofstadter, *Social Darwinism in American Thought* (Beacon Press) is an interesting account of elements in the basic ideology of American business. Robert G. McCloskey, *The American Supreme Court* (Chicago History of American Civilization Series) touches thoughtfully on the issues of this period. *A Hazard of New Fortunes* (Bantam Books, Inc.), a novel by William Dean Howells originally published in 1889, shows insight into the speculative mentality of contemporary Americans. Sigmund Diamond, ed., *The Nation Transformed* (George Braziller) is a useful collection.

SOCIETY IN THE GILDED AGE

54

Industrialization capriciously heaped great wealth in the hands of a few individuals. Like the newly rich everywhere, they had difficulty learning to play their roles. The United States, moreover, lacked an aristocratic tradition; the only model to emulate was European. As a result the holders of American fortunes floundered; the gilt of the age did not cover up their uncertainty.

Their difficulties were symptomatic. American society had never been rigid or orderly. Now deeply divided and changing rapidly, it lacked the cohesive power to hold its members to firm standards of belief or behavior. Each man and each group, in pursuing its own interests, had to judge its rights and obligations and arrive at its own values.

Where there was neither common language nor common understanding there could be no common culture. The efforts of the old leadership to establish control failed. Each sector of the population sought the style of life, and along with it the art and literature, that had meaning for it. Few tastes or emotions were comprehensible to all Americans. Fragmentation was the outstanding characteristic of the society industrialization created.

New Wealth

U NTIL THE CIVIL WAR, Americans recognized a rough equivalence among wealth, virtue, and status. They conceded leadership to the great planters of the South and the great merchants of the North, whose estates and public service earned the respect even of the artisans and the yeomen with divergent economic interests. In the 1850s, the well-established families, rich for several generations, were beginning to display aristocratic pretensions. The Virginia and South Carolina Cavaliers, the Boston Brahmins, and the New York Knickerbockers, for example, claimed first place in their communities by emphasizing not their money but the polished gentlemanly qualities of long lineage, polite manners, and education.

The New Money The upstarts of the postwar decades far outdistanced the old families in wealth, but their dollars lacked respectability. Unlike the riches accumulated generations back from ships or plantations, money gained recently from speculation or grimy factories seemed tainted. The new millionaire, it appeared, had amassed his fortune as an end in itself, without worrying much why. An unabashed scoundrel like Jim Fisk never gave the matter a thought; his wife stayed home while his bank roll bought him his fill of alcoholic, gustatory, and sexual pleasures.

But most men of new wealth were more serious, or if they were not, their wives were. Once they had attained the goal of riches they longed for respectability and status. They then learned that to enjoy the rewards they had to efface the memory of starts behind the dry-goods counter or on the peddler's wagon.

Ostentatious demonstrations of their success were the easiest means of showing what they had become. Their gold was their own and they could spend it as they wished. When William H. Vanderbilt built a mansion on Fifth Avenue worthy of his position, 600 artisans worked a year and a half to get it ready—60 of them stonecutters especially imported from Europe.

Everywhere in the United States success presented the same challenge; the problems of spending an income of $100,000 or $50,000 differed only in degree from those of spending $1,000,000 or $10,000,000. The rapidly accumulating fortunes made any expenditure possible, on lavish homes, elaborate country houses, fashionable clothes, travel, and expensive entertainment. Men who were shrewd judges of value when it came to the price of wheat or iron had no standards by which to appraise the worth of formal gardens or French paintings. They were buying a display and cost did not count. The objective was to gain recognition of what they had become, to obliterate the recollection of what they had been.

New York Chicago, San Francisco, and a few other booming Western cities offered a setting ample enough for the social aspirations of families of wealth; there it was possible to imitate Eastern fashions, while making occasional contacts with similar clans in Saratoga or Newport. But success in Pittsburgh or Cleveland or smaller places often planted a desire to move into the glittering circles of the East. People like Carnegie, Frick, and Rockefeller did not have deep roots in Pennsylvania or Ohio, and they could manage their affairs as easily where the banks were as where the plants were. New York City had the greatest pulling power; it was the nation's financial capital and newcomers found fewer barriers to acceptance in its cosmopolitan life than in the more closely knit communities of Boston and Philadelphia.

Breaking In The upstarts, whose gaudy Fifth Avenue mansions outshone the staid Knickerbocker town houses on Washington Square,

Arthur M. Schlesinger, *Rise of the City, 1878–1898* (New York, 1933) contains a thoughtful general account of the culture of this period.

Parts III and IV of Wayne Andrews, *The Vanderbilt Legend* (New York, 1941) are good on the relationship of culture and society.

Dixon Wecter, *The Saga of American Society* (New York, 1937) is a lively general account.

challenged the primacy of the old leadership. The families formerly in command feared not only the loss of their own position but also the subversion of accepted values. The industrial barons who had scratched their way to the top without scruple and whose antics captured popular attention threatened to make material gain the sole criterion of social worth. There could be no order in a world in which every man was ceaselessly at war with his competitors. Much as she resented it, in the end Mrs. Astor went to call on Mrs. Vanderbilt and thus acknowledged the arrival of the newcomer. But though it might be necessary to make room for the outsiders, it was essential in doing so to be sure that they accepted existing conventions.

Yet the old families lacked the institutional resources with which the European aristocracy retained its pre-eminence. Here were no titles of nobility, established churches, military castes, or royal courts to enforce an appropriate etiquette or sense of rank. Mrs. Astor herself was only two generations away from the German immigrant who had founded the fortune, and few could claim a lineage more distinguished. The example of the English aristocracy, which managed to maintain itself despite the growing democracy of its government, was impressive but could not be imitated. An equivalent was necessary.

Defining Aristocracy

The would-be American aristocracy had to define itself by identifying who was in and who was not, that is, by distinguishing the members of society from the horde of vulgar *nouveaux riches.*

In Boston and Philadelphia, family lines were firm enough so that selection was spontaneous and automatic. But New York required a more deliberate process. In the 1870s, Ward McAllister and a group of twenty-five Patriarchs

Edward C. Kirkland, *Charles Francis Adams* (Cambridge, Mass., 1965) is a thoughtful and interesting biography.

SAMUEL WARD McALLISTER was the perfect middleman for American society in the gilded age. Good family, aristocratic manners deriving from the South, and money endowed him with the attributes necessary to play his role.

He was born in 1827 in Savannah, Georgia, where his father, a lawyer and rice planter, stood at the head of local society. The elder McAllister had demonstrated his national sentiments by marrying a New York girl. At the age of twenty, Ward, as he was later called, went to New York to establish contact with his Northern connections; then he settled in Savannah, where he began to practice law. In 1850, Ward moved with his father to San Francisco, where the latter became a judge and Ward practiced law. Both accumulated substantial fortunes within a few years.

Just before the Civil War, Ward McAllister went East, married well, and settled down on a substantial estate near Newport, Rhode Island. It was then that he understood his mission in life to be to help develop an American aristocracy. In the 1860s he traveled extensively in Europe to observe authentic nobility and prepare himself for the task of elevating the tone of his own society. In the process he hoped to make Newport the pre-eminent resort for people of distinction. By 1870 he was so influential in New York that he dominated the Patriarchs, and in 1890, when he wrote *Society as I Have Found It,* he was the arbiter of the social world. The climax of his career came a few years later when Mrs. William Astor asked him to define the four hundred families worth knowing. He died in 1895, content that his mission had been successful.

Mrs. Astor's Art Gallery, Astor Residence, Fifth Avenue, New York. (Brown Brothers)

were censoring the guest lists of dinners and balls to determine who was eligible. By 1890, McAllister had established the four hundred families who were in society. In other cities, too, formal and informal lists and registers kept account of the admitted and the excluded.

Symbols of Status The would-be aristocracy, unwilling to justify itself by money alone and unable to do so by birth, made taste the symbol of its position. The railroad kings and the barons of coke filled their imitation palaces with paintings, books, and bric-a-brac ransacked from the Old World and there offered lavish entertainment as the etiquette books instructed them to.

Old masters were the best form of display. The cost was high and visible; and they clearly marked their possessor as a person of such means that he could afford them and of such taste that

he would want them. A swarm of dealers in rarities descended upon the cities to supply the desired objects, complete with the warranty of excellence that high price supplied. Old masters and first editions had the greatest worth; tested by time, in short supply and therefore likely to increase in value, these paintings and books also had a gratifying aristocratic, almost feudal, flavor.

Culture thus was a badge of position rather than a means of enjoyment or enlightenment. J. P. Morgan never bothered to inspect the Vermeer for which he paid $100,000. Like a yacht or a home in Newport, paintings were incidentals of a place in society.

Family considerations emphasized the urgency of fixing social status. Fortunes easily won could be as easily lost, and neither the law nor

The Aristocratic Ideal, ca. 1890

The common-schools my father did not care to send his children to; and I have always been glad of it. I don't associate with the laborers on my place, nor would the association be agreeable to either of us. Their customs, language, habits and conventionalities differ from mine; as do those of their children. I believe in school life; and I believe in the equality of men before the law; but social equality, whether for man or child, is altogether another thing . . . .

For me, as I now see it, the absolutely ideal training would have been that described in *School Days at Rugby*. I ought to have been sent away from home and been rubbed into shape among other boys; I should have been made to undergo a severe all-around discipline; I should have been forced to participate in all sorts of athletic games; I ought to have been rounded into shape as much like other boys as a school life could round me.

—Charles Francis Adams, 1835–1915; An Autobiography (Boston: Houghton Mifflin Company, 1916), pp. 15–16, 20–21.

Lawn Tennis. Lithograph, 1887, by Louis Prang & Co. (Library of Congress)

custom provided a mechanism for transmitting positions from one generation to another. In the United States, unlike Europe, no sinecures in the army, the church, or the government bureaucracy took care of privileged children. It was therefore desirable to arrange marriages that would secure the status of aspiring offspring. Not many Americans could emulate Henry Huntington, who endowed his daughter with a gift of a million dollars when she married Prince Hatzfeldt. But a summer in a proper vacation place and access to the correct round of social occasions laid the groundwork for advantageous connections. These considerations became the more important as divorce grew easier, with its attendant expense and publicity and its disruption of family relationships and fortunes.

Aristocracy and Education Concern with social status subtly influenced the development of educational and cultural institutions after the Civil War. Museums and libraries were custodians of the proper standards in art and literature. Their collections were instructive insofar as they defined good taste, and they certified the value of the possessions of the men of wealth who supported them. The colleges were even more important, for they not only established the correct canon of knowledge but also provided a setting within which young men learned to behave like gentlemen and thus prepared themselves for leadership. The classroom equipped the scions of good families with the information, and the clubs or fraternities with the friends and graces they would need in later life. Preparatory schools imitated the Rugby of Dr. Arnold. St. Paul's (1855) and St. Mark's (1865) were already in operation when Endicott Peabody, son of a great banker, established Groton in 1884; through their exclusive halls the select youth moved on the way to superior status.

The most desirable preparatory schools functioned under the auspices of the Episcopal Church, which increasingly drew the elite social groups into its fold. The English connection, the tolerance in doctrinal matters, the hierarchical order, and the moderate ceremonialism of that denomination attracted people with aristocratic leanings. Membership in Fifth Avenue's St. Thomas or in the Back Bay's Trinity Church became as fashionable as a place in Newport.

The number of families struggling actively for places at the pinnacle of society was always small. But they held the attention of the whole country. They were the epitome of success and set the styles for thousands of other Americans who avidly followed their activities in the press.

The tendencies toward stratification appeared everywhere. Local bankers and merchants in smaller communities maneuvered for position, and lawyers and doctors tried to strengthen the dignity, power, and wealth of their professions. Increasingly, people thought of society as ranged on ascending steps; each man sought to protect his space against the climbers from below and at the same time tried to get a foothold in the rank above.

Culture and Society

The struggle for social position transformed many people's ways of thinking about culture. Art ceased to be a medium that expressed and communicated thoughts and emotions and became a symbol of the status of the possessor. The elite groups, with immense fortunes to spend, exerted enormous influence over American taste; and they judged architecture, music, and literature not by the enjoyment these arts gave but by formal rules, established by an authority, preferably with sound European derivations.

The Fine Arts The men grown wealthy from railroads or mines who decided to build new homes or who were on the boards that provided the means for constructing churches, museums, libraries, and colleges could not find any standard of what was appropriate in their own experience. They turned instead to a few respected architects trained at the École des Beaux Arts in Paris who could give them the best that money

A Romantic Heroine, 1884

Fresh young roses of each opening year, fresh with the dew of heaven and the blush of innocence, coming up in this wild garden of a world, what would the gardener do without you? Where would all the beauty and sweetness be found among the thorny bushes and the withering old shrubs and the rotting weeds, were it not for you? Maidens with clean hands and pure hearts, in whose touch there is something that heals the ills and soothes the pains of mortality, roses whose petals are yet unspotted by dust and rain, and whose divine perfume the hot south wind has not scorched, nor the east wind nipped and frozen—you are the protest, set every year among us, against the rottenness of the world's doings, the protest of the angelic life against the earthly, of the eternal good against the eternal bad.

—F. Marion Crawford, *An American Politician* (New York: Regent Press, 1906), p. 36.

could buy. Richard Morris Hunt and his pupils in the firm of McKim, Mead and White gratified their clients by adapting to a variety of novel uses the designs of Renaissance palaces. The Romanesque structures of Henry Hobson Richardson met the same need. These massive arched stone or brick structures, often embellished with ornamental columns and courts, and lavish in the use of space, impressed the onlooker with the princely qualities of their residents or sponsors.

Ceremonial features dominated also the music the elite society accepted as good. The $2,000,000 Metropolitan Opera House of New York was built, in 1883, about its Golden Horseshoe; the boxholders were content to allow the impresario, Leopold Damrosh, to determine what appeared on the stage, as long as they held the limelight. By this time New York and Boston had elaborate symphony orchestras sustained by generous sponsors; and every city of any size was regularly offered concerts by notable European performers. Native composers like John Knowles Paine and George Chadwick set themselves to imitating the European masters—but without notable achievements.

Polite Literature The purchasers of books they did not intend to read were more interested in bindings, title pages, and price than in content. Busy men of affairs left reading to their women, and the literature produced for this audience reflected feminine tastes. F. Marion Crawford, perhaps the most fashionable writer of the 1870s and 1880s, turned out pretty, sentimental romances that beguiled the ladies of leisure. Here ethereal heroines led angelic lives. Here courtly heroes, usually in a remote environment, set all material considerations aside, in devotion to their one true love. These pages carried no hint of such passions as soiled the dirty French novels. But refined readers could respond to the thrill of brutality when made legitimate by religiosity, as in *Ben Hur* by Lew Wallace.

Occasionally, a husband went as escort to the theater, where Bronson Howard's polite parlor comedies held the stage. Augustin Daly and Lester Wallack, the most skillful theatrical managers of the era, in the effort to be socially fashionable while attracting large audiences, emphasized familiar plots, luxurious settings, and famous stars.

The poetry most appreciated was undemanding. The pallid verses of Thomas Bailey Aldrich, E. C. Stedman, and R. W. Gilder produced a soothing effect; they were not intended to move the emotions. Indeed, it was generally enough, for social purposes, to remember the criticism in *The Nation* or *The Atlantic Monthly*, whose pages supplied the necessary subject matter for conversation.

Popular Culture

Culture thus defined did not pre-empt the whole field in the postwar United States. Side by

Formula for a Fashionable Play, 1886

If you want a particular thing done, choose a character to do it that the audience will naturally expect to do it. I wanted a man to fall in love with my heroine after she was a married woman, and I chose a French Count for that purpose. I knew that an American audience would not only expect him to fall in love with another man's wife, but it would be very much surprised if he didn't. . . . Whatever audience you are writing for, your work must be "satisfactory" to it. In England and America, the death of a pure woman on the stage is not "satisfactory" except when the play rises to the dignity of tragedy. The death in an ordinary play of a woman who is not pure, as in the case of "Frou Frou," is perfectly satisfactory, for the reason that it is inevitable. . . . The wife who has once taken the step from purity to impurity can never re-instate herself in the world of art on this side of the grave; and so an audience looks with complacent tears on the death of an erring woman.

—Bronson Howard, *In Memoriam* (New York: The Marion Press, 1910), pp. 94, 100.

side with the architecture, the music, and the literature that the elite possessed and recognized as good, there developed popular forms that the rest of society needed and used—buildings that served a function, music that was sung, and stories that were read, to the authentic satisfaction of ordinary men and women.

The Skyscraper The men who lived in imitation French chateaux or Tudor castles had a different set of standards when it came to buildings in which to display their wares or manufacture their goods. They wanted simple economical structures that would give them the most space at the least cost. They therefore encouraged the use first of cast iron and then of structural steel, which could sustain tall edifices on valuable land. William Le Baron Jenney's ten-story Home Insurance Building in Chicago (1885) demonstrated the feasibility of the skyscraper, which was soon a familiar sight in many other cities as well. Five years later, Louis Sullivan in the Wainwright Building (St. Louis) showed the creative possibilities of the new form.

Readers and Spectators People unconcerned with cultural credentials, too, depended on the test of usefulness. They expected pictures or books to instruct or entertain them. They subscribed to *Life* or *Judge* in order to laugh at the comic drawings or jokes; and they took *Harper's Weekly* or *Frank Leslie's Illustrated Newspaper* to see the affairs of the world in pictures. The circulation of newspapers zoomed, because they provided a happy combination of information and amusement—details of local and national events as well as advertisements, thrilling accounts of crime and disaster, and advice about practical problems.

Popular fiction was instructive insofar as it always proved that virtue triumphed over evil. But it was interesting also because it often dealt with the known perils of urban life or the promises of Western adventure. Charles Dickens was probably the most widely read novelist, with the Reverend E. P. Roe his leading native competitor; both treated the problems of young people making their way in the city, although at different levels of competence. For the popular female audience, there were sentimental domestic tales by Louisa May Alcott or Laura Jean Libbey. And a flood of dime novels fed the great public tales of crime and detection, of Western daring, and of success in business.

There were more spectators than readers in a population still largely unschooled. The drama in the play of luck and skill that determined the winner of an athletic contest was intensified when the rivals struggled for a championship. When the formerly scattered baseball teams organized the National League in 1876,

Bare Knuckles. American primitive painting, *ca*. 1860, by George A. Hayes. (The Granger Collection)

they developed a following deeply involved in their success. The pugilists did the same in systematizing their championship rules.

The drama acted out on the popular stage, too, moved its audience. Authors like Bartley Campbell put together counterparts of the current fiction, emphasizing the virtues of the honest poor, the bravery of the frontiersman, and the guile of the salesman and speculator. The simple plots and the comprehensible rhetoric of these dramas stirred the emotions, and the happy endings left the assurance that all would somehow come out right despite the apparent hardships of the real world.

The stage was the setting also for gaiety and wonder. The old minstrel show and the circus still drew crowds. But elements of both were being combined with features of the English music hall to form the increasingly popular medium of vaudeville. At Tony Pastor's or Keith's, the acrobat, the magician, the singer, the dancer, and above all the rollicking comic each took his turn in amusing the audience.

Here the popular songs gained currency. The sentimental ballads derived from hymns and the funny tunes with Irish or German antecedents clung to the memory, and were replayed from sheet music on the parlor piano or, after 1877, on the cylinders of Thomas Edison's phonograph. The themes were love, absence from home, the death of dear ones, and the frustrations of everyday life.

These songs were not music recognized in the opera house, just as the dime novels were not literature and the drawings in *Life* were not art. The culture defined by society had excluded the

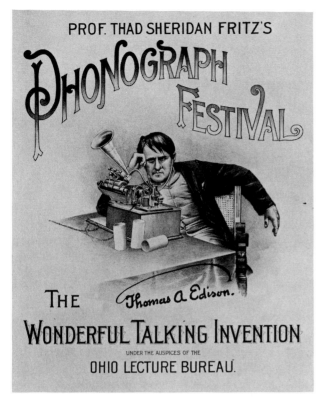

Advertisement for a Phonograph Festival. Lithograph poster, 1890, showing Thomas Edison and his invention. (The Granger Collection)

"Mr. Henry James, as seen by Mr. Max Beerbohm." 1898. (The Granger Collection)

forms that expressed the feelings and thoughts of most Americans.

The Artists

The widening gulf between a narrowly defined culture and the life of the people posed a perplexing problem for creative personalities who could locate audiences neither among the hollow respectables of society nor among the untutored populace. Walt Whitman clung to his Emersonian vision of the common man, pure and perfectible, until his death in 1892. After the Civil War successive revisions of *Leaves of Grass* reflected not only his personal torment but also his confidence in the future. He knew the weaknesses of American society, but insisted that some day all would be well. Others fled—

Henry James, James McNeill Whistler, and John Singer Sargent to Europe, and Emily Dickinson to the secrecy of her own little village.

Still others sought a variety of expedients for getting heard. A few writers found material in local color. Just as the lithographs of Currier and Ives portrayed scenes that appeared to be true and ordinary yet smoothed over the rough features, so Sarah Orne Jewett nostalgically described life in the New England past and Thomas Nelson Page set his novels in the Old South. A sentimental coating flavored also Bret Harte's stories of the West. Even the handful of realistic novelists—Edward Eggleston, W. D. Howells, and Joseph Kirkland—who criticized some aspects of their society, nevertheless labored under the obligation to emphasize the smiling aspects of life. Ed Howe, the one author whose

MARK TWAIN, the name by which Samuel Langhorne Clemens was known as a writer, ruefully observed the changes in his society, not knowing whether to be amused or dismayed by them. He was born in 1835 in Florida, Missouri, and spent much of his youth in nearby Hannibal. His father, a disappointed man who never found the fortune he left Kentucky to seek, died when Sam was twelve. The boy was apprentice to a printer, then drifted as a journeyman all over the country from St. Louis to New York. In 1857 he was piloting a riverboat sailing the Mississippi out of New Orleans. The years of wandering gave him a sharp insight into the character of his countrymen.

When the Civil War put a halt to navigation on the river, Clemens moved to Nevada, where his brother was secretary to the territorial governor. There and in California Clemens began to write and to lecture. His humor caught on. Within a few years he was a success. After the war he traveled to Europe with a group of other Americans, and *The Innocents Abroad* (1869), an account of his encounter with the Old World, established his national reputation. In 1870 he married and settled down.

He enjoyed it all—the success, the popularity of amusing books like *Tom Sawyer* (1876), and the pleasant home his wife made for him. Get-rich-quick schemes tempted him, as they did other Americans. Yet he was deeply critical of his society. Not consistently, but often enough to be disturbing, he kept wondering what had happened to the moral values of the country. In *Huckleberry Finn* (1885), a bitter book beneath its coating of humor, he asked questions more penetrating than those his contemporaries wished to hear. After 1890, personal troubles and disillusion about events in the United States brought despair and then the resignation that clouded the years until his death in 1910.

"American Humor." Mark Twain in a cartoon by Frederick Waddy, 1872. (The Granger Collection)

bitterness defied that convention, found the fewest readers.

Only humor offered a medium through which the artist could speak the truth and yet find numerous listeners, because they did not have to take him seriously. Through the blackface dialect of Uncle Remus, Joel Chandler Harris obliquely criticized the South's failure to deal with its human problems. In the bantering language of Huckleberry Finn, Mark Twain expressed his bitter judgment of the immorality of the gilded age. Such writers, not being fully understood by their audience, could not com-

Justin Kaplan, *Mr. Clemens and Mark Twain* (New York, 1966) is good on the man and his times.

municate with it effectively and hardly comprehended themselves what they were trying to do. The artists sensed the problems of their society, but could not express them clearly; the people read, but did not perceive the seriousness of the joke.

▼

In other parts of the world, industrialization upset even stable, traditional societies. In the United States, where mobility was a habit and change was normal, the transformation of the economy produced widespread social disorder. Competition for the riches now available undermined accepted values and weakened the sense of community.

The victors in the struggle attempted to win recognition as an elite by patronizing a borrowed culture that they expected would sustain their pretensions to aristocracy. The result was estrangement from the artists who might have helped clarify their position and from the people who had a culture, a life, and a society of their own.

Paperbacks for Further Reading

E. Digby Baltzell, *Philadelphia Gentlemen* (Free Press Paperbacks) is a sociological study of that city's leading families, with historical material. Lewis Mumford, *The Brown Decades* (Dover Publications) treats the arts in the thirty years after 1865. Henry-Russell Hitchcock, *The Architecture of H. H. Richardson and His Times* (MIT Press) and Hugh Morrison, *Louis Sullivan: Prophet of Modern Architecture* (W. W. Norton and Company) offer good introductions to one aspect of American culture. Dixon Wecter, *Sam Clemens of Hannibal* (Sentry Editions), Leon Edel, ed., *Henry James* (Spectrum Books), and Arlin Turner, *George W. Cable, A Biography* (Louisiana State University Press) have material on important writers of the period. Constance Rourke, *American Humor* (Anchor Books) is a thoughtful analysis. But the best approach to the culture of the gilded age is through the writings of contemporaries, among them: Mark Twain, *The Innocents Abroad* (Bantam Books) and *The Portable Mark Twain* (Viking Paperbound Portables); Henry James, *The Bostonians* (Modern Library College Editions); William Dean Howells, *The Rise of Silas Lapham* (Perennial Library); Walt Whitman, *The Portable Walt Whitman* (Viking Paperbound Portables); and Edgar W. Howe, *The Story of a Country Town* (Signet Classics).

THE NEW WEST

55

The residents of some parts of the United States resisted the cultural hegemony of Eastern society. The New West and the South, for a time, preserved regional characteristics that distinguished their populations, although toward the end of the century they too felt the impact of national trends.

The long-extended process of settling the continent began to draw to a close after the Civil War. The area of the West then peopled, though intimately linked with the older sections of the country, had a character and an interest of its own. Its turbulent communities were not subject to the control more stable Americans considered desirable, and its institutions were more fluid than elsewhere.

The New West had a marked impact upon the economy. It added to the nation's agricultural strength and provided a great internal market for the products of the expanding factories. In turn, industrialization supplied the transportation, goods, and capital to hasten the spread of population. The process of settlement consequently was extremely rapid, but the speed came at a heavy human cost and left problems that were still unresolved in 1890.

THE WEST, 1860–1890

The Last West

WESTWARD EXPANSION had been a constant factor in American life since the seventeenth century, but the pace had accelerated steadily. It had taken a century and a half to push inward from the Atlantic to the Allegheny Mountains, some 300 miles. It took almost a century to move the next 600 miles to the first tier of states across the Mississippi. But in the forty years after 1850 the whole expanse of 2000 miles to the Pacific was traversed in one vast onrush of settlement.

In the 1850s, the line of settlement had just crossed the Mississippi. In that decade, while the politics of the nation were leading to war, the farmers were moving in a long line between Minnesota and Texas just up to the region of the Great Plains. Smaller groups had made their way by water and overland to outposts along the Pacific, in Oregon, and in California, especially after the gold rush.

The Plains and Mountains Only the Mormons had established themselves in the vast open spaces between the coast and the band of settlement west of the Mississippi in Arkansas, Missouri, and Iowa. The bloody fighting over Kansas had not increased the attractiveness of the region, which was already known as the Great American Desert. The obstacles to traditional agriculture there were formidable. In the Great Plains, the absence of trees deprived the farmer of wood for building, fencing, and fuel, which he had taken for granted in the East. There were few rivers, and the high grass and tough sod resisted the plow. A deficiency of rain parched the soil. Above all, the unfamiliar environment struck

James C. Malin, *Grassland of North America* (Lawrence, Kan., 1947) is an illuminating analysis of the relation of man to environment.

Sand Dunes, Carson Desert, Nevada, 1870. Photograph by T. H. O'Sullivan. (Library of Congress)

The Plains in the 1870s

No one who has not experienced it can dream what it is to live so many years in a glare as we did. Many of the officers were almost blind from time to time, owing to the reflection of the sand over which they marched, and with which they were surrounded in camp and garrison. I once asked a friend who had crossed the plains several times, what she would prefer above everything else on the march. When she replied, "a tree," I agreed with her that nothing else could have been such a blessing.

—Elizabeth B. Custer, *"Boots and Saddles" or Life in Dakota with General Custer*, Jane R. Stewart, ed. (Norman, Okla.: University of Oklahoma Press, 1961), pp. 137–138.

terror in the souls of the men and women who heard stories of the winter blizzards, of the glare of the summer sun, and of the plagues of grasshoppers that periodically swept across the area.

Farther west were the mountain barriers — first the unbroken chain of the Rockies, then beyond the Basin and the Plateau region, the Sierra-Nevada–Cascade system. The lure of gold had drawn the venturesome through these ranges and made the passes familiar, but this was still dangerous terrain for men who wished to make homes for their families. Furthermore, there was no assurance that the Indians would remain on the reservations to which the whites sought to confine them. Real and fancied grievances spurred attacks on travelers and on isolated farmsteads and retarded the arrival of the permanent residents.

By 1890, the advancing settlers had surmounted all these obstacles and had brought the plains under cultivation. Mineral discoveries and

Helena, Montana Territory, June 1870. The discovery of gold in 1864 brought a rush of fortune seekers to the town, formerly known as Last Chance Gulch. (Northern Pacific Railway Company)

a new method of cattle grazing had helped end the Indian danger, while improved transportation had made it possible to market the products raised by new agricultural techniques.

The Mining Frontier The miners were the first to invade the mountains in any number. The gold fever did not abate with the exhaustion of the California diggings. Through the rest of the century, restless prospectors crisscrossed the mountains in quest of the lucky strike. Discoveries of gold and silver in 1859 touched off rushes to the Pike's Peak region of Colorado and to the Washoe district of Nevada; and the same frenzied scenes were repeated in the 1860s in Idaho, Montana, Wyoming, and Arizona and after 1874 in the Black Hills of South Dakota. In all, between 1859 and 1890, miners tore some $2,000,-

T. A. Rickard, *History of American Mining* (New York, 1932) is a rambling but interesting account.

Oscar Lewis, *Silver Kings* (New York, 1947) is a lively description of the men who exploited the mines.

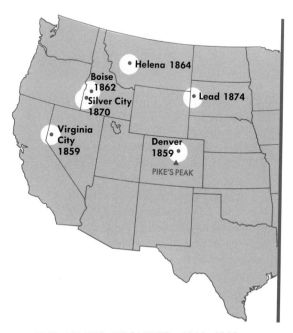

THE MINING FRONTIER, 1860–1890

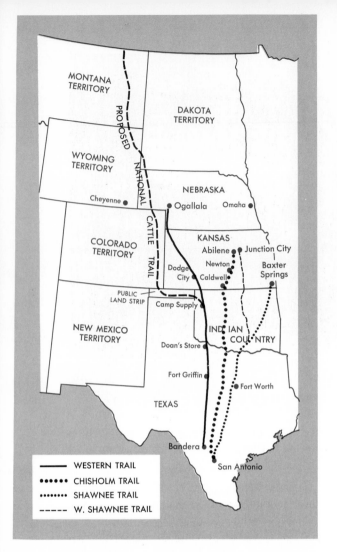

MONTANA
TERRITORY

DAKOTA
TERRITORY

WYOMING
TERRITORY

NEBRASKA

Cheyenne

Ogallala   Omaha

COLORADO
TERRITORY

KANSAS

Abilene   Junction City

Dodge   Newton
City   Caldwell   Baxter
Springs

PUBLIC
LAND STRIP
Camp Supply

NEW MEXICO
TERRITORY

INDIAN
COUNTRY

Doan's Store

Fort Griffin

Fort Worth

TEXAS

Bandera

San Antonio

——— WESTERN TRAIL
•••••• CHISHOLM TRAIL
•••••••• SHAWNEE TRAIL
----- W. SHAWNEE TRAIL

PROPOSED NATIONAL CATTLE TRAIL

CATTLE TRAILS AND COW TOWNS, 1865–1890

000,000 in gold and silver out of the earth, in addition to substantial fortunes in copper, lead, and zinc.

The course of exploitation usually followed the same chaotic pattern. Hundreds of lonely prospectors, guided by hunches and chance, poked through the mountains as long as their stakes endured. When one of these fortune seekers hit upon flecks of gold in some out of the way gulch, he hastened first to lay out his claim, and that at once attracted scores of others. Before long, the tents and huts straggling up the slopes housed a town of 5000 to 10,000. How-

ever, no individual could do more than scratch at the surface with a pick and shovel. To follow the lodes to their innermost recesses, to separate the precious minerals from the quartz, and to ship the gold or silver out required expensive equipment, tunnels, and organization. The discoverers had to sell shares in their claims for the capital. Merchants and saloonkeepers appeared with cash in their fists, and active speculation developed. Usually business acumen proved more important in drawing wealth from the earth than the luck of the first strike.

The most successful bore their gains off to San Francisco, New York, and Europe. But the mineral wealth also built the towns and railroads that served the hordes of digging men and thus created a foundation for the settled society that followed.

The Cattleman's Frontier Another breed of wanderers opened up the Great Plains. Soldiers demobilized after the Civil War were sometimes unwilling to return to the dull routine of civilian life. They might try the diggings for a while or serve as scouts or guides. A few lived by hunting; there was a market for furs and for buffalo meat in army and railway construction camps. Occasionally, bands of desperadoes stepped outside the law and helped themselves by force to the riches others sought by labor. Through the years, adventure-minded Easterners swelled their ranks.

Such people supplied the labor for the range-cattle industry. Already before the Civil War there were great herds on the ample grazing areas of Texas, and after it ranching, using the techniques of branding, roping, and roundups earlier developed by the Mexicans, spread through the Southwest. Some enterprising men began to drive their herds over the long trails to Northern markets, the first terminus being Sedalia, Missouri, on the Missouri Pacific Railroad.

The ingenuity of Joseph M. McCoy, an Illinois meat dealer, put the range-cattle industry

Edward E. Dale, *The Range Cattle Industry* (Norman, Okla., 1930) is a competent study.

A Cattle Chute, Abilene, Kansas. Texas cattle were driven to this early cow town for shipment by rail to Kansas City. From *Frank Leslie's Illustrated Newspaper,* August 19, 1871. (Library of Congress)

on a firm basis. He arranged preferential transportation rates on the Kansas Pacific Railroad and the Hannibal and St. Joseph Railroad, and in 1867 he built yards for the stock at Abilene, Kansas. Thereafter the steers moved regularly to that destination along the Chisholm Trail, which avoided most wooded areas.

The cowboys brought the longhorns in from the open range at annual roundups and drove them in a leisurely march to the shipping points, allowing them to browse in the uninhabited public domain on the way. In the 1870s as many as 350,000 head thus found their way to the slaughterhouses each year.

The long drives became less common in the 1880s. When the herds increased in size, there were conflicts over water rights. As settlers moved in and laid out and fenced farms, they closed off the best routes to the north. The termini shifted further west, to Dodge City and to Cheyenne, but that raised costs. Meanwhile, the refrigerated car, which came into use after 1875, made it possible to ship dressed beef over much longer distances than before. As a result, the slaughterhouses moved westward, closer to the sources of cattle to which the spreading railroad network linked them. Ranching became a stable business.

The long drives created the romantic image of the cowboy. More important, they helped open the region to the settlement that would ultimately close the range. Moving back and forth across the area, the nomadic cowhands passed through the Indian districts and came to know the whole region. The information they spread soon attracted the cultivators.

The Last Stand of the Indians

The intrusion of the white men was a menace to the Indians, of whom there were fewer

Indian Fighting, 1870s

Starting out singly, or by twos and threes, the warriors would suddenly leave the cover of the hillock, and with war whoops and taunts dash over the plain in a line parallel to that occupied by the soldiers, and within easy carbine range of the latter. The pony seemed possessed of the designs and wishes of his dusky rider, as he seemed to fly unguided by bridle, rein, or spur. The warrior would fire and load and fire again as often as he was able to do, while dashing along through the shower of leaden bullets fired . . . by the excited troopers. . . . When the aim of the latter improved and the leaden messengers whistled uncomfortably close, the warrior would . . . cast himself over on the opposite side of his pony, until his foot on the back and his face under the neck of the pony were all that could be seen, the rest of his person being completely covered by the body of the pony.

—George A. Custer, *My Life on the Plains or Personal Experiences with Indians* (New York: Sheldon & Co., 1874), p. 126.

GEORGE ARMSTRONG CUSTER was last in his class when he graduated from West Point. He had never been very lucky. Born in Harrison County, Ohio, in 1839, the son of a farmer, Custer had an unsettled youth, and his blundering continued after he entered the military academy in 1857.

A few days after he received his commission, a court martial found him guilty of failing as officer of the guard to stop a fight. He escaped the consequences, however, because the Civil War was already in progress and officers of any sort were valuable. Gallant to the point of recklessness, Custer attracted the notice first of McClellan and then of Sheridan and moved upward by successive promotions to the rank of major general. This was the most successful period of his life.

With peace, he was reduced to the rank of captain and left with little to do. He thought of resigning to fight with the Mexicans against Maximilian, but remained in the army and joined a cavalry regiment in Kansas. In 1867 he was made the scapegoat for the failure of a campaign against the Indians, but influential friends helped him evade the year's suspension from the army to which he had been sentenced. In the next seven years, various expeditions took him west into the Dakotas. Tall, slender, and strong, he adopted a gaudy costume, lavishly tinseled with gold braid, and highlighted by a cavalier hat and a long scarlet necktie.

Custer's exploration of the Black Hills in 1874 led to the discovery of gold, from which others profited. The influx of white men indirectly led to war with the Sioux a year later. In 1876, Custer was sent at the head of a regiment of 655 men to fight the Sioux and Cheyenne, although President Grant, who disliked him, wished to deprive him of the command. Custer set out in June, heading for the Little Bighorn. There he met an Indian force of about three thousand, and the regiment was wiped out. Custer was blamed by some for recklessness in making the attack too early. The fault, however, seems to have been in planning, for his force was much too small to deal with the Indians.

To some, the West was a source of hope; to Custer, it was cause for disappointment. A variety of experiences awaited the many types of men who opened the vast spaces to settlement.

Apache Prisoners at a Stop on the Southern Pacific Railroad near Nueces River, Texas, 1886. The group was on the way to Fort Sam Houston, San Antonio, Texas, and was eventually taken to Florida. Front row, left to right: Fun and Perico (half brothers of Geronimo), Naiche, Geronimo, Chappo (son of Geronimo), and Chappo's wife. Photograph by A. J. McDonald. (The Smithsonian Institution)

than 250,000 in the Great Plains in the 1860s. The Five Civilized Tribes considered themselves safe in the Indian Territory to which they had been removed in the 1830s, and the sedentary residents of the New Mexico and Arizona pueblos led settled if poverty-stricken lives. But the Sioux, Comanche, Apache, and other nomadic tribes were skilled horsemen who depended for survival on the buffalo, whose meat fed them and whose skin clothed them. Their very existence was threatened by the sportsman or scout who decimated the herds and by the farmer who

fenced in the land. Yet the Indian could no longer retreat farther west. He had no place to go.

Thirty years of intermittent warfare began after 1859, when thousands of miners, and later cowboys and settlers, moved through the plains. The tribesmen, organized in bands of from three hundred to five hundred men, were formidable fighters. Their mobility rendered artillery ineffective against them, and their spirited ponies gave them the advantages of speed and maneuverability. Their stone-tipped arrows were as deadly as the clumsy muzzle-loading guns of the

The Indian Yields, 1877

Tell General Howard I know his heart ... I am tired of fighting. Our chiefs are killed. LOOKING-GLASS is dead. TA-HOOL-HOOL-SHUTE is dead. The old men are all dead. It is the young men who say, "Yes" or "No." He who led the young men is dead. It is cold, and we have no blankets; the little children are freezing to death. My people, some of them, have run away to the hills, and have no blankets, no food. No one knows where they are — perhaps freezing to death. I want to have time to look for my children, and see how many of them I can find. Maybe I shall find them among the dead. Hear me, my chiefs! I am tired; my heart is sick and sad. From where the sun now stands I will fight no more forever.

— Chief Joseph, *Harper's Weekly*, XXI (November 17, 1887), p. 906.

1860s. The officers and troops of the regular army had to learn new tactics; those of the Civil War were futile in this environment.

Occasional pitched battles, such as that at the Little Bighorn in 1876 when General Custer lost his life, were dramatic but not decisive. The Indians hoped to frighten away settlers by raids on wagon trains and homes. The government aimed to force the warriors into submission and confine them on reservations. Both sides were savage, fighting to the death, sparing neither women nor children.

Ultimately the army met the threat by erecting fortified posts from which it could pacify and protect the country. Gradually the superior resources won out. A new carbine increased the effectiveness of the cavalry's fire. The railroad, once built, was not vulnerable to sudden raids. Chief Sitting Bull was still able to lead a Sioux uprising in 1889, but the Indian's power to resist lessened as the settlers multiplied and the buffalo

herds dwindled. In the end the chiefs learned, as one of them explained in Oregon in 1877, that they could fight no more forever.

Repression alone did not solve the problem. The Indians remained an inconvenience even when they were content to stay on the reservation and live off the annuities and rations doled out by the Federal government. The agents sent by the Department of the Interior to supervise and educate them were inefficient and sometimes corrupt; and few of the licensed traders had scruples about cheating the red men. Easterners, safely distant from the frontier, were indignant at the maltreatment revealed in Helen Hunt Jackson's *A Century of Dishonor* (1881). Westerners, avid for the land withheld from settlement, were eager to find some way to dissolve the reservations.

These discordant motives combined to secure enactment of the Dawes Severalty Act in 1887. By this law, the President could end tribal government when he judged any group of Indians ready for assimilation. Each individual would then receive an allotment of land of his own, become an American citizen, and, presumably, settle down to peaceful farming.

The full effects would not be felt until later, for the recipients were not allowed to sell or mortgage their holdings for twenty-five years. But almost at once the new law so diluted the tribesmen's sense of solidarity that they were scarcely capable of further resistance to the schemes of grasping speculators and settlers for obtaining their land. It was indicative of the trend that, in 1889, the areas previously reserved in the Indian Territory (Oklahoma) were thrown open to white settlement.

The Settlers

The miners and the cowboys, the Indians and the army camps were giving way to the advancing host of permanent settlers. Forbidding

Donald Jackson, *Custer's Gold* (New Haven, Conn., 1966), a well-written story of the expedition of 1874, throws light on Custer and on western expansion.

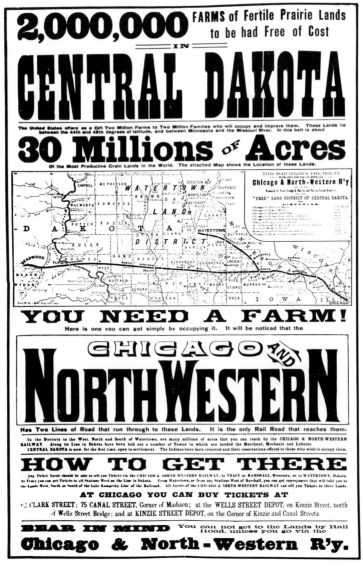

A Chicago and North-Western Railroad Broadside of the 1870s Advertising Free Land. (The Granger Collection)

though they seemed at first, the lands of the West attracted thousands of families ready to make homes there. Many continued to reach their destinations by wagon. But the fact that railroads to the Pacific passed through the region before its permanent residents arrived accelerated the movement. Transportation was far easier and swifter than it had been on any previous frontier.

Breaking the Plains The homestead law (1862) put a holding at the disposal of citizens willing to go through the process of proving a claim, but many found it easier and safer to buy their acres from speculators or from the railroads, which had immense domains to dispose of. The private sale brought an immediate title, could usually be made on credit, and often covered the preferred tracts. The railroads, eager to develop the traffic along their routes, made every effort to attract farmers through agents and advertisements in Europe and the East; and special immigrant fares lowered the cost of bringing families directly to the Great Plains.

The containment of the Indian threat removed an obstacle to settlement; technological innovations and adjustments to the new environment eased the farmers' difficulties. Houses built of sod reduced the need for timber. Barbed wire fencing, invented in the early 1870s in Illinois by Joseph F. Glidden and Jacob Haish, eliminated the need for wood fencing and protected crops against trespassing animals. The Oliver drilled-steel plow cut through the hard-baked topsoil. Irrigation, already practiced by the Mormons, and deep wells powered by windmills compensated for the lack of water. Furthermore, the unencumbered plains offered a particularly auspicious setting for the use of agricultural machinery. Huge combines, some of them powered by steam, were able to reap and bind tremendous crops with relatively efficient use of man power.

A New Agriculture The character of the topography encouraged the appearance in California and in the Great Plains of large bonanza farms, on which entrepreneurs cultivated thousands of acres using gangs of hired hands and numerous machines. A good deal of Eastern and English capital went into such ventures which were expected to profit from the enormous new capacity for production. At Casselton on the Red River, in Dakota Territory, one of these mammoth enterprises occupied 115 square miles and used 600 workers during the harvest. But this was a brief development; by 1890, the rise in land values made it more profitable to divide great units into family-size holdings, which could be operated more intensively.

A steady growth of population accompanied the expansion of agriculture. Kansas and Nebraska, where settlement had begun before the Civil War, each had more than a million inhabitants by 1890. The rest of the area grew, too, and moved swiftly toward statehood, hastened by the calculations of Republican leaders that senators from the region would add to the party's strength. Nevada had had a population of less than 30,000 when it was admitted to statehood in 1864. Three years later, Nebraska became a state. The mining boom justified the grant of statehood to Colorado in 1876, and omnibus bills extended that status to South Dakota, North Dakota, Montana, and Washington in 1889 and to Wyoming and Idaho in 1890. For a time the conflict over polygamy kept Utah a territory, together with Oklahoma, Arizona, and New Mexico.

Western Cities

Towns first appeared to serve the miners and cowhands. Behind the hitching rails that lined the dusty road, saloons supplied the whiskey and prostitutes, and general stores the food and equipment, brought in by stagecoach, that made a hard life tolerable. This was the wide-open West where men took their chances and made their own law. Speculative types like Jim Wardner, tough, quick-drawing fighters like Wild Bill Hickok, devil-may-care youngsters like Jesse James, faced one another in a play for fortune in which anyone might turn up the lucky card. Here at first there was no law except that which the mob or the secret vigilante groups imposed.

Some of these towns faded away when the diggings were exhausted or the drives ended; the false wooden fronts of their deserted buildings blistered quietly in the summer sun. Others grew into substantial cities, as bankers and merchants developed their enterprises and railroads linked them to national markets. Venturesome physicians, lawyers, and preachers established themselves; a communal order took form, and churches, schools, perhaps even an opera house, were built. The rough and ready frontier receded into history.

San Francisco was already a metropolis in 1860, and its 60,000 inhabitants prided themselves on their cosmopolitanism. In 1890, the

Cowboy Saloon in the Former Town of Tascosa, Texas. Tascosa was noted as a tough frontier town in the 1870s and 1880s. (Library of Congress)

JAMES BUTLER HICKOK had his own way of bringing the law to the frontier. A handsome and quiet man, he would nevertheless be known through much of his life as Wild Bill. He had a passion for order, even if force was necessary to attain it. La Salle County, Illinois, where he was born on May 27, 1837, was still frontier when he was a boy. The Indians were a threat, and he spent much of his youth as a hunter. The community's struggle to emerge from the wilderness left its mark on him.

In 1855, at the age of eighteen, Hickok went to Kansas where he joined the free-state elements fighting against slavery. He now first experienced the need to fight for law, and for a time was a constable. He then became a stagecoach driver, first on the Santa Fe Trail and later on the Overland Trail to Oregon. Stories came to be told of his fighting qualities—how he killed a bear with his bowie knife, how he shot down the McCanles Gang. In the Civil War, he was a Union scout.

In 1866 Hickok was back in law enforcement. As deputy marshal in Fort Riley, Kansas, and as marshal in Abilene, he fought thieves, outlaws, and Indians and ruled with an iron hand. He killed the saloonkeeper Phil Coe in an encounter that became a gunfighting classic. For him, need to maintain the law justified violence.

In 1872 William F. (Buffalo Bill) Cody persuaded Hickok to tour the East with him. No doubt the experience of being on show affected him adversely, and the frontier was beginning to outlive its need for gunmen. When he came back to Deadwood in Dakota Territory in 1876, Jack McCall outdrew him.

population was almost 300,000. By then it had acquired a potent rival in Denver, the population of which zoomed from about 4000 in 1870 to more than 100,000 in 1890. Mormon enterprise sustained about 45,000 people in Salt Lake City in 1890; in the Northwest, Seattle and Tacoma were then only slightly smaller, and Spokane had almost reached the 20,000 mark. On the edge of the East, Omaha had become a meat-packing and grain-trading center; its population grew from 30,000 in 1880 to 140,452 in 1890. By the latter date industry was established deep in the interior; Pueblo, Colorado, for instance, was manufacturing steel.

Whether on the Pacific Coast or in the interior, size and time brought the familiar urban problems, compounded by the high costs of labor and materials. Towns were built and re-built to meet the changing needs for housing and municipal services. There was a struggle to curb the individualism of the turbulent characters drawn into the region by the promise of quick and easy fortunes or of adventure. Law and the jury slowly replaced the six-shooter and the lynching party as Westerners created an orderly society. Evidences of recency persisted, however, even in 1890. Life was easygoing among people who were all, more or less, new arrivals and all on their way up. Manners in the mansions on San Francisco's Nob Hill long remained more casual than in the East.

Hostility to the Chinese revealed the survival of violent elements. Cantonese peasants had come to labor on the railroads and in the mines and to perform such humble services as laundering in the mining towns. Their numbers

Chinese in the United States, 1860–1890

Year	Number	Percent Males
1860	34,000	94.9
1870	64,000	92.8
1880	105,000	95.5
1890	107,000	96.4

increased decade by decade, and they found a welcome at first in communities accustomed to differences among the Mexican, Indian, Anglo-American, and foreign-born populations.

There were occasional expressions of unfriendliness to the Chinese in the 1850s, but time intensified rather than relaxed the hostility. The Orientals, unlike European immigrants, rarely brought their families with them or intended to strike roots. Instead, they remained sojourners, striving to accumulate the savings that would take them back to their ancestral homes. The Chinese therefore did not become a part of the communities in which they lived. Their strange appearance and their distinctive customs antagonized the whites, particularly the laborers, who feared their competition. Racist agitation, sparked by Denis Kearney and the Workingmen's Party of California, ultimately led to a series of Federal exclusion laws, beginning in 1882; the Orientals were frequent victims, too, of mob action. The easy tolerance of the earlier period of settlement was giving way to a concern with position as social lines hardened.

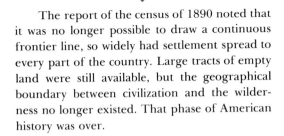

The report of the census of 1890 noted that it was no longer possible to draw a continuous frontier line, so widely had settlement spread to every part of the country. Large tracts of empty land were still available, but the geographical boundary between civilization and the wilderness no longer existed. That phase of American history was over.

The climactic experience of the forty years between 1850 and 1890 had recapitulated a process played out on earlier frontiers. The advance agents—miners, cowboys, and speculators—had opened the area; the Indians had put up only temporary resistance; and agriculture had supplied the basis for thriving permanent communities. But industry and the railroad had sped up the whole cycle and all of American society felt the consequences.

Paperbacks for Further Reading

Walter P. Webb, *The Great Plains* (Universal Library) is a thoughtful and sensitive discussion of the relations between culture and environment. Everett Dick, *Vanguards of the Frontier* (Bison Books) is a social history of the northern plains and the mountains. There are sections on this period in B. H. Hibbard, *A History of the Public Land Policies* (University of Wisconsin Press) and in Roy M. Robbins, *Our Landed Heritage* (Bison Books). Ernest S. Osgood, *The Day of the Cattleman* (Phoenix Books) is a good general description and Andy Adams, *Log of a Cowboy* (Bison Books) is a first hand account. C. H. Shinn, *Mining Camps* (Harper Torchbooks) is a stimulating analysis, and Mark Twain, *Roughing It* (Holt, Rinehart and Winston) contains lively contemporary observations. Stanley Vestal, *Joe Meek* (Bison Books) and Aubrey L. Haines, ed., *Journal of a Trapper* (Bison Books) contain material on the mountain men. William T. Hagan, *American Indians* (Chicago History of American Civilization Series); Wilcomb E. Washburn, ed., *The Indian and the White Man* (Anchor Books); and D'Arcy McNickle, *The Indian Tribes of the United States* (Institute of Race Relations) are general works. Interesting specialized accounts include: Mari Sandoz, *Crazy Horse* (Bison Books); Merril D. Beal, *"I Will Fight No More Forever"* (University of Washington Press); Robert M. Utley, *The Last Days of the Sioux Nation* (Yale University Press). Useful local studies include: Howard R. Lamar, *Dakota Territory* (Yale University Press) and Nels Anderson, *Desert Saints: The Mormon Frontier in Utah* (Phoenix Books).

THE NEW SOUTH

56

The South suffered more than any other section from the effects of the Civil War, and peace brought no end to the trials of the states of the former Confederacy. Reconstruction after 1865 produced its own strains and hardships. A whole generation grew up in an uneasy atmosphere.

Many Southerners therefore welcomed the end of Reconstruction in 1876 with a high sense of expectation. They glimpsed then the possibility of creating a new South stronger than the old. Peace and order would permit them to develop the resources of the section and catch up with the rest of the country.

But there was a profound ambiguity in their outlook. They sought to model the new South on the pattern of the other parts of the nation. Yet at the same time they cherished ideals from their past; above all, the heritage of slavery continued to influence their future. The new South, like the old, had distinctive regional problems and attitudes.

The Redeemers in Control

THERE CAME A TIME IN EACH of the conquered states when the vanquished began to perceive that they might not have to pay the price of defeat. The precise moment varied from place to place, depending on the force of the Federal presence and the strength of the local Reconstruction governments. But sooner or later the failure of experiments in social change, the weariness of the conquerors, and the longing for peace persuaded the former planters and their allies that they could regain control. After 1876, when the last Federal troops withdrew, their ambitions were close to fulfillment. The Redeemers like Wade Hampton were free of external interference.

Political Control   Each state followed its own course within the general pattern. Most often the exhausted communities looked for guidance to their former leaders. For the whites, memory of the lost cause was a unifying force; men who had fought together forgot the agony of battle and recalled its glory and adventure. Respect for the old commanders nurtured political loyalty and elevated Confederate officers to power at every level, at the county seat and at the state capital. As for the Negroes, once the hope of a great new day had vanished, it seemed better to accept responsible orderly rule—even by the masters of the past—than to remain exposed to sporadic violence.

Local control was characteristic of the politics of the region. The emphasis on states' rights reflected not only tradition but also the determination to offset influences from Washington. But Baton Rouge and Montgomery were far from dominating the states of which they were the capitals. In the Louisiana parish or the Alabama county, the judge, the sheriff, the lawyers, and the planters formed tightly knit cliques which elected members of the legislature, administered justice, decided on taxes and public expenditures, and were influential in all other

WADE HAMPTON was almost sixty when, in 1876, he was elected governor of South Carolina. A long career of public service lay behind him, but for a decade he had devoted himself almost entirely to private affairs. Now he agreed to take office in order to help redeem his native state.

Hampton was born in 1818, offspring of a well-known family of planters and merchants. He entered South Carolina College and studied law, then settled down to managing his plantation, with occasional periods of service in the legislature. In 1856 he became a state senator. He had come to doubt the soundness of slavery and believed secession was inexpedient, but he supported the decision to withdraw from the Union once it was made. He fought through the war dutifully, was twice wounded, and by 1862 was a brigadier general.

After the peace, the Reconstruction government, controlled by Republicans, gave Hampton no opportunity to hold office, so he devoted his time to his lands. On the withdrawal of the troops, the old planting families he represented were again able to assert their control. In his two terms as governor, Hampton began restoration of the state's earlier political and social system. He returned to the United States Senate and served there through the 1880s, his greatest effort being the defeat of the Force Bill in 1891. He helped establish white supremacy by evading a general armed conflict with the Negroes and by working out peaceful means of retaining power.

Ironically, the fruits of victory slipped from him in the 1890s. A new element of small white farmers then made their protests heard. Hampton lost his seat in the Senate, and although he held some minor posts thereafter, his influence had faded by the time he died in 1902.

public and private affairs. The rural areas were strong enough to retain a disproportionately large share of political power.

After 1876, the South was solidly Democratic. Past affiliations and the issues of war and peace, as well as the current emphasis upon states' rights, assured that party of control. Republican efforts to maintain a foothold below the Mason-Dixon line were half hearted and ineffectual. Dissidents within the region consequently lacked any organized national support with which to challenge the entrenched local powers.

The result of this tight control was a narrow view of the scope of government, especially after 1876. The influential citizens sought to reverse the spending policies of the Reconstruction regimes in order to lower taxes, which bore most heavily on them. In any case, groups that had their own ways of running their communities saw no need for the expansion of state services. Among the first institutions to suffer were the schools.

Whatever opposition existed came from within the developing single-party framework. A Republican organization survived, sustained by pockets of Federal officeholders, but it had lost hope of carrying elections and accommodated itself to the position of a permanent minority. The only effective dissent came from among the Democrats.

Sources of Conflict Divisions turned on a variety of issues. In the 1870s the memory of prewar alignments was still fresh; in some states, former Whigs and former Democrats then fought for control of the dominant party. Everywhere, ambitious young men, for whom politics was the most likely means of advancement, challenged the position of the old-timers, and personal and factional feuds produced intermittent conflicts that reached from the local courthouse to the state capital. Occasional splits over economic matters sometimes arrayed the country against the city, poor farmers against rich, and those who claimed to speak for the people against the Bourbons, as the conservative Redeemers came

to be called. But until the end of the 1880s these conflicts occurred within the limits of the Democratic party, which was the primary instrument of political control.

The Negro

The presence in the South of about six million Negroes, more than a third of the population of the region, complicated politics, as it did every other aspect of life. The high hopes generated by liberation had proved illusory. The freedmen, lacking land, capital, or skill, now had to make their own way in the face of widespread prejudice against them.

Up from Slavery The great achievement of the Negroes was the formation of stable family units. They resisted every effort to keep them on the old plantations, with all that that implied in terms of dependence; attempts to get them to work for wages were usually unsuccessful. They sought holdings of their own, even if as tenants, because that was the setting of free family life. Slowly they learned the unfamiliar tasks of independent existence, how to buy and sell, how to make contracts, how to plant and pick without the direction of the overseer. They had to put aside the temptation to idleness and the careless habits of the time when their labor belonged to others, and to do so in a discouraging rural environment in which hostile whites stood ready to cheat and exploit them. By 1890, fully 120,000 Negroes were landowners, a small proportion of the families of their race but a respectable one in terms of their start as slaves and in terms of the obstacles they had to surmount.

Timidity and lack of information inhibited their movement; it was safer to face known than unknown difficulties. But in the 1880s some Negroes began to seek opportunity where there was a shortage of hands, in the richer Mississippi delta, in the Southwest, and in the cities. A few began small businesses to cater to their own neighbors, and now and then a craftsman used

Joel Williamson, *After Slavery* (Chapel Hill, N.C., 1965) is an excellent study of South Carolina Negroes.

Southern Freedmen. (Library of Congress)

his skill advantageously. But teaching and the ministry in their own schools and churches were the only professions open to Negroes, and the chances for any improvement in status remained pitifully slim. The educational institutions available to Negro youth therefore tended to lower their sights, concentrating on teaching the simpler manual, agricultural, and commercial subjects appropriate to people with narrow expectations.

Segregation Social disabilities were as important as economic limitations in holding the freedmen back. The stroke of Lincoln's pen did not efface the effects of two centuries of slavery; nor did the Thirteenth or Fourteenth Amend-

ment. Once the Federal troops were gone—and in some places much sooner—the former masters insisted on and received the old deference. The racial etiquette now became general; the worst white was superior to the best black. A pattern of segregation formalized the inferiority of the Negro that had earlier been established by his servitude. He was always to remain apart, stand back, and give way as a constant reminder that freedom had not brought him equality.

There was no sharp line between black and white districts, but Negroes tended to live together in the meaner quarters, and they attended their own schools and usually rode on separate railway cars. Few, of course, had the

Segregation in Practice, 1870

The action was brought by Redding and wife, the plaintiffs, to recover damages for an injury sustained by the wife in the passenger saloon of the defendant. The facts of the case are as follows: While the wife, on the evening of February, 1870, was sitting at the depot of the defendant in Charleston, in the parlor assigned for lady passengers, awaiting the departure of the train for Columbia, which she proposed to take, one Wollen, assuming to have charge of the said room, as the servant of the defendant, informed her that he was instructed to keep negroes out of that parlor; and, on her refusal to leave, he seized and dragged her out with violence—throwing her on her face to the floor. About a month before, the same man had ordered her out of the parlor, saying that his instructions were to keep negroes out; and, on being told by her that she was not a negro, he apologized, and further interference ceased. Martin, who had charge of the whole premises, constituting the depot, testified: "That the first thing Wollen was employed for was to attend the ladies' room, to keep it clean, sweep it out, empty the chambers, and such things. That this was his only employment; and orders had, before that time, been given to make no distinction at all"—meaning between white and colored persons.

—Opinion of Justice J. J. Wright of the Supreme Court of South Carolina in *Redding and Wife* v. the *S.C.R.R. Co.* (Columbia: Republican Printing Company, 1872), p. 3.

The Plight of the Freed Negro. Cartoon, wood engraving by Thomas Nast, *Harper's Weekly*, October 24, 1874. (Library of Congress)

An Alabama Redeemer Appeals for Negro Votes, 1867

My colored friends, we are Southern men, born upon the same soil, live in the same country, and will sleep in the same graveyard when life's troubles are over. . . . It is alike your duty and interest to cultivate friendly relations with your neighbors and former owners, who are today, and even have been, your best friends. . . . I am deprived of citizenship. . . . I am prostrated by the war, but I will assist you all I can. . . . [The Radicals] want office; they want spoils; and they want to retain power. It is quite pleasant and profitable to them. It is not because they love you better than other people. I warn you against [them] and all like [them], at home or abroad. . . . I thank you for the respectful attention you have given me.

—General Clanton in Montgomery, Ala., as quoted in the *Charleston Daily Courier*, May 19, 1867. Cited in Paul Lewinson, *Race. Class, and Party* (New York: Universal Library Edition, 1965), pp. 42, 43.

Negro Self-Help, 1883

There is a society organized among them to look after and provide for the wants of those who are out of a job. That makes them perfectly independent and relieves them from all fear of being discharged, because when they are discharged they go right straight to some of these "sisters." They have a great many societies and they have some funny names for them. They have the society of the "Immaculate Doves," and the society of the "Sisteren," and the society of the "Beloved Disciples," and societies with all kinds of curious names within their church organizations, and those societies undertake to take care of their members. When one dies the members all come out in uniform, men and women, and parade up and down the town with white bonnets and black dresses, and, in fact, whenever they hear of the death of any brother or sister it is just like a "scursion" to them.

—Statement to Senate Committee on Labor and Capital, W. L. Fleming, ed., *Documentary History of Reconstruction* (Cleveland: The A. H. Clark Co., 1906–1907), vol. II, pp. 444–445.

means to venture into good hotels or restaurants. Since the statutes did not yet define a separation, the pattern was not clear or consistent.

No matter what the law said, the violence that assured enforcement of the prescribed rules of behavior was never far below the surface. Even where the Black Codes no longer stood in the statute book, their spirit lingered on. Since judges and juries were entirely white, the Negro found no protection in the law, whether he was accused of crime or was the victim of an attack. Once convicted even of a minor offense, he could in many states be bound into peonage. And always he lived in the shadow of the threat of lynching. Hence he had no means of influencing the state that failed to protect him.

In some places Negroes still exercised the right to vote and held office. They continued to serve in Congress and in the state legislatures of Virginia, North Carolina, South Carolina, and Louisiana. They were likely, in such cases, to act as a political counterweight to the poor whites who ventured to contest the control of the dominant Redeemers. In any event, the Negroes could not work toward ends of their own; at best, they were political tools of the whites, who really held power. With so large a part of its population condemned to inferiority, the South as a whole could not rise very far.

Booker T. Washington's appraisal of the situation seemed realistic. The Negro was a part of the South and would have to learn to live

BOOKER T. WASHINGTON learned that it was possible to rise from slavery, but that there was a ceiling beyond which a nineteenth-century Negro could not climb. He was born a slave in Franklin County, Virginia, in 1856. Sharing a tiny one-room cabin with his mother, his brother, and his sister, until the age of seven he never slept in a bed. Probably his father was white.

Among Booker's earliest recollections was that of his mother praying for freedom. After emancipation she walked west with her children to Malden, West Virginia, where she hoped they would be able to make something of themselves. With the help of Webster's spelling book, she taught Booker to read, and he continued to study while he worked in a salt furnace. Education, he knew, would be his means of advancing.

At the age of sixteen he made his way to Hampton Institute, a teacher-training school for Negroes founded in 1868. He spent three years there, supporting himself by work as a janitor. Although he had learned the brickmason's trade, he determined to be a teacher. After he received his diploma, he held several posts in various parts of the South.

In 1881, on the recommendation of the principal at Hampton Institute, Washington became head of a new Negro normal school in Tuskegee, Alabama. There he found his true vocation. A competent administrator and a persuasive advocate of the Negro's cause, he succeeded in eliciting substantial contributions from white sympathizers. This permitted him to expand the institution, increase its faculty, and train thousands of students in skills that would enable them to be self-supporting.

The price he paid was acceptance of the existing social system with its discriminations against Negroes. In all things that were social, he accepted the separateness of his race, but he insisted that the Negro share in the economic well-being of the region. Given the conditions of the South in the last decades of the century, this was no doubt the only feasible course for the minority.

After 1900, Washington met increasing resistance from a newer generation of Negro leaders, many of them raised and educated in the North. Having themselves never known slavery, they were impatient with his compromises and pushed for a broader concept of equality. When he died in 1915, the Negroes were leaving the South; they were no longer content to recognize the ceiling to their aspirations that he had had to accept.

The Only Trouble Now, 1884

Here is the only thing that we are troubled about now, about civil rights. A colored man and his wife may go to work to get a little home, may go hungry and naked to educate a daughter, the dearest treasure that they have got, and the very moment that she begins to come up there is an inroad made upon her by the whites of this country, and we have got no redress in the world. . . . Now I want as much civil rights and rules to regulate and protect my family as any white man does. . . . That is what we want, to protect the virtue of our girls. That is the rights I want. I don't want no social equality with the white people, and I don't want them to have none with me.

—J. K. Green, Montgomery, Ala., to Senate Committee on Labor and Capital, W. L. Fleming, ed., *Documentary History of Reconstruction* (Cleveland: The A. H. Clark Co., 1906–1907), vol. II, pp. 445–446.

AREA OF TOBACCO

AREA OF COTTON

THE SOUTHERN ECONOMY, 1890

there as best he could, even if that meant acceptance of its disagreeable rules. He would create
a separate communal life, worship in his own
churches, form his own lodges, and read his
own newspapers; he could thus exist with dignity
in the separate orbit white society tolerated.
Whatever the distant future might bring, for
the moment he had to set aside the aspiration
toward social equality and make himself useful
as a farmer or craftsman. Tuskegee and similar
institutions would provide him with the skills
that rendered labor profitable. He would be
able to consider larger goals only after he could
support himself. Given the condition of the
economy of the South, that in itself was no easy
task.

Economic Development

Agriculture The South remained primarily
agricultural. Almost all the Negroes and a great
majority of the whites lived by tilling the soil. The
inefficiencies in their way of doing so condemned
the region to poverty.

In the hills and on the exhausted uplands
the poor whites engaged in haphazard farming
much as they had for the century before the
Civil War. They eked out a meager existence but
could accumulate no surpluses. Always victims
of malnutrition and subject to debilitating illness,
they counted themselves lucky to survive.

The better lands sold at a price too high for
people such as these, and were given over to

"The Cotton Market in New Orleans." Painting, 1873, by H. G. Edgar Degas. (Musée des Beaux-Arts, Pau, France; The Bettmann Archive)

cultivation of the prewar staples. Kentucky was at first the great center of tobacco production, but as the smoking habit spread, there was a rising demand for the leaf best grown in North Carolina and Virginia. Louisiana, by contrast, remained the predominant source of domestic rice and sugar. The output of these three crops rose steadily once the damage of the war had been repaired.

But cotton was king, as it had been in the 1850s. Sustained demand from domestic and foreign textile mills and new uses for cottonseed created an ample market. Fresh lands in eastern Texas entered into use and the older areas were

gradually restored to cultivation. It took about a decade for production to regain its 1860 level of about 4,000,000 bales; then it climbed to about more than 6,000,000 in 1880 and more than 8,000,000 in 1890.

A difficult readjustment accounted first for the delay and then for the sudden spurt. The plantation simply would not work without slavery; it was necessary to find an alternative in various forms of tenantry. The number of holdings therefore rose steadily decade by decade. Divided into small plots, the land went to white and Negro laborers who paid the owner either a fixed rent in money or cotton or a share of the crop—the amount depending on who supplied the tools and equipment. Ultimately a distinction appeared between the white and Negro farmers. The former were share tenants, considered by law owners of the crops from which they paid one-third as rent to the landowners. The Negroes, on the other hand, were generally held to be sharecroppers whose produce by law belonged to the landlord from whom they received their two-thirds as wages. The distinction was significant mainly in defining the inferior status of the former slave.

Under the best of circumstances the tenancy system was inefficient for it had the virtues neither of the large-scale plantation nor of the yeoman farm. The tenant lacked incentive to improve a holding that was not his own; the owner lacked control over production. Agriculture in the South therefore remained backward, unrelieved by the mechanization and scientific techniques that developed elsewhere.

In addition, there were abuses. The tenants, white or Negro, lived from harvest to harvest on credit supplied by the owner or by the middlemen who bought the crop. Debt became a bog from which the cropper could never extricate himself. Year by year he labored harder to increase the yield, often punishing the land in the process. Output rose in the desperate effort to get ahead of the game, but the rewards rarely went to the men who tilled the soil; and the competition between Negro and white tenants inhibited any effort to break out of the hopeless cycle.

Manufacturing The miserable little farms were not, of course, the New South of which there was much talk in these years. The Atlanta editor Henry W. Grady, who helped make the term popular, referred rather to the spirit of enterprise, especially in the border states and in the uplands, which aimed to industrialize the region after the Northern model. The New South was no longer to cling to its rural values

Raymond B. Nixon, *Henry W. Grady, Spokesman of the New South* (New York, 1943) is a competent biography.

Population Residing in Cities of 10,000 or More, United States and Southern States, 1890

Place	Percentage of Total Population
United States	27.59
Louisiana	23.65
Kentucky	13.87
Virginia	12.85
Florida	12.02
Tennessee	10.65
Georgia	9.91
Texas	9.71
South Carolina	6.11
West Virginia	5.85
Alabama	5.23
North Carolina	3.37
Arkansas	3.30
Mississippi	2.64

but was to hasten, by way of the factory and railroad, to catch up with the times.

The growth of Southern cities seemed to justify the optimism of the New South's spokesmen. Atlanta emerged from the ashes of war and grew to a population of 65,533 in 1890. New Orleans, with 242,039 residents that year, remained the queen of the Mississippi; and Louisville, Nashville, Memphis, and Richmond could boast of substantial gains.

However, urbanization scarcely affected the rural character of the region as a whole, and trade remained the primary activity of such cities as did appear. In urban areas bankers, brokers, and merchants carried on the transactions that brought the staples to their markets. A railway boom in the 1880s strengthened the region's transportation system and added to the business of its cities, but with a few exceptions, notably Birmingham (which had a population of only 26,000 in 1890), manufacturing did not thrive there.

The most important industrial development came in the mill towns of the border states and depended upon proximity to raw materials. The enterprise of the Duke family helped establish the cigarette factories of North Carolina, the output of which increased fivefold between 1880 and 1890. New cotton mills raised the number of spindles substantially and for the first time the primacy of Northern textiles was challenged. In comparison with the situation of 1860, these results were gratifying, but they still left the South far behind other parts of the nation. Only a small proportion of the Southern population was employed by industry—in 1890, no more than 3 percent of the labor force, as compared with about 20 percent in the country as a whole.

Further industrial expansion depended upon a supply of capital, which was difficult to recruit. The local entrepreneurs who built the mills had limited resources and banking was slower to develop in the South than elsewhere. Furthermore, neither Northerners nor Europeans were easily persuaded to send their funds into a region that seemed stagnant, was troubled by racial divisions, and had a reputation for repudiating its financial obligations.

Some of the rhetoric of the New South was directed primarily at outsiders in an attempt to persuade potential investors that a spirit of enterprise favored new ventures. The arguments most used stressed the low taxes and the cheap labor of the region, so that even when factories appeared, there were few benefits for the population as a whole. Favorable assessments, purposely kept low to attract new firms, shifted the tax burden from manufacturers to farmers. In general, the desire to lure industry increased the reluctance to raise either wages or the level of public expenditures and thus deepened the backwardness of much of the area.

Whatever manufacturing developed depended on labor drawn from among the poor whites who drifted into the towns. Prejudice and inertia prevented the hiring of Negroes. Moreover, there was a determined effort through state bureaus to attract European immigrants who, it

Broadus and George S. Mitchell, *The Industrial Revolution in the South* (Baltimore, Md., 1930) is a good survey.

was hoped, would add to white strength. But foreigners were reluctant to compete with the native cheap labor or to become involved in existing racial difficulties. The number of newcomers was small.

The Value of Tradition

The growth of some branches of manufacturing had relatively little effect upon the South. The plantation heritage continued to shape social and cultural values. The remnants of the old families clung to their status and set the tone for the newly rich. The lower strata, clearly marked off from one another, resented but at the same time respected the faded elegance of their superiors. All whites were united by a common bond that distinguished them from Negroes, the lowest group of all; the sense of racial unity therefore often offset the economic causes of conflict between rich and poor. As for the Negroes, they had reason to believe that they had less to fear from a conservative man of wealth than from those whites who were almost as poor as themselves.

By the 1880s the dominant Southerners showed less concern with rectifying than with justifying the errors of the past. Slavery had disappeared, but racist theories sustained the belief in Negro inferiority. The great plantation houses, the life of leisure, and the gentlemanly aversion to work remained the ideals of a rural Southern culture distinct from that of the rest of the nation.

The remoteness of these ideals from reality generated nostalgic and lethargic daydreams more often than action. For the majority of poor whites, the only status worthy of their color seemed unattainable and nothing else was worth striving for. Only a few actually bent their efforts toward realizing the goals of the New South. The most energetic and ambitious moved to the cities and to the North. Despite efforts to encourage immigration, the number of Southerners

North-South Migrations, 1870–1890

Year	Number Born in North, Living in South	Percentage of Total Born in North	Number Born in South, Living in North	Percentage of Total Born in South	Net Gain of North
1870	298,000	1.5	1,050,000	8.3	752,000
1880	473,000	1.9	1,112,000	6.7	639,000
1890	635,000	2.0	1,135,000	5.8	500,000

who left the region was substantially larger than the number of outsiders who entered it.

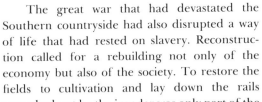

The great war that had devastated the Southern countryside had also disrupted a way of life that had rested on slavery. Reconstruction called for a rebuilding not only of the economy but also of the society. To restore the fields to cultivation and lay down the rails wrenched out by the invader was only part of the task Southerners faced in 1865. They also had to restore communities that once had rested on slavery.

How new would the New South be? The position of the Negro—neither fully free nor fully equal—was the key to the answer. Modernization called for the surrender of prewar habits of thought and action and the recognition by society of the rights of all its members. Though some men understood the need for catching up with their times, few were willing or able to relinquish the past. The South remained preponderantly rural and the legacy of the Civil War and Reconstruction compounded the difficulties from which the farmers of the whole nation suffered.

Paperbacks for Further Reading

Among the general books on the South which throw light on the problems of this period are: Wilbur J. Cash, *Mind of the South* (Vintage Books, Inc.); Charles G. Sellers, Jr., ed., *The Southerner as American* (Dutton Paperbacks); Hodding Carter, *The Southern Legacy* (Louisiana State University Press); and Robert Penn Warren, *Legacy of the Civil War* (Vintage Books, Inc.).

C. Vann Woodward's *Reunion and Reaction* (Anchor Books) and his *Origins of the New South* (Louisiana State University Press) together competently survey the half century after Appomatox. Paul Buck, *The Road to Reunion: 1865–1900* (Little Brown & Co.) describes the general process of reconciliation of North and South.

Vladimir O. Key, Jr., *Southern Politics* (Vintage Books, Inc.) deals with a later period but shows the consequences of nineteenth-century developments. Other works on politics include: Paul Lewinson, *Race, Class, and Party* (Universal Library); Dewey W. Grantham, *The Democratic South* (W. W. Norton & Company, Inc.); Theodore Saloutos, *Farmer Movements in the South* (Bison Books); and T. Harry Williams, *Romance and Realism in Southern Politics* (Louisiana State University Press). Albert D. Kirwan, *Revolt of the Rednecks* (Harper Torchbooks) deals with the poor whites in Mississippi.

Booker T. Washington tells his own story in *Up from Slavery* (Bantam Books, Inc.) and Samuel R. Spencer, Jr., *Booker T. Washington and the Negro's Place in American Life* (Little Brown & Co.) is a good biography. George W. Cable, *The Negro Question* (Anchor Books) contains the insights of a white man. There are useful materials in Harvey Wish, ed., *The Negro since Emancipation* (Spectrum Books). Segregation is the subject of C. Vann Woodward, *The Strange Career of Jim Crow* (Galaxy Books). George B. Tindall, *South Carolina Negroes: 1877–1900* (Louisiana State University Press) and Vernon L. Wharton, *The Negro in Mississippi* (Harper Torchbooks) are excellent local studies.

FARM PROBLEMS

57

After the Civil War farmers everywhere formed a troubled element in American society. Their achievements were impressive. A tremendous rise in output permitted them to supply the growing population and also export great quantities of basic commodities. Furthermore, their purchasing power provided a market for an expanding industry at home. Nevertheless, their complaints grew louder by the decade. In 1890 they were on the verge of revolt.

Agriculture operated under circumstances that varied greatly from one part of the continent to another, but certain difficulties were common to all. Like other sectors of the economy, it was in transition from a simple to a complex form of organization and was increasingly dominated by extended communications and the wide use of capital. Men who continued to regard themselves as simple yeomen had to alter their ways of thinking and acting. The process was painful; hence the protests. But it also laid the foundation for a powerful new mode of production.

Productivity
and Prices

MOST OF THE STATISTICS were encouraging. Decade by decade the number of farms increased, with a great jump from some two and a half million in 1870 to more than four million in 1880. The acres under cultivation multiplied at about the same rate, as did the value of the land, buildings, and machinery. That much was to the good.

The gross-production figures were also heartening. Measured in terms of the bushels of cereal grown or the dollar value of total farm output, American agriculture was doing well in the decades after the Civil War.

Other indexes told a different story. Certainly the harvests of corn and wheat grew steadily more bountiful; at their peaks they were more than three times as large as in 1866. But the price these crops brought in the market declined correspondingly. It was almost the same with cotton and wool; the more the farmers produced, the lower were the prices they received, so the net reward for their efforts was hardly better than before. Their grievances were far from imaginary.

The dilemma was a product of forces Americans considered desirable. Expansion brought under cultivation new areas that competed with the old. The use of machinery, stimulated by the Civil War and by later inventions, raised the level of productivity, and improved methods of transportation created a national, indeed an international, market. Immigration strengthened settlement and tended to sustain land values, but it also put hard-working rivals to the farmers in the fields. The same elements that encouraged higher output created the danger of falling prices.

Fred A. Shannon, *The Farmer's Last Frontier* (New York, 1945) is an adequate survey of agriculture between the Civil War and the end of the nineteenth century.

American Farms, 1850–1890

Year	Number (thousands)	Land, Acres (thousands)	Value: Land and Buildings (millions)	Value: Machinery (millions)
1850	1,449	293	$ 3,270	$152
1860	2,044	407	6,642	246
1870	2,659	407	7,441	271
1880	4,008	536	10,193	406
1890	4,565	623	13,273	494

Production of Cereal Crops, 1850–1890
(in millions)

Year	Cereals, Bushels	Output, Constant Dollars
1850	867	$1,379
1860	1,239	1,985
1870	1,387	2,436
1880	2,698	3,784
1890	3,519	4,604

Grain Harvests and Prices, 1866–1890

Year	Corn, Bushels (thousands)	Price per Bushel	Wheat, Bushels (thousands)	Price per Bushel
1866	730,814	$0.657	169,703	$2.062
1870	1,124,775	.521	254,429	1.042
1880	1,706,673	.39	502,257	.952
1890	1,650,456	.49	449,042	.837
Peak 1889			*Peak 1884*	
2,250,000	.27	571,292	.645

Fibers: Production and Prices, 1850–1890

Year	Cotton, Bales (thousands)	Price per Pound, Cents	Shorn Wool, Pounds (thousands)	Price per Pound, Cents
1850	2,136	–	–	–
1860	3,841	–	–	–
1870	4,352	12.1	162,000	22.2
1880	6,606	9.83	232,500	23.1
1890	8,653	8.59	276,000	17.1

The Grange Awakening the Sleepers. The farmer seeks to rouse the country to the railroad menace. Cartoon from an American newspaper of 1873 inspired by the Vanderbilt system of secret rebates. (The Granger Collection)

Farm Grievances

The Middlemen The farmers often blamed their plight on the high costs of distribution. Too many middlemen stood between the loaf of bread or yard of cloth and the bushel of wheat or bale of cotton. The railroad, the grain elevator, the mill, the gin, the bakery, and a horde of grasping brokers and dealers each took a toll as the commodity moved from producer to consumer. This, it was argued, accounted for the vast differential between the cost to the ultimate purchaser and the price paid the husbandman.

There was some justification to this complaint. Rates were unregulated, and the farmer was in no position to bargain when he had to dispose of his crop; rather than let the produce rot on his hands, he took what he could get in the sale and paid what he had to in fees. The im-

personal corporations with which he dealt charged what the traffic would bear; and the railroads were often tempted, in dealing with the little customer who lacked alternative means of transportation, to make up for what they lost on rebates to big shippers. This situation explained the growing demand for regulation by the government.

An Unpredictable Market Other causes of agrarian difficulties were less close to the surface. American wheat, pork, and cotton went to tables in England and Germany, where they met the competition of grains, meats, and fibers from Argentina, Canada, Egypt, India, Russia, and Australia, countries that were also rapidly raising their output. The price the farmer received in Minnesota or Alabama depended, therefore, on fluctuations in supply and demand on an international market over which he had no power.

84

Some economic theorists argued, as Southerners had before the Civil War, that the high tariff damaged agriculture, which was unprotected, by raising the cost of imported manufactured goods and thus restricting the capacity of foreigners to buy in the United States. But that factor, if important at all, was less consequential than the inability to predict or control the volume of the commodities handled in the exchanges. A bumper crop in the Ukraine or a drought in India could upset the most prudent calculations.

The staple farmer was a small producer engaged in a big business. His individual decision could not influence the general trend; whether he withheld his acres from cultivation or added to them would scarcely alter the supply or affect his return. He tended therefore to struggle for maximum output, which would cushion the effect of a fall in prices and give him the greatest profit in the event of a rise. The result was a supply usually unrelated to demand.

No matter how cautious he was, the farmer could regulate his volume of production only imperfectly. The commodity he sold was seasonable and perishable; it reached the market at the worst possible moment, at the same time as the goods of his competitors. Above all, he had no way of knowing, when he put his plow to the soil, what the situation would be months later when he would finish the harvest. Unable to be foresighted, he had one goal: to raise as much as he could.

Yet agriculture did not absorb the consequences of mistakes as industry did. The manufacturer who guessed wrong or was inefficient went to the wall and left the field to luckier or abler competitors. A fall in prices eliminated marginal producers and thus in time reduced supply. But the farmer, no matter how marginal, hung on; a drop in the price of his products set him to working all the harder. To give up, in his case, was to surrender not merely a business but also a home. He made heartbreaking sacrifices and resorted to desperate expedients to avoid the loss of his land. His problems were due not simply to villainous distributors but to his rela-tionships with a market from which he sought a profit but in which he could not act as other businessmen did.

Cash and Credit The farmer's ambiguous role as both householder and entrepreneur helped explain also the perennial complaint that not enough money was in circulation. Farmers were tempted to ascribe falling prices to contraction in the currency or at least to the failure to expand it sufficiently. Many believed that inflation would raise the value of their goods and ease the burden of their debts. Some farmers considered the efforts to retire the greenbacks a mistake; and the decision to cease coining silver dollars came to be known as the crime of 1873.

The farmers felt strongly about these matters because they were always short of cash. Taxes were not high by later standards, but as long as they rested mainly on real estate, they put a disproportionate burden on landowners. Resentment against taxes mounted when they went to improvements in remote parts of the state or to the discharge of obligations incurred to build railroads, which then exacted high rates.

More important were the charges on the agriculturists' debts. Once made, loans were hard to liquidate, for the interest rates were high — legally 7 to 10 percent a year, often amounting to 20 percent when fees and bonuses were counted in. These fixed costs had to be met before the farmer could touch the proceeds from the sale of his crop. Whether prices were high or low, whether the harvest was good or bad, the lender expected his due, and foreclosure was the penalty for failure to pay.

The volume of farm debt climbed steadily. By 1890, fully 28 percent of all holdings were mortgaged, and that national average was far from revealing the true gravity of the situation. In Kansas, probably half the farm homes were thus encumbered, many by more than one obligation. In addition, numerous families worried

Allan G. Bogue, *Money at Interest* (Ithaca, N.Y., 1955) is a detailed study of farm mortgages which throws light on the farmers' credit problems.

Harvesting on a Bonanza Farm. Drawing by W. A. Rogers, *Harper's Weekly,* August 29, 1891. (Library of Congress)

about notes due and accounts payable on the books of merchants.

The fault was not solely that of the grasping financier. Many obligations were due to local people—shopkeepers, lawyers, and bankers—who had no desire to impoverish their clients. Nor did the more distant mortgage companies earn an exorbitant profit from farm loans. The cost of credit was steep because the risks were high. Furthermore, to make such loans it was necessary to attract Eastern and European capital away from alternative investments in industrial or railroad securities.

The farmer's view was thus accurate only in part. The moneylenders did not thrust debt upon him; he sought it out because the stake was essential to settlement or expansion.

The experience of those who did not become borrowers throws light on the reasons why others did. Debt was rare in such stable agricultural areas as western New York, central Pennsylvania, and eastern Wisconsin, which were beginning to diversify their economies by raising fruit, vegetable, and dairy products and which had put the basic costs of settlement well behind them. Nor were the foreign-born as likely to take loans as the natives; immigrants were traditional in their attitudes to the soil. They valued self-sufficiency and raised their own food by their unaided labor, depending on the market only to dispose of their surpluses. They could therefore absorb the losses of falling prices by tightening their belts.

By contrast, native Americans who were commercial farmers aimed primarily to market a staple. Rather than pay in full for a small holding, they bought the largest tract their credit could afford them. In new areas, they assumed heavy costs in establishing themselves on the chance that future returns would bring them more than a competence. Particularly in the Great Plains, where the basic wood and water were lacking, they needed capital for a start — to buy wire, to sink a well, and to lay in supplies, machinery, and equipment — all long before the first crop came in. They did not hesitate to raise the capital by borrowing. When times were good, such people were as likely to increase as to liquidate their debts; they took the risk of expanding in the hope of still greater gains. Poor times caught them short, as happened to Jerry Simpson. They were, in other words, speculators on future growth, subject to the perils other businessmen faced but without the same flexibility.

Speculation Speculative patterns had long been familiar in American agriculture, but the situation after 1870 was novel in one crucial respect. The eighteenth- and early-nineteenth-century farmer, over his head in debt, could sell out and use the proceeds as a stake in a move farther west. After 1870, the rapid opening of the Great Plains to settlement made immense tracts of land available, and competition among railroads and speculators — to say nothing of government homesteads — drove values down. A foreclosure in Kansas left the dispossessed with nothing, and by 1890 there was no longer a farther frontier to nurture romantic hopes of doing better elsewhere.

Someone had robbed the people of their birthright, the empty spaces that Americans had always assumed would assure them a second chance. The accusation, which grew shriller with time, voiced the protest of the unsuccessful; two-thirds of the homestead claimants before 1890 failed to retain their holdings and were inclined

In 1884, **JERRY SIMPSON** thought he had a fortune just about in his grasp. He sold the farm on which he had worked for five years at Holton, Kansas, and invested his accumulated savings in a cattle ranch near Medicine Lodge in the same state. His experience until then had not been much different from that of thousands of other men who peopled the West.

Simpson was born in 1842 in New Brunswick, Canada, and at some point had moved with his family south of the border. At the age of fourteen, Jerry was on his own. He worked as a cook on a lake boat, served in the Civil War, and settled down to farm, first in Indiana and then in Kansas.

The treacherous climate of the Great Plains destroyed his chance to get ahead. A severe winter wiped out his herd of cattle. Unable to make payments on his mortgage, he lost his holding. He survived on a minor government appointment that brought him $40 a month, and he drifted into local politics. He left the Republican party to join the Greenback movement and then shifted to the Farmers' Alliance, which grew rapidly in the state after 1888. As a Populist between 1890 and 1898, he held office several times and espoused such radical causes as the single tax and easy paper money. The return of prosperity after 1898 ended his political career. In 1902 he became involved in a new land and colonization venture. He died in 1905, never having made his fortune.

to agree that monopolistic speculators had somehow engrossed the land.

Tenantry was a somber measure of the new condition. By 1890, tenants operated almost a fourth of the farms in the United States. The peculiarities of Southern agriculture accounted only in part for this development. Of the roughly one and a quarter million tenant farms in the

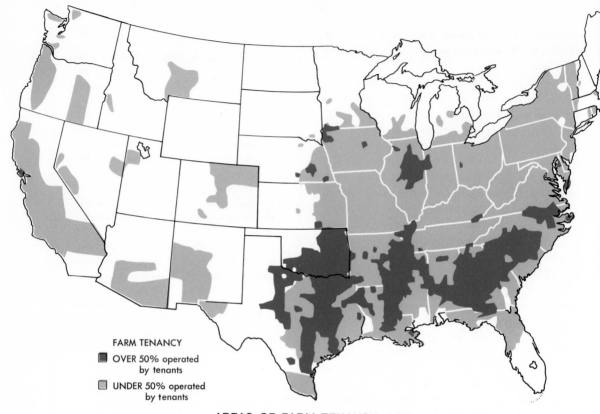

FARM TENANCY

■ OVER 50% operated
  by tenants

□ UNDER 50% operated
  by tenants

AREAS OF FARM TENANCY, 1880

country, almost six hundred thousand were outside the South and were occupied by tenants because of the inability of the men who worked the soil to secure or retain the capital necessary to own it. Sometimes the farms were large tracts held by absentee owners as investments or for speculation, while the renter operated them. Sometimes they were foreclosed farms, whose former proprietors tilled them until they could be sold. By whatever route the independent yeoman drifted into it, tenancy was evidence that he was not holding his own.

Rural Life The grievances of the farmers sprang also from sources that were not purely economic. Farmers who counted on success in the future to justify the ardors of the present had a pervasive and ominous premonition that the future was no longer theirs. Perhaps fortune went now not to him who bent over the plow but to the city slicker whom the country cousin

feared and envied. In that event the farmer's own toil and deprivation were in vain. When young people decided to take jobs in shops and offices rather than stay on the farm, they denied the value of their parents' efforts. The sense of rejection added to the pain of separation and to the worrisome prospect of lonely old age.

There were also local causes of frustration. In the South, racial tensions and social conflicts between the poor whites and the former planters added bitterness to the problems of debt and tenantry. In the older sections, the hilly soil, abused for decades, could not compete with the virgin fields to the west. Almost everywhere in rural New England and in many parts of New York, New Jersey, and Pennsylvania the population declined in an unmistakable sign of decay.

Most important, the Great Plains subjected the people who invaded them to unaccustomed hardships. Periodic droughts, plagues of grass-

Defeat, 1880s

"I hate farm-life," she went on with a bitter inflection. "It's nothing but fret, fret, and work the whole time, never going any place, never seeing anybody but a lot of neighbors just as big fools as you are. I spend my time fighting flies and washing dishes and churning. I'm sick of it all."

Howard was silent. What could he say to such an indictment? The ceiling swarmed with flies which the cold rain had driven to seek the warmth of the kitchen. The gray rain was falling with a dreary sound outside, and down the kitchen stove pipe an occasional drop fell on the stove with a hissing, angry sound.

The young wife went on with a deeper note:

"I lived in La Crosse two years, going to school, and I know a little something of what city life is. If I was a man, I bet I wouldn't wear my life out on a farm, as Grant does. I'd get away and I'd do something. I wouldn't care what, but I'd get away." . . .

She stopped with a bitter sob in her throat. She forgot she was talking to her husband's brother. She was conscious only of his sympathy.

As if a great black cloud had settled down upon him, Howard felt it all—the horror, hopelessness, imminent tragedy of it all. The glory of nature, the bounty and splendor of the sky, only made it the more benumbing.

—Hamlin Garland, *Main-Travelled Roads* (New York: Harper & Row, Publishers, 1922), pp. 80–82.

Life in a Rough Place, 1883

Tell Mrs. Johnson I think if her Nephew was out here, he could get work but he would find it a very rough place and in regards to Christianity, it makes no dif. He would have to do as the rest of the fellows out here. It is all day and Sunday too. He would find the cowboys a hard set to work with. Stock raising out here is so different from what he is used to that experience in that country would do no good out here. All the experience he wants, to know how to throw a rope and ride. They turn there cattle out and in spring and fall they round them up and brand them and turn them out again. Sheep is different. He might find his experience in raising them to help him, but winter herding would be hard on him; it is so cold. I advise her not to let him come to this country unless he goes into business for himself, for they don't have any mercy on any body. The cow boys are all right if you get acquainted with them and treat them all right, but otherwise they are not; and if you bother them it is better if you look a 'letle oud."

—Letters by Otto Merdian, in L. B. Mirrielees, ed., "Pioneer Ranching in Central Montana," *The Frontier*, X (March, 1930), p. 257.

hoppers, and sudden tornadoes swept away the fruits of the labor of years. Nature here was oppressive. Men and women, worn down by hard work, found no relief in the visual bleakness of the landscape. Discouraged by the lack of order, by the isolation from churches, schools, neighbors, and relatives, they succumbed often to sheer loneliness. Weeks passed without the sight of a strange face, without news from the outer world, without variation in a monotonous diet. A visit to town, distant and ramshackle as it was, offered the only variation in the life of toil.

Sod House and Well, Custer County, Nebraska. Photograph, *ca.* 1890.
(The Bettmann Archive)

OLIVER H. KELLEY was too ambitious to remain a farmer. He was willing to work on the land to keep going, but his restless imagination drew him into a variety of ventures that seemed to promise success.

Kelley was born in Boston in 1826, the fifth child of a tailor. He lived in Illinois, Iowa, and Minnesota, and worked as clerk, reporter, and telegraph operator. In 1849 he acquired some land at Itasca, Minnesota, which he farmed, at the same time trading with the Indians and writing.

In 1864 Kelley went to Washington as a clerk for the Bureau of Agriculture, although he retained his farm. In the next two years he made several trips through the country, during which he conceived the idea of forming a fraternal association of farmers. In 1867 he persuaded six people to join with him, and the Grange was born. His work for the organization furthered its spectacular growth.

Kelley, however, could not limit his ambitions. He became interested in Florida land speculation and in 1878 he resigned from the Grange. His business flyers proved unsuccessful; he was living on a pension from the Grange when he died in 1913.

The Granger Program, 1874

GENERAL OBJECTS . . . United by the strong and faithful tie of agriculture, we mutually resolve to labor for the good of our Order, our country, and mankind. . . .

SPECIFIC OBJECTS . . . We shall endeavor to advance our cause by laboring to accomplish the following objects:

To develop a better and higher manhood and womanhood among ourselves. To enhance the comforts and attractions of our homes, and strengthen our attachments to our pursuits. To foster mutual understanding and cooperation. To maintain inviolate our laws, and to emulate each other in labor to hasten the good time coming. To reduce our expenses, both individual and corporate. To buy less and produce more, in order to make our farms self-sustaining. To diversify our crops, and crop no more than we can cultivate. . . . To systematize our work, and calculate intelligently on probabilities. To discountenance the credit system, the mortgage system, the fashion system, and every other system tending to prodigality and bankruptcy . . . .

BUSINESS RELATIONS . . . For our business interests, we desire to bring producers and consumers, farmers and manufacturers into the most direct and friendly relations possible. Hence we must dispense with a surplus of middlemen, not that we are unfriendly to them, but we do not need them. Their surplus and their exactions diminish our profits.

— Declaration of Purpose of the National Grange, 1874, *Proceedings of the Seventh Session of the National Grange of the Patrons of Husbandry* [St. Louis, February 11, 1874] (New York, 1874; no publisher), pp. 56–60.

Farm Organizations

As their common plight became apparent, the farmers reached out to one another for assistance. The habit of voluntary association was strong; numerous lodges and fraternal societies existed and new ones sprang into being every year. Small-town lawyers, petty politicians, and businessmen without capital—energetic promotors of every sort—were constantly generating cooperative schemes for which the agricultural countryside was fertile ground. Once an appropriate plan became available, organization spread rapidly.

The Granger Movement   In 1867, Oliver Hudson Kelley, a clerk in the Bureau of Agriculture, with a small group of friends established the National Grange of the Patrons of Husbandry. The intention was to found a fraternal organization in which men could meet for companionship and mutual aid. In a rural environment that had few institutions even for social encounters, the plan was attractive. In the next two years six granges appeared in Minnesota and four in other states.

Then the popularity of the association skyrocketed. Thousands of little groups spontaneously took up the idea. In 1875, fully 20,000 granges throughout the country had enlisted about 800,000 members. Local offshoots sprouted almost everywhere, but there was an especially heavy concentration in a band of territory that ran from Illinois through Iowa and Wisconsin to Minnesota, areas settled for a generation where farmers had a little time to create solid communities.

Increasing membership tempted some of the grangers into politics. In 1878, many farm-

Everett Dick, *The Sod House Frontier, 1854–1890* (New York, 1937) contains a good account of the social conditions of frontier life.

Solon J. Buck, *The Granger Movement* (Cambridge, Mass., 1913) is the standard account.

Meeting of the Grangers in the Woods near Winchester, Scott County, Illinois. Sketch by Joseph B. Beale, *Frank Leslie's Illustrated Newspaper,* August 30, 1873. (Library of Congress)

ers, persuaded of the need for easier money, backed Greenback candidates in Congressional and state elections. More usually, the grangers tried to make their weight felt through the two major parties. In some places they were able to persuade the legislatures to enact laws establishing commissions to regulate railroad and grain-elevator rates.

Self-help also took the form of a cooperative movement. It seemed plausible to eliminate the middlemen whose profits were blamed for the shrinking margin left the farmer. Grange agents at first arranged to purchase supplies directly from manufacturers and later set up communally owned stores to lower the costs of goods to members. Some granges experimented with producer cooperatives through which they marketed or warehoused their products.

These ventures failed with distressing promptness. Good managers were rare and capital was short; credit was too easily granted to neighbors and debts were hard to collect. Above all, distribution proved to be not merely a device of rapacious middlemen but a necessary and costly service on which the farmers depended.

Nor did politics bring quick relief. In most places, the grangers were not able to control party machinery. Furthermore, agricultural commodities usually moved across state lines and therefore escaped the control of commissions until the Federal government acted.

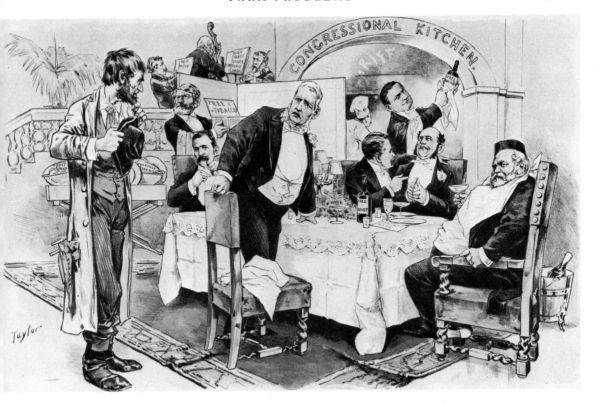

"The Political Poor Relation—An Unwelcome Guest." The farmer looks for his place among the monopolists. Cartoon, 1888, from *Puck*. (The Granger Collection)

Disillusionment set in early. In the 1880s membership in the granges sank precipitously. The local organizations that survived withdrew from both business and politics and confined themselves to social functions. In that more limited capacity they provided useful relief from the tedium and isolation of rural life.

The Alliances In the 1880s the aggrieved farmers in some sections of the country found an alternative to the Grange in the rival organizations that clung to faith in cooperatives and political action. The earliest such group had appeared in Texas in the 1870s. In the next decade it affiliated with similar bodies in nine Southern states and adopted the title The National Farmers' Alliance. In 1888, it combined with the Agricultural Wheel, which had been formed in Arkansas six years earlier; thereafter known as the Farmers' and Laborers' Union, it sought to sponsor cooperatives and improve agricultural techniques. Meanwhile in another part of the country, the Northwest Alliance was also campaigning for cooperatives and for nationalization of the railroad and telegraph lines.

At a meeting in St. Louis in 1889, an effort to unite all these elements failed. The negotiators were in general agreement on a platform that called for reform of the banks, softer money, government ownership of the means of communication, and farm credit, but they could not work out the details of organization. Although the alliances had already gained considerable power in the legislatures of some states in the South and in the Great Plains, their significance did not become clear until the next decade.

▼

In 1890, the farm problem was still far from solution. Agriculture contributed substantially to the nation's economic strength, but the farmer considered his share unsatisfactory. His grievances were a continuing irritant in the political life of the United States.

Those who complained did not fully understand the source of their difficulties and in the search for scapegoats preferred to overlook the fact that more was involved than the greed of railroads and moneylenders. For a long time, American farmers had been torn between the conflicting ideals of the self-sufficient yeoman and the successful businessman. In the speculative haste to expand settlement after 1865, they became dependent upon an intricate mechanism of credit and distribution over which they exercised little control. Some of them were paying the price for the very growth in which they took pride.

Paperbacks for Further Reading

Many of the titles listed in Chapters 55 and 56 are also relevant here. In addition, the following novels give perceptive impressions of rural life in various parts of the United States: Edith Wharton, *Summer* (Scribner Library); Willa Cather, *O Pioneers!* (Sentry Editions) and *My Antonia* (Sentry Editions); Hamlin Garland, *Main-Travelled Roads* (Signet Classics); Mari Sandoz, *Old Jules* (Bison Books); and O. E. Rolvaag, *Giants in the Earth* (Perennial Library) and *Peder Victorious* (Perennial Library).

THE LABORING
CLASSES

58

The laborers of the United States bore the heaviest share of the costs of industrialization. They were divided in interests and in origin and therefore in no position to protect themselves. Only toward the end of the nineteenth century did some of them organize well enough to be able to improve the conditions of their life and labor.

The great majority, however, remained unorganized and gained even fewer immediate benefits from economic change than did the farmers. Workers were available in abundant numbers for all the tasks the entrepreneur set them, but were unable to demand rewards that corresponded to their efforts. They accepted their lot not through docility but because they lacked the means of expressing their desperate grievances and because American society offered them other compensations.

The Cobbler. (Library of Congress)

Types of Labor

Labor in the middle of the nineteenth century was a heterogeneous and ambiguous category. The term did not refer to a uniform group or to a single economic interest. It applied loosely to various types of workers markedly different from one another in origins, in function, and in situation.

The Artisans The artisans were easiest to define for they had a long history in the United States and in 1850 were still in a strong position. The perennial shortage of skills in the New World put a high premium on their services, and their numbers gave them substantial local political weight.

Yet in the two decades after 1870 some of the handicraftsmen proved vulnerable to industrial change. The growth of a national transportation system weakened their command of the local market, and the spread of the factory gradually undermined their competitive position. Before the Civil War the effects had been relatively slight because industrialization came first in textiles and other manufactures that displaced few artisans. After 1865, as the machine advanced into the boot and shoe, the tailoring, and the iron industries, it devalued the skills of thousands of handicraftsmen. In the 1870s and 1880s, as industry grew in scale and in technical complexity, the impact on the artisans became more severe.

There remained places in the economy, however, in which skill still counted and in which the handicraftsmen therefore possessed real bargaining power. The building trades, for instance, held control of their local markets and were not threatened by mechanization; as a result, carpenters, bricklayers, and masons could protect their positions. Cigar makers, printers, and railroad engineers, among others, were in the same enviable position as long as they did not have to compete with machines.

People in these occupations earned enough to support their families in moderate comfort. Their wives stayed home to manage decent households and their children went to school. It was possible to put aside savings for an emergency and even to buy a home. A man could aspire to be his own master and reap the rewards of his labor as long as he did not compete with the factory.

The strength of the artisans lay in the scarcity of their skills. Control over apprenticeship permitted them to regulate entry to each craft so that they could minimize the danger of unemployment through an excess of hands. As a result they were able to push their pay upward by about 25 percent between 1860 and 1890. Since the prices of the goods they consumed fell steadily after 1865, the rise in real wages was considerably higher—in some cases as high as 100 percent. But most of these gains came before 1870, as a result of the Civil War. In the next two decades even the building-trade workers only just about held their own.

The Factory Hands   The situation of factory employees was far less gratifying. It is true that general hourly rates, where comparable, climbed for them too and that they too gained by the falling cost of living, but other factors offset these favorable developments.

Had an imaginative timekeeper been able to categorize the men who passed through the gates of a plant, he would have thought in terms of a pyramid. At the pinnacle he would have visualized a small number of skilled machinists, carpenters, and foremen. Below these would be a larger, but still limited, stratum of the semi-skilled—experienced loom fixers or cutters or last makers. But into the base would be crowded the great mass of the unskilled.

The hands in the last category were marginal; lack of security kept their earning power low. They were the element in the cost of production easiest to manipulate. Charges for rent, upkeep, interest, and raw material were beyond the control of the manager who sought to cut back expenses, and he would hesitate to discharge machinists, who were few in number and difficult to replace. But he could reduce the item for wages simply by laying off laborers who, he knew, would be waiting at his gate when he needed them once more.

For such employees, the hourly rate was important but the number of hours of work available was more important still. Annual incomes varied tremendously and fluctuated widely; estimates are only guesses. In the relatively good years of the 1880s, the unskilled worker who earned more than $400 in twelve months did well; in bad times he was likely to earn much less.

The hazards of unemployment shaped the way of life of unskilled laborers. To increase the chance that some wage would always come in, every member of the family sought a job. In 1890 about a million children and perhaps four times as many women were reckoned in the labor force. The constant threat of a halt in earnings kept consumption to a minimum, yet also encouraged wasteful habits. Those who depended upon the local shopkeeper for credit in hard times could not shop around for bargains but paid what was demanded of them. They did not

Stephan Thernstrom, *Poverty and Progress* (Cambridge, Mass., 1964) is a thoughtful study of social mobility among the laborers of an industrial town.

INDEX OF AVERAGE DAILY WAGES, 1860–1890
(1860 = 100)

All Nonagricultural Employment

Building Trades

Quitting Time at McCormick's Harvesting Machine Company Plant, 1886. (State Historical Society of Wisconsin)

gain as much from falling prices as did the more fortunate with margin.

In the mill towns, usually only one industry and often a single firm controlled all employment. As the impersonal corporation replaced individual ownership, the workingman's helplessness deepened. When production slackened, there were no alternatives; everyone was out of work. The laborer who lived in a company house and was in debt to a company store was immobile and could only wait, in deepening misery, to be taken on again. Local shopkeepers and politicians were frequently sympathetic but were no match for the impersonal absentee corporation.

Urban Labor   In the larger industrial cities the laborer had some choice and could maneuver in a more flexible market, finding a job where he could—in the factory, on the docks, or in the streets. If nothing else turned up, he could take a place in the army of draymen, carters, stevedores, and porters who did the heavy work of business. Or the family could piece together a living in the crowded tenement sweatshops, by sewing trousers or coats. The hard sixty-hour week was tolerable as long as it provided an income. The high cost of living was the problem. Rent, fuel, fares, and food swiftly used up the earnings of the most industrious. In return for their toil, the laborers got the dense quarters of the spreading slums, which took a heavy toll in disease and mortality.

Unemployment sometimes reached into the city too. In good times the solidarity of the family was a source of security, for its pooled earnings kept it going even when individuals in it sickened or lost their places. But in depressions, such as that which struck in 1873, whole families no member of which could locate employment became utterly dependent on charity. Wives and children were then a drag—their deprivations reminded the father of his own failure and their needs competed with his own.

Such circumstances tempted some men to desert and shift for themselves, since they were no help to their dependents anyway. They formed part of an army of migrants who roamed the countryside subsisting on handouts, petty theft, and earnings from odd jobs; by 1880 the tramps seemed a menace to property owners everywhere. Yet the wanderers' prospects for rewarding labor were slim. Agricultural workers rarely got more than $12 a month and board, and they were needed only seasonally. Those who wielded the pick and shovel on railroad and other construction projects usually did not do as well; they received larger wages but consumed them in the purchase of supplies from the contractors' stores. The gangs that laid the tracks or harvested the crops consisted mainly of unattached men without resources whose earnings rarely did more than cover their maintenance and who were stranded at the end of each season no better off than they had been before.

Immigration   The pool of available labor kept expanding through immigration. The foreign-born population of the United States leaped from about four million in 1860 to some nine million in 1890, much of it available for work at the machine or with pick and shovel. The steamship and railroad, which shortened the time in transit and lowered the cost, accelerated the movement from Europe. Arrivals from Ireland, England, Germany, and Scandinavia mounted quite steadily until the peak in 1882, and although some of the newcomers made straight for the farms, a large percentage of them took places in the ranks of industry.

In addition, by the 1880s the mines and factories were beginning to receive hands from eastern and southern Europe. That decade witnessed the arrival of more than 200,000 Italians and almost as many natives of Russia. These

Foreign-born Population of the United States, 1850–1890

Year	Number
1850	2,244,000
1860	4,138,000
1870	5,567,000
1880	6,679,000
1890	9,249,000

Triple-deck Dormitory Cars for Construction Workers on the St. Paul, Minneapolis and Manitoba Railroad, 1887. The cars rode the new track as it was laid. (Minnesota Historical Society)

newcomers had an even harder time than those from northern and western Europe. Religious and social conflict with workers of the older stocks and ignorance of the habits of urban life complicated all the problems of adjustment.

Labor Organization

The Crafts For a long time, the assumption that the heterogeneous army of labor had a common interest confused the section of it able to organize in self-defense. Almost all the associations of workingmen in the nineteenth century consisted primarily of artisans. However, these associations had never been clear on the vital question of how narrowly or how broadly to draw their membership lines. The masons or printers each had a common interest and the bargaining power to improve their own wages and conditions of employment. They understood, too, the desirability of affiliation for

mutual aid and for fraternal and political purposes. A society limited to brothers within a single trade could best serve those ends.

But since early in the century, American artisans had considered themselves also part of a single united body of all labor. A persistent tradition of universality persuaded many that a true union should take in all who toiled with their hands—artisans, factory workers, and the unskilled alike. Not until the 1880s did a succession of issues clarify the position.

Some craft unions were already in existence before 1860; the war increased their membership and strengthened their position. After 1865, such groups as the machinists, blacksmiths, railroad engineers, and carpenters retained their power. Usually these were fraternal societies, as "brotherhood" in their titles often indicated, and they occupied themselves with social activities as well as with efforts to set the rates and conditions of labor. They relied primarily on the

"A Question of Labor." The cartoon (*ca.* 1888) reflects the attitude of unionized American workers toward newly arrived immigrants, who were often hired as strike-breakers. (Culver Pictures)

strike or work stoppage to force employers to come to terms.

But more general organizations to attain broader objectives also attracted the artisans. In 1866, William H. Sylvis of the iron molders formed the National Labor Union to unite the efforts of these groups and to associate them with like-minded farmers and reformers. The Union flourished briefly. Its ideal was the self-employed independent craftsman. It did not like to consider its members as employees, and therefore eschewed such methods as the strike, appropriate to wage earners. Instead, it mounted campaigns against monopoly and the importation of contract labor, and for the eight-hour day and land reform. The one notable achievement it may have influenced was establishment of the eight-hour day for Federal employees in 1869.

The Knights of Labor The National Labor Union faded after a feeble venture into politics in 1872. A more attractive rival, the Noble Order of the Knights of Labor, founded in 1869 by Uriah Stephens, a Philadelphia tailor, had the fraternal features of its predecessors and it admitted anyone who toiled, including Negroes and excluding only lawyers, bankers, liquor dealers, and gamblers. It thus made room for the unskilled as well as the skilled and for professionals and small business men.

The local assemblies, organized sometimes by trade but usually by district, grew steadily in membership in the 1870s. In time, a national General Assembly coordinated activities, but each unit retained a good deal of autonomy. Terence V. Powderly, who became Grand Master Workman in 1879, enunciated the general views of the organization although his power within it was limited. His objective, like that of Sylvis, was to make every man his own master; the Knights of Labor opposed child and prison labor and called for an eight-hour day, arbitration of disputes, an income tax, prohibition, government collection of labor statistics, and the formation of

Jonathan Grossman, *William Sylvis* (New York, 1945) is a competent biography.

TERENCE V. POWDERLY came up the hard way. He was born in Carbondale, Pennsylvania, in 1849, one of twelve children of Irish immigrant parents. His father was a teamster. Although Terence received some schooling, he had to go to work early, holding various jobs on the railroad. At seventeen he was an apprentice to a machinist, and he worked at that trade until he was almost thirty. Once he was a full-fledged craftsman, he joined the machinists' union and did some organizing for it. He also joined the Knights of Labor and rose steadily in the ranks of that organization as it expanded.

Powderly dabbled in politics, and in 1878 was elected on the Greenback ticket as mayor of Scranton, Pennsylvania, a post he held for six years. But he remained deeply involved in the work of the General Assembly of the Knights. By 1883 he was Grand Master Workman of the Order, and for the next decade he markedly influenced its strategy, retaining his interest in both politics and labor. In 1886 he spoke for Henry George in the New York mayoralty campaign. Later he was one of the organizers of the People's party.

Powderly was a reformer of the old type. He viewed the Knights of Labor as a great educational organization and therefore stressed such general objectives as prohibition and alteration of the land and currency systems rather than negotiations for better wages. For the same reason, he preferred arbitration to strikes and insisted that the skilled should aid the unskilled. He looked forward ultimately to the total abolition of the wage system in favor of a scheme of universal cooperation. These goals did not match the immediate aims of the American Federation of Labor in attractiveness and contributed to the decline of the Knights of Labor.

After 1894, Powderly became a lawyer, joined the Republican party, and was rewarded with Federal office. He died in 1924, the same year as his old antagonist Samuel Gompers.

Objectives of the Knights of Labor, 1869

I. To bring within the folds of organization every department of productive industry, making knowledge a stand-point for action, and industrial and moral worth, not wealth, the true standard of individual and national greatness.

II. To secure to the toilers a proper share of the wealth that they create. . . .

III. To . . . [demand] . . . from the various governments the establishment of bureaus of Labor Statistics.

IV. The establishment of co-operative institutions, productive and distributive.

V. The reserving of the public lands . . . for the actual settler. . . .

VI. The abrogation of all laws that do not bear equally upon capital and labor, the removal of unjust technicalities, delays, and discriminations in the administration of justice, and the adopting of measures providing for the health and safety of those engaged in mining, manufacturing, or building pursuits.

VII. The enactment of laws to compel chartered corporations to pay their employees weekly. . . .

VIII. The enactment of laws giving mechanics and laborers a first lien on their work for their full wages.

IX. The abolishment of the contract system on national, State, and municipal work.

X. The substitution of arbitration for strikes. . . .

XI. The prohibition of the employment of children in workshops, mines, and factories before attaining their fourteenth year.

XII. To abolish the system of letting out by contract the labor of convicts. . . .

XIII. To secure for both sexes equal pay for equal work.

XIV. The reduction of the hours of labor to eight per day. . . .

XV. To prevail upon governments to establish a purely national circulating medium, based upon the faith and resources of the nation, and issued directly to the people, without the intervention of any system of banking corporations.

—T. V. Powderly, *Thirty Years of Labor* (Columbus: Excelsior Publishing House, 1890), pp. 243–245.

---

cooperatives. Such general reforms, which bore close similarities to those urged by the grangers, were more attractive to the miscellaneous participants in the Order than more specific labor grievances likely to provoke conflict.

Membership mounted rapidly after 1884, when the Knights, against Powderly's wishes, became involved in a great railroad strike. Seven years earlier the Baltimore & Ohio had attracted national attention by suppressing an effort to halt its operations. The workers had gained widespread community sympathy everywhere, from Buffalo in the east to San Francisco in the west; they nevertheless lost the struggle. The company had secured court injunctions against the strikers and had used troops to prevent interference with traffic. The outcome had demonstrated the difficulty of winning a struggle against a railroad.

The Knights showed it could be done. In 1885 and 1886 they led a successful campaign against the Missouri Pacific and the other lines of Jay Gould and achieved substantial gains for the workers. The appeal for labor solidarity evoked a tremendous response and raised the membership of the Order to 700,000.

In a few years, most of those who had enthusiastically joined drifted away. In 1890, only

Terence V. Powderly, *The Path I Trod* (New York, 1940) is an informative autobiography.

Haymarket Square, Chicago, May 4, 1886. Wood engraving from *Harper's Weekly*, 1886. (Library of Congress)

100,000 names remained on the rolls. Some of those who had left were respectable people worried by the anarchist menace. On May 4, 1886, in Haymarket Square, Chicago, a bomb thrown in the course of a labor meeting protesting brutality against strikers killed several policemen and wounded numerous bystanders. Although the bomb thrower was never identified, a trial found eight anarchists guilty of incitement to violence and four were actually hanged. Testimony seemed to show the infiltration of anarchists into the Knights of Labor and no doubt frightened away some of its membership.

The Order also suffered from the same attrition that drained support away from the granges. People who had joined a few years earlier without any substantial personal reason lost interest as time passed, and some laborers, discouraged by unsuccessful strikes, concluded that such a general organization could do little for them.

The American Federation of Labor   The effects of these setbacks were magnified by the emergence of a new organization which revealed that craftsmen who had the bargaining power of their skill could further their own welfare most effectively by cutting loose from the great mass of unskilled laborers and concentrating on improvement of their own conditions. During the 1870s such craft groups as the typographers and the ironworkers, while not opposed to the Knights of Labor, had sought a mode of common action that would not involve them with the high-flown general idealism of the Order. In

The AF of L Declares War on the Knights of Labor, 1886

The K. of L. have persistently attempted to undermine and disrupt the well-established Trades' Unions, organized and encouraged men who have proven themselves untrue to their trade, false to the obligations of their union, embezzlers of moneys, and expelled by many of the unions, and conspiring to pull down the Trades' Unions, which has cost years of work and sacrifice to build; therefore, be it Resolved we condemn the acts above recited, and call upon all workingmen to join unions of their respective trades, and urge the formation . . . of all under one head, The American Federation of Labor.

—Proceedings of the First Annual Convention of the American Federation of Labor, 1886, quoted in Philip Taft, *Organized Labor in American History* (New York: Harper & Row, Publishers, 1964), p. 115.

1881, a dozen similar unions joined together in the Federation of Organized Trades and Labor Unions of the United States and Canada. That association, however, remained weak and ineffective until 1886.

In that year the issue between the craftsmen and the Knights, between the specific objectives of the skilled and the general goals of all laborers, came to a head. Some socialists, expelled from the cigarmakers' union by Samuel Gompers and Adolph Strasser after a fight on precisely this point, had secured a charter from the Knights of Labor. Such dual unionism, which permitted employers to play one labor organization against another, was a threat to all artisans. When the Knights persisted in recognizing the dissidents, the Federation summoned a conference, which formed a new expanded American Federation of Labor. The AF of L immediately declared war on its rival and called on all union men to withdraw from the Knights.

The new organization grew rapidly in strength. By 1890, its affiliates had fully 550,000 members. Its success was due to more than the effectiveness of Gompers and its other leaders. Its structure and goals attracted the skilled workers. It was a loose federation that left substantial autonomy to its constituent unions, and it concentrated on improving the wages and working conditions of its own members.

The AF of L refused to be distracted by vague reform goals and accepted the existing economic order, on condition only that a fair share be allocated to those it represented. Its methods were in accord with that purpose; it bargained with the bosses, using strikes and boycotts where necessary, and it dabbled in politics only where its immediate interests were at stake. Many of its locals had a strong ethnic character — being predominantly Irish or German or Yankee — and some as a matter of course excluded Negroes, who had occasionally been used as strikebreakers. The craftsmen had thus determined to take care of themselves, as everyone else did. Indeed, the strongest, the railroad brotherhoods, refused even to affiliate with the AF of L.

Labor and Society   Only a tiny fraction of the labor force joined any union at all before 1890. The mass of the unskilled remained unorganized and lived either in utter helplessness or in a state of endemic warfare with their employers. Few factory owners accepted any responsibility toward the men in their plants. The Pullman Company took an unusual step in 1880 when it surrounded its plant near Chicago with brick tenements, athletic grounds, and gardens in the hope that contentment would increase the efficiency of its workers. Abram S. Hewitt, industrialist and political leader, was almost unique in recognizing the legitimacy of unionization.

Philip Taft, *The A.F. of L. in the Time of Gompers* (New York, 1957) is a thorough account.

SAMUEL GOMPERS perceived that industrialization had transformed the situation of labor and that labor organization would have to change too. He was born in 1850 in London, into a Jewish family that had recently migrated from Holland. At the age of ten he was apprenticed first to a shoemaker and then to his father as a cigarmaker. Three years later the family moved to New York, and Samuel went to work at his craft. At the age of seventeen he married, and he seemed destined for the bleak life of toil in which so many other Americans were trapped.

Inquisitiveness and gregariousness set him on another course. He wanted to know; in the evenings he studied at Cooper Union and when it was his turn to read to his fellow employees as they rolled cigars, he often chose the works of Marx, Engels, and Lassalle. His mind was occupied in argument with the theories of the class struggle spelled out in those books, but he never accepted them.

Gompers was a joiner. In meetings of the Odd Fellows and the Foresters, fraternal societies, he learned how to get on with people, and he applied the lessons to the local cigarmakers' union, of which he was a member. The failure of a long strike against the tenement sweating system led to a crisis in the organization and brought Gompers and his friend Adolph Strasser to command. They strengthened the union and brought it into the AF of L. Their basic principle was insistence that there be only one union in each trade so that it would control the labor market.

After 1890 Gompers' role increased in importance. Hostile to all utopian schemes, he insisted that the proper function of a union was to bargain for improvement of the wages and working conditions of its members; he was willing to leave management to the businessmen and politics to the politicians. Concentrating on this narrow role, he guided the AF of L through a period of steady growth, which culminated during World War I.

At the time of Gompers death in 1924, however, the deterioration of the lot of labor raised questions about the applicability of his formula to the problems of the twentieth century.

Abram S. Hewitt on Cooperation, 1880s

This is no dream of an enthusiast, for I am a plain man of business, nor is it an excursion into the realms of Utopia, for I have been trained to weigh and measure the results of human action. It is a sober deduction from the study of the operation of the principle of association, which has crowned this age with material achievements of stupendous grandeur and beneficence, and which is invading and taking possession of every domain of human affairs. It has already begun to organize labor for emancipation from the bondage of ages, and it will be found as easy of application, and as fruitful of benefit, in this final field of action, as it has been triumphant and beneficent in other spheres of social development.

—Allan Nevins, *Abram S. Hewitt* (New York: Harper & Row, Publishers, 1935), p. 431.

A Molly Maguire Ballad, ca. 1875

Kind-hearted Christians, I pray you give attention,
It's of a young man, down in jail he doth lie,
For the shooting of the boss, John P. Jones,
A murderer's death he is doomed for to die.

They say Doyle and Kelly committed the murder,
And that it was plotted by some cruel gang;
And likewise Jimmy Kerrigan that weak-hearted creature
That told all about it, 'fraid he would hang.

In years after this when he will be at his freedom,
When people will see him their blood it will boil.

They will say, "There goes that weak-hearted creature
That swore away the lives of Campbell, Kelly and Doyle."

The Commonwealth lawyers have done hard against them;
The ones that have done it are Hughes and Albright.
They say that the Hibernians are a great band of criminals
That go about robbing and murdering at night.

Now Hughes and Albright, stop throwing your slander
When the whip is in your hand; don't crack her free
Lest early some morning or late in the evening
You may trip on a brick and come down on your knee.

—Quoted in George Korson, *Minstrels of the Mine Patch* (Philadelphia: University of Pennsylvania Press, 1938), p. 263.

Most of his contemporaries rejected the principle of collective bargaining as an interference with the right of contract, and many were callously indifferent to the welfare of the anonymous hands who toiled for them. It was each man for himself, with the government a disinterested onlooker. Massachusetts was almost the only state, for instance, to provide for safety regulations in the use of machinery, and those not very effective ones.

The only recourse of the desperate laborers was ineffectual violence. In the anthracite coal fields of Pennsylvania, the Irish miners organized a secret society within the Ancient Order of Hibernians. The Molly Maguires did not hesitate to use terrorism to protect their interests; for more than a decade after the Civil War, murder and arson were their weapons against enemies. James McParlan, a Pinkerton private agent, finally secured the evidence in 1876 to hang ten of the leaders, and the gang then broke up. Resentment simmered beneath the surface, however, and would burst out again in the 1890s.

Nevertheless, the mass of laborers—skilled and unskilled—did not turn against the system that employed them. Unlike their counterparts in Europe, they did not join revolutionary socialist or anarchist movements or seek to overthrow the order that failed to reward them.

Hope made their lives tolerable. The immigrants, the most deprived sector of the labor force, had fled of their own free will from conditions still more wretched in their old homes. In America, some advance was feasible. Meager though earnings were, some families could accumulate savings and move into petty trade. Rarely was the ascent from rags to riches possible, but even moderate gains kept the spark of

Wayne G. Broehl, Jr., *The Molly Maguires* (Cambridge, Mass., 1964) is a lively narrative.

107

hope alive, and if the laborer himself could not rise, his children might.

Most important of all, life did not consist only of economic relationships. Harsh though the factory was, there were compensations outside it. There were psychic rewards in the absence of rank and in the freedom to create an autonomous social life that satisfied spiritual and emotional wants. Each urban district became a social center with churches and philanthropic and fraternal organizations that gave the laborer a sense of community. In the St. Patrick's Day parade or in the beer garden, he was a man, not just a hand. Let the Astors and the Vanderbilts preen themselves in their gilded palaces, he had a society of his own. It was in this context that he began to conceive of politics as a means of improving his condition.

▼

Hardships in the lives of laborers in the last quarter of the nineteenth century were the price the United States paid for industrialization. The cost fell disproportionately on those least capable of bearing it; only the most skilled were able, in these decades, to act in self-protection. But the institutional looseness of American society kept the burden from crushing the individuality of the oppressed, and incisive questions were being raised about the inevitability of the process.

Paperbacks for Further Reading

Among the general histories that devote some attention to this period are: Henry Pelling, *American Labor* (Chicago History of American Civilization Series) and Joseph G. Rayback, *A History of American Labor* (Free Press Paperbacks). Leon Litwack, ed., *The American Labor Movement* (Spectrum Books) contains an interesting collection of materials. There is also a section on this period in Maldwyn A. Jones, *American Immigration* (Chicago History of American Civilization Series). Two excellent monographs are: Norman J. Ware, *The Labor Movement in the United States, 1860–1895* (Vintage Books, Inc.), which deals mostly with the Knights of Labor; and Henry David, *History of the Haymarket Affair* (Collier Books), which is good on the incident and on its social and intellectual context.

THE CHALLENGE
TO INTELLECT

59

The optimism that had survived the tragedies of the Civil War and the failures of Reconstruction endured through the trials of expansion and industrialization. In the vague balance sheet that men commonly kept in their minds, the gains outweighed the costs. Americans considered the slums of the great cities and the difficulties of life on the Great Plains temporary inconveniences on a course that ultimately led to progress.

There was no complacency about social and personal difficulties but rather confidence in the power of reason to answer every important question. People who believed that all problems could be solved by the correct use of intelligence did not lose heart because of the obstacles they encountered. Rather they sought the means of applying the intellect to the needs of society.

Speeches at the Opening of the Philadelphia Centennial Exposition, 1876. (Culver Pictures)

Education

THE GREAT PHILADELPHIA Centennial Exposition of 1876 was a paean to progress. Its
halls demonstrated how the nation had grown,
materially and culturally, in the century since
Independence. Visitors left with every expectation that still more impressive developments lay
ahead. Thoroughgoing environmentalists, the
American people had faith that proper training
would enable them successfully to surmount
every obstacle. Hence many states had displayed,
in addition to their industrial and agricultural
achievement, the evidence of their advance in
education.

The continued popularity of the lecture
platform was evidence of the assurance that
learning was useful. After 1874, the Chautauqua
movement in upstate New York, with offshoots
throughout the country, offered adults who
could afford them a variety of more extended
courses. The spread of public libraries put books
within the reach of everyone. But increasingly
Americans identified education with the formal
school system, which was intended to equip children with the information and skills they would
need through life.

Education for All?   Despite the lip service to
the ideal of universal instruction, however, there
were wide variations in the amount and quality

of schooling available to young Americans. Elementary education still lagged after the Civil War in spite of the reforms initiated earlier in the century by Horace Mann and his followers. The South, which had been particularly slow in progress, now had to accommodate the offspring of Negroes as well as of whites; and the mushrooming cities in all parts of the country faced a constant demand for new facilities. The teachers and the administrators, like William T. Harris, who were most directly involved, knew the dimensions of the problem; and the National Education Association and the Bureau of Education, created by Congress in 1867, frequently pointed to the urgency of the needs. But professional educators rarely commanded the resources necessary to cope with them.

The steps forward were hesitant. By 1890 about half the states had enacted compulsory education laws that generally required sixteen weeks of attendance for children under fourteen. Even fewer states made any special provision for immigrants or provided free textbooks to students, a consideration of enormous importance for the poor. As a result the schools served only part of the population and not the part that needed them most. Attendance figures mounted encouragingly and passed the twelve million mark in 1890, but the increase just about matched the growth in population; it did not reflect education of a greater proportion of the nation's children.

The delay came from the reluctance to increase expenditures, which fluctuated throughout the period at about $10 a year for each student, not an impressive sum in the light of the rhetoric about the importance of learning. The insistence that governmental costs be kept minimal prevented any increase in budgets beyond that necessary to take in the rising numbers. As a result, the average wage of male teachers did not rise much above $40 a month, and many communities preferred to take on women at a lower cost. In 1890, the average teacher's salary

Merle E. Curti, *Social Ideas of American Educators* (New York, 1935) treats this period in some detail.

Learning at Chautauqua, 1892

Chautauqua sends its little books and papers into stagnant homes from Maine to California, and gives the silent occupants something to think about. . . . Any man who loves knowledge and his native land must be glad at heart when he visits a summer assembly of Chautauqua: there listens to the Orator's Recognition Address; attends the swiftly successive Round Tables upon Milton, Temperance, Geology, the American Constitution, the Relations of Science and Religion, and the Doctrine of Rent; perhaps assists at the Cooking School, the Prayer Meeting, the Concert, and the Gymnastic Drill; or wanders under the trees among the piazzaed cottages, and sees the Hall of Philosophy and the wooden Doric Temple shining on their little eminences; and, best of all, perceives in what throngs have gathered here the butcher, the baker, and the candlestick-maker—a throng themselves, their wives and daughters a throng—all heated in body, but none the less aglow for learning and a good time. The comic aspects of this mixture of science, fresh air, flirtation, Greek reminiscence, and devoutness are patent enough; but the way in which the multitude is being won to discard distrust of knowledge, and to think of it rather as the desirable goal for all, is not so generally remarked by scholarly observers. . . . Minds are set in motion; an intellectual world, beyond the domestic and personal, begins to appear; studious thought forms its fit friendship with piety, gladness, and the sense of a common humanity; a groundwork of civilization is prepared.

—G. H. Palmer, "Doubts about University Extension," *Atlantic Monthly*, LXIX (March, 1892), pp. 369, 370.

Apathy Toward Education, 1877

A plain and candid statement would of necessity be the old story of a tardy Congress and an over-confident, procrastinating people, less appreciative of education, notwithstanding their claims on this score, than proud of their material progress and power. . . .

In view of the amount and incalculable value of the work done by this Bureau [National Bureau of Education], and of the supreme importance of education in a country whose Government is of the people, by the people, for the people, it is surprising that it should be constantly hampered and embarrassed for want of adequate appropriations. . . .

[In the District of Columbia, for instance] there are, in all, 19,489 persons of school age (six to seventeen), as shown by the last census, with but 8520 pupils in average daily attendance, and with sittings for but 9645. Under these conditions it is not very strange that the compulsory law is practically a dead letter.

—U.S. Centennial Commission. International Exhibition, 1876. *Reports and Awards, Group XXVIII*, F. A. Walker, ed. (Washington: Government Printing Office, 1880), pp. 3, 9, 19.

WILLIAM T. HARRIS tried to apply prewar transcendentalist sentiments to the practical problems of modern education. Born on a Connecticut farm in 1835, he went to school sporadically and entered but did not graduate from Yale. He was rebellious and uncommitted, subscribing to one idea and then another; spiritualism, mesmerism, and phrenology all attracted him for a time.

In 1857 he began to teach in the public schools of St. Louis, and in this work found himself. In little more than a decade Harris was superintendent of the city's school system. The practical experience he gained supplemented his reading in the transcendentalist philosophers. Through Theodore Parker, he came to Goethe, Kant, and especially Hegel. He fastened upon Hegelian idealism as a way of supplying philosophical support for the old transcendentalist longing for solidarity. Hegel's belief in the crucial role of the state in connecting the individual with society seemed the essential counterweight to postwar individualism.

Harris attempted to further these ideas in the *Journal of Speculative Philosophy* and, after 1880, at a school in Concord, Massachusetts, where he aspired to be Emerson's successor. The results were disappointing. Americans of that decade were not particularly interested in abstract philosophy.

Through education, ideas could be put into practice, however, for the child became a citizen in the school. Harris achieved his greatest importance in 1899, when he became United States Commissioner of Education, a post he held until 1906, three years before his death. He was important not as a systematic philosopher but as a practical schoolman. His articles and reports helped rationalize the curriculum and focused attention on the importance of the school as an instrument for maintaining social order.

The Teaching Profession, 1877

Teaching in the United States is not recognized fully enough as a distinct profession. It is regarded too much as a stepping-stone to some better and more settled position in life. There are more reasons than one for this state of things. The appointment of teachers depends in too many cases not upon the fitness of the candidates, but upon personal or political reasons. One superintendent says, in regard to favoritism, "Teachers are hired first, and examined afterwards, and woe to that man who refuses a certificate to a friend of some member of the district committee!" But it appears that the superintendents are themselves in some cases in fault; they have absolute control over the teachers, and are by no means always free from political bias; so that many well-qualified persons refuse to become teachers when employment must be purchased at the sacrifice of independence.

—U.S. Centennial Commission. International Exhibition, 1876. *Reports and Awards, Group XXVIII*, F. A. Walker, ed. (Washington: Government Printing Office, 1880), p. 215.

1870s and 1880s, although only a tiny minority of the population attended them.

That the general illiteracy rate dropped to 17 percent in 1880 and to 13 percent in 1890 and that some children of the poor struggled for an education was due not to the ease of access to schooling but to the enormous reward attached to it. The classroom was the least restricted channel of social mobility; anyone who wished to sacrifice immediate income could come and climb a step in the competition for careers. Here ambitious children of artisans and even of immigrant laborers could learn not merely the skills useful to the future clerk or businessman but also how to look and behave like one.

The Colleges   The aspiration toward a rise in status accounted also for the continued proliferation of colleges. Their number almost doubled and their enrollment tripled in the two decades after 1870. This was the one branch of education that grew dramatically, between the Civil War and 1890, relative to total population.

Since the 1850s the states had labored actively to create practical and, particularly, agricultural and mechanical universities. By the Morrill Act of 1862, the Federal government put at their disposal substantial lands, from the sale of which they could derive funds to support such

was only $252 a year. It was not surprising therefore that the usual turnover in staff was about 26 percent annually.

Secondary Education   Relatively greater attention went to the new high schools, which catered to the sector of the population best able to make its wishes felt in politics. These institutions appealed primarily to young people who could not afford to go to an academy or college but who wished to complete an education that would lift them into the middle ranks of society. High schools had appeared in the largest cities in the 1850s, and they spread rapidly in the

High Schools in the United States, 1870–1890

Year	Enrollment	Number of Graduates
1870	80,000	16,000
1880	110,000	23,000
1890	202,000	43,000

Colleges in the United States, 1870–1890

Year	Number	Enrollment	Percentage of Population 18–21
1870	563	52,000	1.68
1880	811	116,000	2.72
1890	998	157,000	3.04

institutions. These schools, like the denominational ones, felt the pressure to change their purposes almost as soon as they opened. Their students did not aspire to careers as farmers or mechanics; nor were the faculties content to teach the skills of the field or shop. The ambitions of both pupils and teachers drew the new colleges into imitations of the old in curriculum as well as in sports, fraternities, and other aspects of student life.

The social prestige of the old college began almost at once to envelop a still newer kind of institution, originally created for an entirely different purpose. In the 1860s there was nothing in the United States to compare with the German universities in which serious scholars pursued advanced studies with impressive results. The prospect of creating their counterparts attracted particularly Americans eager to supply a firm scientific foundation for the professions. But to establish universities in this sense it was necessary to cut away from the schools, which devoted most of their energies to the rudimentary teaching of unruly adolescents. Johns Hopkins (1876) and Clark (1889) were therefore planned as graduate institutions, with an explicit intention of avoiding the task of schooling undergraduates.

They were rather to be centers for the disinterested pursuit of knowledge. Johns Hopkins and its hospital were the model. Here, from the painstaking study of many cases, the researcher drew the data on the basis of which he arrived at a general formula for solving a problem. Here he could test and perfect the cure, so that the continuing interplay of science and practice both advanced the understanding and helped the patient. What was true in medicine was equally true in other fields.

Whatever the intentions of their founders, the graduate universities did not long remain a species apart. Harvard and Yale among the older colleges, and Michigan and California among the state institutions, had the money and the power to assimilate the same objectives; the university became a kind of holding company that carried on simultaneously a variety of different and sometimes contradictory activities—social, cultural, and practical as well as scientific. Control rested somewhat incongruously with boards of trustees designated by the state or by the men of wealth who contributed financial support and who regarded scientific pursuits with mingled faith and distrust. While the universities purported to seek knowledge for its own sake, their ultimate strength rested on the expectation of their students that attendance would carry them forward on the road to success.

Science and Religion

Science too took on a somewhat ambiguous role. It now ceased to be the avocation of amateurs, and became professional, organized by specialized disciplines and subject to its own rules of inquiry and discovery. Men little known to the public, like the astronomer Simon Newcomb and the physicists Josiah Willard Gibbs and Albert A. Michelson, made notable discoveries the importance of which only their peers recognized. Yet the society in the context of which science operated regarded it with both hope and fear—hope for the progress toward which its knowledge might contribute, fear for the unsettling questions it might raise.

Darwinism After the Civil War popular attention focused on the challenge of Darwinism to accepted intellectual assumptions. The implications of the evolutionary propositions put forward in *On the Origin of Species* (1859) now received widespread consideration.

The concept of evolution ran counter to the common literal interpretations of the Biblical description of the origin of the universe and of man's place in it. The world, Darwin had suggested, was not the product of a single act of

Donald H. Fleming, *William H. Welch and the Rise of Modern Medicine* (Boston, 1954) is a fascinating biography that throws light on the role of modern science.

Stow Persons, ed., *Evolutionary Thought in America* (New Haven, Conn., 1950) contains material on a broad range of related subjects.

creation and designed by God to be the stage on which the descendants of Adam would act out the drama of salvation. It was instead the outcome of a slow development, in the course of which humans appeared, like other beings, as a result of a blind process of natural selection. Gone was the assurance of man's uniqueness and of a known beginning and a known end to his history. His animal past reached back through the dim aeons of time; his future was scarcely predictable.

Darwinism bore a still more frightening aspect. If the Bible had been inaccurate, then no authority could be taken on faith. Even the propositions of science had to be constantly tested and retested. Every absolute proposition was questionable, for knowledge itself developed and had validity only within the context in which it was grasped at any given moment. The old certainties were suspect and no new ones replaced them. The evolutionary ideas thus challenged not merely traditional orthodoxy but the doctrinal basis of all religion.

In Defense of Faith   The initial reaction of the devout was a frontal attack on the whole theory of evolution. The conclusions of science could not stand against authoritative judgments of faith. Stated in these terms the argument was lost, for science had acquired such prestige that it readily won the minds of men in any direct confrontation with religion. Colonel Robert Ingersoll, a professed agnostic, easily routed the clergymen who debated him as long as they clung to tradition.

A more subtle defense of religion appeared in the affirmation that there were two kinds of knowledge which did not contradict each other. There was, therefore, no essential warfare between science and theology. To effect a widely desired reconciliation, it was necessary only to read the Scriptures metaphorically and to yield to the claims of science in the areas of its competence. People respected the power of science but they also felt the will to believe; they wished to use the telephone and modern surgery but they were afraid to cut loose from the inherited ideas

of heaven and hell. Henry Ward Beecher and Lyman Abbott explained from their pulpits that evolution simply displayed, in a new and more sublime form, the mysterious way in which God performed His wonders. The American Institute of Christian Philosophy (1881) devoted itself to distributing literature which proved that science and religion were in accord.

The drift away from the literal defense of older views conformed with the long-term tendency to regard religion not as a body of dogma but as a rule of conduct. Since the eighteenth century, ethics not theology had been central to the religious thinking of Americans. They were prepared therefore to redefine the function of the churches in moral terms and thus absorb the shock of evolution.

The Society for Ethical Culture, founded in 1876 by Felix Adler, was an extreme expression of the willingness to dispense with dogma. But the same development appeared in many older denominations, in which the formal aspects of worship yielded in importance to practical acts of benevolence.

The desire to emphasize action rather than creed played a part in formulation of the social gospel that shook American Protestantism in the 1880s. The crying needs of the depressed elements in the population challenged the integrity of Christians who put good works at the center of their religious life. In *Our Country* (1885), Josiah Strong called on his fellow citizens to demonstrate their faith in philanthropy. The quieter preaching of Washington Gladden urged a constant attention to the social mission of the church. Indeed before the decade ended, institutional churches under Episcopal, Congregational, and Baptist auspices were providing their congregations with sewing and manual-training classes as well as with gymnasiums and reading rooms; and theological seminaries emphasized that it was desirable for future ministers to acquire experience in social work and a knowledge of economics.

Henry F. May, *Protestant Churches and Industrial America* (New York, 1963) analyzes the problem in this period.

The Emergence of Social Science

The Study of Man It was recognized that the mastery of knowledge which had brought so many material rewards could also contribute solutions to the problems of human order. The study of society was therefore as important as the study of the physical world; and the same techniques could further understanding in both realms.

Man himself was the basic subject of inquiry. The ethnic diversity of population in the United States early excited interest in anthropology as a means of discovering the basic laws that governed human development. The early students of the subject had devoted their attention especially to physical differences, in the effort to describe the physical types of man. Darwinism supplied a firm intellectual framework for the idea that human beings were divided into separate and unmixable races; all men need not have been the descendants of a single pair of Biblical progenitors but could have evolved as biologically distinct species. The desire to justify the inferiority of the Negro and the Chinese made these views attractive in many parts of the country.

Anthropology yielded valuable social as well as racial insights. The examination of primitive people like the Indians could also make clear the social forces that governed the development of such institutions as the family. The New York lawyer and ethnologist Lewis Henry Morgan thus based his influential analysis of *Ancient Society* (1878) on research on the Iroquois. In an effort to define the factors responsible for progress, the book traced the successive epochs through which people moved from savagery to barbarism to civilization.

History was slower to draw comparable insights from the more recent past. The impressive work of German and English scholars had provided new information on the origin of religious and political institutions, but no American yet matched them in learning or in power of analysis. The narrative tradition, of which Francis Parkman was the ablest expositor, had not yet given way to professional scholarship. The historical activity stimulated by the patriotic celebrations of the centennial of Independence in 1876 were largely antiquarian.

More scholarly investigations were, however, beginning to take form. Herbert Baxter Adams taught his seminar at Johns Hopkins the rigorous methods he had absorbed in Germany and stressed the importance of the continuities that linked present institutions to the germs from which they developed. On a more popular level John Fiske traced the features of American democracy to the German forests, from which he believed they had grown.

Economics The science of economics was to provide answers to the most important questions of contemporary society. Morgan had pointed out that changes in technology had been responsible for the key transitions from one epoch to another. An understanding of the system of production was therefore basic to the ability to formulate all social policy.

A knowledge of the rules that governed the fluctuations in the volume of international trade or in the value of currency was obviously useful in making practical decisions about the tariff or about paper money. Carroll D. Wright even argued that a solution to the labor problem might emerge if only enough information were available; and he and others set themselves the task of collecting the appropriate statistics.

Economists like Richard T. Ely and John Bates Clark asserted that their science offered the means of diagnosing the ills and prescribing the remedies for a society that did not as yet operate in accord with religious values. Economics could show how to alter the system of production from which both the wealth and the poverty of the nation emanated. Ely was among

Milton Berman, *John Fiske: The Evolution of a Popularizer* (Cambridge, Mass., 1961) is a thoughtful biography.

those who formed the American Economics Association with that intention deliberately in view.

Social Policy The developing social sciences stimulated thought and buttressed the preaching of the ministers of the social gospel. Nevertheless, the conclusions derived from studies in these sciences did not win universal assent as did those in the natural and physical sciences. Perhaps the methods were as yet imperfect; perhaps interest, too, often shaped judgment. Whatever the reason, it was possible to arrive at diametrically opposed positions from the same point of departure in Darwinian evolution. William Graham Sumner, for instance, provided a forceful American statement of the principles of Herbert Spencer, supported by Darwin's ideas. The survival of the fittest through which the species developed demanded conflict to eliminate the weak. Government should therefore refrain from any interference with free competition, whether by the tariff or rate regulation or misguided acts of sympathy toward the unfortunate. *Laissez faire* was the only tolerable policy.

By contrast Lester Ward, who started with the same assumptions, argued that the survival of the fittest did not depend simply upon the blind forces of nature. Human intelligence entered into judgments of what was fittest and evolution could be successfully guided toward desirable goals. Knowledge could serve as a basis of positive action. Social science was thus less likely to produce a neat formula than to frame meaningful questions about which people could argue.

Conservative Tendencies

The old order continued to find defenders whose traditional faith enabled them to reject the findings of science. To the Irish and German Catholics, the Scandinavian Lutherans, and the European Jews, the new learning was alien like everything else around them and therefore suspect for its threat to ancestral values.

JOHN FISKE never explained why he decided to change his name. He was born Edmund Fisk Green in 1842 in Hartford, Connecticut. At the age of ten, he lost his father, and he went to live with his grandparents when his mother remarried. No doubt the precocious boy, who learned foreign languages easily, was insecure. He remained so through life, and never found the place he thought he deserved.

He did well as a student at Harvard, but he surrendered orthodox religion there and became a follower of Herbert Spencer. His early espousal of evolution may have kept him from a career as a lawyer or as a professor. Although he gave popular lectures in Cambridge, the only post open to him was as assistant librarian at Harvard.

In 1873, after the publication of his first book, Fiske traveled to Europe, where he met Darwin, Spencer, and Huxley. There he wrote his most influential book, *The Outlines of Cosmic Philosophy* (1874). In the next quarter century he earned substantial popularity as a writer and lecturer.

His work focused on two themes, American history and philosophy. He was not an original scholar in either sphere. His strength lay in stating ideas clearly so that the layman could understand them. Fiske's historical work was intensely patriotic. His successive volumes traced the development of American institutions in a markedly nationalistic tone. They caught on with a public reminded of its origins by the centennial celebrations after 1876.

As a philosopher, Fiske was primarily concerned with assimilating the intellectual consequences of evolution. Although he never returned to an orthodox faith, he handled the new ideas in a manner that made them palatable to religious people. He stressed the optimistic features of evolution and left open the possibility of immortality and of a guiding providence in human affairs. He had the satisfaction of knowing, before he died in 1901, that he had made a deep impression on his fellow countrymen.

117

Business and Religion, 1890

But, we are told . . . . You cannot devote your time and energy to the acquisition of riches and do your duty as a disciple of Jesus Christ. . . . Why not? Do we find men who are diligent in business wanting in patriotism or in family affection? Nay, is it not such men who are most likely to be loyal to family and friends and country? Why may they not be equally loyal to the divine sovereign to whom they have voluntarily sworn allegiance? . . .

If I am gifted with the capacity to organize industrial enterprises, is it not my duty to engage in such enterprises, and to set therein an example of pluck and diligence and energy? In doing so I shall certainly grow rich. . . . And how can I better aid the work of the Master than by earning money thus to devote to missionary enterprises which must be maintained by the contributions of Christians?

—A. B. Lyons, "The Christian's Vow of Poverty," *Thirty Eighth Annual Report of the Hawaiian Mission Children's Society* (Honolulu: Press Publishing Company, 1890), pp. 34, 35.

Mary Baker Eddy (1821–1910), Founder of the Christian Science Church. (The Granger Collection)

Wherever possible, they set up parochial schools to guard the loyalty of their children. Most Negroes, too, preferred the emotional consolation of their churches to the remote abstractions of a science that had little relevance to their situation.

The old verities retained their hold also on many native Americans, particularly in the rural regions of the country. There the circuit rider carried the familiar warnings against sin, and the revivalist issued the strident call to salvation by way of repentance. The evangelist Dwight L. Moody brought the technique into the city, where he found earnest listeners among people born on the farms who wished to hear the good old doctrine. They too were concerned about the souls of their children, as the spread of Sunday schools indicated.

Men disturbed by the social consequences of the new thought also rejected it. The potential radicalism of its approach to social problems concerned those primarily interested in order, who tried to use their churches as a means of restraint.

Both the defenders and attackers of science exaggerated its powers. The millennial quality of the thinking of the times, the expectation that all problems would soon be solved, made many people gullible about panaceas of every sort. Medicine shows and newspaper advertisements still displayed patented remedies, and it was but a short step from the belief that any illness could be cured to faith healing. It was significant that Mary Baker Eddy gave the most popular such sect the name Christian Science, uniting in its title an appeal to both the old and the new. And numerous crusaders and reformers were promising quick solutions to difficult social problems.

▼

The belief that intelligence could cope with the difficulties of a rapidly changing society led to a radical transformation in American ways of knowing. Science took the place of religion as the authority for knowledge of the world and of man's place in it.

The learning of this period was by no means as universally accepted as rhetoric made it seem. Nor did it do all that was expected of it. But the new institutions founded to develop and spread science did take firm root, and they supplied an impressive foundation for later development. Above all, the impact of science made people think about matters they had long taken for granted.

Paperbacks for Further Reading

Frederick Rudolph, *The American College and University* (Vintage Books, Inc.) is good on this period. Richard Hofstadter, *Social Darwinism in American Thought* (Beacon Press) is a thorough analysis; and there is relevant material also in his *Anti-Intellectualism in America* (Vintage Books, Inc.). Edward Lurie, *Louis Agassiz* (Phoenix Books) is a scholarly biography of an important scientist and opponent of Darwinism.

CRITICS AND CRUSADERS

60

The disorder created by industrialization and expansion compounded the social problems left by the war and Reconstruction. The scars visible in both the city and the countryside disturbed Americans but did not shake their faith in progress. Their material and intellectual resources were ample enough, they believed, to deal with all difficulties.

Reform was possible. Since early in the nineteenth century, confidence in man's ability to improve himself had animated numerous organized movements; it continued to do so after the Civil War. Novel conditions changed some of the tactics and objectives, but the sense of urgency and of the possibility of change remained unshaken.

UNTIL 1860, REFORMERS had regarded themselves as fighters in a common cause. Important differences about methods and pace often set various kinds of antislavery or temperance men to bickering with one another, but the bonds of unity among them were strong, for all the efforts to ameliorate the condition of mankind took root in the culture of a society not yet sharply divided against itself.

After the Civil War Americans sometimes still spoke of reform as if it were the homogeneous response to a single impulse. Yet in actuality the term now applied to a variety of quite different desires to alter the features of life in the United States. Civil Service, temperance, and the single tax were all reforms, but each drew its support from limited sectors of the population and each was inspired by distinctive motives. Reform was fragmented, as society and culture were.

Genteel Reformers

Some people considered the outstanding problem of the 1870s to be the subservience of the government to special interests. The evidence was pervasive: corruption in the municipalities and the states, venality in the entourage of President Grant, and the failure to check the depredations of the business barons. The Tweed Ring, which looted New York City, was for reformers the symbol of the age.

The sense of outrage was particularly acute among the members of respectable old families now being rapidly outdistanced in wealth by grasping men of low breeding on the way up. Young Theodore Roosevelt in New York or Henry and Charles Francis Adams in Massachusetts considered themselves patricians, endowed by education with the qualities of leadership if only the society would call upon their services. Since they believed that civilization should unite men so that they could dwell harmoniously together, they most valued order that defined for each individual his appropriate rights and obligations.

Their culture taught the patricians to follow their consciences in doing what was right on behalf of the less-well endowed. Some of them were too fastidious to compete with the roughnecks either in politics or trade; yet others, responding to the call of duty, entered the battle for purity. Uncomfortable under discipline, they were generally independents in politics; those who bolted from the Republican party earned the epithet "Mugwumps."

Reform for them generally meant the neutralization of government. In a democracy, which lacked the stabilizing influence of an aristocracy, the state was too readily corrupted to be charged with more than the bare responsibility for police protection. The prospect that a low politician like Chester A. Arthur could become President by an accident proved that it was necessary to set narrow limits to power entrusted to any officeholder.

Fighting the Spoilsmen Civil Service reform was one means toward that end. A disinterested bureaucracy, composed of men selected for their merit, it was hoped, would replace the political appointees who had swamped the Federal and state agencies since Jackson demonstrated the use of the spoils system. Able public servants, after the British model, would reduce the cost of government and stand up to the scoundrels who sought to pervert it. The change would purify politics by eliminating the corrupt influence of patronage. The shock of Garfield's assassination, in 1881, by a man seeking an appointment added force to these arguments.

The agitation of the Civil Service Reform League, on the Federal level, finally led to the enactment in 1883 of the Pendleton Act, which created a bipartisan commission to administer competitive tests for positions placed on the classified list. The number of such posts expanded steadily in the years that followed, and

Edward C. Kirkland, *Charles Francis Adams, Jr., 1835–1915* (Cambridge, Mass., 1965) is a readable study of a patrician reformer.

George F. Howe, *Chester A. Arthur* (New York, 1934) is a straightforward biography.

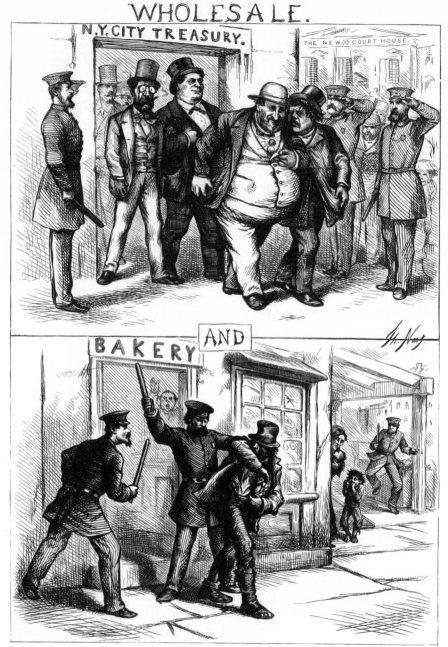

Boss Tweed and His Ring. This is one of many cartoons by Thomas Nast attacking a group of New York City politicians headed by William M. Tweed which gained control of the city's finances and swindled it out of many millions of dollars. From *Harper's Weekly*, September 16, 1871. (The Granger Collection)

CHESTER A. ARTHUR, who received the Republican nomination for the vice-presidency in 1880, was everything the Mugwump Republicans detested. Born in 1830 in Franklin County, Vermont, he was educated at Union College and taught school before entering the practice of law. He was active in the organization of the Republican party and served successfully as quartermaster general of the New York State militia under the Civil War Governor Edwin D. Morgan. He was, in other words, a routine machine politician.

In 1871, therefore, President Grant made him Collector of the Port of New York, then the chief patronage dispensing office in the city. Arthur followed the normal practice of overstaffing his agency with clerks and laborers who then spent most of their time on party duties. High customs receipts provided an ample war chest with which to maintain the party faithful. Arthur was personally honest but devoted to the duty of supporting the New York Republican machine under United States Senator Roscoe Conkling.

Between 1877 and 1880 the antagonism between President Hayes and Conkling caught Arthur in the cross fire. The President ordered Customs House employees to abstain from politics. Arthur, loyal to his chieftain, defied the order. Hayes sought to remove him. Conkling invoked the Tenure of Office Act and prevented the ratification of an alternative in the Senate. As a result Arthur became the symbol of the spoils system when, in 1880, he received the Republican nomination to offset Garfield and mollify Conkling.

Arthur's administration surprised both friends and enemies. He was no worse a President than any other in these decades, but he was able to win over neither the reformers nor the machine stalwarts and was denied renomination. He died in 1886.

New York and Massachusetts adopted a similar practice. The success of the reformers in this endeavor was no doubt partly due to the support of many a politician overwhelmed by the task of dealing with mobs of office seekers.

Economic Liberalism Some reformers worried about those aspects of industrial development which seemed to encourage dishonesty and to limit the free competition that they regarded as essential in a free society. Their criteria were those of traditional morality and of the independent proprietor. Charles Francis Adams, Jr., in 1871 thus revealed the corrupt manipulations of Erie Railroad securities, and Henry Demarest Lloyd in 1881 exposed the maneuvers of the Standard Oil Company. But before 1890, people shocked by the escapades of Daniel Drew or by the deals of John D. Rockefeller faced a dilemma: they did not wish to increase the powers of government, which alone was able to restrain the new capitalists.

Nor was there much headway in the effort to lower the tariff. High protective rates ran counter to the theories of the laissez-faire economists and were evidence of the pressure of special interests. Reform-minded writers periodically took up the pen in a call for downward revision, but however plausible the arguments, they carried little political weight. There were only minor adjustments in 1872 and 1883, and the McKinley Act of 1890 provided for a substantial increase.

Reformers of the Mugwump variety also became involved in movements to improve the sanitary condition of cities and to extend the rights of women, the Negroes, and Indians. Agitation sensitized the conscience of the nation to these problems although as yet it bore meager fruits.

Despite their respectability and the attention they commanded, the crusaders had little leverage on issues that affected substantial groups in the country. They could count on the prestige of social rank and on the influence of such journals as *The Nation* and *Harper's Weekly*, and they enlisted vigorous intellectual support

Reform as Laissez Faire, 1883

Society . . . does not need any care or supervision. If we can acquire a science of society, based on observation of phenomena and study of forces, we may hope to gain some ground slowly toward the elimination of old errors and the reestablishment of a sound and natural social order. Whatever we gain that way will be by growth, never in the world by any reconstruction of society on the plan of some enthusiastic social architect. The latter is only repeating the old error over again, and postponing all our chances of real improvement. Society needs first of all to be freed from these meddlers—that is, to be let alone. Here we are, then, once more back at the old doctrine—*Laissez faire*. Let us translate it into blunt English, and it will read, Mind your own business.

—William Graham Sumner, *What Social Classes Owe to Each Other* (New York: Harper & Row, Publishers, 1883), pp. 119–120.

from such writers as Edwin L. Godkin and Carl Schurz. But criticism from this source was cautious, qualified, and biased by the social perspective of the would-be patricians. All too self-confident of the correctness of their own standards, the reformers were often self-righteous about their own polite affairs and censorious about the cruder business of others. Like Mrs. Sam in F. Marion Crawford's novel, they understood Boston business and called it finance but despised the New York Stock Market and denounced its conduct as gambling. By the same token, gentlemen appointed to office by their friends were not the spoilsmen the nominees of machine politicians were. Such attitudes

Edward L. Godkin, *Problems of Modern Democracy* (Cambridge, Mass., 1966) is a useful collection with an informative introduction by Morton Keller.

limited the attractiveness of the Mugwump appeal.

Above all, genteel reformers had no answers to the questions that occupied the great mass of the population. Injunctions to heed reason rather than brute passion, to do good rather than act by selfish interest, had little meaning to the men in the factories and the homesteads. Critics of other sorts addressed themselves to the problems of life in the cities and on the farms of the nation.

The Urban Challenge

The moral and social hazards of urbanization had already attracted attention before the Civil War. Away from the land, people lost their sense of independence; right and wrong blurred; and there were no restraints on the impulse to greed. It was hard to be a good citizen or a good Christian in the city. Often, too, it was hard to stay alive.

The metropolis became more dangerous as it grew in size. Its bright lights tempted the unwary into careers of crime and prostitution; its shadows only partially concealed poverty and dependency. Since all forms of delinquency were ascribed to the injurious effect of the environment, their very existence showed the need for reform.

In the countryside, the family and the intimate community of which it was a part could deal informally with the problems of the orphans, the aged, the poor, the insane, and the criminal. Often Americans expressed the hope, as did Edward Everett Hale in *Sybaris* (1869), for the development of idyllic villages where neighborliness would resolve all difficulties for the workers who commuted to their factories. But Hale realized that the prospect of turning back the wheels of time was remote and not as attractive in reality as it was in daydreams. The wealthy could escape to their country homes, the middle classes to the suburbs, but the mass of urban residents had to stay where they were.

The Pull of City Life, 1869

As we pile people together in cities — as we separate them from their mother earth — as we make them tenants of one and another landlord, we do our best to unmake the virtues of two centuries' growth, which sprang from the holding of one's own home in fee-simple. . . .

Nobody . . . expects to sweep back these thronging millions from the towns to the prairies by nice little half-column articles in the daily papers, on the joys of Agricultural Life. If the men who write these Idyls like the prairies, why do not they go to them themselves? This is the fierce question which young men from the country and young girls from the country ask — men and girls who have forced their way to the large towns and their excitements and occupations, precisely because their own tastes or aptitudes lay in the direction of commerce or of handiwork or of fine art, and precisely because they did not choose to continue in the duties which the life of a farmer compelled. We cannot undo the eternal laws of our civilization. . . . We cannot have large cities, with the stimulus they give in civilization, and at the same time send all our young people to fence in prairies, and raise breadstuffs.

—Edward Everett Hale, *Sybaris* (Boston: Fields, Osgood & Company, 1869), pp. 123, 127–128.

Philanthropy Within their limited means, the poor tried to help themselves through benevolent and fraternal associations. Usually men of Irish or German or Yankee antecedents banded naturally together to aid members of their own ethnic group, although some societies served a more general clientele. Thousands of voluntary organizations proferred relief to the victims of temporary misfortune; in 1878 there were eight hundred such bodies in Philadelphia alone. But the meager resources available from dues and contributions were inadequate to cope with the problem in normal times and were quickly exhausted in periods of depression when everyone was to some extent dependent.

Promiscuous philanthropy seemed unwise to reformers, for it aimed to demonstrate the benevolence of the donor rather than to improve the lot of the recipient. Soup kitchens took the edge off the tramp's hunger, but might actually blunt his desire to become self-supporting. The careless almsgiver thus unwittingly perpetuated the evil that elicited his generosity.

People who wished to improve society considered a more scientific approach necessary. The Charity Organization Society founded in Buffalo in 1877 created a clearing house that passed on the worthiness of applicants for aid on behalf of all the agencies in that city. It stressed the need for rehabilitating those assisted, by which it meant generally, getting them back to work. Other places quickly copied the practice, which had the added virtue of seeming scientific.

Help in the form of cash payments to the recipients, even when thus safeguarded, was suspect in the eyes of reformers. The money, they thought, might go for liquor or other unworthy expenditures and the individuals who received it remained in a corrupting environment within which improvement was unlikely. It seemed better when feasible to remove those who could not support themselves to institutions under the oversight of people qualified to govern them. The mere fact of dependency was proof of the incompetence of the individual and his family and of the need for incarceration and control. Since the calls for aid increased, the number of public and private asylums for the ill, the poor, the orphaned, the aged, the deaf, the dumb, the blind, and the drunk multiplied. These institutions were expected to carry on the work of reform. If the asylums often looked like prisons, it was because these institutions followed a common model; the criminal, as well as the dependent, was subject to reform, and the de-

Women in the Elizabeth Street Police Station, New York, 1880s. Photograph by Jacob A. Riis. (The Jacob A. Riis Collection, Museum of the City of New York)

A Temperance Crusade. Women in Fredericktown, Ohio, clean out the leading liquor saloon. Cartoon from the *New York Illustrated Times*, 1879. (Culver Pictures)

The Age of Brass, or the Triumphs of Woman's Rights. Lithograph by Currier & Ives, 1869. (Library of Congress)

pendent, as well as the criminal, needed discipline.

Rising costs, however, were worrisome and encouraged experiments designed to get the inmates out on their own as soon as possible. Massachusetts adopted a scheme to put prisoners on probation; New York's reformatory at Elmira consciously worked to effect quick cures of criminality; and there were a variety of efforts to use the labor of convicts, orphans, and paupers on farms and in workshops. Massachusetts was the first to create a state board of charity (1864) to coordinate the work of local agencies and to increase their efficiency.

The role of government nevertheless remained residual. Reformers, like most other Americans, believed that the primary responsibility for relief rested with individuals and voluntary groups. The state intervened only when all other efforts failed. This narrow view of the scope of government action sprang partly from the desire to keep its expenses low, but partly also from a constricted sense of obligation, which reflected the lack of community feeling.

Temperance The ideal laborer took care of his own family. Charity might tide him over in crises or send his children to a camp in the country for a week. But his true salvation lay in learning how better to manage for himself. The ideal reformer best served his function by providing the needy with helpful information and by removing temptation from their paths. Let the workingman only learn to spend his evenings in the library instead of in the saloon and his condition would improve.

In the 1880s the temperance movement devoted itself to exhortation on behalf of these objectives as its role. The failure of prewar efforts to legislate the liquor business out of existence had not dampened the ardor of the prohibitionists. Solidly entrenched in the rural districts, they continued the campaign against alcohol. Though they succeeded, by means of local option laws, to have their way in the countryside, they could not dry out the cities. At

To her closest friends, **FRANCES E. C. WILLARD** was known as Frank. As a girl she hated housework and liked hunting and the outdoor life. She resented the fact that her father would not let her ride horseback and was envious of her older brother. Much of the time she was lonely. She liked to read, but novels were forbidden her by her father.

Frances was born in 1839 in Churchville, New York. Her parents struggled for status and education, and moved to Wisconsin, where she lived until she was eighteen. She overcame her early religious doubts, joined the Methodist Church, and studied at Northwestern Female College in Evanston, Illinois. Briefly she was engaged, but instead of marrying, in 1860 took a job in a county school and held various teaching positions until 1871, when she became president of Evanston College.

A turning point in her life came in 1874 when she joined the temperance crusade in Pittsburgh and delivered her first public prayer on the sawdust floor of a Market Street saloon. She had found her mission. Her zeal made her president of the Chicago branch of the Women's Christian Temperance Union, and she advanced steadily until 1891, when she became President of the World's WCTU.

Frances Willard realized that the temperance question was linked to other issues. Extension of the ballot to women, for instance, was a means of mobilizing support for eradication of the liquor evil. Moreover, abstinence was a step toward encouraging workingmen to use their funds advantageously and thus was connected with the labor movement. Political activity was important to attain any of these ends. She helped organize the Prohibition party in 1882 and the People's party in 1892, and was for a time president of the National Council of Women. She died in 1898, confident that her efforts would soon bear fruit.

most, by insisting on the rigid enforcement of Sunday closing laws, they managed to take the fun out of the workingman's one day of leisure.

It was for his own good, of course. Abstinence would permit him not only to use the nickels wasted on beer for more important expenses but also to conserve his energy so that he could work harder and rise in the world. Sobriety was essential to sound family life and thus to the welfare of society.

Women's Rights The Women's Christian Temperance Union, founded in 1874, linked the causes of prohibition and women's rights. Frances E. C. Willard, later president of the WCTU, explained that mothers and wives best understood the costs of intemperance; given the right to vote, they would purify politics, abolish the saloon, and further the cause of reform in every aspect of life.

The demand for equal rights had a deeper import, however. Well-to-do women, impatient with the domesticity to which society confined them, now sought a wider scope for their activity. They could attend college and hold jobs until they married, but the voluminous skirts that were draped five yards wide over their bustles were symbolic of the male insistence upon removing them from active contact with reality. They protested against the assumption that they were inferior beings, and exclusion from the ballot was a sign of their incomplete citizenship.

Their campaign won only the meager concession in some states of the right to vote in school elections, but temporary defeat left them undaunted. The notorious Victoria Woodhull, candidate for the presidency, was less important than the patient organizers Susan B. Anthony and Elizabeth Stanton who gradually mobilized a powerful army in the National Woman Suffrage Association (formed in 1869). For the time being they threw themselves with increasing vigor into the temperance movement and into good works on behalf of the dependent. The

Mary Earhart, *Frances Willard* (Chicago, 1944) is an informative study.

Victoria Woodhull, in a cartoon by Thomas Nast. Here the course urged by Victoria Woodhull is rejected by the wife with the words, "Get thee behind me, (Mrs.) Satan! I'd rather travel the hardest path of matrimony than follow your footsteps." From *Harper's Weekly*, February 17, 1872. (Culver Pictures)

Erecting the Statue of Liberty. The statue by the French sculptor Frédéric Bartholdi was presented by the French people to the United States in 1885 and unveiled the next year. From the French newspaper *Journal Universel*, 1886. (Museum of the City of New York)

The Effects of Poverty on Progress, 1881

The unequal distribution of the power and wealth gained by the integration of men in society tends to check, and finally to counterbalance, the force by which improvements are made and society advances. On the one side, the masses of the community are compelled to expend their mental powers in merely maintaining existence. On the other side, mental power is expended in keeping up and intensifying the system of inequality in ostentation, luxury, and warfare. . . . Invention may for awhile to some degree go on; but it will be the invention of refinements in luxury, not the inventions that relieve toil and increase power. . . . For as it tends to lessen the mental power devoted to improvement, so does inequality tend to render men adverse to improvement. . . .

What has destroyed every previous civilization has been the tendency to the unequal distribution of wealth and power. This same tendency, operating with increasing force, is observable in our civilization today, showing itself in every progressive community, and with greater intensity the more progressive the community. Wages and interest tend constantly to fall, rent to rise, the rich to become very much richer, the poor to become more helpless and hopeless, and the middle class to be swept away.

—Henry George, *Progress and Poverty* (New York: Appleton-Century-Crofts, 1881), pp. 466–467, 475.

white ribboners doughtily carrying their hymns into the grogshop would soon be a force to reckon with.

Social Reconstruction

On balance, the reformers who wished to improve the conditions of the unfortunate elements of the population were no more able than the Mugwumps to mount a crusade that enlisted the full enthusiasm of the country. Americans were conscious of the ominous problems created by the changes of the postwar period. Industrialization and expansion had not furthered the liberty that Bartholdi's statue memorialized; the huddled masses it welcomed at the entrance to New York harbor deserved something more than the slums that awaited them. Recollections of the old sense of destiny reminded Americans that the richest of nations could not afford to be one of the most sordid. Yet no convincing guideposts marked the path of progress.

Periodically the citizens responded to the suggestion that a total change in the social environment could wipe away their problems. Enthusiasm was quick to swell but also quick to ebb. People were willing to hope that either science or imagination would reveal the proper formula, but the demand for swift results often led to disappointment.

The Single Tax The approach of Henry George was intended to be scientific. As a journalist in California, he had become interested in the relationship between land and wealth, a subject to which he devoted years of study. His *Progress and Poverty* (1879) demonstrated that throughout history progress had brought monstrous wealth to a few and debasing want to the many. That result was due to the operation of laws of political economy as binding as those of physical nature. In the past, a few individuals able to grasp strategic pieces of property had profited from the unearned increment that

growth added to their land. Yet they contributed nothing to the productive system. Their strangle hold on the economy had diverted income from those who needed it most.

Yet the human will was potentially an initiatory force that could redirect progress toward a more desirable goal. A single tax, not on property, but on the unearned increment would restrain monopolists, make other taxes unnecessary, and force capital into its most productive uses. The whole productive system would revive, to everyone's advantage. The idea gained widespread popularity and inspired the next generation of reformers. But although George himself conducted an impressive if unsuccessful campaign, in 1886, for the mayoralty of New York City, there was no meaningful attempt to put the single tax into practice.

Utopia The many novelists who sought a panacea through the imagination had an advantage; they could describe Utopia without detailing the steps necessary to reach it. Of works of fiction on the subject Edward Bellamy's *Looking Backward* (1888) was the most popular; it sold 60,000 copies in the year of publication. The story described an industrialized economy such as that of the United States at the time Bellamy wrote, one which functioned like a department store but was more orderly. Government had turned into a system of economic management, while labor was mobilized and used efficiently in an industrial army that provided adequately for the needs of all.

This and other utopian books stressed the need for the communal solidarity lacking in the contemporary world. Their readers glimpsed in them the outline of a society freed from the strain of competition; in them the individual did not have to stand alone, locked in combat with his rivals. But beguiling as the dream was, it never affected practice. Bellamy's Nationalist clubs briefly gained some adherents and then withered away.

Charles A. Barker, *Henry George* (New York, 1955) is the definitive biography.

The Parable of the Coach, 1888

I cannot do better than to compare society . . . to a prodigious coach which the masses of humanity were harnessed to and dragged toilsomely along a very hilly and sandy road. The driver was hunger, and permitted no lagging. . . . Despite the difficulty of drawing the coach at all . . . the top was covered with passengers who never got down, even at the steepest ascents. These seats on top were very breezy and comfortable. . . . Naturally such places were in great demand and the competition for them was keen, every one seeking as the first end in life to secure a seat on the coach for himself and to leave it to his child after him. By the rule of the coach a man could leave his seat to whom he wished, but on the other hand there were many accidents by which it might at any time be wholly lost. For all that they were so easy, the seats were very insecure, and at every sudden jolt of the coach persons were slipping out of them and falling to the ground, where they were instantly compelled to take hold of the rope and help to drag the coach on which they had before ridden so pleasantly. . . .

But did they think only of themselves? you ask. . . . Had they no compassion for fellow beings from whom fortune only distinguished them? Oh, yes; commiseration was frequently expressed by those who rode for those who had to pull the coach. . . . The desperate straining of the team, their agonized leaping and plunging under the pitiless lashing of hunger, the many who fainted at the rope and were trampled in the mire, made a very distressing spectacle, which often called forth highly creditable displays of feeling on the top of the coach. . . . The passengers would call down encouragingly to the toilers of the rope, exhorting them to patience, and holding out hopes of possible compensation in another world for the hardness of their lot, while others contributed to buy salves and liniments for the crippled and injured. . . .

It must in truth be admitted that the main effect of the spectacle of the misery of the toilers of the rope was to enhance the passengers' sense of the value of their seats upon the coach, and to cause them to hold on to them more desperately than before. If the passengers could only have felt assured that neither they nor their friends would ever fall from the top, it is probable that, beyond contributing to the funds for liniments and bandages, they would have troubled themselves extremely little about those who dragged the coach.

—Edward Bellamy, *Looking Backward* (New York: Ticknor and Company, 1888), pp. 10–12.

Socialism In the 1870s and 1880s industrialism in Europe furnished the soil in which a vigorous socialist movement took root. There was no analogous development in the United States, partly because of a lack of interest among the labor force, partly because Americans, even the reformers, rejected the Marxist concept of class war and insisted on the uniqueness of their country's experience. Various little groups of socialists in the United States persuaded one another without gaining any mass support; they were probably not as influential in the 1880s as in the 1840s. The impassioned anarchists attracted attention only in the aftermath of the Haymarket affair. The apparent injustice of the trial earned an otherwise obscure anarchist sect the sympathy of such men as Henry Demarest Lloyd, whose radicalism deepened thereafter.

Few reformers went that far. The remedies they proposed were less important than their incisive criticism of a society that unjustly tolerated extremes of wealth and poverty. Bellamy's parable of the stagecoach excited the moral sensibilities of thousands of Americans who had passed their youth in the cultural environment of Emersonian transcendentalism and who still believed in the solidarity and mutuality of mankind. The crusaders' exposure of the deficiencies of industrialization struck home. George, Bellamy, and the other generous visionaries of their time bequeathed to the next generation the conviction that a solution to the painful riddle of their society was not impossibly far off.

▼

The postwar reformers were voices of the American conscience rather than mobilizers of effective movements to carry out changes. They were more influential as critics than as crusaders. Their limitations derived from the poverty of their thinking. The Mugwumps, prohibitionists, and philanthropists drew their ideas from the past; the socialists and anarchists, from Europe. Able and well intentioned as they were, the reformers did not look realistically at the economic changes about them or take account of what the deprived people actually wanted. George and Bellamy came closest to doing so; hence their popularity. But they were more attracted by visions of total redemption than by measures for immediate practical reform. They were read for the indignation they expressed about the moral inequities of industrialization, but they provided little guidance for organized political action, which took other forms.

Paperbacks for Further Reading

Edward Bellamy, *Looking Backward* (Dolphin Books and Dolphin Masters) is a basic contemporary document. William Graham Sumner, *Social Darwinism: Selected Essays of William Graham Sumner* (Spectrum Books) gives an insight into the thinking of one kind of liberal, Henry M. Christman, ed., *The Mind and Spirit of John Peter Altgeld* (University of Illinois Press) into the thinking of another. Horace S. Merrill, *Bourbon Leader: Grover Cleveland and the Democratic Party* (Little, Brown & Co.) and Russel B. Nye, *Midwestern Progressive Politics* (Harper Torchbooks) touch on the political aspects of reform. Daniel Aaron, *Men of Good Hope* (Galaxy Books) contains an interesting section on the prophetic agitators. Winthrop S. Hudson, *American Protestantism* (Chicago History of American Civilization Series) and Robert H. Bremner, *American Philanthropy* (Chicago History of American Civilization Series) treat this period briefly. Andrew Sinclair's *The Emancipation of the American Woman* (Harper Colophon Books) and his *Era of Excess: A Social History of the Prohibition Movement* (Harper Colophon Books) are interesting accounts of reform in action.

POLITICS ABOVE
AND BELOW
THE SURFACE

61

Since the eighteenth century Americans had considered politics the appropriate means for making changes in their society. It had been a basic premise of the Republic that informed citizens would act, as interest and reason dictated, through the machinery for arriving at decisions provided by the state. The will of the people could thus make itself felt, while respecting individual rights.

After 1865 faith in government declined, among reformers as among other Americans. A common belief developed that the electoral process was ineffectual and that officeholders were corrupt; it seemed desirable therefore to contract the scope of government as much as possible. Contemporary critics found plenty of evidence to support that view.

Beneath the perceived surface of campaigns and deals, however, the substructure of politics was changing in ways not quite understood at the time. A mechanism was evolving, even if not yet well or properly used, to give the people of the country a voice in the management of their society.

A CENTURY AFTER THE REVOLUTION, observers of the American scene commented frequently on the failure of the political system. The free representative government devised by the men of 1776 had fallen on evil days. Henry Adams, the grandson and great grandson of Presidents, concluded his novel *Democracy* (published anonymously in 1880) with resignation; the hope of the past had proved illusory. Foreigners were no longer impressed with local institutions in the United States as de Tocqueville had been. Perceptive and sympathetic visitors like Lord Bryce, English historian and statesman, were more conscious of the deficiencies than of the virtues of what they saw. A thoughtful young American professor of political science in 1885 explained the failure in the operations of government. Woodrow Wilson's *Congressional Government* expressed a decided preference for the British parliamentary system, which seemed to him both more representative and more efficient than the government of his own country.

The Presidency

The Election Process Most commentators then, and since, described American politics in terms of the recurring cycle of presidential elections. The spectacle after the end of the Civil War was not very edifying. Every four years the people marched to the polls to the sound of wave upon wave of oratory, but the ritual seemed to settle nothing. The candidates were either military heroes or substantial, businesslike lawyers. The issues were rarely clear-cut, and the outcome made little difference in the actual conduct of government.

In 1872, General Grant ran for a second term as President. The corruption that tinged his administration had become common knowledge, and he lacked the administrative ability

Joseph Rogers Hollingsworth, *The Whirligig of Politics* (Chicago, 1963) and George H. Mayer, *The Republican Party, 1854–1964* (New York, 1964) deal with developments in the major parties in this period.

Irresponsible Government, 1885

As at present constituted, the federal government lacks strength because its powers are divided, lacks promptness because its authorities are multiplied, lacks wieldiness because its processes are roundabout, lacks efficiency because its responsibility is indistinct and its action without competent direction. It is a government in which every officer may talk about every other officer's duty without having to render strict account for not doing his own, and in which the masters are held in check and offered contradiction by the servants. . . . Talk is not sobered by any necessity imposed upon those who utter it to suit their actions to their words. There is no day of reckoning for words spoken. The speakers of a congressional majority may, without risk of incurring ridicule or discredit, condemn what their own Committees are doing; and the spokesmen of a minority may urge what contrary courses they please with a well-grounded assurance that what they say will be forgotten before they can be called upon to put it into practice. Nobody stands sponsor for the policy of the government. A dozen men originate it; a dozen compromises twist and alter it; a dozen offices whose names are scarcely known outside of Washington put it into execution.

—Woodrow Wilson, *Congressional Government* (Boston: Houghton Mifflin Company, 1885), p. 318.

and the statesmanship to provide dependable guidance on Reconstruction policies. In the hope of winning over dissident members of the Republican party, the Democrats chose as their standard bearer Horace Greeley, long editor of the New York *Tribune*, a former abolitionist and a reform Republican with high tariff views. They thereby gained some Mugwump votes, but not

Horace Greeley (1811–1872), Journalist and Political Leader. Photographed in 1872 by Napoleon Sarony. (The Granger Collection)

RUTHERFORD B. HAYES was born in 1822 in Delaware, Ohio, the son of a poor but respectable farmer of New England antecedents. He had a good local education but was too poor to go to Yale, as he wished, and graduated from Kenyon College instead. He read law in Columbus, Ohio, and entered practice, first in the rural countryside, then in Cincinnati. He married his boyhood sweetheart and followed the proper road to success. His ideas tended toward agnosticism, but he became a member of the Episcopal Church, joined the Sons of Temperance and the Odd Fellows, and ventured into politics as a Whig. In 1861 he got a commission as a major and fought in the Civil War, advancing to the rank of major general.

In the postwar period Hayes pursued a political career as a Republican. He served for a time in the United States House of Representatives and then became governor of Ohio, where he achieved a reputation as a moderate reformer. The favorable impression he made on the public gave him the nomination for the presidency over James G. Blaine in 1876. As part of the bargain that brought him to office he withdrew Federal troops from the South and ended Reconstruction. He furthered civil service reform and reorganized the Department of the Interior. He favored sound money. Although the Bland-Allison Act passed over his veto, he did arrange for the resumption of specie payments. He did not hesitate to use Federal troops to suppress the railroad riots in 1877. He made it clear at the outset of his term that he would not accept renomination. He left office in 1881, and retired to an estate in Ohio, where he died in 1893.

enough to offset their losses in the South. Grant won by 700,000 votes, a larger majority than he had commanded in 1868.

The events of the next four years raised Democratic hopes; scandals rocked the Administration and the Republicans lost control of the Congress elected in 1874. Yet the voters in 1876 did not have much to choose from; the Republican Rutherford B. Hayes, governor of Ohio, and the Democrat Samuel J. Tilden, governor of New York, were both respectable figures, both lawyers untinged by scandal, both moderately

Hamilton J. Eckenrode, *Rutherford B. Hayes* (New York, 1930) is a competent biography.

JAMES A. GARFIELD led the erratic life of the Ohio frontier for his first thirty years. He was born in 1831 in a poor family of Yankee antecedents. He drifted about, doing odd jobs and acquiring a casual and fragmentary education. He was a teacher at Hiram College in 1859, when he was elected a Republican member of the state Senate. His only distinguishing features were his height and the imposing appearance his beard gave him. He was a lay preacher among the Disciples of Christ and his emotional nature evoked confidence among religious people — particularly, a contemporary observed, among those who did not know him personally.

In 1861, Garfield was a firm believer in coercion of the South. He helped assemble a volunteer regiment, fought in several campaigns, and gained some prominence by his military success. In 1863 he took a seat in the United States House of Representatives. He was regularly re-elected, despite some hints of scandal. In 1880 he was elected to the United States Senate, although he never actually sat.

He went to the Republican convention that year as a supporter of John Sherman. There were suggestions at the time that he was less than enthusiastic in his efforts and aimed for the nomination himself. Whether that was his intention or not, he was the choice of the convention and won the election. His brief term in office was troubled. New scandals arose and the problem of patronage was difficult. He was shot on July 2, 1881, by a frustrated office seeker and died on September 19, having served only four months.

Theodore Clarke Smith, *Life and Letters of James Abram Garfield* (New Haven, Conn., 1925) is the standard biography.

well known outside their own states. They opposed each other publicly on no important issue except that of the future tenancy of the White House.

The election did not yield a clear result. Of the 185 votes required in the electoral college Tilden certainly had 184 and Hayes 166. The 19 votes of South Carolina, Florida, and Louisiana were in dispute; if the Democrats carried any one of those states, the presidency was theirs. The controversy over the rival sets of returns dragged on for months, to be settled only by an understanding in which the Democrats yielded the presidency in return for a promise, duly honored, to end military reconstruction. The arrangement may well have been eased by the lobby for the Texas-Pacific Railroad, which feared the choice of Tilden.

In 1880, both parties placed their bets on generals: James A. Garfield, Republican, and W. S. Hancock, Democrat. The victory went to Garfield. His assassination soon thereafter brought to the White House Chester A. Arthur, but without making any noticeable difference in the conduct of government.

The Democrats at last returned to power when in 1884 Grover Cleveland defeated James G. Blaine, the plumed knight from Maine. They did so partly because of Republican blunders; a tactless allusion to rum, Romanism, and rebellion by one of his supporters may have cost Blaine the Irish votes he hoped to capture in New York City. Minor incidents of this sort were significant because the margin between victory and defeat was always narrow. In 1888, the outcome was reversed when Benjamin Harrison defeated Cleveland's bid for re-election, although he received fewer popular votes.

Sources of Support   The campaigns generated an excitement quite disproportionate to their importance. In most parts of the nation, the contests were largely formal. Sixteen states always voted Republican and fourteen Democratic. South Carolina, Florida, and Louisiana deviated only in 1876 while Reconstruction regimes still held power; thereafter they were

The Assassin Firing the Second Shot at President Garfield. Wood engraving after W. A. Rogers, *Harper's Weekly*, July 8, 1881. (Library of Congress)

The Inauguration of President Harrison, March 4, 1889. (Library of Congress)

STEADFAST REPUBLICAN

UNDECIDED STATES

STEADFAST DEMOCRATIC

DEMOCRATIC EXCEPT IN 1876

NONVOTING AREAS

POLITICAL ALIGNMENTS, 1870–1890

safely Democratic. Only in five states—Connecticut, New York, Indiana, Nevada, and California —were the rival parties so close to one another in strength that their electoral vote might swing to one side or the other. The outcome of every campaign therefore depended on minor shifts in a very few places.

The nominations were much less predictable. In the Republican conventions, powerful chieftains like John Sherman of Ohio, James G. Blaine of Maine, and Roscoe Conkling of New York controlled substantial blocs of delegates. But the great chieftains were rarely able to muster a majority for themselves. The front runner almost always united his rivals against him, and a dark horse was usually better able to reconcile the various elements of the party. Besides, no one wanted as President a man so strong as to dominate the whole government.

The Democrats felt an even greater compulsion to compromise among strong candidates. The rules of their convention called for a two-thirds vote to nominate, and that in itself prevented any quick decision. Furthermore, the party had to maneuver tactfully. Although its greatest strength lay in the South, it always chose a Northern candidate, for it could win only with some help from above the Mason-Dixon line. The Democrats, like the Republicans, therefore gravitated to rather neutral characters, respectable men, preferably with military careers, who had not taken extreme positions on any important issue.

The Campaigns As a result, the campaigns involved not sustained debate on important questions but rather rhetorical appeals to emotion. The Grand Old Party frequently waved the bloody shirt, in an effort to revive the passionate

Convention Oratory, 1876

Our country, crowned with the vast and marvelous achievements of its first century, asks for a man worthy of the past, and prophetic of her future: asks for a man who has the audacity of genius; asks for a man who is the grandest combination of heart, conscience and brain beneath her flag—such a man is James G. Blaine.

For the Republican host, led by this intrepid man, there can be no defeat.

This is a grand year—a year filled with recollections of the Revolution; filled with proud and tender memories of the past; with the sacred legends of liberty—a year in which the sons of freedom will drink from the fountains of enthusiasm; a year in which the people call for the man who has preserved in Congress what our soldiers won upon the field; a year in which they call for the man who has torn from the throat of treason the tongue of slander—

for the man who has snatched the mask of Democracy from the hideous face of rebellions; for the man who, like an intellectual athlete, has stood in the arena of debate and challenged all comers, and who is still a total stranger to defeat.

Like an armed warrior, like a plumed knight, James G. Blaine marched down the halls of the American Congress and threw his shining lance full and fair against the brazen foreheads of the defamers of his country and the maligners of his honor. For the Republican party to desert this gallant leader now, is as though an army should desert their general upon the field of battle.

James G. Blaine is now and has been for years the bearer of the sacred standard of the Republican party. I call it sacred, because no human being can stand beneath its folds without becoming and without remaining free.

—Robert G. Ingersoll, *Works* (New York: C. P. Farrell, 1900), vol. IX, pp. 58–59.

A Politician's Work, 1870s

[Dec. 6, 1873] Went to several of the Departments. Got an appointment for the widow of Mr. Robinson, late a leader of the Disciples Church of this place. . . .

[Feb. 2, 1875] Went to the Treasury with the son of Mr. Parks of Warren to secure him a place in the Marine Hospital Service. I help this man with reluctance, for I think he was opposed to me last year. I ought perhaps to tell him so but I concluded to let it pass and help his boy, as the father has not helped me. . . .

[Oct. 21, 1875] Went to the Interior Department to secure the restoration of Warren Young to his clerkship in the pension office. . . .

[Dec. 28, 1875] Went to the Post Office Department and spent two or three hours in trying to secure a clerkship for Warren Young and a place for Mrs. Lacy, a lady in whom C. has taken so much interest. . . .

[Jan. 15, 1876] Spent several hours at the Departments in securing a place for Warren Young. . . .

[Feb. 5, 1876] Went to the Treasury and War Departments to secure Warren Young a clerkship. . . .

[March 2, 1876] Called at the Treasury to remove a trouble in the way of Warren Young's appointment.

—T. C. Smith, *The Life and Letters of James Abram Garfield* (New Haven, Conn.: Yale University Press, 1925), vol. II, p. 726.

Office Seekers in the Lobby of the White House Awaiting an Interview with President Hayes. Wood engraving, *Frank Leslie's Illustrated Newspaper*, 1877. (Library of Congress)

solidarity of wartime. The Democrats too depended on tradition, alluding to the lost cause just enough to evoke Southern sentiment without creating the suspicion of disloyalty in the North. Gaslight parades, brass bands, and tub-thumping oratory were the standard appurtenances of presidential elections.

Of the postwar Presidents, only Cleveland was outstanding. Grant, Hayes, Garfield, Arthur, and Harrison were moderate men of moderate ability. Content to follow well-tried routines, they were honest by their own lights but rarely took the initiative. They regarded their position mainly as ceremonial, apart from the duty of making appointments; patronage problems consumed a large part of their time. Foreign policy they left to the secretaries of state; legislation, to Congress. It was a sign of how little was expected of the Presidents that Cleveland was considered superior because he was courageous and honest —virtues that might ordinarily be taken for granted in the holder of the nation's highest office.

Party Government

Nevertheless, the gloomy view of American politics was not altogether justified. The Republic was not fulfilling the optimistic expectations of its founders, but neither was it falling victim to the demagoguery that its critics had anticipated. It was adjusting slowly and painfully to new conditions. The forms developed in a small rural society were now being modified to fit one that was large, urban, and industrial.

The Popular Base Popular interest in politics remained high and the number of participants increased steadily. The votes cast climbed

The Democratic Campaign Song, 1876. Cover of song sheet. (The Smithsonian Institution)

by about 10 percent every four years, a rate that kept pace with the growth of population. Fully 80 percent of those eligible cast ballots in 1888, a mark never reached before or since. That was an impressive achievement in view of the number of immigrants in the United States. Nor were intense feelings confined to presidential elections. Contests for other offices were often fought more bitterly because the outcome seemed really to matter. In the struggle for the mayoralty of New York in 1886, for instance, Theodore Roosevelt, Abram S. Hewitt, and Henry George offered the electorate a genuine choice among differing approaches to municipal government. In many states, battles for the governorship and for control of the legislature had the same quality.

At the local level, politics became important to a large part of the population. The tariff, the currency, Indian policy, and relations with Britain—these were complex issues settled in Washington, with effects the citizen felt only remotely. Water supply, transit systems, railroad rate regulation, and factory laws—these were issues settled in the city hall or the state capital, with effects immediately apparent to the voter. There was more excitement about presidential elections, more involvement in the outcome of local campaigns.

The political party was the means of organizing popular support. There remained independents, like the Mugwumps, who refused to bind themselves in a total commitment and preferred to make judgments among the rival candidates and platforms without reference to labels. Occasionally such people combined temporarily to support a nonpartisan ticket in a municipal election. These efforts lacked cohesion and discipline and were rarely successful.

In general, the electorate did not arrive at its decisions on the basis of a rational calculation of interests. Many voters had developed firm loyalties to the political parties. The appeals to the bloody shirt or the lost cause, the great parades, the songs, and the nicknames were manifestations of an identification of the people with the processes of government. The voter as often marked his ballot Democratic or Republican because he happened to belong to one party or the other, as out of an abstract comparison of candidates or platforms. His affiliation reflected his ethnic antecedents, his regional and class position, and his attitude toward the great war, the memory of which long survived.

After 1865 the two parties that reflected these loyalties acquired a permanence and coherence they had not possessed before. No earlier political organization had held its character for more than two decades. Changing conditions had called for realignment in new associations, but the parties that emerged from the war retained their identity through the century that followed.

Attempts to establish others to serve a particular group or further a specific idea proved abortive. Eastern artisans in 1871 formed a National Labor party, which however enjoyed only a brief existence. For a decade after 1874, some artisans and small businessmen sponsored a Greenback party, which bore various titles; in national elections it mustered as many as 300,000 votes, and in the Congressional election of 1878, about a million. But neither it nor the National Prohibition party nor any of the other even more exotic groups exercised any political influence. Their foundations were too narrow to sustain the organization that kept the two major parties going.

Organization The basic units of power operated in the counties. Often well-entrenched machines held control for generations, keeping a tight grip on local offices and also on representation in the state legislature. The effects were most visible in the cities, where the stakes of politics were greatest. Size there made necessary a formal organization not required in the small rural counties. A hierarchy of ward chieftains ruled by a boss became characteristic of urban party structure. New York City's Tammany organization was nationally notorious; its counterparts existed in other communities.

The city machine often attracted unfavorable attention. The population it governed was heterogeneous and therefore subject to divisive contests for control; the boss often resorted to floating blocs of illegal voters and to the judicious distribution of favors in order to win. Furthermore, the urban machine controlled patronage and contracts of enormous value. The great sums expended on public and private building and on the construction and care of streets and bridges, together with various forms of licenses and franchises, were effective means of mobilizing support. They put at the disposal of the boss substantial amounts of money and numerous jobs that cemented the loyalty of his followers.

The corruption involved in such transactions aroused the indignation of Mugwumps and independents and touched off periodic exposés. The

An Anti-Greenback Cartoon from *Puck*, 1878. (The Granger Collection)

avarice of William M. Tweed of Tammany Hall thus led to his exposure and imprisonment. Generally more temperate leaders kept their positions for decades because the reformers were unable to develop durable rival organizations. The well-intentioned crusader, having ousted the boss and seized power, did not know what to do with it and let it slip back into the hands of the machine.

Less visible, but more important, was the apparatus governing the hundreds of rural counties, which outweighed the cities in state politics. At the hub of affairs stood an intimate circle composed of men in whom their neighbors had confidence — the banker, lawyer, editor, or prosperous farmer with time to devote to public business. Connections were personal and informal; Tom Platt, from the corner drugstore in Owego, became the key figure first in Tioga County and then in New York State because of the number of people with whom he was familiar. In a context in which everyone was known, it was not necessary to buy votes and there was

The Marshals Plunder the Public, 1884

The investigation reveals the wonderful unanimity with which these officers of almost every grade and in the several portions of the country have plundered the public Treasury by false, fraudulent, and fictitious charges. . . . They have charged for arrests that were not made; for travel that was not performed; for expenses that were not incurred; for guards that were not employed. They knowingly rendered false accounts against the Government and to the courts; increased accounts after they were made up; made up accounts in the name of fictitious persons; arrested persons upon false charges worked up by themselves; extorted money from private citizens and in ways without number have swindled the Government and oppressed the people.

— House Committee on Expenditures in the Department of Justice. House Report 2164, 48th Cong., 1st sess. (July 3, 1884), p. 1.

usually little margin for doubt in the award of places or contracts. Corruption intruded only with outsiders; there was no harm in mulcting the circus that sought a license. But control was fully as tight as in the great city.

The machines, urban and rural, were intermediaries between the people and politics. The formal agencies of government were remote, whether in Washington or the state capital or the city hall, but the ward or county boss was nearby, worth supporting in return for his intercession when needed. The loyal vote was the token of the citizen's participation in an organization through which he influenced politics.

Local roots, together with federalism, sustained the two-party system. Capture of the White House or the governor's mansion did not bring such total control that the opposition could be eliminated. The grass-roots organizations remained intact. In this period the party in the minority, in a national or state election, still had strength enough in some counties to remain in the battle for power. Only the South approached a virtual monopoly by one party.

The relationship between people and party was much less close above the local level. The legislatures dominated state government through their control over expenditures and over the law-making process. Their members, though elected in the counties, were not subject to the oversight of constituents when away from home, except when it came to local issues. Usually, however, the legislator passed on matters in which his own neighbors had no stake. The vote on an urban franchise bill would not affect the folks back in the county. The vote on a rural road bill would not affect the people back in the city. Why not go along with the instructions of the party leader or the suggestions of a generous lobbyist?

Occasional flurries of reform generated a tighter sense of responsibility. Exposures in the press, pressure from organized groups like the granges, and the appearance of third parties that highlighted specific grievances could bring action in the state capitals. Above all, a governor who wished to be more than a ceremonial figure or a dispenser of patronage could attract the public attention that kept the legislature in line.

The Federal Congress

The legislative process was far more complex on the Federal level. Congress dealt with issues that affected the whole continent, some of them highly technical; a tariff schedule, for instance, contained thousands of different items. Many members had no previous experience with the problems with which they were to deal; and the separation of powers deprived them of the guidance of the administrative departments, particularly in a period of weak Presidents. Moreover, the ability to appeal to the voters was not the same as the ability to make informed decisions on national policy. Under these circumstances, it was a considerable achievement to get any action without splitting the country apart.

The United States Senate was the channel of communication between the states and the Federal government. In order to gain and hold his seat, the Senator needed the support of the organization in the legislature which elected him. He was consequently sensitive to its needs. On the other hand, his six-year term and his influence over Federal patronage gave him some freedom of maneuver and a vantage point from which he could exercise considerable power. Often therefore he was more responsive to the opinions of his colleagues than to those of his constituents.

Both houses of Congress developed internal procedures for getting work done. Debate on the floor lost its earlier importance. Committees structured on party lines handled the business of government. Leadership in the House fell to the Speaker who made committee assignments. In the Senate, a small group of insiders with informal party affiliations to the White House had the same power. These self-contained coteries were efficient, but a good deal of their effort went into river and harbor bills and similar pork-barrel legislation. They had not yet learned to make their proceedings relevant to the interests and ideas of the people with whose consent they ruled.

▼

There was cause for discouragement in a comparison of the visible features of government with their prewar counterparts. There were no Jeffersons or Jacksons after 1865, nor Clays or Websters. Weak executives and irresponsible legislatures yielded far too readily to corruption and too often fell short of the statesmanship the times required. That was one of the reasons why the scope of government failed to expand with the needs of society.

The one hopeful sign was the persistence of popular faith in the methods of politics. Local machinery for enlisting participation in the governmental process developed despite the unsettling effects of expansion and industrialization. The electorate was as yet not well informed and as yet fixed its attention on local issues; but it preserved its party affiliation and the habit of political action and it would respond to later calls to use its latent power for broader purposes.

Paperbacks for Further Reading

Three contemporary accounts are of primary importance. Woodrow Wilson, *Congressional Government* (Meridian Books) is a systematic analysis. James Bryce, *The American Commonwealth* (Capricorn Books) contains the perceptive observations of an Englishman. Henry Adams, *Democracy* (Signet Classics) is a novel based on experience.

Bruce Catton, *U. S. Grant and the American Military Tradition* (Universal Library) and Horace S. Merrill, *Bourbon Leader: Grover Cleveland and the Democratic Party* (Little, Brown & Co.) are biographies that touch on the politics of this period. Leonard D. White, *The Republican Era* (Free Press Paperbacks) contains a department by department analysis of Federal administration. Richard Hofstadter, *The American Political Tradition* (Vintage Books, Inc.) contains a chapter on the spoilsmen. Seymour Mandelbaum, *Boss Tweed's New York* (John Wiley & Sons, Inc.) treats local politics. There is also relevant material in R. G. McCloskey, *American Conservatism in the Age of Enterprise, 1865–1910* (Harper Torchbooks) and in Russel B. Nye, *Midwestern Progressive Politics* (Harper Torchbooks).

David J. Rothman, *Politics and Power* (Cambridge, Mass., 1966) is a penetrating study of the United States Senate between 1869 and 1901.

FOREIGN AFFAIRS

62

Americans emerged from the Civil War with a rudely disordered view of their place in the world. Until 1860, the understanding of the future inherited from the Revolution had oriented their relations with other powers. It had then seemed the Manifest Destiny of the Republic to spread across the hemisphere and ultimately to provide a model for other peoples. Progress everywhere would clear the way.

The war had subjected American institutions to a cruel test. Secession had undermined confidence in the superiority of the government of the United States, and the politics of the 1870s and 1880s did not revive the old faith. Furthermore, the fighting was no sooner over than domestic issues began fully to occupy the attention of the citizens. The men who built the great new factories and settled the West spent little time thinking about events beyond their borders. Economic, cultural, and personal ties with other lands were still strong in a nation actively engaged in trade and receptive to the migration of men and ideas. But Americans were impatient with foreign affairs insofar as involvements abroad diverted energies from the exciting tasks at home.

Settling
the War Issues

The Alabama Claims The Civil War had left residual problems in the relations of the United States with England. British shipyards had supplied the Confederate navy with cruisers like the *Alabama* which had done heavy damage to American merchant shipping. From the perspective of Washington, actions were counter to international law. The British government was therefore to blame for the losses due to its negligence, about $15,000,000. Indeed, Charles Sumner, chairman of the influential Senate Foreign Relations Committee, pointed out in 1869 that the responsibility extended also to the indirect damages that resulted from the prolongation of the conflict as a result of the cruisers' activities. His calculations set the amount at $4,000,000,000.

This grievance combined with other causes of irritation. Resentment was still keen in the United States over the British recognition of Confederate belligerency. An old agreement on the North Atlantic fishery rights had expired, and some Americans considered the time ripe to liberate and annex Canada.

The British were willing to compromise. They had pressing problems in Asia and the Near East, and were just beginning to feel concern about the rise of German power. London assessed correctly the significance of Germany's impressive victory over France in 1870 which enabled Bismarck to consolidate the Kaiser's empire. Furthermore, the English were in no position to defend Canada in the event of a dispute with the United States; and an American law of 1866 which permitted the sale of naval vessels to foreign countries showed that a great sea power might have much to lose in the future by defending the *Alabama* policy. It was better from the British point of view to acknowledge the errors of that policy than to leave a precedent that would enable potential enemies to buy cruisers in wartime.

Canada Events along the northern frontier had revealed that the United States, too, was not eager for a break. The Canadian provinces had long seethed with discontent; a stream of migrants flowed south to the United States and there was much talk of rebellion. The time seemed propitious for annexation.

The opportunity was particularly attractive to Irish-Americans. On the Emerald Isle support grew for repeal of the Act of Union with Britain and for Home Rule. Within the United States, refugees, many of whom had served in the Union armies during the Civil War, formed a government in exile in New York City, began to issue Irish currency, and raised an army through the secret organization known as the Fenian Brotherhood. The Fenians did not, for the time being, expect to launch a transatlantic expedition to redeem the homeland, but they hoped that an invasion of Canada would force the British into negotiations and bring Ireland freedom.

In 1866 one group actually crossed the border, only to meet defeat at the hands of the Canadian militia. Another expedition readied in 1870 met the firm veto of the United States government. The authorities in Washington were unwilling to use force. They had become aware that the Canadians were not eager for annexation, particularly after the grant of dominion status in 1867. A war on this issue would be pointless. The British, for their part, reacted with moderation and displayed a willingness to calm the disturbed relations between the two powers.

The Treaty of Washington of 1871 outlined the terms of agreement. England expressed regret for the *Alabama* damages, and the two countries accepted a general statement of the obligations and rights of neutrality. A mixed commission was to pass on the wartime claims. (Ultimately a tribunal consisting of representatives of England, the United States, Italy, Brazil, and Switzerland set the amount at $15,500,000.) The treaty also established the free navigation

Allan Nevins, *Hamilton Fish* (New York, 1936) covers the foreign policy of the Grant administration.

"*Alabama* and *Kearsarge*." Painting, 1864, by Edouard Manet. This engagement between the Confederate and the Union ships took place off Cherbourg, France, June 19, 1864. (The Granger Collection)

of the St. Lawrence and allowed British and American vessels to fish in the North Atlantic for ten years without regard to national boundaries. Acceptance of the principle of arbitration, as much as the specific terms of the pact, demonstrated the desire to avoid conflict.

Residual anti-English feeling persisted however. The centennial of the Revolution in 1876 revived memories of the hated redcoats and monetary stringency nurtured suspicions of the London bankers. Irish-Americans, moreover, kept alive dislike of the rulers of their homeland. In 1888, therefore, a tactless letter from the British minister Sir Lionel Sackville-West evoked a storm of protest for its expression of a preference for Grover Cleveland and probably threw some marginal votes to Benjamin Harrison.

The Legacy of the Monroe Doctrine

Mexico The tense relations of the United States with France when the Civil War ended arose from Napoleon III's sympathy for the Confederacy and from his ambitions, which conflicted with the interests of the United States in Latin America. He had joined Britain and Spain in intervention in Mexico in 1861, and his troops remained when his allies withdrew. The French had captured Mexico City in 1863 and had installed the Archduke Maximilian of Austria as emperor, encouraging his extravagant dreams of a great realm that would encompass all of Central America.

The venture early ran into difficulty. The stubborn Mexicans under Benito Pablo Juárez refused to accept the alien overlord, who survived only by the power of French bayonets. Napoleon III began to regret the drain on his resources, particularly when the rise of Prussian strength revealed that he would soon have problems closer to home. Furthermore, he had in

hand a succession of warnings from William H. Seward, Secretary of State, that the United States would never recognize a regime imposed from Europe on the Western Hemisphere. After Appomattox the Americans were in a position to take stronger measures. In December 1865 President Johnson stated bluntly that the United States would defend republicanism in the New World against any foreign interference. Two months later he demanded the withdrawal of French troops. Napoleon III complied, and without aid Maximilian's hapless regime collapsed. In 1867 the would-be emperor was executed.

The Caribbean The issue in Mexico was clear. The Monroe Doctrine forbade the extension of European influence in the Americas. In the past that statement of policy had rested upon the assumption that the United States had a long-term interest in preserving the independence of the countries of the Western Hemisphere until some vague future date when all would be part of a common political system. The same statement of policy after 1865 had an ambiguous quality. Did the exclusion of European power mean that the United States would gradually extend its sway over the whole hemisphere?

That question arose with reference to the Dominican Republic. Spain had resumed control of that turbulent little state on the invitation of a local political faction, then had found the trouble of governing not worth the effort and in 1865 had withdrawn. Left to its own devices, the Dominican Republic was incapable of maintaining order; its citizens began to fear annexation by neighboring Haiti.

Meanwhile American fortune hunters planned an ambitious project to exploit the peninsula of Samanà. They were behind the scheme in 1869 for annexing the Dominican Republic to the United States. An American commissioner negotiated a treaty to that effect which the cowed Dominicans ratified in a referendum by a vote of 16,000 to 11. But President

Harford Montgomery Hyde, *Mexican Empire* (London, 1946) is a lively narrative of Maximilian's career.

Dexter Perkins, *The Monroe Doctrine, 1867–1907* (Baltimore, Md., 1937) is the standard account.

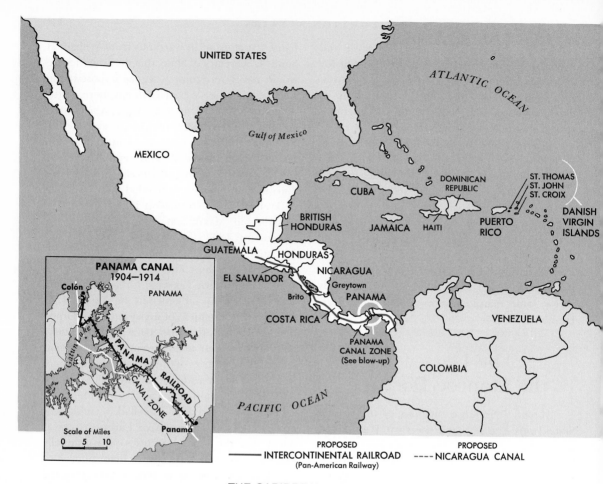

The Caribbean, 1865–1890 map showing United States, Mexico, Gulf of Mexico, Atlantic Ocean, Cuba, Jamaica, Haiti, Dominican Republic, Puerto Rico, Danish Virgin Islands (St. Thomas, St. John, St. Croix), British Honduras, Guatemala, Honduras, El Salvador, Nicaragua, Costa Rica, Panama, Colombia, Venezuela, Pacific Ocean; inset map PANAMA CANAL 1904–1914 with Colón, Gatún Lake, Panama Railroad, Canal Zone, Panamá, Scale of Miles 0 5 10; Greytown, Brito, Panama Canal Zone (See blow-up); Proposed Intercontinental Railroad (Pan-American Railway) and Proposed Nicaragua Canal legend.

THE CARIBBEAN, 1865–1890

The Good Neighbor, 1869

Kindness, beneficence, assistance, aid, help, protection, all that is implied in good neighborhood—these we must give freely, bountifully; but [the Dominican people's] independence is as precious to them as is ours to us, and it is placed under the safeguard of natural laws which we cannot violate with impunity.

—Charles Sumner in the United States Senate. Charles Sumner, *Works* (Boston: Lee and Shepard, 1883), vol. XIV, p. 124.

Grant was unable to secure ratification by the Senate. Led in revolt by Charles Sumner, chairman of the Foreign Relations Committee, the Senate rejected the proposal. Grant then tried to complete the annexation by the device of Congressional joint resolutions, which required only a majority rather than a two-thirds vote. That attempt also failed and the Dominicans retained their independence.

The collapse of the Dominican scheme, as well as of efforts to buy the Virgin Islands, was evidence of American unwillingness to add new territory to the Union. Sumner's opposition was on moral grounds and undoubtedly reflected the old abolitionist stance against expansion during the Mexican War. Other Americans had no in-

JAMES G. BLAINE was a politician who understood the use of power. Born in West Brownsville, Pennsylvania, in 1830, he grew up in the Middle West. After holding several teaching positions he moved to Augusta, Maine, where he entered journalism and politics. A good memory and great personal charm made him an effective speaker, and he advanced steadily in the ranks of the Republican party.

In 1863 he went to the United States House of Representatives, where his influence mounted steadily. By the time he moved to the Senate in 1876 he was a force to be reckoned with. In the factional party infighting, he led the Half Breeds against the Stalwarts, who followed Ulysses S. Grant and Roscoe Conkling. The Mulligan Letters, which implicated Blaine in a railroad scandal, deprived him of the presidential nomination in 1876, and he missed out again in 1880. When nominated four years later, he lost the election to Cleveland.

Blaine served twice as Secretary of State, briefly under Garfield (1881) and for Harrison's full term. Ignorance of diplomatic history and of international law and a lack of discrimination about the subordinates he appointed hampered Blaine in that office. On the other hand, he did have a sense of power and he had inherited Clay's vision of a united Western Hemisphere. Blaine believed that the economic development of the United States required expanding international markets, and he was therefore suspicious of the intentions of Great Britain. He also worried about the implications of possible European control over the Isthmian canal a French company was building across Panama.

He was anxious to nurture the concept of Pan-Americanism, which emphasized the common interests of all the republics of the Western Hemisphere. His tenure as Secretary of State in 1881 was too short to permit any advance toward realizing the idea but he continued to speak and write about it in the next decade. In 1889, when he returned to the office, he was instrumental in calling the first Pan-American Congress, which took the initial halting steps toward establishing the connections he desired. He died in 1893, before he could see the results that would follow.

terest in acquiring islands of dubious value because they could not envisage an appropriate status for them. Every tradition of a free society rejected the prospect of holding colonies as the European nations did. Yet to make the Dominican Republic a territory or state would confer citizenship upon its strange colored population. The domestic Negroes were problem enough to Americans increasingly worried about questions of race. Better to focus all energies on the growing economy of the United States.

The long bloody Cuban rebellion that lasted from 1868 to 1878 attracted sympathy in the United States but led to no intervention. When the Spaniards killed a number of Americans on the gunrunner *Virginius* in 1873, President Grant was willing to settle the matter amicably, and Americans stood by as Spain crushed the rebels.

Secretary of State Seward, whose expansionist views went back to the 1850s, in 1867 secured the right to build a canal across Nicaragua, but no action followed, although a French company was actually at work in Panama. Secretary of State Blaine twice issued calls for a Pan-American Conference; on the first occasion (1881) the meeting never occurred; on the second (1889) it had no immediate results.

David S. Muzzey, *James G. Blaine* (New York, 1934) is a competent biography.

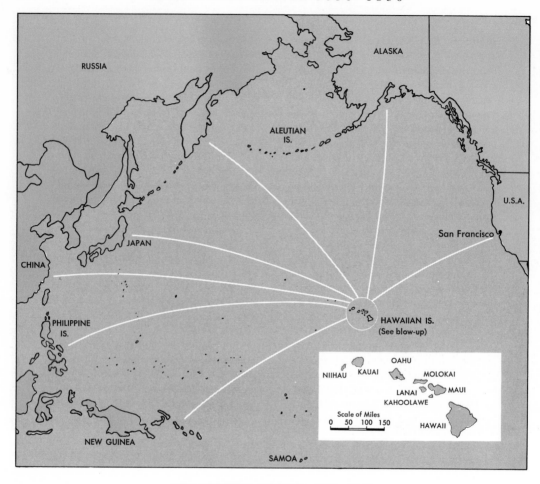

THE CENTRAL PACIFIC, 1870–1890

The Orient

The clash between old conceptions of American destiny and the new desire to attend to business at home confused policy also in the Pacific. To some, Asia was still a fertile field for missionary activities and trade; to others, it was a potential distraction, to be avoided if possible. The familiar expansionist phrases still cropped up in oratory and a few businessmen thought hopefully of the millions of potential customers in the teeming Orient, but to most Americans the lands beyond the Pacific Coast were totally alien and could remain so. There was little concern in these years when the great European powers, drawn by the disintegration of the Chinese state and pushed by the quest for markets, began to extend their control over Asia. Imperialism did not seem to affect the United States.

The country had, however, already acquired interests in scarcely noticed corners of the Pacific. Seward had increased the stake of the United States in the area when he leaped at a suggestion that Russia might be willing to dispose of Alaska. The Secretary of State, convinced that Canada would some day be part of the Union, thought

Ulysses S. Grant and Li Hung Chang, Viceroy of China. Photograph by See Tay, 1879. (Library of Congress)

of the transfer as a means of rounding out possession of the whole continent north of the Rio Grande. But purchase of the Alaska territory for $7,200,000 in 1867 extended the boundaries of the country far into the Pacific. The occupation of Midway Island the same year established a foothold some 3000 miles west of San Francisco.

The United States was nevertheless reluctant to follow up on these steps. American missionary and commercial enterprises had grown steadily in Hawaii since 1820; in the 1870s they dominated the islands. Yet the efforts to tighten the ties between the United States and Hawaii through a reciprocity treaty met with no success until 1875. In that year, a display of interest in the region by Britain and France produced an agreement, which was renewed in 1884, when the United States also received the right to build a naval station at Pearl Harbor.

The sense of hesitation and doubt was even clearer in the case of Samoa. The indigenous chieftains, fearful of English and German designs, were eager for American protection, but the Senate refused to act upon a compact negotiated in 1872. Six years later the Senate ap-

The Hawaiian Achievement, 1860

The Hawaiians are generally considered a Christianized people. They furnish to the world the most complete illustration of successful missionary enterprise, and today, are a ready argument against the common skepticism that the dark skinned races are not susceptible of elevation. The eager reception of the Gospel, forty years ago, by these then barbarous islanders, is a matter of history, and, search where we will, that history finds no parallel.

— A. Francis Judd, "President's Address," *Eighth Annual Report of the Mission Children's Society* (Honolulu: H. M. Whitney, 1890), p. 15.

proved a treaty of friendship which gave Americans the right to use the harbor at Pago Pago. In return, the United States assured the Samoans of its good offices in resolving any dispute with other powers.

In 1879, Britain and Germany secured somewhat more favorable arrangements in Samoa, but for a time the consuls of the three countries worked together in advising the local ruler. Then the two European nations, in an effort to arrive at a general settlement of their colonial disputes, decided that Samoa should become a German mandate. The United States protested but could head off the arrangement only by becoming part, in the Berlin Conference of 1889, of a three-power condominium. Largely against its will, it thus drifted into a relationship which would later make trouble.

Robert Louis Stevenson, *A Footnote to History* (New York, 1900) is a charming account of Samoa in the 1880s, with keen insight into the human aspects of imperialism.

Reluctant Diplomacy

The peripheral nature of foreign affairs was evident in the character of the men who conducted them. Except for Blaine who served two years, the secretaries of state after Seward were no longer, as before, active politicians who might aspire to the presidency. They were competent men performing a task remote from popular interests.

Since American policy was generally passive, there was little need for force to back it up. The level of expenditures for military purposes accordingly ran consistently low. The army had been promptly demobilized in 1865; the residue thereafter existed primarily for service against the western Indians. The navy, regarded as an arm of the coastal defense system, lost strength just as the merchant fleet did. Since this was a period of great change, with steam replacing sails and wooden hulls giving place to steel, the United States fell far behind the European powers.

But even in 1886, when Senator Benjamin Harrison complained of the dangers of weakness, he had in mind the threat to American weakness, he had in mind the threat to American coasts; and in the next few years a good deal of thought went to the possibility of constructing mammoth monitors, great floating fortresses to beat off invasion. The totally defensive cast of these ideas reflected the desirability of keeping costs and taxes low as well as the belief that

Number of Men in Regular Peacetime Military Forces, 1889

Country	Army	Navy	Marines
United States	28,441	8,230	2,080
Austria-Hungary	327,100	8,019	–
France	541,365	28,621	25,339
Germany	491,677	15,573	–
Russia	809,973	29,245	–
Great Britain	149,667	62,400	–
Italy	253,000	12,728	–
Spain	144,664	14,671	7,000

Despite his Virginia ancestry **BENJAMIN HARRISON** was a staunch Republican. Born in 1833, he attended Miami University in Ohio, read law in Cincinnati, and settled down in Indianapolis. He was a member of the Republican party almost from its foundation and held a number of local offices before the Civil War. After secession, he raised an infantry regiment, served as colonel, and participated in several campaigns. He returned to help fight the local Ohio Copperheads, who sympathized with the South, and the conflict increased the depth of his partisan feelings.

After the war a growing law practice made Harrison wealthy. Always a member of the Presbyterian Church, he regularly taught a men's Bible class and was superintendent of the Sunday school. Although he retained an interest in politics, he was unsuccessful in a campaign for the governorship of Indiana in 1876. The taunt, "Kid-glove Harrison, as cold as an iceberg" contributed to his defeat.

In 1881, the state legislature chose him United States Senator and he served one undistinguished term. He was available for the presidential nomination in 1888 and won by a large electoral vote, despite the fact that he lacked a popular majority.

Harrison was a mediocre President. He was content to let his Secretary of State, James G. Blaine, conduct the country's foreign policy, and he exercised no leadership over Congress. Harrison did appoint Theodore Roosevelt as Civil Service Commissioner in an effort to limit the patronage disorders. He took great pride in the navy, in which he had already shown interest as Senator.

Some prominent party leaders opposed his renomination. But as the incumbent President, he was the choice of the convention, and he was defeated by Cleveland. Harrison died in 1901.

the true interests of the United States ended at the oceans' edges.

The great European powers considered the United States a negligible factor in international affairs. By their standards, it was weak, lacking as it did armed power and formal alliances. Conservatives, like Napoleon III, still feared it as a source of republican contagion and a refuge for revolutionaries. But they did not have to take account of it as a force in diplomacy. Only Britain, with its large stake on the North American continent, set any value on the friendship of the United States, but more to prevent a nuisance than out of a serious estimation of its strength.

To the common people of all countries, the United States was still the New World, the land of promise whose open gates and free institutions were the hope of all mankind. But the common people did not form opinion in any chancellery. Among diplomats, Americans bore the reputation of being bumbling amateurs, given to windy rhetoric but incapable of acting. A special Providence, Bismarck noted, took care of fools, drunkards, and the United States.

Shifts in opinion within the country confirmed the minor role it played in world affairs. There was a less boastful attitude than formerly and a growing respect for European culture among the thousands of tourists, scholars, and businessmen who looked to the Old World for esthetic, scientific, and financial capital. Americans were not isolationists by any means, but they were less certain than formerly that they could change the world. Consequently, they preferred to cultivate their own gardens. Individuals might venture abroad to convert the heathen or to paint, build railroads, or sell kerosene, but most of the nation did not feel that it had a stake in these activities and therefore saw no reason to protect or further them.

A new concept of race, in the writings of such men as Josiah Strong, was just beginning to transform the old idea of mission. But the consequences would not become apparent until after 1890.

Conservative Fears of America, 1871

If we, children of old Europe, who cling to the present as the logical natural continuation of the past, who cherish old recollections, traditions, and habits, if we do homage to your success, obtained under institutions which, on all essential points, are contrary to ours, this is a proof of our impartiality. For let us not deceive ourselves, America is the born antagonist of Europe. The first arrivals, the precursors of your actual greatness, those who sowed the seed, were discontented men. Intestine divisions and religious persecutions tore them from their homes and threw them on America's shores. They brought with them and planted in the soil of their new country the principle for which they had suffered and fought—the authority of the individual. He who possesses it is free in the fullest sense of the term. And, as in that sense you are all free, each of you is the equal of every other. Your country then is the classic soil of liberty and equality and it has become so from the fact that it was peopled by the men whom Europe expelled from its bosom. That is why you, in conformity with your origin, and we by a totally different genesis are antagonistic. . . .

All the world admires you. But all the world does not love you. Those among us who judge you from an exclusively European point of view see in you nothing but enemies of the fundamental principles of society. The more they appreciate your work, the more, in fact, they admire, the less they like you. I should add that they fear you. They dread your success as a dangerous example to Europe, and as far as they can they try to stop the spread of your ideas.

—Baron von Hübner, *Promenade autour du monde* (Paris, 1873), vol. I, pp. 305–308.

The Race of the Future, 1885

God, with infinite wisdom and skill, is training the Anglo-Saxon race for an hour sure to come in the world's future. Heretofore there has always been in the history of the world a comparatively unoccupied land westward, into which the crowded countries of the East have poured their surplus populations. But the widening waves of migration, which millenniums ago rolled east and west from the valley of the Euphrates, meet today on our Pacific coast. There are no more new worlds. The unoccupied arable lands of the earth are limited, and will soon be taken. The time is coming when the pressure of population on the means of subsistence will be felt here as it is now felt in Europe and Asia. Then will the world enter upon a new stage of its history—*the final competition of races, for which the Anglo-Saxon is being schooled.* . . .

Then this race of unequaled energy, with all the majesty of numbers and the might of wealth behind it—the representative, let us hope, of the largest liberty, the purest Christianity, the highest civilization—having developed peculiarly aggressive traits calculated to impress its institutions upon mankind, will spread itself over the earth. If I read not amiss, this powerful race will move down upon Mexico, down upon Central and South America, out upon the islands of the sea, over upon Africa and beyond. And can any one doubt that the result of this competition of races will be the "survival of the fittest"?

—Josiah Strong, *Our Country* (New York: Baker & Taylor, 1885), pp. 174–175.

▼

In the 1870s and 1880s, neither preparations for war nor overseas expansion seemed important to Americans. Their business was business — the development of the new productive system. Their energies went into the accommodation of a growing population, the spread of Western settlement and of communications, and the development of industrial and financial institutions. In the social, cultural, and political environment shaped by these forces, the prudent avoided external distractions as far as possible.

Yet detachment was not always possible. The promoters of business and religious ventures kept tugging at their fellow citizens to look abroad. The Monroe Doctrine and the concept of mission still evoked emotional responses. And a few people had already learned of the new concept of sea power that Captain Alfred T. Mahan would expound in a book published in 1890.

Furthermore, the world beyond the oceans was changing swiftly and other countries did not share American reticence about expansion. If the United States did not exercise the responsibilities its power gave it, other nations would fill the vacuum it left. In the quarter century after 1890, it would repeatedly face the problem of how to participate in an international scene dominated by imperialist rivalries without itself engaging in the race for colonies.

Paperbacks for Further Reading

Thomas N. Brown, *Irish-American Nationalism* (Preceptor Books) is a good analysis of immigrant pressures. Albert K. Weinberg, *Manifest Destiny* (Quadrangle Books, Inc.) and Frederick Merk, *Manifest Destiny and Mission in American History* (Vintage Books, Inc.) throw light on this period. Walter LaFeber, *The New Empire* (Cornell Paperbacks) emphasizes business pressure for expansion. A. Whitney Griswold, *The Far Eastern Policy of the United States* (Yale University Press) touches on these years.

THE THRUST OF PROGRESS

1890–1912

VII

THE POPULIST REVOLT

63

In the quarter century after 1890, Americans re-examined critically the society they had developed since the Civil War. They could boast unparalleled material achievements, but many other features of life in the United States were far from satisfactory. Each individual and each group judged the country's deficiencies in the light of its own interests, but all shared an uncomfortable awareness that the great disparity between wealth and poverty, the individualism that tended to become a greedy disregard of the common welfare, and the evasion of accepted rules of behavior were immoral. Through various means, people attempted to bring practice into conformity with their ideals.

In the 1890s the Populist movement drew together many strands of the reform impulse. The agricultural sections of the nation took the most active part in the protest. But Populism expressed the grievances of other elements of the population as well; it aimed not merely to further the interests of farmers but also to purify American society. That was both the source of its strength and the cause of its quick collapse.

Agrarian Grievances

THE 1890s WERE LOUD with the cry of the aggrieved. Advancing industrialization seemed to extend and perpetuate the inequities it had created earlier. People who worked hard and lived frugally nevertheless often found themselves destitute, while exorbitant rewards went to a few. Discontent mounted and protest took a powerful political form.

The Farm Problem The farmers were hard hit. Prices continued their disheartening decline; wheat dipped to a low point in 1894, corn in 1896, and cotton in 1898. The returns on tobacco, beef, and sheep told the same dismal story. One-crop areas, particularly in the South, suffered most. The number of mortgaged holdings rose, but money was tight and interest rates were high. Foreclosed farms as a result soon depressed the value of land. Men who had hopefully taken on debts now saw the future close in about them. All their personal sacrifices had been for nought. There was no place for failures in America.

Forms of Protest As in the past, those in danger tried to organize in self-protection. By 1890, the granges, particularly in the older, better-settled parts of the country, had become social associations and were not appropriate media for vigorous protest. The farmers' alliances were more capable of action; in the West branches had spread in a broad band from Kansas northward into Minnesota and South Dakota. Here, in the recently settled plains, social institutions were informal, the hardships of becoming established were painful, and the penalties of speculative failure were disastrous. In the scattered homesteads, people isolated from one another through much of the year valued the periodic occasions for gathering at the meetings to discuss common grievances. The alliances developed strength also in many areas of the South; they had started in Texas and Arkansas and gradually spread eastward to Georgia and South Carolina, appealing mostly to marginal farmers adversely affected by falling prices and the competition of new methods. As times grew worse, membership rolls swelled.

The men in the alliance lodges often discussed cooperation and the improvement of agricultural techniques. Some found attractive Charles W. Macune's subtreasury scheme. By that proposal, the government could help the farmers store their crops until prices were right, by providing them with warehouses and loans at low interest. The husbandmen could thus resist the unfavorable fluctuations of the markets.

Middlemen and Money But as the alliance members reviewed their grievances it became clear to them that two factors were responsible for the plight of the farmer. The return for his effort was inadequate because the middlemen took too large a toll and because a money short-

The Farmers' Protest, 1891

The hand of the money changer is upon us. Money dictates our financial policy; money controls the business of the country; money is despoiling the people. . . . These men of Wall Street . . . hold the bonds of nearly every State, county, city and township in the Union; every railroad owes them more than it is worth. Corners in grain and other products of toil are the legitimate fruits of Wall Street methods. Every trust and combine made to rob the people had its origin in the example of Wall Street dealers. . . . This dangerous power which money gives is fast undermining the liberties of the people. It now has control of nearly half their homes, and is reaching out its clutching hands for the rest. This is the power we have to deal with.

—W. A. Peffer, *The Farmer's Side* (New York: Appleton-Century-Crofts, 1891), pp. 121–123.

age artificially depressed the prices of the commodities he produced.

The railroads—the most visible intermediaries between farm and city—seemed to farmers great monopolies able to exact from the little man the rates they wished. The solution to that problem was government ownership so that the lines would operate to serve the people.

Alliance members believed, too, that the state could ease the fiscal stringency. The prices of corn and cotton were low because money was dear. The remedy was to increase the supply of currency by the free coinage of silver and by elimination of the bankers' control over the emission of paper. Some alliance members also argued that the prohibition of speculation and a system that gave the farmer credit against the security of his crops would improve his situation in the market and enable him to control the prices he received.

Political Action

To attain these objectives, it was necessary to gain political power either, as in the South, by capturing control of the Democratic party or, as in the West, by setting up independent organizations. Some political activity was already in progress in 1888 and 1889. Then in 1890 the alliances launched a sustained campaign for power, seized control of five Southern state legislatures, and demonstrated notable strength in Kansas, Nebraska, and South Dakota. In addition they elected about fifty congressmen. Suddenly they were a force to be reckoned with.

Allies As they gained prominence, the alliances reached out toward, and attracted, allies. The farmers considered themselves *the people* and identified their interests with those of all who labored honestly. The alliance mem-

Populism is most rewardingly examined through the studies of specific states. Among the best are: James C. Malin, *A Concern about Humanity* (Lawrence, Kan., 1964); Francis B. Simkins, *The Tillman Movement in South Carolina* (Durham, N.C., 1926); and Alex M. Arnett, *The Populist Movement in Georgia* (New York, 1922).

bers were therefore able to make common cause with the surviving Knights of Labor.

The agrarian demand for government ownership of railroads also struck a responsive chord among some socialists. Those who adhered to a strict ideology, notably the followers of Daniel De Leon in the Socialist Labor party, backed away from suggestions for collaboration with middle-class landowners. On the other hand, journalists and intellectuals, less committed to doctrine yet outraged by the contrast between the poverty of the farmers and the wealth of the capitalists, were willing to lend their support to the agrarians. Edward Bellamy, for instance, thought that he could thus edge the country toward his utopia. So too, Henry Demarest Lloyd joined in when his studies of the trusts convinced him of the need for national ownership of the great industries and means of communication.

Other reformers gravitated toward the new core of power taking shape after 1890. Temperance advocates had always been strongest in the rural regions and had all along argued that they were friends of the workingman, whose dollar they wished to divert from the saloon to the bakery. Now it appeared that their battle was the same as that of the farmer. To give wives and mothers the right to vote, the feminists had explained, would further the prospects of prohibition.

There were additional potential recruits. The good-government forces (often derisively labeled the Goo-Goo's) were impatient with the two major parties and had made the corrupt city machines their chief target. Some campaigners for civic purity, too, could take part in a new political movement. A good many people in the East and in the cities were thus ready to enlist under the banner of reform out of a conviction that recent changes had injected immoral elements into American society. A crusade for redemption was necessary.

Program and Techniques The mushrooming movement steadily gathered strength in the six years after 1890. Its outstanding characteristics were the distinctive style in which it summoned its forces to battle, its nationalism, and its hostility to the existing order of society.

Populist rhetoric and techniques owed much to the tradition of religious revivalism. Simple tracts like W. H. Harvey's *Coin's Financial School* (1894) and Ignatius Donnelly's *American People's Money* (1895) expounded the argument in readily comprehensible terms. Didactic novels like Donnelly's *Caesar's Column* (1890) made the same points dramatically.

The books, pamphlets, and magazines delivered a simple message. The greed of the wicked was the source of evil. Damnation awaited the society that failed to repent, but there was a way out. Redemption was available to those who wished to seek it, and the Populists could show the way. A band of fiery orators called upon their audiences to redeem their society. Biblical phrases enlivened their speeches, but they did not hesitate to use also the language of the plain people. Mary Elizabeth Lease, the Kansas Pythoness, warned the bloodhounds of money to beware as she urged the farmers to raise less corn and more hell.

Often the Populists emphasized American distinctiveness. Corrupt institutions and greedy rulers controlled other nations; the United States was different, destined to be pure. Its duty was to fulfill the mission of the Founding Fathers — to assure liberty and justice for all. Under existing conditions, however, the nation was betraying its heritage and its promise.

Often the farmers, estimating the pittance they received for the year's labor, contrasted their condition with that of the fortunate residents of the city. To suffer from the winter's blizzards and the summer's heat, to lose sight of man in the loneliness of the Great Plains, to be hemmed in by the crowded tenant's shack in the South, to lose all to plagues of insects — that was the lot of the tiller of the soil. The life of ease, the unconfined luxury of the gilded mansions, was the reward lavish wealth gave those who lived by the labor of others. It was not surprising that the young men and women, tempted by the fleshpots of Babylon, deserted their families to go off to the metropolis.

The people were not responsible for the corruption of the Republic. The common man — in whom a divine spark dwelt — could solve every difficulty if only he took control. The direct election of Senators, the primary, cooperatives, and government ownership were ultimately means of establishing that control. The voice of the people was the voice of God.

The fault lay elsewhere. The bloated plutocracy that had engrossed the nation's wealth was responsible for the evil that thrived in the cities. It had established a grip on all aspects of life and threatened, unless defeated, to subject the entire country to its will.

As the farmers thought about their own inability to get loans they needed and as they paid out the high interest charged them, they were tempted to accept a simple but imaginary explanation of the means by which the few had subjugated the many. According to this theory, the plutocrats had gained power through an insidious conspiracy of the international bankers — particularly the British and the Jews — whose manipulation of the money supply gave them mastery over the whole economy. The gold standard was the instrument by which it raised and lowered prices, created trusts, and oppressed the farmer, the laborer, and the honest businessman. Only a revived democracy that put power back in the hands of the people could meet the threat.

The People's Party

The Election of 1892 The election of 1892 mobilized the forces of protest. The existing parties seemed to offer the people no genuine choice. Grover Cleveland, attempting to regain office for the Democrats, and Benjamin Harrison, attempting to hold it for the Republicans, were both remote from the positions the alliances and their allies had taken. A new, third party was necessary.

Intense moral fervor animated **JAMES B. WEAVER** in all his actions. He was born in 1833 in Dayton, Ohio, one of thirteen children in a family that soon moved to Iowa. There Weaver grew up and acquired some desultory schooling, and there he would spend almost all his life.

California gold captured his imagination and he went west in 1853. The rapacious society of the Pacific coast horrified him and he soon returned to Iowa, where he worked in a store and, after a brief legal education in Cincinnati, began to practice law.

The new Republican party attracted his attention for it offered him a means of expressing his hostility to slavery. At the outbreak of the Civil War he enlisted, received a lieutenant's commission, fought gallantly in several battles, and emerged a brigadier general. His military record, commanding presence, and gift for oratory promised to open the way to a successful political career, and he held several local offices. But Weaver was a devout Methodist and an ardent prohibitionist. Honest and moral, he refused to play the political game with the Republican party leaders. A falling out in the 1870s drove him into independent action.

Weaver's sympathy for the hard-pressed farmers and laborers led him into the Greenback party, although he was not an extremist on the subject of money. He was elected to the United States House of Representatives in 1878 and again in 1884 and 1886, and ran for the presidency in 1880 on the Greenback ticket and in 1892 as a Populist. In office and during his campaigns, he spoke out for those who failed to receive a fair return for their toil.

He was among the Populists who welcomed fusion with the Democrats in 1896 and supported Bryan. The defeat that year ended Weaver's role on the national scene. He remained in Iowa, to which prosperity returned, and after serving for a while as mayor of the town of Colfax, died in 1912.

The Populists on Finance and Transportation, 1892

[Finance] We demand a national currency, safe, sound, and flexible, issued by the general Government only, a full legal tender for all debts, public and private, and that without the use of banking corporations. . . .

1. We demand free and unlimited coinage of silver and gold at the present legal ratio of 16 to 1.

2. We demand that the amount of circulating medium be speedily increased to not less than $50 per capita.

3. We demand a graduated income tax.

4. We believe that the money of the country should be kept as much as possible in the hands of the people, and hence we demand that all State and national revenues shall be limited to the necessary expenses of the Government, economically and honestly administered.

5. We demand that postal savings banks be established by the Government for the safe deposit of the earnings of the people and to facilitate exchange.

[Transportation] Transportation being a means of exchange and a public necessity, the government should own and operate the railroads in the interest of the people. The telegraph and telephone, like the post-office system, being a necessity for the transmission of news, should be owned and operated by the government in the interest of the people.

—J. M. H. Frederick, comp., *National Party Platforms* (Akron, Ohio: Akron Printing and Publishing Co., 1892), pp. 82–83.

The National Convention of the People's party met in Omaha, Nebraska, in July 1892. It nominated for the presidency James B. Weaver of Iowa, a veteran Greenbacker. The Populist platform attempted to state the objectives of the various groups which through it raised their voices in protest. To ease the burden of debt for the farmers and to raise prices for miners, it promised the unlimited coinage of silver and gold at a ratio of 16 to 1. Labor was assured some restriction of immigration, a limitation on strikebreaking detective agencies, and the eight-hour day on government projects. Nationalization of the railroads, the telegraph, and the telephone, a graduated income tax, and postal savings banks would undermine the monopolies. A single term for the President, direct election of Senators, and the initiative, referendum, and recall would restore the people's control over politics. A forceful statement of principles supplied the foundation for these planks.

A vigorous campaign followed. Although the two-party system proved strong enough to withstand the rising tide of protest, Weaver gained more than a million popular votes and took 22 places in the electoral college. He was particularly strong in the Great Plains and in the silver states and made a good showing in the South. Populist prospects for the future seemed excellent.

The Money Question   In the next four years, fiscal problems absorbed the attention of the nation. The advocates of an expanded money supply and the mining interests, represented by the strategic votes of the mountain states, pressed for even more liberal coinage of silver than provided for in the Sherman Silver Purchase Act (1890). This measure had directed the Treasury to buy 4,500,000 ounces of silver monthly with the intention of maintaining a parity between that metal and gold. Coming at the same time as the prohibitory rates of the McKinley tariff, which lowered total customs receipts, the law

Milton Friedman and Anna J. Schwartz, *A Monetary History of the United States, 1867–1960* (Princeton, N.J., 1963) is an excellent, although technical, treatment.

A National Plea for Silver, 1897

Our commercial power and demands for money exceed those of all Europe combined. The United States holds the key to the situation. We can unlock the vaults and set free the silver of the world. In other words, we can break down the dam that now confines silver by permitting that metal to flow freely into and out of our mints. We can thus establish an international bimetallism that will assure free circulation and glad acceptance to both gold and silver as money throughout the commercial world.

It needs a great, free and independent people such as ours, with our immense territory and resources, a population of over seventy millions — probably nearly eighty millions, and soon to reach one hundred millions — of industrious, enterprising citizens, to take the lead in undoing a great wrong for which in the main, at least, we were responsible. That we will do so in the future, and in the near future, all the indications go to point out as a certainty.

—Richard P. Bland, "Present Status of the Silver Question," *North American Review,* CLXV (October, 1897), p. 475.

drained the nation's supply of gold. By 1891, silver which still commanded $1.00 in gold from the United States, was worth as bullion only 84.76 cents. Whoever could paid silver into the Treasury and drew the more valuable gold out. The situation became more acute after the Panic of 1893 sharply depressed government revenues. Hoarding and withdrawals of gold to Europe then produced a crisis. Between 1890 and 1894, the net gold reserve of the United States dropped from more than $190,000,000 to less than $65,000,000.

As long as Americans operated within an international economy, the standard of which was gold, they could not alone sustain the use

Free Silver: Dubious. "What awful poor wages they get in all those free silver countries, John!" the wife says. "That's so," he replies, "but the politicians say it will be different in America." Cartoon, 1890s, from *Wasp*, a political satire magazine. (From the Ralph E. Becker collection, on loan to the Smithsonian Institution)

of another metal as money. One by one, the few other nations that still coined silver stopped doing so—Tunis in 1891, Austria-Hungary in 1892, and China, Japan, and Russia later in the decade. Only international acceptance of bimetallism could have saved the situation, and the Brussels Monetary Conference in 1893 failed to arrive at such an agreement. As a result the United States Treasury was paying out gold in exchange for the silver no one else wanted.

Soon after taking office in 1893 Cleveland successfully used every political resource of the presidency to persuade Congress to repeal the Sherman Silver Purchase Act, but his effort to replenish the gold reserve in 1894 failed. In February 1895, therefore, he turned to a syndicate led by J. P. Morgan which undertook to buy

a large issue of United States bonds for gold, half the bullion to be drawn from Europe. The bankers profited handsomely by the deal, but the government at last restored confidence in its currency.

The struggle over monetary policy now came to a head. The inflationary elements included farmers, debtors, speculators, and silver miners. In opposition were merchants, creditors, professional people, and other recipients of fixed incomes. But voters rarely aligned themselves solely by a simple calculation of their interests. In a more general way they were likely to support or oppose a stable currency as a part of the total economic system which they either accepted or rejected. And some evaded the choice entirely by taking refuge in the anti-Catholic American

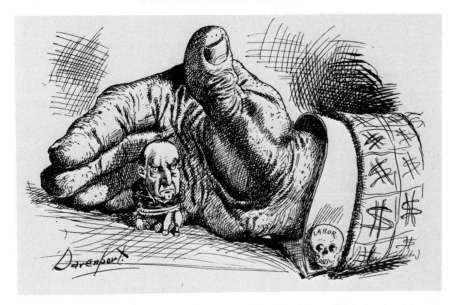

"A Man of Mark"—McKinley as Marc Hanna's Man. Cartoon by Homer Davenport which appeared in William Randolph Hearst's *The New York Journal* in the mid-1890s. (The Granger Collection)

Protective Association, which enrolled almost a million members by 1896. Such people followed the same pattern of escape taken by the Know-Nothings forty years earlier.

The Crisis of 1896 In the congressional elections of 1894 the Populists made some notable gains; they elected six Senators and seven Representatives. They did not, however, do as well as they expected in the state contests. The two major parties, conscious of the strength of the new force, were adopting some features of the Omaha platform. Moreover, once office was within reach, the ambitious were anxious to hasten to it by fusion with the Democrats in the South or with the Republicans in the West.

For the Populists, the results of 1894 were ominous foreshadowings of the situation in 1896. The prospect of capturing the presidency created an irresistible pressure for alliance with one party or the other. Those Populists who were committed to the full Omaha program resisted the temptation, for they realized that coalition was the death knell of their own organization.

They preferred to stand alone; they expected that if they did, the major parties would cling to gold and thus divide the vote of conservatives. Enough aggrieved elements in society would be unwilling to vote for either a gold Democrat or a gold Republican to sweep the Populist candidate into office. But many middle-of-the-roaders among the Populists were reluctant to take that risk and were ready to support an acceptable coalition ticket should either the Republicans or Democrats propose one.

The Republican Convention rejected the bait. The bulldozer carefully manipulated by Marcus A. Hanna, the Ohio coal and iron millionaire, secured the nomination for William McKinley as well as a plank firmly repudiating any measure calculated to debase the currency. The small silver contingent was powerless. Its forty-four delegates led by Senator Henry M. Teller of Colorado withdrew. The Republicans were firmly committed.

The Democrats, who met shortly thereafter, were unwilling to defend Cleveland's unpopular

The Cross of Gold, 1896

You come to us and tell us that the great cities are in favor of the gold standard; we reply that the great cities rest upon our broad and fertile prairies. Burn down your cities and leave our farms, and your cities will spring up again as if by magic; but destroy our farms and the grass will grow in the streets of every city in the country.

My friends, we declare that this nation is able to legislate for its own people upon every question, without waiting for the aid or consent of any other nation on earth; and upon that issue we expect to carry every state in the Union. I shall not slander the inhabitants of the fair State of Massachusetts nor the inhabitants of the State of New York by saying that, when they are confronted with the proposition, they will declare that this nation is not able to attend to its own business. It is the issue of 1776 over again. Our ancestors, when but three millions in number, had the courage to declare their political independence of every other nation; shall we, their descen-

dants, when we have grown to seventy millions, declare that we are less independent than our forefathers? No, my friends, that will never be the verdict of our people. Therefore, we care not upon what lines the battle is fought. If they say bimetallism is good, but that we cannot have it until other nations help us, we reply that, instead of having a gold standard because England has, we will restore bimetallism, and then let England have bimetallism because the United States has it. If they dare to come out in the open field and defend the gold standard as a good thing, we will fight them to the uttermost. Having behind us the producing masses of this nation and the world, supported by the commercial interests, the laboring interests, and the toilers everywhere, we will answer their demand for a gold standard by saying to them: You shall not press down upon the brow of labor this crown of thorns, you shall not crucify mankind upon a cross of gold.

—William Jennings Bryan, *Speeches* (New York: Funk & Wagnalls Company, 1909), pp. 248–249.

"Candidate Billy's Busy Day." William Jennings Bryan is shown in this cartoon as having accepted the nomination of the Populist, Free Silver, and Democratic parties. Pen and ink drawing by G. Y. Coffin, September 13, 1896. (Library of Congress)

administration. They repudiated the sale of bonds to the bankers and demanded stronger antitrust legislation. Above all, thoughts at the Convention turned to the money question. William Jennings Bryan of Nebraska roused the delegates with the religious imagery of his cross-of-gold speech. A wave of emotion spread through the hall at the reminder of the people's martyrdom. The party platform took an unequivocal stand in favor of the free and unlimited coinage of silver at a ratio of 16 to 1 with gold, and Bryan received the nomination, although he accepted a respectable banker as his running mate.

The choice left the Populists scarcely an alternative. To have run their own candidate as some wished would have divided the silver vote and given the election to McKinley. They therefore accepted Bryan at the head of their ticket, but as a token of independence, nominated Thomas E. Watson of Georgia for the vice-presidency.

The issue was clearer to the electorate in this campaign than in any election since 1860. McKinley stood for the *status quo*. No wild experiments were to hamper industrial development that had given Americans the full dinner pail. Bryan voiced the protest of the farmers who toiled to bring the nation's wealth out of its broad and fertile prairies and who resented their subjection to the great cities. Bryan's frenetic campaign carried him over thousands of miles, for scores of speeches; McKinley depended upon the careful organizational work of Hanna and the Republican party, backed up by ample funds.

The outcome was a clear victory for McKinley. In the popular balloting McKinley received about 53 percent of the total, and he captured 271 electoral votes as against 176 for Bryan, taking all the Northern states east of the Mississippi as well as Minnesota, California, and Oregon. The election revealed where the balance of strength now lay. Without support in the

Paolo E. Coletta, *William Jennings Bryan* (Lincoln, Neb., 1964) covers Bryan's career until 1908.

THOMAS E. WATSON was a man swayed by passion. Red-haired and intense, he spoke and wrote with conviction, and even his humor was purposeful. As he grew older, he thought of himself as a prophet not honored in his own country, and his anger at those who rejected his dire warnings mounted.

He spent his boyhood in Columbia County, Georgia, where he was born in 1856. His father fought with the Confederates, was wounded, and came home impoverished. Dreamy and studious, Tom wrote romantic poetry and was uncertain about what he would do. He studied for a while at Mercer University but never graduated, then taught school and read law.

It was at the bar that he found himself. Watson acquired a good reputation and a good income as a criminal lawyer, using his oratorical gifts effectively before juries. His practice exposed him to the injustices of a society that was torn between old illusions and the materialistic, get-rich attitudes of the New South. In the state assembly, where he served in 1882, he broke with established party leaders and thereafter sought to mobilize farmer support for an independent policy.

In 1890, the Farmers' Alliance helped elect him to the United States House of Representatives, where he proved exceptionally able, introducing thoughtful reform legislation. Fraud deprived him of his seat in 1892 and again in 1894. He nevertheless gained wide attention as one of the most thoughtful of the Populist leaders.

In 1896, Watson opposed fusion of the Populist with the Democratic party, for he feared that the silver issue would obscure other aspects of the program and he had reservations about Bryan. He made the race as Populist candidate for the vice-presidency in order to assert the autonomy

(*Continued on next page*)

(Continued from preceding page)

of the party. He ran futile campaigns for the presidency as a Populist in 1904 and 1908.

After 1896 he did a good deal of writing, composing several historical works with a Populist interpretation and commenting on current events in newspapers and magazines. Although Watson grew personally wealthy, his bitterness did not subside. As the South and the country moved toward industrialization, he concluded that the world was plunging hell-

ward and directed his animosity at the Catholics, socialists, Negroes, and Jews who, he thought, had corrupted the nation. He became more parochial and more prejudiced as time went on, as well as more perverse in his hostility to the forces in control of the country. He opposed entry of the United States into World War I and favored recognition of the communist regime in Russia. He was a member of the United States Senate when he died, in 1922, still passionately outraged at the course American development had taken.

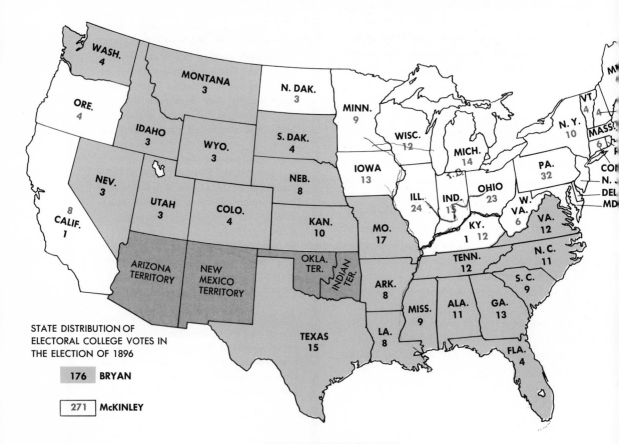

STATE DISTRIBUTION OF
ELECTORAL COLLEGE VOTES IN
THE ELECTION OF 1896

176 BRYAN

271 McKINLEY

THE ELECTION OF 1896

Gold Rush to the Klondike Region, 1898. The miners and prospectors here approaching the Chilkoot Pass were among the 30,000 people who made their way to the region following the discovery of gold at Bonanza Creek in 1896. (Culver Pictures)

industrial regions, to which Bryan was alien, no candidate could carry the presidency.

The Aftermath of Populism

The silver issue died shortly thereafter. Discoveries of gold in Alaska and in South Africa and more efficient mining and refining methods raised the supply of specie, and the United States formally adhered to the gold standard in 1900. An improvement in the balance of trade also helped relieve the monetary stringency.

The Populist party never recovered from the defeat. Traces of its influence survived in the South, where many of its members turned racist in resentful disappointment that the Negroes, whose cooperation they had expected, had instead become tools of the Bourbons. Most whites of all classes now united to disenfranchise the Negroes. Mississippi, South Carolina, and Louisiana pioneered in working out the means of evading the restraints of the Fifteenth Amendment. A requirement limiting the ballot to people whose grandfathers had enjoyed it or calling for the ability to read the Constitution could readily be applied to bar the Negro. These devices spread to most of the former Confederate states.

Meanwhile in the West, with the recovery of agriculture and the return of prosperity soon after 1896, most farmers reverted to their Republican loyalties. The basic conditions favorable to economic growth were still intact and the Populist revolt subsided. Other men under other circumstances would take up some of the issues raised in the protest, but the call for a total recasting of society faded.

▼

The Populist revolt was the initial response of discontented Americans to the effects of massive industrialization. Its failure was due to more than the tactical errors of fusion with the Democrats and concentration on the silver question in 1896. The great strength of Populism had come from the rural regions of the country, and its program had reflected the interests of the independent farmer. It offered no rationally acceptable alternative to the rest of the population, which wished to spread the rewards of industrialization rather than impede or reverse the process.

Yet there was another and more durable aspect of Populism. It enlisted the moral fervor of many citizens not by its program but by its protest. Something was wrong! However faulty the diagnosis, thousands of Americans wished to register their concern with the ills of society. The disparity of incomes, the callous disregard of the welfare of the helpless, and the corruption of politics cried for reform. Such protests would occupy progressives in the twentieth century, but in a different context and with more rewarding results.

Paperbacks for Further Reading

John D. Hicks, *The Populist Revolt* (Bison Books) is a general history. There is a less conventional interpretation in Richard Hofstadter, *Age of Reform* (Vintage Books, Inc.). Theodore Saloutos, *Farmer Movements in the South* (Bison Books) and C. Vann Woodward, *Origins of the New South, 1877–1913* (Louisiana State University Press) deal with the movement in the Southern states, and Russel B. Nye, *Midwestern Progressive Politics* (Harper Torchbooks) handles the Western aspects. Albert D. Kirwan, *Revolt of the Rednecks* (Harper Torchbooks) is an excellent account of Mississippi. C. Vann Woodward, *Tom Watson* (Galaxy Books) is a first-rate biography with good material on the Georgia setting. Paul W. Glad, *McKinley, Bryan and the People* (Preceptor Books) is a lively account of the election of 1896, which is also treated in George F. Whicher, *William Jennings Bryan and the Campaign of 1896* (D. C. Heath and Co.). William H. Harvey, *Coin's Financial School* (Harvard University Press) has been edited with a thoughtful introduction by Richard Hofstadter. George B. Tindall, ed., *A Populist Reader* (Harper Torchbooks) contains selections from the works of other leaders.

THE NEW
AGRICULTURE

64

Subsidence of the Populist revolt was closely connected with a change in the farmers' prospects after 1896. Protest continued, but in a more moderate, less aggrieved form. Almost everywhere the flaming radicalism that had animated the People's party flickered out as agriculture, in which the larger part of the American population still engaged, made a decisive recovery.

The hardships of the 1890s led to a period of experimentation and readaptation. In 1912, some farmers still suffered from difficulties and all were yet to face recurrent depressions, but tremendous growth in the whole economy had enabled them to begin the reconstruction that would restore the strength of agriculture in the United States.

INDEX OF FARM PRICES, 1890–1912
(100 = average for 1910–1914)

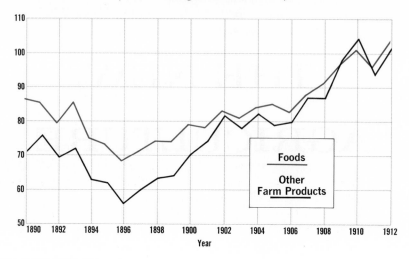

Year

The Demand for Farm Products

THE 1890s WERE YEARS of crisis for American husbandmen. The protests, already sounded before the decade began, then reached a peak of intensity. Low prices and high costs left the farmers an inadequate reward for their labor. Meanwhile the burden of debt grew weightier. The yeoman faced defeat.

Foreign Markets Adverse forces persisted well into the twentieth century. For a time optimists predicted that foreign markets would absorb whatever surpluses the United States produced, but by 1912 those exaggerated hopes were dimmed. American grains and cotton met severe competition from foreign producers as the latter introduced technological advances and lowered their costs accordingly. In addition, Germany and England adopted protectionist policies, as France already had done. As a result the export of American commodities failed to rise significantly.

There is a general account of agriculture in this period in Harold U. Faulkner, *The Decline of Laissez Faire, 1897–1917* (New York, 1962).

The shipment abroad of wheat and other crude foodstuffs had reached a peak in the early 1890s but thereafter it fluctuated in a generally downward direction. The export of meat and other manufactured foods had shown a promising rise between 1870 and 1890 but then leveled off as discriminatory tariffs and inspection laws abroad curtailed the packers' foreign markets. Cotton and tobacco did better. The volume exported moved generally upward but not enough to offset the over-all failure of agricultural exports to climb.

Domestic Markets When the situation of agriculture improved, it was as a result of developments at home. Toward the end of the century a painful readjustment pointed the way toward the restoration of prosperity. The trend of prices was a measure of the extent of recovery. After dropping in the first half of the 1890s the prices of food and other farm products began to rise, and after 1900 they soared. The trend was notable particularly in the prices of corn and wheat, the great staples of the West. As the level rose, the farmer's returns became more ample; and the average value of his land per acre almost doubled between 1890 and 1912, most of the rise coming after 1896. The total worth of the

American Farms and Their Value, 1890–1912

Year	Number of Farms (millions)	Value (millions)	Value of the Average Holding	Farm Laborers (thousands)
1890	4.5	$13,082	$2,907	5,296
1900	5.7	16,615	2,915	5,036
1910	6.3	34,801	5,525	4,465
1912	6.4	44,637	6,974	–

average holding more than doubled between those dates.

The rise in prices was partly, but not entirely, the result of the discovery of gold in Alaska and in South Africa, which no doubt eased the shortage of specie. The experience with corn and wheat showed that the reversal of the earlier trend, despite the contraction of foreign markets, was due to a basic improvement in the condition of the farmer. Agriculture revived after the turn of the century because a radical reorganization enabled it to take full advantage of the economic growth of the nation.

Commercial Agriculture

The independent yeoman who tilled his own family plot remained the ideal figure in the rhetoric of politicians and in popular fiction. In reality, however, he was becoming a figure of the past as agriculture took on a new form modeled after that of industry. The change was neither deliberate nor conscious. Farmers gradually learned that they would profit on holdings of an economical size if they would adopt rational methods, specialize, and utilize the information science put at their disposal.

Efficient Holdings A first step in modernization was liquidation of the marginal producers. For generations the belief had survived that anyone could make it. The willingness to work and an empty tract were enough for a start in farming. Drawn on by the expectation of independent proprietorship, thousands of families had attacked the soil without reckoning the backbreaking costs of the effort. The 1890s were their time of trial; it was then that the desperate residents of the sod huts either failed or pulled through. Those who had overextended themselves or who lacked the resources to absorb the shock of hard times had to stand by as their foreclosed lands went by sale to more fortunate neighbors. The experience was bitter for those who were liquidated, but those who survived gained. And as a result agriculture became more efficient after 1900 than it had been earlier.

The disappearance of large bonanza farms eased the competitive situation. The heavy costs —in capital and labor—of these enterprises discouraged their absentee owners, who preferred to sell off plots when land values rose. More stable, more efficient resident producers took their place.

It is true that the rate of farm tenancy rose from 28 percent in 1890 to 35 percent in 1900 and 37 percent in 1910. But the rise was much lower in the second than in the first decade and in both the increase came primarily in the South, where agriculture still failed to conform to the national pattern. The problems inherited from the plantation and the color line kept that region backward; tenants tilled more than 1,500,000 of its 3,000,000 farms in 1910.

Rationalization In the rest of the country, holdings increasingly took a form susceptible to modernization. The rate of mechanization

Harold Barger and Hans H. Landsberg, *American Agriculture, 1899–1939* (New York, 1942) is a technical study of output, employment, and productivity.

Leo Rogin, *The Introduction of Farm Machinery in Its Relation to the Productivity of Labor* (Berkeley, Calif., 1931) deals with the nineteenth century as a whole.

Modern Steam Thresher with Self-feeder, Stacker, and Bagging Attachment, California, 1905. Photograph by C. H. Graves. (Library of Congress)

George Washington Carver Teaching a Laboratory Class at Tuskegee Institute, *ca*. 1900. (The Granger Collection)

accelerated. New machines, like the steam harvester, widely and skillfully used, reduced the dependency upon hired laborers, whose number declined sharply despite the rise in output. Other improved devices—the silo, the centrifugal cream separator, and the butterfat tester, for instance—also markedly raised efficiency.

Furthermore, farming was less often than earlier a haphazard rule-of-thumb affair. New fertilizers raised yields, and rationalized processes made calculation and planning as important as in manufacturing. Although there had been much talk of it earlier, the scientific method began seriously to affect the conduct of many farms only after 1890. In most states the universities applied the talents of scientists to the specific problems of their area and permitted a more efficient utilization of resources. County agents carried the new techniques from the laboratory and the experimental farm directly to the husbandman and helped increase his productivity.

Since 1887 the national government had also been actively involved in the effort. The Hatch Act, that year, provided funds for research through agricultural experimental stations. Two years later, with the establishment of the Department of Agriculture, Federal activities were coordinated and expanded. And in 1890 the Morrill Act made a substantial appropriation for the instruction of farmers. Science now caught the imagination of the men in the fields, as it raised the returns from their labor.

Specialization Significant shifts in the older patterns of American agriculture furthered its efficiency. A decided change in the location of many crops improved the use of land resources. The center of cotton production moved westward. By 1910 Texas raised greater quantities of that staple than the whole of the old southeast. The areas newly opened had the advantages of unexhausted soil, improved methods, and freedom from the anachronistic habits inherited from the plantation.

Farm Demonstrations in the South, 1909

The plan adopted at the beginning of the work has been found to be so universally successful that it has been continued. Namely: The demonstration of the principal crop by the farmer, on his own farm, at his personal expense, the Agent giving him instructions. As the entire profit belongs to the farmer he is readily convinced of the superiority of the intensive methods, and no amount of argument can change his views. His demonstration is inspected by the cooperators and neighbors at the monthly field meeting with the Agent, where there is ample opportunity for observation and discussion, thus convincing them that they can do as well on their own farms.

In addition to this work we are putting forth a strong effort to arouse and encourage every additional force to adopt and promote better rural methods, by an active cooperation with the State Colleges of Agriculture, State Departments of Agriculture, State Superintendents of Public Instruction, County high schools, rural district schools, country churches, etc., all of which is more or less effective.

The expansion of the Demonstration Work and its hold upon the masses are both surprising and gratifying. One of our chief difficulties at present is our inability to meet the increasing demand for work— it comes from all sources—The people, Members of Congress, Governors and Senators, and with a force that accepts no excuse.

—General Education Board, "Report on Farmers' Cooperative Demonstration Work 1909."

Dairying in the United States, 1890–1912

	1890	1900	1910	1912
Cheese production (million pounds)	318	323	364	–
Milk cows (thousand head)	16,512	17,136	17,125	19,517
Value per head	$22	$31	$35	$39
Milk production (million pounds)	44,807*	62,486†	64,211‡	–
Production of canned milk (million pounds)	44*	206	555	700
Per capita consumption of canned milk (pounds)	–	2.5†	–	7.1
Butter production (million pounds)	1,292	1,540	1,706	–

* 1889   † 1899   ‡ 1909

Time and again, Professor **THEOPHILUS L. HAECKER** told his classes, "Treat the cow kindly, boys. Remember she is a lady —and a mother."

Haecker knew whereof he spoke. He was born in a log cabin in Iowa in 1836, one of twelve children in a German immigrant family. He fought in the Civil War, studied intermittently at the University of Wisconsin, held some minor government offices, and worked on a newspaper. But all along he remained close to the soil and on his Silver Springs Dairy Farm experimented with feeds and breeds. With his neighbors, he set up a cooperative creamery and gained practical experience in its management.

In 1891 he began to teach in the dairying school at the University of Minnesota, where for twenty-seven years he preached the gospel of science applied to agriculture. In special courses for adults he taught farmers the advanced methods of butter and cheese production and kept theory close to practice. Gradually his objection to the multipurpose cow prevailed. For dairying he favored the Holstein, and urged a continuing adjustment of feed to function, so that the type of fodder would be related to tests of the fat content of the milk produced.

In a survey of conditions in 1892, Haecker observed the success of a cooperative run by Danes who imitated the methods of their homeland. Thereafter he campaigned for the establishment of cooperatives throughout the state. By 1918, fully 630 had been formed. Their efficient operation added substantially to farm income. He retired from teaching in 1918 but lived until 1938, by which time his theories had become standard practices fundamental to American dairying.

Fruit Production in the United States, 1890–1912

	1890	1900	1912
Apples (million bushels)	80	205	225
Peaches (million bushels)	36*	49	49
Pears (million bushels)	3*	6†	13
Grapes (thousand tons)	–	650†	1,197
Oranges (million boxes)	–	–	13
Grapefruit (million boxes)	–	–	2

* 1889   † 1899

There were noticeable changes also in grain production. Wheat invaded the Dakotas on a large scale in the 1890s, adding to the areas in nearby western Minnesota, Kansas, and Nebraska suitable to mechanization. By contrast, farmers in Iowa, Illinois, and Indiana were abandoning that crop in favor of corn and hog production. At about the same time, with the closing of the open ranges and the end of long drives, cattle raising shifted eastward in Texas and northward through Kansas to Iowa.

These changes were evidence of a growing diversity and specialization of function. As the marginal farmers dropped away and as the total improved acreage declined after 1900, the producers who survived discovered the advantages of focusing on the crop best suited to their distinctive conditions in terms of soil and markets.

Everywhere some farmers began to explore the possibilities of still more specialized agriculture. Dairying had long been confined to a very limited market area and therefore to small-scale production. The railway and refrigeration permitted expansion just when the urban population, increasingly conscious of diet, raised its

Oscar E. Anderson, Jr., *Refrigeration in America* (Princeton, N.J., 1953) is a good study.

demands for milk and cheese. Scientific methods, such as those advocated by Theophilus L. Haecker, enabled farmers to increase their output. At the same time prices went up. The result aided not only Wisconsin, which became the largest dairying state, but also eastern Minnesota, New England, and New York State, which were close to urban markets.

The cities were responsible for the expansion of truck farming and fruitgrowing. Apples, pears, and oranges now moved in unprecedented quantities to the tables of urban consumers, along an effective distribution system. Meanwhile the desire of many city people for a taste of country life enabled some husbandmen to earn added income by taking in summer boarders in the East or dudes on the ranches of the West.

Ingenious experimenters and scientists developed new crossbred strains particularly appropriate to urban markets—the navel orange, the loganberry, the youngberry, and the grapefruit, for example. The work of Luther Burbank in this field became as well known as that of Thomas Edison in mechanical invention. Vineyards in California and along Lake Erie in New York and Ohio produced increasing quantities of wine. The tonnage of grapes raised in the United States almost doubled between 1900 and 1912.

The effects of the transformation in agriculture were most notable on the Pacific Coast and in the immediate vicinity of the great cities, but to some degree they were also evident in the prosperity of agriculture elsewhere. Cottonseed oil came to provide a significant supplement to Southern farm incomes. In 1876, as in the past, planters depended almost entirely on the sale of the cotton fiber; they sold only 5 percent of their seed for oil production and wasted most of the rest. By 1910, new mills consumed well over 70 percent of the seed. Growing efficiency in the exploitation of old crops and the development of new ones laid a sound foundation for the agriculture of the future.

LUTHER BURBANK was born in Lancaster, Massachusetts, in 1849, the thirteenth child of a farmer. Times were hard for New England agriculture, and though he attended the district school, he was able to go on to the local academy only in the winter when his labor was not needed on the farm. For a while he worked in a factory, but was unhappy away from the world of nature, which fascinated him.

His father died in 1868 and Luther was then on his own. That same year he read in the local library Darwin's study of the influence of domestication on animals and plants, and the book opened a new world to him. He had learned that the forms of nature were not fixed or immutable. Man's ingenuity could alter them.

Burbank took up market gardening for a living, selling his vegetables in the nearby city of Fitchburg. He found time also to experiment and shortly developed a new potato.

In 1875 he sold out and moved to the more congenial climate of California, where three older brothers had already preceded him. He had a difficult time at first, but worked as a laborer and saved enough money to buy 4 acres in Santa Rosa in 1880. There he built a greenhouse and laid out a garden.

Later, when Burbank's fame had spread, the Carnegie Institution tried to persuade him to keep systematic records for scientific purposes, but he was not interested in knowledge in the abstract. His sole desire was by tinkering to make plants grow better in fairer forms. He imported species from abroad, practiced hybridization by trial and error, and worked out a method of grafting seedlings on existing trees so as to produce variations quickly. His most important efforts produced new types of tomatoes, corn, plums, berries, and lilacs. He died in 1926.

American Railroads, 1890-1912

	Miles of Track (thousands)	Ton Miles of Freight (millions)
1890	199	76,207
1900	258	141,597
1910	351	255,017
1912	371	264,081

The Distribution System

A good part of the transformation depended upon a distribution system about which the farmer had formerly complained. An increasingly efficient marketing mechanism now brought the purchasers of his products within easy reach.

The Railroads   The railroad network of the 1890s, as seen on a map, seemed complete; the lines crisscrossed every corner of the country. Yet between 1890 and 1912, the miles of track rose from 199,000 to 371,000. The amount of freight carried increased at an even higher rate between those dates. Construction in those years lacked the drama of the extension of the transcontinentals across the open plains, but it was nonetheless important. Branches reached out into the agricultural counties; double-tracked lines made possible a high volume of traffic; and great new freight yards permitted the effective utilization of equipment. Combined with better, graded roadbeds and sturdier bridges, these improvements increased the railroads' capacity to carry goods. The ton miles of freight shipped quadrupled between 1890 and 1912, and a good part of the increase represented the movement of farm products.

Improvements in the processing and handling of agricultural commodities, too, expanded markets. New mechanized elevators, flour mills, and slaughterhouses efficiently turned wheat and cattle into loaves of bread and sides of beef, which the spreading chain stores and the net-

Rudolf A. Clemen, *The American Livestock and Meat Industry* (New York, 1923) has a section on this period.

The Victory of Western Beef, 1894

Western dressed beef has completely captured New England. The most expert and experienced butchers concede it is an impossibility to kill native steers and compete in price with the imported article. When the fact is shown the observer by careful mathematical computations he begins to appreciate the commercial genius of the men who can kill cattle in far western points, lay the carcass down at the most remote New England crossroads and sell at prices lower than the bare cost of raising and killing the native animal.

—*Butcher's Advocate*, XVIII (November 21, 1894), as quoted in R. A. Clemen, *The American Livestock and Meat Industry* (New York: The Ronald Press Company, 1923), p. 251.

works of commission merchants brought to family tables in every part of the nation. Western meat could be sold in the East more cheaply than it could be raised locally. Cooperatives, especially among fruitgrowers and dairymen, lowered distribution costs.

The growing prevalence of processed foods gave farmers greater control over their markets. The per capita consumption of condensed and evaporated milk, for instance, tripled between 1899 and 1912, while production went up from 44,000,000 pounds in 1889 to 700,000,000 in 1912. Milk and fruit for which there were no buyers at the moment did not have to be poured out or thrown away. Canned, they would last until demand resumed.

Population Growth

The prosperity of the farms owed much to the steady expansion of the domestic market. To the extent that it was freed from dependence upon the fluctuations of foreign markets, agriculture became more calculable and more subject to control by producers. This was the first step toward regulating the output of the farms. The size of the domestic market, in turn, depended upon the continuing rise in population, particularly the portion residing in the cities.

Decade after decade, the census takers counted the increase in the country's inhabitants. The 63,000,000 persons of 1890 became 76,000,000 in 1900 and 92,000,000 in 1910—a rate of increase of about 20 percent for each ten-year period.

In 1910, a majority of the population was still classified as rural, but by then urban residents were only slightly less in number. In the preceding two decades, the rural population had grown from 41,000,000 to 50,000,000; the urban population, from 22,000,000 to 42,000,000, a rise of 91 percent.

Internal Migration The cities did not grow simply from the multiplication of the people already in them in 1890. The increase was the result of migration from within the United States and from outside. Disappearance of the shifting line of westward settlement along which restless Americans had moved in the past had not meant the end of the frontier. The city was the new frontier, drawing newcomers by the prospect of gain, adventure, and freedom. The percentage of Americans born outside the state of their residence remained as high in 1910 as earlier. The migrants were no longer proceeding toward the wilderness; the city had given them another destination. Migration patterns showed heavy losses in rural New York, Pennsylvania, New England, Indiana, Illinois, Wisconsin, Missouri, Kentucky, and Tennessee and gains to the cities close to those areas.

Immigration The cities welcomed also an army of the foreign-born, who more than compensated for the decline in the native birth rate. A new wave of immigration took form in the 1890s and mounted to a peak after the turn of the century. Arrivals were now more numerous

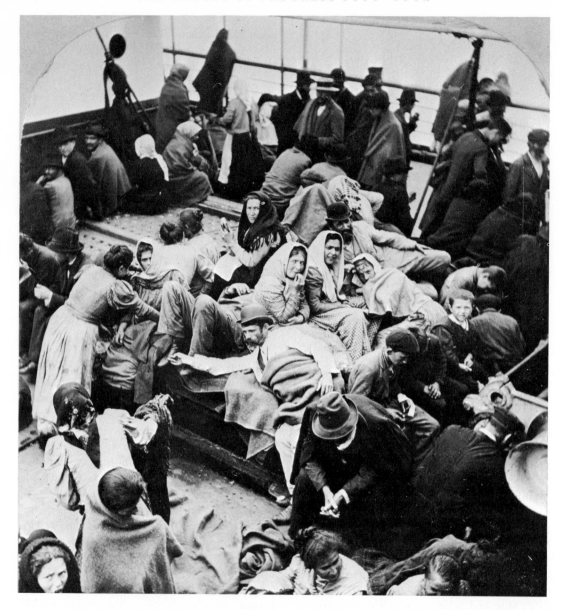

Immigrants Aboard Ship, 1902. Photograph by William H. Rau. (Library of Congress)

The Emigration Fever in Italy, 1906

The emigration this year is assuming extraordinary proportions. The local ticket agencies are continually crowded with people who would like to depart at once, but can not do so, as the steamers are filled up already for the months of February and March. The part of our population, too, that is emigrating is the youngest, sturdiest, and the soundest morally. It can not be said that they are driven out by dire want and necessity; they are lured away rather by the desire to better themselves in the world and make a possible fortune. Whole families, including old folks, women, and children, and young couples but just married are seen bidding farewell to their homes. Many are of a class possessing some little property, the easy so-called borghesi (meaning a lower middle class).

—Report from the Province of Girgenti to the United States Consul in Palermo. *Reports of the U.S. Immigration Commission, 1907–1910. Emigration Conditions in Europe* (Washington: Government Printing Office, 1911), p. 183.

Immigration to the United States, 1890–1912

Year	Number Admitted (thousands)
1890	455
1891	560
1892	579
1893	439
1894	285
1895	258
1896	343
1897	230
1898	229
1899	311
1900	448
1901	487
1902	648
1903	857
1904	812
1905	1,026
1906	1,100
1907	1,285
1908	782
1909	751
1910	1,041
1911	878
1912	838

than ever before. In four of the first ten years after 1900 the number of admissions rose above the million mark, and it rarely sank much below this level in that decade. The total of entries between 1890 and 1912 was 14,600,000.

A variety of sources supplied this vast flow of people. The countries that had produced emigrants earlier in the century continued to do so. Well over 100,000 Germans arrived annually until 1892, and between 30,000 and 40,000 thereafter. A steady stream of newcomers originated in England, Ireland, and Scandinavia. These immigrants were less likely to be peasants than in the past and more likely to be industrial workers. They made straight for the mines and the factories, and so contributed directly to the rise in urban population.

The new arrivals from other, hitherto little-tapped parts of the world were peasants, but they too generally found urban destinations. Southern, central, and eastern Europe and parts of Asia Minor now felt the effects of the economic changes that had earlier transformed the western countries of the Old World. An increase in population crowded the lands and the growth of industry and of large-scale farming forced out the cultivators of small plots. Crop failures and epidemics hastened them on their way. The great majority drifted to the industrial and commercial cities of their own countries; Milan, Vienna, Prague, Budapest, and Warsaw were expanding at unprecedented rates.

But a goodly number of displaced peasants chose to make the longer journey to the New

Children Playing in the Street in Front of a Polish Store, Chicago. (Chicago Historical Society)

World, and railroads and steamships were now available to carry them there with relative speed and at low cost. Once the pioneers discovered the way, their letters and remittances brought friends and relatives along the same path. Out of Italy, particularly its southern regions, came between 100,000 and 200,000 immigrants a year. A conglomerate host of peoples whom Americans generally referred to as "Slavs" also sought opportunity in the New World. Among them were Hungarians, Croatians, Czechs, Slovaks, Rumanians, Poles, Serbs, Macedonians, and Bulgars. From Russia, Germany, and Poland came well over a million Jews, forced to depart by poverty as well as by pogroms and other forms of discrimination. Greece, Armenia, and Turkey contributed lesser contingents, joined by sizable groups from other parts of the world—from Japan until 1907, from Canada after 1903, and from Mexico after 1909.

With relatively few exceptions, the millions of newcomers in the decades after 1890 settled in the cities. There they played an important part in the evolution of American industry, but their first impact was on the capacity for consumption of the urban population. They formed a significant portion of that rapidly expanding domestic market which absorbed the output of the transformed farms of the United States.

▼

A profound reordering of the basic pattern of American agriculture quieted the unrest of the 1890s. Many problems remained. The incidence of debt and tenancy continued high, particularly in the South, which lagged in modernization. Yet in a long-term readjustment the commercial features of agriculture developed, and they would sustain its future prosperity. Though the farm was a family unit and a home as well as a business, the farmer was learning to behave as an entrepreneur. He was painfully finding a place in the industrial world of the twentieth century.

Paperbacks for Further Reading

The situation of agriculture in the 1890s supplied the background for a good deal of speculation about the effects of the end of the frontier on the United States. Much of the discussion revolved about the thesis stated in Frederick Jackson Turner, *Frontier in American History* (Holt, Rinehart & Winston, Inc.). See also the selection of his essays in Frederick Jackson Turner, *Frontier and Section* (Spectrum Books). Other material on the controversy will be found in Ray Allen Billington, ed., *The Frontier Thesis* (Holt, Rinehart & Winston, Inc.); Wilbur R. Jacobs, John W. Caughey, and Joe B. Frantz, *Turner, Bolton, and Webb* (University of Washington Press); and Henry Nash Smith, *Virgin Land* (Vintage Books, Inc.). Chapter 20 of R. E. Riegel, *Story of the Western Railroads* (Bison Books) deals with this period. Suggestions on the history of immigration will be found under Chapter 66.

INDUSTRIAL
INTEGRATION

65

In the first decade of the twentieth century a growing urban population swelled the domestic market and eased the farm problem. The consumers whose purchases of bread and meat sustained American agriculture increasingly derived their incomes, directly or indirectly, from manufacturing. Industry supplied a mounting share of the national wealth and became pivotal to the whole economy.

The gigantic factories which made the goods that clothed, housed, and conveyed the people created formidable political and social difficulties. The industrial organization inherited from the past was inadequate for the new scale of operations. The vastly enlarged size of manufacturing plants persuaded many investors that regularity and integration were preferable to unlimited competition, but efforts to impose orderly patterns on business ran counter to traditional legal assumptions and popular attitudes. The result was a long conflict over the control of the economy which extended through the first half of the new century. The rising output of industry thus created new problems as it helped solve old ones.

AMERICAN INDUSTRY, 1912

Industrial Power

AT THE END of the nineteenth century the awesome capacity for growth of the American economy impressed observers at home and abroad. All the indexes moved upward, and the trend continued without serious interruption to 1912. In the two decades after 1890, the gross national product, measured in constant dollars, more than doubled.

Industrial Output Only part of the increase was due to the rise in population. The fact that the product per capita went up by about 60 percent in the same years showed that the economy was also improving its ability to produce. Not only were more hands at work at the end than at the beginning of the period but superior tools enabled each to turn out greater quantities of goods.

Manufacturing accounted for a widening share of the total output. The basic industrial plant was already in existence in 1890. In the two decades that followed, it expanded, grew more efficient, and accelerated its operations. The volume of its products multiplied by more than 150 percent. In the same period the capital invested in factories and equipment tripled.

The most important branches of manufacturing were those already established before 1890 — on the one hand, the preparation of foods and textiles for consumers and, on the other, of iron and steel. The output of steel reached levels unimaginable a few years earlier; between 1890 and 1912 it multiplied fully eightfold and provided a sturdy foundation for the development of the whole economy.

The most vigorous new industry appeared in response to perfection of the internal combustion engine. Many mechanics were already tinkering with the horseless carriage in the

Robert H. Wiebe, *The Search for Order: 1877–1920* (New York, 1966) is a good general survey.

Henry Ford and His Son Edsel in a 1905 Model F Ford in Front of Their Home on Hendrie Avenue, Detroit. (The Granger Collection)

1890s, but in 1900 they just about managed to sell 4000 cars and trucks in the whole United States. Then came an astounding expansion that raised the total in 1912 to 378,000, worth $400,000,000. Meanwhile, there were developments of future significance in aluminum and chemicals.

The nation's supplies of fuel and minerals kept up with the demands of manufacturers. New discoveries of oil in Texas, Oklahoma, and Louisiana and of vast quantities of iron ore in the Mesabi range of Minnesota amply replenished the resources of the country. And improved methods of extraction raised the yield of the anthracite and bituminous coal fields. In addition, by 1912, Americans were deriving substan-

tial energy from natural gas and from electricity generated by water power. There was no danger that a lack of raw materials would hamper industrial growth.

The Supply of Capital   There was no shortage of capital, once the stringency of the 1890s had been eased. Uninhibited speculation produced a financial panic in 1907, for the looseness of controls still left the banking system vulnerable to abuse by erratic speculative elements, but generally entrepreneurs found money and credit enough for their needs. The balance of international payments had become favorable to the

There is a rather technical discussion of long-term trends in Jeffrey G. Williamson, *American Growth and the Balance of Payments, 1820–1913* (Chapel Hill, N.C., 1964).

Indexes of Manufacturing Production, 1890–1912

(1899 = 100)

1890	71
1900	100
1910	172
1912	194

Steel Production in the United States, 1890–1912

(million long tons)

1890	4
1900	10
1910	26
1912	31

Sources of American Energy, 1890–1912

Year	Bituminous Coal (million tons)	Pennsylvania Anthracite (million tons)	Crude Petroleum (million barrels)	Natural Gas (billion cubic feet)	Iron Ore (million tons)	Electricity from Waterpower (trillion British thermal units)
1890	111	46	45	–	16	22
1900	212	57	63	128	27	250
1910	417	84	209	509	57	539
1912	450	84	222	562	55	615

BALANCE OF INTERNATIONAL PAYMENTS, 1890–1912
Total United States goods and services, in millions of dollars

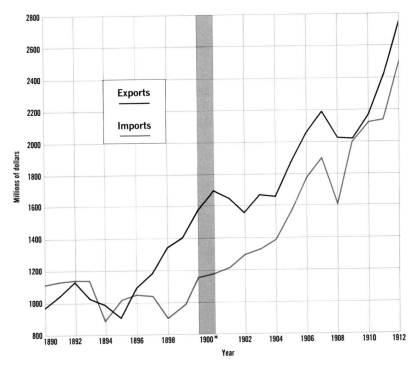

* Two figures are available for 1900, one comparable with earlier, the other with later years.

Pyramid Switchboard and Operators, 1881. (American Telephone and Telegraph Company)

ELBERT H. GARY was born in 1846 near Wheaton, Illinois, where his father was a prosperous farmer. He was brought up to a life of hard work and rigorous living. He attended but did not graduate from college, taught school, and served for two months in the army during the war.

He decided to make law his career. He read in his uncle's office, went to Union College of Law in Chicago, and then entered practice, forming a partnership with his elder brother. In the 1870s and 1880s the midwestern business boom opened ample fields for the ingenuity of attorneys, and Gary earned success, serving both railroads and industry. Often he became a director of the companies he represented, and fortunate investments added to his income from fees. He served two terms as county judge and was for a time mayor of Wheaton.

As a director of the Illinois Steel Company, he participated in the negotiations that formed the American Steel & Wire Company. In 1898 he became president of the Federal Steel Company financed by J. P. Morgan. Gary then moved to New York, where his ability and character made a favorable impression upon the banker. Gary was Morgan's choice to run United States Steel and remained head of that corporation until 1927.

A patient somber man, conscious of his own dignity, Gary was thoroughly conservative and a faithful churchgoer who believed in the literal accuracy of the Bible. To that extent he was a figure of the nineteenth century, but he was more modern in his attitudes toward business. He had no taste for the ruthless competi-

(Continued on next page)

190

(Continued from preceding page)

tion of an earlier generation of industrialists, but instead had a lawyer's wish for neatness and order. He helped found the American Iron and Steel Institute to further the general interests of the industry, and he was ready, at regular dinners, to discuss common problems and policies with rivals. Laborers, he thought, deserved fair wages and the opportunity to purchase stock in the enterprises that employed them. He was willing to consider abolition of the twelve-hour day when the company could afford it. But all such decisions, he believed, were the prerogative of management and he vigorously fought any effort at unionization. When he died in 1927, he had no reason to suspect that he had been mistaken in any of these views.

United States in the mid-1890s and remained so thereafter. The specie drain from which the country had long suffered was no longer troublesome. Meanwhile, the domestic stock of currency, the amount of deposits in commercial banks, the value of life insurance reserves, and the total of outstanding preferred and common stocks all rose, with the result that the means of doing business and of making investments were abundant.

The Problem of Integration Expansion made room for units of production of unprecedented size. The American Woolen Company's Wood Mill at Lawrence, Massachusetts—the largest textile factory in the world—was six floors high and covered 29 acres. The United States Steel plant in Gary, Indiana, on which work began in 1906, was the largest steel plant in the world. Its 70 coke ovens, 50 blast and open hearth furnaces, and scores of auxiliary mills and shops spread across 1250 acres. Production in such gigantic enterprises was on a basis entirely different from earlier models.

All operations changed character. Frederick W. Taylor's system of scientific management, which was widely adopted, emphasized the desirability of accurate records, precise planning, tight controls, and careful organization of each step in fabrication. The corporation became increasingly impersonal, remote alike from its thousands of stockholders and from its employees. Decisions were no longer made on the spot within the plant but in distant offices where the records and the power were. The typewriter, shorthand, and the long-distance telephone had all been invented before 1890, but entered widely into use after that date to meet elaborate business needs.

Managers like Elbert H. Gary of United States Steel considered themselves professional experts who operated by rules rather than by guesswork and who commanded their far-flung empires with precision. Such men valued the order, regularity, and predictability that were the essential ingredients of planning. The existing pattern of unlimited competition seemed to them wasteful, chaotic, and costly. Like the investment bankers and engineers, who also valued efficiency and order, the managers looked forward to a continuing process of integration that would organize every branch of industry in large units, controlled by the men fittest to operate them. The first steps toward integration had already been taken by 1890; shortly the economy was bound to go the whole distance.

The proponents of a rationally ordered industry were willing to accept government regulation as the price for eliminating wasteful competition. The experience of the state railroad commissions and of the Interstate Commerce Commission had shown that such supervision eliminated unsettling rate cutting and helped the truck lines. From this point of view, Federal controls, uniform throughout the country, were preferable to those by the states, which put the large corporation at the mercy of scores of conflicting rules. The essential problem was how to provide for regulation while protecting property

In Defense of Combination, 1897

The conclusion is inevitable to any dispassionate thinker, that we are in danger in this country of going too far in condemning aggregations of capital and hampering their rights of contract in their application to modern commerce; that in this age of steam, electricity, and machinery, such aggregations are a necessity; that they result in the greatest good to the greatest number, and that while all that is unreasonable should be restrained, there is a difference between reasonable regulation and unreasonable restraint of trade, and the right of freedom of contract for labor and for capital should be fostered and not destroyed.

—F. B. Thurber, "The Right of Contract," *North American Review,* CLXV (September, 1897), p. 275.

rights, minimizing political interference, and encouraging the efficient consolidation of industry.

The Dangers of Monopoly

Wealth and the Public Interest The aspirations of managers and bankers for integration encountered massive resistance. The basic objections were moral; the masters of American industry too often used their wealth in lavish living, which shocked Americans who still valued the simple standards of the rural past. Mistrust of the rich, whose corruption turned the city into a modern Babylon, extended far beyond the ranks of the Populists and gained force from the callous disregard some capitalists displayed toward the welfare of the less fortunate. The result was an almost instinctive reaction against

any tendency that might add to the power of the great bankers and industrialists.

To many citizens, furthermore, concentration of economic control in the hands of a relatively few individuals was a threat to democracy. Since the Civil War, government had grown weak because its functions had not expanded to meet the needs of a changing nation. Corporations more powerful than legislatures and a banker who dealt with the President as an equal undermined the foundation of the Republic.

Self-interest added to the hostility to bigness. The small businessmen unable to hold their own against the superior resources of their great competitors complained that unfair tactics rather than more efficient production methods were responsible. And indeed there was enough evidence in the speculative maneuvers and the price- and rate-fixing methods of the times to lend credence to these protests. Thousands of little entrepreneurs—local bankers, manufacturers, and traders of every sort—viewed with suspicion every step toward concentration which limited their own freedom of action. They found willing allies among the farmers and the professional men long accustomed to making a scapegoat of the capitalist.

Such people formed the leadership of most American communities outside the largest Eastern cities. They mobilized potent political support, particularly since their hostility to monopoly evoked recollections of Jackson's war against the Bank and of the Boston Tea Party and thus fell into an authentic national tradition. By 1890, the demand for government action was irresistible. Only a few die-hards clung to laissez-faire theories and remained hostile to corrective legislation.

Antitrust Legislation To define a policy was difficult, however. The states had long carried prohibitions against monopolistic practices on their statute books, and conspiracy was a common-law offense. But the parties damaged could not readily assemble proof, and the operations of the great corporations and pools ran across state lines and thus eluded surveillance

Dealing with Rockefeller, 1893

MR. BEALL: Your connection with Rockefeller began about 1893?

MR. MERRITT: Yes.

MR. BEALL: When was the call loan made?

MR. MERRITT: In 1893.

MR. BEALL: The same year?

MR. MERRITT: Yes.

MR. BEALL: Your business connection with Mr. Rockefeller had then extended over only a few months?

MR. MERRITT: Yes, that is all.

MR. BEALL: At the end of your business connection with Rockefeller did you have the railroads?

MR. MERRITT: No.

MR. BEALL: Did you own the stock?

MR. MERRITT: No.

MR. BEALL: Did you own the iron mines?

MR. MERRITT: No, sir.

MR. BEALL: Did you own the stock?

MR. MERRITT: No.

MR. BEALL: What did you have?

MR. MERRITT: I had a chance to walk from New York to Duluth on the ties; that is all I had. That is all I had in sight.

—House of Representatives, *Hearings before the Committee on Investigation of United States Steel Corporation, 1911* (Washington: Government Printing Office, 1911), no. 26, p. 1926.

Too Much Government, 1897

These results are of small consequence as compared with the immeasurably greater evil of that threatened deadening of individual effort in the business world through the force of paternalistic legislation. The evidences accumulate with each successive session of every legislative body of a lack of the citizen's reliance on self, and in that self-abnegation he is given encouragement by too willing legislators. In the end, however, he must fall back in the struggle for existence upon his own energy, ability, integrity, prudence, and judgment. The danger springs from the discontent bred when at last it is found that the government is powerless to aid and the legislation relied upon, instead of benefiting, has proven to be a hindrance through its attempting to regulate things beyond its province. If the country is to be free from the forces that threaten its political and financial integrity, the first and greatest reform to be entered upon should be the eliminating of unnecessary and unwise legislation. It should be undertaken in order that legislation may no longer menace all lines of business but be restricted to those matters which are proper objects of legislative control.

—James H. Eckels, "The Menace of Legislation," *North American Review*, CLXV (August, 1897), p. 246.

"The Monster Monopoly."
Cartoon of 1884 attacking
the Standard Oil Company.
(The Granger Collection)

and control. Ohio and Pennsylvania, for instance, had not been able effectively to attack the Standard Oil Company, which slipped out of their jurisdiction by securing a New Jersey charter of incorporation.

As in the case of the railroads, Federal action was necessary. In 1890, three years after the Interstate Commerce Act, Congress passed and President Harrison signed the Sherman Antitrust Law. The measure prohibited monopolies and conspiracies in restraint of trade and provided that the Department of Justice or injured parties could prosecute violators in the Federal courts.

Arnold M. Paul, *Conservative Crisis and the Rule of Law* (Ithaca, N.Y., 1960) is a thoughtful study of the judiciary down to 1895.

Passage of the Sherman act evoked relatively little controversy because it established no new principle but simply provided procedures for Federal action. Differences of opinion which reflected differences of interest arose over efforts to administer the law. The crucial issue was how the terms conspiracy, restraint of trade, and monopoly would be defined. Was any step toward business concentration a step toward monopoly? If not, what standards revealed the illegality of a combination?

The courts wrestled with these questions in the decade that followed. At first, ingenious defense attorneys found technical reasons for blocking action, as this was a relatively new field of law, but between 1895 and 1899 the Supreme Court at last faced up to the issue. It then groped tentatively toward a distinction between trade, which was covered by the Sherman act, and manufacture, which was not. In the E. C. Knight case (1895) it held that even control of almost all the sugar refined in the country was not illegal. The company involved was not engaged in commerce but in making sugar. In the Addystone Pipe case (1899), however, the judges held that agreements by a pool to limit the sale of its members' products were illegal. These went beyond the control of manufacturing to the control of commerce.

The distinction drawn in the two cases was scarcely clear-cut. The Court's effort to separate trade, to which the Sherman act applied, from manufacturing, to which it did not, satisfied neither the industrialists, who wished a greater degree of consolidation, nor their opponents, who favored free competition.

Techniques of Combination

Political uncertainty markedly influenced the methods of industrial combination. In the United States, the government was unwilling to sponsor or approve concentration, as some European countries did. It would not even mark out in advance what degree of consolidation was permissible. The entrepreneurs proceeded at their own risk, testing the limits of the law as their business expanded.

Mergers The Sherman act failed to curb the tendency toward bigness. Indeed it probably accelerated the trend. The provisions against conspiracies ruled out use of the pools and trusts of the preceding two decades, arrangements that had in any case proved ineffective. Separate firms could no longer ally themselves in restraint of trade.

But a corporation could not conspire with itself. A single company, no matter how big or how large a share of the market it commanded, was not a conspiracy. The men who, before 1890, thought in terms of formal or informal arrangements among several competitors to control the

The Sherman Antitrust Act, 1890

Every contract, combination in the form of trust or otherwise, or conspiracy, in restraint of trade or commerce among the several states, or with foreign nations, is hereby declared to be illegal. Every person who shall make any such contract or engage in any such combination or conspiracy, shall be deemed guilty of a misdemeanor, and, on conviction thereof, shall be punished by fine not exceeding five thousand dollars, or by imprisonment not exceeding one year, or by both said punishments, in the discretion of the court.

Every person who shall monopolize, or attempt to monopolize, or combine or conspire with any other person or persons, to monopolize any part of the trade or commerce among the several states, or with foreign nations, shall be deemed guilty of a misdemeanor, and on conviction thereof, shall be punished by fine not exceeding five thousand dollars, or by imprisonment not exceeding one year, or by both said punishments. . . .

Any person who shall be injured in his business or property by any other person or corporation by reason of anything forbidden or declared to be unlawful by this act, may sue therefor in any circuit court of the United States in the district in which the defendant resides or is found, without respect to the amount in controversy, and shall recover threefold the damages by him sustained, and the costs of suit, including a reasonable attorney's fee.

That the word "person," or "persons," wherever used in this act shall be deemed to include corporations and associations.

—"An Act to Protect Trade and Commerce against Unlawful Restraints and Monopolies," *United States Statutes at Large*, vol. XXVI (1889–1891), pp. 209–210.

The E. C. Knight Decision, 1895

Commerce succeeds to manufacture, and is not a part of it. . . . The fact that an article is manufactured for export to another State does not of itself make it an article of interstate commerce, and the intent of the manufacturer does not determine the time when the article . . . passes from the control of the State and belongs to commerce. . . . [Otherwise] "Congress would be invested, to the exclusion of the States, with the power to regulate, not only manufacturers, but also . . . every branch of human industry. . . . A situation more paralyzing to the state governments, and more provocative of conflicts . . . , it would be difficult to imagine."

– Chief Justice Melville W. Fuller, 156 United States 1 (January 21, 1895), pp. 12–15.

The Addystone Pipe Decision, 1899

It was the purpose of the combination, to . . . increase the price for which all contracts for the delivery of pipe . . . should be made . . . by abolishing all competition. . . . The direct and immediate result of the combination was therefore necessarily a restraint upon interstate commerce in respect of articles manufactured by any of the parties. . . . Interstate commerce consists of intercourse and traffic between the citizens or inhabitants of different States, and includes not only the transportation of persons and property and the navigation of public waters . . . , but also the purchase, sale and exchange of commodities. . . . If, therefore, an agreement or combination directly restrains not alone the manufacture, but the purchase, sale or exchange of the manufactured commodity . . . , it is brought within the provisions of the statute.

– Justice Rufus W. Peckham, 175 United States 211 (December 4, 1899), pp. 240–241.

production and distribution of goods, after that date began to plan mammoth combinations outside the scope of the Sherman act. In popular usage, these firms, too, would be known as trusts, but in law and practice they were quite different from the trusts of the earlier period.

The simplest form of combination was the merger. One company took over another by buying up its assets. In 1891, for instance, the American Tobacco Company, which had theretofore concentrated on the manufacture of cigarettes, acquired the smoking-tobacco factories of Marburg Brothers and the Gail & Ax Company in return for a payment in cash and some of its own common stock. This method was feasible in relatively small deals that required no large outlay of money and no substantial dilution of control. The number of recorded mergers in manufacturing and mining mounted rapidly to a peak in 1899, then declined.

The Holding Company Another procedure by which to achieve the same end came into use in the 1890s. The New Jersey corporation law of 1889 made available an effective technique of combination. Enterprises chartered under its terms were not themselves required to operate plants but could simply hold the stocks of other corporations doing business anywhere. Such holding companies could form extensive multi-layered pyramids, since their subsidiaries in turn could own or control scores of smaller firms.

The American Sugar Refining Company, organized in 1891, was one of the first to use the holding company technique. Itself the successor to a trust that had held twenty refineries throughout the country, it acquired controlling interests in its five leading competitors a year later and for a time accounted for almost 90 percent of the national output of sugar.

In the next decade the advantages of the device attracted imitators in many other fields. The process was cumulative; a combination once formed could itself be assimilated in a larger grouping. The peak came between 1899 and 1901, when American Copper, American Smelting and Refining, Standard Oil, Consolidated Tobacco, and United States Steel all sprang into being. By 1904 it was estimated that the 318 important holding companies in the United States controlled 5288 plants and were capitalized at well over seven billion dollars.

The United States Steel Company, formed in 1901, was the largest and most powerful of these enterprises. It absorbed eleven corporations, including Carnegie Steel, each of them itself swollen by previous combinations. Capitalized at more than a billion dollars, its subsidiaries operated 785 plants—blast and open-hearth furnaces; Bessemer converters; rail, plate, and rod mills; wire, tube, and bridge factories; iron ore and coal mines; coke works, railroads, and quarries.

Capitalist Rivalries

The necessary capital resources for these combinations were available in the financial institutions which had developed before 1890 but which expanded rapidly thereafter. The assets of commercial banks soared from less than $5,000,000,000 in 1890 to about $21,500,000,000 in 1912. Deposits in savings banks almost doubled in the same period, while the assets of life insurance companies rose from $771,000,000

to $4,400,000,000. A good part of these sums was, directly or indirectly, available for investment.

The Bankers The catalysts in the process of concentration were the investment bankers, familiar with the securities of competing companies, able to sell the stocks and bonds of new enterprises, ready to guarantee the necessary funds to further consolidation, and eager both for the orderly arrangement of the economy and for the business of floating new stock issues. The bankers often demanded places on the boards of directors of the firms they created, partly out of a sense of responsibility to the investors who followed their lead, partly out of the desire for power. They were then in a position to influence policy, to plan new steps of consolidation, and to draw upon the resources of the corporations in whose control they shared. When the same individual or the members of the same banking house served on the board of more than one corporation, they provided a means of coordination. Such interlocking directorates could control whole sectors of the economy.

The rewards of the successful were tremendous. J. P. Morgan and Company was the prime architect of United States Steel and of some of its subsidiaries such as National Tube. In return for his promotion and underwriting services, the banker received directly or indirectly some $150,000,000.

Such payments added water to the stock of the holding company. The capitalization usually included an amount large enough to cover the estimated value of the component companies and the expenses of underwriting and managing the consolidation. The market value of the stocks was therefore often below their par value, and the value of the assets was lower still. The constituent companies of United States Shipbuilding, organized in 1902, were capitalized at about $20,000,000 and owned plants valued at $12,000,000 with a working capital of about $5,000,000. The holding company issued stocks and bonds to the amount of almost $68,000,000 —a substantial difference, magnified when a

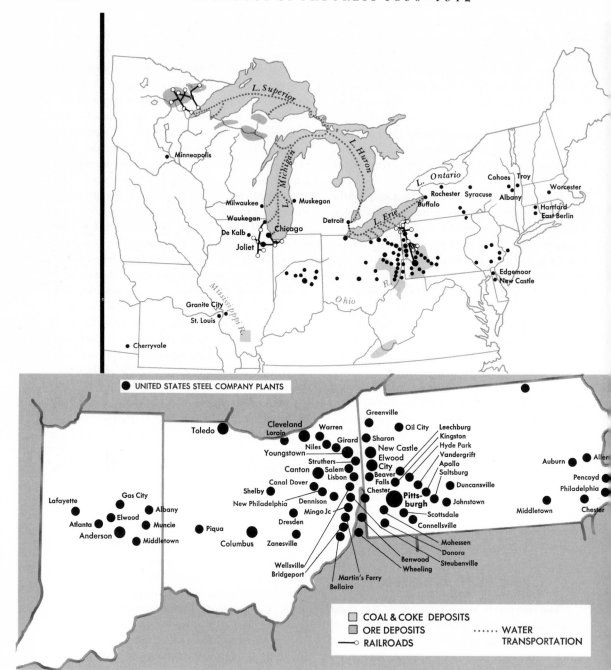

THE UNITED STATES STEEL COMPANY, 1904

The New York Stock Exchange, *ca.* 1907. The picture was taken with a camera hidden in the photographer's sleeve before picture-taking was allowed in the Exchange. (Library of Congress)

receivership later revealed that even the original values were inflated. This was an extreme case, but even more moderate promoters left themselves ample margins.

The magnitude of the stakes engendered intense rivalry, as competing capitalists strove to carve out baronies for themselves. The investment bankers established alliances with the men in control of the great enterprises in the effort to mobilize economic strength. Although the boundary lines were not distinct, several complex groupings had taken form at the opening of the twentieth century.

Rockefeller and Morgan   John D. Rockefeller and his Standard Oil associates had had the longest experience in the manipulation of great enterprises, and their control of 80 to 90 percent of the nation's oil business put enormous sums at their disposal. In addition, their role in the National City Bank and in the Equitable and

JOHN D. ROCKEFELLER was not troubled by doubts. A simple faith, derived from his Puritan forebears, taught him that wealth came as a result of God's will. It was every man's duty to work as hard as possible and to amass what he could.

Rockefeller was born in 1839 in Richford, New York, where his father owned a farm and also dabbled in various business ventures. The boy early learned the gospel of effort and savings, and after the family moved to Cleveland, Ohio, he finished high school and then went to work. He held his first job, with a commission merchant, for more than three years, accumulating the capital he needed to go into business for himself.

In 1863, Rockefeller perceived the potentialities of oil and set up a refinery. Cleveland was strategically located near the fields and served by excellent lake and rail transport. In addition, Rockefeller's attention to detail led him to seek out the best methods and to take advantage of every opportunity for expansion. Growth at first was vertical; he bought the timber to build his own barrels, owned a fleet of lighters and tankers and a drayage service, and manufactured the acid the refinery required. After the incorporation of the Standard Oil Company of Ohio, he sought also combinations that would reduce competition, trying in turn all the devices — pools, trusts, mergers, and holding companies. He let nothing stand in the way of additions to his fortune.

His drive to command and his success blackened his popular reputation. After 1881 he was the target of numerous attacks and of hostile legal action. Imperturbably, he continued to amass wealth. His headquarters after 1883 were at 26 Broadway in New York City. Rockefeller did not enjoy society or the gay life in town; he devoted himself to the management of his affairs until 1897, when he began to retire.

He lived on until 1937. In the last forty years of his life his fortune was of itself growing toward the billion mark. A devout Baptist, he then gave thought to using his riches to good effect and to improving his reputation. He turned over more than $550,000,000 to philanthropy, mainly for educational purposes. And with the advice of the public relations expert Ivy Lee, he created an image of a benevolent old man giving away dimes in the Florida sun. By then the days of his power were over.

Mutual life insurance companies added to the capital they commanded. An alliance with the Widener and Elkins interests involved them in United Gas Improvement of Philadelphia and other public utilities. An association with Jay Gould gave them a voice in the affairs of the Missouri Pacific; Wabash; and Chicago, Milwaukee, and St. Paul railroad systems; and in American Telephone and Western Union. The Standard Oil crowd also dominated the great copper, smelting, mining, and tobacco corporations, and they had a share in United States Steel.

Their only peer was J. P. Morgan and Company, with its tight connections with the First National and Chase National banks, the Guaranty Trust, and the New York Life Insurance Company. Morgan interests were also preeminent in steel, shipping, and rubber and were solidly entrenched in the New Haven; Chicago, Burlington and Quincy; Northern Pacific; Southern; and the Atlantic Coast Line railroads.

Allan Nevins, *Study in Power* (New York, 1953) is a sympathetic biography of John D. Rockefeller.

An alignment of Edward H. Harriman with Kuhn, Loeb and Company held power over the Union Pacific, the Southern Pacific, and Illinois Central railroads and the Pacific Mail Steamship line. Other smaller groups held lesser positions of influence. In addition, scores of banks in Boston, Philadelphia, Chicago, and San Francisco as well as New York orbited as satellites around the great centers of financial gravity, contributing their local resources to the force of one element or another, deriving some share of profit as a reward.

There were thus grounds for the fear or the hope, depending upon the point of view, that control of the whole productive system would soon focus in the hands of a few men. Yet by 1912, it had become apparent that there were limits to the process of concentration. Other forces were then beginning to offset the economic power so eagerly accumulated.

The Limits of Concentration

Excessively integrated enterprises sometimes toppled because they lacked a firm economic base to support their top-heavy capitalization. This was the case in shipbuilding; there simply were not enough orders to generate the profits that could reward investors. Not every activity could support a holding company pyramid.

Errors of judgment were expensive. Morgan, in 1902, established the International Mercantile Marine with the intention of uniting all the important North Atlantic shipping companies. The original plan embraced the Cunard Line which, however, refused to join and fought back with the aid of a British government subsidy. As a result the International controlled only about 40 percent of the traffic and lost out in the competition, so it could pay no dividends.

Furthermore, it sometimes proved difficult to organize the efficient management of very large enterprises with the means available in 1900. The great life insurance companies, for instance, wrote policies in all the states and in many foreign countries. They had to deal with scores of governments and operate through thousands of agents. They were responsible for investing hundreds of millions of dollars in reserves and had to maintain connections with dozens of banks and trust companies. The magnitude of the task set a brake on any inclination to consolidate.

Above all, unforeseen economic changes disordered the best-laid plans. In the 1890s the American Sugar Refining Company expanded until it commanded almost 90 percent of the output. Then the development of beet sugar reduced its share to less than half. In the same way, the discoveries of Western oil after 1900 shook the Standard Oil monopoly. And the great new industries like autos and aluminum, which grew in importance after 1912, escaped the control of the masters of the old holding companies.

The great economic empires built in the generation after 1890 did not widen to take in the new areas of production. The Morgans and Rockefellers lacked the power to push concentration any further. After 1900, they encountered increasing political and social resistance to integration. The depressed condition of labor, broad cultural changes, and progressive ideas fired the hostility of Americans to further centralization. An equilibrium then developed between the integration and dispersal of economic energies.

The two decades after 1890 witnessed few great technological innovations such as had transformed American industry in the half century before that date. This was a period of exploitation of starts already made. Its attention focused on the problems of organization. The enlarged scale of manufacturing, along with the rising output and profits of the factories, made the question of the future control of the nation's economy pressing. Was the productive system

Morton Keller, *The Life Insurance Enterprise, 1885–1910* (Cambridge, Mass., 1963) is an excellent, readable account.

to consist of thousands of small entrepreneurs or of a few great centralized combinations?

The government was not prepared to give an answer because its role since the Civil War had been largely negative. It could forbid unlawful actions; it could not point positively to desirable directions of development. As a result the process of concentration proceeded in a trial-and-error fashion, guided by the ambitions of promoters and bankers until they gradually began to learn the social and political limits of their potential power.

Paperbacks for Further Reading

Samuel P. Hays, *The Response to Industrialism: 1885–1914* (Chicago History of American Civilization Series) is a brief general survey. Robert A. Lively, *Shaping the Industrial Republic* (McGraw-Hill Paperback Series) contains an interesting collection of documents. Alfred D. Chandler, Jr., *Strategy and Structure: Chapters in the History of the Industrial Enterprise* (Anchor Books) includes several thoughtful essays. Sigmund Diamond, *The Reputation of the American Businessman* (Harper Colophon Books) treats Morgan, Rockefeller, and Ford, among others. Edward C. Kirkland, *Dream and Thought in the Business Community, 1860–1900* (Quadrangle Books, Inc.) is sympathetic; Robert G. McCloskey, *American Conservatism in the Age of Enterprise, 1865–1910* (Harper Torchbooks) is less so; and Matthew Josephson, *The Robber Barons* (Harvest Books) is hostile to business. Willard L. King, *Melville Weston Fuller* (University of Chicago Press) deals with an influential justice; and there is a general discussion in Carl Brent Swisher, *The Growth of Constitutional Power in the United States* (Phoenix Books).

THE TOILING
MASSES

66

Most Americans measured the performance of industry not in abstract terms but in terms of the effect on the life of the people. In the first decade of the twentieth century, only a meager share of the rewards of economic development reached the growing army of industrial laborers. There was some relief from the harsh conditions of the 1890s, but the level of remuneration remained pitifully low and the conditions of work were incredibly harsh. The miserable lot of the wage earners was eloquent testimony that the merits of capitalism had not helped the whole population.

A sense of desperation spread through the great cities. Labor organization provided protection for only a small minority of the toilers. The rest drifted toward a state of open warfare against society. Violence was frequent and radical leaders sounded the call to social revolution. Only flimsy supports seemed to keep the communities from collapse.

Children Working in a Vegetable Cannery, 1912. Photograph by Lewis W. H. Hine. (The Granger Collection)

Industrial Poverty

UNINTERRUPTED INDUSTRIAL expansion called for a constant increase in the labor force. The number of persons employed in manufacturing, mining, and construction more than doubled in the twenty years between 1890 and 1910. The rate of rise for this group was higher than for the population as a whole. But the growing demand for hands did not bring a corresponding improvement in the condition of the workers. Employers continued to economize on payrolls. Believing that labor was the most manageable element in the cost of production, they strove to keep wages as low as possible.

The Worker's Share As a result, in the 1890s the percentage of the gross national product that reached the labor force probably shrank. In manufacturing, the work week remained between fifty and sixty hours and the ten-hour day was normal. The average hourly salary was about twenty cents; the unskilled received still less. Not many men without special qualifications could take home as much as nine dollars a week. Furthermore, long layoffs were usual, so only the very fortunate worked every week of the year. Annual earnings in factories averaged about $400. Women, children, the unskilled, and farm hands received less. A serious depression in 1893 hit workers hard. In the next year aver-

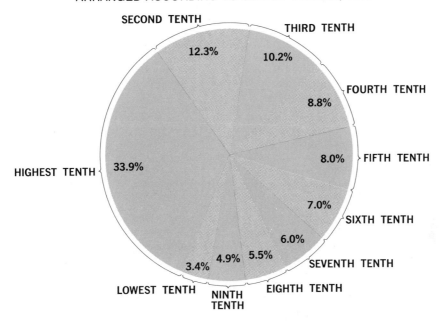

PERCENTAGE OF NATIONAL INCOME
RECEIVED BY SPECIFIC PROPORTION OF RECIPIENTS
ARRANGED ACCORDING TO SIZE OF INCOME, 1910

SECOND TENTH 12.3%

THIRD TENTH 10.2%

FOURTH TENTH 8.8%

FIFTH TENTH 8.0%

SIXTH TENTH 7.0%

SEVENTH TENTH 6.0%

EIGHTH TENTH 5.5%

NINTH TENTH 4.9%

LOWEST TENTH 3.4%

HIGHEST TENTH 33.9%

Consumption Expenditures of Urban Workers, 1901

	Annual Income					
	Under $200	$200 to $300	$300 to $400	$400 to $500	$500 to $600	$600 to $700
Number of families in sample	32	115	545	1,676	2,264	2,336
Average number of persons in family	3.2	3.4	3.8	3.8	3.9	3.9
Total average expenditures	$196	$312	$389	$466	$540	$612
Food	100	148	187	218	249	266
Rent	33	56	73	87	100	113
Fuel	13	19	23	26	27	28
Light	2	4	4	5	6	7
Clothing	17	27	39	53	65	79
Other	31	59	63	77	93	119

Child Labor, 1904

Hundreds of small boys work for Mr. Borden, and many of them toil ten hours a day without a thread of clothing on their bodies. No one except employees is allowed to enter the works, and therefore when it was stated before a woman's club in New York, last week, that naked babies were at work in the Fall River mills, much interest was aroused. . . .

They work in the big tanks called "lime keer," in the bleach house, packing the cloth into the vats.

This lime keer holds 750 pieces of cloth, and it requires one hour and twenty minutes to fill it. During that time the lad must work inside, while his body is being soaked with whatever there is of chemicals which enter into the process of bleaching, of which lime is a prominent factor.

The naked bodies of the children who do this work day after day are never dry, and the same chemicals which effect the bleaching process of the gray cloth naturally bleach the skin of the operator, and after coming out of the vats the boys show the effects in the whiteness of their skins, which rivals the cotton cloth.

—James F. Carey, "The Child Labor Evil," in Robert Hunter, *Poverty* (New York: The Macmillan Company, 1907), p. 357.

A Helpful Child, 1906

Little Anetta Fachini, four years old, [was] working with her mother making artificial flowers, . . . in her squalid tenement home at eleven o'clock at night. . . . The frail little thing was winding green paper around wires to make stems for artificial flowers to decorate ladies' hats. Every few minutes her head would droop and her weary eyelids close, but her little fingers still kept moving—uselessly, helplessly, mechanically moving. Then the mother would shake her gently, saying: "*Non dormire, Anetta! Solamente pochi altri—solamente pochi altri.*" ("Sleep not, Anetta! Only a few more—only a few more.")

And the little eyes would open slowly and the tired fingers once more move with intelligent direction and purpose.

—John Spargo, *The Bitter Cry of the Children* (New York: The Macmillan Company, 1906), pp. 146–147.

age annual factory earnings sank to $386, and the marginal laborers found it difficult to secure any employment at all.

There was some improvement after 1900. A perceptible rise in wage levels helped all categories of labor except during the depression of 1907. But even at best, the worker's share of economic growth was small.

Americans now discovered the extent of poverty in their midst. Some poor had always been with them, explained away as the products of personal failure or misfortune. But in 1904 Robert Hunter's widely read book, *Poverty*, pointed out that more than 10,000,000 persons in the United States did not earn enough to support themselves. The simple fact was that the wages of labor were inadequate to sustain a decent family life.

As in earlier years, families compensated for the deficiencies in their budgets by drawing upon the labor of several members. Children took jobs as soon as they could and women willing to accept lower wages could sometimes get places when men could not. Some girls found a growing number of openings as typists in offices and behind the counters of shops, but the largest demands for their services were in the factories. These extra hands, which supplemented the earnings of the husband or father, helped keep the wheels of industry turning.

Immigrant Labor A large part of the labor force consisted of immigrants. The newcomers eased the problems of employers. The Atlantic crossing was easier and cheaper than previously,

An Immigrant Family Doing Piecework in Their Tenement Home, New York, *ca.* 1900. (The Granger Collection)

so the movement to America was closely attuned to the needs of industry. The number of entries rose during expansive years, when there was a rising demand for hands. In depression, when there was a superfluity of labor, arrivals declined and some of the unemployed returned to their former homes. Entrepreneurs could thus be sure that there would always be enough men for their factories yet had no need to worry about supporting those not needed.

The immigrants themselves suffered from their strangeness. Often they became victims of labor contractors. The padrone, or boss, was a fellow countryman who may have advanced the cost of passage but who, in any case, knew English and could locate a job for the greenhorns whose wages he collected while he provided for

their subsistence. Some Greeks and Italians, ignorant of their rights, worked for years in a kind of peonage with hardly any reward.

Whatever their nationality, the men just off the boats were helpless. To survive, they needed jobs at once, at any pay and under any conditions. They and their families sewed away in their crowded homes hour after hour for the pittance each shirt or jacket brought them. Or they tended machines in the sweatshops, where employers exacted the full measure of effort in return for tiny wages. Or they enlisted, as before, in the army of construction workers, laying rails, carrying the hod, digging ditches. The majority, however, passed through the gates of the mines and mills to do the hard, unskilled work an expansive industry demanded. By 1912, some 60 percent of the miners and some 58 percent of the iron and steel workers were foreign-born, and an additional 15 to 20 percent were their native-born children.

The strangeness of much of the labor force intensified its economic problems. Conflicts between the older "English-speaking" Irish, Scottish, Welsh, and English workers and the newer "Slavs," as the southern and east Europeans were called, often inhibited cooperation. The established Pennsylvania miners tried to protect their own interests by a law requiring a two years' apprenticeship, but the newcomers served their time and earned the right to work. Some employers played upon the latent hostilities among the ethnic groups by mixing their workers to get them to compete with one another. But even managers who did not resort to such tactics approved of the docility of hands who could not

David Brody, *Steelworkers in America* (Cambridge, Mass., 1960) discusses the conditions of work as well as organization.

argue or insist upon their rights. It was now possible to dilute the skills required in the plant, using foreigners for the bulk of the routine tasks while a few mechanics tended the machines. As a result, costs sank to gratifyingly low levels.

Urban Life

Problems Urbanization complicated the life of the laborer. The difficulties of providing housing and supplying necessary services to the population of the great cities often determined the quality of the wage earner's life. Families were jammed into tenements, built row upon row in dense slums that created novel problems of physical existence. Hard work, poor sanitary conditions, and inadequate diet left many vulnerable to disease. And poverty and overcrowding bred crime and prostitution.

The effort to improve city life enlisted tremendous constructive energies. Immense amounts of capital and labor went to build thousands of houses, lay miles of sewers and water pipes, extend trolley tracks, and dig subway systems. These decades witnessed, in addition, an attempt to impart beauty and order to the city by providing parks, monuments, and recreational space in a comprehensive planning process. In 1912, the achievements were impressive, but so too was the amount yet to be done.

Communities The urban population continued to develop its own communal organizations. In each of the great cities, thousands of unaffiliated men and women went their lonely ways in the rooming-house districts, struggling to avoid the misfortunes that would cast them upon the human junk heaps of New York's Bowery or Chicago's Madison Street. Their defenselessness emphasized the importance of association. Only mutual aid could furnish insurance against the risks of life in the city wilderness. Churches and philanthropic, fraternal, and cultural societies supplied help in maintaining an orderly family life as well as in meeting the crises of illness or unemployment. Such voluntary or-

Hester Street, New York, in the early 1890s. Photograph by Jacob A. Riis. (Museum of the City of New York)

Children Playing in the Street near a Dead Horse. (Library of Congress)

ganizations drew the like-minded together and therefore followed ethnic lines. The foreign-born were particularly sensitive to the need for associations, which the shock of migration made clear to them.

The extent to which neighborhoods were homogeneous depended upon the size of the communities, the character of available housing, and the physical layout of the cities. In Manhattan, settlement was so dense that most groups occupied distinct ghettos close to their own shops, churches, and other institutions. In smaller towns, residential lines were less clear. But everywhere, informal cooperation was the means by which the laborers tried to cushion the hardship of adjustment to industrial life.

Labor Organization

The organized labor movement took little direct interest in the fate of the great mass of the workers. After 1890 the Knights of Labor dwindled into impotence, and the skilled craftsman felt no sense of identity with the hordes of unskilled aliens whose presence he regarded as a threat to his own standard of living. The fact that employers tried to use immigrants and Negroes as strikebreakers added to the resentment. Some unions sought to end immigration and to exclude Negroes from desirable jobs.

The AF of L Actually, the craftsmen fared relatively well. Since they formed only a small proportion of the hands in a factory or on the job, their wages could rise without an appreciable increase in total production costs. But their position depended also upon the scarcity of their particular skills and upon the ability to bargain for themselves alone. On both counts they believed it necessary to separate themselves from the unskilled.

The unions that were combined in the American Federation of Labor grew rapidly between 1898 and 1903, when their membership mounted from about 300,000 to about 1,500,000. Then it leveled off; in 1912, the total had risen to only 1,800,000, despite the contin-

ued increase in the size of the labor force. The core of craftsmen, once organized, lacked interest in spreading the benefits of affiliation to outsiders. In fact, the advantages of going it alone persuaded some of the most skilled crafts, like the railroad brotherhoods, to refuse to associate even with the AF of L. Membership in such independent unions rose from about 200,000 in 1897 to about 635,000 in 1912.

Early in the 1890s, Gompers and the original founders of the AF of L faced a sharp internal conflict about objectives. Socialists attempted to enlist the movement in a broad struggle for reform, using political methods such as were at the time shaping the Labour party in England. This effort met determined resistance and failed. From the conflict emerged the philosophy of business unionism articulated by Samuel Gompers. According to this view, the function of the labor organization was neither ideological nor social. Whatever opinions its members held or whatever activities they pursued as individuals, the union was not to concern itself with broad issues of social or political policy. Its purpose —pure and simple—was improvement of the wages and working conditions of its own members.

This definition of union policy sharpened the division between the skilled craftsmen and the mass of laborers. The AF of L rejected overtures from the Knights of Labor for cooperation between the two organizations, and the AF of L's constituent unions each negotiated for itself with its own employers. As a result, the percentage of labor organized remained small. In 1912, out of a total labor force of about 25,000,000, only 2,400,000 belonged to unions. The great majority of American workers thus lacked the means of self-protection.

Efforts to organize the hands in the largest industries therefore were tardy and unsuccessful. Perhaps not even the aid of the craftsmen would have helped, given the determination of employers to resist and the great resources at their disposal. As it was, the mass of laborers had slight bargaining power. Corporations willing

Denying the Right to Strike, 1894

A strike is essentially a conspiracy to extort by violence. . . . I know of no peaceful strike. I think no strike was ever heard of that was or could be successful unaccompanied by intimidation and violence. . . . The strike has become a serious evil, destructive to property, destructive to individual rights, injurious to the conspirators themselves and subversive of republican institutions. . . . Whatever other doctrine may be asserted by reckless agitators, it must ever remain the duty of the courts, in the protection of society, and in the execution of the laws of the land, to condemn, prevent, and punish all such unlawful conspiracies and combinations.

—Federal Judge Jenkins of the Wisconsin Circuit Court, *Federal Reporter*, vol. LX, pp. 821–823, as cited in Almont Lindsey, *The Pullman Strike* (Chicago: University of Chicago Press, 1942), p. 157.

to conciliate the few skilled union members had little to fear from the thousands of dispensable unskilled, to whose cause the state was neutral or hostile.

The Homestead Strike The only weapon available to labor was the strike, an unequal contest between the companies, whose profits could sustain a prolonged stoppage, and the employees, whose hungry families set a limit to the time the breadwinners could remain without wages. Determined resistance on the one side and bitter despair on the other frequently led to the use of force. Violence permeated American labor relations and the great strikes of this period quickly deteriorated into open warfare. The employers brought in strikebreakers, whom they protected with armed guards, while private company detectives and spies sought to weaken the workers' will to resist. The laborers retaliated by destroying property and assaulting the scabs. Each side sought to use the law on its own behalf, but capital generally exercised the more persuasive power over governors and judges.

Two great strikes in the 1890s exemplified the issues involved. The handling of the strike at Andrew Carnegie's steel plant in Homestead, Pennsylvania, cast a somber shadow across his protestations that the interests of capital and labor were identical. He was in Scotland when the strike broke out in 1892, but his rags-to-riches reputation and his repeated paeans to democracy called national attention to the efforts of his employees to advance their own interests. Henry Clay Frick, in actual charge of the company, brought in strikebreakers and imported 300 armed Pinkerton detectives to protect them. Infuriated strikers fired upon the barges that carried the Pinkertons up the Monongahela River and a full-scale battle followed. Ultimately state troopers restored order. That permitted the scabs to operate, ended the strike, and destroyed the union.

The Pullman Strike Two years later the Pullman strike, too, showed the limits of an industrialist's philanthropy and elicited even more direct government intervention. George M. Pullman had built a model town for his employees on the outskirts of Chicago. In 1894, when he deemed it desirable, he cut wages although the charges in company-owned houses remained unchanged. He, like most other employers, refused to discuss the issue with the workers who struck. The American Railway Union, led by Eugene V. Debs, came to the support of the strikers and refused to handle Pullman cars. Since the railroads insisted on attaching those cars to the trains, a good part of the nation's transportation came to a halt.

The Federal courts then intervened. A blanket injunction, issued like other injunctions without a jury trial, forbade the union officers to

Leon Wolff, *Lockout: The Story of the Homestead Strike of 1892* (New York, 1965) is an interesting narrative.

Injustice turned **EUGENE V. DEBS** from an ambitious bureaucrat into a passionate agitator. He was born in Terre Haute, Indiana, in 1855, one of ten children of Alsatian immigrants. At the age of fifteen he left school to work in a railroad shop, and a few years later he became a locomotive fireman. Although the job seemed a dead end and he left to clerk in a wholesale grocery, he did not lose interest in the men on the trains. He helped organize a lodge of the Brotherhood of Locomotive Firemen in 1875 and edited its magazine.

A nice white collar career then lay ahead of him. In 1879 he was chosen city clerk and soon moved up also in the union hierarchy. In 1885 he gained election to the state legislature. Meanwhile he was thinking ahead to one big labor organization that would replace the craft unions that divided the railroad workers. In 1893, his ambition approached fulfillment when he helped organize, and became president of, the American Railway Union.

A year later he was trapped in an unexpected crisis. The Pullman strikers appealed to the ARU for support, and although Debs feared it was inexpedient to help, the Union convention voted to do so. It was then his responsibility to lead the struggle. He was convicted of contempt of court for defying a strikebreaking injunction and served six months in jail.

Prison made Debs a socialist—not that he ever mastered Marxist theory but as a protest against the injustices of American capitalism. In 1896, he supported Bryan and in 1900, 1904, 1908, 1912, and 1920 he campaigned strenuously for the presidency as a declared socialist. Votes for Debs rose to almost a million in 1912. He did not expect, even then, to win, but he regarded his efforts as educational, designed to call popular attention to abuses in the economy.

The socialists denounced entry of the United States into World War I, and Debs spoke out bitterly against the prosecution of dissenters. For these utterances he was convicted of violation of the Espionage Act, and in 1918 was sentenced to ten years' imprisonment. Released in 1921, he continued his agitation until his death in 1926. His last years were confused. He hailed the Russian Revolution but criticized the assassination of the czar and could not decide whether the repressive acts of the Soviet Union were justified or not. The world of the 1920s was moving in a direction he did not understand.

obstruct the mails by interfering with the movements of the railroads. Debs refused to obey. A train was derailed in a riot. President Cleveland thereupon ordered out a regular army regiment, although Governor John Peter Altgeld of Illinois insisted that martial law was not necessary. The trains moved, Debs went to jail, and the strike collapsed. Employers learned that an injunction from a compliant judge could, in effect, end a work stoppage.

The ground for the injunction was the argument that the strike was a conspiracy in restraint of trade, within the meaning of the Sherman Antitrust Act. Pushed further, the same proposition hobbled the power of labor organizations to fight employers. Using the same legal justification, an unorganized Danbury, Connecticut, firm sued the hatters' union, which had launched a movement to persuade consumers not to purchase the firm's hats. In 1890, the Supreme Court found the union boycott a combination contrary to the Sherman act and therefore illegal. The members, held liable for the damages assessed against the union, were ruined.

Radicalism

Socialism The apparent helplessness of the laborers of the United States offered a tempting opportunity to radicals who sought a total overturn of the existing economic and social system. An American branch of the Second (Socialist)

Even when **JOHN PETER ALTGELD** was a success, late in life, the sadness of his pallid face showed that he knew what suffering was. Born in Germany in 1847, he was brought to Ohio as an infant by his illiterate father. Until he was twenty-one, John Peter worked like a slave on his brutal father's farm, with a brief period of duty during the Civil War his only taste of freedom.

In 1869 he left home. For five years, he drifted about, working as a common laborer, teaching school, studying law. In 1874, he was elected county attorney in Andrew County, Missouri, and a year later he moved to Chicago. At that point his English was still imperfect, but he worked hard at his practice, saved, and made some good investments in real estate.

Altgeld never lost the recollections of the poverty of his youth. Contact with the poor led him to publish a study of American penal institutions, in the course of which he made clear the handicaps endured by the laborers in the United States. His concern with oppression, in turn, thrust him into politics. He was elected to the Cook County Superior Court in 1884, and in 1892 became the first Democrat to be chosen governor of Illinois since the Civil War.

Two crises brought him widespread attention. An appeal for clemency led him to restudy the conviction of the Haymarket anarchists. He concluded that their trial had been a miscarriage of justice and pardoned the survivors. Quietly he bore the storm of outrage from conservatives who accused him of undermining the country's institutions. He met even more vilification when he denounced President Cleveland's use of the regular army to maintain order during the Pullman strike. However, neither party loyalty nor deference to the respectable citizens turned him from his commitment to equal justice for the oppressed laborers.

In the election of 1896 Altgeld helped swing the Democrats to Bryan and supported the silver plank. The general debacle that year ousted Altgeld from office although he ran well ahead of the national ticket. In the years that followed he continued to advocate reform measures, and opposed imperialism. His fortune melted away, and he died disappointed, in 1902, too early to see the victory of the causes for which he had fought.

The Pullman Strike, 1894. Regular troops firing into the mob at Loomis and 49th Street, Chicago, July 7. Drawing. (Brown Brothers)

213

Meeting of the Industrial Workers of the World in Union Square, New York, 1900s. (The Granger Collection)

International had flourished in the late 1880s, but factionalism after 1890 made it ineffective. The dominant group, followers of Daniel de Leon, were intellectuals, quite theoretical in approach and unable to establish rapport with the workers. More familiar with the fine points of Marxist writings than with the actual desires of the poor, they fixed their attention on ultimate revolution and scorned palliative reforms. They first cooperated with the Knights of Labor, then set up a Socialist Trade and Labor Alliance, and finally tried to filter into the American Federation of Labor. They were rebuffed in all these efforts.

The Pullman strike gave them a leader. Imprisonment converted Debs to socialism. In 1897, he founded the Social Democratic party, and thereafter was its perennial presidential candidate, attracting a broadening circle of adherents. The number of votes he received rose steadily, but the basic organization of labor was not changed. The socialists penetrated only a few unions; they failed to reach the unskilled; and they catered increasingly to reform-minded middle-class people.

The Wobblies Searching for a means of reaching the rank and file of labor, Debs joined other radical leaders in 1905 in establishing the Industrial Workers of the World, an organization which aimed explicitly to recruit the unorganized. The IWW was to be one big union and include the unskilled as well as the skilled. In the seven years that followed, it gained strength, particularly in the Western mines and lumber camps and among dock and migratory farm workers, but its membership did not rise above 100,000.

Ira Kipnis, *The American Socialist Movement, 1897–1912* (New York, 1952) is a critical history.

214

Membership Certificate, United Mine Workers of America. Lithograph, 1899. (Library of Congress)

The Wobblies were openly revolutionary, rejected capitalism, and summoned the workers to a class war. A pronounced anarchist strain in their thinking made them hostile to all authority, and they did not hesitate to use violence when it was to their advantage. In 1905 Wobbly members were accused of assassinating Frank Steunenberg, governor of Idaho, during a bitter strike a few years earlier. Although they were acquitted, the case brought them nationwide notoriety. The IWW took part in violent battles in Goldfield, Nevada (1906), in McKees Rocks, Pennsylvania (1909), in Lawrence, Massachusetts (1912), and in Passaic, New Jersey (1912). These disturbances and the uninhibited statements of flamboyant leaders like Big Bill Heywood terrified property owners. When the McNamara brothers—who were not Wobblies but officers of the AF of L Structural Iron Workers Union—confessed to dynamiting the Los Angeles *Times* building in 1910, the nation seemed to be on the verge of a social cataclysm.

Efforts at Peace

Class War   Although disaster did not come, there was a basis to the fears of respectable Americans. Social conditions were deteriorating to a point at which it was no longer safe to take the docility of the population for granted. Deepening class divisions were bringing the United States close to the tense revolutionary situation of the Europeans.

A slackening of social mobility in these years gave warning of worse to come, for the hope of advancement had sustained social discipline in the past. Laborers doomed to remain in their depressed state and deprived of the prospect of improvement for their children might well respond to the slogans of incendiary agitators. The integration of business and the spread of large organizations inhibited the upward movement of the ambitious through trade. At the same time, the growing rigidity of the professions narrowed the channel of advancement that education offered. Success was not a goal available to everyone. Negroes, immigrants, and working people in general started with such heavy handicaps that they might well decide the race was not worth running.

The prospect of continuing warfare foreshadowed the deterioration of social relationships that Ignatius Donnelly had described in *Caesar's Column* and Jack London in *The Iron Heel*. Frightened citizens voted to build armories and strengthen police forces to protect lives and property in the event of insurrection. State police forces, such as Pennsylvania formed in 1905, were not susceptible to local control and were considered even more reliable.

The Public Interest   The imminent class war convinced many responsible Americans that a new approach to labor was necessary. For decades, state bureaus had been collecting statistics on the subject, and by the 1890s economics was a recognized academic discipline. Surely, Carroll D. Wright and others argued, there must be a scientific solution, if only the labor problem were put in the hands of experts who could conciliate the rival parties.

In the aftermath of the Pullman strike, Ralph M. Easley, a newspaperman, had formed a civic federation in Chicago to further the cause of industrial arbitration. In the next few years he gained the support of labor leaders like Gompers and of manufacturers like Hanna, and in 1900 he established the National Civic Federation to provide a forum in which the best brains of the nation could settle the labor problem.

The Coal Strike   Peace was a long way off, but the willingness of some capitalists to admit that there was a public interest in their managerial decisions was an important first step. The anthracite coal strike of 1902 revealed the extent to which assumptions had changed in the eight years since the Pullman strike. When the United Mine Workers went out for improved conditions

James R. Leiby, *Carroll Wright and Labor Reform* (Cambridge, Mass., 1960) traces the development of the public interest in labor reform.

Robert J. Cornell, *The Anthracite Coal Strike of 1902* (Washington, 1957) treats the affair in detail.

The Public Interest in Labor Peace, 1895

The attitude of labor toward capital, disclosed in its readiness to strike sympathetically; the determination of capital to crush the strike rather than to accept any peaceable solution through conciliation, arbitration, or otherwise; the certainty with which vast strikes let loose the disreputable to burn, plunder, and even murder . . . are all factors bearing upon the present industrial situation which need to be thoroughly understood by the people and to be wisely and prudently treated by the government. . . .

However men may differ about the propriety and legality of labor unions, we must all recognize the fact that we have them with us to stay and to grow more numerous and powerful. Is it not wise to fully recognize them by law; to admit their necessity as labor guides and protectors, to conserve their usefulness, increase their responsibility, and to prevent their follies and aggressions by conferring upon them the privileges enjoyed by corporations, with like proper restrictions and regulations? The growth of corporate power and wealth has been the marvel of the past fifty years. Corporations have undoubtedly benefited the country and brought its resources to our doors. It will not be surprising if the marvel of the next fifty years be the advancement of labor to a position of like power and responsibility. We have heretofore encouraged the one and comparatively neglected the other. Does not wisdom demand that each be encouraged to prosper legitimately and to grow into harmonious relations of equal standing and responsibility before the law? This involves nothing hostile to the true interests and rights of either.

—United States Strike Commission, *Report on the Chicago Strike of June–July, 1894* (Washington: Government Printing Office, 1895), pp. 19, 48.

New Yorkers in Line to Buy Coal During the Coal Strike, 1902. (The Granger Collection)

217

and union recognition, George F. Baer, president of the Reading Railroad, took the conventional boss's position. He denounced the agitators and assured his employees that their welfare rested in the hands of the Christian men to whom God had given control of the property interests of the country.

But Theodore Roosevelt did not send in the troops as Grover Cleveland had. With the advice of members of the National Civic Federation, the President forced arbitration on the mine operators and brought the strike to an end after five months. He acted less to support the miners than out of concern for the effects on consumers of a coal-less winter. Nevertheless the result was to strengthen the union — one of the few to enlist members broadly in a mass industry.

In 1910, after a bitter strike, the International Ladies Garment Workers Union arrived at a protocol with the association of manufacturers which provided permanent machinery for arbitration and conciliation. In this case, the plight of the female workers earned the support of many prominent women and the fact that a majority of both employers and employees were Jews helped make an agreement possible.

Success in both the anthracite and garment workers' strikes did not transform the condition of the laborers involved. The gains in wages and hours of toil were small and security was still a distant goal. The victories were significant because they were the first steps toward recognition of the legitimacy of the trade union.

Even in 1912, the unions had hardly begun to organize the labor force. Nor had they gained a significant redistribution of the products of the economy. The dominant groups in American society were only beginning to perceive that deprivation created dangerous class antagonisms. Violence still seethed beneath the surface and only a tenuous network of cultural and social restraints preserved discipline. The situation was ominous. The discontent of the industrial workers mounted as the grievances of the farmers subsided, and it forced even the most optimistic Americans to wonder whether the democracy they had inherited could survive the strains that accompanied industrial development.

Paperbacks for Further Reading

Henry Pelling, *American Labor* (Chicago History of American Civilization Series) touches briefly on this period. Oscar Handlin, *The Uprooted* (Universal Library) is a general interpretation of the character of immigration. There is some material on the new immigrants in Maldwyn A. Jones, *American Immigration* (Chicago History of American Civilization Series) and in Carl Wittke, *We Who Built America* (Press of Western Reserve University). Moses Rischin, *The Promised City* (Corinth-Citadel Press) is a careful study of the Jews in New York. Oscar Handlin, ed., *Immigration as a Factor in American History* (Spectrum Books) is a useful collection of primary materials.

Jane Addams, *Twenty Years at Hull-House* (Signet Classics) is a vivid contemporary account. Other material on urban life will be found in Robert Hunter, *Poverty* (Harper Torchbooks) and in Constance M. Green, *American Cities in the Growth of the Nation* (Harper Colophon Books). Almont Lindsey, *The Pullman Strike* (Phoenix Books) is an excellent narrative. C. E. Warne, ed., *Pullman Boycott of 1894* (D. C. Heath and Co.) assembles relevant material. Harry Barnard, *Eagle Forgotten* (Charter Books) is a fine biography of Altgeld, and Ray Ginger, *Eugene V. Debs* (Collier Books) treats its subject sympathetically.

CULTURE:
OFFICIAL AND
POPULAR

67

Deep social divisions among the population widened the gap between the official and the popular cultures of the United States at the end of the nineteenth century. The factory workers did not share the modes of expression, the ideals, or the attitudes of the owners. Their cultures were as separate as their experiences.

The effort of the families of great social and economic power to secure recognition of the primacy of their aristocratic culture proved a signal failure. They were unable to develop the forms that would legitimate their riches and their pretensions to political leadership. The rest of the population was unresponsive to their claims, and by 1912 their own children were beginning to question the values of their parents' aristocratic society.

The lack of a common language in art, literature, or music made it difficult to bridge the gaps among various groups of Americans and left the creative personalities of these years without a sure sense of who their audiences were. The failure of communications impeded the effort of Americans to deal with their pressing problems.

Family Responsibility, 1901

The first requisite in a healthy race is that a woman should be willing and able to bear children just as the men must be willing and able to work and to fight. All the other problems before us in this country, important though they may be, are as nothing compared with the problem of the diminishing birth rate and all that it implies. When a race commits suicide it is not of the slightest consequence what are the qualities which it would have possessed if it had lived.

—Theodore Roosevelt to Hugo Munsterberg, June 3, 1901, in E. E. Morison, ed., *Letters of Theodore Roosevelt* (Cambridge, Mass.: Harvard University Press, 1951), vol. III, p. 86.

The Life of a Race, 1903

So far as present facts go the probability is against natural selection in the case of fertility in man. The contrary hypothesis, that a stock like an individual has a birth, growth, senescence and death; that, apart from the onslaughts of rivals or the privations of a hard environment or the suicide of universal debauchery, races die a natural death of old age, lends itself very well to the interpretation of human history and perhaps to the history of animal forms as well.

—Edward L. Thorndike, "The Decrease in the Size of American Families," *Popular Science Monthly*, LXIII (May, 1903), p. 70.

"The National Bloodstream"

IN THE 1890s Americans worried, for the first time in their history, about the quality of the nation's human stock. Would succeeding generations contain the same number of talented people as preceding ones? Was it necessary to select among the hordes of immigrants seeking admission to the country? Were men of all antecedents equally capable of becoming good citizens? These questions, which acquired urgency, reflected a deep concern with the problems of family and race.

The Family Anxieties about the quality of family life came to the surface in their most evident form in the prolonged discussion of the rising divorce rate. In 1890 there had been 1 divorce for every 16 marriages; in 1900 the ratio was 1 to 12, and it continued to climb in the next decade. By 1912 it was higher in the United States than anywhere in the Western world. Such instability was considered evidence of weakness in a basic social institution.

The related problems of family size and social purity were less openly discussed. In the highly competitive economy a proper start was essential, and a father with too many offspring could not equip all of them with the skills or capital needed to do well in the contest. The need for prudence led to various ill-informed experiments with birth control, but the result seemed to be that people of restraint failed to reproduce themselves while the irresponsible multiplied. Furthermore, the fall in the urban birth rate seemed associated somehow with the spread of prostitution.

The danger to the family had grave personal and national implications because it was still a critical educational agency and because it located the individual in society. The gilded age had touched off a competition for place that made proper family connections a valuable asset, and in a heterogeneous population heritage was

The Matter of Race, 1896

The matter of race which separates the Englishman from the Hindoo and the American from the Indian . . . is something deeper and more fundamental than anything which concerns the intellect. . . . When we speak of a race, then, we do not mean its expressions in art or in language, or its achievements in knowledge. We mean the moral and intellectual characters, which in their association make the soul of a race, and which represent the product of all its past, the inheritance of all its ancestors, and the motives of all its conduct. The men of each race possess an indestructible stock of ideas, traditions, sentiments, modes of thought, an unconscious inheritance from their ancestors, upon which argument has no effect. What makes a race are their mental and, above all, their moral characteristics, the slow growth and accumulation of centuries of toil and conflict. These are the qualities which determine their social efficiency as a people, which make one race rise and another fall, which we draw out of a dim past through many generations of ancestors, about which we cannot argue, but in which we blindly believe, and which guide us in our short-lived generation as they have guided the race itself across the centuries.

—Henry Cabot Lodge, *Speeches and Addresses, 1884–1909* (Boston: Houghton Mifflin Company, 1909), pp. 262–263.

important to people who wanted order in their communities.

Racism The concern about good family had a broader significance as well. Darwinian ideas and the new science of genetics persuaded many Americans that it was vital to preserve the integrity of good stock, human as well as animal. The races of man were biologically distinct and were constantly locked in struggle. Haphazard mixture was considered dangerous because it diluted the strong stock with the weak.

At nearly all levels of society, people insecure about their status sought refuge in racist theories. The existence of lower groups condemned to inferiority by birth provided some reassurance to established families worried about keeping up their position, to the newly rich worried about being accepted, to the farmers worried about losing their land, and to the craftsmen or clerks worried about sinking into the ranks of unskilled labor.

Tracing their own heritage back to the Anglo-Saxons who had brought free institutions from the German forests first to England and then to the New World, some Americans connected social and cultural traits with biological inheritance. As a result, they took a sympathetic view of the Southern effort to confirm the Negro's inferiority by segregation, which the Supreme Court legitimatized in *Plessy* v. *Ferguson* (1896); and they became heavily involved in the movement to restrict immigration. Since they were sincere in the belief that southern and eastern Europeans were less competent than northern, they agitated, as yet unsuccessfully, in favor of a literacy test.

Social Mobility

Aristocracy The concern with family deepened the emphasis after 1890 upon preserving social divisions. The old families that had struggled to make themselves an aristocracy had the greatest stake in the matter. By now they had developed social and cultural institutions to mark

"Unrestricted Immigration and Its Results—A Possible Curiosity of the Twentieth Century. The Last Yankee." Cartoon from *Frank Leslie's Illustrated Newspaper*, 1889. (Library of Congress)

Segregation Confirmed, 1896

We cannot say that a law which authorizes or even requires the separation of the two races in public conveyances is unreasonable, or more obnoxious to the Fourteenth Amendment than the acts of Congress requiring separate schools for colored children in the District of Columbia, the constitutionality of which does not seem to have been questioned, or the corresponding acts of state legislatures.

We consider the underlying fallacy of the plaintiff's argument to consist in the assumption that the enforced separation of the two races stamps the colored race with a badge of inferiority. If this be so, it is not by reason of anything found in the act, but solely because the colored race chooses to put that construction upon it. . . . The argument also assumed that social prejudices may be overcome by legislation, and that equal rights cannot be secured to the negro except by an enforced commingling of the two races. We cannot accept this proposition. If the two races are to meet upon terms of social equality, it must be the result of natural affinities, a mutual appreciation of each other's merits and a voluntary consent of individuals.

—*Plessy* v. *Ferguson*, 163 United States 537 (1896).

A Society Wedding, 1905

The Van Osburgh marriage was celebrated in the village church near the paternal estate on the Hudson. It was the "simple country wedding" to which guests are conveyed in special trains, and from which the hordes of the uninvited have to be fended off by the intervention of the police. While these sylvan rites were taking place, in a church packed with fashion and festooned with orchids, the representatives of the press were threading their way, note-book in hand, through the labyrinth of wedding presents, and the agent of a cinematograph syndicate was setting up his apparatus at the church door.

—Edith Wharton, *The House of Mirth* (New York: Charles Scribner's Sons, 1905), p. 139.

themselves off and an explicit ideology explained and justified their role.

Some members of this group were optimists. Theodore Roosevelt and Henry Cabot Lodge, influenced by the model of the English ruling class, believed that strong educated leadership dedicated to the public service could persuade the populace to follow. Men of good breeding — which combined birth, culture, and knowledge — who set aside all selfish interests and did what was right could guide the democracy in the common welfare.

Others had doubts. Often they felt that they had become strangers in the land of their forefathers. Henry and Brooks Adams, for instance, arrived at the pessimistic conclusion that the ideals of the Republic were unattainable. A rule in history set limits on men's ability to act. The United States had reached a phase in which either order or popular government would have to give way. Industrialization and the growth of

cities had turned the country in the wrong direction, for it was as a result of these developments that the orderly rural and aristocratic virtues had begun to decay. Little could be done to alter that fundamental change without sapping the strength the country needed in the face of a hostile outer world.

There might be hope, they believed, if an elite group would gain sufficient power to control the future or if a great military establishment would restore discipline and purpose. But neither the political nor the business leaders of the country were aware of the problem, and there was no realistic prospect of its solution.

Discrimination Whether they were optimists or pessimists, Americans who bore aristocratic obligations also felt the need to maintain their distinctiveness and to use the culture they controlled to influence the rest of the population. They found numerous allies at every social level because many Americans, conscious of rank, made deliberate efforts to strengthen the lines that separated them from those below.

The exclusions were both economic and ethnic. Licensing laws attempted to bar outsiders from the practice of desirable professions and of skilled trades. The obstacles were especially formidable when it came to visibly alien groups — Negroes and Orientals, Jews and Catholics, Slavic and Mediterranean immigrants. A crazy-quilt pattern of discrimination made it more difficult for these people than for others to advance. The developing discriminatory practices put a premium upon any kind of linkage with the uppermost social elements, and acceptance of the official culture was the most prevalent means of establishing such a connection.

The Official Culture

The official culture was the means of validating the position of people concerned about their status. By 1890, the uppermost group had already defined the correct clubs, colleges,

Pessimism is the subject of Frederick C. Jaher, *Doubters and Dissenters* (New York, 1964).

"Long Branch, New Jersey." Painting, 1864, by Winslow Homer. (Museum of Fine Arts, Boston)

schools, pictures, and books, which were the symbols of its own lofty place. Its standards and tastes remained frozen. Furthermore, its institutions increasingly commanded the respect of all ambitious Americans. The Metropolitan Opera and the Metropolitan Museum of Art stood for music and art even in the minds of men who never occupied a box at the opera or passed through the halls of the museum.

Elite Education Only a few could gain access to the restricted cultural heights. Places in the proper clubs, schools, or even churches were hard to come by because scarcity contributed to their value. In 1908 there was a long waiting list for admission to the class that would enter St. Mark's School in 1920. Those who could not actually join the elite could emulate the more successful. Throughout the country, the fashions, attitudes, and tastes of the smart set exerted the same attraction.

The educational system transmitted social values to widening circles. The college directed the minority of the population it served toward gentlemanly or ladylike ideals. Laboratories and libraries played a relatively small role compared with the informal life of fraternities, sororities, and athletics. The respected professor was generally one who, without nonsense, rapped out what was correct in literature, economics, or geology.

The high school was an even more important medium for diffusion of the dominant social and cultural influences, for it was now the normal channel through which aspiring young people advanced in life. The number of secondary schools and of the students registered in them grew between 1890 and 1912, and pressure from the colleges imposed a uniform pattern on

Aline Saarinen, *The Proud Possessors* (New York, 1958) is a lively description of the art collectors.

the curriculum. A Committee of Ten appointed by the National Education Association in 1892 and led by President Charles W. Eliot of Harvard outlined the courses appropriate for high schools. Since admission to college was the measure of the value of secondary education, the Committee's recommendations soon dominated high school programs throughout the country and spread the canon of official culture through American society.

Fine Arts The social context profoundly influenced the arts. By 1890 the Emersonian generation had disappeared. The important figures of the next two decades were men trained after the Civil War whose views reflected the cultural assumptions of the gilded age.

The growing cities, which demanded an increasing number and variety of new buildings, offered challenging opportunities to architects. Most of the construction remained in the hands of contractors, for whom cost was the sole consideration and who ran up homes and factories without giving much thought to appearance or setting. But wealth, pride, or public spirit created a desire for distinguished mansions, churches, or institutions. The architects who assumed these assignments were now formally organized in associations which certified that they knew beauty and could create it. The designs they produced took account of the site, of the neighboring structures, and indeed of the whole urban layout.

The Chicago World's Columbian Exposition of 1893 dramatically influenced the trend. Daniel H. Burnham, who was primarily responsible for the plan, adopted a monumental style that imitated the Renaissance. Along a broad esplanade that ran back from the lake shore rose a dazzling white city that offered beholders a startling contrast with the grime of Chicago. The phenomenal popularity of the exposition standardized the concepts of architecture and

Henry James, *Charles W. Eliot* (Boston, 1930) treats these issues fully.

Charles Moore, *Daniel H. Burnham, Architect* (Boston, 1921) is a competent biography.

DANIEL H. BURNHAM was good at drawing but for a long time did not know what to do with his talent. Born in 1846 in Henderson, New York, he went as a boy with his family to Chicago. He disappointed his parents by failing to be admitted to an Eastern college, and was no more successful in his efforts at business. After a try at gold mining in Nevada, he returned to Chicago and in 1872 found work in an architectural office.

There he met John W. Root, a skilled draftsman, and the two opened their own office. A commission to build a house for the manager of the Chicago stockyards proved fortunate for Burnham, who married the client's daughter before the task was finished. In any case, the great fire of 1872 provided abundant assignments for every architect, and Burnham and Root got their share of the good contracts, including several in the 1880s for skyscrapers.

The assignment as chief of construction for the Chicago Columbian Exposition (1893) gave Burnham the opportunity to realize his dream of a grand project with works of architecture, sculpture, painting, and landscaping designed about a single theme. The success of the exposition brought him enormous prestige, which he used to advance his ideas throughout the country. He helped devise the city plans for Washington, Chicago, Manila, and San Francisco, and his work markedly influenced other architects. President Taft in 1910 appointed Burnham chairman of the National Commission of Fine Arts, a post he held until his death in 1912.

Burnham's tastes remained those he had expressed in the Chicago exposition. He emphasized above all a pleasant visual exterior, which he imagined could best be attained by adapting classical precedents to present uses. When he joined some of his colleagues in establishing the American School of Architecture, it seemed to them altogether appropriate to locate the institution in Rome, where the most suitable models were. Until well into the twentieth century, his ideas shaped the practice of American architecture.

urban layout for the next two decades. In 1900, the replanning of Washington, D. C., showed the strength of its influence. The city and its buildings were to be visually attractive rather than functional. Monumental avenues and façades were more important than interiors or the ability to move people and goods about.

The effects were far-reaching. Obsessed with the need to avoid all that was earthy, architects diligently imitated the accepted European styles — classical for public buildings, Gothic for schools and churches. The monument to the former was the exact replica, scaled down, of the Parthenon, erected for the Nashville exposition of 1897. The ultimate expression of the latter was the determination of Ralph Adams Cram to construct the Cathedral of St. John the Divine in New York not only in the Gothic style but also by medieval methods.

The desire for imitative adornment altered the character also of business buildings. In a working alliance, engineers made intelligent use of interior space in the new skyscrapers, while architects were permitted to plaster classical façades onto the exterior. The severe simple lines of the 1880s disappeared beneath the grotesque new embellishments. Cass Gilbert adorned the Woolworth Building, the tallest of the period, with an elaborate Gothic exterior.

City planning, in response to society's tastes, proceeded from the perspective of the rider in a carriage who wished a fine view as he passed by. The layout of Washington and of the park systems in New York, Brooklyn, Buffalo, and Chicago reflected this bias. The fact that people lived and worked in these cities had only subsidiary importance. The suburbs, which lay outside the concern of the planners, spread without control and with no effort to establish a rational relationship to the center.

Aristocratic social pressures subjected also the official literature, music, and theater of the period to the genteel tradition and confined them to European forms. The academic critics like Charles Eliot Norton, Irving Babbitt, and William Lyon Phelps emphasized the classics

Image of the Fair, 1905

Both the Black City and the White City were lapped by the waves of Michigan whose blue-green waters penetrated deep into the heart of each city. In the one case the waters were bordered by ugly docks and warehouses, spanned by hideous bridges, and defiled by the city's foulness, while they flowed under a murky sky. In the other, they were lined by fairy architecture, immaculate docks and strips of verdure and crossed by graceful bridges, while the clearness of an azure sky found reflection in the pure waters. The White City was the symbol of regeneration.

— Charles Zueblin, *A Decade of Civic Development* (Chicago: University of Chicago Press, 1905), pp. 62–63.

Avoiding the Earthy, 1902

A building . . . of public character . . . [should be] large, substantial, white and pure; as becomes a vision half of heaven and half of earth, with detached columns and perhaps sculptured figures standing clear against the sky. So rose the Acropolis over Athens. . . . A dozen modern structures carry out the idea. Build them of dark material and they must glower heavily over the city; build them of white marble, in chaste design, and their beauty is not incongruous in the ugliest industrial city. . . . There must be nothing of the earth earthy in the structure that then meets our eyes.

— Charles M. Robinson, *The Improvement of Towns and Cities* (New York: G. P. Putnam's Sons, 1901), pp. 16–17.

Woolworth Building, New York, Designed by Cass Gilbert and Erected in 1912.
(Museum of the City of New York)

Bicycling on Riverside Drive, New York. Drawing by W. A. Rogers, *Harper's Weekly*, June 15, 1895. (Library of Congress)

to the exclusion of modern writers, and as teachers they set the taste of the time in a rigid mold. The pallid compositions of Arthur Foote and Mrs. H. H. A. Beach were the standard of good native music; it took a foreign visitor, Anton Dvořák, to discover the beauty of the Negro spiritual. Meanwhile the vacuous polite comedies of Clyde Fitch held the stage for which the plays of George Bernard Shaw were considered too daring. A stern rebuff awaited every departure from the accepted norms. Richard Strauss's *Salome* was too outrageous to survive more than one performance in 1907, and Edward A. MacDowell, who was sensitive to the live music of contemporary Europe, had to resign his post at Columbia University.

Popular Culture

Quite another culture served the needs of people for information, self-understanding, and entertainment. Even some men and women anxious about their social status were not content

with good music, literature, or art. They sought emotional and intellectual satisfaction elsewhere.

The leisured found ample opportunities for expression—as participants or spectators in athletics, in gardening and bicycling, in excursions to the beaches, in religious revivals, or simply in listening to the band concerts in the park or sitting at the soda fountain. True, there was no social distinction in activities many could share, but there was pleasure not often found in the more narrowly defined culture.

Some media satisfied a particular sector of the population. Each ethnic group developed its own press, stage, and music, sustained by informal organizations and marked by a high degree of spontaneity. Often the participants were amateurs who wrote and played for the joy of it. But even paid or professional performers were responsive to audiences on whose pennies and dimes they depended.

Other media had a more general appeal. Now was the high point in the vogue of the dime novel. Prentiss Ingraham, whose career ran across this period, turned out fully six hundred, in two hundred of which Buffalo Bill was the hero. Westerns and detective stories, too, were staples of the best-seller lists, with Owen Wister and Zane Grey the most popular American authors.

Newspapers that attracted readers from all groups achieved an enormous circulation. In New York, William Randolph Hearst's *Journal* and Joseph Pulitzer's *World* competed successfully for readers by supplying not only news but also literature and entertainment. To communicate with a heterogeneous and barely literate public, they simplified the language, used bold headlines, and stressed stories with human interest. They emphasized pictures. Photographs and drawings illustrated the news; clear editorial cartoons conveyed opinions; and "The Yellow Kid," "Mutt and Jeff," and other comics created a new form for simple stories. Hearst, in addition, developed strength by establishing a chain of similar papers across the country.

The variety format permitted vaudeville and popular magazines to offer something to everyone. By the end of the nineteenth century, vaudeville had become stable and widespread chains carried the troupes through extensive tours. The moving pictures occasionally put on as part of the show in the next decade did not yet seem substantial enough to threaten the older form of entertainment.

In the 1890s cheap methods of engraving and printing enabled a few periodicals to reach out for a mass audience. *Munsey's* at a dime and the *Saturday Evening Post* at a nickel, along with numerous rivals, purveyed pictures and stories as well as instructive articles in a manner so attractive that a perceptive observer concluded that they were the era's true instruments of education. The offerings of the popular stage and press were usually routine and repetitious, but the connection with the audience was authentic and created an opportunity for genuine art and particularly for comedy.

Frank Luther Mott, *Golden Multitudes* (New York, 1947), a general analysis of best sellers, covers this period.

The Yellow Kid, Comic Strip Character Originated by R. F. Outcault. Cover illustration, 1894. (The Granger Collection)

Within this context, too, appeared a new kind of music to dance and sing to. With the birth of ragtime, jazz achieved a place in the American idiom. No one claimed that this was good music as Mrs. H. H. A. Beach's was, but jazz meant something to the people who heard it.

The Dilemma of the Artist

The sharp division between the accepted and the popular cultures of the United States deepened the predicament of the creative personalities who held to high standards and yet

Popular Education, 1907

McClure's Magazine, the *American Magazine*, *Collier's Weekly*, and in its fashion, the *World's Work*, constitute together a real popular university along this very line. It would be a pity if any future historian were to have to write words like these: "By the middle of the twentieth century the higher institutions of learning had lost all influence over public opinion in the United States. But the mission of raising the tone of democracy, which they had proved themselves so lamentably unfitted to exert, was assumed with rare enthusiasm and prosecuted with extraordinary skill and success by a new educational power; and for the clarification of their human sympathies and elevation of their human preferences, the people at large acquired the habit of resorting exclusively to the guidance of certain private literary adventures, commonly designated in the market by the affectionate name of ten-cent magazines."

—William James, *Memories and Studies* (New York: Longmans, Green and Co., 1911), pp. 323 ff.

sought an authentic audience. Architects like Louis Sullivan and Frank Lloyd Wright who wished to move outside the limits of pallid monumentalism found it increasingly difficult to obtain commissions. The same wealthy clients built the skyscrapers and the great homes and also determined the tastes for government and institutional buildings. Sullivan, whose Transportation Building had been the one notable structure of the Chicago exposition, drifted futilely. Wright's commissions in these years were confined to small structures.

Expatriation A growing number of expatriates thought they could express themselves better in Europe than at home. A variety of different motives drew them across the ocean. They

had in common the lack of any ties to hold them in the United States. Painters like John Singer Sargent and James McNeill Whistler continued to work in a transatlantic setting even when their clients were American. Mary Cassatt lived in France to be close to the impressionists, whose work influenced her own. Henry James, whose novels never ceased to reflect the cultural problems of the country of his birth, nevertheless did his writing in England.

An internal migration carried young writers and painters to marginal bohemian neighborhoods in New York City, Boston, Chicago, and San Francisco, where they could evade the artificial restraints of society. To the sensitive and imaginative, the life of the slums appeared more genuine and more human than that of respectable districts, which seemed desiccated and empty of feeling. There was a tendency to idealize the poor as victims of injustice, and the ethnic culture of the immigrants seemed to have firmer roots than the official culture that imitated the European.

The Revolt Against Formalism The desire to describe the life of common men and women was part of a revolt against the formal rules of the official culture. In literature, the Russian and French novelists offered models for the realistic treatment of the serious problems of life, without sentimentality or palliation. Hamlin Garland's *Main-Travelled Roads* (1891) exposed the drab life of people trapped in endless rural toil. H. H. Boyesen's *The Mammon of Uprighteousness* (1891) and P. L. Ford's *The Honorable Peter Stirling* (1894) dealt with the corrosive effects on humans of business and politics, while Stephen Crane's *Maggie: A Girl of the Streets* (1893) showed the influence of poverty on morality.

In the next decade, a few naturalistic writers made it their task to describe the basic drives that shaped human actions and emotions. Frank Norris in *McTeague* (1899) and *The Octopus* (1901) thus examined the context of man's struggle for existence in a panoramic sweep that was both social and personal. Theodore Dreiser's

Sister Carrie (1900) ventured to touch sexual themes that had theretofore been excluded from polite literature, and Jack London treated the animal aspects of human nature. These writers rejected not only the intellectual assumptions but also the stylistic canons of genteel literature. Their style owed much to the newspapers, in the use of colloquial sentences and in the attempt to approximate the speech of the people.

Comparable tendencies were apparent in the painting of John Sloan, George W. Bellows, and Thomas Eakins, who looked for subjects in the society of the bar and the prize-fight ring. In music and sculpture the control of the techniques was too firmly in academic hands to permit extensive experimentation. At the end of the first decade of the twentieth century, the new departures were just beginning to bear fruit.

JACK LONDON had a birthright in bohemia. His youth was hidden in the obscurity of the poor and placeless. Born in San Francisco in 1876, he was early cast adrift and had merely a smattering of grammar school education. By the time he was seventeen he had delivered newspapers and worked on an ice wagon and in a cannery. He may also have sailed about the Bay, pirating oysters. He was certainly familiar with the tough Oakland waterfront and an accomplished boozer. Somehow he had taken, too, to reading in the public library when he was not loafing.

In 1893 he took a memorable voyage on a sealing vessel and then tried to settle down, supporting himself by doing odd jobs while he made a stab at writing for the newspapers. Times were tough, however, and he was soon on the road again; he served a month in a Niagara Falls jail for vagrancy. Back in California, he got a job as janitor, studied in high school, and in 1896 spent a few months at the University in Berkeley.

London had by then become a socialist and from a reading of Herbert Spencer had derived a vague understanding of the concept of survival of the fittest. More important, an unsuccessful venture to the Klondike during the gold rush the next year gave him the material he would exploit in fiction in the decade that followed. In 1900 *The Son of the Wolf* brought him fame, and a succession of other novels earned him a substantial income.

Still, he was not able to put his life in order. He married in 1900, was divorced in 1905, and remarried the same year. He traveled to London and made a vain effort to sail around the world in a 45-foot yacht. Everywhere, he carried his unhappiness with him. The proud house he built on his ranch burned down and he stopped writing. Alcohol did not help his recurrent fits of depression and his frequent illnesses. He died in 1916 as he had lived—unsettled.

A good deal of his writing was autobiographical, and even what was not bore the marks of his waterfront upbringing. London observed a savage world, in which toughness alone counted and in which mollycoddles always suffered. Man's animal nature was not far beneath the surface, and only those who bit and scratched their way ahead survived. He expected socialism to supply the iron discipline to keep primitive passions in check. This he had learned in California as well as in Alaska.

The Ecstasy of the Primordial Beast, 1903

All that stirring of old instincts which at stated periods drives men out from the sounding cities to forest and plain to kill things by chemically propelled leaden pellets, the blood lust, the joy to kill—all this was Buck's, only it was infinitely more intimate. He was ranging at the head of the pack, running the wild thing down, the living meat, to kill with his own teeth and wash his muzzle to the eyes in warm blood.

There is an ecstasy that marks the summit of life, and beyond which life cannot rise. And such is the paradox of living, this ecstasy comes when one is most alive, and it comes as a complete forgetfulness that one is alive. This ecstasy, this forgetfulness of living, comes to the artist, caught up and out of himself in a sheet of flame; it comes to the soldier, war-mad on a stricken field and refusing quarter; and it came to Buck, leading the pack, sounding the old wolf-cry, straining after the food that was alive and that fled swiftly before him through the moonlight. He was sounding the deeps of his nature, and of the parts of his nature that were deeper than he, going back into the womb of Time. He was mastered by the sheer surging of life, the tidal wave of being, the perfect joy of each separate muscle, joint, and sinew in that it was everything that was not death, that it was aglow and rampant, expressing itself in movement, flying exultantly under the stars and over the face of dead matter that did not move.

—Jack London, *The Call of the Wild* (New York: The Macmillan Company, 1903), pp. 90–91.

"McSorley's Bar." Painting, 1912, by John Sloan. (The Detroit Institute of Arts)

Novelists like Norris and London had acquired some following, but whether the revolt against the formal culture would succeed in the other arts was still in doubt.

▼

The cultural confusion at the turn of the century prevented society from facing the grave problems before it in any unified fashion. The would-be aristocracy failed to win the cultural assent of the whole population, which remained apart in modes of expression as well as in ideas. The lack of communication among the country's disparate groups markedly hampered the effort to apply scientific knowledge to the great social and economic problems of the times.

Paperbacks for Further Reading

The development of racism and of the movement to restrict immigration are the subjects of Oscar Handlin, *Race and Nationality in American Life* (Anchor Books); John Higham, *Strangers in the Land* (Atheneum Publishers); and Barbara M. Solomon, *Ancestors and Immigrants* (Science Editions Paperbacks).

Thomas Beer, *The Mauve Decade* (Vintage Books, Inc.) and Lloyd Morris, *Postscript to Yesterday* (Harper Colophon Books) treat the general cultural setting. Thorstein Veblen, *The Theory of the Leisure Class* (Mentor Books) is an incisive critique by a contemporary. Two quite different autobiographies throw light on these years. Henry Adams, *The Education of Henry Adams* (Sentry Editions) contains the introspective recollections of the historian; Edward Bok, *The Americanization of Edward Bok, An Autobiography* (Pocket Books, Inc.) is by a popular editor. Among the useful biographies are: W. A. Swanberg, *Dreiser* (Bantam Books, Inc.) and C. Hartley Grattan, *The Three Jameses* (New York University Press).

There is helpful material on architecture in Hugh Morrison, *Louis Sullivan* (W. W. Norton & Company, Inc.); in Montgomery Schuyler, *American Architecture and Other Writings* (Atheneum Publishers); and in Don Gifford, ed., *The Literature of Architecture* (Dutton Paperbacks).

Contemporary fiction is particularly illuminating in this period. Among the most enlightening novels are: Henry James, *The Ambassadors* (Holt, Rinehart & Winston, Inc.); Henry James, *Selected Fiction* (Dutton Paperbacks); Edith Wharton, *The Age of Innocence* (Signet Classics); William Dean Howells, *A Hazard of New Fortunes* (Bantam Books, Inc.); Frank Norris, *The Octopus* (Riverside Editions); and Jack London, *Great Short Works of Jack London* (Perennial Library).

THE PROGRESSIVE
IDEA

68

The events of the second half of the nineteenth century challenged the inherited American faith in progress. The Civil War and the failure of Reconstruction had demonstrated that there were limits to the capacity of men to solve all their problems rationally. Industrialization and expansion soon thereafter had created imposing new difficulties, which a divided culture magnified.

Most Americans did not lose confidence, however. Their society had faults, but democracy was not therefore to be abandoned, as some would-be aristocrats urged. Reform was possible. Science and technology had already produced immensely beneficial results. By the correct use of intelligence, men could discover how to surmount the difficulties in the way of improvement. That premise certainly was basic to the progressive idea which took form toward the end of the century.

New Ways of Knowing

A s THE TWENTIETH CENTURY approached, the prevailing intellectual outlook of the country was optimistic. It drew support from the scientific development of the previous century. A new way of thinking, too, supported the general faith in progress.

Pragmatism In the 1880s, Charles S. Peirce had begun to reconsider long-accepted philosophical premises about how people made their meanings clear. Knowledge, he asserted, was not the end result of deductions from abstract or ideal systems. Rather, it emanated from experience, from the test of encounters with facts and events.

William James, a physician turned psychologist, developed these principles further. His own work, before 1890, had begun to convert psychology from a cluster of subjective theories into a laboratory science. His studies had persuaded him that any organ could best be understood in terms of its function, for that explained its structure and its relationship to the rest of the body — the eye was comprehensible as a means of vision. Then he generalized: all phenomena are knowable in terms of the way in which they work.

Joined to Peirce's ideas, this insight suggested that the path to knowledge was always by experiment. The truth of a concept was discoverable from its consequences rather than from the extent to which it matched any abstract proposition. James's widely read books *The Will to Believe and Other Essays* (1897) and *The Varieties of Religious Experience* (1902) applied his position forcefully to the apparent conflict of religion with science. Religion and science, James explained, served different functions. The one provided emotional satisfaction; the other organized information about the natural world. Both were valid.

At about the same time the philosopher John Dewey was rethinking the problems of education. Rejecting the formal curricula that imposed a fixed body of knowledge upon the

Faith in Progress, 1901

The drama was over. The fight of Ranch and Railroad had been wrought out to its dreadful close. . . . Into the prosperous valley, into the quiet community of farmers, that galloping monster, that terror of steel and steam had burst, shooting athwart the horizons, flinging the echo of its thunder over all the ranches of the valley, leaving blood and destruction in its path. . . . The ranches had been seized in the tentacles of the octopus; the iniquitous burden of extortionate freight rates had been imposed like a yoke of iron. . . .

But the WHEAT *remained.* Untouched, unassailable, undefiled, that mighty world-force, that nourisher of nations, wrapped in Nirvanic calm, indifferent to the human swarm, gigantic, resistless, moved onward in its appointed grooves. Through the welter of blood at the irrigation ditch, through the sham charity and shallow philanthropy of famine relief committees, the great harvest of Los Muertos rolled like a flood from the Sierras to the Himalayas to feed thousands of starving scarecrows on the barren plains of India.

Falseness dies; injustice and oppression in the end of everything fade and vanish away. Greed, cruelty, selfishness, and inhumanity are short-lived; the individual suffers, but the race goes on. Annixter dies, but in a far distant corner of the world a thousand lives are saved. The larger view always and through all shams, all wickednesses, discovers the Truth that will, in the end, prevail, and all things, surely, inevitably, resistlessly work together for good.

— Frank Norris, *The Octopus* (New York: Doubleday & Company, Inc., 1901), pp. 650–652.

William James (1842–1910), American Psychologist and Philosopher. (Brown Brothers)

Through much of his life ill health and periodic bouts with depression forced **WILLIAM JAMES** to examine his own consciousness. He was well equipped for the inquiry into the state of his feelings, and he hit upon explanations that were intellectually valuable to his contemporaries.

He was born in 1842. His grandfather, a wealthy Albany merchant, had left an estate large enough to support the next two generations in comfort. William grew up in a family dedicated to ideas, for his father was a religious philosopher converted to Swedenborgianism and acquainted with the leading transcendentalists. There was a good deal of travel in Europe and education through informal reading for both William and his brother Henry. William emerged from adolescence uncertain about his career. He tried painting for a year, then entered the Lawrence Scientific School. Finally he went to the Harvard Medical School, from which he received a degree in 1869, but he interrupted his studies for trips abroad and for rest and he never practiced. Meanwhile his brother Henry moved on to his career as a novelist.

In 1872, William became an instructor in physiology at Harvard. Increasingly his interests turned to psychology, however, and ultimately he began to teach that subject in the Department of Philosophy. The shift in interest became more pronounced with the passing years, until his death in 1910.

James dealt with some of the classical problems of philosophy but his unusual approach to the subject exerted a pronounced influence on his thought. He did not begin with a concern about metaphysics. Rather, as a physician, he probed such questions as the relation between physiology and psychology, the connections between sensations and emotions, and the functions beliefs served in the psyche of believers. He found the answers in his own experience and framed them in terms comprehensible to many Americans.

Pragmatism, as he stated it, called for an empirical approach to knowledge and emphasized voluntarism and pluralism in social behavior. Its stress on individual freedom, tolerance, and humanitarianism made it an appropriate philosophy for progressives. James did not offer his readers a set of absolute dogmas but the assurance that it made sense to use experience to make the world better.

student, he argued that learning came through doing—through activities related to the world outside the school. By emphasizing the connection between truths and their uses, Peirce and James helped him develop an intellectual foundation for the conception of progressive education. Furthermore, Dewey argued, since the environment was always changing, all statements of truth were tentative and the instruments for apprehending it had to be constantly reconstructed.

These ideas—generally referred to as pragmatism—exerted an influence far beyond the circles that read philosophy because they corresponded with long-term tendencies in American thought. Since the eighteenth century, practicality had been a popular test of knowledge among people who regarded religion as ethics and education as a means of getting ahead. Moreover, pragmatism was compatible with the theories of evolution, which had gained increasing acceptance since the 1870s. Ideas and institutions evolved through time because what was appropriate to one environment was not appropriate to another. The pragmatic method was thus progressive, for it welcomed change and explained how to direct it intelligently. Men need not be trapped by a fatalistic determinism. They could assert themselves to direct their development consciously.

Social Science Pragmatism supplied a general tool for progressive thought but it did not propound a homogeneous doctrine or program. The challenge to unite knowledge and action stimulated scientists, technicians, clergymen, and journalists to examine the world about them critically and to do something about their observations. Each group responded in terms of its own experience.

Already before 1890 many social scientists were seeking to improve the human condition. Older economists, political scientists, and sociologists like Richard T. Ely and Lester Ward found

themselves in accord with younger colleagues like John R. Commons, Edward A. Ross, Thorstein Veblen, and J. Allen Smith in their faith in the practical application of the results of learning. The new University of Chicago (1891) added significantly to the resources for research and teaching available in the older graduate schools.

Most of these scholars argued vigorously against the idea, sustained by William Graham Sumner, that evolution proceeded by laws beyond human control and that only free competition could assure the survival of the fittest. The dominant assumption of progressive social scientists was more optimistic. Man's will and intelligence could influence his development.

The writings of Oliver Wendell Holmes showed the extent to which evolutionary ideas had begun to influence lawyers and judges. The law, Holmes argued, was not the product of absolute principles but of social forces; its life was not logic but experience. It therefore advanced with history.

For Holmes as for most of his contemporaries, economic forces were primary. Deficiencies in the system of production explained all other social shortcomings. But the University of Pennsylvania economist Simon N. Patten demonstrated that existing resources were sufficient to produce an abundance of goods and abolish poverty. Once that was achieved, political and social reform would follow. It remained only to work out the appropriate mechanisms. That was the task of social science.

Agents of the Progressive Idea

The Engineers A variety of agents diffused and applied the knowledge science made available. Engineers believed that this was their special role. Just as in the practice of the factory

---

Gay Wilson Allen, *William James* (New York, 1967) is a competent biography with much interesting material from family papers.

James W. Hurst, *Justice Holmes on Legal History* (New York, 1964) is a good introduction to the law of this period.

the technicians who knew how, were able to organize the machines that led to greater output, so too many different kinds of specialists could reorganize the basic institutions of society.

Social Work Expertise was particularly necessary in dealing with social disorder. A relatively new group of trained social workers were eager to take on the assignment. Educated women like Jane Addams, determined to have careers, found this a satisfactory life's calling and threw tremendous energy into their efforts. As the social workers gained recognition as a profession, they gained confidence that they could resolve the problems that confronted them. They made a conscious effort to define the goals of social action properly and to apply scientific rules to the cases they treated.

The Clergy Progressive ideas lent meaning also to the activities of clergymen who were no longer content to serve the God of business or to remain aloof from the affairs of the world. Washington Gladden and others had already been preaching the social gospel. Now the challenge to prove religion by its works directed renewed attention to the situation of the poor. The Baptist Walter Rauschenbusch made social reform the central conception of Christianity. The continued popularity of Charles Sheldon's *In His Steps* (1897) showed the relevance of its injunction to measure contemporary social conditions by the standards of Christ.

Ministers, moreover, went beyond the duty of preaching a change of heart to their congregations. Some Protestants, like Charles Stelzle, actually went down to work in the slums and their reports aroused public concern. Jews like Stephen S. Wise and Catholics like John A. Ryan also spread the sense of a need for action among their coreligionists.

Muckrakers Active journalists enlisted in the progressive cause. Henry D. Lloyd's *Wealth Against Commonwealth* (1894) called attention to the misdeeds of big business, as did Ida M. Tarbell's *History of the Standard Oil Company*

Robert D. Cross, *The Emergence of Liberal Catholicism in America* (Cambridge, Mass., 1958) is an excellent analysis.

The God of Business, 1899

Sunday brought me the queerest experiences of all—a revelation of barbarism complete. I found a place that was officially described as a church. It was a circus really, but that the worshipers did not know. There were flowers all about the building, which was fitted up with plush and stained oak and much luxury, including twisted brass candlesticks of severest Gothic design.

To these things and a congregation of savages entered suddenly a wonderful man, completely in the confidence of their God, whom he treated colloquially and exploited very much as a newspaper reporter would exploit a foreign potentate. But, unlike the newspaper reporter, he never allowed his listeners to forget that he, and not He, was the center of attraction. With a voice of silver and with imagery borrowed from the auction room, he built up for his hearers a heaven on the lines of the Palmer House (but with all the gilding real gold, and all the plate-glass diamond), and set in the center of it a loud-voiced, argumentative, very shrewd creation that he called God. One sentence at this point caught my delighted ear. It was apropos of some question of the Judgment, and ran:—

"No! I tell you God doesn't do business that way."

He was giving them a deity whom they could comprehend, and a gold and jeweled heaven in which they could take a natural interest.

—Rudyard Kipling, *American Notes* (Boston: Brown & Co., 1899), pp. 96–97.

Ida M. Tarbell (1857–1944), American Author. Photographed in 1919. (The Granger Collection)

(1904). Magazines like *McClure's*, *Everybody's*, and *Collier's* provided outlets for the writings of muckrakers, who exposed to public indignation the misdeeds of politicians and businessmen. The economic, political, and social ills of American life were analyzed in magazines and in books. Sometimes the works, like those of Upton Sinclair, were disguised as fiction; sometimes, like those of Lincoln Steffens and Ray Stannard Baker, they were composed as reports of careful research and observation.

Progressive Goals

No unified, coherent program emerged from the writings of the disparate groups except insofar as they all assumed that progress was possible and desirable. Proposals inherited from the Populists, the Mugwumps, the socialists, and earlier reformers mingled with responses to immediate local conditions. A few tendencies were general but by no means led to unanimous agreement on detailed proposals.

Purifying Politics Momentum from the past carried some causes forward—temperance and women's rights, for instance. Others acquired a new urgency from the increased stakes of industrialization. Political corruption now involved not only great sums of money but the control of railroads, utilities, and other enterprises that affected the whole economy. A widespread progressive assumption held that the party system was at fault for the ills of government. The remedy, therefore, was to put power directly in the hands of the people by enabling them to review judicial decisions, to bypass the legislature through the initiative and referendum, and to remove offensive officials through recall. The primary and the direct election of Senators were intended to broaden the majority's role in the electoral process.

The Underprivileged No simple solutions were at hand for the problems of the underprivileged groups in the society. Reformers found no easy formula for dissolving the discriminatory practices that ran counter to the ideal of equality of opportunity. Progressives agreed on the desirability of assimilating the immigrants already in the country and broadening their opportunities for advancement. But there were sharp divisions over the issue of whether to restrict the number of new arrivals or to continue the traditional policy of open gates. Some progressives, moreover, accepted the racist view that all men were not equally capable of becoming Americans.

The doubts were even more pronounced when it came to the Negro. The right of Negroes to vote in the states of the former Confederacy practically disappeared, and their situation everywhere was deteriorating. Race riots in Evansville, Indiana (1903), and Springfield, Illinois (1908), showed the intrusion of the problem north of the Mason-Dixon Line. A horrible eruption of violence in Atlanta (1906) forced Negroes to consider measures of self-defense. But only a few progressives ventured to think of either equality or integration as immediate goals for the descendants of the slaves.

Reformers preferred to believe that all social difficulties were subsidiary to the economic one. Just as Booker T. Washington argued that the Negro's first step was the acquisition of skills to raise his occupational level, so progressives maintained that development of a more efficient productive system was the first step toward social justice.

Economic reform focused on two distinct but related objectives. Geographers and geologists like E. C. Semple and Charles R. Van Hise explained the necessity for planned use of the nation's resources, while the historian Frederick Jackson Turner pointed out that the frontier, critical in the nation's past, no longer existed. Conservation was therefore essential, a proposition supported also by naturalists like John Muir, who deplored the disappearance of the country's wildlife.

Conservation and planning emphasized the importance of efficiency. Some progressives, like Veblen, argued the need for eliminating the wasteful features of American life. Others, like

Reflections on the Atlanta Riot, 1907

It is possible that you have formed at least a good idea of how we feel as the result of the horrible eruption in Georgia. . . . But, listen: How would you feel, if with our history, there came a time when, after speeches and papers and teachings you acquired property and were educated, and were a fairly good man, it were impossible for you to walk the street (for whose maintenance you were taxed) with your sister without being in mortal fear of death if you resented any insult offered to her? How would you feel if you saw a governor, a mayor, a sheriff, whom you could not oppose at the polls, encourage by deed or word or both, a mob of "best" and worst citizens to slaughter your people in the streets and in their own homes and in their places of business? Do you think that you could resist the same wrath that caused God to slay the Philistines and the Russians to throw bombs? I can resist it, but with each new outrage I am less able to resist it.

—R. S. Baker, "Following the Color Line," *The American Magazine*, LXIII (April, 1907), p. 574, quoting a letter from a Negro.

Louis D. Brandeis, wished to liberate industry from the grip of rapacious trusts. Still others, like Herbert Croly, thought greater integration desirable. But whatever the means advocated, there was agreement that a more efficient productive system would make more goods available and thus advance the position of labor and solve the problems of the underprivileged elements in the population.

Voluntary Action

Philanthropy Progressives sought to act through both private and governmental means. The older philanthropic organizations broad-

Visiting Nurse Applying Surgical Dressing, 1912–1914. (Chicago Historical Society)

ened their scope, began to use professional personnel, and altered their goals from charity to reform. In addition, new agencies undertook to deal with the poor of the slums. The Neighborhood Guild of New York (1886) and Hull House of Chicago (1889) adopted from England the techniques of the settlement house in which college people attempted to uplift the lives of the poor by living among them. By 1895, there were fifty such groups in the country and the number grew thereafter.

These enterprises at first had access only to limited funds. Philanthropy was an act of individual generosity and donors had very narrow notions of the amount necessary to support it. Attitudes changed, however, at the turn of the century. Andrew Carnegie, for instance, began to ponder the implications of the great fortune he had accumulated. Since striving and hard work were the desirable activities of life, a great inheritance was a genuine disadvantage. Men who had earned riches were obligated to use them while still alive. He who dies rich dies disgraced, Carnegie wrote. Shocked at the bitterness of the Homestead strike and anxious to withdraw from business, he sold his assets and systematically devoted himself to giving away some two hundred million dollars for education, research, and peace. In the two decades after 1892 John D. Rockefeller was similarly occupied, although not yet on so wide a scale.

These were still isolated figures. Most wealthy men had acquired their fortunes too recently to think lightly of disposing of them, and they were only slowly learning the social obligations of their positions. Even those who did give were guided by their own tastes and judgments rather than by the needs of society. Libraries and medical research were certainly useful but they did not cope with the issues the progressives considered most urgent.

Reform Many private organizations therefore conceived it their task not so much to administer programs as to urge them upon government. They lobbied both for regulatory laws and for the expenditure of public funds to attain their objectives. Most of the groups were nonpartisan, that is, worked outside party lines. Some of them had defensive ethnic aims, like the American Jewish Committee (1906) or the National Association for the Advancement of Colored People (1910). But most of them focused upon some particular social cause, as did the National Consumers' League (1898), the National Child Labor Committee (1904), and the American Association of Labor Legislation (1906).

The Role of Government

Since their primary task was to reverse the post-Civil War trend toward narrowing the scope of government, the progressives expended their efforts alike upon the local, state, and Federal levels.

Municipal Reform The municipalities at first presented the greatest problems. Government in the United States was least successful locally, yet decisions made at this level most directly affected the mass of the people, and their results could be demonstrated quickly.

The city, it was now clear, was a permanent feature of American society. However the people clung to rural ideals, they would have to learn to improve the quality of urban life. By 1895, reform organizations operated in some one hundred and fifty cities in thirty-one states. Within a few years, the National Municipal Asso-

ciation, the American Society for Municipal Improvement, and the League of American Municipalities were coordinating efforts and exchanging information. In some places local research bureaus were investigating operations with the aim of suggesting reforms.

The initial objective was to end corruption. The old political machines, entangled in patronage and graft and allied with crime, vice, and intemperance seemed the main obstacles to progress. Occasionally, the progressives were able to attract a wide following by showing the extent to which corruption affected the residents of the slums. For instance, the Lexow investigation of New York City in 1894 revealed, as the Reverend Charles H. Parkhurst had charged, that crime victimized the poor and threw their daughters into prostitution. Revulsion at the findings ousted the Tammany machine temporarily. There followed one of several periodic efforts to clean up the police force and improve municipal services.

To consolidate temporary gains, progressives tried to set the administration of the cities on an efficient basis, hoping to run them like businesses, free of political distractions. In the aftermath of a great flood, Galveston, Texas, in 1900 put control in the hands of a small commission responsible for the economical operation of all departments. In the next twelve years, more than two hundred cities adopted the same form and Staunton, Virginia, and Sumter, South Carolina, began to experiment with city managers patterned after corporation presidents.

Measures that aimed only at efficiency through eliminating corruption and lowering costs could not, however, long sustain the loyalties of a large part of the population that paid no taxes. Insofar as they eschewed conventional political methods and divorced themselves from party connections, the progressives were more effective as critics in opposition than as administrators in power. Furthermore, their link with such causes as prohibition cast them in the role of gloomy puritans forbidding people to enjoy what little leisure they had.

Clifford W. Patton, *The Battle for Municipal Reform* (Washington, 1940) is a brief but informative account that focuses on the 1890s.

Bandit's Roost, Mulberry Street, New York. Photograph by Jacob Riis. (Museum of the City of New York)

Samuel M. Jones ("Golden Rule Jones") and Brand Whitlock of Toledo and Tom L. Johnson and Newton D. Baker of Cleveland demonstrated that a progressive city administration could produce results more positive than mere economy. Municipal ownership of public utilities, or at least strict regulation, lowered costs for the workers. Cheap ice and better milk improved their diets. Tenement-house inspection laws, park concerts, playgrounds, and kindergartens offset some of the brutishness of life in the slums.

Such measures roused the enthusiasm of social workers, who began to serve as representatives of the poor and in some places developed political power that rivaled that of the machines.

State Action The municipalities, however, were instruments of the states. Many crucial decisions were made in the state capital rather than in the city hall. On this level, too, progressives attempted to modernize the machinery of government. When new states were admitted (Utah in 1896, Oklahoma in 1907, and New

SAMUEL M. JONES was a self-made man who refused to forget his origins. Born in 1846 in a tiny peasant village in Wales, he migrated with his parents to New York State in 1849. His father eked out a livelihood as a tenant farmer and by labor in a quarry. At the age of ten, Samuel went to work, to contribute his mite to the family income.

News of the discovery of oil brought him to Pennsylvania in 1865, where he held various jobs as driller, pipe liner, and pumper and saved enough to go into business on his own. After the opening of new fields in Ohio, he moved first to Lima and then to Toledo, where he prospered by manufacturing oil-well machinery.

In his factory Jones hung a placard, "Golden Rule," as a reminder of what he ought to do unto others. He employed no timekeeper, installed an eight-hour day, refused to cut wages or employ children, gave his workers paid vacations, Christmas bonuses, and the opportunity to buy stock, and encouraged a cooperative medical insurance plan. He even favored trade unions. The hall, park, and playground he supported all bore the title, Golden Rule.

In the 1890s he found time to crusade for his distinctive idea of a cooperative commonwealth in which the state would own the trusts and operate industry for the benefit of all. These ideas seemed respectable when stated not by a "wild-eyed radical" but by a successful businessman who actually lived by the precepts of the golden rule.

In 1897 Jones was elected mayor of Toledo, and he held the office until his death in 1904. He brought to government the same energy and the same devotion to the golden rule that had helped him in business. The merit system, the eight-hour day, and decent wages raised the morale of municipal employees. He took the clubs away from the police and forbade them to make arrests on mere suspicion. He gave the people kindergartens, playgrounds, and free concerts, and he fought the traction company that ran the street railways. The politicians writhed, but Jones kept the support of labor and of the mass of voters and demonstrated the progress that was possible at the local level.

Mexico and Arizona in 1912) or when old ones revised or amended their constitutions, there were determined drives for the adoption of devices like the initiative and referendum. Indeed, by 1912, twenty-nine states had provided for the direct election of United States Senators.

The more important reforms were substantive. Some progressives like William S. U'Ren of Oregon filtered into positions of influence in the legislatures, but control of those bodies usually remained in the hands of the rural political organizations hostile to any change. The governor, however, was more responsive to progressive programs since he owed his position to popular election. Governor Altgeld of Illinois early showed the way. Theodore Roosevelt and Charles Evans Hughes in New York, Robert M. La Follette in Wisconsin, Joseph W. Folk in Missouri, Albert B. Cummins in Iowa, and Hiram Johnson in California followed. The climactic election of 1910 which brought Woodrow Wilson to power in New Jersey and John Dix in New York showed the extent to which progressives had gained popular support. These governors used the patronage to control the legislatures and drew upon the universities and intellectuals for ideas and administrative talent.

The power thus mobilized secured the enactment of laws to conserve natural resources,

George W. Chessman, *Governor Theodore Roosevelt* (Cambridge, Mass., 1965) is a good analysis of progressive state politics.

Parks and Patriotism, 1904

The creation of civic centers arouses civic pride and patriotism. They give the city character, dignity, and expression. Here is something which the masses can appreciate and enjoy, something which expresses power, greatness, and ideality, and to which they can point with pride. It is not too much to say that one important reason why politics is so perverted is that the city appears to the great masses of the people only through the policemen—as a restrictive power, and not as a constructive and vitalizing force. Being so distant and apparently so unrelated to their interests, they oppose any seeming attempt to increase the police power, and indifferently bestow their suffrages upon the politician who sends them turkeys upon Thanksgiving Day, who pays their rent when hard pressed, and attends the funeral when the baby dies. Yet these very masses are most easily influenced by visible improvements of a constructive character, and their patriotism is quickly and often permanently aroused by civic progress.

The truth of these statements will, I am sure, be vouched for by those who work in the populous centers of our cities. Even the establishment of a small park or playground has had a wonderful effect. How much greater would be the uplifting influence if the public and semi-public buildings—the court-houses, schools, libraries, baths, offices of the administrative departments, fire stations, settlements, theaters, etc.—were grouped in and about these parks, and the city government thus brought close to the citizen and expressed concretely! Would he not be interested in its operations and be led to see that he is a part of the city and that its welfare depends upon his actions?

—Milo R. Maltbie, "The Grouping of Public Buildings," *The Outlook*, LXXVIII (September 3, 1904), pp. 40–42.

Popular Concert in Tompkins Square, New York. Drawing by T. de Thulstrup, from *Harper's Weekly*, September 12, 1891. (Library of Congress)

245

Democracy in Wisconsin, 1912

Democracy not only produced the expert, it elevated him to office. It recognized the necessity of research, of training, of science, in the highly complex business of government. One of the first acts of the Socialist administration in Milwaukee was the organization of a bureau of economy and efficiency to aid its officials in their work. It sent to the university for an instructor to train its aldermen in problems of city administration. The legislative reference bureau, the railroad commission, the board of public affairs, the industrial commission, are all filled with experts or professors from the university. Forestry, agriculture, and road building have been recognized as requiring the aid of the scientist.

Democracy, too, began to use its powers to serve, to serve people as well as business, to serve humanity as well as property. Democracy has begun a war on poverty, on ignorance, on disease, on human waste. The state is using its collective will to promote a program of human welfare.

Wisconsin is dispelling the fears of those who distrusted democracy. It is demonstrating the possibility of using the state as an instrument for the well-being of all people. It is laying the foundations for a commonwealth whose ideal it is to serve.

—F. C. Howe, *Wisconsin: An Experiment in Democracy* (New York: Charles Scribner's Sons, 1912), pp. 190–191.

to develop water power, to guard against impure foods, and to expand public education. Strong railroad and public utility commissions fixed rates in the consumers' interest. Wisconsin went so far as to introduce an income tax. The states also took the first tentative steps to protect labor against exploitation. In doing so they had to be wary of courts inclined to hold as unconstitutional statutes that infringed upon the rights of contract and of private property. The Ritchie case (1895) and the Lochner case (1905) had on those grounds invalidated efforts to limit the hours of certain workers. Nevertheless, by 1912 progressive states had used their police power to set maximum hours and minimum wages for women and children, and some had provided for compensation for injured workmen.

The Progressive Nation Important problems remained outside the scope of state action. For example, only the Federal government could deal with the great interstate trusts or exert any control over an economy that was continental in scope. Yet the progressive impulse was weak in the Washington of the 1890s, which took a narrow view of the role of government. The controversies over the currency, the tariff, and civil service reform directed attention to inessentials, and emotion dominated the election of 1896. Since 1888, when the parties had begun to collect national war chests, campaigns had grown more expensive and increasingly dependent on great donors like the merchant John Wanamaker and the banker August Belmont. Behind McKinley stood Marcus A. Hanna. "Czar" Thomas B. Reed of Maine, Speaker of the House, and Senator Nelson Aldrich of Rhode Island, together with their allies in both parties, kept firm hands on the machinery of Congress and were not easily moved by calls for reform.

In the desire to strengthen the Federal government, progressives often appealed to national solidarity. They found it pragmatically useful to link patriotism and reform. *Looking Backward* had already done so before 1890, and Bellamy continued to argue in the same vein. Indeed, the association of nationalism and progress, which had long been traditional in American thought, was particularly effective in the 1890s. The final reconciliation of North and South then extinguished the smoldering embers of sectional hatred and generated a strong emotional upswell of loyalty.

But the appeal to common action had unanticipated implications. The people called to unity gave their own meanings to nationalism and those varied according to the diverse social and cultural assumptions of the population. The differences would become apparent with the revival of the concept of mission, which had lain dormant during the post-Civil War decades while Americans concentrated their energies on internal problems.

▼

The internal problems of the United States were far from solved in 1898. The Populist revolt was subsiding, but the reorganization of agriculture and industry was just beginning, with economic, cultural, and social effects that were still unclear. The progressive idea had evoked some political action on the state and local, but not on the Federal level, when war in 1898 impelled Americans to look once more beyond their continental boundaries.

Paperbacks for Further Reading

Richard Hofstadter, *The Age of Reform* (Vintage Books, Inc.) is a provocative general interpretation. Morton White, *Social Thought in America* (Beacon Press) is a lucid analysis. Henry Steele Commager, *American Mind* (Yale University Press) is more superficial. Louis Hartz, *The Liberal Tradition in America* (Harvest Books) sets this period in a general context. There are also challenging ideas in C. M. Destler, *American Radicalism, 1865–1901* (Quadrangle Books, Inc.); and Arthur Mann, ed., *The Progressive Era* (Holt, Rinehart & Winston, Inc.) brings together a useful selection of interpretations.

There are brief essays on individuals in David Mark Chalmers, *Social and Political Ideas of the Muckrakers* (The Citadel Press). Arthur Mann, *Yankee Reformers in the Urban Age* (Harper Torchbooks); Russel B. Nye, *Midwestern Progressive Politics* (Harper Torchbooks); and George E. Mowry, *The California Progressives* (Quadrangle Books, Inc.) deal with various sections of the country.

There are materials on the religious element in progressive thought in Robert Cross, ed., *The Church and the City* (Bobbs-Merrill College Division); John T. Ellis, *American Catholicism* (Chicago History of American Civilization Series); Aaron I. Abell, *American Catholicism and Social Action* (University of Notre Dame Press); and Thomas T. McAvoy, *The Americanist Heresy in Roman Catholicism* (University of Notre Dame Press). Robert H. Bremner, *American Philanthropy* (Chicago History of American Civilization Series) and Samuel R. Spencer, Jr., *Booker T. Washington* (Little, Brown & Co.) touch on other aspects.

Among the useful general collections of primary materials are: David A. Shannon, ed., *Progressivism and Postwar Disillusionment* (McGraw-Hill Paperback Series); Arthur and Lila Weinberg, eds., *The Muckrakers* (Capricorn Books); and Ray Ginger, ed., *Altgeld's America* (Quadrangle Books, Inc.). The books of William James with the greatest bearing on the progressive movement are *Pragmatism and Other Essays* (Washington Square Press, Inc.); *The Will to Believe and Human Immortality* (Dover Publications, Inc.); and *The Varieties of Religious Experience* (Collier Books).

Among the works on politics, the following are especially enlightening: Moisei Ostrogorski, *Democracy and the Organization of Political Parties* (Anchor Books), by a perceptive foreigner; Lincoln Steffens, *Shame of the Cities* (American Century Series), by a leading muckraker; William L. Riordon, *Plunkitt of Tammany Hall* (Dutton Paperbacks), by a local boss; and the section in Oscar Handlin, *Immigration as a Factor in American History* (Spectrum Books).

Morris Janowitz, ed., *W. I. Thomas on Social Organization* (Phoenix Books) contains the selected papers of an influential sociologist. Jane Addams, *Twenty Years at Hull-House* (Signet Classics) and her *Democracy and Social Ethics* (Harvard University Press) contain interesting reflections of contemporary social thought. Frederick W. Taylor, *Principles of Scientific Management* (W. W. Norton & Company, Inc.) and Henry D. Lloyd, *Wealth vs. Commonwealth* (Spectrum Books) expose quite different views of the economy.

IMPERIALISM

69

Before the Civil War, Americans had not limited their thoughts about the future to the area within the existing borders of the United States. They had expected expansion to remain a constant factor in their experience and had framed their concepts of Manifest Destiny in global terms.

After the war many could no longer cling to the old certainty. The course of history no doubt assured the future grandeur of the United States, but the difficulties of governing Boston or Georgia created doubts about the ability to rule additional territories effectively. The problems of the Indian, the Negro, and the immigrants created a reluctance to incorporate into the country other peoples distinguished from the majority by cultural or racial differences. Many Americans thought it better to lessen outside contacts and to reduce the role of the United States in world affairs.

Yet as the century drew to a close, progressives and other Americans felt a renewal of the expansion impulse. Soon a new war endowed the United States with an unexpected empire and its attendant problems.

"According to the ideas of our missionary maniacs, the Chinaman *must* be converted, even if it takes the whole military and naval forces of the two greatest nations of the world to do it." Cartoon from *Puck*, 1895. (The Granger Collection)

Varieties of Imperialist Sentiment

Foreign Burdens A variety of sources—religious and economic as well as military—fed the impulse to overseas expansion in the 1890s. Immigration, travel, and the flow of books and ideas had all along sustained close cultural and social ties between the United States and the world beyond its borders. Humanitarian interests served the same function. Americans thus sympathized with the suffering Armenians, as they had earlier with the Greeks and Hungarians. Immigrants identified with their former countrymen, and this deepened that sense of compassion.

The firmest connections were religious. American missionary enterprise was almost a century old. Many denominations had extensive establishments all over the world, supported by and reinforcing the concept of mission. The members of numerous congregations and parishes throughout the country sustained the missionaries, who labored not only to convert the natives but also to advance their material welfare —setting up schools and hospitals, and providing training in crafts and agriculture. These institutions created an American presence in almost every sector of the globe.

Overseas Markets The economic stake in expansion changed character significantly in the last two decades of the nineteenth century. Earlier the overseas businessman had been a merchant, his role primarily that of intermediary whose vessels passed through alien ports without establishing close contacts with the natives. Now industrialists and investors began to take a direct interest in the potentialities of large overseas markets. The millions of lamps of China seemed

The White Squadron, Pacific Fleet, 1899. The *Chicago, Newark, Atlanta, Concord,* and *Yorktown*. (Official U.S. Navy Photo)

ready to consume endless barrels of American kerosene, and ingenious American tools and machines found a very large part of their market abroad.

  Some American businessmen would have liked to extend the trading area of the United States by extending the influence of their government in Asia and Latin America, as Europeans were doing. But if that were not possible, they wanted at least to preserve equal commercial opportunities by preventing foreign rivals from acquiring special economic privileges or concessions.

  The Ideology of Power New military calculations fed the interest in overseas expansion. American soldiers, professional and amateur, had had twenty-five years of peace by 1890. Those still in the ranks who had nothing better to do than chase scattered bands of Indians across the Great Plains often read with envy

about the activities of European colonizers. As the uneventful years went by, the aging officers thought wistfully of the glory and promotions to be gained on the field of battle. They were therefore receptive to the argument, occasionally heard in the 1890s, that the martial spirit was essential to the moral strength of the nation.

  Furthermore, naval theory supplied a military justification for expansion. Captain Alfred T. Mahan, a careful student of history, showed the crucial importance of sea power in history. And sea power meant the ability to keep in being a great fleet capable of defeating in pitched battle any possible antagonist. Mahan argued that sea power had determined the outcome of the American Revolution and of the War of 1812 and that it remained the critical military factor as the twentieth century approached. But in the modern era of iron-clad or steel warships fueled by coal, it was more difficult to keep a fleet in being in far-flung parts of the world than in the days of wooden sailing ships. Naval bases and coaling stations were essential. Hence sea power depended upon a world-wide chain of colonies.

Mahan's followers were few in number but extremely influential by virtue of their positions. His ideas were particularly attractive to such patricians in politics as Theodore Roosevelt and Henry Cabot Lodge. An imperial role would enable them to emulate the British aristocracy they admired and envied. The naval bill of 1890, which provided for three great battleships, was the first step toward construction of the fleet Mahan advocated.

Missionaries, businessmen, and military theorists found ultimate justification for expansion in their reading of Darwinian evolution. Human progress came through a struggle in which the fittest survived. John Fiske and Josiah Strong were among the writers who explained that the rule was as true for races as for individuals. As the world grew smaller, it was inevitable that the United States expand lest it be crushed. Racist ideology enabled the supporters of expansion to bring the traditional conception of mission up to date. It was the duty of the Anglo-Saxons, particularly of the branch in the United States, to conquer inferior peoples and rule them for the good of all.

The United States and the World   By the 1890s, Americans who believed that their country should play an important role in world affairs considered action urgent. Britain and France had long been rivals in the Mediterranean. Now the contest between them spread around the world. They and Germany, Russia, Italy, Japan, and even Belgium were carving out portions of Africa and Asia. Spurred on by the desire for markets and investments, some of these powers were rising in prominence also in the economy of Latin America. Soon the globe would be divided into tight spheres of influence, from which American trade and ideas would both be excluded. Brooks Adams, contemplating the

Tyler Dennett, *Americans in Eastern Asia* (New York, 1922) discusses missionary activities.

The Immediate Need for Expansion, 1897

I believe we should build the Nicaraguan canal at once, and in the meantime that we should build a dozen new battleships, half of them on the Pacific Coast; and these battleships should have large coal capacity and a consequent increased radius of action. I am fully alive to the danger from Japan, and I know that it is idle to rely on any sentimental good will towards us. . . . We should act instantly before the two new Japanese warships leave England. I would send the *Oregon,* and, if necessary, also the *Monterey* (either with a deck load of coal or accompanied by a coaling ship) to Hawaii, and would hoist our flag over the island, leaving all details for after action. . . .

I fully realize the immense importance of the Pacific coast. . . . But there are big problems in the West Indies also. Until we definitely turn Spain out of those islands (and if I had my way that would be done tomorrow), we will always be menaced by trouble there. We should acquire the Danish Islands, and by turning Spain out should serve notice that no strong European power, and especially not Germany, should be allowed to gain a foothold by supplanting some weak European power. I do not fear England; Canada, is a hostage for her good behavior; but I do fear some of the other powers.

—Theodore Roosevelt to Captain Alfred Mahan, March 3, 1897, in E. E. Morison, ed., *The Letters of Theodore Roosevelt* (Cambridge, Mass.: Harvard University Press, 1951), vol. I, p. 607.

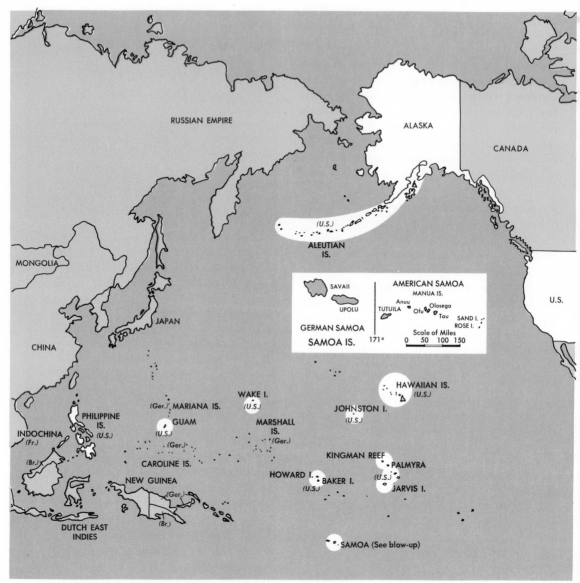

AMERICAN INTERESTS IN THE PACIFIC, 1890–1900

state of affairs in *The Law of Civilization and Decay* (1895), concluded gloomily that perhaps it was already too late to defend the country's interests.

Diplomatic Uncertainties

Americans accustomed to looking westward thought readily of expansion across the Pacific. The romantic concept—westward the course of empire—coincided with long-standing American interest in the Orient. Furthermore, the base in Alaska acquired unexpected importance with the discovery of gold there at the end of the century.

Hawaii Missionary activity and substantial investments gave the United States a considerable stake in the kingdom of Hawaii. In addition, the lease of Pearl Harbor as a naval station in 1887 established an American force on the islands. The expansion of Britain, France, Germany, and Japan further west in the Pacific was accordingly a subject of concern. Natives in all the islands lacked the capacity to resist. There was a distinct danger therefore that one or another of the great powers might covet Hawaii and simply annex it. The growth of Japanese immigration to Hawaii, which already contained numerous Chinese, threatened to extend the Mikado's influence there.

Americans in Hawaii favored annexation by the United States. Resistance to their plans by Queen Liliuokalani and her arbitrary efforts to curb the legislature in January 1893 evoked a revolt, which had the tacit support of John L. Stevens, minister of the United States in Honolulu, and of the Department of State. A new provisional government forthwith proposed a treaty of annexation.

President Harrison left office, however, before the Senate could ratify it. Cleveland resolutely refused to accept the arrangement,

Ethel M. Damon, *Sanford Ballard Dole and His Hawaii* (Palo Alto, Calif., 1957) is a sympathetic account of American interests in the islands.

which he believed to be the product of a plot between the rebels and officials in his predecessor's administration. A provisional government therefore held power in Hawaii, waiting for a change of sentiment in Washington that would permit annexation.

International Morality, 1893

Believing, therefore, that the United States could not, under the circumstances disclosed, annex the islands without justly incurring the imputation of acquiring them by unjustifiable methods, I shall not again submit the treaty of annexation to the Senate for its consideration. . . .

It has been the boast of our Government that it seeks to do justice in all things without regard to the strength or weakness of those with whom it deals. I mistake the American people if they favor the odious doctrine that there is no such thing as international morality; that there is one law for a strong nation and another for a weak one, and that even by indirection a strong power may with impunity despoil a weak one of its territory.

By an act of war, committed with the participation of a diplomatic representative of the United States and without authority of Congress, the Government of a feeble but friendly and confiding people has been overthrown. A substantial wrong has thus been done which a due regard for our national character as well as the rights of the injured people requires we should endeavor to repair.

—President Cleveland's Message Withdrawing the Hawaiian Annexation Treaty, in J. D. Richardson, *A Compilation of the Messages and Papers of the Presidents, 1789–1897* (Washington: Government Printing Office, 1898), vol. IX, p. 470.

STEPHEN GROVER CLEVELAND was a man of stubborn integrity. Nothing could weaken his determination to do what was right—not money or popularity or the opinions of others. He was therefore often out of step with his times.

Cleveland was born in the Presbyterian parsonage at Caldwell, New Jersey, in 1837. The family moved to upstate New York. Then his father died and Grover went to work to help support his mother and two brothers. He studied law on his own and began to practice in Buffalo.

His entry into politics was through law enforcement, first as assistant to the district attorney and then as sheriff of Erie County. In those positions he began the battle against corruption which he continued when he became mayor of Buffalo in 1881. A year later, running as an "un-owned candidate," he became governor of New York and extended his reputation as a reformer.

In 1884 Cleveland was the Democratic candidate for the presidency. Running against James G. Blaine, he attracted Mug-wump support, to which he added when the Chicago *Tribune* reported that he was the father of an illegitimate child. His reaction—"*Tell the truth!*"—probably earned him more votes for his honesty than he lost by the scandal. He failed to be re-elected by a narrow margin in 1888 but returned to the White House in 1892.

During his second term Cleveland felt compelled to take unpopular stands on several issues, among them the end of silver purchases, the gold deal with Morgan, and the dispatch of troops during the Pullman strike. He proceeded unperturbedly along his own course. Adhering firmly to his convictions, he resolutely opposed any tendency toward imperialist expansion in Hawaii and in Cuba. Before he left office in 1897 he had infuriated the opposition and his own party had repudiated him, but he was content in the certainty that he had done right. He retired to Princeton, New Jersey, where he died in 1908, by which time he had the satisfaction of knowing that his reputation had risen in the esteem of the public.

President McKinley revived the issue soon after his inauguration in 1897, believing the matter urgent because of Japan's victory over China in 1895. The Senate, however, remained recalcitrant and he did not press for action. Not until after the outbreak of war with Spain did a joint resolution extend American sovereignty over the islands (July 7, 1898). The annexation significantly extended the boundaries of the United States a thousand miles westward into the Pacific and gave the country a stepping stone for a further approach to the Orient.

The Venezuela Crisis The same hesitant policy was characteristic of the uneasy relations of the United States with Latin America. The interests of American citizens in the Western Hemisphere had grown steadily, and although

the Monroe Doctrine had not been seriously invoked for years, it retained important emotional connotations. Americans were nevertheless unprepared for the crisis that erupted in 1895 as a result of an old boundary dispute between Venezuela and British Guiana.

This miserable controversy had dragged on for years. The discovery of gold in the 1880s raised the value of the disputed area, and Britain, which was the preponderant power in the Caribbean, threatened to settle the matter by force. During his first term in office Cleveland had offered to arbitrate but had been rebuffed by the British. Now he became belligerent. With his approval, Secretary of State Richard Olney declared in a firm—indeed intemperate—message (July 20, 1895) that the Monroe Doctrine made the United States practically sovereign in the hemisphere and demanded a peaceful

Allan Nevins, *Grover Cleveland* (New York, 1932) tells the full story of Cleveland's foreign policy.

"Keep off! The Monroe Doctrine *must* be respected." Cartoon from *Judge,* 1896. (The Granger Collection)

settlement. When Lord Salisbury, the British Prime Minister, rejected the contention with equal firmness, a break appeared imminent. In December 1895 Cleveland received enthusiastic Congressional approval for the proposal to appoint an investigating commission and to back up its recommendations by force if necessary.

The crisis eased in January 1896. Kaiser William II's telegram of congratulations to the Boer President Kruger, who had just suppressed an English uprising, then revealed to the British how isolated they were among the great powers. Germany, which had embarked in an active race for colonies and naval strength, was a more serious threat to the British than the United States. Salisbury determined to seek a rapprochement with the Americans and agreed in principle to arbitrate. Only the desire for peace in London prevented a serious disruption in Anglo-American relations. The English could not have predicted that the arbitration decision, in 1899, would favor them.

Cleveland's action was a sign of the erratic character of American policy. He may have intended to twist the lion's tail—to defy Britain—in order to gain the political support of the Irish-American Democrats who had always been suspicious of him, but he was a man of integrity, and domestic considerations alone would not have induced him to take so grave a step.

The crisis was the result also of the inability to define either the meaning of the Monroe Doctrine or the nature of the American interest in Latin America. The United States had a growing stake in the Caribbean. Would its manifest destiny lead to expansion in that direction? In 1897, there was as yet no answer.

The Problem of Cuba

Cuba would clarify the American role in the Caribbean. Since the Ostend Manifesto (1854), sentiment in favor of annexation had subsided. The United States had problems enough in its

Cuba in the Frying Pan. "The duty of the hour: to save her not only from Spain but from a worse fate." Cartoon from *Puck*, 1898. (The Granger Collection)

own South without adding a large alien population, much of it Negro, living by a plantation economy. American investments in the island had grown but the investors, primarily concerned with the maintenance of order, wished simply to strengthen the Spanish government and to maintain peace.

The Struggle for Independence The outbreak of revolution in 1895 created a problem. The Junta in New York which directed the struggle under José Martí attracted widespread support in the United States. The rebels seemed to be progressives trying to shake off colonial controls and to replace a monarchy with a republic. Furthermore, residual anti-Catholicism identified Spain with the tortures of the Inquisition and the insurgent Cubans with the historic battle for liberty.

President Cleveland took a position that was entirely legalistic. He refused to intervene and he did what he could to prevent filibustering

Ernest R. May, *Imperial Democracy* (New York, 1961) is a careful study of the diplomacy of the Spanish-American War.

expeditions. On the other hand, he announced that he would protect the rights of American citizens in Cuba and urged Spain to accept mediation in order to avoid a costly, fruitless conflict. But he could not prevent Americans from purchasing the bonds of the Junta or from supplying the rebels with arms. And he could not stay the tide of newspaper reports that stirred the sympathies of the American people.

The distant Spanish government was incapable of dealing with the problem. The queen was concerned only with saving the dynasty. Her cynical ministers were absorbed in elaborate parliamentary maneuvers. The army was a power in its own right and exaggerated its strength. The officials accustomed to exploiting the Cubans were a potent force against change. In the end, all of them preferred to lose the island with dignity rather than accept compromises that involved a loss of face.

The first Spanish response to the Cuban uprising was brute force. General Valeriano Weyler, the military commander, rounded up

WILLIAM McKINLEY was rather short and a developing paunch tempted cartoonists into portraying him in a Napoleonic pose. The characterization was far from accurate. He did rise from private to the rank of major in the Civil War, and he did lead the nation into the conflict with Spain which left the United States an empire. However, he took these steps not through ambition but prayerfully, because it was his duty to do so.

McKinley was born in 1843 in Niles, Ohio, where his father was an iron founder. He was able to attend Allegheny College and taught school for a while before enlisting. When he was mustered out, he studied law and began to practice in Canton, Ohio. He married the banker's daughter and entered politics. In 1876 he was elected to the United States House of Representatives, where he served with one brief interruption until 1891. He distinguished himself only by sponsoring the high tariff law that bore his name.

He had, however, acquired the potent support of Marcus A. Hanna, who thrust him first into the governorship of Ohio in 1891 and then into the Republican presidential candidacy in 1896. McKinley spent most of the campaign at home. His stand on silver had, in the past, been ambiguous, and he preferred now not to be drawn into a public debate but to let the platform speak for him against Bryan.

The new President in 1897 was not well prepared to meet the diplomatic issues before the United States. He had little experience with foreign affairs, and he designated as Secretary of State seventy-four-year-old Senator John Sherman, whose seat in the Senate thereupon became available to Hanna. But McKinley had no intention of taking a firm diplomatic line, preferring in this as in other matters to follow 'opinion in Congress and in the country. As a result the nation entered the war of 1898 without a clear concept of what was involved.

On September 6, 1901, less than a year after his re-election, McKinley was assassinated by a deranged anarchist, Leon Czolgosz, and died eight days later. Appropriately, his last words were, "It is God's way. His will, not ours, be done."

---

the civilians, confined them in concentration camps, and treated anyone who remained at large as a rebel. The rising death toll and the ruined economy did not sap revolutionary resistance but did confirm American impressions of the cruel Spaniards. Meanwhile the morale of the occupying army sank and the prospect of crushing the revolt receded.

McKinley's Policy When McKinley took office, no end of the wretched business was in sight. The new President had no desire for war, but he was sensitive to the mounting opinion in Congress that the United States could not indefinitely tolerate the disorder at its doorstep. Through 1897 he played for time, hoping that Spain would recognize the inevitable. Meanwhile lurid newspaper dispatches whipped up popular demands for intervention. The competing Hearst and Pulitzer papers in New York City took the lead in spreading the atrocity stories that enhanced their sales.

Early in 1898 the situation deteriorated rapidly. On February 9, Hearst's publication of an undiplomatic letter by Dupuy de Lôme, Spanish minister in Washington, casting aspersions on President McKinley, touched off excited demands for his recall. A few days later, the battleship *Maine* exploded in the harbor of Havana with the loss of 260 lives. Although there was never decisive proof of the cause of the disaster, public opinion blamed the Spaniards. McKinley had to act, much as he was reluctant to do so. He gave notice to Spain that it could avoid war only by meeting three conditions. It would have to proclaim an armistice, end the concentration camps, and accept the mediation

The Sinking of the *Maine*, as Featured in Hearst's *New York Journal* on February 17, 1898. (The Granger Collection)

of the United States even though that might lead to independence for Cuba.

When the queen temporized and tried to get the Pope and the European powers to intervene, McKinley finally made up his mind. On April 11, he set forth the problem in a message to Congress, which eight days later enacted a resolution calling for recognition of the independence of Cuba and the use of American force if necessary to oust the Spaniards. The Teller Amendment to that resolution disclaimed any intention of acquiring control of the island for the United States, but war was inevitable.

The Spanish-American War

The flare-up of patriotism in the spring of 1898 created the sense of unity and solidarity Americans had sought since the Civil War. The bitter memories of the past and the sharp internal divisions of the present were alike forgotten in the face of a common enemy. The issues in terms of which the country entered battle harked back to traditional national themes. A colonial struggle for independence, the rights of a small nation against a large oppressor, resistance to a backward, feudal regime—all these features of the conflict heightened the sense of popular involvement.

The Course of War The enemy was sufficiently weak to compensate for failures of American military leadership, lack of preparation, and endless inefficiency. Although there was no systematic scheme for mobilization, it was not difficult to recruit an army of volunteers. Part of the fleet was archaic but the navy easily defeated the enemy. It was a splendid little war in which the mute agony of battle was quickly forgotten. The struggle was over in three months, at a cost of some 5000 American lives, fewer than 400 of them lost in battle. (Disease proved more lethal than enemy bullets.)

Frank Freidel, *The Splendid Little War* (Boston, 1958) is a colorful narrative of the fighting.

The Mute Agony of Battle, 1898

The trail was already crowded with stretcher-bearers and with wounded men who could walk. . . . One's sense seemed to demand that these men should cry out. But you could really find wounded men who exhibited all the signs of a pleased and contented mood. When thinking of it now it seems strange beyond words. But at the time—I don't know—it did not attract one's wonder. A man with a hole in his arm or his shoulder, or even in the leg below the knee, was often whimsical, comic. "Well, this ain't exactly what I enlisted for, boys. If I'd been told about this in Tampa, I'd have resigned from th' army. Oh yes, you can get the same thing if you keep on going. But I think the Spaniards may run out of ammunition in the course of a week or ten days." Then suddenly one would be confronted by the awful majesty of a man shot in the face. Particularly I remember one. He had a great dragoon moustache, and the blood streamed down his face to meet this moustache even as a torrent goes to meet the jammed log, and then swarmed out to the tips and fell in big slow drops. He looked steadily into my eyes; I was ashamed to return his glance. You understand? It is very curious—all that.

—Stephen Crane, "War Memories," *Anglo Saxon Review*, III (December, 1899), p. 27.

Only in the Far East, which received little advance public attention, had there been serious American preparation for the fighting to come. Assistant Secretary of the Navy Theodore Roosevelt and a few like-minded men understood that a war with Spain might present the opportunities for developing an imperial interest. Roosevelt happened to be in charge of the Department of the Navy when the crisis neared its climax, and he ordered Commodore George Dewey, in command of the Pacific squadron, to attack the

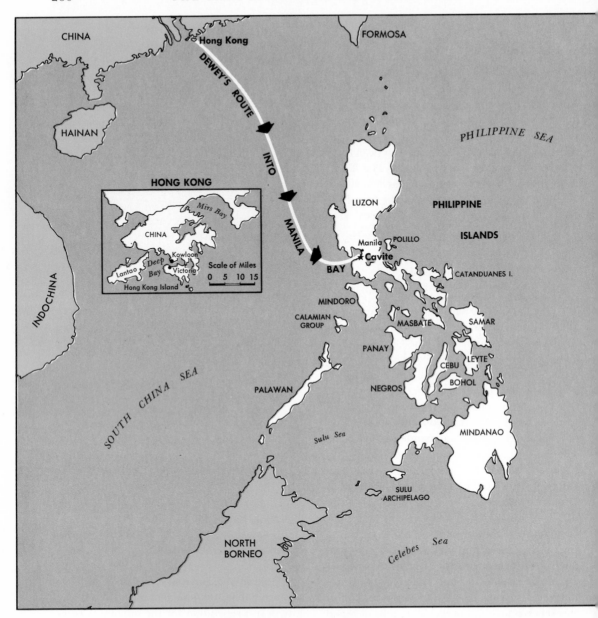

CHINA

HAINAN

INDOCHINA

Hong Kong

FORMOSA

DEWEY'S ROUTE

INTO

MANILA

BAY

PHILIPPINE SEA

LUZON

PHILIPPINE

ISLANDS

Manila
Cavite
POLILLO

CATANDUANES I.

MINDORO

CALAMIAN
GROUP

MASBATE

SAMAR

PANAY

CEBU
LEYTE

NEGROS
BOHOL

PALAWAN

MINDANAO

SOUTH CHINA SEA

Sulu Sea

SULU
ARCHIPELAGO

NORTH
BORNEO

Celebes Sea

HONG KONG

CHINA

Mirs Bay

Kowloon

Lantao
Deep
Bay
Victoria

Hong Kong Island

Scale of Miles
0 5 10 15

THE PHILIPPINES, 1897–1901

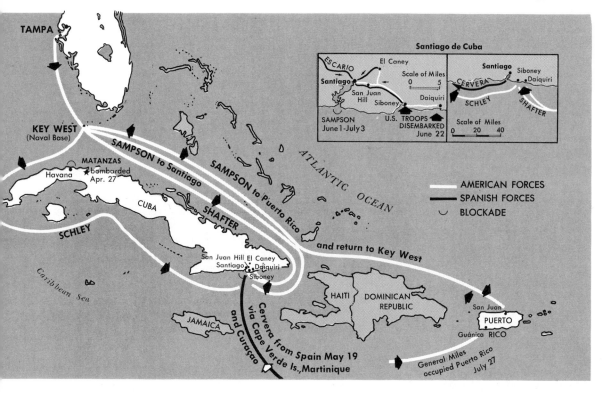

THE WAR IN THE CARIBBEAN, 1898

Spaniards in the Philippines as soon as possible. On May 1 Dewey easily destroyed the enemy fleet in Manila Bay and soon thereafter established a foothold on the island of Luzon.

The main scene of the war, however, was Cuba. On July 3 a fleet of Spanish warships tried to slip out of the harbor at Santiago where they had been blockaded. The waiting American force easily destroyed them. Meanwhile a motley expeditionary army brought over from Florida had invested the city after the battle of San Juan Hill. Santiago soon surrendered, and a small detachment took possession also of Puerto Rico. But there was no effective plan to complete the conquest of Cuba. Fortunately for the United States, no plan was necessary. Without naval power to connect them with their homeland, the Spaniards were no longer able to resist.

The Terms of Peace By an armistice, signed on August 12, 1898, Spain gave up all claims to Cuba and ceded Puerto Rico and Guam to the United States. The fate of the Philippines was left to the formal peace conference. The Treaty of Paris later that year provided for the sale of the Philippines to the United States for $20,-000,000. The great Spanish empire that had endured since the days of Columbus had finally been dissolved.

The war left undecided the question of whether victory would lead to the creation of an American empire. Those who confidently expected that the acquisition of territories as a result of the war would be but an initial expansive step encountered unexpected difficulties. For one thing, the Filipinos were by no means eager simply to exchange masters. Dewey had

Theodore Roosevelt and His Rough Riders on San Juan Hill. Photograph by William Dinwiddie, 1898. (Library of Congress)

encouraged Emilio Aguinaldo, the Filipino leader, to come to Luzon to raise a local revolt against the Spaniards. A movement for independence gained support and led to a clash with the American troops that had occupied Manila. A bitter guerrilla war broke out and dragged on until 1901.

The awareness that a conflict to liberate Cuba had turned into one to make a colony of the Philippines mobilized a determined group of American anti-imperialists in opposition. Some were dubious that the little brown men could ever be more than a burden to the nation. Others insisted that the whole enterprise was contrary to American interests and traditions. Andrew Carnegie, Charles W. Eliot, and Carl Schurz were among those who could not square colonialism with Americanism.

The ratification of the Treaty of Paris in the Senate and McKinley's decisive victory in the election of 1900 were not signs of the victory of imperialist sentiment. Both events were due, in part at least, to the inept political maneuvers of the Democratic standard-bearer, William Jennings Bryan. Bryan, who had supported the war but favored Philippine independence, adopted a complicated strategy. Eager to see peace restored, he did not urge defeat of the treaty but instead planned to campaign to free the Philippines after acquisition by the United States.

Imperialism, however, was not the only issue in the election of 1900. Prosperity had returned

Might and Right, 1900

"Can we not govern colonies?" we are asked. The question is not what we can do, but what we ought to do. This nation can do whatever it desires to do, but it must accept responsibility for what it does. If the Constitution stands in the way, the people can amend the Constitution. I repeat, the nation can do whatever it desires to do, but it cannot avoid the natural and legitimate results of its own conduct. . . . It is of age and it can do what is pleases; it can spurn the traditions of the past; it can repudiate the principles upon which the nation rests; it can employ force instead of reason; it can substitute might for right; it can conquer weaker people; it can exploit their lands, appropriate their property and kill their people; but it cannot repeal the moral law or escape the punishment decreed for the violation of human rights.

— William Jennings Bryan, *Speeches* (New York: Funk & Wagnalls Company, 1909), vol. II, pp. 37–38.

---

and lent substance to the Republican claim to credit for the workingman's full dinner pail and the farmer's rising prices. Bryan was not able to improve on his showing in 1896. But McKinley's victory was far from a clear ratification of the imperialist policy; the future of American expansion was still in doubt when he began his second term in office.

▼

Americans had never been able to separate themselves entirely from the external world, but toward the end of the nineteenth century, the expansion of Europe and the development of imperialism changed the nature of their involvement. A vigorous minority urged the United States to follow the fashion of the other great powers. The Spanish-American War was the expansionists' opportunity.

The imperialists did not realize that the United States was economically and politically unprepared to hold colonies. The great markets for its capital and its manufactures were at home and there would be little gain from overseas possessions. Furthermore, the attempt to use democratic means to govern the dependencies created contradictions in imperialist policy. The war left the United States with the responsibility for governing an empire, a task it soon found uncongenial.

Paperbacks for Further Reading

Julius W. Pratt, *Expansionists of 1898* (Quadrangle Books, Inc.) analyzes the causes of the war with Spain. Walter Millis, *The Martial Spirit* (Compass Books) is a general survey of the war, on which there is also material in H. Wayne Morgan, *America's Road to Empire* (John Wiley & Sons, Inc.). There is a brief account of diplomacy in H. S. Merrill, *Bourbon Leader: Grover Cleveland and the Democratic Party* (Little, Brown & Co.).

A GREAT POWER

70

In the first decade of the twentieth century the United States was a great power. By the indexes of population and wealth, of steel production and strength of communications, it was more than a match for Britain, Germany, or Japan. Yet it did not behave in the predictable fashion of its peers. Its armed forces were small and its colonial empire was not as large as that of Belgium or Portugal. Its actions often puzzled the statesmen forced to take note of it.

The country's internal institutions accounted for the peculiarity of its diplomacy. The President of the United States was not as free to make foreign policy as the Prime Ministers of Britain or France. McKinley, Roosevelt, and Taft each in turn discovered that they needed the acquiescence of a population that was uncertain about the way in which to use power. Americans had no desire for isolation and wished to make their influence felt throughout the world, but they were reluctant to become the masters of colonies. That hesitancy was a handicap in an era when imperialism was the usual policy of a great power.

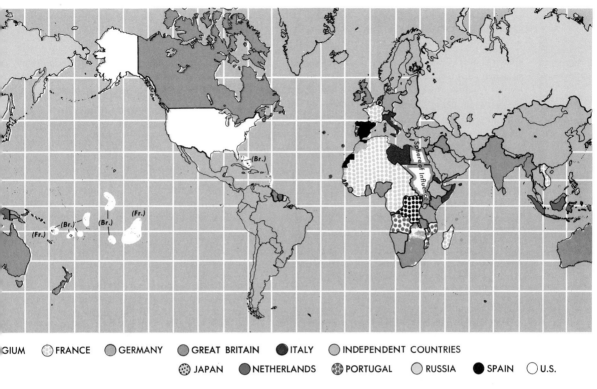

GIUM ○ FRANCE ○ GERMANY ○ GREAT BRITAIN ● ITALY ○ INDEPENDENT COUNTRIES

⊙ JAPAN ● NETHERLANDS ⊛ PORTUGAL ○ RUSSIA ● SPAIN ○ U.S.

THE WORLD IN 1890

The Obligations of Power

A World Power When an assassin's bullet struck down President McKinley and brought Theodore Roosevelt unexpectedly to the White House in 1901, the United States occupied a world situation radically different from that of five years earlier. It had become a great power, with possessions far removed from its continental base.

It had not, however, developed either the apparatus or the frame of mind of a great power. It lacked a professional diplomatic corps. Interested men of wealth like Henry White and party politicians represented the country abroad and shaped policy at home. In 1909 the State Department, reorganized for the first time in forty years, employed only thirty-five officers. The navy had grown in size since 1890 but the stand-

ing army was small and Congressmen and people alike were reluctant to approve any increase in the military establishment. Above all, there was widespread uncertainty about the future role of the country. Would it compete with the other powers in the global struggle for space? Or would its attention revert inward? Or would it seek some as yet unexplored means of making its force felt in world affairs?

Roosevelt's contacts with imperialist circles in the 1890s inclined him toward the first of these choices. His cultural and social interests were broad and he considered himself a political realist who talked softly but carried a big stick. Yet he discovered limits to his capacity for action, and those limits also influenced his successor William Howard Taft.

Canal Diplomacy The Caribbean was central to American policy in the opening decade of

Allan Nevins, *Henry White* (New York, 1930) is a sympathetic biography.

265

HENRY WHITE regarded diplomacy as an activity appropriate to his status in society. In its pursuit he enjoyed a pleasant life abroad while being useful to his country. Born in 1850 into a wealthy Baltimore family, he spent the five years between 1865 and 1870 in Europe. Sojourns in France, Italy, Germany, and England taught him not only languages but also the habits and style of life of the gentry.

In 1879 he married Margaret Stuyvesant Rutherford, who urged him to take up a career. After casting about, White finally requested an appointment from President Arthur, who in 1883 named him secretary of the legation in Vienna. A year later, he moved to London where he remained for almost ten years, standing at the elbow of successive ambassadors who depended upon his advice.

Cleveland replaced him in 1893 with a deserving Democrat, but White was still able to serve unofficially as Secretary of State Olney's agent during the Venezuela crisis. The growth in the volume and importance of diplomatic business after 1898 made a man of White's experience indispensable. He served in the next ten years as first secretary in the delegation to England, then as ambassador to Italy, and finally to France. He also represented the United States at various international conferences.

In 1918, White accompanied President Wilson to Paris as a delegate to the Peace Conference and became an eloquent advocate of the League of Nations, but he failed to win the support of enough Republicans to secure American adhesion. This was the last battle of the respected elder statesman of American diplomacy. He lived in retirement until his death in 1927.

the twentieth century, not only because of its proximity and its association with the Monroe Doctrine but also because it was the passageway between the east and the west coasts of the United States. Since the middle of the nineteenth century, with the development of California, the possibility of a route by way of a crossing in Central America had grown in importance. The plans for a canal acquired additional strategic significance with the increase in the size of the navy. When the influence of Mahan shifted emphasis from gunboats that would guard the coasts to a fleet capable of fighting anywhere around the world, the ability to move easily and quickly from the Atlantic to the Pacific became critical. An American link between the two oceans became a military necessity.

The old Clayton-Bulwer Treaty (1850) that provided for joint Anglo-American control of any future canal was not a serious obstacle. Britain followed through on the logic of its decision in the Venezuela crisis to seek an entente with the United States. In 1901, by the Hay-Pauncefote Treaty (ratified 1902), the English gave up their right to participate in control of the canal. Thereafter they reduced their military establishment in the Caribbean, content to recognize that area as an American sphere of influence.

The two possible routes lay through Nicaragua or through the Isthmus of Panama, which was part of Colombia. A French company, under Ferdinand de Lesseps who had directed construction of the Suez Canal, had secured a concession from the latter country but had failed in its venture. Bankrupt, it now sought some way of salvaging part of its immense investment, and the United States government was the most likely purchaser. The company therefore was eager to have Colombia transfer the authority to build to the Americans.

The Hay-Herrán Treaty of 1903 met its wishes. That agreement authorized the United States to buy the company's assets and build the canal in return for a substantial monetary payment to Colombia. But the Senate of that coun-

Construction of the Panama Canal, 1904–1914. (Brown Brothers)

try refused to ratify, expecting that the French concession would soon expire, at which time Colombia could claim a larger payment from the United States.

Roosevelt was furious at what he considered the corrupt blackmailing tactics of the Colombians. He could have turned to the alternative Nicaragua route, but had he done so, the French company and the local interests on the Isthmus would have suffered. They therefore organized a revolt, proclaimed the independence of Panama, and promptly negotiated the Hay-Bunau-Varilla Treaty with the Americans.

The treaty gave the United States the right to build and fortify the canal, and handed over sovereignty to a zone 10 miles wide along the route in return for $10,000,000 in gold and, after nine years, $250,000 annually. The agree-

ment also established an American protectorate over the new government. The French company received $40,000,000 for its property.

Roosevelt had been no passive bystander during the revolt. American ships off Colón prevented the Colombians from suppressing the uprising. He did not hesitate later to say simply that he took Panama. His action met general approval at home and evoked no surprise abroad. Americans were not reluctant to use force when it was clearly in their interest to do so.

The Roosevelt Corollary Power, however, brought responsibilities that were undefined and

Charles S. Campbell, Jr., *Anglo-American Understanding, 1898–1903* (Baltimore, Md., 1957) discusses the resolution of differences between 1898 and 1903.

Dwight C. Miner, *The Fight for the Panama Route* (New York, 1940) focuses on the Hay-Herrán Treaty.

therefore made the citizens of the United States uneasy. The Monroe Doctrine had enunciated as American policy the rule that no European power was to extend its control over New World territory. But the weak states that ringed the Caribbean were unstable, corrupt, subject to frequent revolutions, and unreliable in international relations. Did the Monroe Doctrine shield them against any sanctions, give them in effect a license to do what they wished, secure in the knowledge that the United States would defend them against retaliation?

The issue first arose with regard to Cuba. The Teller Amendment had assured its independence, but the history of the Dominican and Haitian republics in the nineteenth century had demonstrated that the population might suffer as much from the exploitation of native as of foreign regimes. Those little nations remained sources of disturbance in the region and potential victims of European intervention. It was only reasonable to protect Cuba from the same dangers.

The Platt Amendment to the army appropriation bill of 1901 reaffirmed the independence of Cuba. The island was to revert to the control of its people when they adopted a constitution and signed a formal treaty with the United States. The treaty was to include a guarantee against any foreign colonization, control, or military establishment except for the lease of a naval base to the United States. Cuba was to refrain from borrowing beyond its resources, and the United States reserved the right to intervene to protect the island's independence and to safeguard life, property, and individual liberty. American troops withdrew in 1902 and the required treaty was ratified in 1903.

Twice in the next decade American forces occupied the island. In 1906 the threat of chaos after a national election led to intervention, as did a local revolt in 1911. In each case, the United States withdrew with the restoration of order.

While the Cuban problem unfolded, the issue of European intervention took another

The Roosevelt Doctrine, 1904

If a nation shows that it knows how to act with reasonable efficiency and decency in social and political matters, if it keeps order and pays its obligations, it need fear no interference from the United States. Chronic wrongdoing, or an impotence which results in a general loosening of the ties of civilized society, may in America, as elsewhere, ultimately require intervention by some civilized nation, and in the Western Hemisphere the adherence of the United States to the Monroe Doctrine may force the United States, however reluctantly, in flagrant cases of such wrongdoing or impotence, to the exercise of an international police power. If every country washed by the Caribbean Sea would show the progress in stable and just civilization which, with the aid of the Platt Amendment, Cuba has shown since our troops left the island, and which so many of the republics in both Americas are constantly and brilliantly showing, all questions of interference by this nation with their affairs would be at an end.

—Theodore Roosevelt, Annual Message to Congress, December 6. Congressional Record, 58th Cong., 3d sess., vol. XXXIX, p. 19.

form in Venezuela. Roosevelt then significantly broadened the scope of the Monroe Doctrine. The dictator of that country, Cipriano Castro, had borrowed freely from Europeans and refused either to pay or to arbitrate their claims. Toward the end of 1902 Germany and Britain, later joined by Italy, blockaded the coast and temporarily occupied Venezuelan territory. Roosevelt sympathized with these countries but, fearing that the occupation might become permanent, demanded and secured arbitration (1904). American naval maneuvers off Puerto

"The World's Constable." In this cartoon on the Roosevelt corollary to the Monroe Doctrine, the United States, represented by T. R., is seen as policeman arbitrating disputes among nations. From *Judge*, 1905. (The Granger Collection)

Rico undoubtedly helped persuade the Europeans to withdraw.

Trouble next broke out in the Dominican Republic, which had also defaulted on its debts. Again Roosevelt considered it necessary to forestall European intervention. He authorized an agreement with the Dominicans in 1905 by which the United States collected the customs and allocated a portion to the liquidation of the country's foreign debt. In justifying his actions in Venezuela and the Dominican Republic Roosevelt added a corollary to the Monroe Doctrine. The rule that prevented the great powers from interfering with any nation of the Western Hemisphere obligated the United States to remove the causes of their grievances. Its role was that of a policeman maintaining good order.

The Policeman's Role Actions under the Roosevelt corollary were disturbing to many Americans. Even though they came with the consent of the occupied countries, they involved control of territories that were not part of the United States. Many considered the policeman's role incompatible with their conceptions of freedom, and the Senate delayed its approval of intervention in the Dominican Republic for fully two years. Indeed in 1908 when Liberia, fearful of British and French designs, suggested an American protectorate, the United States preferred to call an international commission to straighten out the African nation's finances.

The steps taken by the United States were far removed from the imperialist practices of other great powers at the time. The United

States did not retain possession of the places its troops entered. Nor did it press negotiations for acquisition of the Danish West Indies (later the Virgin Islands) from Denmark in 1903. Roosevelt at one point thought of intervening in Nicaragua, but instead set to work to persuade it to federate with the other Central American republics. After he and President Díaz of Mexico mediated a local war involving Guatemala, El Salvador, and Honduras in 1906, a conference took the first steps toward establishing such a union. The effort led to nothing because of the persistent internecine rivalries. And a deteriorating situation in Nicaragua induced President Taft to send the marines there in 1911.

The Retreat from Imperialism

It was clear that whatever other involvements it assumed, the United States wanted no more colonies. The Senate had ratified the Treaty of Paris ending the war with Spain by a margin of only one vote, and the country immediately began to discover the cost of its new acquisitions.

The Territories The juridical status of the areas acquired by war was obscure and remained so despite a long line of Supreme Court decisions in the Insular Cases beginning in 1901. Cuba, while the United States occupied it, and the Philippines and Puerto Rico were not incorporated territories in process of becoming states, as were Hawaii, Alaska, Arizona, and New Mexico. Goods from unincorporated territories — there was a reluctance to call them colonies — were subject to the tariff. Yet neither were such places foreign. Congress could, if it wished, make their residents citizens. The Constitution protected the inhabitants insofar as fundamental rights were concerned, but not in such procedural rights as trial by jury. Americans were unwilling either to consider the people of the new possessions equals or to deal with them

candidly as subjects. A tangle of improvisations was the outcome.

The adjustment in each possession was different. Though the Teller Amendment guaranteed the independence of Cuba, the brief occupation of the island was expensive. Before the American forces under General Leonard Wood withdrew, they had begun to put the finances of the island in order, to build schools and railroads, and to control yellow fever. The American connection proved so salutary that it created attractive opportunities for economic development. Investments by citizens of the United States grew, but by 1912 those by natives and Europeans were fully as large. After centuries of stagnation, the island's economy revived, although not enough to produce political stability.

In Puerto Rico, which had become a possession of the United States, there was no discernible movement for independence, and poverty was so great that the island could hardly stand alone. The Foraker Act of 1900 provided for a kind of territorial government with a governor and executive council appointed by the President of the United States and a legislature elected by the people. But it was not clear whether Puerto Rico was permanently integrated with the United States or not, and if it was, how.

The Philippines In the Philippines there was a struggle for independence. The harsh measures used to crush Aguinaldo, who fought on desperately until his capture in 1901, left a queasy feeling among Americans. William Howard Taft had established a civil government in the islands, confirmed by an organic act in 1902. After 1907 the Filipinos elected their own legislature, and the United States spent millions on roads, health, and education. It had gained a military base by the acquisition, but also a ward, expensive to maintain and requiring defense in a remote part of the world. Independence was only a matter of timing.

By the end of Taft's presidency there was a firm resolve against further adventures of the same sort. Within the Western Hemisphere the United States would continue to fulfill the polic-

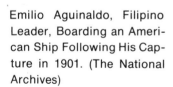

Emilio Aguinaldo, Filipino Leader, Boarding an American Ship Following His Capture in 1901. (The National Archives)

ing function it had assumed. There and elsewhere, however, it would acquire no more colonies. In Asia and Europe, the diplomacy of the book and the dollar would replace that of the sword. Private missionary, educational, and business enterprises would maintain mutually advantageous connections between the United States and the rest of the world.

The Problems of the Pacific

In Asia, the United States was committed to the defense of the Philippines. It also shared a joint protectorate over Samoa with Germany after the withdrawal of the British in 1899. The most extensive American interests, however, were religious and economic, represented by hundreds of missions and sales offices that stretched from Japan to Turkey. Without interference they could perfectly well compete for souls and trade. But the spread of European spheres of influence put Americans under a severe disadvantage. Other countries actively

supported their nationals by giving them special privileges in colonies and protectorates. The United States did not. Therefore Americans, to prevent the spread of colonialism in which they could not participate, sought to maintain the territorial integrity and independence of the feeble states susceptible to conquest.

The Open Door To many Americans China seemed in danger of becoming a victim. Shaken by the loss of the war with Japan in 1895 and governed by corrupt officials, its society was just beginning painfully to modernize. Greedy foreigners, attracted by its wealth, were already exploiting its people and carving out exclusive spheres of influence for themselves.

The future of China worried the British too. Hard-pressed by competition in Africa with the French and in Persia with the Russians, concerned about naval and commercial rivalry with Germany, and tied down in a costly war with the Boers, the English wanted to preserve the status quo in the Orient. In line with their general policy of Anglo-American rapprochement, they preferred to do so in association with the United States. A preliminary British sugges-

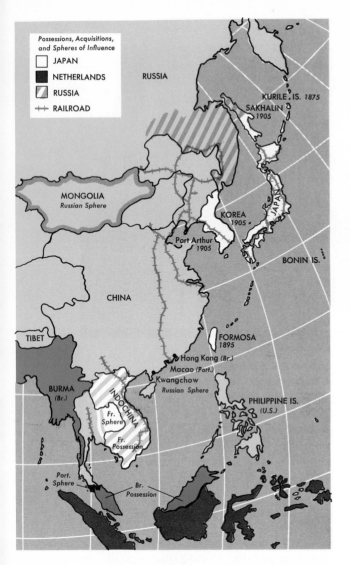

CHINA AND SOUTHEAST ASIA, 1895–1912

Adams almost a century earlier, determined to act independently. In the open-door notes (September 6–November 17, 1899), addressed to Great Britain, Russia, Germany, France, Japan, and Italy, Hay called for equality of tariffs, railroad charges, and port dues in all of China, including the existing spheres of interest.

The Boxer Rebellion Antiforeign violence soon revealed to Americans the desirability of cooperation. Encouraged by the Dowager Empress, the Boxers, a fanatical nationalistic society, rose up to exterminate the intruding Christians. In June and July 1900 the Boxers massacred more than 200 missionaries and laid siege to the legations in Peking. The United States sent 5000 troops to cooperate with Japan and the Europeans in capturing Peking and the surrounding territory.

In order to limit the scope of intervention, Hay, with British encouragement, declared in a circular of July 3, 1900, that it was the policy of the United States to preserve Chinese territorial and administrative integrity and to safeguard the principle of equal and impartial trade in all parts of the Empire. As a result, settlement of the Boxer problem did not lead to the dismemberment of China, although the imperial government was required to punish the responsible officials and to pay a substantial indemnity to the countries that had suffered losses. (The United States returned a large part of its share, which became a fund to support Chinese students in the United States.)

Only Russia was recalcitrant. The troops it had sent into Manchuria remained there, while the Tsar, despite Hay's protests, sought various commercial, mining, and railroad concessions. These broad ambitions led in 1904 to the Russo-Japanese War, during the course of which American sympathies lay with the smaller power. After the initial Japanese victories on land and at sea, Roosevelt offered to mediate. Under his auspices, negotiators from the two powers met in Portsmouth, New Hampshire, and on Sep-

tion for cooperation, in March 1898, evoked no response. President McKinley's attention then was riveted on Cuba.

The acquisition of the Philippines brought China to the forefront of American attention. John Hay, who had become Secretary of State in 1898, was alive to the problem and among his advisers were the American William W. Rockhill and the Englishman Alfred E. Hippisley, who had had long experience in the Orient. Hay knew the British position but, like John Quincy

Tyler Dennett, *John Hay, from Poetry to Politics* (New York, 1934) is an excellent biography.

A deep interest in Asia drew **WILLIAM W. ROCKHILL** into diplomacy. Born in Philadelphia in 1854, he lived much of his life abroad. He studied at the French military academy in St. Cyr, held a commission in the French army, and served for three years as an officer in Algeria. He was thus far from a typical American.

Rockhill had become interested in the Orient while in Paris and had there begun to study the Tibetan language. In time his curiosity about the Far East would also bring him a knowledge of Chinese and Mongolian. The desire to know more about that exotic region undoubtedly attracted him to the American diplomatic service. In 1884 he became secretary of the legation in Peking, and two years later went as chargé d'affaires to Seoul. Between 1888 and 1892 he conducted two expeditions, on behalf of the Smithsonian Institution, to Mongolia and Tibet.

From 1893 to 1909 he was almost continuously in the employ of the State Department as its Asian expert. He drafted Hay's notes on China and went as a special agent to the Far East to help settle the Boxer incident. Between 1909 and 1913 he served in the embassies in Moscow and Constantinople, but his interests remained fixed on the Orient. In 1914 he became personal adviser to President Yüan Shih-k'ai of China but died that year on the way to take up the post.

The Open Door, 1899

Earnestly desirous to remove any cause of irritation and to insure at the same time to the commerce of all nations in China the undoubted benefits which should accrue from a formal recognition by the various powers claiming "spheres of interest" that they shall enjoy perfect equality of treatment for their commerce and navigation within such "spheres," the Government of the United States would be pleased to . . . [secure] assurances from the other interested powers that each within its respective sphere of whatever influence—

First. Will in no way interfere with any treaty port or any vested interest within any so-called "sphere of interest" or leased territory it may have in China.

Second. That the Chinese treaty tariff of the time being shall apply to all merchandise landed or shipped to all such ports as are within said "sphere of interest" (unless they be "free ports"), no matter to what nationality it may belong, and that duties so leviable shall be collected by the Chinese Government.

Third. That it will levy no higher harbor dues on vessels of another nationality frequenting any port in such "sphere" than shall be levied on vessels of its own nationality, and no higher railroad charges over lines built, controlled, or operated within its "sphere" on merchandise belonging to citizens or subjects of other nationalities transported through such "sphere" than shall be levied on similar merchandise belonging to its own nationals transported over equal distances.

—Secretary of State John Hay to Ambassador Andrew D. White. W. M. Malloy, comp., *Treaties, Conventions, International Acts, Protocols and Agreements* (Washington: Government Printing Office, 1910), vol. I, pp. 246–247.

The 9th United States Infantry in the Court of the Forbidden City, Peking, China, During the Boxer Rebellion, 1900. (Library of Congress)

The Russo-Japanese Peace Envoys as Guests of President Roosevelt on Board the Yacht *Mayflower*, Portsmouth, New Hampshire, 1905. From left to right: Count Sergei Witte, Baron Roman Rosen (Russian ambassador to the United States), Theodore Roosevelt, Marquis Jutaro Komura, and Baron Kogoro Takahira (Japanese minister to the United States). (Brown Brothers)

tember 5, 1905, signed a treaty that ended the war.

Japanese-American Relations The Japanese then seemed on the verge of an understanding with the United States that would parallel their formal alliance with Britain (1902). They had made substantial gains at Portsmouth, not only in prestige but also in recognition of their privileged position in Korea. Moreover, by the treaty, Russia ceded to Japan half the island of Sakhalin and agreed to withdraw from Manchuria.

But powerful, although not altogether rational, forces kept disturbing Japanese-American relations. Hostility to the Japanese immigrants in California flared up in 1905, when a corrupt municipal administration in San Francisco used the issue to draw attention away from its own misdeeds. Racist fears conjured up the nightmare of a yellow peril at war with the whole white Christian world. Insulting laws, enacted under the sway of these emotions, confined Japanese children to segregated schools. These measures and later prohibitions of land ownership inflamed the Japanese at home, some of whom came to feel that they had been cheated at Portsmouth: they now insisted that they should have got the whole of Sakhalin and Manchuria as well. Some military and industrial groups thereafter regarded the United States as the chief obstacle to Japanese expansion in the Far East.

Under these circumstances a formal treaty was impossible, although the two governments still wished to cooperate. Three informal executive agreements attempted to ease the difficulties. In the Taft-Katsura memorandum (July 29, 1905) and the Root-Takahira Agreement (November 30, 1908) the United States and Japan undertook to respect each other's positions in the Pacific and to preserve the territorial integrity of China, at the same time recognizing the principle of equal economic opportunity for all nations. Meanwhile, by the Gentlemen's Agreement (1907) President Roosevelt undertook to secure repeal of the offensive California school

Roger Daniels, *The Politics of Prejudice* (Berkeley, Calif., 1962) discusses the anti-Japanese movement.

The Taft-Katsura Understanding, 1905

Secretary Taft observed that Japan's only interest in the Philippines would be, in his opinion, to have these Islands governed by a strong and friendly nation like the United States, and not to have them placed either under the misrule of the natives, yet unfit for self-government, or in the hands of some unfriendly European power. Count Katsura confirmed in the strongest terms the correctness of his views on the point and positively stated that Japan does not harbor any aggressive designs whatever on the Philippines; adding that all the insinuations of the yellow peril type are nothing more or less than malicious and clumsy slanders calculated to do mischief to Japan.

Second, Count Katsura observed that the maintenance of general peace in the extreme East forms the fundamental principle of Japan's international policy. Such being the case, he was very anxious to exchange views with Secretary Taft as to the most effective means for insuring this principle. In his own opinion, the best and in fact the only means for accomplishing the above object would be to form good understanding between the three governments of Japan, the United States and Great Britain which have common interest in upholding the principle of eminence. The Count well understands the traditional policy of the United States in this respect and perceives fully the impossibilities of their entering into a formal alliance of such nature with any foreign nation, but in view of our common interests he could see why some good understanding or an alliance in practice if not in name should not be made between those three nations insofar as respects the affairs in the far East. With

(Continued on next page)

(Continued from preceding page)

such understanding firmly formed general peace in these regions would be easily maintained to the great benefit of all powers concerned. Secretary Taft said that it was difficult, indeed impossible, for the President of the United States of America to enter even to any understanding amounting in effect to a confidential informal agreement, without the consent of the Senate, but that he felt sure that without any agreement at all the people of the United States were so fully in accord with the policy of Japan and Great Britain in the maintenance of peace in the far East that whatever occasion arose appropriate action of the Government of the United States, in conjunction with Japan and Great Britain, for such a purpose could be counted on by them quite as confidently as if the United States were under treaty obligations to take.

Third, In regard to the Korean question, Count Katsura observed that Korea being the direct cause of the war with Russia it is a matter of absolute importance to Japan that a complete solution of the peninsula question should be made as the logical consequence of the war. If left to

herself after the war Korea will certainly draw back to her habit of improvidently entering into any agreements or treaties with other powers, thus resuscitating the same international complications as existed before the war. In view of the foregoing circumstances Japan feels absolutely constrained to take some definite steps with a view to precluding the possibility of Korea falling back into her former condition and of placing Japan again under the necessity of entering upon another foreign war. Secretary Taft fully admitted the justness of the Count's observations and remarked to the effect that, in his personal opinion, the establishment by Japanese troops of a suzerainty over Korea to the extent of requiring that Korea enter into no foreign treaties without the consent of Japan was the logical result of the present war and would directly contribute to permanent peace in the East.

—Memorandum of a Conversation between William Howard Taft and the Prime Minister of Japan, as quoted in D. B. Goebel, *American Foreign Policy* (New York: Holt, Rinehart and Winston, Inc., 1961), pp. 189–190.

---

regulations while the Japanese promised informally to halt the migration of laborers to the United States.

How valid these understandings would prove was uncertain. In 1909 Japan rejected an American proposal for international supervision of Manchurian railroads. However, it did participate with the United States in an International Financial Consortium (1910–1911) by which banking groups from various countries attempted to straighten out Chinese finances. Whether the commitment to preserve the territorial integrity of China had the same meaning in Tokyo as in Washington remained to be seen.

The United States Among the Powers

The power of the United States revealed in the war with Spain created some uneasiness in Europe. The country's ability to muster military and naval strength far beyond its shores, dramatized by the practice cruise of its great white fleet around the world in 1907, showed that it was now a force to be reckoned with. Yet the occasional concern among the statesmen of the Old World about the American peril was due less

The Root-Takahira Agreement, 1908

1. It is the wish of the two Governments to encourage the free and peaceful development of their commerce on the Pacific Ocean.

2. The policy of both Governments, uninfluenced by any aggressive tendencies, is directed to the maintenance of the existing status quo in the region above mentioned, and to the defense of the principle of equal opportunity for commerce and industry in China.

3. They are accordingly firmly resolved reciprocally to respect the territorial possessions belonging to each other in said region.

4. They are also determined to preserve the common interest of all powers in China by supporting by all pacific means at their disposal the independence and integrity of China and the principle of equal opportunity for commerce and industry of all nations in that Empire.

5. Should any event occur threatening the status quo as above described or the principle of equal opportunity as above defined, it remains for the two Governments to communicate with each other in order to arrive at an understanding as to what measures they may consider it useful to take.

—Secretary of State Elihu Root to the Japanese Ambassador. W. M. Malloy, comp., *Treaties, Conventions, International Acts, Protocols and Agreements* (Washington: Government Printing Office, 1910) vol. I, pp. 1046–1047.

The Gentlemen's Agreement, 1907

An understanding was reached with Japan that the existing policy of discouraging the emigration of its subjects of the laboring classes to continental United States should be continued, and should, by cooperation of the governments, be made as effective as possible. This understanding contemplates that the Japanese Government shall issue passports to continental United States only to such of its subjects as are nonlaborers or are laborers who, in coming to the continent, seek to resume a formerly acquired domicile, to join a parent, wife, or children residing there, or to assume active control of an already possessed interest in a farming enterprise in this country; so that the three classes of laborers entitled to receive passports have come to be designated "former residents," "parents, wives, or children of residents," and "settled agriculturists." With respect to Hawaii, the Japanese Government of its own volition stated that, experimentally at least, the issuance of passports to members of the laboring classes proceeding thence would be limited to "former residents" and "parents, wives, or children of residents." The said government has also been exercising a careful supervision over the subject of emigration of its laboring class to foreign contiguous territory.

—Report of the Commissioner-General of Immigration, 1908. Department of Commerce and Labor, *Reports, 1908* (Washington: Government Printing Office, 1909), pp. 221–222.

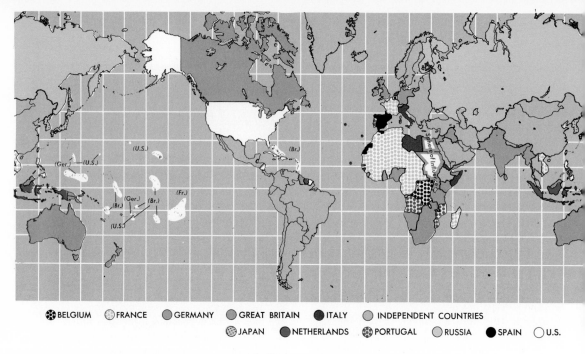

THE WORLD IN 1912

to fear of the United States than to uncertainty about its intentions.

Since 1890, the great powers had been occupied in perfecting the system of alliances by which they expected to protect their imperial and dynastic interests. Britain and Japan, Britain and France, France and Russia, and Germany, Austria, and Italy had aligned themselves in defensive and offensive agreements. The United States stood apart, unwilling to align itself with any group. It participated in some international conferences but without adhering to the rules of the diplomatic game. At The Hague in 1898 and 1907 it worked to create and strengthen a permanent court of international justice, which others did not take seriously. During the Franco-German crisis of 1905 over Morocco, Roosevelt was instrumental in summoning the Algeciras conference, which met the next year to settle the dispute. Much as Roosevelt liked to think of himself as a world statesman, he did not perceive that the English and French used the occasion to reinforce their entente. By 1912, diplomats everywhere knew that the United States had power. They did not know what it wanted to do with it. That uncertainty would plague them in the five critical years that followed.

The United States had grown too fast to play its role adequately. In the nineteenth century the concept of American mission had remained theoretical except at the borders that felt expansionist pressure. But at the end of the nineteenth century, distant parts of the world were no longer far away and the nation, unprepared to exercise its power, faced a future it did not recognize. The imperialist minority, which knew what it wanted, had its way in 1898, but the nation drew back from this policy thereafter. The country remained deeply involved in world affairs, yet uncertain about what its interests were and about how to use its influence.

Paperbacks for Further Reading

A. Whitney Griswold, *The Far Eastern Policy of the United States* (Yale University Press) covers this period. There is an incisive discussion of diplomacy in Howard K. Beale, *Theodore Roosevelt and the Rise of America to World Power* (Collier Books). Richard W. Leopold, *Elihu Root and the Conservative Tradition* (Little, Brown & Co.) also treats these issues.

THE REPUBLICAN
ROOSEVELT

71

The man and the moment coincided when McKinley's death brought Theodore Roosevelt to the presidency in September 1901. In domestic as in foreign affairs, T. R. was a catalyst. Because he had strong views on the economic and social issues before the nation, he dramatized the problems on which decisions were necessary and he focused discussion at points on which action was possible. He did not always have his own way on these matters but he created conditions favorable to moderate legislation. The conflicts he repressed erupted in the administration of his successor, however, and produced a situation in which the country had to make a fundamental choice about the future role of the government in the economy.

As a boy, **THEODORE ROOSEVELT** — asthmatic and nearsighted — strove to impress his father and, despite his later achievement, never shook off the need to prove himself. Born into a good New York family in 1858, Theodore graduated with honors from Harvard and then read law for a while, until he decided he was not really interested in it. History fascinated him then and later, but although in 1882 he published a book on the War of 1812, he decided not to specialize in this field lest he become one of the little men who taught in colleges.

Instead, he entered politics, served in the state assembly, and ran a creditable though unsuccessful race for the mayoralty of New York in 1886. In 1889 President Harrison named him a member of the Civil Service Commission, from which post he went on to become president of the New York City Board of Police Commissioners. In each of these offices he established a reputation as an honest and competent reformer. Meanwhile a succession of books about history and about outdoor life in the West made his name familiar to the public.

At the outbreak of the Spanish-American War, Roosevelt resigned his post as Assistant Secretary of the Navy to serve in the field at the head of a cavalry regiment, the Rough Riders. He came home a hero, maneuvered the Republican party into nominating him for the governorship of New York, and enhanced his reputation in that position.

The state party leaders, anxious to be rid of him, moved him into the vice-presidency, and McKinley's assassination brought him to the White House. Roosevelt loved every minute of his strenuous presidency. He was a world figure and knew that he played a historic role at home and abroad.

He was only fifty when he left office and time rested heavily on his hands. He traveled, hunted, and wrote, but all the time glanced back at Washington, where his successor fell short of his expectations. Personal and political considerations combined to draw Roosevelt back into the Bull Moose campaign in 1912. After 1913, Wilson earned his displeasure even more than Taft had. The United States, T. R. thought, should have entered the war much sooner than it did, and his failure to receive a military command in 1917 disappointed him. He died in 1919 — out of it.

Political Leadership

WELL BEFORE THE ELECTION of 1900, Roosevelt's ebullient personality had made a deep impression on Americans. He had a knack, so natural that it was unconscious, for attracting public attention as an officeholder, as an author, and as a soldier. Widely read, he had opinions on everything and a self-confidence so evident that it erased the initial impression of his stubby figure and squeaky voice. This advocate of the strenuous life threw himself with zest into every conflict, whether for simplified spelling or the exposure of nature fakers. Though he never doubted the correctness of his own position, he was sensitive to the ideas of others and, as a politician, had learned the art of compromising for the sake of what was possible.

In 1900, he accepted the nomination for the vice-presidency reluctantly, aware that this was usually an obscure post, and he was fidgety during his months in that office. When an assassin's bullet made him chief executive, he determined, first, to earn his own election in 1904 and, second, to create a record that would give him a distinguished place in history.

Tactics Roosevelt was intensely partisan. He did not underestimate the strength of the Democrats in opposition, although he was inclined to consider them all scoundrels, as he did anyone who disagreed with him. But he knew that if he could mobilize the support of his own party, he could carry through an effective program. To do so, he had to steer a perilous course between a highly vocal progressive wing, with which the public identified him, and the Old Guard, which controlled the machinery of Congress and whose leaders — Marcus A. Hanna, Nelson W. Aldrich, and Speaker Joseph Cannon — did not trust him. The new President announced cautiously that he would adhere to McKinley's policies and retain his predecessor's cabinet. By doing so, Roosevelt hoped to dispel anxieties about the future that might antagonize any of the elements he planned to bring into his following.

The Election of 1904   At once, however, he began to use the patronage to strengthen his position throughout the country, and he kept his image large in the public eye by vigorous action and even more vigorous pronouncements. By 1904, it was impossible to deny him the Republican nomination, particularly since Hanna, the only conceivable contestant, died shortly before the convention. The Democrats cooperated by nominating Alton B. Parker, a lackluster conservative New York banker, who proved no match for Teddy. Roosevelt carried every state outside the South and won by a wide popular majority. He then had the mandate he sought. Satisfied, he announced that he would not stand for election again and returned to the tasks he had begun in his first term.

Roosevelt's Domestic Policy

The Square Deal   Roosevelt's objective was a square deal for all. The government, he thought, was fundamentally a referee in the great game in which men played to win. As such, its first obligation was to be fair so that no competitor could violate the rules or gain an unfair advantage over his antagonists. Each person deserved

an opportunity to do his best and each was to be judged on his own merits.

An incident early in his first term illustrated the manner in which he applied the concept of the square deal. In 1901 the President invited Booker T. Washington to dine with him in the White House; Roosevelt saw no reason why he should not recognize a Negro leader as he would any other person whose support he sought. When the news touched off a wave of hysterical racist protest in the South, the President defended his action. But he did not repeat it. Thereafter he conferred informally with Washington. He did what was proper, but only after weighing the costs, and he rarely went beyond the line of what was politically feasible.

Roosevelt was readiest to sponsor reforms that were not controversial. Journalistic exposures of the meat-packing industry, particularly in Upton Sinclair's novel *The Jungle* (1906), created a wave of popular sentiment in favor of government inspection. Since the larger and more respectable packers were anxious for standards that would protect them against less scrupulous competitors, it was not difficult to secure the enactment in 1906 of the Pure Food and Drug Act and of the Meat Inspection Act. The two measures aimed to protect consumers against adulterated and unsafe processed foods and patent medicines. Characteristically, Roosevelt evaded a threatened battle over the side issue of the costs of inspection. Yielding to the packers' protests against a fee levied on them, he persuaded Congress to triple the appropriation so that the job could be done without a fight.

The problems of labor were more difficult. Roosevelt was far from wishing to pamper the workers, but he thought they too deserved a square deal and he knew that some employers refused it to them. His intervention in the coal strike of 1902 was at first motivated by concern about the shortage of fuel as winter approached. In the effort to be impartial, he refused the owners' request for Federal troops to police the mines and urged labor to moderate its demands. But by the time he got J. P. Morgan to persuade

Booker T. Washington with President Theodore Roosevelt at Tuskegee Institute. (Brown Brothers)

Meat Inspection, 1906

For the inspection of meat to be sold in the city and state the whole force in Packingtown consisted of three henchmen of the local political machine! And shortly afterward one of these, a physician, made the discovery that the carcasses of steers which had been condemned as tubercular by the government inspectors, and which therefore contained ptomaines, which are deadly poisons, were left upon an open platform and carted away to be sold in the city; and so he insisted that these carcasses be treated with an injection of kerosene—and was ordered to resign the same week! So indignant were the packers that they went farther, and compelled the mayor to abolish the whole bureau of inspection; so that since then there has not been even a pretence of any interference with the graft. There was said to be two thousand dollars a week hushmoney from the tubercular steers alone; and as much again from the hogs which had died of cholera on the trains, and which you might see any day being loaded into box-cars and hauled away to a place called Globe, in Indiana, where they made a fancy grade of lard.

—Upton Sinclair, *The Jungle* (New York: Grossett & Dunlap, Inc., 1906), pp. 113–114.

the mineowners to compromise, he had gained additional insight into the hardships of the workers and the stubbornness of the industrialists.

In his second term, therefore, he sponsored a variety of measures to manifest the concern of the Federal government with the lot of the people who toiled in the mills and the mines. He asked for an investigation of child labor and secured a law providing for compensation for accidents on common carriers. An act of Congress in 1908 was the first step toward regulating the hours of trainmen on interstate railways. The common conception of what the government could do was still narrow but was beginning to widen.

Trust Busting Roosevelt was far less decisive when it came to the most critical economic issue of the time, that of industrial integration. He took office as the combination movement reached its peak. Popular sentiment against the trusts had risen to fever heat and the muckrakers kept it glowing. Professional people, small businessmen, and farmers—numerically the weightiest elements in the Republican party—feared that the Sherman act was inadequate and demanded that something more be done. Roosevelt's public utterances frequently echoed this sentiment. The abuses of shortsighted industrialists revolted him, and he had no desire to fight their battle. On the other hand, he opposed government ownership and considered it unrealistic to attempt to break the great business aggregations into smaller units. Insofar as they strengthened the economy, he was willing to tolerate the trusts, provided they were subject to strict oversight so that they operated in the public interest.

Publicity, in his view, was more helpful than prosecution. A Bureau of Corporations in the Department of Commerce and Labor (1903)

received the task of collecting information about the large enterprises in the hope that exposure would secure voluntary compliance with the antitrust law on the part of industrialists. Yet Roosevelt was willing to invoke the law when necessary. He brought suit against the Northern Securities Company, a mammoth effort to unite the railways of the Northwest under James J. Hill and J. P. Morgan. The Supreme Court in 1904 ordered the company dissolved. The judges held that although a holding company was not itself a conspiracy, the process of forming one was illegal if the intent was to restrain trade. The decision was the signal for further prosecutions. In the next four years, T. R.'s administration secured indictments against twenty-five trusts, including those in beef, oil, and tobacco. Yet Roosevelt did not attack indiscriminately. In 1907, when he feared a deepening of the financial crisis, he acquiesced in Morgan's acquisition of the Tennessee Coal and Iron Company for United States Steel, a move that reduced competition in the steel industry.

Railroad Regulation It was not enough, in the case of railroads, simply to proceed against efforts at monopoly. The issue of regulation had remained alive despite the Interstate Commerce Act. The Commission created by that measure

---

T. R.'s Trust Policy, ca. 1904

"Th' trusts," says he to himself, "are heejous monsthers built up be th' inlightened intheprise iv th' men that have done so much to advance progress in our beloved counthry," he says. "On wan hand I wud stamp thim undher fut; on th' other hand not so fast."

—"Mr. Dooley," as quoted in E. E. Morison, ed., *The Letters of Theodore Roosevelt* (Cambridge, Mass.: Harvard University Press, 1951), p. 199 n.

Hans B. Thorelli, *The Federal Antitrust Policy* (Baltimore, Md., 1955) deals competently with the problem until 1903.

Gabriel Kolko, *The Triumph of Conservatism* (New York, 1963) presents a challenging interpretation of the economic issues of this period.

"The Lion-Tamer." Theodore Roosevelt is portrayed bringing into line the trusts in beef, oil, steel, coal, sugar, and copper and ready to take on any more as they appear on Wall Street. Cartoon by W. A. Rogers, *Harper's Weekly*, 1904. (Culver Pictures)

was without any real power, and it had been able to do little to curb the abuses of the carriers. The grievances of the 1880s and 1890s were still unredressed in 1901.

Two laws passed with Roosevelt's support were the first steps toward reform. The Elkins Act (1903) in effect forbade rebates by ordering the railroads not to depart from their published rates. The carriers had no objections for they hoped the measure would shield them from the piratical practices of large shippers. The President doggedly used the law to prosecute corporations that accepted rebates. A fine of $300,000 imposed on the American Sugar Refining Company showed the seriousness of the government's intentions.

Yet the highly competitive atmosphere encouraged evasion. Each firm was out to get what it could for itself, and if rebates were illegal, it could bargain for other indirect favors. Moreover, the decisive power to set rates still remained in the hands of the individual roads. The struggle between progressives, who wanted strict

government regulation, and conservatives, who were satisfied with the *status quo*, continued after passage of the Elkins Act.

Roosevelt mediated. By hinting that he might push the extreme progressive demands, he won the backing of Senator Nelson W. Aldrich and other Old Guard Republicans who needed his support on the tariff. At the same time Senator Robert M. La Follette and his progressive allies came along because they realized they would get no law at all without the President's approval.

The Hepburn Act (1906), which resulted from these maneuvers, was a compromise. It extended the Interstate Commerce Commission's jurisdiction to cover storage facilities, pipelines, express companies, and refrigerated and sleeping cars. More important, it permitted the Commission to set maximum rates. The Commission was not, however, allowed to establish its own valuation of railroad properties. In judging what charges would produce a fair return on investment, it therefore had to accept the carriers' valuations. Furthermore, the courts could entertain appeals — on procedural grounds — from the Commission's decisions and delay enforcement by injunctions. These were concessions to the conservatives. But the act did not extend the scope of the judicial review to substantive issues, and it put the burden of proof on the carriers — concessions to the progressives.

Neither the Elkins Act nor the Hepburn Act was very radical. Both aimed at equitable competitive conditions and both satisfied the more reasonable railroads and shippers who accepted regulation as a means of assuring fair terms of rivalry. Yet these were steps toward a more active involvement of the Federal government in the control of the economy.

The Tariff and Conservation   In some matters Roosevelt considered discretion the better part of valor. He knew, for instance, that the tariff had developed into a maze of provisions for serving special interests and that it had little economic justification. The Dingley Tariff, enacted in 1897 in the full flush of Republican victory, contained the highest rates theretofore imposed, but it remained in force while Roosevelt held office. He preferred a pattern of reciprocity, by which the United States would lower its trade barriers in return for similar action by other powers, but he was unwilling to risk the political turmoil a change would have involved. Instead he used the threat of revision as a club to bring Congressmen in line behind his other measures.

Roosevelt's conservation efforts were somewhat more successful although he avoided head-on collisions with the opposition. The preservation of the country's natural resources was close to his heart. For him, as for many of his countrymen, conservation had two aspects — efficient utilization of the nation's soil, minerals, and forests and protection of wildlife and scenic areas. While he judiciously labored for both, he did not stir up the speculators who favored quick and easy exploitation.

A succession of conferences publicized his position and the legislation he requested did not damage existing vested interests. The Newlands

The Creed of Conservation, 1908

We are coming to recognize as never before the right of the Nation to guard its own future in the essential matter of natural resources. In the past we have admitted the right of the individual to injure the future of the Republic for his own present profit. In fact there has been a good deal of a demand for unrestricted individualism, for the right of the individual to injure the future of all of us for his own temporary and immediate profit. The time has come for a change. As a people we have the right and the duty, second to none other but the right and duty of obeying the moral law, of requiring and doing justice, to protect ourselves and our children against the wasteful development of our natural resources, whether that waste is caused by the actual destruction of such resources or by making them impossible of development hereafter.

—President Theodore Roosevelt to the Governors' Conference. *Proceedings of a Conference of Governors in the White House Washington, D.C., May 13–15, 1908* (Washington: Government Printing Office, 1909), p. 10.

Reclamation Act (1902) set aside funds from the sale of public lands for purposes of irrigation and established the Reclamation Service in the Department of the Interior. The President also increased the size of the national forests from 43,000,000 to 194,000,000 acres, which he put under the United States Forest Service. Characteristically, when an amendment to the agricultural appropriation bill in 1907 forbade him to add to the size of the national forests, he did not make an issue of the matter but hastened to complete the planned increase before the bill became law.

The Taft Administration

Roosevelt left office on a wave of popular approval, although his actual power had faded during his last year in office. He had satisfied the progressives without alienating the conservatives, and his genuine domestic and foreign achievements created a firm public impression of a man who got things done. Furthermore, he had been able to designate his own successor, Secretary of War William Howard Taft, the long-time trouble shooter, for whose abilities he had tremendous respect. The Democrats once again nominated Bryan. The Republicans held the White House, although not by as large a margin as in 1904. Taft announced that he intended to follow Roosevelt's policies, and the former President left to hunt big game and travel abroad, confident that the country was in good hands.

Roosevelt's Heir Taft was able, but differences in personality and in the political context frustrated his intentions to follow Roosevelt's policy. Amiable and reasonable, Taft nevertheless was unable to project the authority of his office. Not taken seriously as a leader, he was usually content to allow Congress to go its own way without undue pressure.

The times called for a forceful President even more than they had before 1908. Conservatives and progressives alike had exhausted the willingness to compromise. The Republican Old Guard controlled Congress and was in no mood to be managed as it had been by Teddy. At the same time, progressive sentiment was rising. In the House George W. Norris of Nebraska and in the Senate Robert M. La Follette of Wisconsin demanded forceful action. They and their allies had all along been suspicious of Roosevelt, but knowing his popularity had feared to attack him. His heir did not enjoy the same immunity. The

Henry Pringle, *Life and Times of William Howard Taft* (New York, 1939) is an excellent biography.

Kenneth W. Hechler, *Insurgency* (New York, 1940) is an adequate analysis of the movement in Congress.

The jovial appearance of **WILLIAM HOWARD TAFT** belied his character. He was irritable, vacillating, and a confirmed procrastinator, and these traits handicapped him as a political leader despite his integrity and his administrative ability.

Born into a prominent Cincinnati family in 1857, he studied at Yale and entered a career in the law. In 1887 he was appointed to the supreme court of Ohio and three years later became Solicitor General of the United States. His ability earned him a place on the circuit court, where he served for eight years.

In 1900 Taft went to the Philippines to be head of the civil government. He helped pacify the islands and put their institutions on a sound basis. The excellence of his performance induced President Roosevelt to call him back in 1904 to serve as Secretary of War. In the next four years Taft proved to be the trouble shooter of the administration, so T. R. considered him best qualified to step into the presidency in 1909.

Taft was conscientious but he lacked the imagination to cope with the rising demands of the progressives or to satisfy his predecessor. Above all, Taft believed in the sanctity of the law, no matter what the human costs of sustaining it. During the Pullman strike he deplored the fact that the military had killed only six of the mob. That was hardly enough to make an impression! Roosevelt's proposal for the recall of judicial decisions horrified Taft and ended any chance of reconciliation between the two men. The division between them threw the election of 1912 to Wilson.

Between 1913 and 1921 Taft taught law at Yale. He then became Chief Justice of the United States Supreme Court, taking a moderate position between its more liberal and more conservative wings. He retired in 1930 and died the same year.

William Howard Taft (1857–1930) with his sons Charles, left, and Robert, the future Senator. Photographed in 1909. (The Granger Collection)

progressives were impatient with the kind of mediation that Roosevelt had practiced, and would have been restive even had Taft possessed the agility to imitate his predecessor. Those who had held back under T. R. were ready to unleash their pent-up criticisms against Taft when he took office. The choices Roosevelt had dexterously avoided, his successor would have to make.

Economic Issues Taft's economic policy in most instances measured up to progressive standards. He initiated twice as many antitrust cases as Theodore Roosevelt had, including some against the very largest corporations. A suit directed against the Standard Oil Company led to its dissolution in 1911 and gave the Supreme Court the opportunity to enunciate a principle that T. R. had earlier stated somewhat differently. In that case and in a judgment against the American Tobacco Company the same year, the Court held that all combinations which had the effect of reducing competition were not in themselves illegally in restraint of trade. Some were tolerable because they arose out of the desire for

"Baby, Kiss Papa Good-by." Theodore Roosevelt is seen leaving his policies to Taft as he sets out from the White House. Cartoon from *Puck*, February 24, 1909. (The Granger Collection)

more efficient operations. But others were illegal because they achieved their dominant positions through rebates, unfair price war, and other predatory practices that revealed an intent to monopolize the market. In practice, this Rule of Reason permitted public action against offensive trusts without excluding every form of economic combination. The crucial question was, who was to administer the Rule. Taft, like the Court, believed that the decision should lie in the hands of the judiciary. Roosevelt preferred that it rest with the executive through the Bureau of Corporations.

Congress under Taft carried forward the still unfinished business of railroad regulation, although he did not take as active a role in formulating legislation as Roosevelt had. The Mann-Elkins Act (1910) established the jurisdiction of the Interstate Commerce Commission over all communications and strengthened it by allowing it to suspend rates. The old provision against differentials in charges for long and short hauls was also confirmed. In addition, Taft sponsored a variety of measures that carried Roosevelt's square deal further. He extended the merit system in the Civil Service and called for an income tax. He was responsible for setting up a Children's Bureau in the Department of Labor. And he approved the creation of parcel post and postal saving systems, both desired by the rural population.

Banking and the Tariff Good intentions, however, led Taft to a dead end when it came to banking and the tariff. To relieve the financial stringency caused by the panic of 1907, the Aldrich-Vreeland Currency Act (1908) had loosened the conditions under which banks could issue notes and had authorized the appointment of a National Monetary Commission to recommend reform of the currency system. That body suggested that a central bank controlled by financiers would give the currency elasticity. Congress refused to enact the Aldrich bill (1912), based on the Commission's report, and left the impression that the President had wished to hand control of the nation's money over to the bankers.

Nor was Taft able to engage in the evasive maneuvers that carried Roosevelt to safety through the tricky tariff issue. Progressive criticism of the excessively high rates of the Dingley Act persuaded Taft to call a special session of Congress in 1909. Like the progressives, he hoped for downward revision. The House bill made some reductions and provided for an inheritance tax to offset the expected loss of revenue. The Old Guard went to work in the Senate, however. As in the past, each economic interest lobbied to protect its own products. No one stated the case for reduction forcibly. The sum of amendments reversed the character of the bill that had left the House and the inheritance disappeared. The Payne-Aldrich Act set higher rates than the Dingley Act, and when Taft signed it he gained the enmity of the progressives.

The impression that Taft had sold out to the Old Guard persisted despite his constructive action in creating a tariff board to provide accurate knowledge about the effects of the duties. Nor could he shake off his hard luck in this matter. In 1911 he negotiated a reciprocity agreement with Canada which antagonized the Western farmers, who feared the competition from imported grains, and which bore no results because the Canadians in the end rejected it.

Conservation The same ill fortune plagued Taft when it came to conservation policy. True, he created a Bureau of Mines and set aside substantial forest and oil reserves. But one incident, not very important in itself, earned him a reputation as a traitor to the cause.

Secretary of the Interior Richard A. Ballinger had leased some water-power sites in the Northwest and some coal lands in Alaska to private interests. He may have shown poor judgment in making these arrangements, but there was no suggestion of corruption about them. Nevertheless, Gifford Pinchot, chief of the Bureau of Forestry in the Department of Agriculture and personally close to Theodore Roosevelt, attacked the leases as unwise and hinted at corruption. Pinchot refused to let the issue die after the President exonerated Ballinger. Taft's sense of propriety as well as the nature of the case led him to support Ballinger and to dismiss Pinchot. The result was an outcry from the progressives which lasted through the election of 1912.

Taft's alienation from the progressives cast a shadow over his political future, for their strength in both parties continued to rise through his term in office. They made impressive gains in the Congressional and state elections of 1910, whether running as Republicans or Democrats, and pressed their demands with increasing vigor. In 1910 and 1911, Norris and other Republicans in the House of Representatives rebelled against Speaker Joe Cannon, complaining against his control of committee assignments. As a result he was stripped of that power and the committees were made elective. Although in the long run the outcome was a seniority system no more progressive than the one it replaced, the uprising showed the strength of the forces that could be mobilized against the Old Guard, with which Taft in 1912 was identified.

Gifford Pinchot, *Breaking New Ground* (New York, 1947) gives his side of the controversy.

The Speaker's Power, 1910

After months of earnest discussion, investigation and deliberation, this body of men came to the conclusion that no change would be of any real or permanent value to the country that did not take from the Speaker the wonderful influences over the individual members that his office gave him. It was well known that members thought more of an important committee assignment than of anything connected with their official life. The Speaker, under existing rules, had the sole power of making such appointments, and by virtue thereof he controlled to a great extent the political destiny of every member. By this authority he rewarded the faithful and punished those who refused to obey.

This, then, was the secret of the Speaker's power. It enabled him to influence the individual member, to intimidate the Committee, to control the House, to hold up the President, and to defy the country. The insurgents decided that whatever changes in the rules might be desirable, the one that should take away from the Speaker the authority to appoint the standing committees was vital and should be insisted upon.

—George W. Norris, "The Secret of His Power," *La Follette's Weekly Magazine*, II (January 8, 1910), p. 8.

▼

Taft's failure was more than personal. He lacked the popular support and the tactical skill of Theodore Roosevelt and so was unable to evade the thorny political decisions for which the progressive idea called. But his task was also more difficult. Roosevelt's administration had begun to explore the problems of bringing Federal action to bear upon the economic and social dilemmas of industrialization. Roosevelt could follow a middle course, antagonizing neither the conservatives nor the progressives. Taft had to face those problems squarely. By the time he entered the White House, progressives had had more than a decade of experience with these issues in the states and municipalities as well as in Congress. They were ready to make demands that were not as susceptible to compromise as in 1901. Even a more expert politician than Taft would have had a hard time avoiding an alignment with either the progressives or the Old Guard. The campaign of 1912 would reveal more clearly still how much progressive sentiment had grown.

Paperbacks for Further Reading

Henry F. Pringle, *Theodore Roosevelt* (Harvest Books); John M. Blum, *The Republican Roosevelt* (Atheneum Publishers); George E. Mowry, *Theodore Roosevelt and the Progressive Movement* (American Century Series); and William H. Harbaugh, *The Life and Times of Theodore Roosevelt* (Collier Books) present varying interpretations of T. R. Richard W. Leopold, *Elihu Root and the Conservative Tradition* (Little, Brown & Co.) deals with the problems of the Roosevelt and Taft administrations. Upton Sinclair, *The Jungle* (Signet Classics) gives a good indication of the background of the Pure Food and Drug Act.

THE DECISIONS
OF 1912

72

The presidential election of 1912 bore striking similarities to that of 1860. A split in a major party produced an exciting four-cornered campaign and projected a new and relatively unknown personality to the center of the political scene. Each election followed a decade of agitation with the future of American society at stake. The outcome in 1912 did not lead to a war as had that in 1860, but it did go a long way toward shaping national institutions in the twentieth century.

The campaign of 1912 hinged upon two decisions. The first, made by Roosevelt before the election, depended on the belief that the developing progressive movement had enlisted the support of a majority of Americans. The second decision, made by the voters during the election, clarified the issues and pointed the direction in which progressivism would evolve in the future.

ROBERT M. LA FOLLETTE was a progressive in whom the pioneer sense remained strong. He was born in 1855 in a log cabin in Dane County, Wisconsin, and endured a youth of hardships. He worked his way through the state university, studied law, and began to practice in Madison in 1880.

That same year he was elected district attorney of Dane County and began a career in politics. A skilled speaker, he became well known in his region, which sent him to the United States House of Representatives in 1884. He was twice re-elected. In 1890, however, he met defeat in a Democratic landslide touched off by resentment at the high tariff of that year and by Republican sponsorship of a state law requiring all schools to use English in teaching the most important subjects.

In the next decade, La Follette seemed to have reached a dead end. The Republican leaders had lost interest in him and he failed in his efforts to gain a state office. But his political ideas were maturing and he was building a following. When he became governor in 1901, he had a program ready. He had become convinced of the need for the primary, for the taxation and regula-

tion of corporations, and for the use of experts in government. He vigorously fought for these goals against the opposition of conservatives in the legislature and established Wisconsin's reputation as a progressive state.

In 1905 he went to the United States Senate, where he remained for the rest of his life, fighting the same battles on the Federal level. He had become suspicious of Theodore Roosevelt's tendency to compromise when the Republican Convention, the year before, had seated a conservative delegation in place of the progressive group La Follette headed. The designation of Taft in 1908 seemed a step backward, and the events of the next four years strengthened La Follette's resolution to lead an independent progressive movement. Ironically, the outcome was the nomination of Roosevelt. La Follette thereafter continued to labor for reform in the Senate, collaborating with Wilson for a time. He opposed the declaration of war in 1917, however, and voted against the League of Nations and the World Court. In 1924 he finally achieved the candidacy for the presidency on a third-party ticket that gained about 5,000,000 votes. He died a year later.

The Republican Division

THE ELECTION OF 1912 became critical when the Republican party split. The two-party alignment had grown steadily stronger after the Civil War. Since the Populist challenge of 1892 no significant political force had emerged outside the ranks of the two major parties. Furthermore, the four presidential elections after that date had shown a solid Republican majority. Only internal dissent cast doubt upon the outcome of the campaign of 1912.

The Progressive Revolt The Republican progressives in Congress, emboldened by success in the election of 1910, raised the first open challenge to Taft's bid for re-election. They felt that their moment had come and thought that they had little to fear by way of retaliation from the easygoing President. In January 1911 they formed the National Progressive Republican League with the understanding that it would work within the GOP framework for the nomination of Senator Robert M. La Follette.

Belle and Fola La Follette, *Robert M. La Follette* (New York, 1953) is a full biography.

La Follette began his grass-roots campaign in December 1911. In a succession of long, carefully prepared speeches, he called for a more vigorous antitrust policy as well as for the primary, the initiative, referendum, and recall, and a comprehensive roster of other progressive objectives. La Follette, however, collapsed under the strain of his exertions. On February 12, 1912, during a speech attacking the money trust in Philadelphia, he suffered a nervous breakdown and was no longer in the running.

Roosevelt in the Field   At this point Theodore Roosevelt's intentions acquired the utmost importance. The organization created by La Follette was adrift. The ex-President was better able to capture it than anyone else. Very quickly he was convinced that it was his duty to do so.

In part, the decision was personal. Roosevelt had tired of big game hunting and of desultory travel around the world. He had neither the patience nor the zest for the writing that had occupied him before he entered the White House. He was still young—only fifty-four in 1912—and unable to reconcile himself to the fact that his career was over. An itchiness for action drew him back into the political arena.

Furthermore, his resentment against Taft had been steadily rising. Opinionated and emotional, Roosevelt was perhaps bound to judge any successor harshly. But differences over patronage and pique over the outcome of the Ballinger-Pinchot controversy brought his anger to the boil. Taft's action in initiating a prosecution of the United States Steel Corporation only intensified T. R.'s conviction that the country was in improper hands. After all, Roosevelt himself had assured J. P. Morgan that acquisition of Tennessee Coal and Iron would lead to no reprisals.

The New Nationalism   Less personal reasons also induced Roosevelt to try to recapture the mantle of leadership he had passed on to his friend in 1908. Convinced that Taft could not win, Roosevelt feared that victory would then go to William Jennings Bryan or to some other wild Democrat, to the infinite damage of the Repub-

Roosevelt on Taft, 1910

For a year after Taft took office, for a year and a quarter after he had been elected, I would not let myself think ill of anything he did. I finally had to admit that he had gone wrong on certain points; and I then also had to admit to myself that deep down underneath I had all along known he was wrong, on points as to which I had tried to deceive myself, by loudly proclaiming to myself, that he was right. I went out of the country and gave him the fullest possible chance to work out his own salvation. . . .

I was able to hold the Republican party in power only because I insisted on a steady advance, and dragged them along with me. Now the advance has been stopped, and whether we blame the people on the one side, or the leaders on the other, the fact remains that we are in a very uncomfortable position.

—Theodore Roosevelt to Henry Cabot Lodge, May 5, from *Selections from the Correspondence of Theodore Roosevelt and Henry Cabot Lodge, 1884–1918* (New York: Charles Scribner's Sons, 1925), vol. II, p. 380.

lic. In that view of the matter, Teddy was fighting not so much against his former friend as against a potential and dangerous Democratic President.

Finally, since he had left office, Roosevelt had developed views of the presidency and of the important economic issues before the nation that had been only latent with him while he occupied the White House. He was seeing less of old advisers like Elihu Root, who was now in the Taft entourage. T. R. had new friends and discussions with them provided a novel context for his ideas. Wealthy men like George W. Perkins, a Morgan partner and formerly head of New York Life Insurance Company, Frank A. Munsey, the newspaper publisher, and T. C. Du Pont,

GEORGE W. PERKINS was a progressive reared in a business environment. Born in Chicago in 1862, he had a middle-class upbringing and aimed to follow his father's line, life insurance. At the age of fifteen, he left school to take a job as office boy for the New York Life Insurance Company and remained in the employ of that firm for more than twenty-five years.

Perkins rose steadily in the ranks of the bureaucracy until he became president. He transformed the agency system, providing more centralized controls and greater incentives for the company's employees. He also broadened its activities overseas. In his years with the company, it gained steadily in strength and in resources.

The investment decisions he had to make brought him into contact with bankers, whom he impressed with his skill, shrewdness, and amiability. In 1901 he joined J. P. Morgan and Company and thereafter participated in forming the International Harvester, the International Mercantile Marine, and the Northern Securities companies, each an intricate combination. He also helped reorganize United States Steel.

These experiences convinced him of the value of the corporation as an instrument of cooperation to replace the outmoded and wasteful competition of the past. He therefore found himself in accord with the ideas that Herbert Croly and Theodore Roosevelt were also expressing. Perkins left J. P. Morgan and Company in 1910 in order to devote himself to implementing his views, and in 1912 he became an enthusiastic supporter of the Progressive party.

Thereafter, he performed occasional services for the government and for philanthropic organizations, and in 1916 helped bring many progressives back into the Republican fold. He died in 1920.

Combination in the Public Interest, 1911

The effort to restore competition as it was sixty years ago, and to trust for justice solely to this proposed restoration of competition, is just as foolish as if we should go back to the flintlocks of Washington's Continentals as a substitute for modern weapons of precision. The effort to prohibit all combinations, good or bad, is bound to fail, and ought to fail; when made, it merely means that some of the worst combinations are not checked and that honest business is checked. Our purpose should be, not to strangle business as an incident of strangling combinations, but to regulate big corporations in thoroughgoing and effective fashion, so as to help legitimate business as an incident to thoroughly and completely safeguarding the interests of the people as a whole.

— Theodore Roosevelt, "The Trusts, the People and the Square Deal," *The Outlook.* XCIX (November 18, 1911), p. 653.

the powder manufacturer, argued that the day of free competition and the individual entrepreneur was over. Only the great corporation could organize modern business effectively. The whole society would benefit so long as these entities behaved in an orderly responsible manner. Roosevelt had also read Herbert Croly's *Promise of American Life* (1909), which made a similar point but gave it a somewhat different emphasis. The great corporation was the key agency of modern times but it was to serve as an instrument for attaining goals set by the state. Both variations were extensions of positions that Roosevelt had taken pragmatically as President.

John A. Garraty, *Right-Hand Man: The Life of George W. Perkins* (New York, 1960) is an adequate account.

There is a good provocative discussion of Croly in Charles Forcey, *Crossroads of Liberalism* (New York, 1961).

"The New Nationalism. Do you follow me, Sam?" Theodore Roosevelt in a contemporary cartoon from *Life*. (Culver Pictures)

Although many people were discussing the importance of the corporation in modern life, no responsible politician had given it adequate recognition. The antitrust clamor that accompanied the usual expressions of the progressive idea was drowning out the most valuable answer to the nation's problems. Roosevelt believed that he alone could make the people listen. In August 1910, in a speech widely interpreted as an attack on Taft, he issued a call for a New Nationalism. On this platform he would fight in the two years that followed.

The theme was the use of Hamiltonian means—a strong directing government—for Jeffersonian ends—the common welfare. In that light, the trust-busting days were over. Large organizations were a necessary and useful part of American life if controlled by a government whose power increased correspondingly. Therefore, the babbling of the muckrakers was as dangerous as the stubbornness of the intransigent industrialists. The trusts were neither to be smashed nor yielded to. The nation could safely encourage their development and harness them to socially useful purposes through the power of the Federal government. This conviction animated Roosevelt's activities in 1912, first in the quest for the Republican nomination and then in the campaign for the presidency as an independent.

The Decision to Run   In the spring of 1912, with La Follette out of the way, Roosevelt began the search for delegates. He made only slight headway. Although Teddy attracted the Republican rank and file, he had less success with the leaders, who were responsive to calls for solidarity and to the presidential patronage. The party regulars whom he had often crossed in the past now showed their solidarity with Taft.

Taft himself was first hurt and then outraged by Roosevelt's defection. Angered by the betrayal at the hands of a friend and convinced that his antagonist had lost all sense of balance, he set to work cementing the loyalty of the delegates. When the Republican Convention met in June in Chicago, Taft had a majority and was nominated on the first ballot. The President's followers controlled the Convention machinery and were able to increase Taft's margin by awarding all the contested delegations to him.

The Election of 1912

The Rival Candidates When Roosevelt lost the nomination the first of two critical decisions was made; the voters would make the second on election day. Roosevelt determined to bolt. All his life he had been a regular who had spurned the Mugwumps and independents for their lack of realism. Now, out of personal rage at having lost and out of the conviction that he alone could lead the nation in the correct direction, he determined to form a new party. He would lead a crusade for national redemption.

That announced intention influenced the deliberations of the Democratic Convention, which met in Baltimore. For the first time in many years the party had a chance of winning, given it by the Republican division. But it could not win except by nominating a progressive who would draw votes away from the two wings of the GOP. If it selected a standpat old-line Democrat, it might itself lose votes to Roosevelt. That consideration influenced crucial blocks of delegates at the Convention.

William Jennings Bryan, the peerless loser, had by then gone to defeat three times; he would not again be a candidate but he would influence the choice. The leading contenders were Woodrow Wilson of New Jersey, Oscar W. Underwood of Alabama, and Champ Clark of Missouri. The party rule requiring a two-thirds majority for nomination delayed the choice until the Bryan followers had made up their minds. Ultimately Bryan concluded that Clark was too close to Tammany of New York and cast his influence to Wilson, who had earned a reform reputation as president of Princeton University and gov-

There is a full account of the election of 1912 in Volume I of Arthur S. Link, *Wilson* (Princeton, N.J., 1947).

ernor of New Jersey. The nomination went, on the forty-sixth ballot, to Wilson, who then led a united party into the campaign.

On August 5, 1912, the new Progressive party met in Chicago. It was a foregone conclusion that it would nominate Roosevelt and that he would accept. Hiram W. Johnson of California was his running mate. The Republican Convention had been the first skirmish at Armageddon. The conviction that they battled for the Lord imbued the Progressives with religious fervor and inspired them to go forth zealously in the search for converts.

The Convention consisted of a host of strange delegates, each in his own way, like Teddy himself, feeling strong as a Bull Moose. There were relatively few politicians in the hall but a great many reformers and social workers — not the type of comrades in arms with whom Roosevelt had earlier been accustomed to work. The participation of a few friends like George W. Perkins was, however, reassuring. Nor did the platform adopted altogether express Roosevelt's views. He was far from accepting every plank on it, but he was confident that he could shape it to his will. In any case the party was the only medium through which to make his influence felt.

A fourth candidate was in the field, Debs. For the first time the Socialists seriously challenged the dominant political groups. The party in the past had gone through the motions of nominating a candidate, not in the expectation of gaining a substantial number of votes but in the vague hope that campaigning would have an educational effect. The number of votes it gained had risen from about 100,000 in 1900 to about 400,000 in 1904, partly because of effective recruitment and partly because the candidacy of Alton B. Parker in that year had alienated some progressive Democrats. The Socialist vote did not rise above that level in 1908. By 1912, however, Eugene V. Debs was a national figure with a devoted following. And honest and efficient Socialist administration of such municipalities as Milwaukee and Bridgeport left the

Woodrow Wilson Campaigning, 1912. (Brown Brothers)

The Bull Moose Movement and Taft-Roosevelt Controversy. Roosevelt, as the Progressive ("Bull Moose") party candidate, opposed Taft in the election of 1912. A contemporary cartoon. (The Bettmann Archive)

Reform Socialism, 1912

In all of our large industrial concerns—stock companies, railroads and trusts—business is managed and carried on by a few paid officials. These men might just as well be paid by the state, or the nation (as the case may be), to carry on the enterprise in the interest of the people, as paid by a few wealthy men to carry it on for their individual profit. . . .

The Socialist party proposed to supplement our political democracy by industrial democracy.

No one dreams of abolishing private property. On the contrary, we propose to secure private property to every citizen, to the many million men and women who under the present system have no chance of ever having any. Productive capital only is to be owned in common, by the nation, the State or the municipality as the exigencies of the case may require. Business will be carried on for use and not for profit. . . .

The Capitalist system has undoubtedly done some good in this world. The Capitalist system was useful. It has concentrated economic forces and has made possible the production of wealth on a very large scale.

The Capitalist system was a step in the evolution to freedom, but only a step. It has now outlived its usefulness. It has become oppressive to the great majority of the people. Therefore it must pass away.

—Victor L. Berger, "Socialism, the Logical Outcome of Progressivism," *The American Magazine*, LXXV (November, 1912), pp. 20, 21.

Eugene V. Debs Campaigning, 1912. (Brown Brothers)

impression that this party too was progressive, but merely more advanced than the others.

The Platforms The rival platforms revealed the points of similarity and difference among the parties. Some divergencies were almost ritual in character. The Socialists asked for government ownership, the Democrats for lower tariffs, the Progressives for initiative, referendum, and recall. Differences on these matters were genuine although they were hardly likely in any realistic sense to enter significantly into the development of policy.

More significant were the variations of opinion on the basic economic issue of the future character of the productive system. Beyond the surface similarity of the calls for control of the trusts and for broadened responsibilities of the government were vital disagreements about the future shape of industrial organization. The campaign brought these issues to the attention of the citizens.

As between the Progressives and the Republicans, the division was over method and pace. Taft was not a die-hard member of the Old Guard but he was a lawyer who cherished a deep respect for constitutional guarantees. The courts, as in the Standard Oil case, were, for him, the best instruments for determining the reasonableness of combinations. He regarded measures on behalf of labor and the dependent elements in the population desirable, but only if framed within the limits of existing rights established by the Constitution.

Roosevelt sought greater executive power. His distrust of the judges and his support of the concept of recall of judicial decisions emanated from his own experience as President and from the doctrines of the New Nationalism. A powerful Bureau of Corporations with an over-all view of the whole economy could best judge the reasonableness of combinations and guard the public welfare by the licensing power. Quick action on behalf of labor was also essential, as a matter of justice as well as of prudence, to avoid divisive class conflicts.

The difference between the Progressives and the Democrats was more fundamental. Roosevelt was willing to accept a degree of eco-

No Masters for the People, 1913

At the least, under the plan I am opposing, there will be an avowed partnership between the government and the trusts. I take it that the firm will be ostensibly controlled by the senior member. For I take it that the government of the United States is at least the senior member, though the younger member has all along been running the business. But when all the momentum, when all the energy, when a great deal of the genius, as so often happens in partnerships the world over, is with the junior partner, I don't think that the superintendence of the senior partner is going to amount to very much. And I don't believe that benevolence can be read into the hearts of the trusts by the superintendence and suggestions of the federal government; because the government has never within my recollection had its suggestions accepted by the trusts. On the contrary, the suggestions of the trusts have been accepted by the government. . . .

I don't care how benevolent the master is going to be, I will not live under a master. That is not what America was created for. America was created in order that every man should have the same chance as every other man to exercise mastery over his own fortunes.

—Woodrow Wilson, *The New Freedom* (New York: Doubleday & Company, Inc., 1913), pp. 202–203, 207.

when he met Louis D. Brandeis, a lawyer who had spent much of the previous decade fighting the public utilities. Brandeis persuaded the Democratic candidate that bigness was itself an evil, a source of inefficiency and corruption tending naturally toward monopoly. The remedy was contraction of the role of government, except as a means of maintaining competition and protecting the weak against the strong. The ideas of the New Freedom, which Wilson shaped along these lines, were particularly attractive to agrarians in the South and West, where he expected to find much of his support.

The Election of Wilson   The outcome of the election showed that the Republican split had been decisive. Taft carried only Vermont and Utah, the most loyal of GOP states. Roosevelt carried Michigan, Minnesota, Pennsylvania, South Dakota, and Washington, along with part of the electoral vote of California. Wilson won by taking the solid South and enough of the Northern states to give him an overwhelming majority in the electoral college. The new President also carried into office a Democratic Congress, but his popular vote was smaller than that of Bryan in 1908, an indication that he had lost some former Democrats to Roosevelt. Outside the South, Wilson did not gain a popular majority in any state. It was significant, too, that Debs amassed almost a million votes, double his total in 1908. Part of the increase was due to the spread of socialist ideas, but much of it was a protest against the disorder into which the other parties had fallen.

The Nature of the Choice

Roosevelt's bolt—the first decision of 1912—had made it certain that all the candidates would be progressives of some sort. Wilson's election—the second decision—determined the direction in which progressives would move in the immediate future. Roosevelt intended to lead the nation toward an increased use of centralized

nomic concentration under government control unthinkable to Wilson, who feared that the paternalistic combination between money and government which T. R. envisioned would lead to slavery and enchainment of the people. Only free enterprise, according to Wilson, could preserve American liberty. He had not given much thought to these issues until August 1912,

THE ELECTION OF 1912

| | Popular Vote (thousands) | | | | Electoral Vote | | |
STATE	Wilson	Roosevelt	Taft	Debs	Wilson	Roosevelt	Taft
Vermont	15.3	22.0	23.3	.9	–	–	4
Other New England	363.9	259.0	311.4	89.0	40	–	–
New York	655.4	390.0	455.4	63.3	45	–	–
New Jersey	178.2	145.4	88.8	15.8	14	–	–
Pennsylvania	395.6	447.4	273.3	83.1	–	38	–
Border States*	1,261.6	517.4	654.7	114.3	93	–	–
South	690.4	112.0	77.2	42.6	93	–	–
Michigan	150.7	214.5	152.2	23.2	–	15	–
Minnesota	106.4	125.8	64.3	27.5	–	12	–
North Dakota	29.5	25.7	23.0	6.9	5	–	–
South Dakota	48.9	58.8	–	4.6	–	5	–
Other Midwestern†	1,712.2	1,190.8	1,061.4	296.6	112	–	–
Utah	36.5	24.1	42.1	9.0	–	–	4
Other Mountain‡	229.9	150.2	147.9	51.0	26	–	–
California	283.4	283.6	3.9	79.2	2	11	–
Oregon	47.0	37.6	34.6	13.3	5	–	–
Washington	86.8	113.6	70.4	40.1	–	7	–

* Arkansas, Delaware, Kentucky, Maryland, Missouri, North Carolina, Oklahoma, Tennessee, West Virginia

† Illinois, Indiana, Iowa, Kansas, Nebraska, Ohio, Wisconsin

‡ Arizona, New Mexico, Idaho, Wyoming, Montana, Colorado, Nevada

governmental power in domestic as well as in foreign affairs. He had also acquired a distrust of the established political processes and of the courts and was therefore likely to seek greater executive action. Furthermore, he believed that men of intelligence, education, and wealth could best serve the interests of the country by virtue of their wisdom and disinterestedness. Roosevelt in 1912 had thus come close to the position of the Adams brothers, who wished a greater political role for the natural aristocracy of talent.

In sending Wilson to the White House, the nation rejected that course. The new President had no wish to centralize power. Although he had serious objections to the system of Congressional government as it had existed before 1901, he had no desire to expand presidential strength beyond the point it had reached in 1912. He respected states' rights and the estab-

The general social context of progressivism is presented in Harold U. Faulkner, *The Quest for Social Justice* (New York, 1931).

lished party organizations, and was reluctant to stretch the limits of constitutional action even for desirable ends.

Most important, Wilson and the Southern and Western agrarians who would staff his administration judged social policy from the viewpoint of the small proprietor and the independent farmer. Jeffersonians, not only in ends but also in means, they considered restraint on bigness the most effective protection for individual liberties. The New Freedom aimed to rectify the injustices industrialization had caused, by a return to the earlier values of economic and political democracy. The attempt to apply these values to practice would be the primary task of Wilson's first years in office.

▼

The election of 1912 was ultimately significant for its confirmation of progressive primacy and for its definition of what progressivism meant. The political maneuvers of the preceding two years had in effect excluded any conservative from candidacy and had presented the electorate with a choice among various shades of reform opinion. The result, which was not altogether conscious or deliberate, was the selection of the candidate who favored the containment of large enterprise. Wilson's election averted the strengthening of government which under Roosevelt might have led to a substantial increase in the power of the centralized state. Instead, there was renewed emphasis on competition and decentralization.

Since 1890, the nation had passed through radical changes that impelled its citizens toward forceful political action. The first impulse, the Populist revolt, had run its course, and massive agricultural and industrial innovations had begun to transform the life of the nation. But in the twentieth century, the country assumed the responsibilities of a great power and faced a restive population calling for reform. A fundamental alteration in the structure of politics became possible. The decision of 1912 was to avoid such an alteration and to continue to work for progressive ends within the familiar and accepted forms.

Paperbacks for Further Reading

Richard Hofstadter, *Age of Reform* (Vintage Books, Inc.) and Eric F. Goldman, *Rendezvous with Destiny* (Vintage Books, Inc.) survey the progressive movement generally. There is also some information in Daniel Aaron, *Men of Good Hope* (Galaxy Books). Theodore Roosevelt, *The New Nationalism* (Spectrum Books) is a statement of T. R.'s position in 1910. There is a useful collection of material in Richard Hofstadter, ed., *The Progressive Movement, 1900–1915* (Spectrum Books). Herbert Croly, *The Promise of American Life* (Bobbs-Merrill College Division) and Robert M. La Follette, *La Follette's Autobiography* (University of Wisconsin Press) are important primary sources. Divergent interpretations are assembled in Arthur Mann, ed., *The Progressive Era* (Holt, Rinehart & Winston, Inc., American Problem Studies) and in E. C. Rozwenc, ed., *Roosevelt, Wilson, and the Trusts* (D. C. Heath and Co.).

THE QUEST

FOR AN OLD ORDER

1912–1929

VIII

THE NEW

FREEDOM

73

Wilson's first four years in the White House were the culmination of the progressive movement. His administration did not depart radically from past patterns of development but was part of a long slow response to industrialization. Like those that preceded it, it was concerned with the creation of a political and social apparatus to deal adequately with the consequences of economic change.

The election of 1912 had brought to office the New Freedom rather than the New Nationalism. In making that choice the voters had rejected Theodore Roosevelt's proposals for centralizing power but had at the same time revealed their desire to extend the activities of government for the protection of the individual. With the presidency Wilson assumed the responsibility of fulfilling that mandate, and a succession of vigorous measures were proof of his ability to do so. Although a tragic war and a disappointing peace interrupted his work, the progressive idea, as his administration interpreted it, bequeathed a permanent legacy to the postwar generation. The shortcomings of his approach would not be apparent until later.

WOODROW WILSON spent much of his life struggling to do right in politics. He wished to act and yet also to adhere to moral principles. His efforts proved tragic, both for himself and for his country.

He was born in Staunton, Virginia, in 1856 but spent most of his youth in Georgia. His father was a Presbyterian minister and raised the family in respectable poverty. Wilson's first ambitions were for a legal career. He studied at Davidson College and at Princeton and attended the law school of the University of Virginia. His attempt to set up practice in Atlanta in 1882 was a dismal failure, however, and induced him to turn to scholarship.

Wilson went for advanced training to the new Johns Hopkins University, where Herbert Baxter Adams had organized a graduate seminar after the German model. In 1886 Wilson received the Ph.D. degree for his book, *Congressional Government: A Study in American Politics* (1885). There followed sixteen years of teaching at Bryn Mawr, Wesleyan, and Princeton. But Wilson was impatient with cloistered scholarship. In 1902 he became president of Princeton. His desire to reform that institution produced some changes and brought him to public attention.

In 1910 he moved on to politics and was elected governor of New Jersey on the Democratic ticket. He proved an energetic reformer. Cutting loose from machine support, he sponsored primary, corrupt practices, and public utility regulation laws and within two years was an aspirant for the presidency. The division within the Republican party brought him to the White House in 1913.

His talents and training equipped Wilson to lead the Administration successfully in domestic affairs. In these matters he profited also from a quarter century's experimentation with progressive reform. But he had little experience in foreign policy, and the national tradition in that area was uncertain. On the one hand, he did not wish to rest diplomacy on the basis of material interest; on the other, he found no way of avoiding compromises of expediency. He therefore failed either to keep the United States out of war or to establish an enduring peace. During his final effort to persuade his countrymen to ratify the Treaty of Versailles and accept membership in the League of Nations, he collapsed. He lived on until 1924, while Americans, temporarily at least, sought a return to normalcy.

The Purpose of Power

THE ELECTION OF 1912 had clarified the political intentions of Americans. The new conditions created by industrialization required expansion of the role of government. It was not so much that the state was to direct economic and social development but that it was to maintain free competition and protect the rights of individuals.

Political Preparations The new administration took office with a sense of determination and with wide popular support. Important reform measures soon dealt with the major problems of economic life. The nation felt the throb of a sense of purpose. People were confident that the President would be able to achieve the goals of the New Freedom of which he had spoken.

Wilson was by no means the aloof scholar of the ivory tower. He had been trained in a school of politics—the university—as hard and realistic as that of any state legislature. There and as governor of New Jersey he had learned to be practical, to define his objectives, to frame them in plausible terms, and to use what means were necessary to attain them. His earlier studies as a political scientist and his experience in academic and state politics had persuaded him that forceful executive action was essential to achieve worthwhile results. He entered the White House determined to be a strong President, as Roosevelt had been. He proved an adept and persuasive leader.

Wilson selected the members of his cabinet to pay off obligations and to balance sectional and economic interests. He had little respect for William Jennings Bryan, whom he nevertheless made Secretary of State as a reward for help in securing the nomination. William G. McAdoo, a New York corporation lawyer who had managed the 1912 campaign, became Secretary of the Treasury. Similar political considerations influenced the award of most other places. The cabinet, in the President's scheme of things, was to administer the departments and maintain contact with the public. It would not actively create policy.

For that purpose Wilson turned instead to a group of intimate advisers, who formed a dependable "kitchen cabinet." George Harvey, president of the Harper & Brothers publishing firm and a man well-known in New York financial circles, was a respected friend of long standing. Edward M. House was a Texan in whose personal judgment Wilson placed great confidence. Joseph P. Tumulty, an Irish-American politician, had been Wilson's secretary in New Jersey and had served him loyally; he came to Washington to act in the same capacity. In addition, Wilson enjoyed the support of influential Congressional leaders who steered his measures through their respective chambers—Carter Glass of Virginia and Oscar W. Underwood of Alabama in the Senate, and Champ Clark of Missouri in the House.

In an effort to assert his authority, the President resumed the practice, in abeyance for more than a century, of delivering his messages to Congress in person. Furthermore, he took an active interest in the use of patronage as a means of developing and controlling a following. He was to be a party leader as well as a forceful chief executive.

John M. Blum, *Joe Tumulty and the Wilson Era* (Boston, 1951) is an excellent biography.

A Changing Order, 1913

We have come upon a very different age from any that preceded us. . . . There is a sense in which in our day the individual has been submerged. In most parts of our country men work, not for themselves, not as partners in the old way . . . , but generally as employees . . . of great corporations. . . . There is something very new and very big and very complex about these new relations of capital and labor. A new economic society has sprung up, and we must effect a new set of adjustments. . . .

American industry is not free as once it was free; American enterprise is not free; the man with only a little capital is finding it harder to get into the field, more and more impossible to compete with the big fellow . . . because the laws of this country do not prevent the strong from crushing the weak. . . .

What this country needs above everything else is a body of laws which will look after the men who are on the make rather than the men who are already made. . . . The originative part of America, the part of America that makes new enterprises, the part into which the ambitious and gifted workingman makes his way up, the class that saves, that plans, that organizes . . . that middle class is being more and more squeezed out. . . .

We stand in the presence of a . . . silent revolution, whereby America will insist upon recovering in practice those ideals which she has always professed, upon securing a government devoted to the general interest. . . . The whole stupendous program must be publicly planned and canvassed. . . . The habit of co-operation and of compromise which has been bred in us by long years of free government . . . will enable us to win through to still another great age without violence.

—Woodrow Wilson, *The New Freedom* (New York: Doubleday & Company, Inc., 1913), pp. 5, 8, 15, 17, 30–32.

LOUIS D. BRANDEIS was a successful attorney when, in mid-career, he decided to make the people his clients. He was born in 1856 in Louisville, Kentucky, to which his parents had come as refugees from Germany. Louis studied in the local schools, then for three years attended the *Realschule* in Dresden, Germany, and finally took a law degree at Harvard in 1878.

After a year of practice in St. Louis, he entered a Boston law firm and soon had among his clients such industrial giants as the United Shoe Machinery Company. The Homestead strike of 1892 first made him sensitive to the problems of labor, which increasingly occupied his attention in the next quarter century. Thoroughly familiar with the intricacies of corporate finance, he was able to support his arguments with authoritative factual data as well as with citations to the law.

His greatest battles maintained the interests of the people against the power of the trusts. Fearing the concentration of control in the hands of insurance companies, he worked out a plan that allowed Massachusetts savings banks to write life insurance. He fought a long-term lease of the Boston subways to private interests and secured an arrangement favorable to the municipality. He forced a sliding-scale rate upon the gas company and helped prevent J. P. Morgan from absorbing the Boston and Maine into the New Haven Railroad.

These experiences persuaded him that bigness itself was a danger because it encouraged monopoly and submerged the talents of millions. His writing significantly influenced Wilson in 1912 and 1913, while the New Freedom was taking shape.

Brandeis brought these views to the Supreme Court. He and Oliver Wendell Holmes were often a dissenting minority in the two decades after 1916, although not for identical reasons. He was not the legal scholar Holmes was, but his mastery of social data and his awareness of the needs of the laboring people enlivened his progressive opinions. When he retired from the Supreme Court in 1939, the New Deal had begun to implement some of his ideas. He died in 1941.

Basic Ideas Power was important not as an end in itself but as a means. Wilson aimed to be a reformer and early set out to implement his goals. His inaugural address in 1913 had stated the issue. The country had to adjust to the complex new relations created by industrialization and the development of the corporation. Government had to intervene in a heartless economic system to keep competition free, to encourage originative entrepreneurs, to limit special privilege, and to maintain a basic fairness and decency in American life.

Where it mattered Wilson was courageous and ready to defy hostile opinion. Political considerations led him to prefer James C. McReynolds of Tennessee over Louis D. Brandeis, first for the attorney-generalship (1913) and then for the Supreme Court (1914). But in 1916 the President felt strong enough to nominate Brandeis to the Supreme Court, and he fought for confirmation despite a barrage of criticism directed at the appointment of a Jew and a liberal. Wilson would not mediate with political or religious prejudice. On somewhat the same grounds he vetoed a bill to enact a literacy test that would have restricted immigration, pointing to the extent to which the measure contradicted American ideals.

On the other hand, Wilson's heritage and the prominence of Southern Democrats in his administration were responsible for a substantial setback to the cause of Negro rights. He permitted open segregation in government offices. Furthermore, the loss of control over Federal

Alpheus T. Mason, *Brandeis: A Free Man's Life* (New York, 1946) is a competent study.

The Mission of the Nation

In two particulars . . . this bill embodies a radical departure from the traditional . . . policy of this country, a policy in which our people have conceived . . . the very mission and spirit of the Nation in respect of its relations to the peoples of the world outside their borders. It seeks to all but close entirely the gates of asylum which have always been open to those who could find nowhere else the right and opportunity of constitutional agitation for what they conceived to be the natural and inalienable rights of men; and it excludes those to whom the opportunities of elementary education have been denied, without regard to their character, their purposes, or their natural capacity. . . .

The literacy test and the tests and restrictions which accompany it constitute an even more radical change in the policy of the Nation. Hitherto we have generously kept our doors open to all who were not unfitted by reason of disease or incapacity for self-support or such personal records and antecedents as were likely to make them a menace to our peace and order or to the wholesome and essential relationships of life. In this bill it is proposed to turn away from tests of character and of quality and impose tests which exclude and restrict; for the new tests here embodied are not tests of quality or of character or of personal fitness, but tests of opportunity. Those who come seeking opportunity are not to be admitted unless they have already had one of the chief of the opportunities they seek, the opportunity of education. The object of such provisions is restriction, not selection.

—President Wilson's Veto Message of January 28, 1915. Albert Shaw, ed., *President Wilson's State Papers and Addresses* (New York: George H. Doran Company, 1918), pp. 95–96.

patronage weakened the surviving Republican elements in the South, who were almost alone responsive to the needs of the Negro. In the eight years of his tenure of office, Wilson did nothing to call attention to the problems of the least privileged group in the population.

Income Tax Two Constitutional amendments ratified in 1913 significantly strengthened Wilson's hand as he began to implement his program. For almost a half century there had been no changes at all in the nation's frame of government. Then the Sixteenth and the Seventeenth amendments showed the strength of the progressive impulse. The Sixteenth, first passed by Congress in 1909, permitted the Federal government to tax incomes and thus opened a source of revenue that would have enormous importance in the future. The Seventeenth, passed by Congress in 1912, provided for the direct election of Senators. While it did not at once alter the character of the upper house, it did develop in that chamber a sensitivity to popular opinion.

With the psychological support of these measures, Wilson was able to turn forcefully to the economic issues reviewed in the campaign. The election rhetoric had complained that the trusts were not sufficiently regulated, that the financial system was in disorder, and that the tariff was too high. It was the responsibility of the Administration to deal with those matters.

Underwood Tariff The tariff received first attention because here progressive complaints and traditional Democratic policy coincided. Congress, dominated in both branches by Democrats, proceeded to enact a measure that almost eliminated protective features and concentrated on revenue. The Underwood Tariff of 1913 reduced the duties on some 900 items and raised those on only 86. Most rates were set on an *ad valorem* basis—that is, as a percentage of value—in order further to lower them; and the graduated income tax compensated for the revenue lost as a result of revision. The outbreak of war in Europe in 1914, which curtailed imports and stimulated exports, spared the country a test of

The Progressive Amendments, 1913

ARTICLE XVI

The Congress shall have power to lay and collect taxes on incomes, from whatever source derived, without apportionment among the several States, and without regard to any census or enumeration.

— Passed by Congress July 12, 1909; ratified February 25, 1913.

ARTICLE XVII

The Senate of the United States shall be composed of two Senators from each State, elected by the people thereof, for six years; and each Senator shall have one vote. The electors in each State shall have the qualifications requisite for electors of the most numerous branch of the State legislatures.

When vacancies happen in the representation of any State in the Senate, the executive authority of such State shall issue writs of election to fill such vacancies: *Provided*, That the legislature of any State may empower the executive thereof to make temporary appointments until the people fill the vacancies by election as the legislature may direct.

This amendment shall not be so construed as to affect the election or term of any Senator chosen before it becomes valid as part of the Constitution.

— Passed by Congress May 16, 1912; ratified May 31, 1913.

the effects of the new tariff. But the pledge of the 1912 platform had been honored. A Tariff Commission, created in 1916, was to keep Congress informed of desirable changes in the rates.

The Federal Reserve System The problems of banking were more complex. The panic of 1907 had exposed the deficiency of existing arrangements. At moments of crisis the currency was inelastic, incapable of expanding to meet a sudden need for credit. National banks could invest their assets either in loans to business or in government bonds. The banker who wished to increase the amount available to private borrowers had to get the necessary funds by disposing of some bonds. But in that event the law compelled him to reduce the amount of notes his bank emitted. On the other hand, he could increase the amount of notes in circulation only by raising his holdings of government bonds, thereby contracting the funds available for loans. As a result, every panic had a cumulative effect. Furthermore, the banks were unable to mobilize their resources and to protect one another against runs, which would ultimately threaten them all.

The banker-dominated central system recommended by the National Monetary Commission in 1912 attracted little support, for it was considered while the hearings of a Congressional committee under the chairmanship of Arsène P. Pujo were throwing light on current banking practices. Pointing to the numerous connections among bankers and to their influence on other financial institutions, railroads, and industry, the Pujo committee charged that a money trust dominated the American economy. The widely circulated accusations made it unlikely that control of the national currency would be placed directly in the hands of the bankers.

The solution that resulted from a year of deliberation was a compromise among the various interests exerting pressure on Congress. Wilson took an active part in reconciling diver-

Paul M. Warburg, *The Federal Reserve System* (New York, 1930) contains a discussion of its origins.

Louis D. Brandeis, *Other People's Money* (New York, 1914) summarizes the results of the Pujo investigation.

gent points of view. The Federal Reserve Act (December 23, 1913) created twelve districts with a central, Federal Reserve bank in each. The Federal Reserve banks, the capital of which private national and state banks contributed, cleared checks, rediscounted loans, and printed paper currency. To coordinate operations among the several districts, the act set up a government agency, the Federal Reserve Board, which was to establish general policies and provide a medium for communication among the banks and between them and the United States Treasury.

The new system was an improvement over the old. It provided more fluid credit, since the Federal Reserve banks would make loans to the member banks. Furthermore, the currency was somewhat more elastic than before because the Federal Reserve banks could issue notes not only against their holdings of government securities, as the national banks previously had, but also against rediscounted commercial paper.

The issue of control, however, remained ambiguous. Each Federal Reserve bank was directed by a committee of nine, of whom six were designated by the member banks and three by the Federal Reserve Board. The Board itself consisted of the Secretary of the Treasury and seven others, appointed for fourteen-year terms so as to be immune from political influence. The result was a system of mixed private and public power. The regional central banks were dominated by the bankers but subject to the general supervision of a government board. The quality of that oversight was yet to be tested, but the law took the first step toward a more rational pattern of currency and credit.

The Clayton Antitrust Act In 1914 Wilson turned to the problems created by the integration of industry. He followed largely along the path already marked out in the preceding twelve years. The Bureau of Corporations gave way to a presidentially appointed Federal Trade Commission (1914). The new agency was to collect and disseminate information as its predecessor had and, in addition, could prevent unfair com-

The Money Trust, 1913

Far more dangerous than all that has happened to us in the past in the way of elimination of competition in industry is the control of credit through the domination of [the money trust] . . . over our banks. . . . There can be no hope of revived competition and no new ventures . . . that could live against existing combinations, without the consent of those who dominate these sources of credit. A banking house that has organized a great industrial or railway combination or that has offered its securities to the public, is represented on the board of directors and acts as its fiscal agent, thereby assumes a certain guardianship over that corporation. In the ratio in which that corporation succeeds or fails the prestige of the banking house and its capacity for absorbing and distributing future issues of securities is affected. If competition is threatened it is manifestly the duty of the bankers from their point of view of the protection of the stockholders, as distinguished from the standpoint of the public, to prevent it if possible. If they control the sources of credit they can furnish such protection. It is this element in the situation that unless checked is likely to do more to prevent the restoration of competition than all other conditions combined. This power standing between the trusts and the economic forces of competition is the factor most to be dreaded and guarded against by the advocates of revived competition.

—U.S. House of Representatives, *Report of the Committee . . . to Investigate the Concentration of Control of Money and Credit* (Washington: Government Printing Office, 1913), pp. 159–160.

Early Federal Reserve Problems, 1915

Intradistrict clearings.

Plan for settlements between Federal reserve banks.

Cipher and cable codes.

Relation between the Federal reserve banks and the national bank examiners.

Rediscounts between Federal reserve banks.

Membership by Federal reserve banks in the American Bankers' Association and State bankers' associations.

Foreign exchange.

The printing and use of Federal reserve bank notes.

Uniform statements to be exchanged between Federal reserve banks.

The abrasion of gold coin.

Member banks' certification of eligibility on commercial paper.

Chattel mortgages.

—Agenda, Conference of Federal Reserve Governors, March 11, 1915. *Federal Reserve Bulletin* (Washington: Government Printing Office, 1915), vol. I, no. 1, May 1915, p. 15.

petition by issuing cease and desist orders against offending corporations. Although these orders were subject to review in the courts and in practice depended upon complaints, this was a substantial expansion of government power.

The Clayton Antitrust Act of 1914 aimed to plug the gaps in the Sherman act's prohibition of restraint of trade. The new law, which forbade interlocking directorates, also restricted price fixing and such exclusive contracts as might diminish competition. But this measure was no easier to enforce than the Sherman act; nor were its strictures against combinations that limited competition clear enough to make a difference.

The Toilers' Welfare

Labor Wilson was solicitous also about the interests of the farmers and laborers, who had provided him with substantial support. Although he had not previously given the matter much thought, he revealed his attitude at the very start of his administration when he appointed William B. Wilson Secretary of Labor at the suggestion of the AF of L. This was the first time a union man had appeared in the cabinet. Furthermore, the Clayton act nullified the decision in the Danbury hatters' case by explicitly excluding labor from the definition of a conspiracy in restraint of trade. The administration thus mollified the unions, which were thereafter freer to organize than before.

Wilson's administration took the first gingerly steps toward regulation of the conditions of work by the Federal government. He had earlier been dubious of the constitutionality of such measures, which he had considered within the province of the states. But once in office, he perceived the need for some action and found adequate justification for it in the power to regulate interstate and foreign commerce. On those grounds he approved the La Follette Seaman's Act (1915), which set the minimal conditions of labor in the Merchant Marine. On the same basis, he signed the Adamson Act (1916), which established the eight-hour day on interstate railroads, and a child labor act (1916), later declared unconstitutional by the courts, which forbade the flow in interstate commerce of goods made by the labor of persons less than fourteen years of age.

The Farmers Agriculture was generally prosperous, and Wilson was unwilling to tamper with the really depressed sectors of the agricultural labor force, the sharecroppers and farm tenants, particularly in the South. But the commercial farmers received assistance. Laws that extended the scope of agricultural demonstra-

There is a good discussion of the child labor law in Claude G. Bowers, *Beveridge and the Progressive Era* (Boston, 1932).

Charles Evans Hughes Campaigning for the Office of Governor of New York, 1906.
(Brown Brothers)

tions, aided farm education, and set warehousing standards were all designed to increase the scientific and businesslike character of farming. For the same reason, the government finally moved to ease the credit requirements of the agricultural entrepreneurs, although in this matter, too, Wilson had to overcome his original scruples regarding the constitutionality of such measures. In 1916, the Federal Farm Loan Act set up a counterpart of the Federal Reserve system. Twelve land banks in the various regions of the country were specifically charged with the responsibility of providing flexible long-term loans to agriculture. In the same year, the Rural Post Roads Act set the precedent of Federal aid for highway construction.

The Election of 1916

Wilson's first administration seemed to confirm the progressive hypothesis about the means of reforming the American economy. None of the actions was radical. Nor, except in the case of the tariff, did any depart markedly from the starts made by Roosevelt and Taft. But together they formed a coherent program for which wide popular support could be mobilized.

As a result, the Republicans in 1916 felt constrained to nominate a progressive, Supreme Court Justice Charles Evans Hughes, who had earned a reputation as a reform governor in New York and as investigator of the life insurance business. The Progressive party, without Roosevelt as its standard-bearer, suffered heavy losses in the Congressional election of 1914 and disappeared two years later, when the campaign resumed its normal two-party form.

The contest between Wilson and Hughes was practically issueless, because the objectives of the two candidates were so similar. Wilson won with 9,000,000 popular votes as against 8,500,000 for Hughes and with 277 electoral votes as against 254. In the same year, the Democratic majority in the Congress was also confirmed.

State Action

Fully as important as events in Washington were those in the state capitals. The police power of the state legislatures was less encumbered by constitutional restraints than that of Congress and in many parts of the country progressive administrations reformed the structure of government and enacted measures to protect the least powerful elements in society.

Efforts to modernize state constitutions continued. New York, for instance, held a convention in 1915, Massachusetts in 1916. Moreover, the earlier experiments with new modes of municipal administration continued. In many states, too, long-drawn-out reform campaigns now approached consummation. Prohibition had thus become effective by 1915 in a majority of the nation's counties either by state-wide law or by local option.

More important was a concerted drive to protect industrial laborers. Americans were no longer callously indifferent to the accidents that maimed or killed thousands annually. Statutes compelled employers to guard against fires and dangerous machinery. Some states went further and created a general liability of manufacturers to maintain safe conditions in their plants. From there it was but a short step to requiring proper ventilation, washing facilities, and lunchrooms. Furthermore, the most advanced states not only provided for inspection but gave industrial commissions or boards judicial powers to enforce such regulations. Finally, compulsory workmen's compensation laws granted those injured some monetary help.

A growing concern with the welfare of women and children produced a flood of legislation. Compulsory school-attendance laws kept some young people out of the factories, while a variety of statutes limited the hours and the conditions under which they could work. Be-

Compensation Legislation, 1917

The real compensation period began in 1911 when 10 States enacted such laws. Each year since then additional States have fallen in line until at present, as already noted, 40 States and Territories have enacted compensation legislation.

This rapid growth of compensation legislation, involving, as it has, the almost simultaneous enactment of laws in a number of States, has operated to prevent the adoption of any one form of law as a type, so that although a single fundamental principle underlies the entire group of laws of this class, its expression and application present great diversity of details in the different States. . . .

The compensation States contain approximately 77 percent of the persons gainfully employed in the United States and include practically all of the industrial States. There seems to have been no causal connection between the need for compensation laws and the sequence of their enactment. Of the 10 States enacting such laws in 1911, 3 were manufacturing States on the Atlantic coast, 4 were agricultural or semi-industrial States in the Mississippi Valley, and 3 were primarily agricultural or mining States west of the Rocky Mountains. The 12 noncompensation States remaining include 10 Southern States, North Dakota, and the District of Columbia.

—Carl Hookstadt, "Comparison of Workmen's Compensation Laws of the United States up to December 31, 1917," *Bulletin of the United States Bureau of Labor Statistics, No. 240* (Washington: Government Printing Office, 1918), pp. 11–12.

Seamstresses at Work, New York, 1908–1912. There is evidence here of safety measures: the fire extinguisher, the door marked "Exit," and the sign indicating the weight the floor will safely sustain. (Brown Brothers)

tween 1911 and 1913, about thirty states passed such laws. New York, among other states, also regulated the hours of employment of women and required that they receive rest periods, seats with backs, and special working conditions after childbirth. By the end of 1916 nineteen states and the District of Columbia had enacted such provisions. About a dozen states sought to control exploitation by setting a minimum wage for women and children. In 1911, Illinois pioneered in a still more novel measure. It authorized the payment of mothers' pensions to widows with dependent children, thus departing from the traditional assumption that every household would support itself. Old-age pensions (Arizona, Alaska, 1915), however, ran into constitutional difficulties in the courts.

Some states, and many municipalities as well, continued the effort to provide parks and recreational facilities and tried to preserve their natural setting and wildlife. But in the states the significant advance of the years between 1912

Child at Work in a Canning Factory, 1900–1910. (Brown Brothers)

and 1917 was the increasing concern with human resources and the determination to control industry toward that end.

As inauguration day approached in March 1917, Woodrow Wilson could take some satisfaction in the direction of national development during his first term. He had broken the long hold of the Republicans on Federal office and had restored the vitality of the two-party system. He had helped express the progressive idea in action. A solid legislative program had asserted the public interest in banking and economic development, and, joined to far-reaching state action, had offered some protection to the vulnerable people in the population. To that extent he had begun to make the New Freedom a reality.

But as his second term opened, Wilson was aware that events beyond the nation's borders had brought his administration to a diplomatic crisis. Since 1914, he had had to worry about the great war that raged across Europe. Now he and his country were about to take the fateful step that plunged them decisively into world history.

Paperbacks for Further Reading

Arthur S. Link, *Woodrow Wilson and the Progressive Era* (Harper Torchbooks) is a general survey. John M. Blum, *Woodrow Wilson and the Politics of Morality* (Little, Brown & Co.) is a perceptive analysis of the man and his times. Arthur S. Link, *Wilson: The New Freedom* (Princeton University Press) is a more detailed account. Eric F. Goldman, *Rendezvous with Destiny* (Vintage Books, Inc.) and William E. Leuchtenburg, *The Perils of Prosperity* (Chicago History of American Civilization Series) set this period in a longer time perspective. There is an interesting essay on Brandeis in Paul A. Freund, *Supreme Court of the United States* (Meridian Books). Edward S. Corwin, *The President* (New York University Press Paperbacks) throws light on Wilson's conception of the office.

Primary sources on these years include: Alfred B. Rollins, Jr., *Woodrow Wilson and the New America* (Dell Publishing Co., Inc.); Woodrow Wilson, *The New Freedom* (Spectrum Books); and Walter Lippmann, *Drift and Mastery* (Spectrum Books).

THE ROAD
TO WAR

74

In the last decade of the nineteenth century, technology and expansion had drawn the far corners of the world closer together. Thereafter the United States drifted inward from the outer edge of an international order, the center of which was Europe. Americans did not then know it, but the collapse of that old system in 1914 would alter their position in international affairs. The balance of power which had made the coexistence of sovereign states possible had teetered for years under the strain of the patriotic, colonial, commercial, and military rivalry engendered by imperialism. The specific causes of conflict were settled, but they generated alliances that confronted each other inflexibly in August 1914, when an assassin's shot plunged Europe into a disastrous war.

The United States was entirely unprepared for the event. The initial reaction was horror and a determination to remain apart. Neither the President nor his critics nor the country at large understood that the United States had already become a world power. The force it commanded would not remain permanently idle. The issue which no one faced was whether to use that force wisely and reasonably or blindly and without deliberation.

WILLIAM JENNINGS BRYAN had a clear image of America. Year after year, when he returned from his Chautauqua tours, he felt he had not only spoken to but had also listened to the people. He did not realize how much the country was changing during his lifetime.

He was born into the small-town world of Salem, Illinois, in 1860. His father was prosperous enough to send him to Illinois College and to law school. Bryan then practiced for three years in Jacksonville, Illinois, before moving in 1887 to Lincoln, Nebraska. Oratorical ability and an affable personality drew him into politics. At the age of thirty he was elected to the United States House of Representatives, where he served for four years. In 1894, he failed in his quest for a seat in the Senate.

By then he had become well known throughout the state as a speaker and as a writer for the newspapers. All along he had been an advocate of silver, and his appeal for bimetallism won him the Democratic presidential nomination in 1896. He led the ticket again in 1900 and 1908. In 1912 he helped swing the nomination to Wilson. His reward was the post as Secretary of State.

Bryan had visited Europe and toured the world, but he had no familiarity with diplomacy and was equipped for the office only with good intentions. Since 1898 he had been an anti-imperialist, and he earnestly wished for peace. In critical matters, however, the President set policy and the Secretary of State had little influence. Bryan approved of Wilson's attitudes toward Mexico and China, and he had the President's support in negotiating a series of arbitration treaties. But the two men divided on the war in Europe, and Bryan resigned rather than take the responsibility for involvement. Subsequent events seemed to confirm his forebodings about the danger of foreign entanglements.

Bryan remained a loyal Democrat but his sights thereafter turned inward. As the nation changed in the twentieth century, his insistence upon preserving the old values grew more rigid. He became a fervent prohibitionist and a religious fundamentalist. His last battle was against the concept of Darwinian evolution. He died in 1925, having just finished prosecuting a case against a Tennessee high school teacher who taught the forbidden doctrine.

International Morality

WOODROW WILSON ENTERED office determined to set his foreign policy apart from that of his predecessors. Not for him the saber rattling of Theodore Roosevelt or the dollar diplomacy of William Howard Taft. A more enlightened, less assertive attitude, Wilson hoped, would thereafter guide the United States in its relations with other powers. This determination received the enthusiastic assent of Secretary of State William Jennings Bryan, whose commitment to peace was even deeper than the President's.

Wilson had not given much thought to foreign policy before 1912. Like most Americans, he had concentrated his attention on domestic issues. He assumed that the same standards applied in one sphere as in the other. The moral criteria of honor, decency, fairness, and solicitude for the rights of others were sufficient guides abroad as at home. In dealing with Congressmen and other politicians, of course, Wilson had learned to qualify ideals with realistic calculations, for he was well aware of the way in which interest and prejudice influenced men's actions. Because he was less experienced in foreign affairs, he was less capable of displaying the same sensitivity and flexibility in that area.

NEV.

UTAH

CALIF.

COLO.

KAN.

MO.

ARIZ.

N.M.

OKLA.

ARK.

San Diego

Scene of
Villa's Raid,
March 9,
1916

Columbus

El Paso

Ciudad Juárez

Carrizal

TEXAS

LA.

Chihuahua

Santa Ysabel

San Antonio

Parral

▌ AMERICAN
PUNITIVE
EXPEDITION
APRIL 1916

Tampico

Gulf of Mexico

PACIFIC OCEAN

Mexico City ★

Vera Cruz

**Occupied by
U.S. Forces,
April 21, 1914**

TROUBLE WITH MEXICO,
1910–1917

Overseas Entanglements

China In the Far East, Wilson considered moral gestures adequate. He therefore ended the International Financial Consortium, which Taft had sponsored to finance Chinese railroads, because it seemed to be an interference in the affairs of another nation. Intervention was particularly reprehensible in a country which in 1911 had ousted an ancient despotism to become a republic. In 1915 when the preoccupation of the Europeans elsewhere encouraged Japan to demand a virtual protectorate over China, Wilson reaffirmed the open-door policy and announced that the United States would tolerate no diminution of the territorial integrity of the Celestial Empire. He gave little thought to the means of implementing that policy, however.

Latin America Such pronouncements had little consequence in the remote Orient; closer to home the implications were more serious, especially when they were not thought through. Having announced in a speech at Mobile, Alabama, that human rights, not material interests, were the chief concern of American foreign policy, Wilson in 1914 felt obliged to negotiate a treaty giving a $25,000,000 indemnity to Colombia as reparation for Roosevelt's role in the Panama affair. But he then discovered to his embarrassment that the Senate would not ratify it and the matter remained in abeyance until 1921.

Moral criteria were no easier to apply elsewhere in Latin America. The Caribbean nations,

Sumner Welles, *Naboth's Vineyard, the Dominican Republic, 1844–1924* (New York, 1928); Charles C. Tansill, *The Purchase of the Danish West Indies* (Baltimore, 1932); and Arthur C. Millspaugh, *Haiti Under American Control, 1915–1930* (Boston, 1931) treat Wilson's Caribbean policy competently.

Francisco "Pancho" Villa (center) and Emiliano Zapata (at Villa's left), Mexican
Revolutionists, in the Presidential Palace, Mexico City, 1914. (The Granger Collection)

left to themselves, often sank into riotous disorder, from which their own people were the
worst sufferers. If the United States remained
correctly aloof, it would invite either anarchy or
intervention by the European powers. Somewhat
incongruously, Wilson kept a force of marines in
Nicaragua and sent similar expeditions into the
Dominican Republic and Haiti. In 1917 he completed the purchase of the Danish West Indies
(Virgin Islands) to help protect the Panama
Canal, which had been opened in 1915. Despite
the excellence of his intentions, therefore, he
found himself acting in the Western Hemisphere much as Roosevelt and Taft had.

Mexico Wilson's greatest diplomatic difficulty lay just south of the border. In 1910, a
revolution had overthrown the dictatorship of
Porfirio Díaz, who had ruled Mexico for decades.
In the long period of unrest that followed, the
central government disintegrated and various

generals formed their own armies in an effort
to seize power.

The United States was concerned not only
as a neighbor of the disorderly area but also
because its citizens had invested about a billion
dollars in oil, silver, railroads, and land there.
President Wilson refused either to recognize the
de facto government in control or to intervene
to establish what he considered a good one. To
accept the legitimacy of Victoriano Huerta, who
had gained office by murdering his predecessor
Francisco Madero, was out of the question. The
United States would deal only with a regime
installed by the popular will, not with one maintained by force. But it would not act forcefully
to encourage the appearance of an appropriate
kind of authority. The policy was one of watch-
ful waiting.

Yet nonintervention alone would not topple
Huerta, who could get arms from Europe, while

his opponents, Venustiano Carranza and Pancho Villa, could not. By the end of 1913 Wilson had come around to the belief that a little intervention was justified. Early the next year he opened the flow of supplies to Huerta's enemies and in April 1914 he seized upon a flimsy pretext to occupy the port of Vera Cruz.

Luck was with Wilson. True, Mexicans of all parties resented the invasion of their territory by foreigners. But mediation by Argentina, Brazil, and Chile helped to extricate the United States from its dilemma, and while discussions proceeded in the summer of 1914, Carranza succeeded in ousting Huerta.

The new Mexican chief was no more willing than the old to let the United States determine the legitimacy of his regime. When it became clear that Carranza would not respond to advice, Wilson decided that Pancho Villa was the true representative of the people. That was his worst mistake, for Villa lost the struggle for power in Mexico and then determined to embroil the United States by savage raids across the border. An American punitive force under General John J. Pershing set out in pursuit in the spring of 1916. It failed to find Villa but almost plunged the two countries into a war neither wanted. Although Theodore Roosevelt, among others, urged a more belligerent policy, Wilson drew back and negotiated a settlement. The last American troops pulled out of Mexican territory in February 1917. By then the crisis in Europe had first claim on the President's attention.

Noninvolvement had not been successful in Mexico. Neutrality was a difficult role for a great power, however well intentioned. By the time the United States began to use its power, the situation was beyond its control and it exerted little influence upon the outcome of events. Yet between 1914 and 1917 President Wilson pursued almost the same policy in Europe.

The Problems of Neutrality

The war for which Europeans had long prepared came unexpectedly in 1914. The balance of power which had maintained the peace for more than forty years was so delicate that any disturbances set off a chain of reactions.

The Alliances   The great states served complex interests. In all but France, historic dynasties provided continuity of leadership and ambition. All depended for security on elaborate military establishments. Only England did not maintain a large conscript army and it compensated by its tremendous navy. All sought security through alliances, open and secret. Only Austria had avoided the imperialist quest for colonies, and it ruled Slavic, Hungarian, and Bohemian subject peoples close to home. Nationalism was an explosive force in all countries, a source of irrational emotion the leaders could stir up but not control.

The crisis was touched off when a Serbian nationalist assassinated an Austrian archduke. The European states were then locked in alliances and committed to plans that left them no freedom of action. Vienna could not allow the incident to go unpunished lest other aggrieved revolutionaries pull the empire apart. Hence the ultimatum to Belgrade. Russia could not desert its Serbian ally without the loss of influence in the Balkans and Eastern Europe. Germany had to support Austria—and France had to do the same for Russia and England for France. And once the costs were paid in blood and ravaged lands, people and statesmen alike expected and demanded rewards that corresponded with their sacrifices.

American Neutrality   The outbreak of fighting in the Old World shocked Americans. Dismay deepened with news of the heavy casualties, of the tragic destruction of resources, and of the atrocities that accompanied the conflict. Ameri-

George M. Stephenson, *John Lind of Minnesota* (Minneapolis, 1935) has a good account of American policy toward Mexico.

Alex M. Arnett, *Claude Kitchin and the Wilson War Policies* (Boston, 1937) traces opinion on neutrality in Congress.

EUROPEAN ALLIANCES, 1914

cans could not understand how modern civilized nations had become involved in a senseless war. They therefore approved of President Wilson's declaration of neutrality and his injunction to his fellow citizens that they remain neutral in thought as well as in deed. The desire to stand apart from the fighting emanated from two sources, from a powerful sentiment for peace and from the consciousness that the sympathies of the nation were divided.

Since 1900 pacifism had gained support in the United States. The World Peace Foundation and the Carnegie Endowment for International Peace, both founded in 1910, had substantial resources, and numerous church organizations actively participated in the same work. In 1913,

eighty American peace societies made their voices heard against war. There was widespread approval of the treaties Secretary of State Bryan negotiated with thirty-five countries that provided for conciliation of all disputes. To the citizens who approved of these efforts, neutrality seemed the worthiest course for the United States.

Public Opinion Furthermore, noninvolvement would avoid significant internal divisions of opinion. Many Americans had close ties with friends and relatives in the contending armies of Europe. Numerous German-Americans felt sentimental attachments to the Fatherland. Millions of Irish-Americans were bitterly hostile to England, which was suppressing the home

321

rule movement in Ireland. Enmity to Russia inclined many American Jews to Germany, for the Kaiser had been far more tolerant toward their coreligionists than the Czar. In addition, altogether apart from ethnic affiliation, many people had a deep respect for German culture, science, and education.

On the other hand, the Allies had the support of influential groups. The British-born were particularly effective in swaying opinion because they did not seem foreign and their identity was not clearly apparent. Sympathy with France sent some aviators abroad in the Lafayette Escadrille, a group of American volunteers in the French service. Once Italy entered the war, thousands of Italian-Americans became emotionally involved.

Moreover, many native Americans without recent transatlantic connections gradually acquired a feeling of sympathy toward the Allied cause. For two decades there had been a steady decline in Anglophobia, as relations between the United States and England became closer. Children of the 1880s still thrilled with patriotic horror at the misdeeds of the redcoats. But thereafter memories of the Revolution faded, while commercial and cultural ties grew firmer. The effect was the greater because it was not recognized. Wilson himself, for instance, was not aware of the extent to which his regular reading of English newspapers and magazines shaped his ideas. The British exerted a significant influence over the news sources, even apart from their overt propaganda.

During the first year of the war, neutrality was a formula that prevented a clash between divergent opinions and it satisfied pacifists and other Americans uncommitted to either side. News of the calamitous battles that tore Europe apart only increased the sense of gratitude that the United States was spared.

Involvement

Wartime Trade   Yet the United States could not long remain neutral, as smaller countries like Norway or the Netherlands did. Imperceptibly it drifted toward participation. As soon as war broke out, the Allies sent agents to the United States to buy munitions and other supplies. Such sales did not seem unneutral. The Germans, after all, could also make purchases. In practice, of course, the Allies had the shipping and the naval power to carry their purchases to Europe and the Germans did not.

In time, too, the Allies requested and received commercial loans. Before taking action, the bankers consulted the President who decided, against Bryan's objection, that such borrowing in the course of business was not a departure from neutrality. Yet the loans created a vital American interest in an Anglo-French victory. The prosperity of the American economy was closely tied to the fate of the Allies.

Neutral Rights   The consequences quickly became apparent in the attempt of the United States to maintain its rights as a neutral at sea. In this matter, both contending sides were at fault, yet the United States did not react consistently to violations of its neutral rights. In dealing with England there was a will to adjustment; with Germany, a determination to hold to a rigid line.

Great Britain had never accepted the American interpretation of neutral rights. At the outbreak of war it immediately established a blockade of the German coast and began to halt vessels the cargoes of which might be contraband destined for its enemies. Britain also cut off supplies of food to the Central Powers and used the American flag on its own merchant vessels. This was the situation of the 1790s all over again. But this time there was to be no War of 1812. The United States protested against these violations of international practice but refrained from pressing the matter very far. Sir Edward Grey, Foreign Secretary in the liberal cabinet, made enough concessions to avoid a break.

The Submarine Issue   The German problem was that of countering British superiority at sea. The Kaiser's military planners had thought it all

America's Protest, 1915

If the commanders of German vessels of war should act upon the presumption that the flag of the United States was not being used in good faith and should destroy on the high seas an American vessel or the lives of American citizens, it would be difficult for the Government of the United States to view the act in any other light than as an indefensible violation of neutral rights which it would be very hard indeed to reconcile with the friendly relations now so happily subsisting between the two Governments.

If such a deplorable situation should arise, the Imperial German Government can readily appreciate that the Government of the United States would be constrained to hold the Imperial German Government to a strict accountability for such acts of their naval authorities and to take any steps it might be necessary to take to safeguard American lives and property and to secure to American citizens the full enjoyment of their acknowledged rights on the high seas.

— The Secretary of State to U.S. Ambassador Gerard in Germany, February 10, 1915. Department of State, *Papers Relating to the Foreign Relations of the United States*. 1915, Supplement: *The World War* (Washington: Government Printing Office, 1928), p. 99.

An Unneutral Ambassador, 1916

As the world stands, the United States and Great Britain must work together and stand together to keep the predatory nations in order. A League to Enforce Peace and the President's idea of disentangling alliances are all in the right direction, but vague and general and cumbersome, a sort of bastard children of Neutrality. *The* thing, the *only* thing is — a perfect understanding between the English-speaking peoples. That's necessary, and that's all that's necessary. We must boldly take the lead in that. I frankly tell my friends here that the English have got to throw away their damned arrogance and their insularity and that we Americans have got to throw away our provincial ignorance ("What is abroad to us?"), hang our Irish agitators and shoot our hyphenates and bring up our children with reverence for English history and in the awe of English literature. This is the only job now in the world worth the whole zeal and energy of all first-class, thoroughbred English men. *We* must lead. We are natural leaders. The English must be driven to lead.

— Walter Hines Page to Edwin A. Alderman, June 22, 1916, quoted in B. S. Hendrick, *The Life and Letters of Walter Hines Page* (New York: Doubleday & Company, Inc., 1924), vol. II, pp. 144–145.

out in advance. They did not expect to match the Royal Navy in size, but they hoped to develop enough deterrent power to keep it bottled up in its bases. Meanwhile, their land armies could swiftly sweep across France and bring the war to a quick conclusion.

It had not worked out that way. The British fleet did spend most of the war at anchor, but victory eluded the Germans. The war lengthened. To bring it to a close, the Germans resorted to a novel weapon, the submarine, to raid the commerce that kept England supplied. In February 1915, they proclaimed a war zone around the British Isles within which they warned that they would sink enemy vessels on sight.

The United States considered this measure a violation of international law, and Wilson forcefully warned the Germans against the consequences. He thereby lost some of his freedom of maneuver, for if Berlin refused to yield, he would have to take some action lest his future statements be discounted as meaningless bluff.

Secretary of State Bryan was dubious; he suggested that the United States forbid travel by Americans on enemy ships in order to avoid a possible incident. But Under Secretary of State Robert Lansing and the ambassador in London, Walter Hines Page, were already in their hearts committed to the British cause, and Wilson himself was unwilling to deviate from the line of strict legality.

The incident against which Bryan had warned came on May 7, 1915, when a German U-boat sank the British Cunard Liner *Lusitania.* Fully 600 crewmen and 1200 passengers, among them 100 Americans, went down in the disaster. The Germans had warned against travel on the ship, which carried munitions, but American opinion was nevertheless shocked. The sense of revulsion made credible all the stories about German atrocities that British propaganda had industriously been spreading. A consequential body of opinion shifted against the Kaiser.

Wilson wished to retain an even balance. He protested vigorously, warning the Germans that he would hold them strictly accountable for future losses of American lives. On the other hand, he announced that the United States would not fight out of pride alone, but would do whatever it could to maintain both the peace and the law. When the Germans justified submarine warfare as self-defense, Wilson prepared a rebuttal so vigorous that Bryan resigned rather than send it. The effect was to remove one of the brakes on Wilson's action. Lansing, who became Secretary of State, was an interventionist.

In the spring of 1916, the Germans announced after a year of negotiation with the United States that they would suspend submarine warfare. They did so less out of solicitude for Wilson's feelings than because they expected

(*Right.*) Advertisement for the *Lusitania* and Warning of the Imperial German Embassy to Travelers Sailing on Ships Flying the Flag of Great Britain or Its Allies. From the New York *Herald*, May 1, 1915. (The Granger Collection)

OCEAN STEAMSHIPS.

CUNARD

EUROPE VIA LIVERPOOL

LUSITANIA

Fastest and Largest Steamer now in Atlantic Service Sails
SATURDAY, MAY 1, 10 A. M.
Transylvania, Fri., May 7, 5 P.M.
Orduna, - - Tues., May 18, 10 A.M.
Tuscania, - - Fri., May 21, 5 P.M.
LUSITANIA, Sat., May 29, 10 A.M.
Transylvania, Fri., June 4, 5 P.M.

Gibraltar—Genoa—Naples—Piraeus
S.S. Carpathia, Thur., May 13, Noon

ROUND THE WORLD TOURS
Through bookings to all principal Ports of the World.
Company's Office. 21-24 State St., N. Y.

NOTICE!

TRAVELLERS intending to embark on the Atlantic voyage are reminded that a state of war exists between Germany and her allies and Great Britain and her allies; that the zone of war includes the waters adjacent to the British Isles; that, in accordance with formal notice given by the Imperial German Government, vessels flying the flag of Great Britain, or of any of her allies, are liable to destruction in those waters and that travellers sailing in the war zone on ships of Great Britain or her allies do so at their own risk.

IMPERIAL GERMAN EMBASSY

WASHINGTON, D. C., APRIL 22, 1915.

that the summer campaign they were about to launch would bring them victory. Again they were disappointed, and as the winter deepened with no end to the fighting in sight, the arguments of the Kaiser's naval strategists in favor of resuming submarine warfare gained cogency.

Wilson Halting U-boat Destruction. Cartoon by Rollin Kirby, New York *World*, 1916. (The Granger Collection)

Wilson's Logic, 1916

But in any event our duty is clear. No nation, no group of nations, has the right while war is in progress to alter or disregard the principles which all nations have agreed upon in mitigation of the horrors and sufferings of war; and if the clear rights of American citizens should ever unhappily be abridged or denied by any such action, we should, it seems to me, have in honor no choice as to what our own course should be.

For my own part, I cannot consent to any abridgment of the rights of American citizens in any respect. The honor and self-respect of the nation is involved. We covet peace, and shall preserve it at any cost but the loss of honor. To forbid our people to exercise their rights for fear we might be called upon to vindicate them would be a deep humiliation indeed. It would be an implicit, all but an explicit, acquiescence in the violation of the rights of mankind everywhere, and of whatever nation or allegiance. It would be a deliberate abdication of our hitherto proud position as spokesmen, even amidst the turmoils of war, for the law and the right. It would make everything this Government has attempted, and everything that it has achieved during this terrible struggle of nations meaningless and futile.

—President Wilson to Senator Stone, February 24, 1916. Department of State, *Papers Relating to the Foreign Relations of the United States*. 1916, Supplement: *The World War* (Washington: Government Printing Office, 1929), pp. 177–178.

The Break with Germany

The Search for Peace Meanwhile, Wilson labored desperately for peace. In the fall of 1916 he campaigned for re-election in good conscience under the slogan, "He kept us out of war." By then he realized that he was committed at least to the prevention of an Allied defeat, and the only way to avoid American involvement was to achieve a negotiated settlement between the contending powers before it was too late. He had sent his closest adviser, Colonel House, on a mission through the belligerent capitals in search of a formula for peace without a victory. House hoped for a settlement, for he too knew that otherwise the United States would ultimately have to join the Allies. He wished at least to secure a statement of war aims from both sides to lay the groundwork for a future just peace. He was disappointed. Berlin was somewhat more receptive to his plea than London, but in neither capital was there a willingness to forgo the expectation of gains from the war for the sake of early peace.

Nor did Wilson's personal appeal for peace elicit a response. He summoned the fighting parties to lay down their arms. He was unheeded except by the people who longed for peace but whose voices were not heard in the chancelleries of Europe.

The Coming of War As 1917 opened, the crisis approached its climax. In January the Germans announced that they would shortly resume submarine warfare. In protest, Wilson severed diplomatic relations (February 1917). His commitment to strict accountability he felt was binding. To retreat from that position, he feared, would sacrifice legality and also diminish the likelihood that the United States would be able to influence the future terms of settlement. In addition, some aggressive Americans, among them Theodore Roosevelt, were criticizing the President's dilatory responses and pressing for action. And those who thought entry into the war was only a matter of time had begun a widespread preparedness campaign.

The Zimmermann Telegram (released March 1, 1917) added to public excitement. The German attaché had approached the Mexican government with a proposal for an alliance. In the event of war, he suggested, the Mexicans were to intervene on the side of the Germans in return for the southwestern territory of the United States taken from them in 1846. The revelation of this note by the British, who had intercepted it, further inflamed American opinion.

For the President, legality and the shape of the future remained the decisive considerations. He might have chosen the alternative of armed neutrality, provided American vessels with weapons, and fought back in self-defense, as John Adams had against France in 1798. Instead, Wilson chose war despite his anguish and trepidation. He did so partly because he did not know the full cost and thought that the Ameri-

EDWARD M. HOUSE had English roots, the tenacity of which he himself did not realize. He was born in Houston, Texas, in 1858, the son of a prosperous planter and merchant. His father, an immigrant from Britain, sent Edward back to the old country to school.

When his father died in 1880, House, then a student at Cornell, returned to manage the plantation. After ten years he sold it and thereafter enjoyed an income large enough to enable him to live in leisure. He traveled frequently and made firm friendships in Washington, New York, Boston, and the European capitals. In the 1890s he enjoyed managing the campaigns of successive Texas governors and played a role of some importance as their behind-the-scenes adviser.

House first met Wilson in 1911 and the two immediately hit it off well. House helped Wilson to line up the presidential nomination and later to select his cabinet. Thereafter he was the President's most important counselor on foreign affairs. House occupied a pivotal position since he was also a friend of Sir Edward Grey, the British Foreign Secretary.

The summer of 1914 found the Texan in Europe attempting to ease Anglo-German tension. At the outbreak of war, he favored neutrality, as Wilson did, but he realized much sooner than the President that the United States would be involved. His efforts to mediate in 1915 and 1916 were motivated by the awareness that only an end to the fighting would spare his country from taking part.

After 1917 House worked with the Allies to arrange the details of American participation. At the same time he organized "The Inquiry," a semiformal group that discussed the terms of the peace settlement. During the conference that drew up the Treaty of Versailles and planned the League of Nations, he stood at Wilson's right hand, and he felt the country's failure to ratify as keenly as the President. Wilson's illness ended his friend's role. House lived on until 1938, just a year before the Europe he had struggled to save once more went up in the flames of war.

The Zimmermann Telegram, 1917

We intend to begin on the lst of February unrestricted submarine warfare. We shall endeavor in spite of this to keep the United States of America neutral. In the event of this not succeeding, we make Mexico a proposal of alliance on the following basis: make war together, make peace together, generous financial support and an understanding on our part that Mexico is to reconquer the lost territory in Texas, New Mexico and Arizona. The settlement in detail is left to you. You will inform the President of the above most secretly as soon as the outbreak of war with the United States is certain and add the suggestion that he should, on his own initiative, invite Japan to immediate adherence and at the same time mediate between Japan and ourselves. Please call the President's attention to the fact that the ruthless employment of our submarines now offers the prospect of compelling England in a few months to make peace.

—Zimmermann to the German Minister in Mexico, January 19, 1917. Department of State, *Papers Relating to the Foreign Relations of the United States.* 1917, Supplement 1: *The World War* (Washington: Government Printing Office, 1931), p. 147.

can role would be mostly that of supplying ships, arms, and money. Primarily, however, he decided to fight because he realized that only by becoming a belligerent could the United States act as a great power, influence the peace, and convert a European struggle for national gain into a crusade to make the world safe for democracy. When the Germans refused to withdraw the submarine, which was proving increasingly effective, he acted. On April 6, 1917, Congress, in response to his request, declared war on Germany.

▼

A variety of factors explained the American decision. Wilson's commitment to strict legality, the effectiveness of British propaganda, the economic ties of the United States with the Allies, and the cultural and social sympathies among their peoples help account for abandonment of neutrality.

Another factor complicated the decision. Americans were slow to recognize that the United States had any stake in the outcome. For more than two years they clung to neutrality while in actuality they drifted toward commitment to an Allied victory. As a result, they lost the freedom of decision. When the Germans decided to risk unrestricted submarine warfare, the Americans had to come in. It was then too late to achieve internal agreement about the country's objectives in the struggle, or to exact from the Allies desirable terms of participation, or even to secure binding pledges about the shape of the peace to come. The power Americans would display in the fighting would not help them at the conference table.

Paperbacks for Further Reading

Arthur S. Link, *Wilson the Diplomatist* (Quadrangle Books, Inc.) is a collection of general essays. Howard F. Cline, *The United States and Mexico* (Atheneum Publishers) examines Wilson's policy of recognition, and Robert E. Quirk, *An Affair of Honor* (W. W. Norton & Company, Inc.) is on the occupation of Vera Cruz. William L. Langer, *European Alliances and Alignments* (Vintage Books, Inc.) is an excellent analysis of the prewar systems. Barbara W. Tuchman, *The Guns of August* (Dell Publishing Co., Inc.) deals with the outbreak of war in Europe. Ernest R. May, *The World War and American Isolation* (Quadrangle Books, Inc.) is a balanced account of the issues of diplomatic neutrality. Herbert J. Bass, *America's Entry into World War I* (Holt, Rinehart & Winston, Inc.) and Daniel Smith, *The Great Departure* (John Wiley & Sons, Inc.) present various interpretations of the causes of American involvement. Randolph S. Bourne, *War and the Intellectuals* (Harper Torchbooks) contains contemporary reflections on the problem.

MAKING WAR

75

Because the United States was ill prepared for a war it thought would not come, it had to improvise hastily all the means of fighting it. Readiness for combat, in the twentieth century, involved not only assembling an army but also organizing the vast industrial apparatus for supplying it. To sustain the costs, it was also necessary to mobilize the psychological support of civilians.

Furthermore, the scenes of battle were in Europe, thousands of miles away, so transportation became a problem of critical dimensions. To draw together all the required resources called for extreme measures, the shock of which left permanent marks on American society.

The *New York American* Announcing Entry of the United States into World War I, April 6, 1917. (The Granger Collection)

The State of Preparation

BY THE STANDARDS of the European competence, the United States was totally unprepared for war. In August 1914, the army had
numbered about 5000 officers and 90,000
enlisted men, with about 100,000 more in the
militia and 66,000 in the navy. The Defense Act
of June 1916 raised the size of the army to
175,000 men. This fragmentary force bore the
task of guarding American interests around
the world.

Furthermore, industry, although highly
developed, was not ready for war. Hundreds
of different companies went their own way, using
methods designed for competition rather than
cooperation. Apart from a few weak trade associations, no instruments were available for
coordinating the activities of separate firms.
Indeed, government policy down to 1917 had
aimed primarily to prevent collusion in the
market place out of fear of restraint of trade.
In 1916, the pressures on the economy of orders
from the Allies and the possibility that the
United States might enter the war led to creation
of the Council for National Defense, consisting of cabinet members and representatives
of industry and labor. This advisory body had
achieved little and was in no position seriously
to plan for war by the time the declaration came
in April 1917.

Frederick L. Paxson, *America at War, 1917–1918* (Boston,
1939) is a straightforward general account.

Making Cannons, World War I. (Culver Pictures)

Most Americans were psychologically unprepared. The battles, they thought, would be easy—fought mostly by Europeans. This generation had only the pleasant recollections of the painless victories against Spain in Cuba and the Philippines. The Civil War had faded into a sentimental mist created by popular history and fiction which obliterated all the tragic features of the fighting. Innocently, almost gaily, the citizens of the Republic assumed a burden the weight of which they were yet to learn.

Mobilizing
the Economy

The Needs The Allied missions that arrived promptly after the entry of the United States into the war revealed the full urgency of the situation, however. After almost three years of

bitter struggle, French and British resources were depleted. The United States would have to help finance the war. Its industry would have to equip the fighting men. Its transport system would have to carry troops and materials to the ports and to Europe. And a full American army would have to take a place on the battlefield. Wilson's government hastily addressed itself to the task of meeting these needs in 1917.

Economic Reorganization Precisely because the peacetime organization of American society was so loose and decentralized, the shift to emergency conditions seemed to require tight controls exercised from Washington. The existing government departments were inadequately staffed for the purpose and a good deal of the work necessary to the war effort fell to specially created agencies. In the absence of a competent

Bernard M. Baruch, *American Industry in the War* (New York, 1941) emphasizes Baruch's role.

bureaucracy, businessmen were hurriedly called to take office, usually at a nominal salary of a dollar a year. Haste led to inefficiency and waste, yet there was no time to spare.

The Council for National Defense, the only existing body available to act, appointed boards to supervise the transition to a war economy in industry, food, trade, railroads, and shipping. But these improvised groups had little power and produced no results. They depended on the willingness of entrepreneurs to forgo profits for the sake of the common interest and, in effect, penalized the patriotic and rewarded the greedy.

By the summer of 1917, for instance, the railroads' efforts at voluntary collaboration had broken down. The transportation system was in a tangle. There was a shortage of freight cars and shippers were clamoring for space. Yet despite the increase in their business, the roads were losing money. The crisis impelled the government to take over. On December 26, 1917, President Wilson, by proclamation, assumed control of the nation's railroads, which he placed under the authority of Secretary of the Treasury McAdoo. The government operated the roads throughout the war, paying the owners a fee for their use. By the same token, the post office department assumed responsibility for operating the telephone and telegraph service.

Federal control in those cases was relatively easy. The personnel remained the same, with the presidents of the carriers acting as regional directors. The change did permit a high degree of standardization of equipment; twelve uniform types, for instance, replaced the 2000 different kinds of freight cars in service before the war. It was also possible to consolidate services, improve efficiency, and increase the volume of goods carried. Nevertheless, the shipping space available proved inadequate and a system of permits was necessary to assign priorities for essential commodities.

Faith in private ownership and mistrust of bureaucracy, however, made Americans unwilling to let the government operate the whole economy. Instead, the United States set up a number of agencies to supervise the private enterprises that remained under the management of their owners. The Fuel Administration, organized in August 1917, allocated essential supplies of coal, while other bureaus undertook to assure an equitable distribution of sugar and food. Ultimately, the War Industries Board, set up in March 1918 and directed by Bernard M. Baruch under authority of the President, assumed the power to plan the whole economy. The Overman Act of May 1918 subsequently gave the President almost unlimited control over the productive system, which he could exercise through the Board.

The achievements of American agriculture and industry under these circumstances were impressive, particularly since both had already been under stress before 1917 from the pressure of Allied orders. In the five-year period from 1913 to 1918, the production of steel increased by a third, rising from about 3,000,000 to more than 4,000,000 long tons. The ton miles of freight carried by railroads mounted by the same proportion, and the value of exports leaped from $2,000,000,000 to $6,000,000,000.

But the absence of prior planning was costly. It produced inequities in rewards since there was no effective restraint upon profiteering. And it led to severe inflation, to which rising prices and heavy government spending both contributed. Price controls were weak. The index of consumer prices rose from 100 in 1914 to 149 in 1918. For the time being an increase in the earnings of labor kept pace with the rise, but a disagreeable postwar situation was in the making.

Shipping The lack of preparation created immediate shipping difficulties. Since the Civil War the United States had consistently neglected its merchant marine. Lines subsidized by foreign governments had almost entirely displaced American vessels in the transatlantic business, and the sudden demand for wartime shipping precipitated a grave crisis.

In September 1916, the Congress made a gesture toward solving the problem by creating

Wilson often referred to **BERNARD M. BARUCH** as "Dr. Facts." Long experience had taught Baruch the importance of hard data. He knew how to find out, how to remember, and how to apply his information.

Baruch was born in Camden, South Carolina, in 1870. His father had migrated from East Prussia fifteen years earlier, had practiced medicine, and had served in the Confederate army as a surgeon. The family moved to New York in 1881, where Bernard received most of his education, graduating from The City College in 1889. He held a variety of jobs, tried his luck unsuccessfully in the Colorado gold fields, and then settled down to work with a brokerage firm in New York.

Baruch advanced and in 1896 had a share in A. A. Housman & Company, but all along he speculated on his own and did well. He bought a seat on the stock exchange, and at the age of thirty was a millionaire. He was willing to take risks, but on the basis of facts, and he became intimately familiar with the intricate structure of American industry.

A Democrat and a liberal contributor to party campaign funds, Baruch had met Wilson before 1912. The President appointed him a member of the Advisory Commission of the Council for National Defense in 1916 and in March 1918 made him chairman of the all-important War Industries Board.

Baruch's ability compensated for his dictatorial manner. He really knew the capacity of the nation's industry, laid out a master blueprint for mobilizing its resources, and cut through red tape to get supplies manufactured. He performed so well that Wilson took him as economic adviser to the Paris Peace Conference.

In the 1920s, Baruch withdrew from public attention. He understood the importance of coping with the vexing farm problem of that decade. But the Republican administrations had little regard for his views until the Depression, when Hoover called on him to aid in organizing the Reconstruction Finance Corporation.

After 1933, he was an elder statesman, consulted by Franklin D. Roosevelt on economic issues and called back into government service during World War II. In 1946, President Truman named him United States representative on the United Nations Atomic Energy Commission, where he labored in vain to achieve agreement on the control of nuclear weapons. He died in 1965.

the United States Shipping Board with an allocation of $50,000,000 to buy or build merchant vessels. The agency had scarcely got organized by the time the country entered the war. The Board then created the Emergency Fleet Corporation to act for it and by the time of the armistice had acquired almost 9,000,000,000 tons of shipping.

The ultimate success in assembling supplies and transferring them to Europe did not obscure some serious failures in the war effort. The United States, for instance, was quite unprepared when it came to new weapons. It did not build its share of aircraft and was often dependent upon the Europeans for artillery and tanks.

The Emergency Fleet Corporation was able to construct less than 500,000 tons of shipping. Agricultural output grew by 24 percent but that was still inadequate to feed the troops and civilians in Europe and at home, with the result that Americans learned to go through breadless days.

Furthermore, the whole operation of harnessing the economy to war was expensive. The dollar-a-year men who came down to run the agencies did not forget the companies that still usually paid their salaries. And the general abandonment of competitive bidding in favor of cost-plus contracts substantially added to the burden. This was the price of mobilizing a decentralized economy and subjecting it to common decisions in a period of crisis.

Financing the War

The cost of the war was substantial. The United States itself expended about $22,000,000,000 and, in addition, loaned fully $10,000,000,000 to its allies. Total Federal government expenditures in the three years from 1917 to 1919 ran about $33,000,000,000 as against receipts of less than $10,000,000,000. The resulting deficit of more than $23,000,000,000 had an inflationary impact.

To counteract that tendency, there was a determined effort to sell war bonds directly to the public. Four Liberty Loans (and a Victory Loan after the peace) drew out of circulation $21,448,000,000 that might have contributed further to inflation. To diffuse these bonds to their 65,000,000 purchasers, 75,000 four-minute men made 7,550,000 speeches, using every technique of salesmanship to convince audiences totaling 315,454,000 persons of the justice of the war against the venomous, bacterial German *Kultur*. This campaign of persuasion left a deep imprint upon American society.

Taxes paid for a smaller share of government expenditures than loans. An excise supplemented the revenue from the tariff, and the levy on incomes rose substantially. In 1916, the latter had ranged from a minimum of 2 percent to a maximum of 13 percent. By the end of the war, the minimum had become 12 percent, the maximum 65 percent. A corporation tax and a levy on excess profits, which went as high as 70 percent, added further to the burden. No taxpayer would escape the consciousness of American involvement in the war, no matter how much he profited from it.

Over There

Man Power In contrast to the complexity of the economic and fiscal problems, it proved surprisingly easy to mobilize the armed forces and get them into battle. By the time of the armistice, the United States had put 4,750,000 men under arms. Almost 2,000,000 youths had entered the ranks through voluntary enlistment, but as in earlier wars, the draft was the primary means of recruitment. The Selective Service Act of May 18, 1917, set up machinery under which 24,000,000 men registered. Through this mechanism some 2,800,000 draftees were inducted into the army. There was no procedure for substitutes as there had been in the Civil War but the calls met little resistance. Fewer than 4000 persons claimed the status of conscientious objectors. Hastily organized camps gave the recruits a smattering of training before they entered the trenches.

Assembling the man power was merely the first step in the task of putting an army in the field. It was necessary to ship 2,000,000 men and 5,000,000 tons of supplies in a hurry to Europe. Vessels were scarce and German submarines were a continuing threat. The navy managed to send 300 warships across the Atlantic to combat the menace. A carefully planned system of convoys permitted the United States to transfer its army without the loss of a single troop ship. A mine barrage laid by the Navy across the North Sea contributed to the containment of the German attack.

In October 1917, there were already some Americans in the trenches in France. Their presence was largely symbolic. To the weary French and British, they offered psychological assurance that help was on the way. Although the number of Yanks mounted steadily, they did not play a substantial part in the fighting until July 1918. But in the last five months of the war their addition to the Allied forces proved a consequential element in the ultimate victory.

Halting the Germans By the time the Americans arrived, the Eastern front had collapsed. The Russian Revolution (March 1917), which the United States had originally welcomed, weakened resistance to the Germans even while the

Frank Freidel, *Over There* (Boston, 1964) tells the battle story.

Scout Plane in Flight over the Front. (The National Archives)

new Provisional Government determined to fight on. But the Bolsheviks, who seized power in November 1917, decided to make peace. In the Treaty of Brest-Litovsk with Germany, they laid down their arms and surrendered an enormous expanse of Russian territory. The outcome of the war was to be decided in the West.

In March 1918, the Germans began their final spring offensive, using the men and weapons they were able to transfer from the East. By now the battles followed a well-established pattern. Maneuver and grand strategical schemes and new weapons such as the tank and the airplane were of slight importance. The opposing armies were dug in in trenches so that the defense always had the advantage. The attackers moved forward in wave after wave. The decisive element was the naked weight of fire power. Each spring an offensive had taken off. Hard fighting had followed through the summer and the fall and then, regrouping in winter.

The Americans in France, 1918

June 1, 1918. — A perfect June Day — and three red roses blooming in the garden in the very center of the arched bush over the gate. . . . And, yet, not far, that awful battle. We can know very little of it; this morning's bulletins may be interpreted as meaning that the offensive is slowing up at the wings, if not at the center. However, it is not ever much one learns from the *communiqués.* Nell and I go downtown usually after tea; there is a great crowd — French, English, Australian, Scotch, Belgian, American standing there reading the bulletins; and for the first time since I have been at Havre I read on those bulletins something that pleased me. It was the brief announcement of the splendid conduct of the Americans at Cantigny. I thrilled with pride. Oh! If we only had them all over here! . . .

June 14, 1918. — I went to look at the *communiqué.* The news good.

American troops pour through by the thousands, several regiments each day. Splendid big handsome fellows, and the young officers so fine, so straight, so serious, so clear eyed. They come from the boats in the morning, and afternoon and evening they march to the trains, bands playing, flags flying. Only a moment ago the strains of a band came to our ears, and while at tea we heard one. They sing, too, late at night. The sight of them cheers the French immensely, and they wring praise even from the English. To see it is significant, sublime, moving beyond words. I am always near tears. And how proud I am! Proud to be American.

— Allan Nevins, ed., *The Journal of Brand Whitlock* (New York: Appleton-Century-Crofts, 1936), pp. 483, 485.

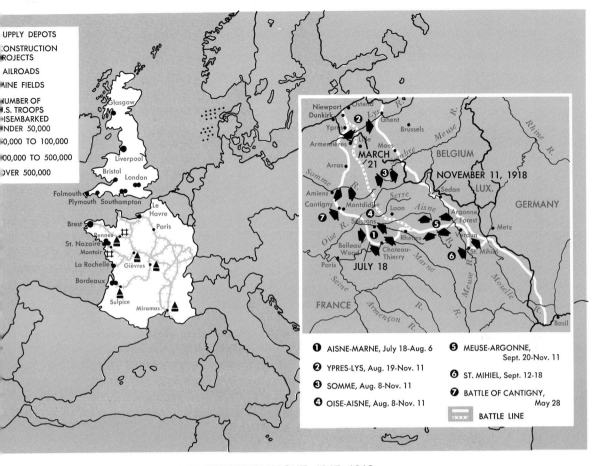

Glasgow

Liverpool

Bristol
London

Falmouth
Plymouth Southampton

Brest
Le
Havre
Rennes Paris
St. Nazaire
Montoir
La Rochelle Gièvres
Bordeaux

Sulpice
Miramas

Niewport Ostend R.
Dunkirk Lys
Ghent
Ypres Brussels
Lille Mons
Armentieres Meuse R.
Arras BELGIUM
MARCH
21 NOVEMBER 11, 1918
Somme R. Sedan LUX.
Amiens Laon GERMANY
Cantigny Montdidier Aisne
Soissons Argonne
Forest Metz
Oise R. Rheims Verdun
Belleau Marne St. Mihiel
Wood Chateau-
Thierry
Paris Meuse R.
JULY 18 Moselle R.
Seine Rhine R.
FRANCE Armençon R.
Basil

❶ AISNE-MARNE, July 18-Aug. 6   ❺ MEUSE-ARGONNE,
                                                                    Sept. 20-Nov. 11

❷ YPRES-LYS, Aug. 19-Nov. 11   ❻ ST. MIHIEL, Sept. 12-18

❸ SOMME, Aug. 8-Nov. 11   ❼ BATTLE OF CANTIGNY,
                                                                    May 28

❹ OISE-AISNE, Aug. 8-Nov. 11   ▭▭▭ BATTLE LINE

THE WESTERN FRONT, 1917–1918

Battery C, 6th Field Artillery, Montsec in the Distance. This battery fired the first shot for the United States on the Lorraine front and also defended Soissons. (The National Archives)

JOHN J. PERSHING was a professional soldier trained for command in an era when executive ability was more important in a staff officer than gallantry in action. He was born in 1860 in Linn County, Missouri, where his father farmed and worked on the railroad. As a boy, Jack saw the fighting men struggle home from Appomattox. The memory left him no desire to be a soldier.

But the poor young man could not pass up an opportunity for an education. An appointment to West Point drew Pershing into a military career. Commissioned in 1886, he served in campaigns against the Apache and the Sioux in New Mexico, Arizona, and Dakota. In 1891 he was detached to act as military instructor at the University of Nebraska and while there earned a law degree. He never practiced, however. He went on to teach tactics at the United States Military Academy and served with the Tenth Cavalry in Cuba in 1898.

His career as an administrator began shortly thereafter, when he organized the Bureau of Insular Affairs. There followed periods of duty in the Philippines and as military attaché in Tokyo. In the latter capacity he had the opportunity to observe the Japanese army in Manchuria during the war with Russia. While he was a member of the general staff, he married (1905) the daughter of the wealthy rancher, Senator Francis E. Warren of Wyoming—popularly known as "the greatest shepherd since Abraham"—and then led a successful campaign against the Moro tribesmen in the Philippines.

By then Pershing had acquired a considerable reputation. Nicknamed "Black Jack" for his success with Negro troops, he was a martinet when it came to discipline and had the sense of organization that enabled him to command a large army.

He suffered a shattering personal tragedy in 1915 when his wife and three daughters lost their lives in the burning of the Presidio in San Francisco where he was commandant. He conducted the successful operations against Pancho Villa in Mexico and was selected commander in chief of the American Expeditionary Force in 1917. Here his organizing ability manifested itself and contributed to the quick mobilization of American power in France. He returned a hero and served as chief of staff in 1921 before retiring. He died in 1948.

In the climactic German effort between March and July 1918, General Erich Ludendorff repeatedly struck the Allies—near Amiens, in Flanders, at Chemin des Dames, and at the Marne. By then there were 300,000 Americans in France, serving in the Allied armies under Marshal Ferdinand Foch, the commander in chief. The Americans participated in the fighting at Cantigny, Château-Thierry, and Belleau Wood. And in the battle of the Marne (July 15–18) they helped prevent a breakthrough in the final German offensive.

The Allied Offensive In preparation for the counteroffensive, the Americans organized a separate command. General John J. Pershing in August 1918 took command of the first American army prepared to fight as a unit. Its initial assignment was elimination of the salient of St. Mihiel. A four-day battle, in which 500,000 Americans participated, achieved that objective in September at a cost of 7000 casualties.

Later that month the Americans formed part of a multipronged offensive designed to end the war. Their sector took them through the Argonne Forest along the Meuse River. On September 26, a forty-day battle began, in which the Americans suffered 117,000 casualties. The German army was decimated; its capacity for resistance, finished. The Kaiser's allies also collapsed. Bulgaria surrendered at the end of September, and Austria and Turkey soon thereafter. On November 11, 1918, the Germans

The Argonne Region, September 28, 1918. Ammunition, guns, and other supplies are going forward, while caissons, ambulances, and empty trucks stream back. (The National Archives)

signed an armistice that amounted to complete capitulation.

Costs: Physical and Spiritual

Casualties In the war, the Americans suffered 50,000 deaths in battle and 57,000 from disease. Some 237,000 were wounded. These were the measurable casualties. The cost to the United States in money was heavy, but not beyond the capacity of the nation to endure.

Harry R. Rudin, *Armistice, 1918* (New Haven, Conn., 1944) is a detailed monograph.

Other charges, however, were less readily absorbed. They, too, were the product of lack of preparation for the kind of conflict the war would be. President Wilson had felt a foreboding of the damage that might ensue, even as he led the nation into battle. Shortly before the declaration he expressed the fear that the war would witness the end of American liberties. Precisely because he lacked confidence that those freedoms would endure, he took no effective steps to protect them.

The War of Words Wilson understood that the war was fought for the minds of men as well as on the battlefields. Immediately after entry of the United States into the conflict he created the Committee on Public Information under

The Military Costs of War, 1914–1918

(in thousands)

Country	Men Mobilized	Killed	Wounded
Germany	11,000	1,773	4,216
Russia	12,000	1,700	4,950
France	8,410	1,358	4,266
Austria-Hungary	7,800	1,200	3,600
Great Britain	8,904	908	2,090
Turkey	2,850	325	950
Italy	5,615	650	947
United States	4,750	107	237

George Creel, assigning to it the task of spreading favorable propaganda and attacking the enemy. It mobilized artists to prepare patriotic posters and writers to put into more sustained form the emotional appeals that the orators condensed into a few minutes. Using scores of languages, it printed 75,000,000 pamphlets at home and abroad.

Creel and the Committee aimed at moderation. In line with the official position that the United States was fighting to end war and to make the world safe for democracy, there was some effort to distinguish between the German people and their government. Nevertheless, the result of the Committee's work was an upsurge of popular irrationality. Wilson himself sometimes grew shrill as he demanded that the German empire, a thing without conscience or honor, be crushed. And he warned against dissenters who might obstruct the crusade.

Others were carried away with hatred. The German nation itself was infamous, greedy, sensuous, and bloodthirsty, a popular preacher told Congress. All traces of the vile influence were to be eradicated—Teutonic music and literature banned, the language excluded from school curricula, and sauerkraut renamed liberty cabbage.

James Robert Mock and Cedric Larson, *Words That Won the War* (Princeton, N.J., 1939) analyzes the work of the Committee on Public Information.

Wilson's Anguish, 1917

FOR NIGHTS, he said, he'd been lying awake going over the whole situation; over the provocation given by Germany, over the probable feeling in the United States, over the consequences to the settlement and to the world at large if we entered the mêlée. . . .

He said he couldn't see any alternative, that he had tried every way he knew to avoid war. "I think I know what war means," he said, and he added that if there were any possibility of avoiding war he wanted to try it. "What else can I do?" he asked. "Is there anything else I can do?"

I told him his hand had been forced by Germany, that so far as I could see we couldn't keep out.

"Yes," he said, "but do you know what that means?" He said war would overturn the world we had known; that so long as we remained out there was a preponderance of neutrality, but that if we joined the Allies the world would be off the peace basis and onto a war basis. . . .

The President said a declaration of war would mean that Germany would be beaten and so badly beaten that there would be a dictated peace, a victorious peace.

"It means," he said, "an attempt to reconstruct a peacetime civilization with war standards, and at the end of the war there will be no bystanders with sufficient power to influence the terms. There won't be any peace standards left to work with."

—Frank I. Cobb, *Cobb of the World* (New York: E. P. Dutton & Co., Inc., 1924), pp. 268–269.

Free Speech in Wartime In the face of the devilish foe, no dissent was tolerable. Restrictive legislation seriously narrowed the scope of personal liberties. The Espionage Act of June 15, 1917, provided heavy penalties for acts or advocacy of acts that threatened American security. Shortly thereafter the Trading with the Enemy Act added other controls; treasonable utterances were barred from the mails, and letters to or from foreign countries were subjected to censorship. The Sedition Act of May 16, 1918, went even further in punishing those who disagreed with the government's policy. The capture of the Russian Revolution by the Communists touched off a red scare in the United States. The anarchists and socialists who had been preaching class war for a decade now seemed formidable enemies, as dangerous at home as the Huns were abroad.

Mounting hysteria raised the demand for conformity. Patriots were expected to be 100 percent Americans. Disagreement was a crime and even criticism of the Allies was suspect. The Department of State instructed the press that news unfavorable to England gave aid and comfort to the enemy, and a Federal judge explained, in banning "The Spirit of 1776," a film, that any statement derogatory to Great Britain violated the Espionage Act. The post office excluded from the mails publications it deemed unpatriotic; and the Department of Justice began a sustained drive against those suspected of holding unpopular opinions. In September 1917, it launched a series of raids against the IWW, and by February 1918 had jailed some two thousand Wobblies. The prosecutions drew no precise lines among various types of dissenters. Eugene V. Debs, Victor Berger, and other Socialists were the victims of wartime hatreds equally with pacifists, anarchists, labor leaders, and people charged with German sympathies.

In addition, some states passed espionage acts of their own. In 1918 and 1919 many of them adopted statutes against advocacy of criminal syndicalism—defined as the doctrine that approved violence as a means of attaining in-

Purifying American Music, 1918

Deception, intrigue, and cunning will work for a time with the unsophisticated. This sort of thing has been going on in the United Stated for many years, but at last the mask that has hidden the insidious German propaganda that has been woven into our whole educational system has been lifted and the whole scheme is being revealed in its true light.

Not only have our school-books been filled with matter that has sounded the praises of everything that is German, but it has been threaded into our school music-books and sent out on the wings of song. German music, German opera, German songs translated without changing the substance, and directed and sung by Germans, have been taken up and carried along by American supervisors who never suspected any evil designs of Germany to make America German in thought and feeling.

In all the many courses laid down in the many "systems" of music-books used in our public schools, adaptations from the German, with words translated to fit them instead of the reverse order as it should be, are given prominence, not because they are better music or more adaptable to our nationality than the music of our American composers, but for the obvious reason of making our musical supervisors, superintendents, and boards of education think so, and to make it appear that German music is more pleasant to the taste.

—Des Moines *Capital,* as quoted in *Literary Digest,* LVI (March 30, 1918), p. 30.

dustrial or political ends. Meanwhile, laws and local vigilantes did not scruple to take direct action when they thought it necessary. The dangerous reaction that Wilson had feared had occurred.

The Effects At the war's end it was difficult to assess the losses and the gains. The casualties were genuine enough and a large national debt was evidence of the financial outlay caused by the fighting. But the country was prosperous. Agricultural output had risen; manufacturing had gained new markets; and wages had increased. The position of Samuel Gompers in the Council for National Defense showed the respectability of labor and the membership of the American Federation of Labor attained unprecedented heights. Yet the emotional outbursts of opinion at home were an ominous indication of changes in the country, the character of which was not yet evident. The full consequences of the crusade to make the world safe for democracy would depend on the nature of the peace that emerged from the war.

Wilson, the Congress, and the American people had been able to overcome some of the handicaps created by their unreadiness for war. They had mobilized industry and man power, shipped an army overseas, and got it to fight creditably. But Americans found it more difficult to surmount their subtle psychological unpreparedness for a role as a world power. Unable to deal reasonably with the domestic consequences of the war, they would also prove incapable of accepting the peace that emerged from it.

Paperbacks for Further Reading

There is a thoughtful discussion of some of the issues in René Albrecht-Carrié, *The Meaning of the First World War* (Spectrum Books). Marc Karson, *American Labor Unions and Politics* (Beacon Press) is about labor during the war. The effects on civil liberties are treated in William Preston, Jr., *Aliens and Dissenters* (Harper Torchbooks); and Samuel Konefsy, *The Legacy of Holmes and Brandeis* (Collier Books) deals with the decisions in the sedition cases.

LOSING THE PEACE

76

The nature of its involvement in the war limited the extent to which the United States could influence the character of the treaty of peace. The nation had drifted into battle without deliberation or preparation. Its goals were vague and undefined. Moreover, it took up arms without knowing in advance whether the countries that shared the struggle also shared its objectives. In any case, the passions raised by war were not conducive to the formulation of a just peace.

As a result, President Wilson suffered at the conference table a defeat that nullified his hopes for a world free of armed conflict and safe for democracy. His goals were so remote from those of the Allies that there could be no effective bargaining between them. In the end, he was compelled to bring home a treaty that his countrymen would not accept.

The Secret Treaties, 1915–1917

Date	Participants	Chief Provisions
March 1915	England, France, Russia	Dismemberment of the Turkish empire with Constantinople to Russia
April 1915	England, France, Italy	Italy to acquire parts of Austria, Albania, Turkey, and the Dodecanese Islands along with assurance of control of the Adriatic
August 1916	England, France, Romania	Romania to take Transylvania from Hungary
February 1917	England, France, Russia, Italy, Japan	Supplanted an Anglo-Japanese agreement of 1915. German islands north of the equator to Japan, south of that line to England. Japan to acquire German rights to the Shantung Peninsula (China)
March 1917	France, Russia	Russia to get German Poland; France, Alsace-Lorraine
August 1917	France, England, Italy	Partition of Asia Minor

War Aims

Secret Treaties The Allies knew exactly what they wanted. Long before the assassination at Sarajevo they had considered the possibility of an outbreak of war and had begun to map out the results each power expected. The course of the conflict sharpened their views. Between March 1915 and March 1917 five secret treaties among England, France, Italy, Romania, and Japan set the outlines of the future. Since partnership in the conflict with Germany did not altogether dispel the habitual mistrust of diplomats for one another, behind-the-scenes negotiations continued; and a sixth agreement was reached without consulting the United States well after it had entered the war.

There was nothing sentimental about these understandings, which sliced up the territory of the losers in the interest of the victors. The statesmen who haggled over the terms had in view simply the fulfillment of the national, dynastic, and imperialistic ambitions of their countries. The prospective conditions for peace were no worse than those the Germans might have imposed had they won, but neither were they any better.

The Allied leaders, moreover, had spent four years drumming up hatred of the enemy. As losses mounted on both sides, the tone of the propaganda became more bitter and more vindictive. The fighting no longer affected only limited groups of warriors; it drew into its orbit the whole population. The people, driven to increasingly painful sacrifices, yielded to rage, and their uneasy rulers, worried lest popular passion turn into revolution at home, made a scapegoat of the devilish enemy, who was to blame for all evil. The fate of the Tzar was an omen of what the abused masses might do if the foe did not supply an adequate outlet for their anger. Whether Lloyd George actually intended to hang the Kaiser or not, he found the

The concluding chapter of Alan J. P. Taylor, *Struggle for Mastery in Europe* (New York, 1954) gives the context of the secret treaties.

slogan useful in appeals to the electorate. Then, too, some leaders ended by believing their own propaganda about the malevolent Hunnish culture of the Germans.

The American Objectives Wilson's conception of the peace was quite different from that of the Allies. His was a war to end war. He had called frequently for a settlement that would establish permanent good relations among the nations, all in the future governing themselves democratically within boundaries set according to the principle of self-determination. A just treaty would eliminate future causes of conflict. A vindictive one would obstruct progress toward that goal.

On January 8, 1918, Wilson enunciated the fourteen points he considered essential to end wars and to make the world safe for democracy. He emphasized extension of the areas of freedom, disarmament, the liquidation of imperialism, national self-determination, and an association of nations to maintain peace. These objectives were poles removed from those of the Allies.

Wilson had done nothing in advance to remove this potential cause for misunderstanding. He knew the Allied aims and had learned the terms of the secret treaties before the United States entered the war. That was why he refused to ally himself formally with Britain and France. By fighting the war and negotiating the treaty as an "associated power" of the Allies, he hoped to keep the United States pure of their corrupt motives. However, by doing so he lost the opportunity to compel the Allies, who were desperately eager for his aid, to modify their objectives. At the peace conference, where he expected the correctness of his views to prevail, the consequences would be tragic.

Wilson's stance also compelled him to deceive the American people. The citizens, who knew nothing of the treaties, were repeatedly soothed by his assurances of the lofty aims of the war. They would react in shocked indignation when they finally learned the terms of the Treaty of Versailles.

The Fourteen Points, 1918

I. Open covenants of peace, openly arrived at, after which there shall be no private international understandings of any kind but diplomacy shall proceed always frankly and in the public view.

II. Absolute freedom of navigation upon the seas, outside territorial waters, alike in peace and in war, except as the seas may be closed in whole or in part by international action for the enforcement of international covenants.

III. The removal, so far as possible, of all economic barriers and the establishment of an equality of trade conditions among all the nations consenting to the peace and associating themselves for its maintenance.

IV. Adequate guarantees given and taken that national armaments will be reduced to the lowest point consistent with domestic safety.

V. A free, open-minded, and absolutely impartial adjustment of all colonial claims, based upon a strict observance of the principle that in determining all such questions of sovereignty the interests of the populations concerned must have equal weight with the equitable claims of the government whose title is to be determined.

VI. The evacuation of all Russian territory. . . .

VII. Belgium, the whole world will agree, must be evacuated and restored, without any attempt to limit the sovereignty which she enjoys in common with all other free nations. . . .

VIII. All French territory should be freed and the invaded portions restored, and the wrong done to France by Prussia in 1871 in the matter of Alsace-Lorraine, which has unsettled the peace of the world for nearly fifty years, should be righted, in order that peace may once more be made secure in the interest of all.

(Continued on next page)

(Continued from preceding page)

IX.   A readjustment of the frontiers of Italy should be effected along clearly recognizable lines of nationality.

X.   The peoples of Austria-Hungary, whose place among the nations we wish to see safeguarded and assured, should be accorded the freest opportunity of autonomous development.

XI.   Rumania, Serbia, and Montenegro should be evacuated; occupied territories restored; Serbia accorded free and secure access to the sea; and the relations of the several Balkan states to one another determined by friendly counsel along historically established lines of allegiance and nationality; and international guarantees of the political and economic independence and territorial integrity of the several Balkan states should be entered into.

XII.   The Turkish portions of the present Ottoman Empire should be assured a secure sovereignty, but the other nationalities which are now under Turkish rule should be assured an undoubted security of life and an absolutely unmolested opportunity of autonomous development, and the Dardanelles should be permanently opened as a free passage to the ships and commerce of all nations under international guarantees.

XIII.   An independent Polish state should be erected which should include the territories inhabited by indisputably Polish populations, which should be assured a free and secure access to the sea, and whose political and economic independence and territorial integrity should be guaranteed by international covenant.

XIV.   A general association of nations must be formed under specific covenants for the purpose of affording mutual guarantees of political independence and territorial integrity to great and small states alike.

—Woodrow Wilson, *The Fourteen Points.* H.R. Doc. 765, Serial No. 7443, 65th Cong., 2d sess. (Washington: Government Printing Office, 1918), pp. 3–7.

The Treaty of Versailles

Preparations   The German offer to surrender had been based on the Fourteen Points, but discussion of Wilson's statement by the victors revealed significant differences of opinion among them before the armistice. The British would not accept the American concept of the freedom of the seas, and the French insisted on receiving reparations for the damage they had suffered. Wilson, at the time, was unwilling to argue these points. He preferred to leave these matters to future decision, counting on the support of world popular opinion to help him convince the Allies.

He did have his way, however, about the procedure by which to prepare the treaty. The French had suggested that the great powers arrange the terms in advance and present them to the others for acceptance. Wilson, his imagination already seized by the association of nations mentioned in the Fourteen Points, insisted that all twenty-seven countries which had broken with Germany participate. Moreover, he intended to head the American delegation in person, putting the weight of his moral authority behind a just settlement.

The Conference   The Peace Conference met in Paris on January 18, 1919. It continued its sessions until the end of June, when the Treaty of Versailles was finally signed. The gathering quickly proved too large to work effectively and it delegated the task of drafting the terms to a council of ten on which the United States, Britain, France, Italy, and Japan were represented. However, the critical decisions were made by four men, Wilson, Georges Clemenceau of France, David Lloyd George of Great Britain, and Vittorio E. Orlando of Italy. The future lay in their hands.

In the bitter, protracted wrangling over terms Wilson proved incapable of converting the

John M. Keynes, *Economic Consequences of the Peace* (New York, 1919) is brilliantly written, though biased.

The Big Four at Versailles. Left to right, Lloyd George of Great Britain, Orlando of Italy, Clemenceau of France, and Wilson. (UPI)

others. At one time, he considered an appeal over their heads directly to their peoples. When he returned to the United States briefly in February 1919, he still hoped to soften the views of Orlando, Lloyd George, and Clemenceau. He was, after all, a popular international figure on whom the hopes of the whole world rested.

The Peace Terms In the end, Wilson yielded. As a politician, he knew the necessity of compromise and once he discovered the strength of his opponents' position, he edged toward it, hoping to receive useful concessions in return. His bargaining power was not great, however. The fighting was over and Germany was crushed. The Allies, who outvoted him, no longer needed American help. As a last resort they could actually make peace without him. The final draft of

the treaty was therefore far removed from the Fourteen Points.

The Kaiser had long since abdicated and his empire had collapsed. The German people, whom President Wilson had not considered responsible for the sins of their rulers, had formed a democratic republic. Yet their delegates received the opportunity neither to discuss nor to modify the terms thrust upon them. They were forced to acknowledge that Germany was to blame for all the losses and damages caused by the war, and they assumed the liability for reparations to the victors, the amount later to be calculated to cover the whole cost of the fighting.

In addition, Germany was stripped of its fleet and its army. Its colonial possessions went

EUROPE 1914

EUROPE 1920 ▶

✿ CORDON
  SANITAIRE

NOTE:
THE GREEN TONE ON
EUROPE 1914
WHEN ENLARGED IN
PROPER JUXTA-
POSITION ON
EUROPE 1920
SHOWS A COMPLEX
OF ADDED
BOUNDARIES.

THE PEACE SETTLEMENTS, 1918–1920

to its enemies, under the thin disguise of mandates on behalf of the League of Nations. Germany also suffered substantial territorial losses. Alsace-Lorraine went to France; and Silesia and Posen, to a restored independent Poland, along with a corridor to the sea. Danzig unwillingly became a free city, and the Saar was to be held by the French until 1935. In the Far East, Japan appropriated the German-held Shantung Peninsula despite the protests of China. These changes were made without consulting the inhabitants, as the principle of self-determination might have required.

Subsidiary Treaties Decisions reached in Paris and later embodied in treaties with Germany's allies came closer to honoring that principle. The Treaty of St.-Germain with Austria (September 10, 1919), of Neuilly with Bulgaria (November 27, 1919), of Trianon with Hungary (June 4, 1920), and of Sèvres with Turkey (August 10, 1920) created a cluster of new states in Eastern Europe and the Balkans. Here, self-determination coincided with England's desire to dissolve the Austro-Hungarian empire and with France's wish to create a *Cordon Sanitaire* to prevent the westward spread of Communism. The boundaries of the new countries were based on imperfect knowledge of the areas and, in any case, destroyed the economic unity of the region. Substantial minorities were left in Yugoslavia, Czechoslovakia, Romania, Greece, and Poland, for the population of Eastern Europe in actuality was too heterogeneous to permit strict adherence to the principle of national self-determination.

The League of Nations Wilson could console himself with subsidiary successes. The German colonies were not legally transferred to their new owners. They were assured independence at some future unspecified date and meanwhile were to be administered as mandates for their own good by their new rulers. In return for the promise of a defensive treaty with the United States (which the Senate never ratified) and upon the guarantee that the area would remain demilitarized, France yielded on its claim to the German Rhineland, which Clemenceau had coveted. Italy was denied the city of Fiume.

Such minor gains alone would not have made the outcome of the conference palatable to Wilson. One greater success did so. The agreement on a permanent international association, in his eyes, compensated for all the concessions he had had to make. Provision for the League of Nations was an integral part of the Treaty of Versailles. Time and again as he gave way on particular points, he consoled himself with the reflection that the new organization would provide a permanent means of adjusting any future difficulties.

The League was to consist of an Assembly in which all nations were represented, but its powers were only advisory. A Council of nine, consisting of Britain, France, the United States, Italy, Japan, and four other countries, would have greater authority. It could mediate disputes and establish a world court. In addition, a permanent Secretariat would provide means of communication, and the International Labor Office would disseminate information. Significantly, the conference refused Japan's request that the Covenant of the League recognize the principle of racial equality, lest such a provision arouse the colonial populations. But most of the Covenant consisted of statements of good intentions. Article 10, however, did provide for action to halt aggression and for sanctions against any disturbance of the integrity of existing nations. That machinery of maintaining the peace, for Wilson, justified everything else about the treaty. In the end, even that prize slipped from his fingers.

The Struggle for Ratification

The Failure of Presidential Leadership The Treaty of Versailles failed of ratification in the United States. Wilson had entirely overlooked this possibility. He had assumed that he could control the Senators of his own party, and he

William E. Borah (1865–1940). (Brown Brothers)

had expected little opposition from the Republicans. Since 1915, the League to Enforce Peace, of which Taft was President and the aims of which Senator Lodge endorsed, had been working toward ends similar to Wilson's. It had not occurred to him that there would be serious questions about the agreement he brought back from Paris.

The President did not understand the factors that steadily built up sentiment against him. He had blundered in the fall of 1918 when he had called for the election of a Democratic Congress, hoping to capitalize on wartime sentiment for party purposes. Censorship and stifling of dissenting opinion had closed off the information that might have warned him of the danger of his course. The campaign revealed a good deal of discontent to which he was inattentive. The results of the balloting were Republican majorities in both houses of Congress and alienation of the leaders of the opposition party. Theodore

WILLIAM E. BORAH was a loner. All his life he resented restraints and he never acknowledged that his ideal of the unconfined individual might be inappropriate to the twentieth century.

He was born in Jasper Township, Illinois, in 1865. His father was a successful farmer, a stern disciplinarian, and a devout Presbyterian. William rebelled. He ran away from home to be an actor, then wandered about, studied intermittently at the University of Kansas, and secured admission to the bar of that state in 1887. Hard times drove him west. He settled in Boise, Idaho, developed a profitable practice, married the governor's daughter, and entered politics.

Borah gained national fame as prosecutor of the IWW leaders accused of murdering Governor Steunenberg in 1905, and in 1907 he was elected to the United States Senate. There, as earlier, he refused to be a party regular. He was a Republican but had supported Bryan in 1896 and remained a staunch silver man. He sponsored bills to improve labor conditions, and favored the income tax and the direct election of Senators. On the other hand, he opposed conservation, upheld Taft on the tariff, and refused to bolt the party in 1912 although T. R. was his hero.

Borah's dislike of bureaucracy and centralization led him to oppose most of Wilson's domestic program after 1913. He voted not to confirm Brandeis' nomination to the Supreme Court, supported prohibition, and opposed women's suffrage. At heart, he wished the country to remain as he thought it had been in the nineteenth century—free and individualistic.

His dislike of change evoked his irreconcilable hostility to the League of Nations. He had never gone abroad and saw no reason for involvement in alien affairs. Rejection of the Treaty of Versailles seemed the high point of his career. He lived for twenty years more, favoring progressive measures that conformed with his vision, opposing others. He died in 1940, a year before the United States finally discovered it could not remain apart from the affairs of the world.

Roosevelt triumphantly proclaimed that the country had repudiated the President's leadership. Wilson had included no Republican Senators in the delegation he took to Paris, and he identified himself so closely with the treaty he brought back as practically to invite opposition.

Hostility to the Treaty Objections developed in the United States as soon as the terms were known. Many Americans without any particular political commitment were shocked to discover that the war they had fought to spread democracy had turned into a sordid contest for French and English gains. The settlement, they predicted, would not end war, for it contained the seeds of future difficulties. The loss of the support of responsible and respectable progressive leaders particularly damaged the President. Oswald Garrison Villard of the influential journal *The Nation* and Senators Norris, Borah, and Johnson—among others—turned against him. These were not partisan politicians but independents whose views carried weight throughout the country.

In addition, some ethnic groups resented specific features of the treaty for reasons of their own. German-Americans regarded the war-guilt clause as an unwarranted slur upon the German people. Irish-Americans, still emotionally involved in the Emerald Isle's struggle for home rule or independence, feared that Article 10 might some day compel the United States to aid Britain in repressing an Irish rebellion. If that contingency was remote, they pointed out, a strict reading of Article 10 would certainly prevent Americans from aiding the Irish against the English. Italian-Americans were dissatisfied with the inadequate gains of their former home country. Among Armenian-, Ukrainian-, and Lithuanian-Americans, and among other groups as well, disappointment that results did not match their limitless expectations generated hostility to the treaty.

Republican Tactics These scattered grievances acquired significance because the Republi-

Marian C. McKenna, *Borah* (Ann Arbor, Mich., 1961) tells the story of his life.

Doubts About Article 10, 1919

Looking at this article as a part of a perpetual league for the preservation of peace, my first impression was that the whole article ought to be stricken out. If perpetual, it would be an attempt to preserve for all time unchanged the distribution of power and territory made in accordance with the views and exigencies of the Allies in this present juncture of affairs. It would necessarily be futile. . . . It would not only be futile; it would be mischievous. Change and growth are the law of life, and no generation can impose its will in regard to the growth of nations and the distribution of power, upon succeeding generations.

—Elihu Root to W. H. Hays, quoted in Philip C. Jessup, *Elihu Root* (New York: Dodd Mead & Company, Inc., 1938), vol. II, pp. 392–393.

cans made defeat of the treaty a partisan issue. Ratification would strengthen Wilson and the Democratic party. While the GOP leaders were patriotic and believed sincerely that they acted in the national interest, they saw no reason to accommodate themselves to objectionable provisions when they might profit from opposition.

The alignment of forces in the Senate, where the decision rested, reflected both principle and party politics. Almost all the Democrats favored the treaty, whether out of loyalty to the President or out of conviction. Thirteen progressive Republicans were among the irreconcilables, who were absolutely opposed. Sick of the war and of its results, they wished an end to foreign entanglements and considered the League a device of the Allies to perpetrate an unjust peace. They would not reconcile themselves to any version of the treaty that tied the United States to the League.

HENRY CABOT LODGE kept his mind firmly closed. Family, education, and experience had taught him what was right. He saw no need for examining other opinions.

Lodge was born in 1850, just when the Boston Brahmins were beginning to recognize their gentlemanly identity. He passed through Harvard and its law school without distinction. A taste for polite scholarship led him to the assistant editorship of the *North American Review* and to a Ph.D. in political science (1877). In the next few years he wrote and taught history at Harvard.

Before the age of thirty he decided that his career was to be in politics. He was a staunch Republican and supported Garfield in 1880 and Blaine in 1884, somewhat to the distress of his Mugwump friends. After a brief period of service in the Massachusetts legislature, Lodge went to Washington, where he served in the House of Representatives from 1887 to 1893 and thereafter in the Senate.

Although he took some interest in civil service reform, immigration restriction, and other domestic issues, his chief concern was foreign policy. A thorough imperialist, he early sought to strengthen the navy and consistently argued for an aggressive national role. He viewed with disdain all proposals for international arbitration or disarmament.

He was close to Theodore Roosevelt until 1912 and like T. R. had a deep distrust of what he regarded as Wilson's sentimentality and moralism. Lodge favored early intervention in the war against Germany, which, he thought, should be an opportunity to expand the world-wide influence of the United States. The peace terms seemed to him too lenient, and he considered it folly to link the League of Nations to the Treaty of Versailles.

The election of 1918, which gave the Republicans a majority in the Senate, made Lodge chairman of the Foreign Relations Committee. He devised the strategy that prevented ratification. Since many Republicans supported the idea of a league, he sought to throw the onus for rejection on the Democrats and did so by attaching to the treaty reservations unacceptable to Wilson.

Lodge was instrumental in securing the nomination and election of Harding in 1920. He died in 1924, content with the world he thought he had preserved.

The balance of power between these two groups was in the hands of the large body of Republican Senators who were committed in principle to an international association but either disliked particular features of the treaty or resented Wilson's desire to take credit for it. Since they were unwilling to take the responsibility for rejecting the treaty, they would not vote flatly against it. Instead, they argued in favor of approval with reservations. Ratification under those terms would demonstrate that Wilson had been soft as a negotiator and would convert the improved treaty into a Republican achievement. On the other hand, if the Democrats refused to accept the reservations, the blame for failure of the League would fall on Wilson's own party.

The definition of the appropriate reservations and the general management of the struggle fell to Henry Cabot Lodge, chairman of the Senate Foreign Relations Committee and a bitter enemy of the President. The personal hostility between the two men contributed to the inability to reach a compromise. Through the summer of 1919 Lodge conducted hearings that publicized all sorts of objections to the treaty. In response,

John A. Garraty, *Henry Cabot Lodge* (New York, 1953) is a competent biography.

Henry Cabot Lodge (1850–1924). (The National Archives)

Wilson undertook a tour of the country to stir up support. On September 25, 1919, while delivering a speech in Boulder, Colorado, he suffered a stroke and thereafter was an invalid, cut off from most contacts with the public and with politicians.

Lodge was thereafter in a position skillfully to maneuver toward the President's defeat. His primary objective was to hold the Republicans together and to prevent the waverers from accepting the treaty as it stood. He did so by proposing fourteen reservations to the treaty. Mostly these provisos were thoroughly innocuous, like affirmations of the Monroe Doctrine and of the sovereign rights of the United States. Although they were scarcely necessary—since the Covenant recognized those rights—they offered the Republicans an opportunity to stand in favor of a proper League and a proper treaty. Yet Lodge, at least, knew that Wilson could not accept the reservations. Having compromised so much, he could compromise no further, particularly because to do so would be to acknowledge that he had failed to protect American interests fully in Paris. Yet if the President remained intransigent, the disciplined Republicans, acting with the irreconcilables, could prevent ratification.

"The Accuser." Cartoon by Rollin Kirby in the New York *World*, March 22, 1920, three days after the Senate returned the Versailles Treaty unratified to President Wilson. (The Granger Collection)

Defeat The Republicans were correct in their calculations. The Democrats joined the irreconcilables in beating down the reservations, so the Senate had to vote on the treaty as submitted. On November 19, 1919, it defeated the treaty by a vote of 55 to 39. An effort in March 1920 to secure a reconsideration also failed to gain the necessary two-thirds majority. The United States therefore did not become a party to the Treaty of Versailles or a member of the League of Nations.

For Wilson, this was the final defeat. In the gloom of his final illness he learned that the League too, the one saving element that he had hoped would justify the treaty and the war, went down to defeat. The sacrifices had all been in vain.

▼

The meaning was ill-omened. Until the 1890s Americans had never considered themselves apart from the rest of the world. Their destiny was linked with that of men everywhere. Cultural and economic ties with Europe were intimate, and there was a confident expectation that political relations would become closer as other nations advanced toward democracy. The experiment in imperialism at the turn of the century had been confusing, because it made the United States party to a kind of domination most Americans did not wish to exercise. After 1900,

therefore, they had attempted to withdraw from colonialism, but they still hoped to play an important role in world affairs.

The world war and its aftermath challenged that assumption. President Wilson led his countrymen into a crusade for ideals that they regarded as part of their national heritage. The crusade did not succeed. The effort to redeem Europe for democracy and freedom failed. Some Americans thereafter rejected the outside world. American values, they believed, were safe only within the United States, and the country could best defend them by isolating itself from contacts with the corrupt outer world. The two decades that followed would test the feasibility of that effort at withdrawal.

Paperbacks for Further Reading

Two books by Thomas A. Bailey give a balanced account of the Treaty of Versailles and its rejection: *Woodrow Wilson and the Lost Peace* (Quadrangle Books, Inc.) and *Woodrow Wilson and the Great Betrayal* (Quadrangle Books, Inc.). Ralph Stone, ed., *Woodrow Wilson and the League of Nations* (Holt, Rinehart & Winston) contains a useful collection of interpretations. There are also materials on the issue in T. P. Greene, ed., *Wilson at Versailles* (D. C. Heath and Co.). J. C. Vinson, *Referendum for Isolation* (University of Georgia Press) is a helpful monograph on Article 10. J. M. Blum, *Woodrow Wilson and the Politics of Morality* (Little, Brown & Co.) is particularly good on the closing years of Wilson's administration and life.

Herbert C. Hoover, *The Ordeal of Woodrow Wilson* (New York, 1958) is an interesting account.

ISOLATION AND GLOBAL RESPONSIBILITY

77

In the 1920s, substantial numbers of Americans came to believe that isolation was the only safe policy for their country. They rejected any new ties with the outside world and sought to dissolve existing connections. The nation, in their view, was to confine its energies within its existing continental limits.

Yet the United States had inherited from the past continuing responsibilities abroad, and actual ties with the outer world did not simply dissolve. Americans had genuine economic, cultural, and religious interests in Asia, Africa, Latin America, and Europe. Their country therefore could not altogether withdraw from external contacts. As a result, in shaping foreign policy throughout the decade, the United States confusedly tried to reconcile the divergent tendencies toward isolation and involvement.

Isolationist Trends

The United States and the League The election of 1920 brought power to a Republican administration headed by an undistinguished politician, Warren G. Harding. The new President had refused to take a clear position on the question of the League but his plea during the campaign for a return to normalcy reflected the desires of many who would vote for him. He and they wished to return to the uncomplicated life of the prewar days.

Once in office, therefore, Harding made no effort to revive the Treaty of Versailles. Instead, the United States unilaterally proclaimed an end to the state of war with Germany (July 2, 1921), and it signed separate treaties with the other countries with which it had severed relations. Several efforts to secure American adhesion to the Permanent Court of International Justice (World Court) organized under the League of Nations failed, none of them having received the enthusiastic support of the Administration. The United States did maintain observers at the League of Nations, with which it occasionally coordinated policies, but the country was not an active participant in the association's affairs. Nor did there seem a prospect that it would become one. Europe seemed to many Americans beyond redemption.

Detachment The apathy toward foreign affairs of large parts of the American public revealed the growth of isolationism. The Rogers Act of 1924, which organized the professional Foreign Service, reflected the general willingness to leave these matters, remote from the concerns of the ordinary citizen, to the career diplomats.

Internal economic pressures reinforced postwar disillusionment. As their overseas markets shrank, farmers lost interest in events outside the country. The return of the Republicans to office led to an immediate general demand for a reversal of the Underwood Tariff. The Fordney-McCumber (1922) and the Hawley-Smoot (1930) acts drastically raised the rates and ex-

Unregenerate Europe, 1921

The war was a gigantic folly and waste. No one will deny that. But it was not so foolish nor so wasteful as the peace which has followed it. The European governments, . . . would have us believe they are mere victims of the war. They say nothing of what the war did for them. We might remind them that they profited as well as lost by the war. Many of them were freed from age long tyranny. They got rid of kaisers and saber clattering aristocracies. They were given freedom, and their present state shows how little they have known how to profit by it. They have been given new territories and new resources, and they have shown how little they deserve their good fortune. The last three years in Europe . . . have been marked by new wars and destruction, by new animosities and rivalries, by a refusal to face facts, make necessary sacrifices and compromises for financial and economic recovery, by greedy grabbing of territory and new adventures in the very imperialism which brought about the war.

It is well for Americans and their representatives to keep this in mind. . . . America would be foolish to contribute to the support of present methods or give any encouragement to the spirit which now prevails in the old world.

—From the *Chicago Tribune*, November 13, 1921, in *A Century of Tribune Editorials* (Chicago: Chicago Tribune, 1947), p. 92.

(*Left*) "But, Monsieur, where does it bend?" France asks. Cartoon by Rollin Kirby on the Fordney-McCumber tariff, New York *World*, October 4, 1927. (The Granger Collection)

(*Right*) "Playing No Favorites." By restricting immigration and imposing a tariff, Uncle Sam feels that he has done his bit for labor and for capital. Cartoon from the Chicago *Tribune*, ca. 1924. (Culver Pictures)

tended coverage to a broad range of agricultural commodities. The extreme protective features of both measures revealed a fixed determination to keep foreign goods out of American markets.

Immigration Restriction After the war the United States also decided to end foreign immigration. The literacy test, finally introduced over President Wilson's veto (1917), had not had the effect its proponents anticipated. The immigrants proved able to surmount this hurdle and when the war ended the flood of arrivals resumed. Entries, which had fallen precipitously during the war, started their upward climb once more in 1920, and in 1921 they totaled more than 800,000.

The unguarded gates seemed more dangerous than earlier. The wartime calls for conformity to 100 percent Americanism, the fear of foreign conspiracies, the suspicion of radicals

seeking to overthrow the government as they had in Russia, and the spread of racist beliefs coalesced in a determination to reverse the historic policy of unrestricted immigration. The postwar difficulties of organized labor lent plausibility to the argument that newcomers who competed with natives for jobs were no longer an economic asset as they had been in the expansive frontier days. Increasingly, public sentiment demanded a sharp reduction in the number of total admissions, combined with a device to make certain that those admitted would be of racially superior stocks.

The solution was the national-origins quota system originally proposed by the Reverend Sidney L. Gulick, a Protestant missionary who had worked in Japan. Seeking to end discrimination against Orientals, he suggested a limit on all immigration—European as well as Asian—in conformity with the percentage of each nationality already in the United States. That formula would curtail the total admitted, remove a special stigma from the Orientals, and maintain the existing distribution of blood stocks.

The Johnson Act of 1921 set the quota of each national group at 3 percent of its number resident in the United States in 1910. A new Immigration Act of 1924, for the time being, reduced the rate to 2 percent and shifted the base year back to 1890. However, the same law also provided for a permanent procedure that would become fully operative in 1929. There was to be a ceiling of about 150,000 immigrants a year. Assuming that the character of the population was unalterably fixed, the law called for a statistical analysis to ascertain the exact proportions of the various bloods that flowed in American veins through birth or descent. Each nationality would receive a quota equivalent to that percentage of the total of 150,000 to be admitted each year. The arrangement allocated most places to countries like Germany, which no longer needed them, and least to countries like Italy and Greece, where potential immigrants were numerous. The result was to curtail the flow almost entirely, except from the independent nations of the Western Hemisphere to which the law did not apply. The new policy thus expressed the desire for isolation, as the old one had taken involvement for granted.

The Ties of Culture and Trade

Other forces almost as powerful sustained a continuing connection between the United States and the external world. Negroes, for instance, although cut off from contact with Africa for centuries, exhibited a growing interest in the dark continent. The established Protestant missions continued, indeed accelerated their work. At a conference at Lake Mohonk, New York, in October 1921, they participated in forming the International Missionary Council to coordinate the overseas efforts of Protestants in various countries. In addition, Catholics in the United States, no longer content simply to support the activities of the international Society for the Propagation of the Faith, launched ventures of their own overseas. The American Joint Distribution Committee aided the distressed

Immigration Quotas, 1924–1929

	Under the 1924 Act (2 percent of 1890)	Under the National Origins System (1929)
Germany	51,227	25,957
Great Britain	34,007	65,721
Ireland	28,567	17,853
Sweden	9,561	3,314
Norway	6,453	2,377
Poland	5,982	6,524
Italy	3,845	5,802
All Others	25,025	26,166
Total	164,667	153,714

Immigration to the United States, 1911–1930

Year	All Countries	Europe
1911	878,587	764,757
1912	838,172	718,875
1913	1,197,892	1,055,855
1914	1,218,480	1,058,391
1915	326,700	197,919
1916	298,826	145,699
1917	295,403	133,083
1918	110,618	31,063
1919	141,132	24,627
1920	430,001	246,295
1921	805,228	652,364
1922	309,556	216,385
1923	522,919	307,920
1924	706,896	364,339
1925	294,314	148,366
1926	304,488	155,562
1927	335,175	168,368
1928	307,255	158,513
1929	279,678	158,598
1930	241,700	147,438

Jews of Eastern Europe, while American Zionists helped the settlements in Palestine. Secular connections supplemented the religious ones. The China Medical Board set up by the Rockefeller Foundation (1915), for example, undertook to help develop Western medicine in the Orient.

Nor did the nation's economic situation permit it to stand apart. The war had fundamentally altered the financial position of the United States. Until then, it had always been in debt to the more advanced economy of Europe. In 1914, it owed some $3,500,000,000 to foreign creditors. In 1919 the relationship was reversed. The United States was owed some $12,500,000,000. Furthermore, in the same interval American exports mounted from a value of little more than $2,000,000,000 to almost $8,000,000,000. The total declined thereafter as other countries also adopted restrictive commercial policies, but exports remained above the level of imports, and the Department of Commerce under Herbert Hoover tried to raise the amount still further. As a result, the balance of payments continued to favor the United States and added to the indebtedness of foreigners to it.

The high tariffs in the United States prevented its foreign debtors from selling it the goods that would repay the principal owed to it or even contribute to interest charges. As a result, the funds owed Americans remained overseas and were available for investment there. American corporations began to open branch plants in foreign countries. Such direct investments abroad more than doubled, rising from $3,700,000,000 in 1919 to $7,300,000,000 in 1929. At the same time, individuals in the United States began to buy the securities of foreign corporations and governments. The amount so invested tripled in the same interval, rising from $2,500,000,000 to $7,700,000,000. These funds, distributed everywhere, but especially in Canada, Europe, and Cuba, created ties of the most intimate sort. Furthermore, they were cumulative in nature, for the returns the investments earned often were reinvested abroad.

War Debts   Complicating the economic relations of the United States were the intergovernmental debts that had survived from the war. The $10,000,000,000 Americans loaned during the conflict were not repaid. By 1929 accumulated interest charges had raised the total to $11,600,000,000. The simple fact was that the sums were too large to be liquidated, and the Allies had no intention of paying them.

Since no great power wished to plead poverty, England and France sought to justify their delinquency by linking their debts to German reparations, although there was no juridical basis for the connection. In 1921, a conference had fixed the total of reparations at $33,000,000,000, and the French and the English announced, against the protests of the United States, that they would make payments on their obligations only to the extent that they received installments from Germany. Since that country was bankrupt and passing through a calamitous inflation, the likelihood of any repayment was slim. In fact, the Germans defaulted in January 1922, and the French in retaliation marched into the Ruhr. Meanwhile, payments on debts to the United States stopped.

To unfreeze the process of clearing all these obligations was difficult because nationalistic tariff barriers and other restrictions on trade impeded every transfer of funds. The United States was as culpable as others in this respect, although it had the greatest stake in a freer economic order. But political isolation immobilized it.

Twice the United States attempted to unclog the international system of payments. The Dawes Plan (1924) and the Young Plan (1929) aimed to get a flow of funds moving. These arrangements reduced the amount of reparations somewhat and provided American loans to aid German reconstruction. It was expected that the Germans would then be able to pay some of the reparations to the Allies, who in turn would repay some of their debts to the United States. A relatively small amount of American money went into motion in this circular fashion, but had practically no effect.

Disarmament and Asia

The Arms Race Americans who resented the unwillingness of the foreigners to pay the war debts often complained that France, England, and Italy were misappropriating their resources on armaments. The defeat of Germany did not lead to a complete relaxation of tensions or to the conversion of swords into plowshares. Instead, each victorious power retained a large army and navy to which it devoted a substantial part of its budget. It seemed plausible to suppose that disarmament would be advantageous to all. If the former Allies ceased to compete with one another, their relative strength would remain the same while the level of expenditures would sink. The logic was hard to dispute. Its validity had been recognized since the first Hague Conference (1899). Although few useful results had followed from that conference, the return of peace justified a new effort toward disarmament.

Disarmament was popular in the United States for both domestic and foreign reasons. The high rate of expenditures seemed profligate to Americans who remembered the low prewar military and naval costs. A reduction in such expenses would permit the government to lower taxes, balance the budget, and pay off the national debt. The objectives were so universally accepted as desirable that even the potent lobbyists of the Navy League and the armaments manufacturers could hardly argue against them. With demobilization, the size of the army was reduced gratifyingly, but a similar reduction in the navy waited upon an international agreement.

Americans believed, too, that there were good diplomatic reasons for disarmament. Not only would the European powers that pleaded poverty be better able to repay their debts but they would also strengthen their economies by eliminating a useless expense. Such reform was particularly desirable at a time when the aggrieved European working classes were on the verge of revolt and when communism, which had already swept across Russia, threatened the West.

The China Problem To some extent, the problem of disarmament was linked to the situation in Asia. Revolution had not solved the problems of China. The chaotic republican government was incapable of controlling the country, which seemed on the verge of breaking up as regional war lords set up their own despotic satrapies. Around the borders the imperialist powers stood poised, prepared to pick up as many of the fragments as possible.

Pragmatically, the situation was ripe for an agreement among the three great powers in the area, all of which had been allied in the war against Germany. British interests concentrated on the south, spreading out from Hong Kong and Canton to the interior. Japanese designs were on Korea, Manchuria, and the north. In the center, the vast Yangtze Valley was available to the penetration of the Americans.

However, the United States was not in a position to agree to a deal. Anti-imperialist sentiment, expressed in the Jones Act of 1916 which promised the Philippines their independence, was now reinforced by isolationism. Short of washing their hands of the area entirely, American statesmen could only reaffirm both the open-door policy and their pledge of support for the territorial integrity of China. Hence the ambiguity of all understandings, such as the Lansing-Ishii Agreement (1917) with the Japanese, who sought a simple clear-cut division of the spoils.

The Washington Conference Since the United States was not a member of the League, it had to improvise a means for handling the problems of disarmament and Asia. In February 1921, Congress adopted a resolution, introduced by Senator Borah, which asked for an international conference to consider the two subjects. In response, the United States, England, France, Japan, Italy, Belgium, Portugal, the Netherlands, and China met in Washington in November 1921.

The Lansing-Ishii Agreement, 1917

The Governments of the United States and Japan recognize that territorial propinquity creates special relations between countries, and, consequently, the Government of the United States recognizes that Japan has special interests in China, particularly in the part to which her possessions are contiguous.

The territorial sovereignty of China, nevertheless, remains unimpaired and the Government of the United States has every confidence in the repeated assurances of the Imperial Japanese Government that while geographical position gives Japan such special interests they have no desire to discriminate against the trade of other nations or to disregard the commercial rights heretofore granted by China in treaties with other powers.

The Governments of the United States and Japan deny that they have any purpose to infringe in any way the independence or territorial integrity of China, and they declare, furthermore, that they always adhere to the principle of the so-called "open door" or equal opportunity for commerce and industry in China.

Moreover, they mutually declare that they are opposed to the acquisition by any Government of any special rights or privileges that would affect the independence or territorial integrity of China or that would deny to the subjects or citizens of any country the full enjoyment of equal opportunity in the commerce and industry of China.

[Secret Protocol]

In the course of the conversations between the Japanese Special Ambassador and the Secretary of State of the United States which have led to the exchange of notes between them dated this day, declaring the policy of the two Governments with regard to China, the question of embodying the following clause in such declaration came up for discussion: "they (the Governments of Japan and the United States) will not take advantage of the present conditions to seek special rights or privileges in China which would abridge the rights of the subjects or citizens of other friendly states."

Upon careful examination of the question, it was agreed that the clause above quoted being superfluous in the relations of the two Governments and liable to create erroneous impressions in the minds of the public, should be eliminated from the declaration.

It was, however, well understood that the principle enunciated in the clause which was thus suppressed was in perfect accord with the declared policy of the two Governments in regard to China.

—W. M. Malloy, *et al., Treaties, Conventions . . . and Other Agreements* (Washington: Government Printing Office, 1910–1938), vol. III, p. 2720; *Foreign Relations of the United States: The Lansing Papers* (Washington: Government Printing Office, 1940), vol. II, p. 450.

The Washington Conference, 1921, to Discuss Problems of the Far East and the Limitation of Naval Armaments. The American delegation is seated at the table, on the right; Henry Cabot Lodge is at the center with Elihu Root at his right and Charles Evans Hughes at his left. (The Granger Collection)

The gathering, in which Secretary of State Charles Evans Hughes took an active part, hammered out three agreements. A five-power treaty took a useful first step toward limiting naval armaments. The great battleships were the most expensive items in military budgets, and they were in addition so visible that nations did not have to trust one another blindly to be sure agreements relating to them would be honored. The pact limited such capital ships according to a ratio of 5 each for the United States and Great Britain, 3 for Japan, and 1.75 each for France and Italy. The signatory countries accepted a ten-year moratorium on new construction and left for future negotiation the reduction of other armaments. In both a four-power treaty and a nine-power treaty the signatories agreed to maintain the *status quo* in the Far East and to make no changes there by force of arms.

These treaties proved to be the only important steps toward a relaxation of international tensions. A conference on armaments at Geneva in 1927, designed to carry the work forward, failed, and another in London in 1930 made only minor modifications to the Washington agreements.

Dexter Perkins, *Charles Evans Hughes and American Democratic Statesmanship* (Boston, 1956) is a readable biography.

Betty Glad, *Charles Evans Hughes and the Illusions of Innocence* (Urbana, Ill., 1966) focuses on the Washington Conference.

CHARLES EVANS HUGHES long intended to become a minister. Though he followed another course, the commitment to morality endured. Austere, efficient, and averse to any appeal to passion, he was an easy mark for satirists, who nicknamed him "Charles the Baptist," "the animated feather duster," and "the human icicle." But he adhered to his own standard of ethics through his long career in public service.

Hughes was born in Glens Falls, New York, in 1862. His father, a Baptist preacher, had immigrated from Wales seven years earlier. Charles was a precocious boy who entered college at the age of fourteen; he graduated from Brown, taught school for a while, and in 1884 took a law degree at Columbia. He became a member of a good firm and lived quietly in the next two decades.

He entered New York politics in 1905, through his service as counsel first with a committee to investigate gas rates and then with the "Armstrong commission," which studied the practices of life-insurance companies. These assignments revealed to him the problems attendant upon the development of great corporations and brought him widespread public attention. In 1906 he was elected governor of New York on the Republican ticket, and he pushed through a creditable program of progressive reforms. Named to the United States Supreme Court four years later, he was liberal in his decisions, especially in the affirmation of the right of government to regulate industry.

After his disappointment in 1916 when he failed to win the presidential election by a narrow margin, he returned to private practice. Harding called him back to Washington to be Secretary of State in 1921. Hughes succeeded in managing the Washington Conference, a task that called for great tact both in dealings with foreign diplomats and in relations with Congress.

Hughes left office in 1925. President Hoover appointed him Chief Justice in 1930. He presided over the Supreme Court in the difficult decade when it passed on New Deal issues. Despite the acrimonious political controversy created by the need for redefining government power and private rights, he held the Court together and maintained its prestige. He retired in 1941 and died in 1948.

The Kellogg-Briand Pact It was easier to secure general pledges of good intentions than consent on practical details. In the Pact of Paris of 1928, Secretary of State Frank B. Kellogg and French Foreign Minister Aristide Briand agreed to outlaw war as an instrument of national policy. Sixty other nations quickly associated themselves with that undertaking by voluntary statements. The pact was evidence that the peoples of the world, even the statesmen, longed for peace, but it had no sanctions behind it and would not in the future significantly restrain the signatories.

Robert H. Ferrell, *Peace in Their Time* (New Haven, Conn., 1952) deals with the Kellogg-Briand pact.

Nationalism and Internationalism

Within the United States, as in other parts of the world, nationalism was stronger than the desire for peace. Far from persuading the peoples of the world to live harmoniously together, the war had stirred passions that drove men to separatism and mistrust of their neighbors. Americans were singularly inept in responding either to the need for compromise with a powerful Asian country or to the challenge of the one powerful international movement of the 1920s — communism.

Japanese-American Relations One feature of the Immigration Act of 1924, for instance, undid much of the work of the Washington Conference. Since the Gentlemen's Agreement of 1911, the number of Japanese who came to the United States had averaged fewer than 8000 a year, and many of those had stayed only temporarily. Yet hostility to the Japanese in California—partly political and partly racist—remained strong. Ironically, the quota system as enacted, despite Sidney L. Gulick's intention, entirely barred Orientals. Congress deliberately excluded aliens ineligible for citizenship. By doing so, it closed the gate to the Japanese and to other Asians, for the courts had already ruled that such people even when admitted in the past did not have a right to naturalization.

This unilateral abrogation of the Gentlemen's Agreement stirred up a storm of anti-American indignation in Japan, weakening the forces there that favored good relations with the United States. The ultimate result was a strengthening of the militaristic element, with consequences that would begin to be apparent in the next decade. The offensive section of the Immigration Act ran counter to the wishes of the Secretary of State. His party controlled Congress, yet he was unable to influence legislation that directly affected foreign policy.

Soviet Problems Indecisive diplomacy, vacillating before the contradictory pressures of nationalism, isolationism, and the desire for peace, accounted for the unwillingness to recognize the existence of the Soviet Union. The United States had broken off diplomatic relations with Russia after the Communists signed the Treaty of Brest-Litovsk and pulled out of the war. The Americans thereafter were unwilling either to accept the legitimacy of the new regime or to join the Allies in bringing it down. The small American forces in Murmansk and Archangel were withdrawn in June 1919. Wilson took no action, the next year, on the suggestion for a settlement with the Soviets made by his emissary

William C. Bullitt. American troops participated with the Allies in a joint expedition to Siberia and then retired in 1920. The Republican Presidents thereafter simply preferred to evade the issue through the formula of nonrecognition, leaving unsettled the questions of debts owed the United States and the status of the Communist International.

Latin America The same confusion of purposes was evident closer to home. Wilson had repudiated the methods of the big stick in the Western Hemisphere and his Republican successors had no desire to revert to force in the area. Yet they, too, found it difficult to adhere to these intentions.

The United States had recognized the Carranza regime in April 1917 in the hope that it would restore stability to Mexico. A variety of claims by Americans for damages and for land expropriated remained outstanding and were still unsettled when another revolution in 1920 brought General Álvaro Obregón to power. All these questions then rose to the surface along with the problems created by nationalization of the oil industry. The United States resisted demands by infuriated investors for intervention. Instead, patient negotiations led to recognition by the United States in 1923 in return for Mexico's undertaking to settle the claims. A year later a new government seized office and refused to honor the agreement. Negotiations guided by Ambassador Dwight W. Morrow produced a final compromise in 1928.

The Caribbean countries were still unstable. American troops kept order in Haiti throughout the period and in the Dominican Republic between 1916 and 1924. The protectorate established over Nicaragua in 1914 endured until 1933. In Cuba a disputed election in 1917 brought in forces from the United States which were not removed until 1922. In each case, left alone, native chieftains proved corrupt and brutal, ready to help themselves from the public treasury and unscrupulous in manipulating the

Rodman W. Paul, *The Abrogation of the Gentlemen's Agreement* (Cambridge, Mass., 1936) is a good brief study.

Harold G. Nicolson, *Dwight Morrow* (New York, 1935) is an excellent biography.

DWIGHT W. MORROW had the knack of getting many different kinds of people to trust him. He was willing to listen and usually quickly found the common ground on which to resolve conflicting interests. That trait, which stood him in good stead as a diplomat, was the product of his legal training.

He was born in Huntington, West Virginia, in 1873 and grew up in western Pennsylvania. He studied at Amherst College where he was a classmate of Calvin Coolidge, attended Columbia Law School, and then joined a good New York firm. His work with important corporate clients gave him an insight into business and brought him to J. P. Morgan's attention. In 1914, while Morgan was involved in financing the purchase of Allied war materials, Morrow went to work for him and thereby also acquired some diplomatic experience.

Morrow learned in these years that capitalists could not expect to regard their overseas investments as sacrosanct. They would have to take account of the needs and interests of the people of the countries into which their funds had gone. Persuasion and mutual understanding were better protection for property than guns. He brought these insights to bear upon the problems of Mexico, to which President Coolidge sent him in 1927. The revolutionary government south of the border was expropriating the property of the oil companies and of the large landowners and was persecuting the Catholic Church. Some Americans as a result advocated intervention. But Morrow's mediation produced an acceptable solution that cleared the way for the subsequent improvement in relations between the two republics.

Elected United States Senator from New Jersey in 1930, Morrow served only briefly. He died in 1931 before he could contribute to solution of the new economic problems the Depression created.

ballot boxes. The United States sought only to help maintain order so that its citizens could do business with security. Unwittingly, it found itself on that account supporting dictators—Gerardo Machado in Cuba, Anastasio Somoza in Nicaragua, and Rafael Trujillo in the Dominican Republic—a curious outcome of the effort to make the world safe for democracy.

▼

The great war bequeathed to Americans a mixed legacy: on the one hand, a desire for peace; on the other, conditions that tended toward renewed conflict. The war had been far more expensive than the statesmen in Paris imagined. It left the world divided among nationalistic states arrayed suspiciously against one another, all heavily armed. To abate the resulting tensions was beyond the skill of the leaders of the 1920s.

The United States was in much the same position as the other powers. Its people wanted to avoid war, but they were also jealous of their national sovereignty. And in the case of the United States there was an additional, confusing illusion. The experience of the war and of the unsuccessful peace generated the belief that the two oceans and a separate history would permit the country to remain aloof from the world's disorders. Already in the 1920s there were reasons to doubt the adequacy of the isolationist view. The next decade would test it more severely.

Paperbacks for Further Reading

Selig Adler, *The Isolationist Impulse* (Free Press Paperbacks) deals with the twentieth-century reaction to world affairs. Herbert Feis, *The Diplomacy of the Dollar 1919–1932* (W. W. Norton & Company, Inc.) treats the economic aspects of foreign policy in the 1920s. R. F. Smith, *The United States and Cuba* (College and University Press Services) covers the period after 1917. George F. Kennan's two volumes, *Russia Leaves the War* (Atheneum Publishers) and *The Decision to Intervene* (Atheneum Publishers) deal with Soviet-American relations to 1920.

SOCIAL

DISORDER

78

The change in the way in which Americans appraised their relations with the outer world was linked to the spreading disorder within their own society. In earlier times, while they had been confident about the excellence and durability of their own institutions, nationalism had been compatible with involvement. Citizens of the United States had had no doubt that their own democratic form of life was best not only for themselves but also for other peoples. The isolationism of the 1920s was, among other things, a sign of the loss of certainty about the basic features of American society.

An old order was passing. Industrialism, urbanization, and the mere increase in the magnitude of the numbers involved complicated all human relationships and led to the breakdown of the inherited system of social control. Progressive reform measures solved some problems but also created new ones. The family, the church, and other community organizations adjusted painfully and not always adequately to the shifting needs of their members. The resulting tensions persuaded some Americans that only resistance to further change would save them. Others dared still to look optimistically toward an unknown future rich in promise for the nation.

Average Annual Death Rates per 100,000 Population for Selected Causes, United States, 1900–1929

Cause of Death	1900–04	1910–14	1915–19	1920–24	1925–29
All causes	1622	1385	1434	1198	1179
Typhoid Fever	26	18	12	7	5
Childhood diseases	65	46	37	34	20
Diarrhea, enteritis	115	88	69	43	29
Pneumonia, influenza	184	142	257	141	131
Tuberculosis	184	147	139	97	80
Cancer	67	76	80	86	94
Cardiovascular-renal	359	371	381	369	407
Syphilis	12	15	18	17	16
Motor-vehicle accidents	–	2	8	12	21
Other accidents	79	79	70	58	56

Source: From Mortimer Spiegelman, *Significant Mortality and Mobidity Trends in the United States Since 1900* (1966), p. 6, American College of Underwriters, Bryn Mawr, Penn.

Family Tensions

The Health of the People   Contemporaries who examined recent social trends in the 1920s found encouragement in some of the developments of the twentieth century. There had been a notable fall in the death rate and a consequent rise in life expectancy. Some of the improvement had been due to advances in medicine—the decline in the mortality from diptheria and other childhood diseases, for instance. But the sharp reduction in the number of deaths from typhoid, diarrhea, pneumonia, and tuberculosis owed little to physicians or drugs. It stemmed rather from a notable improvement in living and working conditions. Moreover, the rise in the figures for cancer and heart disease reflected the circumstance that the population was living to a greater age than formerly.

Two trends were sinister, the increase in mortality from syphilis and the fact that the rise in the number of accidents due to automobiles more than made up for the decline of those in industry. Both trends were connected with new social problems.

The Bonds of Matrimony   The family, as it had been traditionally conceived in the United States, no longer seemed capable of anchoring its members firmly in society. Divorce had attracted some public attention between 1880 and 1912, but it was then still an unusual phenomenon. Most fatherless households were the product of desertion or disaster. In the 1920s the incidence of divorce rose so that there was almost one such separation for every five marriages. Relaxation of the laws in some states eased the process for all who could afford it. Meanwhile, the age of first marriage dipped somewhat, an indication that bonds which could be lightly dropped were more readily assumed than formerly. The greater willingness both to enter and to leave matrimony showed that the family was becoming a transient means of gratifying personal needs rather than a permanent organization of households within society.

The New Women   The effects were apparent in the growing autonomy of American women. By 1917 they had already gained the vote in many states and the Nineteenth Amendment

Recent Social Trends in the United States (New York, 1933), the report of the President's Research Committee, deals with many of the subjects of this chapter.

Mrs. Norman Whitehouse Speaking for the Suffragettes, 1913. (Library of Congress)

removed the remaining restraints throughout the nation. The number of female wage earners mounted after 1910 and education at every level was accessible to women.

Women found a new freedom in society. The inhibitions that had earlier hemmed in their behavior ceased to exist. Their habits as well as their clothing revealed that they no longer thought of themselves simply as wives and mothers, but as persons the equal to men.

Liberation had connotations that the feminists of the nineteenth century hardly imagined. Equality included an end to the double standard in sexual relations. The decade before 1912 had already caught glimpses of the new woman, in actuality and in popular fiction. After the war she became a recognized type—free of ladylike delicacies, subject to the same passions as men, able like them to drink and drive and dance with only such restraints as she herself chose. The steady diffusion of birth-control devices, openly discussed after 1914 by Margaret Sanger's American Birth Control League, enabled the flapper to retain her freedom after one or several marriages.

The Nineteenth Amendment

The right of citizens of the United States to vote shall not be denied or abridged by the United States or by any state on account of sex.

The Congress shall have power by appropriate legislation to enforce the provisions of this article.

—Passed June 5, 1919; ratified August 26, 1920.

To a friend who chided her for the lack of a sense of humor, **MARGARET SANGER** replied, "I am the protagonist of women who have nothing to laugh at." She spoke from experience. Her Irish mother had died of tuberculosis after bearing eleven children.

Margaret was born in Corning, New York, in 1883. Her father chiseled tombstone angels for a living. He was a radical who espoused socialism, the single tax, and woman's suffrage, and he taught Margaret to think for herself. Having decided on nursing as a career, she found a place in a New York City hospital and in 1900 married William Sanger, an artist. In the next ten years, she recovered from a touch of tuberculosis, bore three children, and became familiar with the radical circles of the city. She also did some nursing in the slums of the lower East Side.

In 1912, she decided that her efforts to relieve the misery about her were useless. There could be no order in the lives of families unable to control pregnancy. She returned from a trip to Europe in 1914 to establish a birth-control league and to found a magazine. Her slogan was: "No gods; no masters." She was at once in trouble with the law, for the Comstock Act of 1873 declared that any information about contraception sent through the mail was obscene. Despite efforts to prosecute her, she established a pioneer clinic and published *What Every Girl Should Know* (1916) and *What Every Mother Should Know* (1917).

Margaret Sanger met opposition from the conservative churches and also from doctrinaire socialists, who considered birth control a palliative that would dull the revolutionary zeal of the masses. Nevertheless she persisted through the 1920s, maintaining the clinic, lecturing, sponsoring conferences, and writing about the issue. As she became aware of the world-wide implications of population growth, she took to travel to make her views known, and by the time she died, in 1966, she had become a familiar figure in Asia and Europe.

Though Margaret Sanger met with little success in securing the repeal of hostile legislation in the United States, the practice of birth control spread rapidly after 1920 and was tolerated, if not encouraged, by the law.

Flaming Youth Children, too, were individuals and treated as such. American parents had always been permissive and remained so after 1912, but the change in the family situation gave fresh significance to the familiar indulgence of their offspring. The sense of orientation within a fixed unit weakened. Furthermore, as the school-leaving age rose and more children pursued their education beyond the elementary level, a large proportion of them drifted away from the family context. The judgments and values of teachers and peers became more important than those of parents. The establishment of children's clubs like the Boy Scouts (1910) had somewhat the same effect in drawing the young into activities unconnected with the family.

The consequences varied according to social and economic status. The upwardly mobile children of laborers often established themselves by widening the distance between them and their parents. The offspring of Negroes, who had begun the migration to Northern cities during the war, were particularly vulnerable to disorganization because of their poverty and because of the prejudice against them. By contrast, middle class youths centered their lives on the school, which not only trained them to

Flaming Youth. Cover of *Life*, September 30, 1926. (The Granger Collection)

get ahead but also organized their social, athletic, and cultural activities.

Progressive education, which extended the ideas of John Dewey to create a child-centered institution, in the 1920s affected only a minority of students. But the tendency in all schools to relax the traditional curriculum, to broaden the range of subjects, and to loosen discipline reduced the adjustments demanded of the pupil and encouraged him to go his own way. Even aristocratic families, which retained the greatest control over offspring, could not keep them bound to the rules. Revolt against the laboriously contrived conventions of the previous period erupted shortly after 1910 and raged furiously in the 1920s.

By then it was expected that flaming youth would kick over the traces. The normal boy rebelled against his parents and resisted the pressures of society. Distinctive juvenile courts showed that young people were not to be subject to the same rules as their elders. So too, in the popular novels of Booth Tarkington, Penrod constantly questioned the proprieties, and increasingly, girls were portrayed as tomboys who associated with their brothers on terms of complete equality. Nor could it be assumed as in the past that age would lead to conformity.

The bonds that united the family therefore seemed restrictive to all its members. The individual's highest obligation often bid him defy social convention in order to fulfill himself. Marriage was no longer the first step in the formation of a family but the climactic point of romantic love, to be consummated despite any barriers of class, race, religion, or group, as Eugene O'Neill in *All God's Chillun Got Wings* (1924), Anne Nichols in *Abie's Irish Rose* (1922), and scores of sentimental movies demonstrated.

Communal Restraints

Communal restraints were inadequate to contain the tendencies toward fragmentation. The formal society of the best families ceased to hold the respect of its own members, particularly following the postwar downfall of the European aristocracy after which Americans had carefully modeled themselves. When authentic dukes lost their dignity, the pretensions of imitators collapsed.

The Effects of Urban Life The general conditions of American life had weakened among many groups the discipline once centered in the family. The growth of industrialization had isolated the individual wage earner. Whether he stood at a machine in the factory or behind the counter in a shop, he did his own work and earned his own income. The cluster of economic relationships once focused on the household disappeared.

The steady movement from farm to city exaggerated the trend. In the metropolis, the members of the family dispersed each day, not to see one another except evenings and on holidays; and different uses of leisure often separated them even then. Apartment dwelling set the home in a novel environment—providing a convenient mode of sheltering cliff dwellers who sought little contact with relatives or neighbors.

Often the suburbs, too, lost their communal character. The bungalow, which originated in California, spread after 1915 to other parts of the country. This style of building offered low-cost accommodations to people who escaped the crowded urban center but who rarely struck deep roots anywhere. In any case, the large distances over which the city spread and frequent moves by individuals made it difficult to maintain intimate relationships, broke up familiar communities, and prevented families from acquiring attachments to any particular place. It took a powerful ethnic tradition or a rural setting to permit communities to resist the trend toward disorganization.

Crime The lack of discipline left many individuals disoriented and uncontrolled. Without authoritative criteria for what behavior was proper, each person made his own decisions. The increase in delinquency of various types was one of the results.

There was a disturbing rise in crime. Observers were most distressed by its organized forms. The gangs that controlled vice and gambling in the tenderloins of the large cities grew in power. Some of them entered the service of labor unions, which occasionally provided a useful base for racketeering. After the enactment of prohibition, the illegal traffic in liquor provided another attractive field of operations. Access to guns and the mobility of the automobile often permitted criminals to outdistance the primitive police forces, particularly when the latter were corrupt or hampered by venal politicians.

Al Capone, Dutch Schultz, and Legs Diamond recruited their followers from among the marginal elements of the population. The gangs provided a means for organizing the youth neglected by respectable society. They attracted men who turned the dominant social standards of acquisitive success against the established order.

Crime, however, extended beyond the violence of hoodlums. A succession of scandals showed the disregard for honesty in business and politics. The oil magnates who bribed public officials were as ruthless and self-seeking as

There is a lively account of crime and politics in Lloyd Lewis and H. J. Smith, *Chicago* (New York, 1929).

A "Distillery," Washington Street, New York, 1924. Izzy Einstein and Moe Smith, prohibition agents, raid the premises, where even fake labels were manufactured. (UPI)

The Funeral of Angelo Genna, Notorious Gangster, Chicago, May 30, 1925. (UPI)

(manly strength or courage)

Al Capone. They, too, were pursuing their own ends without recognizing any social limitations. When Dr. S. Parkes Cadman, a popular preacher, endorsed the statement that Moses was a great real-estate promoter and when Bruce Barton's *The Man Nobody Knows* (1925) explained that Jesus was the founder of modern business, and his disciples, a board of directors, there was at least the suggestion that any man was justified in getting what he could.

Widespread hedonism in every aspect of American life reflected the disillusion with old standards. In the 1920s many people who earlier had been taught that what was worth doing was worth doing well, reflected on the manifest injustices of their society and on the fiasco of the war and concluded that what could not be done well was not worth doing at all. Pleasure justified easy-money speculation and encouraged the horde of gamblers who took risks in securities, in real estate, and in business. Religion rarely imposed restraints for it no longer wielded credible sanctions with which to sustain the guidelines to ordinary behavior.

Social Service The older forms of voluntary action grew in ways that limited their effectiveness. The amounts expended on philanthropy *(HUMAN WELFARE)* did not absorb a substantial part of the income of society, and a large portion of them went to gratify the social and cultural wishes of the giver rather than to meet the real needs of the poor. When great centralized fund-raising campaigns took form, donors treated their contributions as a kind of tax rather than as a mode of involvement in the community. Furthermore, increasing centralization and professionalization widened the distance between welfare agencies and their clients. The social workers as a group regarded themselves as professionals dealing clinically with problems rather than as individuals directly involved in them.

Roy Lubove, *The Professional Altruist* (Cambridge, Mass., 1965) discusses the development of social work as a profession.

The Struggle for Morality

MORAL CONDUCT (VIRTUE)

These signs of the times shocked Americans who still had faith in the old standards. Men and women in the rural districts of the South and West and in the respectable middle-class neighborhoods of the cities felt an aching desire to preserve the old-time values. The unabashed pursuit of pleasure, the striving for gain, and the decay of family and communal responsibilities were all sinful. Any measures to restrain evil and purify men were justified even if they involved the unlimited expansion of the power of government.

Prohibition Temperance reform absorbed much of this emotion after 1912. Local option and state-wide prohibition had already dried up a good part of the country by the time the Eighteenth Amendment was ratified early in 1919. But the intensity of temperance sentiment became even more evident thereafter. The Volstead Act of October 1919 adopted a definition of intoxicating liquor that forbade all but the weakest beer, and efforts at enforcement were so rigid as to evoke a reaction within a decade. By 1928, the conflict between wets and drys had become one of the central issues of American politics.

Fundamentalism The crusaders for virtue expected the support of religion. The shocking moral lapses of the time were, they thought, due to a drift away from the fundamentals of faith. The cure lay in a return to the old-time worship and to the certainties of the past. To wildly enthusiastic crowds, Billy Sunday, once an outfielder for the St. Louis Browns, preached a modern revivalism. Aimee Semple MacPherson in southern California delivered an undemanding message of redemption to thousands, while new Pentecostal sects heard the awesome word of God—unequivocal, unchanging, and clear in its condemnation of evil. Within the established Protestant denominations, too, sizable groups

A Prohibitionist Call for Authority, 1916

"Personal Liberty" is at last an uncrowned, dethroned king, with no one to do him reverence. The social consciousness is so far developed, and is becoming so autocratic, that institutions and governments must give heed to its mandate and shape their life accordingly. We are no longer frightened by that ancient bogy—"paternalism in government." We affirm boldly, it is the business of government to be just that—paternal. *Nothing human can be foreign to a true government.*

—*Gospel of the Kingdom,* July 1916, as quoted in J. H. Timberlake, *Prohibition and the Progressive Movement, 1900–1920* (Cambridge, Mass.: Harvard University Press, 1963), p. 27.

The Eighteenth Amendment

After one year from the ratification of this article, the manufacture, sale, or transportation of intoxicating liquors within, the importation thereof into, or the exportation thereof from the United States and all territory subject to the jurisdiction thereof for beverage purposes is hereby prohibited.

The Congress and the several states shall have the concurrent power to enforce this article by appropriate legislation.

This article shall be inoperative unless it shall have been ratified as an amendment to the Constitution by the legislatures of the several states, as provided in the Constitution, within seven years from the date of submission hereof to the states by Congress.

—Passed December 17, 1917; ratified January 29, 1919.

battled vigilantly for the fundamentals of faith against the modernist heresy.

In July 1925 there was a significant test of these sentiments in Dayton, Tennessee, in the trial of John T. Scopes, a young high school teacher who had disobeyed the state law forbidding the teaching of Darwinism. The fact that he was defended by Clarence Darrow and prosecuted by William Jennings Bryan attracted international attention. The case was a test of modernism and fundamentalism. The outcome, conviction of Scopes, revealed the determination of a substantial part of the population to defend the literal word of the Bible against science. Significantly, the legislature had passed the law regarding Darwinism by majorities of 71 to 5 in one house and 24 to 6 in the other. Its members, like Bryan, were more interested in the rock of ages than in the age of rocks.

CLARENCE DARROW came naturally by his radicalism. His father was a small-town preacher who left the pulpit because he ceased to believe, and he transmitted a skeptical agnosticism to his son. Clarence was born in 1857 and grew up in Kinsman, Ohio. After some desultory schooling, he read law, was admitted to the bar, and practiced in the neighboring towns until 1887, when he moved to Chicago. By then he had become familiar with the ideas of Henry George and John P. Altgeld and was a confirmed reformer.

Darrow worked as an attorney in several fields. He had some remunerative corporate clients such as the Chicago & Northwestern Railroad. He prepared the briefs that secured amnesty for the Haymarket anarchists, and served on several occasions as counsel for the city of Chicago.

(Continued on next page)

Ray Ginger, *Six Days or Forever?* (Boston, 1958) tells the story of the Scopes trial.

(Continued from preceding page)

After 1894, when he defended Eugene V. Debs in the Pullman-strike trial, he handled numerous labor cases. He acted on behalf of the miners in the strike of 1902 and defended the Wobblies accused of the murder of Governor Steunenberg in 1906. But these phases of his practice ended in 1911, when he was charged with suborning perjury in the course of the trial of the McNamara brothers.

Thereafter—until his death in 1938—Darrow made an entirely different career for himself in criminal law. He lost only one of the fifty murder cases in which he acted for the defense. He had a command of the usual lawyers' tricks. He kept on good terms with the judges, built up favorable publicity in the press, and took care in the selection of juries. His shambling figure, the slight drawl in his speech, and the liberal use of familiar jokes generated confidence in the court room and made his statements credible. But more important was the logical structure of his arguments. No matter how hopeless the prospect of his clients—for example, in the famous Leopold-Loeb murder trial—he tried to show that the accused were not at fault. They may have pulled the trigger, but they had no control over their actions. Men, he insisted, behaved in response to social, biological, and psychological forces of which they were themselves unaware and for which they were not responsible. When the jury brought in the verdict "not guilty," it accepted the accuracy of this portrayal of the human condition.

Darrow was therefore the perfect antagonist for Bryan in the Monkey Trial. The defense argued the case for man, the product of physical evolution. The prosecution insisted that God had created man in His own image, a moral being. The trial thus posed a problem that troubled a whole generation.

William Jennings Bryan (seated, left) and Clarence Darrow (arms folded) at the Scopes Trial, July 1925. (UPI)

Resisting Conspiracies

The Plots of the Foreigners The people who yearned for the old morality often wondered where in the course of events their country's history had gone wrong. As earlier, many fixed the blame on an alien conspiracy. Populist fears of a bankers' plot and suspicions of anarchist designs, sparked by prewar labor violence, were still remembered. Prosecutions under the Espionage Act had sensitized Americans to the danger from German sympathizers, slackers, and pacifists. The experience of Russia showed how a small minority could destroy a government and seize power for its own ends. Attorney General of the United States A. Mitchell Palmer, an aspirant for the presidential nomination, in 1919 rounded up thousands of suspected communists, deported hundreds of them, and set off a red scare that extended into the 1920s.

Numerous groups, such as the American Legion, kept vigilant watch over tendencies toward disloyalty. The mayor of Chicago repeatedly warned the king of England against any effort to subvert the Republic.

The Klan The fear of conspiracy evoked a counterconspiracy. The Ku Klux Klan began in 1915 in Atlanta, Georgia, as an effort to revive the secret Reconstruction organization of that name. But until 1920, it remained simply another one of those fraternal orders that Americans showed a great propensity for joining. Then the Klan spread, even more rapidly in the North than in the South. Before scandal and internal conflict wrecked it after 1924, it had enrolled some 4,000,000 members; it had gained practical control of Indiana and Oregon, and had become a powerful force elsewhere. In its stand for the maintenance of a traditional way of life it was determined to use violence and secrecy if necessary.

David M. Chalmers, *Hooded Americanism* (Garden City, N.Y., 1965) is a general history of the Klan with a section on this period.

Its most important target was the Catholic Church. Latent hostility to the Pope and to the foreigners who, it alleged, had brought his rule to the United States now came into the open. The Klan considered Catholics the ignorant tools of priests, party bosses, and gangsters, the foes of prohibition, and the agents of an international conspiracy. It therefore wished to deprive them of the ballot and to let none but genuine Americans stand on guard.

Fear of international connections also contributed to the growth of anti-Semitism. Prejudice against the Jews had become virulent after the turn of the century. Already identified with the international bankers, they became more conspicuous and more suspect with the rapid increase of immigration from Eastern Europe. In 1915 an unfounded murder accusation against Leo Frank and his subsequent lynching in Georgia spread across the nation lurid images of the vicious Jews. Two years later prejudiced and ill-informed writers associated them with Russian communism. Then the forged Protocols of the Elders of Zion revealed that all these elements were part of a conspiracy in which both bankers and communists collaborated to give the Jews mastery of the whole world. Henry Ford for a time took this accusation seriously and his *Dearborn Independent* diffused it throughout the nation.

The Negroes were less important to the Klan because they were no threat. Outbreaks of violence in East St. Louis (1917) and in Chicago (1919) demonstrated that whites in the North had the power to terrorize colored newcomers. In the South the situation of the Negroes seemed less hopeful than at any time since emancipation. A rigid pattern of segregation firmly held them in a subordinate position. The Klan included the Negroes in its category of inferiors but it had no fear of their conspiracies.

Racism The Klan put into practice the racist convictions that many other Americans shared passively. The ideas were clear: since mankind was divided into unalterably different species, society was obliged to preserve the lines among them and prevent the dilution of superior by inferior strains. Biological and historical science seemed to support these beliefs. Genetics, as then taught, showed that physical characteristics passed through the blood stream from generation to generation. Examination of the past revealed to some thinkers that the Aryan race had been the sole civilizing force in man's evolution. Europeans like Count Gobineau and Houston Stewart Chamberlain had already explained its contributions to progress. But it remained for Americans to clarify the danger of mixture with the lower types of man. Madison Grant, in *The Passing of the Great Race* (1916), showed that all the institutions and ideas his countrymen valued had been the product of pure Aryans, who were now being threatened from below.

Klan membership and racist thinking were alike reactions to the tensions created by the failure of the old order. These were substitutes for the sense of solidarity and cohesion society now lacked. In a world of strangers who no longer enjoyed dependable intimate relationships with one another, individuals could discover their lost common brotherhood in no other way than by the exclusion of outsiders. Quotas that limited access of the underprivileged to education or that barred them from desirable residences and occupations now applied to many white Americans the kind of segregation with which Southern Negroes were already familiar.

The Solidarity of Self-Defense

The more conservative forces in the United States were socially inert. The political leaders and men of wealth made little effort to restrain the new tendencies. It would have taken all their prestige and power to do so, and the will to make the attempt was lacking.

The groups under attack devoted much of their energy to self-defense. The Knights of Columbus, the American Jewish Committee,

Immigration a Menace, 1916

These immigrants adopt the language of the native American, they wear his clothes, they steal his name and they are beginning to take his women, but they seldom adopt his religion or understand his ideals and while he is being elbowed out of his own home the American looks calmly abroad and urges on others the suicidal ethics which are exterminating his own race. . . .

It is evident that in large sections of the country the native American will entirely disappear. He will not intermarry with inferior races and he cannot compete in the sweat shop and in the street trench with the newcomers. Large cities from the days of Rome, Alexandria, and Byzantium have always been gathering points of diverse races, but New York . . . will produce many amazing racial hybrids and some ethnic horrors that will be beyond the powers of future anthropologists to unravel.

One thing is certain; in any such mixture, the surviving traits will be determined by competition between the lowest and most primitive elements and the specialized traits of Nordic man; his stature, his light colored eyes, his fair skin and light colored hair, his straight nose and his splendid fighting and moral qualities, will have little part in the resultant mixture.

—Madison Grant, *The Passing of the Great Race* (New York: Charles Scribner's Sons, 1918), pp. 91, 92.

and the National Association for the Advancement of Colored People mobilized the resources to refute polemical slanders and to maintain their legal rights in the courts. But people slurred by prejudice and barred from equality of opportunity responded also by creating nationalistic movements of their own. The causes of their homelands enlisted the support of Irish- and Italo-American organizations. Zionism evoked the sympathy of some Jews. And Marcus Garvey was able to recruit many Negroes in a forlorn "Back to Africa" movement.

There was something synthetic in all these tendencies, among the victims as well as among the prejudiced. Nationalism did not solve the problem of restoring social order; it evaded it. That effort to unify the people disoriented by life in the twentieth century offered little to the men and women who wished to be individuals and not simply parts of a mass movement.

▼

In the 1920s the culminating effects of the great changes of the preceding half century became apparent. Industrialization and urbanization had long been undermining the inherited structure of family and community life. The shock of the war exposed and extended weaknesses that had already developed, and created, as a first response, the desire to restore the lost order.

But social disorder also raised provocative intellectual questions about the relations of the individual to society. Americans sought answers to those questions within the variety of cultural contexts that influenced the country's heterogeneous population, with results that were sometimes frustrating, sometimes rewarding.

Paperbacks for Further Reading

Frederick Lewis Allen, *Only Yesterday* (Perennial Library) is a popular history of the 1920s. Clarence S. Darrow, *The Story of My Life* (Scribner Library) is a revealing autobiography. There are treatments of the problems of race and immigration restriction in Oscar Handlin, *Race and Nationality in American Life* (Anchor Books) and in Thomas F. Gossett, *Race* (Schocken Books, Inc.). Herbert W. Schneider, *Religion in Twentieth Century America* (Atheneum Publishers) covers the subject in general. Liston Pope, *Millhands and Preachers* (Yale University Press) has an excellent analysis of the social context of fundamentalism, which extends into the 1930s. Lawrence A. Cremin, *The Transformation of the School* (Vintage Books, Inc.) is a study of progressive education. Roy Lubove, *Community Planning in the 1920s* (University of Pittsburgh Press) focuses on the Regional Planning Association. There is a good deal of useful material in the sociological literature of the decade. Among the best works are: Robert E. Park, *The City* (Phoenix Books); Allison Davis and Burleigh and Mary Gardner, *Deep South* (Phoenix Books); Louis Wirth, *The Ghetto* (Phoenix Books); Caroline F. Ware, *Greenwich Village* (Harper Colophon Books); Frederick M. Thrasher, *The Gang* (Phoenix Books); E. Franklin Frazier, *Negro Family in the United States* (Phoenix Books); and Robert S. and Helen M. Lynd, *Middletown* (Harvest Books). There are related materials in Roy Lubove, *The Urban Community* (Prentice-Hall, Inc.) and George E. Mowry, ed., *The Twenties* (Spectrum Books). The fiction of this period is also instructive, particularly: Sherwood Anderson, *Winesburg, Ohio* (Compass Books); John Dos Passos, *U.S.A.* (Sentry Editions); and *Main Street* (Signet Classics), *Babbitt* (Signet Classics), *Dodsworth* (Dell Publishing Co., Inc.), and *Elmer Gantry* (Dell Publishing Co., Inc.), all by Sinclair Lewis.

THE INDIVIDUAL
AND HIS
CULTURE

79

The difficult personal and social adjustments to industrialization and urbanization had a profound effect on all levels of American culture. The efforts to define official standards suffered shocks that left merely a façade standing in 1929. Meanwhile, technological innovations created new media which brought popular culture to a vast audience.

Detached from both popular and official culture, the creative personalities sought and found new means of giving form to their ideas and emotions. The result was a remarkable renaissance in literature and the arts, in the course of which perceptive men strove again to understand the meaning of America and the place of the individual in it.

Cultural Transition

BETWEEN 1912 AND 1929, the official culture gained such strength as was measurable in the new buildings of universities and the high fees of theatrical and opera stars. Millionaires still derived satisfaction from the old masters and rare books that Lord Duveen and A. S. W. Rosenbach sold them, if not from the tedious offerings Giulio Gatti-Casazza, the general manager, set before them on the stage of the Metropolitan Opera House. Yet the roots were shallow and the evidence of hollowness was already visible, although the collapse would not come until the great depression after 1929.

Only science remained impregnable. Its practical results in industry and in medicine bore such prestige that its premises won acceptance as a matter of course. It gained support from the new foundations and from its position both in the universities and in industry. Nobel prizes were awarded to A. A. Michelson (1907), Alexis Carrel (1912), Theodore W. Richards (1914), Robert A. Millikan (1923), and Arthur H. Compton (1927). The causes of hookworm and yellow fever were discovered. The substantial achievements of science seemed to validate its claims.

By contrast, official literature, art, and music became increasingly academic and derivative, more devoted to criticism than to original creation. The sponsors of a static American culture based on classical models lost the support of Europe, which now moved toward radical new forms. Nor could the laboriously acquired interest in good music or good art be transmitted to the next generation. The holders of the boxes at the opera found themselves out of touch both with the advanced tastes of Paris and London and with the hedonistic desire for fun of their own children.

The disillusionment and rejection of authority which followed the war widened the gap. Still entrenched in the universities and a few other institutional strongholds, the custodians of the official culture—such people as Henry van Dyke of Princeton, Irving Babbitt of Harvard, William Lyon Phelps of Yale, Paul Elmer More and Stuart P. Sherman of *The Nation*, and Ralph Adams Cram, the architect—maintained the old standards, but with steadily diminishing influence.

New Media for Popular Culture

Popular culture enjoyed no such immunity to change for it had to relate itself to the needs and emotions of the people on whose patronage it depended. Furthermore, practitioners who lived by attracting audiences were attentive to the financial implications of technological innovations. They welcomed new media capable of serving a massive public.

Regrets About the Present Age, 1913

The civilization characteristic of Christendom has not disappeared, yet another civilization has begun to take its place. We still understand the value of religious faith; we still appreciate the pompous arts of our forefathers; we are brought up on academic architecture, sculpture, painting, poetry, and music . . . . On the other hand the shell of Christendom is broken. The unconquerable mind of the East, the pagan past, the industrial socialistic future confront it with their equal authority. Our whole life and mind is saturated with the slow upward filtration of a new spirit—that of an emancipated, atheistic, international democracy.

—George Santayana, *Winds of Doctrine* (New York: Charles Scribner's Sons, 1913), p. 1.

David Wark Griffith (left), Mary Pickford, Charlie Chaplin (seated), and Douglas Fairbanks, April 17, 1919. They are signing the incorporation papers of United Artists, a company for producing and distributing pictures. (The Granger Collection)

Adapting a Classic for the Movies, 1923

The "conference" consisted of the managing director, two directors, the publicity manager, the studio manager, the cashier, two typists, the producer and myself. And, with the exception of the producer, not one of them had read the book!

I read the script, and a "discussion" followed, the following being some of the points raised by the assembled "experts":

"The story was gloomy — suggest introducing a low-comedy character.

"Make two of the secondary characters marry, in order to 'introduce a bit of romance' into it.

"Shift the period to present day, in order to save expense!

"Eliminate the death of the central character, and make him recover at the last moment!"

When in the course of the very heated discussion on these suggestions I pointed out that the public would never stand such liberties being taken with a famous classic, I was informed condescendingly, that the public, for the most part, had never read the book, and so wouldn't know, and that the author was dead and couldn't object! I then asked, very pertinently, why the book had been selected for filming, and was told because it was out of copyright, and the title would be a "draw." After which it was decided to change the title!

—W. J. Elliott in the *Daily News*, October 1923, as quoted in C. E. M. Joad, *The Babbitt Warren* (London: Routledge & Kegan Paul, Ltd., 1926), pp. 75–76.

DAVID WARK GRIFFITH instinctively knew that the screen was not a stage. He thereby helped create a new art.

Griffith was born in La Grange, Kentucky, in 1880, the son of an impoverished Confederate officer. Meager schooling left him with the desire to be an author, but he depended on menial jobs to stay alive. He hesitated to take road-show roles lest he besmirch the family name as an entertainer. When hunger forced him to become an actor, he did so under a pseudonym.

In 1907 he tried to sell a movie scenario to the Edison Company, was turned down, and instead had to accept a bit part wrestling with a stuffed eagle in a thriller. He never left the movies and soon was directing important pictures. Griffith's most important innovation was to make the camera mobile. The first movie makers had anchored the camera so that it faced the set of each scene, and this limited the scope of what the lens could take in. Griffith opened up the action. His moving camera shifted its perspective, recorded close-ups and distance, and followed along after people and vehicles in motion. It did not have to confine itself to visual images of the stage.

The new medium expanded in size, length, and complexity. The climax came for Griffith in *The Birth of a Nation* (1915), a lurid Reconstruction tale in which the Ku Klux Klan put the "bestial" Negroes in their place. Made at a cost of $100,000 the film grossed some $18,000,000. Griffith was totally unaware of his prejudices and astonished at the accusations of bigotry that greeted *The Birth of a Nation.* To show his good intentions, he made an even larger film, *Intolerance,* in which four parallel historical stories proved that injustice never paid. *Intolerance* was not as popular as its predecessor, but it showed a masterly ability to bring spectacles to life.

Thereafter Griffith made such sentimental tear jerkers as *Way Down East* (1920) and *Orphans of the Storm* (1922). In all, he turned out 432 movies and developed such stars as Mary Pickford and the Gish sisters. But he was unable to adjust to the new requirements of sound after 1930, and his fortune and reputation both dwindled. He was quite forgotten by the mass audience of the "talkies" when he died in 1948. Yet the techniques he developed remained the basic tools of the cinema art.

The Movies The popular stage of the past, whether vaudeville or drama, had suffered from the smallness of its audience, confined as it was to a single building where the performance was repeated. The development of motion pictures did away with that limitation. The actor played his part once before the camera, yet hundreds of audiences and thousands of people would see the film. After 1912, conditions were ripe for development of the movies. Electricity was in use even in small centers of population, and almost everywhere theaters and other halls were available for exhibitions.

Entrepreneurs, often men with no previous connection with entertainment, were quick to seize the opportunity. By the outbreak of the war, a steady flow of films was reaching a large audience. In the 1920s a colossal business took form. Its center shifted from the east coast to California, where the climate and the natural setting made outdoor production dependable. Extensive networks of producers, distributors, and chains of movie houses, financed by bankers, yielded substantial profit. But the motion picture had also become a medium of great versatility capable of serving audiences of unprecedented size.

Performers and subject matter were drawn from the popular stage. Sentimental dramas of love and family life were the staples of the serious film in which Gloria Swanson or Lillian Gish or Mary Pickford suffered and suffered

Lewis Jacobs, *Rise of the American Film* (New York, 1939) is a clear narrative.

until all came right in the end. In exuberant westerns the good strong men pursued the Indians and bandits in a predictable triumph of virtue. David Wark Griffith freed the screen from the limitations of the stage, using the camera imaginatively to produce lavish spectacles like *The Birth of a Nation* (1915) and *Intolerance* (1916). Meanwhile Mack Sennett and Charlie Chaplin had refined the techniques of the comedy they knew from vaudeville. By 1929, the dream palaces of the land offered something for everyone.

The Popular Press   An expanding audience altered the character of metropolitan journalism. By the beginning of the century Hearst and Pulitzer had already discovered the uses of sensationalism, of pictures, and of human interest features. Pulitzer, however, soon withdrew from the contest for circulation. His New York *World* became a sober, crusading newspaper, and its sales dropped off in consequence. Hearst, on the other hand, continued the pursuit of the widest audience, adding units to his chain as he competed with a new rival, the Scripps-Howard papers.

After the war, an English model showed the feasibility of a small newspaper format, heavily illustrated and simple to read. The *New York Graphic*, which specialized in lurid "composographs"—imaginatively modified photographs—went to extremes, but hardly outdid its rivals. The tabloid soon seized a good part of the urban market, taking readers away from the older ethnic newspapers because it made few demands on literacy.

This form of publication shaded over into the magazine field. *True Story* (circulation almost 2 million) was the most successful of a host of periodicals which catered to popular tastes in a simple, direct, and comprehensible manner. They shared a common formula that combined sex and violence with clear moralistic injunctions.

Radio   A still newer medium had just taken

form in 1929. The first radio broadcasts were arranged by curious amateurs and by the Radio Corporation of America, which wished to provide listening material that would persuade people to buy its sets. Talent was recruited haphazardly and generally unpaid. The presumption was that ultimately a non-profit-making educational organization would control the air waves. In 1923, however, WEAF, the telephone company's New York station, began to sell fractions of time to advertisers and thus uncovered a potential source of revenue. But even when the National Broadcasting Company (1926) and Columbia Broadcasting System (1929) networks were formed, resources were still too slim to give broadcasting the force it would acquire in the next decade.

Fun for All   Between the popular and the official cultures a middle ground emerged, as promoters sought the widest possible audiences and as the upper classes aimed to share the fun of the lower. The breakdown of social authority permitted popular tastes to permeate all levels of the population. The movies emerged from the dingy nickelodeon to appear at elegant uptown houses, and the radio carried identical sounds to the drawing room and the tenement kitchen. The cabaret, which had first appeared early in the century, became the night club and the speak-easy. There and on the stage of Earl Carroll's musical reviews and Florenz Ziegfeld's follies, entertainers from out of the slums appeared before audiences in which gangsters and newly rich butter-and-egg men rubbed elbows with scions of the Four Hundred.

Jazz was the most important language in the night spots and in the hundreds of country clubs scattered across the nation. The blues gradually supplanted ragtime in these years, but for most listeners both were music to dance to as well as to sing to. The simple lyrics reiterated a romantic theme with a few variations— love was the sole desire of man. Meanwhile the syncopated rhythms moved the embracing bodies about in the fox trot, the Charleston, and the stepped-up waltz.

There is an interesting account of work for a tabloid in Emile Gauvreau, *My Last Million Readers* (New York, 1941).

Fun from the Slums, 1924

If whites bored me, it was because they bored themselves. They seemed to get little fun out of life and were desperately lonely. Often when I worked in night clubs I'd look around at those pale faces and weary eyes and I'd think, "They are only here to kill time." In spite of the countless advantages they enjoyed as the master race they looked fed up with everything and as though they hated life itself. When you worked in front of them you had to do the whole job.

But in the Negro night clubs the customers worked with you. They had come to the spot to cut loose, and even if you were lousy they had a good time. High spirits weren't forced on them. They came in with bounce and éclat, checking their troubles at the door.

As far as I could see, the white man was full of mental pains and psychic aches. He had all but forgotten what it was like to breathe freely and with pleasure. If he came to night clubs it was only to escape whatever the hell it was that ailed him. And I couldn't help wondering, if he was really like that, what good were all his fine homes and jobs, trips to Florida, silk hats, and his poses of superiority?

—Ethel Waters, *His Eye Is on the Sparrow* (New York: Doubleday & Company, Inc., 1951), p. 194.

Flappers in a Charleston Contest at the Parody Club, New York, January 22, 1926 (UPI)

The athletic field, or at least the grandstand, was the other common cultural arena. Formerly aristocratic sports like tennis, golf, and collegiate football acquired a popular following, and gentlemen began to make an appearance at prize fights and professional baseball games. The idea of a contest that yielded a winner and a loser was itself exciting to people who thought of life as a striving for success. But attention focused also on the star. Babe Ruth, Red Grange, Jack Dempsey, Bobby Jones, Bill Tilden, and Helen Wills satisfied the craving for a heroic individual able to assert his personality within the rules of the game.

In the process of diffusion, popular culture lost some of its authenticity. Promoters who invested millions in a movie or a prize fight could not depend on chance for the audience that would earn them a profit. The aggressive advertising techniques their press agents and public-relations men employed went beyond the point of making the event known. Contrived occasions called notice to the star or contest, and the event itself was often shaped to attract attention. The popular arts thereby became part of a general world of ballyhoo that extended over the whole realm of entertainment, and also over business and society.

An Intellectual Community

The weakening of the official culture and the diversion of the attention of most of the population to pleasurable distractions liberated the generation of rebellious intellectuals that matured after 1910. Creative artists now acquired support, independent resources, the ability to criticize themselves, and some backing from Europe.

Stimuli from Europe The Great Armory Show of 1913 provided Americans with an opportunity to see at first hand some of the important transatlantic developments in painting. The French impressionists were a revelation

to viewers in the United States, reared on the pallid and traditional canvases of the museums. The interest then aroused remained alive to the vigorous movements that surged through the art of Europe in the decades that followed.

Contact with the new trends in the Old World was stimulating in every field of expression. The music of Debussy and Stravinsky, the architecture of Gropius, the drama, novels, and poetry of Ibsen, Strindberg, Dostoevski, Shaw, Joyce, and Rimbaud stirred and encouraged Americans who had been seeking their own ways of breaking out of the stifling genteel culture about them.

The Old World also generated exciting new ideas. Nietzsche and Freud in different ways pointed to the importance of irrational, emotional elements in man's nature. Modern astronomy and physics, as interpreted by such writers as H. G. Wells, opened up a universe vast in its space and time dimensions, one that operated not by rigid Newtonian laws but indeterminately by the principles of relativity. Suddenly the thinking, feeling individual had a totally new environment to respond to and to describe.

Avant-garde Media Americans who wished to write or paint or compose now had the instruments at hand. The ambitious young people who flocked to New York and, to a lesser extent, to Chicago found a community in existence, the foundations of which the Bohemian avant-garde had already built during the preceding generation. The setting for discussion, for mutual criticism and admiration, sustained their morale; and outposts of expatriates in London and Paris maintained the connection with Europe.

The resources of the creative community were adequate to support its own media of expression, particularly since it sometimes attracted the interest of patrons with wealth. A sprinkling of little magazines left the presses, publications that aimed not at large circulations or commercial success but at proclaiming the editor's attitudes and ideas. *Poetry, The Dial, Hound and Horn,* and *The Masses* gave space to new writers and to discussion of the arts uninhibited by the

HENRY L. MENCKEN was born in Baltimore in 1880 and grew up in a convivial German-American family. Educated in private schools, he went to work at nineteen as a reporter for the *Baltimore Herald*. In 1906 he transferred to the staff of the *Baltimore Sun* and retained a connection with that newspaper for forty years. His more important role, however, was as literary critic and magazine editor, first for *The Smart Set* (1908–1923) and then for *The American Mercury* (1924–1933). Through those journals he markedly influenced the thinking of postwar Americans.

Mencken had some familiarity with the literature of continental Europe, and he had picked up a smattering of Nietzschean philosophy. From these sources he drew material to support his own thoroughly individualistic ideas. All institutions were suspect because they tended to restrain and pervert man. Jeering at the conformists, he made self-expression the supreme value. A master of the quip, he attracted the attention of a large audience, which half agreed with him and was delighted to see its own prejudices pricked.

He directed his barbs at the *Boobus Americanus* and all his pish-posh. Mencken was W. C. Fields in print. Everything was a racket—God, marriage, education, radio, children, communism, astronomy, and the movies. A good politician was no more conceivable than an honest burglar, and the churches grew more sordid and swinish as they grew more prosperous.

Mencken's literary taste was capricious, but his unrelenting opposition to what was respectable helped ridicule out of existence a good deal of the trash that passed as literature under the cloak of the genteel tradition. For the same perverse reasons, he helped nurture the underdog writers, among them Sinclair Lewis, Theodore Dreiser, Willa Cather, Ezra Pound, and F. Scott Fitzgerald.

The Depression muted Mencken's influence. It was hard to pass off the unemployed or Hitler with a joke. He continued to write for the *Baltimore Sun* until he suffered a stroke in 1948, but his erratic opinions evoked no response. He lived on until 1956, but remained always a man of the 1920s.

---

criteria of official culture. Similarly, little theaters, like the Provincetown Playhouse, offered a stage for drama not bound by the usual conventions.

Links to the Public With surprising speed, a variety of intermediaries found larger audiences for the products of new writers. Critics like H. L. Mencken and George Jean Nathan at first were interested mostly in attacking the smug, tight-laced genteel culture which they called "Puritan." But they were willing to make allies of any rebels against that culture and occasionally promoted the work of dissident novelists and playwrights. As a result, thousands of Americans who bought *The Smart Set* or *The American Mercury* to read the latest sallies against the "booboisie" of Main Street made the acquaintance of Ezra Pound or Robinson Jeffers. *The New Yorker*, which prided itself on standards that were not those of the old lady from Dubuque, was also receptive to new writing. With such wide recognition, F. Scott Fitzgerald, Sinclair Lewis, and Ernest Hemingway were able to find places on the best-seller lists or in the slick pages of the well-paying magazines. Their writings were occasionally selections of the Literary Guild and the Book of the Month Club, not to be read perhaps but at least to be displayed. By the same token, the Theatre Guild brought to Broadway the advanced dramas of Eugene O'Neill, among others.

Carl R. Dolmetsch, *The Smart Set* (New York, 1966) is a good history and an anthology.

The Smart Set, Cover, October 1914. Illustration by James Montgomery Flagg. (New York Public Library)

Freedom of Form

This context endowed the creative artist with unusual freedom. An audience was available for those who wanted one, and some writers, like Fitzgerald and William Faulkner, were uncertain about the degree to which to cater to it. Others made a virtue of their lack of popularity. As Ezra Pound pointed out, the dedicated poet or painter did not depend on mass support. He could write or paint to satisfy himself and the community within which he worked. He could let go and make what he felt, create for self-expression and spontaneity rather than out of adherence to formal rules.

Experimentation Opportunities for experiment were unlimited. The inner needs of the artist took precedence over external structure. The techniques of one medium influenced the practitioners of another. Impressionist paintings played upon the imagination of imagist poets. The Dos Passos novels used flash backs borrowed from the movies. The newspapers fashioned the contours of Hemingway's prose. E. E. Cummings went beyond free verse to the total destruction of the conventional line. Indeed, novelty sometimes became an end in itself, so strong was the imperative to be smart and original.

Yet the net effect of the experimentation was stimulating and constructive, for each talent was able to locate its own mode of expression. Robert Frost and William Carlos Williams fixed their vision on the setting of the small community, while Carl Sandburg attempted to encompass the metropolis. T. S. Eliot tried to capture in his verse the patterns of city speech, while Frost set down the country idiom. The variety of available forms and the tolerance of innovation left few voiceless who had anything to say.

A Renaissance The greatest achievements were in literature. Whitman and Poe, Mark Twain, Henry James, Hawthorne, and Melville gave the United States a tradition that twentieth-century writers respected. Furthermore, whatever the other faults from which it suffered, the educational system offered talented young writers some training in their craft. The resulting renaissance produced major poets in Frost, Pound, and Eliot and a half dozen others only slightly less gifted. Prose fiction was powerful but less consistent. Still, the imperfections in the work of Theodore Dreiser, John Dos Passos, Ernest Hemingway, Sinclair Lewis, and Sherwood Anderson detracted only slightly from the value of their contributions. The ambitious dramas of Eugene O'Neill already hinted at the

Lawrance Roger Thompson, *Fire and Ice* (New York, 1942) is an interesting study of Robert Frost.

The Poet and the People, 1915

The artist is *not* dependent upon his audience. This sentence is Whitman tired. You have only to compare Whitman to my mutton-headed ninth cousin, or to any other American of his time who had the "great audience," to see the difference of result. . . .

The artist is not dependent upon the multitude of his listeners. Humanity is the rich effluvium, it is the waste and the manure and the soil, and from it grows the tree of the arts. As the plant germ seizes upon the noble particles of the earth, upon the light-seeking and the intrepid, so does the artist seize upon those souls which do not fear transfusion and transmutation, which dare become the body of the god. . . .

It is true that the great artist has in the end, always, his audience, for the Lord of the universe sends into this world in each generation a few intelligent spirits, and these ultimately manage the rest. But this rest—this rabble, this multitude—does *not* create the great artist. They are aimless and drifting without him. They dare not inspect their own souls.

It is true that the great artist has always a great audience, even in his life time; but it is not the *vulgo* but the spirits of irony and of destiny and of humor, sitting within him.

—Ezra Pound, "The Audience," *Poetry*, V (October–March, 1914–1915), pp. 29–30.

quality of the superior work he was to produce in subsequent decades.

The results in other fields were more fragmentary. The painters did not connect themselves with a native tradition, but struck out in new directions. The expressionist John Marin contrived a technique that conveyed to canvas the visual impact both of the natural and the urban landscape. Charles Sheeler abstracted the shapes of the city into severe geometrical patterns. The photographer Alfred Stieglitz freed himself of the rigid realism of the camera and learned to portray personal character and social setting on film.

The situation of the creative personality was most difficult in the arts that depended for fulfillment on institutions still controlled by custodians of the official culture. Charles Ives composed music of great originality and beauty but no orchestra performed his symphonies; he sang to himself. Frank Lloyd Wright had a considerable reputation among architects, but the important commissions went to others. Nevertheless, in these laggard fields, too, resistance was weakening, and the cultural revolution was only temporarily postponed.

The Lone Hero

In the 1920s, it was no more accurate than before to pretend that a single culture served the vast population that was America. The effort to impose on the nation a defined set of uniform standards had failed, and a variegated pattern had evolved to meet the needs of diverse social, sectional, and ethnic groups. The man who enjoyed the comics in Hearst's *New York Evening Journal* had little in common with one who enjoyed the poetry of E. E. Cummings.

Yet there were connections. Some ideas and emotions bore a meaning and evoked a response even among people unfamiliar with the idiom of the particular culture in which they were stated. E. E. Cummings was an admirer of the

John I. H. Baur, *Revolution and Tradition in Modern American Art* (Cambridge, Mass., 1951) is a comprehensive analysis.

Charles A. Lindbergh with the Plane He Flew to Paris, May 1927. (The National Archives)

Journal's Krazy Kat. Everyone understood Charlie Chaplin's tramp, although not all in the same way.

Individualism Two themes had general currency. The Kat and the tramp, the heroes in Hemingway and Fitzgerald, are all defiant individuals, generally at war with the ludicrous conventions of their society. They have their own standards and they seek fulfillment through doing what is right, just as the cowboy does in the movie. Whatever the odds against them, they will fly their own course. They may lose in the end, but the flight is worth making. And the value of having won lies not in the reward but in the process of winning.

Hence, Charles A. Lindbergh captured the imagination of the whole generation when, in May 1927, he flew alone nonstop from New York to Paris in 33½ hours. He was the greatest

Rejecting Main Street, 1920

It is an unimaginatively standardized background, a sluggishness of speech and manners, a rigid ruling of the spirit by the desire to appear respectable. It is contentment . . . the contentment of the quiet dead, who are scornful of the living for their restless walking. It is negation canonized as the one positive virtue. It is the prohibition of happiness. It is slavery self-sought and self-defended. It is dullness made God.

A savorless people, gulping tasteless food, and sitting afterward, coatless and thoughtless in rocking-chairs prickly with inane decorations, listening to mechanical music, saying mechanical things about the excellence of Ford automobiles, and viewing themselves as the greatest race in the world. . . .

Such a society functions admirably in the large production of cheap automobiles, dollar watches, and safety razors. But it is not satisfied until the entire world also admits that the end and joyous purpose of living is to ride in flivvers, to make advertising-pictures of dollar watches, and in the twilight to sit talking not of love and courage but of the convenience of safety razors. . . .

Not individuals but institutions are the enemies, and they most afflict the disciples who the most generously serve them. They insinuate their tyranny under a hundred guises and pompous names, such as *Polite Society*, the *Family*, the *Church, Sound Business*, the *Party*, the *Country*, the *Superior White Race;* and the only defense against them, Carol beheld, is unembittered laughter.

—Sinclair Lewis, *Main Street* (New York: Harcourt, Brace & World, Inc., 1948), pp. 265, 267, 430.

hero in the history of the human race, according to the sober judgment of the New York *World.*

Isolation   Loneliness is a theme related to individualism. What a need for love and communal solidarity the printed page and flickering images express! Never far beneath the surface of the lines in Frost and Eliot is the cry of the individual who is incomplete for want of love. This, on another level, is the unabashed message of scores of hack movies and of countless stories in the pulp magazines. The price of being a hero is rejection of Main Street, of home and family, of church and clan, of all the associations that pin a man down yet lend him support.

Often as a result there arose a question about the nation and the times. Looking back, it seemed to the most sensitive of the writers that it had been the promise of America to liberate the individual, to offer him the hope of fulfillment. But the process had also destroyed the sheltering community and disordered the imprisoning family. With freedom came solitude and uncertainty. Was it the meaning of progress thus to set men adrift alone?

▼

Social disorder, hastened by the war and the postwar reaction, produced the conditions under which Americans were able to perceive and understand their situation. The collapse of cultural authority stimulated the writers and artists to look afresh at human relations and their social context. New modes of expression and freedom to experiment permitted them to probe the unexplored questions of their society. The popular culture was, at the same time, dealing with these issues in its own way.

Social disorder thus created the means for examining and understanding its own conse-

quences. It brushed away the facile optimism of the preceding half century and laid bare the question of man's destiny in the New World as it had not been raised since the Revolutionary generation. Their enlightenment faith had assured the contemporaries of Jefferson that man's will could transform the world. The proper organization of free government could create order in society, and a productive system could draw upon a beneficent nature to satisfy all man's needs. The men of the 1920s could take no such comfort in what was going on in their political and economic systems.

Paperbacks for Further Reading

Frederick Lewis Allen, *Only Yesterday* (Perennial Library) touches on cultural trends. Gilbert Seldes, *The Seven Lively Arts* (Perpetua Books) deals with the movies; and Foster Rhea Dulles, *A History of Recreation* (Apollo Editions, Inc.) treats sports. Alfred Kazin, *On Native Grounds* (Anchor Books) and Frederick J. Hoffman, *The Twenties* (Free Press Paperbacks) discuss the literature of this period. Henry F. May, *End of American Innocence* (Quadrangle Books, Inc.) analyzes intellectual tendencies between 1912 and 1917. Frederic Ramsey, Jr., and Charles E. Smith, eds., *Jazzmen* (Harvest Books) contains materials on popular music.

Among the literary biographies are: Barbara and Arthur Gelb, *O'Neill* (Delta Books); Edgar Kemler, *The Irreverent Mr. Mencken* (Little, Brown & Co.); Arthur Mizener, *The Far Side of Paradise* (Sentry Books) on Fitzgerald; and Mark Schorer, *Sinclair Lewis* (Delta Books). Andrew Turnbull, ed., *The Letters of F. Scott Fitzgerald* (Delta Books) contains much interesting information. James T. Farrell, ed., *Theodore Dreiser* (Dell Publishing Co., Inc.) and Charles Poore, ed., *The Hemingway Reader* (Scribner Library) are useful anthologies. Most of the works of the writers referred to in this chapter are available in numerous paperback editions.

THE POLITICS OF
NORMALCY

80

Although the decade was one of transition, American politics in the 1920s did not face the issues of the period head on. A new generation had appeared on the scene with a viewpoint somewhat different from that of the preceding one. Operating in a world radically altered by war and by internal social change, it could not simply duplicate the programs of the progressive era. It was shaping new attitudes which the depression of 1929 would only partly obscure.

The return to normalcy that Warren G. Harding advocated in 1920 did not materialize. There was no reverting to 1912, much less to 1900. The changes of two decades could not be undone. Behind the familiar cycle of recurring elections, a transformation in the structure of government was taking place. Whether this transformation, which emphasized individualism rather than community needs, was capable of dealing with the postwar social and economic problems was a question that the depression of 1929 would soon answer.

National Politics

Basic Structure A new political generation became prominent in the 1920s. Theodore Roosevelt was dead; Taft had withdrawn to the Supreme Court; and Wilson was in retirement. A few senators maintained the links with the prewar world. But the influential politicians of the decade were relatively new men.

They inherited a stable party system with established procedures for nominating candidates, conducting campaigns, distributing offices, and managing legislative business. Radio, the one innovation of the period, did not significantly alter political practice before 1929. Furthermore, there was no desire to review the dramatic issues of the progressive era or to refight the questions raised by the war or the peace settlement. On the surface, therefore, politics bore a placid appearance.

Federal elections ran a predictable course. After the Republicans healed the split of 1912, they were once more the majority party—thirty-two states voted regularly for the GOP presidential candidate. Six states of the former Confederacy were as loyal to the Democrats. In four (Kentucky, Tennessee, Wisconsin, and Oklahoma) local issues cast doubt upon the outcome in one of the three contests. But only in 1928, in Massachusetts, Rhode Island, Virginia, North Carolina, Florida, and Texas, was there a change with national significance.

The Harding Administration In 1920, both presidential aspirants were Ohio politicians. Warren G. Harding and James M. Cox ran traditional campaigns, which avoided such prickly questions as adherence to the League of Nations. Harding's plea for a return to normalcy expressed the weariness of many Americans with wartime problems and their longing for a return to the good old days. He garnered sixteen million votes against Cox's nine.

Andrew Sinclair, *The Available Man* (New York, 1965) is a well-written biography of Harding.

WARREN G. HARDING was tall, handsome, convivial, and a good fellow. When he played in the Marion (Ohio) cornet band in the 1880s, he was known as a gay blade and he was not averse to a bit of fun even as Senator and President. There was no harm to him, only a woeful inadequacy for the position he held.

He was born in 1865 on a farm in Morrow County, Ohio. His ambitious father studied medicine and moved to Marion, the county seat, where Warren spent most of his life. Harding went to school some and tried to study law but he had no patience with the books; after selling insurance for a while, he settled down to journalism. He married the banker's daughter; his paper, the *Star*, prospered; and little business deals brought him shares of the local lumber and telephone companies. He was an inveterate joiner and was well liked by everyone. His friends pushed him into politics, for which he had little taste; he served first in the state legislature, then as lieutenant governor.

Harding was not himself very ambitious, but his personality was an asset in the tough infighting of Ohio politics and his pal, Harry M. Daugherty, kept thrusting him forward. In 1914, Harding was elected to the United States Senate, a position he rather liked. Business was undemanding and there were enough genial people around to make up a lively poker game. He voted the straight party line and did not allow his own taste for a drink now and then to stand in the way of support of the Eighteenth Amendment.

In 1920 when the Republican Convention got down to choosing a candidate, Harding was available. The party leaders, after eight years out of power, were eager to win, and they wanted no ideological

(Continued on next page)

(Continued from preceding page)

carry-overs from the 1912 split to spoil their chances. Harding was their man. Nominated on the tenth ballot, he ran a front-porch campaign, straddled the issue of the League of Nations, and exuded an aura of old-fashioned folksiness that reassured Americans tired of Wilson's demanding ideas.

He tried to be a good President, but really did not know how and was not willing to work at the job. He let his subordinates go their own way, while he enjoyed himself after his own fashion. He had some intimation that a scandal might break when he set out on a transcontinental tour in 1923, and was disturbed by a long message in code which reached him in Alaska. On August 2, 1923, in San Francisco, he died suddenly of an embolism.

Presidential Vote, 1920–1928

	1920		1924		1928	
	Popular	*Electoral*	*Popular*	*Electoral*	*Popular*	*Electoral*
Republican	16,143,407	404	15,718,211	382	21,391,993	444
Democratic	9,130,328	127	8,385,283	136	15,016,169	87
Socialist	919,799	–	–	–	267,835	–
Progressive	–	–	4,831,289	13	–	–

Harding's administration was uneventful. What credit it deserved for the Washington Conference was due to Secretary of State Charles Evans Hughes; what blame it earned for the excessively high rates of the Fordney-McCumber Tariff was due to Congress. The President himself took the burdens of his office lightly. Legislation he left to the House and Senate, administration to the members of his cabinet, while he prepared to enjoy the rewards of office, among them the fun and games of a house on K Street, where the atmosphere was less austere than in the White House.

Unfortunately, not all his appointments were good ones. In gratitude for services back in Ohio, he named as Attorney General Harry M. Daugherty, later implicated in deals of dubious legality. On a whim, Harding set at the head of the Veterans Bureau Charles R. Forbes, who managed in two years to waste some $200,000,-000 and to commit enough misdeeds to guarantee him a stay in Leavenworth pentitentiary.

Secretary of the Interior Albert B. Fall would also serve a jail sentence for handing over the naval oil reserves at Teapot Dome to private companies in return for a bribe. These scandals caused some public distress but not enough to damage the GOP.

The Election of 1924 Harding's death (August 3, 1923) brought to the White House Vice President Calvin Coolidge. A furious clash within the opposition party helped him gain a full term in the election of 1924. The Democratic Convention that year divided over the question of whether to condemn the Ku Klux Klan. The Southerners and Westerners, who supported William G. McAdoo, preferred not to take a stand that might cost them votes in their regions. The urban Easterners, who backed Governor Alfred E. Smith of New York, insisted on an explicit repudiation of the hooded order out of deference to their Catholic constituents. A nar-

William A. White, *A Puritan in Babylon* (New York, 1935) is a sympathetic biography of Coolidge.

A Commentary on the Tea-pot Dome Scandal. Cartoon from the Chicago *Tribune*, 1924. (Brown Brothers)

IT'S WASHDAY EVERY DAY IN WASHINGTON

row majority decided to keep the platform silent, but neither aspirant could get the two-thirds vote required for nomination. After a deadlock that lasted through 102 ballots, the weary delegates turned to a dark horse, John W. Davis. The subsequent Democratic campaign suffered from the bitterness left by the Convention battle.

The same campaign witnessed the last significant third-party nomination. Robert M. La Follette, running on the Progressive and Socialist tickets with the endorsement of the American Federation of Labor, received almost five million votes and carried Wisconsin, but his effort made no difference in the ultimate outcome.

The Election of 1928 Coolidge's years in office were uneventful. His concern with econ-

omy and tax cuts led him to veto bills favored by the farmers and veterans, but he might well have secured a renomination in 1928 had he actively sought it. He did not choose to run and there was no movement to draft him for the race. Instead, the Republican party turned to his Secretary of Commerce Herbert Hoover, a Wilsonian who had earned a progressive reputation during the war and who campaigned as a forward-looking engineer able to solve the country's problems scientifically.

Al Smith was the Democratic candidate. There was no acrimony about the nomination as there had been four years earlier. Smith, as governor of New York, had continued to attract favorable national attention and he had mollified

393

CALVIN COOLIDGE was a Yankee who believed in minding his own business. He was born in 1872 at Plymouth in Windsor County, Vermont, where his parents kept a general store. He attended the local school and St. Johnsbury Academy and graduated from Amherst College in 1895. He then read law in Northampton, Massachusetts, and remained there to practice, dealing with local cases—mortgages, bankruptcies, estates, and debts.

He had early been interested in politics, and moved into local affairs as a lawyer. He served as mayor of Northampton and in the state legislature, rising steadily through the ranks of the Republican party, controlled in the state by United States Senators Murray Crane and Henry Cabot Lodge. In 1918 Coolidge became governor after having served successfully as president of the state senate and as lieutenant governor.

Coolidge won national fame during the Boston police strike, which he suppressed by calling out the state guard. That action earned him the vice presidential nomination, and he was elected in the Harding victory. As President, following Harding's death, he minded his own business, was unsmirched by the scandals of his predecessor's administration, and won election to the office in 1924. In the summer of 1927 he made up his mind not to seek renomination, but he probably would have accepted another term. Hence his statement, "I do not choose to run for president in 1928." In 1929 he retired to Northampton, where he died in 1933.

Coolidge was an able administrator but his refusal to question the old verities limited his capacity for action. He did not marry until the age of thirty-three, and was moody, secretive, and stingy. At the start of his career he had supported the gold standard, eulogized the great corporations, and defended the courts, for he believed that morality was the essential element of statesmanship. Yet he closed his eyes to the scandals of the Harding administration. Since he considered it more important to kill bad bills than to pass good ones, his energies went mostly to keeping things as they were. Within a year after Coolidge left office, the Depression destroyed the order in which he had faith.

---

the opposition. Furthermore, the decline in the strength of the Klan eliminated the religious question from the Convention's consideration.

Anti-Catholicism was nevertheless a factor in the campaign. Smith's opposition to prohibition, his New York accent, and his undisguised urban manners were taken in the rural regions of the country as signs of his Tammany and Romanist affiliations. Bigoted attacks stirred up prejudice and pushed Virginia, North Carolina, Florida, and Texas out of the Democratic ranks for the first time in many years.

The Republican triumph did not, however, depend on the transfer of the votes of those states. Hoover's majority was so large (21,000,000 to 15,000,000 popular votes; 444 to 87 in the electoral college) that he would have won without them. The country enjoyed a high level of prosperity and Hoover's progressive record was impressive. He took office with the support of a comfortable majority in Congress and with the confidence of the country.

The wide margin of Smith's defeat concealed the significance of the fact that his vote almost doubled that of Davis in 1924. The shift of Massachusetts and Rhode Island to the Democratic column pointed to the source of the added support. The Republicans did just about as well in those states as they had earlier. But a hoard of new voters flocked to the polls—urban immigrants or their children, laborers expressing their solidarity with the governor of New

Popular Vote for President, 1924–1928

(in thousands)

Year	Massachusetts Republican	Democratic	Rhode Island Republican	Democratic
1924	703	280	125	76
1928	775	792	117	118

York who was one of their own kind. The full meaning of their participation in national politics would become apparent in the next decade.

State and Local Government

State Actions The pattern of elections on the state level was essentially similar to that on the Federal, but the achievements were more substantial. The progressive movement had cleared legislatures of the pervasive corruption of the past, and strong, determined governors addressed themselves to the critical postwar problems. The disproportionate representation of the rural districts in the legislatures was offset by progressive influences, and did not impede action as it had earlier and would again.

The states devoted a good deal of attention to consolidating the pioneer work of the years before 1917. New statutes regulating industrial working conditions surmounted the constitutional hurdles set up by the courts. Improved workmen's compensation laws and more adequate provision for the care of dependents showed an increasing awareness of the necessity for guarding against the hazards of modern society. New York State in 1926 gave a fresh turn to the problem of housing the poor by granting tax concessions and the power of condemnation to cooperative and limited-dividend corporations. Concern about forest, wildlife, and water-power resources led to stronger conservation measures in many states.

For the first time, there was a substantial increase in the support to public education. The number of children enrolled in elementary and secondary schools rose, along with the percentage between the ages of five and seventeen. Furthermore, the greater length of the term and the increase in the average number of days attended reflected an important improvement in quality. Americans were now willing to spend money for education. State and local expenditures increased more than fourfold between 1912 and 1929. The higher outlays did more than accommodate a larger number of pupils. The amount spent on each child multiplied almost as fast. To provide the necessary funds, the states were willing to raise taxes and some of them undertook to draw upon levies on income.

Municipal Problems The situation of local government was more complex than that of the states. Experiments with commission and city-manager forms continued to spread in small and middle-sized communities. But in the large metropolitan areas, the number and size of which increased, the formal political system remained unchanged. Intermittent reform movements did not shake the power of the machines. Too often the mayors were amiable scoundrels like James Michael Curley of Boston and James J. Walker of New York, or hard-fisted despots like Frank Hague of Jersey City, or blatant demagogues like "Big Bill" Thompson of Chicago.

The Level of Education, 1912–1929

	1912	1929
Public school enrollment (millions)	18	25
Percentage of population aged 5–17 in public school	72	81
Length of term (days)	158	171
Average days of attendance	115	141
High school graduates (thousands)	180	600
Percentage of age group	10	29
Estimated receipts of elementary and secondary schools (million dollars)		
State	75	340
Local	346	1,700
Total expenditures of all schools	482	2,200

They enjoyed the support of one or several ethnic groups, usually had a working arrangement with local labor leaders, sometimes operated in a tacit alliance with crime and vice gangs, and dispensed patronage and favors with feudal benevolence. Opposition to the bosses was by no means dead, but it lacked the means of mobilizing popular support.

Paradoxically, Americans in the postwar decade gave more thought to the problems of city planning than earlier. Yet they were inclined to write the metropolis off as hopeless. Some planners dreamed of breaking up the large cities into smaller communities. Others sought to bypass the existing municipalities by establishing quasi-governmental authorities appointed by the states, charged with specific functions and isolated from local political control. The Port of New York Authority, for instance, was created in 1921 with power to build and operate facilities in the harbor. Before long, other communities set up similar bodies for one objective or another.

Such agencies served two purposes. The large cities had outgrown their political boundaries, yet the surrounding suburbs to which many former residents had fled resisted efforts at incorporation, preferring their own low tax rates and superior services. The new authorities and commissions reduced the pressure toward engulfing the outlying districts and also evaded the risk of domination by the popular machines. These quasi-governmental bodies were symptomatic of a general tendency to put less faith in the machinery of democratic elections and more in the service of technical experts.

Government by Experts

The Business of Governing From the progressives of the first two decades of the century Americans had learned that government was a science and, like any other, was best left in the hands of trained experts. The political system had outgrown the informal town meeting, as business had the country store. Only men edu-

cated to understand the intricate machinery could administer either industry or government.

The expert had the additional virtue of disinterestedness. All political decisions were subject to the pressure of rival interests. The farm bloc in Congress was only the most visible of many organized efforts to exert influence on government. In Washington, in the state capitals, and in the corridors of scores of city halls, energetic lobbyists urged the causes of industry, labor, agriculture, and reform. The expert could appraise these forces with scientific precision and engineer an operation efficiently calculated to provide the maximum satisfaction.

In the 1920s, the faith in the expert that had already influenced municipal government extended to other areas as well. Soon after the war, New York, Massachusetts, and other states, on the basis of recommendations from reconstruction commissions, reorganized and streamlined their administrative agencies, centralizing responsibility in the governor and aiming for nonpartisan efficiency.

National Administration The great change on the Federal level was the creation of the Bureau of the Budget (1921) to consolidate the appropriation process, which until then was dispersed in many different Congressional committees. Together with a General Accounting Office, headed by the Comptroller General, the new bureau assumed broad fiscal oversight of all expenditures, which were thereafter to be made within a planned framework.

Secretary of Commerce Herbert C. Hoover and Secretary of the Treasury Andrew W. Mellon were pre-eminent among the officials presumed to have distinctive competence because their careers had not been political. Their reputations were those of experts—Hoover's as an engineer and as a wartime food administrator, Mellon's as a banker. They sought not only to manage their departments economically but also to reduce the debt and taxes and to provide in-

Charles G. Dawes, *First Year of the Budget of the United States* (New York, 1923) treats the problem.

Herbert C. Hoover (left), Henry Ford, Thomas A. Edison, and Harvey S. Firestone, Fort Myers, Florida, February 1929. (UPI)

formation and other services as aids to business. Meanwhile the multiplication of independent agencies since the creation of the Interstate Commerce Commission had put considerable executive and judicial power into the hands of nonpolitical experts who operated by codes of administrative law far removed from popular law and popular wishes.

The Progressive Legacy

The shift of influence from the elected legislator to the scientific administrator conformed to tendencies implicit in the progressive idea since the very start of the century. But new conceptions of psychology, society, and politics hastened the development.

The Nature of Man and of Society   The psychologists challenged the validity of the nineteenth-century democratic assumption that any man could solve his own problems by the application of correct reason. During the war the army intelligence tests had shown wide disparities in the level of personal competence. William McDougall, concerned about the relationship of these performances to heredity and eugenics, argued (1921) that America was not safe for democracy.

The theories which held that reason exerted only a limited influence on man's actions deepened these doubts. In *Behavior* (1914), John B. Watson explained that humans could be conditioned to make unreflective responses to predetermined stimuli, and the advertising of the

397

Conscious Purpose and Tradition, 1914

Men have to substitute purpose for tradition: and that is, I believe, the profoundest change that has ever taken place in human history. We can no longer treat life as something that has trickled down to us. We have to deal with it deliberately, devise its social organization, alter its tools, formulate its method, educate and control it. In endless ways we put intention where custom has reigned. We break up routines, make decisions, choose our ends, select means.

The massive part of man's life has always been, and still is, subconscious. The influence of his intelligence seems insignificant in comparison with attachments and desires, brute forces, and natural catastrophes. Our life is managed from behind the scenes: we are actors in dramas that we cannot interpret. Of almost no decisive event can we say: this was our own choosing. We happen upon careers, necessity pushing, blind inclination pulling. If we stop to think we are amazed that we should be what we are. And so we have come to call mysterious everything that counts, and the more mysterious the better some of us pretend to think it is. We drift into our work, we fall in love, and our lives seem like the intermittent flicker of an obstinate lamp. War panics, and financial panics, revivals, fads sweep us before them. Men go to war not knowing why, hurl themselves at cannon as if they were bags of flour, seek impossible goals, submit to senseless wrongs, for mankind lives to-day only in the intervals of a fitful sleep. . . .

Mastery means . . . the substitution of conscious intention for unconscious striving. Civilization, it seems to me, is just this constant effort to introduce plan where there has been clash, and purpose into the jungles of disordered growth. But to shape the world nearer to the heart's desire requires a knowledge of the heart's desire and of the world. You cannot throw yourself blindly against unknown facts and trust to luck that the result will be satisfactory.

1920s increasingly applied the techniques he suggested. McDougall's *The Group Mind* (1920) also called into question the rationality of behavior by pointing out that people responded less often to logical precepts than to instincts.

The concept of instincts also entered into the thinking of Thorstein Veblen, whose writings after 1914 emphasized the nonrational elements in society. He remained an evolutionist who believed that institutions had to adjust to circumstances. But he pointed to the cultural lag created by the popular, unreasoning resistance to change and urged that it was the duty of technologists and engineers to manipulate development in the proper direction.

These views strengthened the propositions Walter Lippmann stated in his *A Preface to Politics* (1913) and his *Public Opinion* (1922). In a subtle criticism of popular democracy Lippmann combined ideas derived from the English theorist Graham Wallas with certain Freudian conceptions and with instinct psychology. Government, he argued, was not a distinctive area set off from other human experiences but part of the total life of the community. People did not make decisions rationally on isolated issues but responded according to preconceived opinions or stereotypes based on emotion and interest. They therefore needed the guidance of exceptional, inventive individuals who could make the correct policy choices. The historical writings of Charles A. Beard added to the persuasiveness of these theories by demonstrating the economic basis of past political development. In addition, they undermined the fetishistic faith in constitutionalism by showing the self-interest behind the actions even of the founding fathers.

In the context of the new conceptions, the appeal to reason of the conventional progressives of the first decade of the century seemed naïve and inconsequential. In 1924 La Follette was already old-fashioned, and Wilson seemed a figure from the past. Indeed, the very label progressive dropped out of use in favor of the term liberal.

The impulse toward reform still drew the support of influential writers, journalists, and politicians but there was a significant alteration in emphasis. There was no need to fight for the scientific method and the use of experts since conservatives and businessmen, too, had adopted the cause. The remaining tasks for liberals were exposure of error and corruption and the defense of individual liberty.

Debunking The foibles of the Harding administration stimulated the continued activity of muckrakers. The material generated by those misdeeds was ample enough to feed Congressional investigating committees, newspapers, magazines, and novels. Old hands like Upton Sinclair broadened their attacks on established institutions to include industry, journalism, and education. Popular biographies such as the life of Washington by Rupert Hughes (1926) and of Grant by W. E. Woodward (1928) pulled national heroes off their pedestals, while Elmer Davis in *The Giant Killer* (1928) revealed the Biblical feet of clay of King David. Numerous revisionist histories explained the needlessness of the World War, the Spanish-American War, and the Civil War and deflated the reputations of Wilson and Lincoln. In good part, the circulation of *The American Mercury* depended on the desire of its subscribers to see the inside story of their national institutions exposed.

Individual Liberty Individualism was the link between liberalism and the dominant ideas of the 1920s. The community was, according to those ideas, a threat to personal freedom and its encroachments were zealously to be resisted. Prohibition became the central issue of much political discussion during the decade, for both to its traditional supporters and to its liberal opponents it was a symbol of the effort to establish communal control over personal behavior. That was also why this decade lost interest in health and unemployment insurance and old-age pensions. These measures were objectively no less necessary than previously but they threatened to make the individual dependent upon society for security and therefore seemed less desirable in the new intellectual context.

By contrast, civil liberties acquired unprecedented importance. John Dewey and others had already formed the American Association of University Professors (1914) to battle for academic freedom. A reaction against wartime repression and the Red scare produced a broad definition of personal rights in Zechariah Chafee, Jr.'s *Freedom of Speech* (1920), and Justices Holmes and Brandeis, who had dissented in the sedition cases, became the heroes of the generation. The American Civil Liberties Union, formally founded in 1920, gained steadily in strength and energetically defended dissenters of every kind. It also challenged every form of censorship and fought bigotry.

The liberals found cases enough to keep them busy. The labor leaders, Thomas J. Mooney and Warren Billings, languished in a California jail, serving life sentences for bombing the San Francisco Preparedness Day parade of 1916, despite evidence that they were victims of a frame-up. Similar doubts existed about the conviction (1921) of Nicola Sacco and Bartolomeo Vanzetti of the murder of a paymaster in

Zechariah Chafee, Jr., *Free Speech in the United States* (Cambridge, Mass., 1941) is a thoughtful revision of the book first published in 1920. Herbert B. Ehrmann, *The Untried Case* (New York, 1933) is a brief history by one of the defense counsel.

Nicola Sacco (right) and Bartolomeo Vanzetti (center) in Court. (Brown Brothers)

South Braintree, Massachusetts, a year earlier. By the time they were executed in 1927, a wave of protest had challenged the justice of their trial. Liberals generally believed that the verdict of guilty rested not on the evidence but on prejudice against immigrants and anarchists.

Sympathy for the victims of conservative attacks also drew the liberals to the defense of organized labor, the socialists, and the communists. In addition, the interest in scientific planning seemed a link to the new society emerging in the Soviet Union. John Reed and Lincoln Steffens, among others, were inspired by the spectacle of a revolution that tore down an ancient tyranny to liberate the individual. Few Americans actually joined the various radical party groups that took form in the United States. But many liberals argued in favor of recognition of the Soviet Union and defended the rights of the Reds in the United States to freedom of speech and association.

Triumph, 1927

If it had not been for these things, I might have lived out my life talking at street corners to scorning men. I might die, unmarked, unknown, a failure. Now we are not a failure. This is our career and our triumph. Never in our full life could we hope to do such work for tolerance, for joostice, for man's onderstanding of man as now we do by accident. Our words—our lives—our pains—nothing! The taking of our lives—lives of a good shoemaker and a poor fish-peddler—all! That last moment belongs to us—that agony is our triumph.

—Bartolomeo Vanzetti, Statement after sentencing. M. D. Frankfurter and Gardner Jackson, *Letters of Sacco and Vanzetti* (New York: The Viking Press, Inc., 1928), frontispiece.

The Purpose of Law, 1921

The final cause of law is the welfare of society. The rule that misses its aim cannot permanently justify its existence. "Ethical considerations can no more be excluded from the administration of justice which is the end and purpose of all civil laws than one can exclude the vital air from his room and live." Logic and history and custom have their place. We will shape the law to conform to them when we may; but only within bounds. The end which the law serves will dominate them all. . . . I do not mean, of course, that judges are commissioned to set aside existing rules at pleasure in favor of any other set of rules which may hold to be expedient or wise. I mean that when they are called upon to say how far existing rules are to be extended or restricted, they must let the welfare of society fix the path, its direction and its distance. We are not to forget, said Sir George Jessel, in an often quoted judgment, that there is this paramount public policy, that we are not lightly to interfere with freedom of contract. So in this field, there may be a paramount public policy, one that will prevail over temporary inconvenience or occasional hardship, not lightly to sacrifice certainty and uniformity and order and coherence. All these elements must be considered. They are to be given such weight as sound judgment dictates. They are constituents of that social welfare which it is our business to discover. In a given instance we may find that they are constituents of preponderating value. In others, we may find that their value is subordinate. We must appraise them as best we can.

— Benjamin N. Cardozo, *The Nature of the Judicial Process* (New Haven, Conn.: Yale University Press, 1925), pp. 66–67.

In the context of these issues, the courts often seemed reactionary, more likely to safeguard the privileges of property than personal freedom. Yet the judges were also becoming aware that the law existed to further the welfare of society. Three cases between 1923 and 1925 paved the way to a fuller defense of liberty against state action as well as against Federal action. Two of them held unconstitutional statutes forbidding the teaching of foreign languages or the operation of private and parochial schools. In ruling that these laws interfered with the right of parents to direct the education of their children, the Supreme Court argued that the states were answerable in the Federal courts for such violations of individual liberty. *Gitlow* v. *New York* stated the basic principle explicitly: the Fourteenth Amendment made binding upon the states the same restraints that the Bill of Rights placed upon the Federal government. A generation later that principle would be the foundation for still wider expansion of the conception of liberty.

After the World War, the political system was in transition. Most of the work of the progressive era was finished, but the new tasks were not yet fully defined. The ability and the means were available to meet the novel needs of society through government action. But the existing machinery was not adequate to the purpose and the liberal heirs of progressivism were slow to define the proper objectives. Their achievements were on the state or local rather than on the national level. The result was not the great overarching reforms of the first fifteen years of the century but rather a cluster of smaller changes that dealt with immediate issues. It would take the shock of a great depression to bring serious thought about the problems of the economy and of the society to the forefront of men's minds.

Paperbacks for Further Reading

John D. Hicks, *Republican Ascendancy* (Harper Torchbooks) is a general survey. There is also some material on politics in Frederick Lewis Allen, *Only Yesterday* (Perennial Library). Samuel Hopkins Adams, *Incredible Era* (Capricorn Books) is a sensational account of the Harding administration. Burt Noggle, *Teapot Dome* (W. W. Norton & Company, Inc.) is more scholarly. Oscar Handlin, *Al Smith and His America* (Little, Brown & Co.) treats the decade of the 1920s. Edwin O'Connor, *The Last Hurrah* (Bantam Books, Inc.) is a novel about municipal politics in these years. There is a good discussion on the significance of the election of 1928 in Samuel Lubell, *Future of American Politics* (Harper Colophon Books). Irving Howe and Lewis Coser, *The American Communist Party* (Frederick A. Praeger, Inc.) discusses the radicalism of the period. Robert P. Weeks, *Commonwealth vs. Sacco Vanzetti* (Prentice-Hall, Inc.) assembles the material bearing on the case, which is also discussed in Felix Frankfurter, *Law and Politics* (Capricorn Books) and in Louis Joughin and Edmund M. Morgan, *The Legacy of Sacco and Vanzetti* (Quadrangle Books, Inc.). Samuel Konefsky, *Legacy of Holmes and Brandeis* (Collier Books) analyzes the Gitlow case; and there is material on legal developments in Benjamin N. Cardozo, *Nature of the Judicial Process* (Yale University Press) and in Alexander M. Bickel, *Unpublished Opinions of Mr. Justice Brandeis* (Phoenix Books).

ECONOMIC
CHANGE

81

American entrepreneurs before 1929 proceeded under the assumption that the economy was simply developing along the familiar lines of the past. Once the war was over they settled down to enjoy the rewards of virtue and good management. In the 1920s, prosperity seemed to justify their confidence.

Contemporaries, however, were not in a position to perceive the full implications of the changes that were altering both the country's relationship to the world and the character of the domestic market. In view of a new technology and the reorganization of industry the economy depended more than formerly upon a population with sufficient purchasing power to consume the products of the farms and factories. Yet limited incomes kept a substantial number of Americans out of the ranks of the buyers. This situation existed well before 1929, but only after a great depression would it be recognized.

Prosperity

THE PROSPERITY OF THE 1920s was due to a rapid expansion of manufacturing activity. In the course of the decade industrial production just about doubled, and the national income and the gross national product rose at gratifying rates. Making allowance for population increases and price changes, the real income per capita still showed an impressive movement upward. The trend derived from a favorable position in international capital markets and from a tolerant public attitude toward business, as well as from improved technology.

American Capitalism Until the World War, American investments overseas had grown slowly. The incentives at home were so large that capitalists rarely had reason to export their capital. Actually, foreigners were more likely to invest within the United States, which therefore was on balance still a debtor to others.

The war changed all that. The sums owed abroad were liquidated as foreign investors sold their American securities for the dollars their countries needed. At the same time public and private loans made the United States a creditor. The new tendency persisted through the 1920s. The war debts were not repaid. Instead, more American capital flowed out during that decade through loans to governments, through investments in foreign enterprises, and through the erection of American branch plants overseas. In addition, an excess of exports over imports added to the amounts due the United States. The historic shortage of capital was over. A mature economy generated surpluses available for widespread investment and for speculation.

Supplies of money and credit were ample. The Federal Reserve system, which expanded the base of the currency from government bonds alone to commerical paper also, made the supply more flexible in periods of expansion. Since each Federal Reserve district had some autonomy,

George Soule, *Prosperity Decade: From War to Depression, 1917–1929* (New York, 1947) is a good general survey.

Gross National Product (billion dollars, 1929 prices)	
1912–1916 (average)	62.5
1917–1921 (average)	71.9
1922	75.8
1923	85.8
1924	88.4
1925	90.5
1926	96.4
1927	97.3
1928	98.5
1929	104.4

controls were not wholly centralized. The New York investment banks of the former generation therefore lost some of their power. New firms established themselves easily and the great corporations became less dependent than earlier on financial intermediaries.

Productivity, 1929

The years 1922 to 1929 witnessed a marked increase in the physical volume of production. . . . There have been prosperous periods in the past which may have surpassed these rates of increase but none so far as the committee can learn which has shown such a striking increase in productivity per man-hour. . . . And these increases in productivity have been joined to a corresponding increase in the consuming power of the American people. Here has been demonstrated on a grand scale the expansibility of human wants and desires.

—Committee on Recent Economic Changes, National Bureau of Economic Research, *Recent Economic Changes in the United States* (New York: McGraw-Hill, Inc., 1929), vol. I, p. 3.

A Sunday Afternoon in Forest Park, St. Louis, Missouri, 1920s. (The Granger Collection)

Speculation Easy money encouraged a wave of speculation which continued down to 1929. While the Federal government had no desire to direct the economy, its fiscal policies, unintentionally but effectively, stimulated the boom. The steady reduction of the national debt and of Federal expenditures as well as substantial tax cuts in 1921, 1925, and 1926 added to the funds in private hands available for investment.

The values of most kinds of property spiraled upward under pressure from the unbounded American faith that economic growth could make anyone rich. An enormous real estate boom inflated the prices of urban land throughout the nation. Florida and California, which seemed susceptible to sudden development, went to extremes and suffered occasional relapses but not enough to extinguish the underlying optimism.

A great construction boom, too, stimulated speculation. The total value of new building, in constant dollars, doubled between 1915 and 1929. Meanwhile the automobile accelerated the demand for new highways. The number of vehicle miles traveled rose about fourfold between 1921 and 1929 alone. The value of roads and streets laid out each year tripled between 1915 and 1929, a good part of it derived from Federal grants-in-aid.

Much of the urban construction of the late nineteenth century had to be replaced because it had become obsolete either through original deficiencies in planning, through changes in the character of the cities, or through shifts in population from one neighborhood to another. Transit facilities, public utilities, and schools as well as new residences absorbed tons of steel and concrete and gave employment to thousands of

405

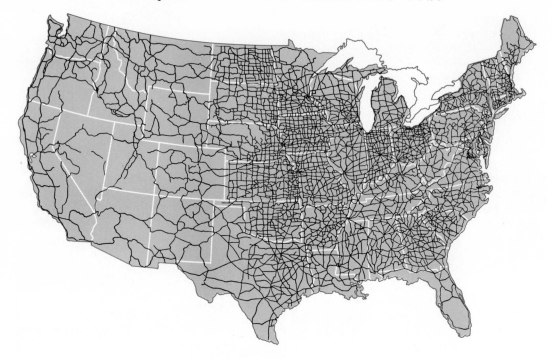

THE FEDERAL ROAD SYSTEM, 1925

workers. The rise in the standard of living and the pent-up demand of the war years, when there had been relatively little construction, touched off a wave of speculative building after 1918. The number of housing starts climbed in the 1920s, reflecting the prevailing confidence in continuing growth.

By far the most important manifestation of unrestrained speculation was the boom in securities. The number of shares traded mounted rapidly and their prices rose to levels totally unjustified by earnings or dividends. Loose credit practices permitted speculators to deal on margin, investing relatively little cash in short-term turnovers of large blocks of stock. The firms on the New York Stock Exchange in 1929 carried about half their accounts on this basis. Brokers' loans for margin accounts climbed from $2,800,000,000 at the beginning of 1927 to $3,500,000,000 at the end and rocketed to $6,000,000,000 by the summer of 1929.

Many banks encouraged the expansive tendency. Some of them entered the business of selling securities through affiliates and thus profited directly from sales. Others, lured by

Stock Prices, 1928–1929

Corporation	Opening March 3, 1928	High* Sept. 3, 1929
American Can	77	181⅞
American Telephone	179½	335⅝
Anaconda Copper	54½	162
Electric Bond	89¾	203⅝
General Electric	128¾	396½
Montgomery Ward	132¾	466½
Radio Corporation of America	94½	505
Union Carbide	145	413⅝
United States Steel	138⅛	279⅛
Westinghouse	91⅝	313

*Adjusted to take account of splits

high interest rates, became lax in extending credit. The Federal Reserve Board felt some uneasiness about these developments but took no effective action to curb them. In fact, in August 1927 it lowered the discount rate from 4 to 3.5 percent. Easy loans encouraged stock purchasers. Prices promptly shot upward. The sky was the limit!

The Modern Corporation Renewed faith in the corporate organization of business fed excessive expectations about the capacity of American industry to grow. The corporation was now far removed from its nineteenth-century antecedents, not only in size but also in character. The individual entrepreneur was a figure of the past. The modern corporation was autonomous, managed by a bureaucracy under the indirect control of the stockholders. Its object was not personal profit but productive growth.

The hostility of the old trust-busting days subsided. In the 1920s there were few prosecutions under the Clayton Act despite the intentions of its framers. Capitalists like John D. Rockefeller, aware that they could not disregard the views of the man in the street, hired Ivy Lee and other public relations experts for advice on how best to gain popularity. The concern with opinion was itself an indication of a new sense of public responsibility. John Maurice Clark's influential *Social Control of Business* (1926) explained that monopoly was not a danger. Although the day of *laissez-faire* was over, Clark asserted, the state was a clumsy means of control and it was better to let the large, organized interests of the country balance one another to advance the general welfare.

In a context tolerant of bigness, the refusal of the Supreme Court in 1920 to order the dissolution of the United States Steel Corporation touched off a chain of mergers and combinations. The judges held in that case that mere size or command of a large part of the market was not itself evidence of restraint of trade. Mean-

Ray E. Hiebert, *Courtier to the Crowd* (Ames, Iowa, 1966) is a study of Ivy Lee and the development of public relations.

while some states sanctioned branch banking, and chain stores increased the number of their outlets—the A & P from 5000 in 1922 to 17,500 in 1928. These tendencies toward consolidation aroused the trepidation of only a few liberals. Most Americans took comfort from the rising level of corporate profits and dividends.

New Industrial Developments

Power and Aluminum New industries, protected by the tolerance for bigness, displayed the dramatic growth that seemed to justify the confidence in the future. The use of electric power, for instance, had grown slowly down to the first decade of the century, then expanded rapidly, drawing upon both coal and water for generating energy. The number of customers rose, the use per customer doubled, and the total production mounted more than fivefold between 1912 and 1929. The companies that produced and distributed power promised fortunes to investors. Samuel Insull and others assembled vast holding companies to tie the operating networks together and, in the process, created great opportunities for the manipulation of stock values.

The use of electricity enabled the aluminum industry to pass through a spectacular rise. Primary production rose about sixfold between 1912 and 1929. That rapid expansion, virtually confined to a single company, encouraged widespread expectation of unlimited future profits. The Aluminum Company of America, controlled by the Mellon interests, had a practical monopoly of ingot production, and through its Canadian affiliate, Aluminium, Ltd. (1928), cooperated with a world-wide cartel.

The Automobile The most important of the new industries was the manufacture of automobiles. Production had grown slowly in the first decade of the twentieth century, when techniques in the United States were less advanced than those of Europe, and a substantial number of vehicles were imported.

Business shaped the world of **ANDREW W. MELLON.** He was born in 1855 in Pittsburgh, where his father was a well-known lawyer and entrepreneur. By the time Andrew entered the Western University of Pennsylvania, his father had formed a banking house and was making loans to the booming industries of the region. Andrew did not bother to finish his studies but went into business while still a youth. At nineteen he had entered the family bank and at twenty-seven was managing it.

The opportunities for investment were rich. Mellon acquired shares of the Aluminum Company of America, of the Carborundum Company, and of Gulf Oil, which made important strikes in Texas and Oklahoma. He also had interests in steel, coke, and other property. Business was his life. He had few indulgences other than a game of poker with men like Frick or Westinghouse. He did not marry until he was forty-five, and that unhappy experience ended in divorce. He was active in behind-the-scenes Pennsylvania Republican politics, but was completely unknown to the public when named Secretary of the Treasury in 1920.

In his view, the function of government was to serve business. In the decade he held office his primary concern was to reduce the national debt, which he lowered from $24,000,000,000 to $16,000,000,000 between 1921 and 1929. At the same time he wished to push down taxes. The income tax he believed was a means of rewarding one class and punishing another. The rates went down and the excess-profits tax disappeared. Mellon expected to compensate for the loss of revenue by cutting back on expenditures and therefore opposed the veterans' bonus and the McNary-Haugen bills, which would have cost money. He took pride in the steadily declining budget. These economies, however, contributed to speculation and ultimately to the depression.

After the panic of 1929 Mellon was suspicious even of Hoover's moderate measures for recovery and in 1932 was sent as ambassador to London to get him out of the way. His whole order was gone and he watched the New Deal with dismay and bewilderment. In 1937, when he died, he was one of the defendants in an antitrust suit against the Aluminum Company.

The innovations of Henry Ford then quickly altered the whole industry. Ford aimed to produce a cheap car to be sold at a relatively low price to a mass market. He standardized the parts and the manufacturing process, introduced the assembly line, and kept his margin of profit to a minimum. As a result he was able to lower the price of his Model T from more than $900 in 1909 to $360 in 1917, while raising annual sales from 18,000 to 785,000. As output rose, he plowed the profits back and enlarged the plants. Most manufacturers depended upon scores of suppliers who furnished the numerous parts of the car, but Ford perceived the advantages of large-scale, integrated production and soon expanded vertically. His manufacturing network reached out to include the plantations that supplied rubber for the tires, the mills that furnished the steel, and dispersed plants that assembled the Model T's.

With his success, Ford's capacity for innovation ran out. He remained an individual entrepreneur who had built a better mousetrap and held to it. His accounting practices were primitive, and although he used some advertising, he relied on the product to sell itself. In 1921 he still accounted for 55 percent of all American automobile sales, but he would not hold the lead long.

In 1908, William C. Durant had begun to put together the General Motors Corporation, through mergers, but he was essentially a finan-

Allan Nevins and Frank E. Hill, *Ford* (New York, 1957) deals with the automobile industry between 1915 and 1932.

The American Automobile Industry, 1911–1929

Year	Factory Sales Automobile	Factory Sales Trucks	Total Registrations	Value of Exports (million dollars)
1911	199,319	10,681	639,500	16
1912	356,000	22,000	944,000	26
1913	461,500	23,500	1,258,060	33
1914	548,139	24,900	1,763,018	35
1915	895,930	74,000	2,490,932	70
1916	1,525,578	92,130	3,617,937	123
1917	1,745,792	128,157	5,118,525	124
1918	943,436	227,250	6,160,448	101
1919	1,651,625	224,731	7,576,888	156
1920	1,905,560	321,789	9,239,161	303
1921	1,468,067	148,052	10,493,666	84
1922	2,274,185	269,991	12,273,599	103
1923	3,624,717	409,295	15,102,105	171
1924	3,185,881	416,659	17,612,940	210
1925	3,735,171	530,659	20,068,543	318
1926	3,692,317	608,617	22,200,150	320
1927	2,936,533	464,793	23,303,470	389
1928	3,775,417	583,342	24,688,631	502
1929	4,455,178	881,909	26,704,825	541

cial manipulator and in November 1920 he over-played his hand. The Du Pont interests took over, with the aid of J. P. Morgan, and installed an entirely new management, committed to centralized policy but decentralized administration.

The men like Alfred P. Sloan who developed the General Motors organization adopted Ford's production techniques but were more sensitive than he to market needs and better able to anticipate future developments. They integrated horizontally in addition to vertically. They were therefore able to produce a variety of models under different names in order to blanket the whole range of potential purchasers. Furthermore, to sustain demand, they introduced periodic model changes, or planned obsolescence to reduce the disturbing fluctuations in the flow of cars out of the factory. As a result they not only outdistanced Ford and took the lead among producers but also in the end forced him to follow their practices.

Consumer Durables Automobiles were the products of a new sector of American manufacturing. Like radios and refrigerators, automobiles were sold to consumers, though at a relatively high price. Destined for the consumer and yet durable, such goods differed both from the products of heavy industry like steel, which went mostly to producers, and also from clothing or shoes, which were used up as they were bought. The nineteenth-century precursors of the new category—furniture, pianos, and sewing machines—had enjoyed limited markets. Now novel sales techniques expanded the number of potential buyers and sharply raised the level of production.

The manufacturers of durable goods established networks of distributors throughout the country to assure adequate markets. Extensive advertising campaigns used a variety of media to make their product names familiar to the public and to sustain demand. Finally, in alliance with

The Magnavox Reproducer and the Magnavox Power Amplifier

"These two devices have revolutionized Radio"

MAGNAVOX Radio equipment takes the feeble sound vibrations produced by your receiving set and builds them up into full, round tones in exact accordance with the original broadcasted speech or music.

The development of the Magnavox is one of Radio's spectacular achievements.

Magnavox R3 Reproducer and 2 stage Power Amplifier, as illustrated . . $90.00

R2 Magnavox Reproducer with 18-inch curvex horn: the utmost in amplifying power; requires only .6 of an ampere for field . $60.00

R3 Magnavox Reproducer with 14-inch curvex horn: ideal for homes, etc. $35.00

Model C Magnavox Power Amplifier insures getting the largest possible power input for your Magnavox Reproducer . . 2 stage $55.00
3 stage 75.00

Magnavox Products can be had from good dealers everywhere. Write for new booklet.

THE MAGNAVOX CO.
Oakland, Cal.
New York: 370 Seventh Ave.

MAGNAVOX Radio
The Reproducer Supreme

[1923]

Advertisement for a Magnavox Radio, 1923. This appeared during the first boom period in radio sales (1922–1924). (The Bettmann Archive)

410

ALFRED P. SLOAN was a heavy-duty trouble shooter. He focused his interests on his work, read little but corporate reports, went to bed early, carried a home-made sandwich to his office, and maintained an inhuman detachment from the people around him. He got the job done.

Born in New Haven, Connecticut, in 1875, he grew up in Brooklyn, New York, and at the age of twenty earned an engineering degree from M.I.T. A friend of his father got him a job with the Hyatt Roller Bearing Company, where he soon became partner and general manager. Sales to the auto companies brought him in contact with Durant, who took him on when the fledgling United Motors acquired Hyatt. Sloan became vice president of General Motors in 1918 when Durant formed that greater empire.

Two years later, Durant having overextended himself, General Motors passed into Du Pont control, and Sloan took charge of operations. In 1923, he was president. In the next decade he introduced the innovations that gave his corporation primacy in the industry. He decentralized management, giving the division chiefs heavy responsibilities but retaining control over general policy and finances in a central committee. He realized that auto purchasers wanted more than transportation, and provided them with closed bodies and numerous styles at all price levels, along with installment credit, trade-ins, and annual model changes. Within a few years he had outdistanced Ford, and he was never overtaken. He also expanded into appliances and established branches overseas.

The company survived the difficulties of the 1930s, but Sloan failed to understand why increased productivity did not in itself solve all problems. He refused to deal with the unions until the sit-down strikes of 1936, and a year later he retired as president. He muttered thereafter against the wishful thinking of such panaceas as wage-and-hour laws and lived on to be surprised at the prosperity after 1940 that defied his prescriptions. He died in 1966, having accumulated a fortune of $250,000,000, a good part of which he gave away.

finance companies they provided credit to enable consumers to make purchases without an immediate heavy outlay of cash. The practice of installment selling spread widely in the optimistic 1920s, as the amount required for down payment sank. By 1929, well over three billion dollars was outstanding for such loans, about half the total being for cars. In that year 70 percent of automobile sales in the United States were on installments. Since capital was liberally available, although at high cost, the ability of the manufacturers to finance distribution sustained a high level of production.

This whole development depended upon a climbing rate of consumption. The goods turned out on the assembly lines had to be bought at home. Exports of manufactures were substantial but not a significant part of total production. In 1929, for example, the value of American cars exported was merely one-seventh of the total sold. Only within the United States was there a mass consumer market capable of absorbing the products of industry. There were indications, however, that that market was in danger. Some sectors of the economy were not feeling the full effects of prosperity and some were already depressed.

The Lag in Agriculture

The omens of a slowdown were unheeded in the postwar decade. The population still increased—from 91 million in 1910, to 105 million in 1920, to 122 million in 1930. But the rate of increase was lower than ever before as a result of the declining birth rate and the end of immigration. These dynamic factors in past growth were now lacking.

The expansion of settlement had also ceased to be important, not so much because there was no longer a frontier line, but because American agriculture was in a precarious state. The farmers had done remarkably well between 1900 and 1920. The war added to their prosperity. Since there was not enough food either at home or abroad, all the techniques of government persuasion directed them to raising their output. During the first year of peace, famine ravaged much of Europe so that the pressure toward producing greater crops persisted. The acres under cultivation increased, and the widespread use of machinery raised the level of productivity substantially.

There were signs of trouble when a drought hit the Great Plains in 1919. Then after 1920 grain and cotton from overseas producers flooded world markets and drove the inflated wartime prices down. Furthermore, restrictive economic policies in Europe put barriers in the way of the flow of American commodities abroad. The result was a serious surplus that further depressed returns to the farmers. The consequences became evident during the 1920s in the fall in the value of agricultural land, in the rise in the number and amount of farm mortgages with their burden of interest payments, and in the increase in tenancy. Once again a cry of protest rose from the rural countryside.

The farm population declined somewhat (from 31 million in 1920 to 30 million in 1930) and 13,000,000 acres were abandoned during the decade. But recollections of the good times just a few years earlier and the lack of alternative opportunities induced most families to cling to their holdings and to seek political solutions to their dilemma. The Congressional farm bloc managed to get the Agricultural Credits Law enacted in 1923 in the hope of making loans easier. But President Coolidge twice vetoed the McNary-Haugen bills (1927 and 1928), which would have enabled the government to sell surplus commodities abroad for whatever they would bring and make up the difference between the foreign and domestic prices by an equalization fee, or tax, on American consumers. An agricultural marketing act in 1929 had hardly taken effect before depression overwhelmed the whole economy.

The crux of the farm problem was the inability of the domestic market to consume the output of agriculture. The nationalistic policies of the United States and of other countries made the hope of increased exports illusory. Yet the American population was not growing fast enough to absorb the surplus. Indeed, changing dietary habits actually reduced the per capita consumption of grains among the most prosperous parts of the population.

Backward Economic Areas

There were additional soft spots in the economy. Aging plants and changing economic conditions prevented industry in New England and in the old South from sharing the prosperity of other parts of the country. The merchant marine collapsed after a brief interlude of expansion during the war. The Jones Act (1920) provided an indirect subsidy from the government and the Shipping Board survived as a regulatory agency but the tonnage registered under the American flag declined. The railroads, restored to private ownership by the Esch-Cummins Act (1920), retained their importance as carriers but no longer presented attractive investment opportunities. Despite efforts at modernization through electrification and the use of diesel locomotives, the confidence of the prewar era in limitless railroad expansion was gone. Ominously, passenger revenues declined, and those from the haulage of freight just about remained constant although neither the truck nor the airplane was yet a serious competitor.

Labor

The Decline of the Unions The relatively depressed state of labor compounded all these difficulties. Many managers of industry were still unprepared to concede the right of the workingmen to organize. In 1913, bitter strikes by textile operatives in Paterson, New Jersey, and by miners in Colorado failed, and the IWW entered upon a decline accelerated during the war. Many of the gains won before 1919 quickly evaporated. In the great steel strike of that year the corpora-

tions set out to destroy the union and lower costs, using the issue of Red control to gain public support. A long conflict led finally to the collapse of the steelworkers' organization.

Meanwhile the new mass industries like autos and aluminum remained totally unorganized, and the AF of L lost more than a million members in the decade after 1920. The shift in textiles from New England to the South was also a shift from a unionized to an un-unionized area. The new immigration law ended the influx of foreign workers. But the northward movement of Negroes and poor whites brought to Detroit, Chicago, and other cities large numbers of unskilled laborers difficult to organize.

The Government's Role As a result, labor found itself more helpless than it had been since the start of the century. The Department of Labor, after its organization in 1913, did little to assist and the La Follette Seaman's Act (1915) and the Railway Labor Board affected only declining branches of industry. On the other hand, the courts used injunctions freely to break strikes and held unconstitutional Federal laws restraining child labor and setting minimum wages for women in the District of Columbia. Local officials were generally unsympathetic to workers.

Internecine warfare, touched off by the efforts of communists and other radicals to gain a foothold within the declining unions, further sapped the strength of the workers, as did the intrusion of gangsters in some locals.

A few corporations assisted their employees both out of enlightened benevolence and out of the desire to inhibit unionization. Company unions, stock ownership, and profit-sharing plans, aid toward education and home purchase, cafeterias, medical service, vacations, recreation facilties, group insurance, and pensions were among the schemes of amelioration some large corporations adopted in the 1920s. Control of

Paul M. Angle, *Bloody Williamson* (New York, 1952) is the story of the Herrin massacre, a violent labor incident in a coal-mining section of Illinois.
Lewis Lorwin, *American Federation of Labor* (Boston, 1933) touches on this period.

Why the Steelworkers Struck, 1919

"Those damn guineas are making more money than they ever made in their lives, they buy stocks, they buy washingmachines and silk stockings for their women and they send money back to the old folks. While our boys were risking their lives in the trenches, they held down all the good jobs and most of 'em are enemy aliens at that. Those guineas are welloff, don't you forget it. The one thing they can't buy is brains. That's how those agitators get at 'em. They talk their language and fill 'em up with a lot of notions about how all they need to do is stop working and they can take possession of this country that we've built up into the greatest country in the world . . . . I don't hold it against the poor devils of guineas, they're just ignorant; but those reds who accept the hospitality of our country and then go around spreading their devilish propaganda . . . My god, if they were sincere I could forgive 'em, but they're just in it for the money like anybody else. We have absolute proof that they're paid by Russians reds with money and jewels they've stole over there; and they're not content with that, they go around shaking down those poor ignorant guineas . . . . Well, all I can say is shooting's too good for 'em."

—Opinion of Ted Healy, Pittsburgh editor, in John Dos Passos, *The Big Money* in the trilogy *U. S. A.* (New York: Random House, Inc., 1939), pp. 133–134.

The Causes of the Steel Strike, 1919

We find the grievances to have been real:

(a) The average week of 68.7 hours, the twelve-hour day, whether on a straight twelve-hour shift or on a broken division of 11–13 or 10–14 hours, the unbroken 24-hour work period at the turn of a shift and the underpayment of unskilled labor, are all inhuman.

(b) It is entirely practicable to put all processes requiring continuous operation on a straight eight-hour basis as is illustrated by the Colorado Fuel and Iron Company. These processes require the services of only a fraction of the workers.

(c) The "boss system" is bad, the plant organization is military and the control autocratic. The companies' claims, that they accord the right to join unions and the opportunity of conference, are theoretical; neither is allowed in practice.

(d) The use of "under-cover" men is severely condemned. It breeds distrust, breaks down morals and stimulates ill-will; it is undemocratic and un-American.

(e) The refusal of the United States Steel Corporation to confer, to accept mediation and its attitude of hauteur as shown by its refusal to follow the recommendations of the War Labor Board incited labor strife and because of the strength and influence of this Corporation, forms one of the greatest obstacles to a just settlement of industrial grievances and unrest at this time.

—*Report of the Steel Strike of 1919 by the Commission of Inquiry, the Interchurch World Movement with the Technical Assistance of the Bureau of Industrial Research* (New York: Harcourt, Brace & World, Inc., 1920), pp. 247–248.

these arrangements rested, however, not in the hands of the workers but of the managers.

Labor's Share Although average earnings — hourly, weekly, and annual — remained near the levels they had reached during the war, the laborers were not in a position to share generously in the profits of prosperity. Unemployment was considerable, the rate ranging from 5 to 12 percent and a great pool of marginal labor floated around the edges of the economy. These people could survive, but they could not join the ranks of those who consumed the products industry produced.

▼

A set of new relationships within the economic system developed in the 1920s, when industrial expansion depended upon mass markets. But the assumptions of the owners and managers of the productive system remained unchanged: each individual could pursue his own interest although that left some with little power to consume. The consequences of that internal contradiction would become clear after 1929, when a depression of great magnitude undermined the economy and the assumption on which it rested.

The problems of the economy reflected the problems of the society and revealed the limitations of the progressive victory of 1912. Americans who voted for the New Freedom still sought an order that would subject the individual to few controls by either government or other communal institutions. The expansive entrepreneur of the 1920s thrived by this rugged individualism which, however, did not altogether square with the realities of the new industrial economy. He was ill prepared for the test that lay before him.

Paperbacks for Further Reading

William E. Leuchtenburg, *The Perils of Prosperity* (Chicago History of American Civilization Series) is a general survey. Alfred D. Chandler, Jr., *Strategy and Structure* (Anchor Books) contains a discussion of industrial organization in the 1920s. Irving Bernstein, *The Lean Years* (Penguin Books, Inc.) is a vivid history of the American worker between 1920 and 1933. David Brody, *Labor in Crisis* (J. B. Lippincott Co.) deals with the steel strike of 1919.

THE END OF

THE OLD ORDER

1929–1947

IX

THE GREAT
DEPRESSION

82

The panic of 1929 brought a phase of American history to a close. It revealed the internal contradictions of the existing economic and social order and created a complex and interlocked set of problems which would occupy the United States in the ten years that followed. Preoccupation with these internal questions strengthened isolationist sentiment. Americans had so much to think about at home that they could spare little attention for foreign affairs. Events in Europe and Asia nevertheless produced the climax of the decade — a great war that completed the destruction of the old order.

The depression and the war challenged American society. Did it possess the resilience to develop a new economic and social system amid the ruins of the old? Could it resolve the earlier contradictions and yet sustain the basic institutions and values of the Republic? After 1932, the nation slowly set out in search of answers to these questions.

Panic

The Big Losers, 1929

Price per Share on the New York Stock Exchange

Company	High, September 3	Low, November 13
American Can	181⁷/₈	86
General Electric	396¹/₄	168¹/₂
Montgomery Ward	137⁷/₈	49¹/₄
Radio Corporation	101	28
Union Carbide	137⁷/₈	59
Westinghouse Electric	289⁷/₈	102⁵/₈
Electric Bond & Share	186³/₄	50¹/₄

Dangers Ahead There had been signs of weakness in the economy well before 1929. A good part of the productive system depended upon a high rate of consumption, yet much of the population suffered from low incomes. Furthermore, the speculative boom inflated values and credits and linked prosperity to future expectations rather than to current realities. The ability to keep business going rested on the faith that prices would continue to rise.

Warnings about the vulnerable features of the American economy passed unheeded. It was true that housing starts had fallen, and farmers and laborers were far from prosperous. Frequent bank failures were indications that credit was overextended. Moreover, every student of economics knew about cycles. Declines inevitably followed sharp climbs. Worried about the trend, the Federal Reserve Board in February 1929 raised the discount rate to put the brakes on speculation. But confidence persisted that the productive system was basically sound and was capable of underpinning whatever excesses appeared from time to time. The slight decline in the indices of economic activity between June and October 1929 seemed undisturbing.

Crash Disillusionment came that fall. The American economy collapsed because its internal weaknesses prevented it from absorbing the initial shock.

At the end of the summer the stock market reached a vulnerable high point. In September and October prices wavered as investors wondered whether still another rise lay ahead. Then on October 23, 1929, a decline set in. On the next day — Black Thursday — there was panic. Selling got out of hand, and no purchasers were to be found. The dip in prices reduced the margin of speculators who had bought securities with borrowed funds. The banks called their loans and forced sales followed. That put additional pressure on the market, and the decline became a disaster. Efforts by the pillars of the financial community to halt the panic failed. On October 29, 1929, 16,410,030 shares were traded on the New York Stock Exchange, and the average value of fifty key stocks fell forty points. By mid-November, industrial securities had lost nearly half their worth, and the Dow-Jones index had dropped from 327 to 199. Within a month, a large part of the paper values of the preceding decade had been totally wiped out.

The people who had put their faith in speculation felt the impact first. As the value of securities fell, the banks contracted their credit and that caused further declines. The squeeze soon affected the funds for other forms of investment. Commercial paper became difficult to negotiate; the supply of money tightened; and manufacturers had to cut back production. Many operating companies retrenched because the holding companies with which they were connected lost fluidity. At the same time funds for private loans to customers abroad were no longer available, and there was a consequent curtailment of the export of such key commodities as cotton, wheat, and tobacco.

The Federal Reserve System was unequal to dealing with the situation. During the 1920s it had been able to direct the flow of money to facilitate expansion. But in 1929 and 1930, when the economy was contracting, the Federal Re-

Broadus Mitchell, *Depression Decade, 1929–1941* (New York, 1947) is a general economic history.

Alfred L. Bernheim, *The Security Markets* (New York, 1935) contains a clear, not too technical, discussion.

Until 1929, the life of **HERBERT C. HOOVER** was a continuous success story. Born in West Branch, Iowa, in 1874, he was left an orphan at the age of 10 and lived with a succession of uncles. At sixteen he decided to become a mining engineer and worked his way through Stanford. The degree, at first, did him little good. He was a laborer and office boy until 1897, when he went to Australia where he managed a mine. He spent much of the next two decades abroad, directing mines and railways in China and running a firm of consulting engineers in London. In the process he became wealthy.

When the war broke out in 1914, Hoover was in London and he took over the arrangements for getting American citizens out of Germany. In 1915 he became chairman of the Commission for Relief in Belgium. Two years later, President Wilson asked him to head the Food Administration. After the peace, Hoover worked with a group that planned the economic restoration of Europe.

By then he had political ambitions. Shortly before the party convention of 1920, he announced that he had always been a Republican. He served as Secretary of Commerce under Harding and Coolidge. His reputation for efficiency helped him to secure the presidential nomination and to win the election in 1928.

The disaster of the depression completely unsettled him. The failure of the economy to recover was not his fault, but the experience embittered him. His rigid mind, set to the defense of past errors, remained closed to fresh views of the situation. After he left office, any government action seemed like socialism or fascism. The aging ex-President became a familiar figure at Republican party conventions, where he announced the old gospel and opposed any involvement in the international affairs of the 1930s: Hitler would not attack the West nor would Japan threaten the United States. In 1941, Hoover calculated that it would take at least ten years to train five million men and to build the ships to carry an army to Europe. As victory approached in 1945, he denounced military alliances and a postwar organization to enforce the peace. He died in 1964, convinced that he had been right and that the world had gone wrong.

serve Board did not act. Instead of unfreezing the supply of credit, it allowed interest rates to rise. Thereupon money became still more difficult to get; bank failures increased; and the whole economy slowed down.

The Immediate Effects The debilitating consequences rippled outward. Agriculture, already depressed, slumped precipitously for there was no money to move crops to market; and the market itself was contracting because consumers were tightening their belts. The new Federal Farm Board, organized under the marketing act of 1929, tried to stabilize prices but accomplished little other than to lose $676,000,000 in three years. Gross farm income fell from $14,000,000,000 in 1929 to $11,000,000,000 in 1930 and to $6,500,000,000 in 1932. Since taxes and interest rates rose in the same years, the net income from agriculture slipped in 1932 to about one-third of what it had been in 1929. Lenders were unwilling to renew mortgages as they fell due. In 1932, more than half the total farm debt was in default, and desperate farmers were on the verge of revolt.

The situation in industry was as bad. Orders fell off, production slowed down, and factories laid off their hands. Unemployment rose until in 1933 about one-third of the population lacked jobs. Workers without earnings dipped into savings, reduced their expenditures, and tried to borrow. Many went hungry.

The process of retrenchment operated at every level. A large share (about one-third) of total personal income went to people of wealth (about 5 percent of the population). Since this group was most involved in speculation, the collapse of the stock market significantly influenced consumption. Those whose paper fortunes disappeared in the panic were not able to make the purchases they had optimistically planned; and the contraction of credit slowed down installment buying. The economy headed downward on a slope along which there was no apparent plateau.

Hoover's Response

Herbert Hoover, who had taken office in March 1929, was determined to be a forceful and vigorous President. He had noticed the danger of excessive speculation soon after his inauguration and had privately asked the Stock Exchange to dampen enthusiasm. Once the panic began he wished to act, but the basic pattern of his assumptions limited the alternatives available to him.

Encouragement to Industry Hoover was not content to let the depression follow its own course, as some of his *laissez-faire* advisers urged him to do. He considered it his duty to encourage American industry to resume production. To that end he sought to make it advantageous for entrepreneurs to take risks, to sustain the buying power of the consumers, and to develop export markets.

A tax cut seemed desirable to increase the reward of manufacturers willing to start their factories going once more. Hoover hoped that the reduction in government expenditures to balance the budget, even though it would lead for the moment to further economic contraction, would create incentives for private capital and would ultimately renew the vigor of industry. Meanwhile, he urged businessmen to keep prices and wages up so that the flow of purchases would resume.

As Secretary of Commerce and as President, Hoover believed that foreign markets were essential to American growth, and he suspected that inability to expand the volume of exports had contributed to the panic and the depression. International trade therefore deserved attention. The Hawley-Smoot Tariff had certainly not eased the flow of goods. But the President thought that the confusing pattern of reparations and war debts was the most serious impediment to the recovery of commerce. A moratorium (June 1930), therefore, waived payments on all such obligations for one year in the hope that relief from these burdens would help revive the European economies. A month later a standstill agreement halted collections on private international debts.

Little good came of these measures. The depression was world-wide. The breakup of the Hapsburg empire, whatever its political justification, had destroyed the economic unity of Central and Eastern Europe. Austria, a truncated head without connections to the body of the hinterland which had formerly sustained it, fell into economic collapse. The failure of the great Vienna Credit Anstalt in 1931 affected creditors throughout Europe, who felt financial stringency that forced them to liquidate their holdings of American securites. Each nation raised its trade barriers and some devalued their currencies, so the hope of revival of international commerce faded.

When the slump continued and worsened, the President in 1932 recommended loans to relieve homeowners and the creation of the Reconstruction Finance Corporation, a temporary government pump-priming agency with substantial capital. Designed to ease the credit stringency, the RFC was to supply banks, insurance companies, and large industries with the loans they were unable to get through normal channels. Hoover hoped that such relief would stimulate recovery throughout the economy.

To maintain confidence, he continued to make optimistic statements, belied by his evident gloom. Recovery was just around the corner. The fundamental business of the country was on

There is a good survey by the National Industrial Conference Board in *A Picture of World Economic Conditions at the Beginning of 1932* (New York, 1932).

a sound basis. The nation required only faith and
confidence to bring the depression to an end.

Fundamental Assumptions Hoover and many
other Americans were mistaken. They sup-
posed that the decline was just an inevitable
swing in the business cycle. Once prices fell far
enough, they believed, buyers would resume
their purchasing, sales would pick up, production would expand, prices, profits, and wages
would rise, and prosperity would return. Pa-

tience and confidence would permit the compen-
sating mechanisms of the free market to operate.
It followed from these premises that a large part
of the difficulty was simply psychological. Soothing words were therefore useful to induce timid
investors and buyers to expend their remaining
funds.

Hoover's strategy of recovery, furthermore,
aimed to bring prosperity back by providing relief at the top of the economic system. Aid to an
individual might tide him over from meal to
meal; that was a task for municipal or private
philanthropy. The Federal government, however, was to administer such assistance as would
start the wheels of industry turning and provide
jobs for millions. In time, the rewards would
dribble down to the masses.

Even if the long-term strategy had been
effective, it demanded immediate sacrifices from
a large part of the population. The mass of the
unemployed men whose families lacked food
and the farmers unable to dispose of their products were not willing to accept the assurance
that their suffering was all in a good cause. Their
profound dissatisfaction led to a demand for
more direct forms of relief. On that account
alone the prospect of restoring confidence by
appeals to hope was slight.

In the bitter winter of 1930–1931, the hard-
pressed cities slashed relief funds, and the unemployed, who now numbered more than six
million, bleakly wondered how two or three
dollars a week would feed their families. The
huddled bread lines lengthened, and a profound
sense of despair spread through the land. To
add to the woe, drought parched the Southwest.
In this atmosphere the call for faith had a hollow
ring.

There seemed no bottom to the economic
pit out of which the climb should once more
have begun. A brief revival early in 1931 was
disappointing, as was a similar flash of hope in
the autumn of 1932. The collapse of the Insull
public-utilities empire in April 1932 had ruined

Albert U. Romasco describes the public reaction to
Hoover's policies in *The Poverty of Abundance* (New York, 1965).

420

Bread Line, East 25th Street, New York, December 25, 1931. Men wait to enter the Municipal Lodging House, where on this Christmas Day 10,000 persons, including 100 women, were fed. The police glee club and band provided entertainment. (UPI)

The failure of the companies of **SAMUEL INSULL** in April 1932 ruined thousands of investors who had put their faith in his enterprise. The collapse of his empire left the pitiful old man a fugitive through most of his remaining life. He died in 1938 with twenty cents in his pocket.

Insull was born in London in 1859, the son of a craftsman. He held a succession of odd jobs until 1879, when he became bookkeeper for the London manager of Thomas A. Edison. Two years later, Insull came to the United States to be Edison's manager, and in the next decade participated in the developments that finally led to the formation of General Electric Company.

Insull, however, was convinced that the future lay in the generation and sale of power rather than in the manufacture of equipment, and in 1892 he undertook the management of a small utility in Chicago. He experimented with large central generating stations that would feed local distributors. When the invention of the Curtis turbine in 1903 permitted the transmission of electricity over considerable distances, Insull spread a network out of Chicago. In 1912 he organized the Middle West Utilities, a holding company, which ultimately controlled assets of some two billion dollars and through operating subsidiaries served 1,718,000 customers.

Although he retained his primary interest in electricity, his enterprises included gas and traction systems, and in the 1920s he set up two great investment companies in which he concentrated ownership of all his subsidiaries. The crash of 1929 weakened the foundations of this elaborate structure. To prevent the dumping of large holdings of shares on the open market, which would depress the price further, Insull bought some $56,000,000 worth of securities, financing the purchase by loans from New York and Chicago banks. He counted on a rise in values to bail him out. Instead, the stock market decline of September 1931 caught him short. His creditors refused to renew their loans, and Insull was ruined.

There followed a long investigation of public-utility holding companies and various indictments of Insull on charges of fraud. He fled to Greece and Turkey, was extradited, tried and acquitted, but spent most of the rest of his life abroad. Of his private fortune, which at one time was estimated as high as $300,000,000, nothing remained.

Security Values, 1929–1933

	September 1929	January 1933
Dow-Jones Industrial Index	364.9	62.7
Dow-Jones Utilities Index	141.9	28.0
Dow-Jones Railroad Index	180.0	28.0
Aggregate Value 50 Industrials (million dollars)	20,995.0	4,730.0

thousands of investors and had intensified the sense of doom. All the indices of economic health continued to drift downward until the spring of 1933. Since the panic of 1929 wages and farm income just about halved, unemployment had tripled, and stock prices had fallen about 80 percent. The classical assumptions about the way in which recovery should have come seemed more remote from realization early in 1933 than they had been in 1929.

The Democrats Take Control

The election of 1930 reflected widespread disillusion with President Hoover's management both of the government and of the economy. In the new Congress, the Democrats had a majority in the House and, with the Western agrarians, controlled the Senate. The result, on some issues, was a stalemate. The Congressional leaders, for instance, proposed that the Federal government take a direct hand in relief and expand public works to create employment. Hoover believed that the first suggestion went beyond constitutional limits and that the second threatened the budget balance.

In the summer of 1932, tempers grew heated. An army of 20,000 veterans marched upon Washington demanding immediate cash payment of the bonus Congress had promised would be paid them at a future date. Camping on the Anacostia flats, they created a nuisance and were visible evidence of the nation's distress. The President ordered the regular troops

to disperse the protesters, an action that seemed to many Americans symbolic of his lack of compassion. Nor did he gain in stature by dismissing the veterans' grievances as communist-inspired.

The Election of 1932 The continuation of the depression enhanced the value of the Democratic presidential nomination. Victory in the election was almost certain. The candidate of 1928, Al Smith, believed that he deserved another chance. But he had a potent rival in his former protégé, Franklin D. Roosevelt, governor of New York State since 1928. Roosevelt had developed a wide following, particularly among Southern and Western Congressional leaders reluctant to carry once more the burden of supporting a Catholic candidate. Through an alliance with John N. Garner of Texas, Speaker of the House and beneficiary of the support of William Randolph Hearst, Roosevelt overcame the difficulty posed by the two-third's rule. The combination secured Roosevelt the nomination and made an effective ticket that alienated no one, not even for the moment Smith's friends.

The Republicans had no alternative but to renominate Hoover, despite his shrinking popularity. He ran a tired, defensive campaign that attempted to justify his administration. The contest skirted the most important issues. There was much discussion of the repeal of prohibition, a question on which neither candidate took a forthright position. Roosevelt attacked the Republicans and promised to reduce government expenditures, aid the unemployed, regulate the security market, and provide farm relief, but there was little indication in his statements of what he would actually do.

The country did not demand that Roosevelt be specific. It was in no mood to listen to Hoover's assurance that the United States was the world's biggest business. It wanted action on behalf of the forgotten man, and it did not care whom Roosevelt had in mind when he used the phrase. Every man was forgotten!

The outcome of the election was a foregone conclusion. Hoover carried only Pennsylvania, Delaware, Connecticut, Vermont, New Hamp-

The Burning of the Bonus Army's Encampment, Anacostia Flats, Summer 1932. (The National Archives)

shire, and Maine, while Roosevelt took the 472 electoral votes of the other states. The popular majority was equally decisive, twenty-two million for the Democrats as against fifteen million for the Republicans. The election was not a test of sentiment on programs or policies. It was an expression of discontent with the existing conduct of the nation's affairs.

The Bank Crisis During the winter of 1932–1933 the economy continued to slither downward. Uncertainty about the intentions of the President-elect, the long interval until March during which Hoover — though repudiated — was still head of the government, and further deterioration of the situation in Europe hurt business and agriculture. After the turn of the year, the loss of confidence produced a full-scale bank-ing crisis. Panicky depositors withdrew their savings, and one institution after another closed its doors. As the inaugural day in March approached, there was a general collapse of the private financial system of the United States. One of the new President's first duties would be to deal with this problem.

Roosevelt met the crisis with a vigor and optimism that immediately won the hearts of his countrymen. Often he used the same words as Hoover, abjuring fear, calling for confidence, but where his predecessor was tired and dispirited, F. D. R. was buoyant and ebullient. Above all, he got matters moving. In the first hundred days of his term in office he demonstrated a refreshing capacity for action. And in the next six years he proved receptive to new ideas, flexible in attitude, and ready to experiment. Under his leadership, the economy moved through a significant transformation.

The Nature of the Depression

The Elusive Recovery Yet the New Deal did not end the depression. In 1939, there was still no assurance that the defects of 1929 had been rectified. The economy had followed a wavering course. The level of business activity and of national income had risen unsteadily between 1933 and 1937, although the progress was more marked in consumer than in producer industry, and construction had lagged seriously. Then followed a serious recession in 1937 which lasted into the summer of 1938, with manufacturing, exports, and prices slumping once more. The recovery of 1939, while welcome, was not firm enough to assure Americans that their troubles were over.

The long-term economic failure of the decade revealed the full impact of the great depression. In the ten years after 1929 the real national output of all goods in the United States rose by only 6 percent and that was entirely due to an increase in the labor force. Per capita output in the same interval declined by 1 percent. Industry achieved this dismal record despite the fact that it was profiting from numerous technological innovations. The modernization of plants continued, as managers sought to cut costs. But such improvements no longer came within the context of an expanding productive system and in fact sometimes exerted a negative effect. In 1937, for instance, the production of automobiles had regained the 1929 level, but advancing mechanization enabled the companies to achieve this with substantially fewer hands.

The Workless and the Farmers The most visible form of the failure was unemployment. Throughout the decade, the number of jobless never sank below one-sixth of the potential labor force, with the result that a large part of the population was unable to consume and much of it was literally destitute. In 1939, a relatively good year, 9.5 million people could not find work.

Almost as important an indication of the defects in the economy was the persistence of the farm problem. The depression in agriculture was already almost a decade old in 1929. It deepened in the next four years, and prolonged drought and dust storms in 1934 and 1935 intensified the misery. Between 1933 and 1937 there was a rise in farm prices and incomes but only enough to get back to the 1930 level. In 1938 and 1939 there was another slip and another recovery but no escape from the difficulties that had burdened agriculture since 1920 — excess production, low prices, inadequate income. The tenants evicted by the thousands who drifted hopelessly west were the most miserable victims. But the husbandmen who clung to their titles were hardly more fortunate. As they fed their surplus corn to the fire for warmth or watched the wind blow the topsoil away, they saw the dream of independence vanish. For the farmers, as for the unemployed, the great depression endured through the whole decade.

The End of Expansion A variety of factors prolonged the depression. The prices of important commodities did not respond to the slackening demand as classical economic theory assumed that they would. Each producer, seeking to protect himself, should have competed more intensely for customers. But the great industrial corporations had substantial reserves and usually faced limited competition. As a result, they did not lower prices but rather cut back on production. Buyers, therefore, were not tempted into the market and demand did not revive. Instead, the lowered output made less employment necessary and further contracted potential purchasing power.

Moreover, Federal fiscal policy failed to stimulate the economy, at least before 1935. The

John L. Shover, *Cornbelt Rebellion* (Urbana, Ill., 1965), an account of the Farmers' Holiday Association, also gives a picture of agricultural discontent.

An Abandoned Tenant House, Hall County, Texas, June 1937. Photograph by Dorothea Lange. (Library of Congress)

Federal Reserve Board ultimately reduced the rediscount rate in order to make borrowing more attractive. But the operations of the Federal Reserve banks continued to have a depressing effect upon credit, which remained linked to fixed reserves.

Hoover's efforts to limit government spending gave way, after 1933, to the freer policies of the New Deal. The Republican policy was to draw funds out of the economy; the New Deal pumped money in, but its efforts were too small and too intermittent to be effective. Neither policy generated enough demand to counter the tendencies of the productive system to contraction. Foreign and domestic markets failed to expand. World-wide exports from the United States fell fully 80 percent between 1929 and 1939 and left no illusion that foreign sales would be a source of salvation. Nor was the domestic scene more encouraging. The rate of population growth had slackened. Absolute numbers were rising so slowly that the number of prospective consumers failed to expand.

The end of immigration in 1925 also had a depressing effect. Until then the movement of people to the United States had fluctuated with the ebb and flow of economic activity, rising in prosperity, falling in depressions. The newcomers came when they were needed, stayed home when they were not. Restriction by the 1930s had nullified this force. By 1939, many Americans were aware that all the frontiers had disap-

426

Eviction in the 1930s

And at last the owner men came to the point. The tenant system won't work any more. One man on a tractor can take the place of twelve or fourteen families. Pay him a wage and take all the crop. We have to do it . . . .

The tenant men looked up alarmed. But what'll happen to us? How'll we eat?

You'll have to get off the land. The plows'll go through the dooryard.

And now the squatting men stood up angrily. Grampa took up the land, and he had to kill the Indians and drive them away. And Pa was born here, and he killed weeds and snakes. Then a bad year came and he had to borrow a little money. An' we was born here. There in the door—our children born here. And Pa had to borrow money. The bank owned the land then, but we stayed and we got a little bit of what we raised . . . .

And now the owner men grew angry. You'll have to go.

But it's ours, the tenant men cried. We—

No. The bank, the monster owns it. You'll have to go . . . .

But if we go, where'll we go? How'll we go? We got no money.

We're sorry, said the owner men. The bank, the fifty-thousand-acre owner can't be responsible. You're on land that isn't yours. Once over the line maybe you can pick cotton in the fall. Maybe you can go on relief. Why don't you go on west to California? There's work there, and it never gets cold. Why, you can reach out anywhere and pick an orange. Why, there's always some kind of crop to work in. Why don't you go there? And the owner men started their cars and rolled away.

The tenant men squatted down on their hams again to mark the dust with a stick, to figure, to wonder. Their sunburned faces were dark, and their sun-whipped eyes were light. The women moved cautiously out of the doorways toward their men, and the children crept behind the women, cautiously, ready to run. The bigger boys squatted beside their fathers, because that made them men. After a time the women asked, What did he want?

And the men looked up for a second, and the smolder of pain was in their eyes. We got to get off. A tractor and a superintendent. Like factories.

Where'll we go? the women asked.

We don't know. We don't know.

And the women went quickly, quietly back into the houses and herded the children ahead of them. They knew that a man so hurt and so perplexed may turn in anger, even on people he loves. They left the men alone to figure and to wonder in the dust . . . .

—From *The Grapes of Wrath* by John Steinbeck. Copyright 1939, © 1967 by John Steinbeck. Reprinted by permission of The Viking Press, Inc.

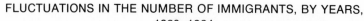

FLUCTUATIONS IN THE NUMBER OF IMMIGRANTS, BY YEARS, 1820–1924

Source: Harry Jerome, *Migration and Business Cycles* (New York: National Bureau of Economic Research, 1926), p. 34.

peared, and they believed, as a result, that the expansive phase of their productive system had come to a close.

The persistence of the depression which began with the panic of 1929 revealed that the American economy had moved into a new phase. This was no temporary setback such as had punctuated economic growth in 1819, 1837, 1857, 1873, or 1893. Recovery did not come of itself or even as a result of the remedies applied in the 1930s.

The conditions that in the past had sustained expansion no longer existed. The free land of the open West, a rapidly expanding population, unlimited immigration, fluid social and economic institutions, and risk-taking entrepreneurs energetically dedicated to production, all had ceased to stimulate the society as they had earlier. Any hope of bringing back the past or restoring those conditions was vain.

But it was not vain to try to create new forms appropriate to the twentieth century which would enable the productive system to resume its expansion. The New Deal imperfectly and hesitantly began the search, and the shock of war after 1939 carried the effort forward.

Paperbacks for Further Reading

J. K. Galbraith, *The Great Crash 1929* (Sentry Editions) is a brief popular analysis. Arthur M. Schlesinger, Jr., *Crisis of the Old Order* (Sentry Editions) is well written and more detailed. Harris G. Warren, *Herbert Hoover and the Great Depression* (W. W. Norton & Company, Inc.) is sympathetic to Hoover. Irving Bernstein, *The Lean Years* (Penguin Books, Inc.) extends the description of the conditions of labor into the depression period. Alfred B. Rollins, Jr., *Depression, Recovery and War* (McGraw-Hill Paperback Series) and David A. Shannon, *The Great Depression* (Spectrum Books) are useful collections of documents.

THE NEW DEAL

83

The New Deal was a creative response to the long crisis in American economic development. The program devised under the leadership of Franklin D. Roosevelt aimed at the same time for industrial recovery, for relief of the millions of needy, and for reform of the whole productive system. It did not succeed fully in attaining any of its objectives, and it was often chaotic and incoherent. Yet it served two important functions. It started the process of rethinking the relationship of government to the economy, and it imbued the people with a sense of hope so that they could pass through the trials of the years after 1933 without succumbing to despair. That was no mean achievement in a decade when other countries were surrendering their faith in democracy.

JUST OILING THE CLOCK A BIT.

One View of Roosevelt's Brain Trust. Cartoon from *St. Louis Daily Globe-Democrat*, May 1, 1934. (Franklin D. Roosevelt Library)

The New Administration

The Cabinet Roosevelt took office without any clear plan for dealing with the deepening depression. In the months between the election and the inauguration Hoover made some effort to coordinate policies with his successor. But Roosevelt was unwilling to take responsibility in the absence of real power.

In the clumsy interval between November 1932 and March 1933 the President-elect gave careful thought to the cabinet he would bring into office with him. Its membership reflected more his political debts than his intentions for the future. Secretary of State Cordell Hull, Secretary of the Navy Claude A. Swanson, and Secretary of Commerce Daniel C. Roper were Southern Democrats whose collaboration had been important in securing the nomination.

Secretary of the Treasury William H. Woodin was a businessman whose appointment was to placate the financial interests of the country. Secretary of Agriculture Henry A. Wallace and Secretary of the Interior Harold L. Ickes were progressive Republicans designated to gain mid-Western support.

Two members were personally close to the President. Postmaster General James A. Farley, Roosevelt's right-hand man in the campaign for nomination and election, kept an eye on political connections and had general oversight over the patronage. Secretary of Labor Frances Perkins, the first woman in the cabinet, was a social worker who had headed the state labor department while Roosevelt was governor of New York. The

Frank Freidel, *Franklin D. Roosevelt* (Boston, 1952); Volume I deals primarily with the pre-presidential career of its subject, but gives a good picture of F. D. R.

Searle F. Charles, *Minister of Relief* (Syracuse, N.Y., 1963) treats Hopkins and the depression.

When **FRANKLIN D. ROOSEVELT** was a student at Harvard, his remote cousin Theodore was President of the United States. Franklin was born at Hyde Park in 1882, tutored at home, and sent at fourteen to Groton School. In those respects his early life was very much like his cousin's. The parallels would continue, whether out of conscious emulation or simply out of the logic of the situation into which both men were born.

Franklin Roosevelt studied law for a while, then married a cousin and settled in New York City. In 1910, he was elected to the state senate and two years later went as a delegate to the Democratic National Convention, where he supported Wilson. The rewards were soon forthcoming. From among various possibilities offered him, Roosevelt selected the post of Assistant Secretary of the Navy, a position Theodore had once held.

After the war Franklin Roosevelt returned to New York politics, aiming unsuccessfully for the Democratic nomination for the United States Senate. He secured the vice-presidential nomination in 1920 and went down to defeat along with Cox.

Stricken by polio in 1921, he was left crippled for life and had to struggle under grave handicaps to continue his career.

He did not surrender his hopes, however. Until 1928, he held an undemanding job as vice-president of The Fidelity and Deposit Company of Maryland in New York, but his interests still focused on politics. In 1924 he placed Al Smith's name before the Houston Democratic Convention; and that year he entered a law partnership with Basil O'Connor. In 1928, Roosevelt was selected to run for governor of New York to balance a ticket headed by the Catholic Smith. Roosevelt was elected and served two terms with distinction.

Shrewd political maneuvers secured him the presidential nomination in 1932, but he seemed then, in the words of Walter Lippmann, a pleasant man who, without any important qualifications for the office, wished very much to be President. Upon F. D. R. fell the major responsibilities for dealing with the depression. His four terms in office were without precedent, and when he died in 1945 he was attempting to guide the nation through the greatest war in its history.

cabinet members, who often worked at cross purposes, were not likely to furnish the President with a coherent program.

Advisers and Doers Roosevelt—like Wilson and Jackson—depended on an informal kitchen cabinet, early labeled the brain trust because most of its members came from university life. Lacking the binding commitments of the professional politician, they were able to act for the President with vigor and to move across the traditional lines of the bureaucracy. Among Roosevelt's advisers were Ed Howe, his personal secretary, Raymond Moley, Harry L. Hopkins, Rexford G. Tugwell, and Samuel I. Rosenman. Others answered the call from time to time when the White House required their services. In addition, an army of new men took over important administrative posts to fill the vacancies created by the departure of Republicans and by the establishment of new agencies. Roosevelt was not averse to appointing a personal friend or a rich party supporter, as when Henry M. Morgenthau, Jr., replaced Woodin as Secretary of the Treasury (1934). But the President also wished to bring in bright young officials capable of generating new ideas.

In consequence, Washington hummed with schemes for remaking the government and the country. In the first hundred days of the administration an enormous amount of work was done,

When **HARRY L. HOPKINS** was putting in eighteen hours a day on his job, he explained, "Do you know a better way to die?" He paid the price in 1946, when he died at the age of fifty-six.

He was born in 1890 in Sioux City, Iowa, where his father was a harness maker. The family was hard hit in the depression of 1893, and the automobile did the harness business no good. Harry grew up in tight circumstances, but graduated from Grinnell College in 1912. From his mother, who was active in Methodist home missionary work, he acquired a sense of social service. He took a position directing a boys' camp and then moved into social welfare work, holding various posts in New York and New Orleans. Dealing for two decades with the dependent elements of the urban population, he acquired a sense of the suffering that suffused the slums and practical experience in dealing with poverty.

In 1931, when the depression deepened the problem of unemployment, Governor Roosevelt appointed Hopkins director of the New York State Emergency Relief Administration, in a desperate effort to stave off mass hunger. Two years later, F. D. R., then President, asked him to head the Federal Emergency Relief Administration. Thereafter the two men worked intimately together, in foreign as in domestic affairs. To Hopkins, relief meant not only a dole to keep men from starving but also work to preserve their spirit. As Works Progress Administrator between 1935 and 1938, he built thousands of schools, bridges, and public buildings and gave meaningful employment to millions. Although he was not unmindful of the political implications of the jobs at his disposal, his administration was untainted by scandal. He was appointed Secretary of Commerce in 1938, but illness compelled him to resign in 1940.

The war called him back to Roosevelt's side. In 1941 Hopkins helped launch the lend-lease program, which sent supplies to Britain, and thereafter he was the President's closest adviser. Hopkins sat on the various boards during the war, became familiar with the vast bureaucratic network, and wielded Roosevelt's authority to break log jams and get decisions made. He also served as the President's personal emissary in dealing with the Russians and the British. He thus persuaded Stalin to break the deadlock over the United Nations at the San Francisco Conference and made the preliminary arrangements for the meeting at Potsdam. But his usefulness ebbed with Roosevelt's death, and less than a year later he followed his chief.

and despite disappointments and setbacks energy did not flag in the years that followed. The vibrant personality of the President conveyed to his followers an inspiring sense of the importance of their jobs. And his fireside chats drew enthusiastic public support. Successive elections therefore showed that he had no cause for worry either about his own hold on office or about Democratic control of Congress. With only occasional lapses he was able to get done what he wished.

A Choice of Programs

Roosevelt did not bring a consistent political or economic philosophy to the White House. Nor did the brain trust supply him with one. His approach was pragmatic. He was willing to try anything if it had a prospect of success. This hit-and-miss tactic had its share of failures, but it engendered an atmosphere of constant activity and of positive achievement.

Planning The New Deal drew upon a progressive heritage that contained incompatible elements. From the New Nationalism, the experience of the World War, and the writings of the engineers came an emphasis on rational planning. By 1932, Veblen and the technocrats had expanded Lester Ward's vision into a comprehensive scheme for centralized social control. Furthermore, exaggerated impressions of the success of Soviet planning emphasized the desirability of analogous measures in the United States. Roosevelt's Commonwealth Club speech in San Francisco (1932) had explained that the end of the expansive frontier, which had made the individualistic methods of the past feasible, now called for assertion of the government's power to direct the economy.

It followed that the concentration of industry was not a danger so long as it proceeded under public supervision and control. *The Modern Corporation and Private Property*, an influential study by Adolph A. Berle and G. C. Means (1932), showed, even more persuasively than John Maurice Clark had, that the great combinations were efficient institutions that could serve social purposes.

Planning required erection of a wall around the economy within which rational estimates of resources, needs, and future program could be calculated. Tariffs were not bad if devised for that purpose rather than to protect selfish interests. Unregulated foreign trade, on the other hand, subjected domestic producers to the mercurial fluctuations of world markets. Moley's statement of this position attracted the support of some agricultural and business spokesmen.

Competition Quite another approach stemmed from the ideas of the New Freedom. The basic economic difficulties derived from the failure to enforce the Sherman and Clayton acts. The monopolistic trusts, able to maintain high prices despite falling demand, inhibited the consumption that would restore industrial activity. The government was to deprive the great corporations of the unfair advantages that enabled them to stifle competition. It was also to rehabilitate the purchasing power of the

A Reappraisal of Values, 1932

A glance at the situation today only too clearly indicates that equality of opportunity as we have known it no longer exists. Our industrial plant is built; the problem just now is whether under existing conditions it is not overbuilt. Our last frontier has long since been reached, and there is practically no more free land. More than half of our people do not live on the farms or on lands and cannot derive a living by cultivating their own property. There is no safety valve in the form of a Western prairie to which those thrown out of work by the Eastern economic machines can go for a new start. We are not able to invite the immigration from Europe to share our endless plenty. We are now providing a drab living for our own people . . . .

All this calls for a re-appraisal of values. A mere builder of more industrial plants, a creator of more railroad systems, an organizer of more corporations, is as likely to be a danger as a help. The day of the great promoter or the financial Titan, to whom we granted anything if only he would build or develop, is over. Our task now is not discovery or exploitation of natural resources, or necessarily producing more goods. It is the soberer, less dramatic business of administering resources and plants already in hand, of seeking to re-establish foreign markets for our surplus production, of meeting the problem of underconsumption, of adjusting production to consumption, of distributing wealth and products more equitably, of adapting existing economic organizations to the service of the people. The day of enlightened administration has come.

—Franklin D. Roosevelt, Commonwealth Club Address, September 23, 1932, in *The Public Papers and Addresses of Franklin D. Roosevelt* (New York: Random House, Inc., 1938), vol. I, pp. 750–752.

population. Furthermore, international trade would expand sales if tariffs were lowered by agreements that opened foreign markets to American products. Justices Louis D. Brandeis and Felix Frankfurter, both close to the President, argued this position forcefully.

Still another approach led to prosperity by way of inflation. Bryan and the Populists had already explained that easy money would raise farm prices, help debtors, and put the means of making purchases in the hands of potential consumers. Professors James H. Rogers and George F. Warren supplied the intellectual justification for this policy, and the radio priest, the Reverend Charles Coughlin, mobilized wide public support for it. On the other hand, Lewis Douglas and Bernard Baruch took a more orthodox stand.

Then, too, people close to Roosevelt like Frances Perkins and Harry Hopkins argued for welfare measures that would aid the depressed wage earners to consume. With money in the hands of the unemployed, the aged, and the underpaid the surpluses of agriculture and industry would soon be used up.

The President never made a clear-cut choice among these diverse ideas, some contradictory, some overlapping. He was more sympathetic to planning and currency manipulation in the first two years of his administration than later. But elements of all these approaches entered into the programs devised by the New Deal to relieve the needy, to recover prosperity, and to reform the economy.

Financial Institutions

Banking On inauguration day in March 1933, the closed banks presented an immediate crisis. The flow of money and credit had stopped, while Hoover, at the end of his rope, felt that he could do nothing. At the moment Congress might well have agreed to nationalize the whole system.

Roosevelt restored confidence. An emergency act, passed within seven hours of introduction, set up a procedure for rescuing the sound institutions. The banks began to reopen and business resumed. This was also the occasion for significant reform. The Glass-Steagall Act (1933, amended in 1935) established the Federal Deposit Insurance Corporation as a means of preventing future runs, and it effectively barred the banks from the business of selling securities through affiliates. Elimination of the Secretary of the Treasury and the Comptroller from the Federal Reserve Board made that body less political, and its Federal Open Market Committee received the power to alter reserve requirements and thus to shape the credit policies of each of the districts.

Meanwhile the President tried inflation. In April 1933 he decided to go off the gold standard, and Congress obliged by invalidating all requirements for payments in gold in public and private contracts. In the fall he bought gold on the world market in the mistaken expectation that a rise in price levels would follow. Not until January 1934 did he halt these purchases. Congress then stabilized the value of the dollar in specie at 59.06 per cent of its former worth and set the price of gold at $35 an ounce. Being still hopeful that tinkering with the currency would raise commodity prices and eager to win support from Western mining interests, Roosevelt approved a Silver Purchase Act in June 1934. (He had already been buying the metal, above market price, since December 1933.) All this manipulation, however, failed to affect prices.

Speculation The security acts of 1933 and 1934 dealt with abuses in the stock markets, which were thereafter to be licensed by the Securities and Exchange Commission. Corporations were required to make accurate information available to investors, and the Commission put stringent controls on trading practices. In 1936, a commodities commission received similar power to police the commodity exchanges, and in 1940 investment trusts were subjected to the oversight of the SEC. These measures left the management of capital in private hands but asserted the concern of the government in the orderly conduct of activities that vitally affected the national economy.

Planning and Regulation

NRA Industrial recovery in 1933 seemed to depend on liquidation of the surpluses that had halted manufacturing. The experience of the World War and the proposals of various trade associations for suspension of the antitrust laws suggested to the President the idea of providing industry with the machinery for self-regulation, price fixing, and planned production. To offset that concession to business, he asked for protection of labor and for a public works program to raise purchasing power.

The National Industrial Recovery Act of June 1933 allowed councils in each industry, representing government, management, labor, and consumers, to adopt enforceable codes governing all the conditions of production, including the quotas allocated to each firm. The National Recovery Administration under General Hugh Johnson approved more than five hundred such codes and launched an immense publicity program to popularize the Blue Eagle that signified adherence to the plan.

The NRA promptly ran into difficulties, however, for many companies simply took it as cover for fixing prices and avoiding competition. Roosevelt was secretly relieved when the Supreme Court, in the Schechter Poultry case (May 1935) declared the law unconstitutional on the grounds that it transferred legislative functions to the President and that it made improper use of the Federal power over interstate commerce. A similar fate met the Bituminous Coal Conservation Act (1935) which attempted to impose planning on a single industry.

TVA The one great success in planning was regional. Two government plants for the manufacture of nitrates, built during the World

Modern Guilds Under NIRA, 1933

In my Inaugural I laid down the simple proposition that nobody is going to starve in this country. It seems to me to be equally plain that no business which depends for existence on paying less than living wages to its workers has any right to continue in this country. By "business" I mean the whole of commerce as well as the whole of industry; by workers I mean all workers, the white collar class as well as the men in overalls; and by living wages I mean more than a bare subsistence level — I mean the wages of decent living.

Throughout industry, the change from starvation wages and starvation employment to living wages and sustained employment can, in large part, be made by an industrial covenant to which all employers shall subscribe. It is greatly to their interest to do this because decent living, widely spread among our 125,000,000 people, eventually means the opening up to industry of the richest market which the world has known. It is the only way to utilize the so-called excess capacity of our industrial plants. This is the principle that makes this one of the most important laws that ever has come from Congress because, before the passage of this Act, no such industrial covenant was possible . . . .

If *all* employers in each trade now band themselves faithfully in these modern guilds — without exception — and agree to act together and at once, none will be hurt and millions of workers, so long deprived of the right to earn their bread in the sweat of their labor, can raise their heads again. The challenge of this law is whether we can sink selfish interest and present a solid front against a common peril.

It is a challenge to industry which has long insisted that, given the right to act in unison, it could do much for the general good which has hitherto been unlawful. From today it has that right.

— Statement by President Franklin D. Roosevelt, June 16, 1933, in *The Public Papers and Addresses of Franklin D. Roosevelt* (New York: Random House, Inc., 1938), vol. II, pp. 251–252.

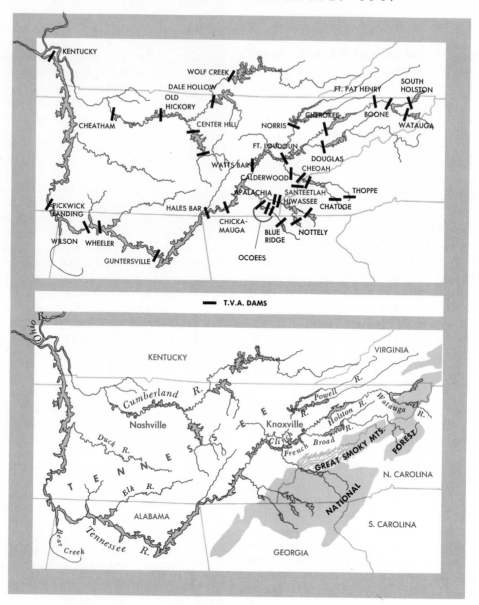

TVA, 1930–1940

War at Muscle Shoals on the Tennessee River, had long been a cause of controversy. Senator George W. Norris had hoped the government would retain and operate them along with Wilson Dam, from which they drew power. But Coolidge and Hoover had vetoed bills to that effect, preferring to sell out to private owners. In May 1933, the Tennessee Valley Development Act put the plants and the dam in the hands of a public Authority which was to use them for flood control, for the generation of power, and for the economic development of the whole region. The success of this measure in salvaging both the natural and the human resources of the area encouraged the construction of the Hoover (1936), Bonneville (1937), and Grand Coulee (1942) dams. But Roosevelt's suggestion in 1937 of six regional developments in other parts of the country bore no fruit. By then planning had lost its attractiveness and the emphasis in Congress had shifted to competition.

Regulation A growing demand for the protection of small business reflected the disillusion with planning. The Robinson-Patman (1936) and the Miller-Tydings (1937) acts forbade manufacturers to discriminate among dealers and authorized the setting of minimum resale prices in order to limit the cut-rate bargains chain stores and other large distributors could offer. At about the same time the Temporary National Economic Committee began an intensive study of monopolistic practices, and the Antitrust Division of the Department of Justice, under Thurman Arnold, put teeth in the Sherman and Clayton acts.

With the loss of faith in planning, attention shifted to more effective regulation of transportation and power as a means of ensuring fair competition. The Public Utility Holding Company Act of 1935 gave the Federal Power Commission the right to set rates, prohibited most pyramiding, and subjected securities of such enterprises to the control of the SEC. Another law, the same year, extended the power of the ICC to cover trucks and buses. Supervision of air traffic, at first governed by air-mail contracts, in 1938 was entrusted to a Civil Aeronautics Authority. Meanwhile, in 1936, the United States Maritime Commission assumed responsibility for subsidizing and governing American shipping. Thus the end of the NRA did not signify a weakening of government but rather a changeover from positive planning to regulation.

Agriculture

Roosevelt hoped that the general revival of the economy would in the long run help every element in the population. But he was also acutely conscious of the short-run needs of the farmers, who had suffered from the depression for decades and who wielded formidable political power.

Concern for the farmers' well-being influenced several facets of the New Deal, including flood control, rural electrification, encouragement of homesteading, and efforts to dispose of commodity surpluses. But two goals remained consistently in view: the attainment of parity and reduction of the burden of debt.

Parity Parity involved a commitment to restore to farmers the purchasing power they had enjoyed between 1909 and 1914. The New Deal expected to attain that goal partly through inflation and partly through induced scarcity. A law of May 12, 1933, administered by the Agricultural Adjustment Administration, attempted to persuade the producers of cotton, wheat, corn, hogs, rice, milk, and tobacco to take some 30 percent of their acreage out of cultivation. In return they would receive payments from a tax on the goods processed from those commodities. In June 1936, the Supreme Court held the measure unconstitutional, as a misuse of the tax power and as an invasion of an area reserved to the states.

The Federal government continued the same policy, however, under cover of various acts for soil erosion and conservation until 1938, when Congress passed the second AAA in a form

Murray R. Benedict, *Farm Policies of the United States* (New York, 1953) is a careful analysis.

Parity, 1933

To establish and maintain such balance between the production and consumption of agricultural commodities, and such marketing conditions therefor, as will re-establish prices to farmers at a level that will give agricultural commodities a purchasing power with respect to articles that farmers buy, equivalent to the purchasing power of agricultural commodities in the base period. The base period in the case of all agricultural commodities except tobacco shall be the prewar period, August, 1909–July, 1914. In the case of tobacco, the base period shall be the postwar period, August, 1919–July, 1929.

— First Agricultural Adjustment Act, *United States Statutes at Large,* 73d Cong., 1933–1934, vol. XLVIII, part I, *Public Laws,* p. 32.

that survived the scrutiny of the courts. That law retained the principle of the parity price, permitted the allocation of quotas to growers, and created an "ever-normal granary" within which surpluses would be accumulated, both to remove them from the market and to guard against future shortages.

Debt   To relieve the burden of debtors, the New Deal in 1933 expanded existing facilities by creating the Farm Credit Administration with power to make liberal loans. A year later, three mortgage laws assisted landholders who were in trouble and enabled those bankrupt to repurchase their property over a six-year period at interest of 1 percent. Although the courts held some features of that arrangement unconstitutional, it was thereafter practically impossible to foreclose a farm. Private lenders abandoned the field of agricultural finance to the government.

The New Deal legislation helped some farmers but did not solve the farm problem. The acres plowed under and the little pigs slaughtered

kept agricultural prices and incomes up by inducing scarcity, just as cutbacks did in industry. But scarcity did not restore the balance between the supply of commodities and the demand for them. Subsidy payments from the processing tax enabled marginal producers to remain on the land where it was not difficult to evade quota restrictions, while the same levy raised prices to the consumer and constricted demand.

Furthermore, the neediest elements of the rural population—migratory workers, tenants, and croppers—not being landowners, received practically no aid at all. The Rural Resettlement and Farm Security administrations (1935, 1937), designed to move such people from submarginal land, operated under severe restrictions and had little effect.

Labor Under the New Deal

Roosevelt was also aware of the needs of his urban following. During the campaign when he had spoken about the plight of the forgotten man, he had in mind the small entrepreneur, but after the election the phrase more often applied to the destitute unemployed. Although the President was no sentimentalist, he considered it unjust to force those who could find no work to stand on the corners selling apples. Furthermore, as governor he had understood that municipalities close to bankruptcy could not provide adequate relief. The Federal government had to create employment and provide industrial laborers with some economic security.

Work   It was all very well in 1933 to set up a National Employment Service to support and coordinate state activities. But private industry did not have the jobs to offer. The government therefore had to make work. The Civilian Conservation Corps (1933) enrolled some 300,000

David E. Conrad, *The Forgotten Farmers* (Urbana, Ill., 1965) discusses the problems of the Southern sharecroppers under the New Deal.

Civilian Conservation Corps Work in Progress, the Adirondacks, 1935 (Culver Pictures)

young men in useful projects such as planting trees in drought areas, and a provision of the NIRA appropriated $3,300,000,000 for public works. (The amount actually spent was double that sum.) In 1935 the Works Progress Administration continued the policy, expending in the seven years of its existence some $10,500,000,000 on buildings, roads, bridges, airports, housing, and slum clearance and employing at its peak in 1938 about 3,800,000 people.

Apart from its political utility in winning mass support for the New Deal, the effort was an effective palliative. It put men to work. Any job had more dignity than the idleness of subsisting on relief. The WPA also had pump-priming consequences. Purchases made with the government checks restored demand for the products of agriculture and industry and revived production, although Roosevelt's caution about spending prevented him from getting the maximum results from the policy.

Security The plight of the laborers called attention to their perennial insecurity. For those who could not find work, the Federal Emergency Relief Administration (1933–1935) appropriated $3,000,000,000 in direct aid through state and local agencies. It was supplemented in 1935 by the social security and railroad retirement systems, which provided old-age pensions, aid to dependent children and to the destitute aged, and unemployment insurance. Though payments and the numbers covered were relatively small, these measures were a radical break with the past.

439

Social Security Board Poster, 1936. (Social Security Administration)

National Labor Relations Act, 1935

It is hereby declared to be the policy of the United States to eliminate the causes of certain substantial obstructions to the free flow of commerce . . . by encouraging the practice and procedure of collective bargaining and by protecting the exercise by workers of full freedom of association, self-organization, and designation of representatives of their own choosing, for the purpose of negotiating the terms and conditions of their employment or other mutual aid or protection . . . .

Employees shall have the right to self-organization, to form, join, or assist labor organizations, to bargain collectively through representatives of their own choosing, and to engage in concerted activities, for the purpose of collective bargaining or other mutual aid or protection . . . .

It shall be an unfair labor practice for an employer . . . to refuse to bargain collectively with the representatives of his employees.

—*United States Statutes at Large*, vol. LXIX, part I, pp. 449–453.

The scope of legitimate government action widened. In 1933, the New Deal had been willing to go no further in providing housing than to help home owners refinance their mortgages. In 1937, the Wagner-Steagall law authorized the United States Housing Authority to make loans to municipalities for local public housing projects. Similarly, after a timid experiment in the Walsh-Healey Act (1936), the Fair Labor Standards Act (1938) proceeded to ban child labor and to set maximum hours (44 a week) and minimum wages (25 cents an hour) for the production of goods in interstate commerce.

Unionization A successful drive to win recognition for labor's right to organize enabled workers to improve their status and thus re-duced their dependency. The improvement originated in Article 7A of the NIRA, which guaranteed collective bargaining to labor. The Wagner-Connery Labor Relations Act of July 1935 confirmed that assurance and set up the National Labor Relations Board to hear complaints and punish violations.

The benevolent attitude of government gave a marked impetus to the campaign to unionize heavy industry. In November 1935 the AF of L overcame the hesitations of the craft unions and permitted a Committee for Industrial Organization to launch a drive that would take in all workers regardless of skill. The resistance of employers in the steel and automobile industries was broken when, in 1937, striking workers seized the plants. Public indignation roused by the simultaneous revelation, through the La Follette Committee, of the corporations' unscrupulous labor practices kept the police or troops from interfering. When the old leadership of the AF of L, worried by the aggressive tactics of the new unions, tried to curb them, they broke away. In 1938 the Committee for Industrial Organization under John L. Lewis split off as a separate federation, the Congress of Industrial Organizations (CIO). A year later, its membership was near that of its conservative rival, and the unskilled laborers for the first time had gained an effective voice.

Compensatory Spending

The startling array of programs set in motion between 1933 and 1939 was expensive. The direct outlays by the Federal government, the grants to the states, and the increased size of the bureaucracy made heavy drains on the budget and worried the President, who had entered the White House with a promise to reduce expenditures. He tolerated deficits because there was no alternative, and when conditions seemed to improve early in 1937, he cut back on spending, an action that promptly produced a recession. He did not realize that he had unwittingly hit upon an important tool for managing the economy which the English economist John Maynard Keynes described systematically in 1936.

Empirically and inconsistently, the New Deal had begun to use fiscal policy as a means of directing the productive system. Spending, financed by the income tax and by deficits, pumped funds into the economy and partially revived business. A later generation would profit from the experiment and learn to use the instrument more skillfully.

Kenneth D. Roose, *The Economics of Recession and Revival* (New Haven, Conn., 1954) contains a good analysis of the recession of 1937.

The New Deal was a cautious, experimental approach to restoring some communal control over the economy. Committed to no consistent philosophy, the administration nevertheless understood that the government had to act. Roosevelt's program developed by trial and error, and it had its share of failures as well as successes. It did not solve the immediate problems of the depression. But it did produce important social and economic innovations that preserved the faith of Americans in their system at a time when other countries were abandoning democracy. It also sparked intellectual speculation about issues, the solutions to which awaited another war.

Paperbacks for Further Reading

Arthur M. Schlesinger, Jr., *The Coming of the New Deal* (Sentry Editions) is a well-written, sympathetic account. Basil Rauch, *History of the New Deal* (Capricorn Books) is a straightforward narrative. Dexter Perkins, *The New Age of Franklin Roosevelt* (Chicago History of American Civilization Series) is a brief survey. James MacGregor Burns, *Roosevelt* (Harvest Books) is an interpretive biography. Material on the social context may be found in Frederick Lewis Allen, *Since Yesterday* (Bantam Books, Inc.).

There is a good selection in Franklin D. Roosevelt, *Selected Speeches* (Holt, Rinehart & Winston, Inc.), edited by Basil Rauch. Frances Perkins, *The Roosevelt I Knew* (Harper Colophon Books) is the best account by a friend of the President. Eleanor Roosevelt, *This I Remember* (Dolphin Books and Dolphin Masters) is also useful. Robert E. Sherwood, *Roosevelt and Hopkins* (Universal Library) is informative on the collaboration.

There is a thoughtful chapter on the New Deal in Louis Hartz, *Liberal Tradition in America* (Harvest Books). David E. Lilienthal, *TVA — Democracy on the March* (Quadrangle Books, Inc.) explains the program of the TVA. The productive system is informatively discussed in Alvin H. Hansen, *American Economy* (McGraw-Hill Paperback Series); and Robert A. Lively, *The South in Action* (University of North Carolina Press), a study of freight rates, illustrates regional problems.

Morton Keller, ed., *The New Deal* (Holt, Rinehart & Winston, Inc.), and Frank Freidel, ed., *The New Deal* (Spectrum Books) contain collections of views on the policy of the 1930s.

NEUTRALITY

84

In the 1930s the United States consciously sought to draw back from any deep involvement in world affairs. The primary problems were domestic; all else was a distraction. This was the high point of American isolation.

Yet outside the borders of the United States, a series of international conflicts was building up toward a climax that would plunge the world into a second global war in 1939. In the face of the repeated threats to peace, isolation amounted to being a policy of drift.

Isolation and Neutrality

New Deal Attitudes The New Deal started with a bias toward isolation. Although Roosevelt had been a Wilsonian, he did not refer to the League of Nations during his campaign and made no effort to revive the question of American membership. He viewed with indifference a new and unsuccessful effort to secure American adherence to the World Court in the spring of 1935. His only gesture toward internationalism was acquiescence in Secretary of State Hull's project for reciprocal trade agreements. An act of 1934 authorized tariff reductions of up to 50 percent based on such pacts. But this was a minor deviation from the general policy of noninvolvement.

The President's isolationist course stemmed from a variety of factors. The problems of the depression were so imposing that domestic considerations absorbed most of his energy. Events beyond the oceans seemed annoying distractions. Furthermore, the initial emphasis on planning in the recovery program produced a tendency to think in terms of a self-contained national economy that foreign connections would needlessly complicate. Secretary of Agriculture Wallace's influential *America Must Choose* (1934) argued the case for a middle way between complete isolation and internationalism. The trade he advocated, however, was not to be conducted blindly by individuals but managed through bilateral barter in accordance with a national economic plan. The New Dealers, like planners in other countries, tended to believe that adequate controls over the productive system were possible only with autarchy.

Americans also felt an aversion to the corruption and decadence of Europe. Like the expatriates returning from exile, the people washed their hands of the Old World and its vices. The foreigners had led the United States into the error of war in 1917 and had perverted the peace in 1919. Now they refused to pay their debts. Never again! A plague on all their houses, was the dominant attitude.

The effects emerged in the London Economic Conference of 1933, originally called while Hoover was still President, to lower trade barriers and to restore the international economy. When the delegates met in June 1933, hope for recovery through planning and inflation was still fresh. Roosevelt, then subject to the strong influence of Raymond Moley, disregarded the wishes of Secretary of State Hull and refused to agree to any scheme for stabilizing world currencies that limited American freedom of action. The assembly dissolved without results.

A Clean Slate The isolationist mood generated a desire to write off embarrassing commitments inherited from the past. The United States was to disentangle itself from outmoded doctrines and connections that might make trouble in the future.

The persistent refusal to recognize the Soviet Union was one such posture, meaningless while the world was moving into a dangerous period in Europe and Asia. The United States continued, however, to do business with the Reds as with other foreigners. On November 16, 1933, regular relations with the Soviet Union were resumed in return for promises by the Russians to refrain from propaganda in the United States and to negotiate the outstanding claims between the two countries. Roosevelt did not thereafter insist that these promises be kept, although his ambassador in 1935 thought Soviet violations justified a break in diplomatic relations. The President was far from being a sympathizer with Communism but he was reluctant to let moral judgments influence foreign policy. The United States was to be distantly polite to all countries without approving or disapproving of their regimes.

There are good surveys of the diplomacy of the 1930s in Selig Adler, *The Uncertain Giant* (New York, 1966) and Richard W. Leopold, *The Growth of American Foreign Policy* (New York, 1962).

Herbert Feis, *1933: Characters in Crisis* (Boston, 1966) contains an interesting account of the London Economic Conference.

"Good farming, clean thinking, right living" —that was the slogan of *Wallaces Farmer* for many years, and it was also the aim of **HENRY A. WALLACE**. World affairs in the 1930s and 1940s were, however, uncongenial to right living.

Wallace was born in Adair County, Iowa, in 1888. After attending the public schools and graduating from Iowa State College, he worked for his father's *Wallaces Farmer* and experimented with hybrid corn, developing a popular new strain. When his father went to Washington as Secretary of Agriculture in Harding's cabinet, Henry took over management of the family journal and became widely known in the region.

He was always a maverick. In 1928 he bolted the Republican party to support Al Smith, and in 1932 he campaigned for F. D. R. and helped swing Iowa to the Democrats. His independence and insistence upon going his own way had deep religious sources. He refused to smoke or drink, drew readily upon Biblical phrases, and had a mystical faith in the efficacy of his own conscience.

While he was in charge of the Department of Agriculture (1933–1940), he bent his efforts to saving the farmer. Much of his thinking in the 1930s focused on the effects of American foreign policy on agriculture. But in 1940, when he moved to the vice presidency, he turned his attention to wider horizons. He knew the costs of war and became convinced that only a close *rapprochement* with the Soviet Union would avoid future difficulties. Yet having had little experience with foreign affairs, he underestimated the gravity of the problem. That was one of the reasons why Roosevelt eased him out of the vice-presidency in 1944.

Wallace then became Secretary of Commerce, although Congressmen suspicious of his eccentricities insisted first on taking the Reconstruction Finance Corporation out of the Department. As American policy hardened in the face of Russian aggression, Wallace insisted more stridently that concessions would lead to peace. The difference in policy finally led to his resignation in 1946. Two years later he ran for the presidency on the Progressive party ticket, mobilizing in his support a motley group of Communists, fellow travelers, and liberals. He earned little more than a million votes and had no influence on the outcome of the election.

Thereafter he was out of things. He left the Progressive party in 1950 and voted for the Republicans in 1956 and 1960 and for the Democrats in 1964. Only his faith in the soil was rewarded. On his farm in South Salem, New York, he experimented with chickens, strawberries, and gladioli. He died in 1965.

Although Roosevelt understood that the United States had a special relationship with the nations of the Western Hemisphere and although he had no wish to flout the star-spangled emotions attached to the Monroe Doctrine, he did intend to reinterpret the obligations assumed between 1895 and 1920. He wished to be not the paramount power in the New World but simply a good neighbor.

The Republican administrations of the 1920s, in their dealings with Mexico and the Caribbean, had already implicitly repudiated Theodore Roosevelt's corollary to the Monroe Doctrine. Franklin Roosevelt did so explicitly. At the Montevideo Conference (1933), the United States and the Latin American countries undertook not to intervene in one another's affairs or to seek special privileges for their citizens abroad. At the Buenos Aires Conference (1936), they agreed that the whole area shared a distinctive American system unlike that of Europe, and a gathering at Lima (1938) spelled out the means of cooperation. These negotiations transformed the Monroe Doctrine from

Declaration of Lima, 1938

1. The intervention of any State in the internal or external affairs of another is inadmissible.

2. All differences of an international character should be settled by peaceful means.

3. The use of force as an instrument of national or international policy is proscribed.

4. Relations between States should be governed by the precepts of international law.

5. Respect for and the faithful observance of treaties constitute the indispensable rule for the development of peaceful relations between States, and treaties can only be revised by agreement of the contracting parties.

6. Peaceful collaboration between representatives of the various States and the development of intellectual interchange among their peoples is conducive to an understanding by each of the problems of the other as well as of problems common to all, and makes more readily possible the peaceful adjustment of international controversies.

7. Economic reconstruction contributes to national and international wellbeing, as well as to peace among nations.

—Declaration of Principles, Approved December 24 as quoted in S. S. Jones and D. P. Myers, *Documents on American Foreign Relations January 1938–June 1939* (Boston: World Peace Foundation, 1939), p. 46.

a statement of United States policy into one sustained by all the nations of the Hemisphere. Meanwhile, the marines left Haiti and the protectorate over Cuba came to an end.

Neutrality An investigation of the munitions industry conducted by the Nye Committee of the Senate (1934–1936) shocked the country and aroused a demand for legislation to prevent involvement in a future war. Although the Committee found no evidence that a conspiracy of the merchants of death had dragged the country into war in 1917, it exposed the hidden aspects of Wilson's diplomacy, revealed the high profits of some armament firms, and showed the extent to which lobbyists for the companies had worked to keep the arms race going. As a result, many citizens demanded laws to offset the forces that had drawn the United States into war in 1917.

GERALD P. NYE was born in Hortonville, Wisconsin, in 1892 and spent most of his youth in the vicinity. After leaving high school, he edited a local newspaper owned by his father and then moved to North Dakota, where he worked for similar publications. When the postwar depression hit the wheat areas, he became a vigorous supporter of the Nonpartisan League, and he campaigned for La Follette in 1924.

Nye's political career began in 1925 when he was appointed to fill an unexpired term in the United States Senate. Elected to a full term the next year, he won prominence in investigations of misdeeds in the sale of public lands and in the use of campaign funds. Vigorous opposition to the World Court and to President Coolidge also endeared him to his constituents.

(Continued on next page)

(Continued from preceding page)

Nye was intelligent but half educated; everywhere he saw signs of conspiracies by which the interests attempted to rob and mislead the people. He opposed monopolies, chain stores, and branch banking and called for steep inheritance and income taxes. He therefore looked askance at the unfamiliar aspects of the New Deal. The NRA Blue Eagle was, to him, a bird of prey gorging upon the masses.

In 1934 he became head of a Senate committee to investigate the munitions industry. The hearings exposed some dubious practices in the business, but they did not prove that the munitions manufacturers had conspired to cause war. Nevertheless, the sensational publicity evoked support for the neutrality legislation of the years that followed. Nye became a hero for pacifists, liberals, and radicals. He was unable to differentiate among those who hailed him. He accepted the Cardinal Newman medal, spoke to Coughlinites, Communist-front organizations, and the German-American Bund, yet retained a broad following among Americans committed to an isolationist policy.

As the war approached, his attacks on Roosevelt's policy grew more extreme. In 1941, Nye criticized movies that took an unfavorable view of Hitler, and at the news of Pearl Harbor he announced that the United States had been maneuvered into the incident by the President in accordance with a British plan. The war upset his isolationist assumptions, but he still voted against the United Nations. By then, however, events had passed him by. He was defeated in a bid for re-election in 1944. Honest and able, he was incapable of adjusting to a world he did not understand.

The Neutrality Act of August 31, 1935, forbade the sale or transport of munitions to belligerents during a state of war. It also permitted the President to warn Americans against travel on belligerent vessels in order to avoid a repetition of the *Lusitania* incident. It thus discarded the concept of neutral rights for which Americans had argued since the Revolution. The next year Congress, still thinking of the precedent of 1917, forbade private loans to countries at war. Finally, the law of May 1, 1937, codified existing prohibitions, allowed exports to countries at war only on a cash-and-carry basis, and made travel on belligerent vessels flatly illegal.

The basic assumption of the neutrality legislation was nonintervention. Whatever happened outside the borders of the United States was not a valid concern of the nation. The United States was not to discriminate between aggressors and the helpless victims of aggression, but to look inward and take care of its own affairs.

Totalitarianism

Events across the oceans were making a policy of neutralism illusory. A series of crises tested the conscience of the nation and raised serious doubts about the morality and feasibility of isolation.

The Wave of the Future In the past, Americans had never had reason to doubt that they represented the future. Throughout the world they had confronted outmoded monarchies or Asiatic despotisms. In the 1930s, however, they faced the novel challenge of new undemocratic regimes that nevertheless claimed to be further advanced than the United States on the road to progress.

Fascism and communism flourished in the disordered societies of Europe. The peace settlement imposed by the short-sighted and vindictive victors of the World War was, to some extent, responsible for the subsequent difficulties of the continent. But the new philosophies of the state made the situation still more precarious by per-

Hatred of War, 1936

We shun political commitments which might entangle us in foreign wars; we avoid connection with the political activities of the League of Nations; but I am glad to say that we have cooperated whole-heartedly in the social and humanitarian work at Geneva. Thus we are a part of the world effort to control traffic in narcotics, to improve international health, to help child welfare, to eliminate double taxation and to better working conditions and laboring hours throughout the world.

We are not isolationists except in so far as we seek to isolate ourselves completely from war. Yet we must remember that so long as war exists on earth there will be some danger that even the Nation which most ardently desires peace may be drawn into war.

I have seen war. I have seen war on land and sea. I have seen blood running from the wounded. I have seen men coughing out their gassed lungs. I have seen the dead in the mud. I have seen cities destroyed. I have seen two hundred limping, exhausted men come out of line—the survivors of a regiment of one thousand that went forward forty-eight hours before. I have seen children starving. I have seen the agony of mothers and wives. I hate war.

I have passed unnumbered hours, I shall pass unnumbered hours, thinking and planning how war may be kept from this Nation.

I wish I could keep war from all Nations; but that is beyond my power. I can at least make certain that no act of the United States helps to produce or to promote war. I can at least make clear that the conscience of America revolts against war and that any Nation which provokes war forfeits the sympathy of the people of the United States.

—President Franklin D. Roosevelt, Speech at Chautauqua, August 14, in *The Public Papers and Addresses of Franklin D. Roosevelt* (New York: Random House, Inc., 1938), vol. V, pp. 288, 289.

mitting powerful nations to mobilize their resources for aggression.

The essence of totalitarianism was complete subordination of the individual to the state. Each person was simply a constituent unit with no inviolable rights whatever. A variety of programs rested on this basic premise, but their political forms were very much the same. Rejecting the liberalism of the past, the totalitarian powers dispensed with parliamentary government, democracy, and constitutions. They stressed the military virtues and the necessity of following a great leader. Above all, they were expansive. They went beyond other nationalist regimes in the disregard for all historical limits. No matter how large its territory, the nation needed more. Aggression was a positive good because it furthered the interests of the state and developed the virtue and fortitude of its members.

Fascism The Fascist party in Italy first applied these concepts. Mussolini's illegal seizure of power by his march on Rome (1922) gave him control of the government with the collaboration of the monarchy. Drawing on his socialist background for the specific ingredients of his policy, he proceeded to mobilize the state on corporate lines, so that every individual became a part of some government organization. At the same time Il Duce promised his Black Shirts dominion over a new Roman Empire.

Adolf Hitler, Munich, November 8, 1942. He addresses party members on the anniversary of the eve of the 1923 Nazi *Putsch*. (UPI)

Socialism and nationalism were also powerful in Germany, where Adolf Hitler became Chancellor on January 30, 1933. His Nazi party added to its antidemocratic ideology the element of racism—the German "folk" was a pure Nordic stock, with all others inferior. As the greatest losers from the war, his countrymen were at first drawn to his movement by the desire for revision of the unjust Treaty of Versailles.

Communism Communists rejected nationalism. Yet in the 1930s, the Soviet Union, too, moved toward totalitarianism. A disregard for democratic and parliamentary methods had enabled the Communist party to seize control of the feeble republic that succeeded the government of the Tzar. But in the 1920s, the links in the Communist party to the humane socialism of the nineteenth century were stronger than among the Fascists. Maxim Gorky and others at the time perceived that the machinery for dominating the state which Lenin had created could, in other hands, become instruments of

despotic power. Stalin demonstrated the validity of such fears. He seized control after Lenin's death, liquidated the opposition led by Leon Trotsky, and by 1932 was in unchallenged command.

The tragic failure of Stalin's economic plans after that date drove him to violence. The party apparatus grew increasingly terroristic, and the great show trials of 1936 and 1937, with their trumped-up charges, strengthened his grip on the country.

Soviet totalitarianism was unique in its international connections. From Marxism, it inherited a faith in the solidarity of the working classes everywhere, and it dominated the Third International, branches of which operated throughout the world. In the United States, the Communist party attracted some Americans disillusioned with capitalism, but its popular base was weak and it splintered into rival factions. In Western Europe it possessed considerable strength. It served the Soviet state as a cover for espionage rings, and it provided a convenient means of influencing foreign policy, at least in France. It could count everywhere on loyal supporters willing to alter their own attitudes to correspond with those of Moscow. Few Americans, or for that matter, Europeans, knew what was going on in the Soviet Union. Few believed that it had become a dictatorship.

Japan Another variant of totalitarianism gradually appeared in Japan as the military clique took over. In the 1920s liberal elements were still in the ascendancy in the Japanese Diet, but the predominant position of the Emperor and the relative autonomy of the armed forces even then limited their power. The American abrogation of the Gentlemen's Agreement and other rebuffs during that decade nullified the hope of the Japanese liberals for a *rapprochement* with the West that would enable them to contain the military. In the 1930s, expansion further weakened the civilian elements in the Mikado's regime. The militarists imposed increasingly strict controls on political expression. Totalitarianism at home and expansion abroad went hand in hand.

Outside the borders of the United States, therefore, four great aggressive powers readied themselves for war. Americans, secure in the confidence that they could stand apart, whatever conflagration destroyed the rest of the world, insisted that these developments were not their concern. Events were soon to demonstrate the magnitude of their error.

War in Asia

Manchuria The first serious conflict erupted in the Far East. The Roosevelt administration inherited the problem of Manchuria. In September 1931, the Japanese army invaded that Chinese province and in March 1932 set up a puppet regime there under Henry Pu-Yi, the last Manchu Emperor. These actions ran counter to American commitments to the open door and the territorial integrity of China, and they violated the Nine-Power Treaty signed at the

Japanese Troops in Shanghai, 1932. A naval landing party with the most modern weapons guards the approach to a bridge leading to the Kiangwan sector of the city. (Brown Brothers)

Washington Conference, as well as the Kellogg-Briand Pact. Secretary of State Henry L. Stimson proclaimed the concept of nonrecognition (1932). According to the Stimson Doctrine, the United States would refuse to recognize the legality of any conquest made by the use of force.

English interests were also involved, especially after the Japanese occupation of Shanghai (January 1932). But Britain faced serious problems at home and abroad, and was therefore ready to accommodate itself to the facts of the

Dorothy Borg, *The United States and the Far Eastern Crisis of 1933–1938* (Cambridge, Mass., 1964) treats the evolving problems of American policy.

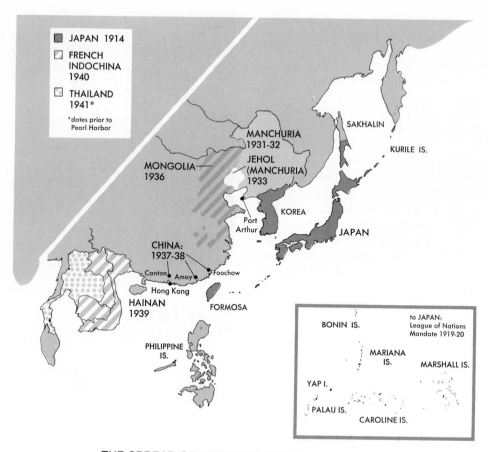

THE SPREAD OF JAPANESE POWER, 1914–1921

Japanese conquest, relying upon the long-standing friendly relations between the two powers to minimize friction. The British might have been willing to back some form of American action, but Stimson's protests were verbal only. The United States preferred to leave more decisive measures—such as economic sanctions—to the League of Nations, of which it was not a member and which it could not support. There was no action.

China   Emboldened by the knowledge that they would meet only verbal criticism, the Japanese withdrew from the League (March 1933) and proceeded to implement their scheme for the conquest of all East Asia, within which they expected to build a vast empire as their "co-prosperity" sphere. A clash at the Marco Polo Bridge in Peking in the summer of 1937 offered them an excuse to invade China, and a full-fledged, but undeclared, war thereafter existed. At one point the fighting actually touched the United States, when the Japanese deliberately hit the American gunboat *Panay* in the Yangtze River (December 1937). Tokyo apologized and paid reparations. But neither the League nor an international conference in Brussels was able to halt the fighting.

Waldo H. Heinrichs, Jr., *American Ambassador* (Boston, 1967) deals with Japanese policy in a biography of Joseph C. Grew, Ambassador to Japan (1932–1941).

The Epidemic of World Lawlessness, 1937

It seems to be unfortunately true that the epidemic of world lawlessness is spreading.

When an epidemic of physical disease starts to spread, the community approves and joins in a quarantine of the patients in order to protect the health of the community against the spread of the disease.

It is my determination to pursue a policy of peace and to adopt every practicable measure to avoid involvement in war. It ought to be inconceivable that in this modern era, and in the face of experience, any nation could be so foolish and ruthless as to run the risk of plunging the whole world into war by invading and violating in contravention of solemn treaties the territory of other nations that have done them no real harm and which are too weak to protect themselves adequately. Yet the peace of the world and the welfare and security of every nation is today being threatened by that very thing.

No nation which refuses to exercise forbearance and to respect the freedom and rights of others can long remain strong and retain the confidence and respect of other nations. No nation ever loses its dignity or good standing by conciliating its differences and by exercising great patience with and consideration for the rights of other nations.

War is a contagion, whether it be declared or undeclared. It can engulf states and peoples remote from the original scene of hostilities. We are determined to keep out of war, yet we cannot insure ourselves against the disastrous effects of war and the dangers of involvement. We are adopting such measures as will minimize our risk of involvement, but we cannot have complete protection in a world of disorder in which confidence and security have broken down.

If civilization is to survive the principles of the Prince of Peace must be restored. Shattered trust between nations must be revived.

Most important of all, the will for peace on the part of peace-loving nations must express itself to the end that nations that may be tempted to violate their agreements and the rights of others will desist from such a cause. There must be positive endeavors to preserve peace.

—President Franklin D. Roosevelt, Address at Chicago, October 5. Department of State, *Peace and War. United States Foreign Policy, 1931–1941* (Washington: Government Printing Office, 1943), pp. 386–387.

The desire for noninvolvement plunged American policy into the deepest ambiguity. In 1934, the grant of independence to the Philippines was a sign of the desire to extricate the United States from Pacific involvements. Yet Roosevelt was unwilling to concede to Japan the right to dominate northern China and the other parts of Asia from which it drew the materials its industry needed. He therefore encouraged the Chinese to resist and held inflexibly to the doctrine of nonrecognition. Missionary interests and liberals antagonized by the character of the Japanese government supported that position.

On the other hand, the United States did nothing practical to halt the Japanese advance.

The State Department ruled that the neutrality laws did not apply to the undeclared war and supplies of fuel oil and scrap iron essential to the Japanese continued to move across the Pacific. This laxity had the justification of expediency: interruption of these supplies might have goaded the Japanese into still more aggressive action. But it also reflected isolationist sentiment unwilling to recognize the necessity for involvement.

Roosevelt was confused. He wished to shun entangling diplomatic commitments. Yet events in Europe as well as dangers in Asia were pointing to war. On October 5, 1937, at Chicago, he called for a quarantine of all aggressors, but he

[handwritten annotation: Capable of being understood in more than one way.]

451

A Spanish Loyalist Dies, 1936. (Robert Capa, Magnum)

made no recommendation for action and the public remained apathetic. The only outcome of his concern was a move toward rearmament. In 1939, the United States had not defined a clear policy for furthering American interests and world peace, either by an accommodation with the Japanese or by forceful measures to halt their aggression.

The Peace of Europe

The consequences of isolation were as damaging in Europe as in Asia. The first test of policy came when Mussolini invaded Ethiopia. In October 1935, the League of Nations called ineffectively for sanctions against Italy, and American cooperation was halfhearted. The United States disapproved of the abortive Anglo-French Hoare-Laval Plan (December 1935), which aimed to appease Mussolini, but it was unwilling to go beyond a moral embargo to stop him. Increased shipments of American oil fueled Italian ships and planes. In the end the Fascists had their way.

Spain The outbreak of civil war in Spain clarified the issue of nonintervention. The effort to build a democratic republic on the ruins of the corrupt monarchy that had fallen in 1931 offered genuine hope for future progress until Fascist conspirators unleashed a civil war in July 1936. Although Francisco Franco, who took command of the rebels, had indigenous support as well as some mercenary troops, his chances of success depended on aid from his friends in Germany and Italy. Hitler and Mussolini sent abundant equipment to Spain, along with units of their own armed forces.

Popular opinion in France and England strongly favored aid to the legitimate government of the Spanish republic, but the statesmen of those countries were unwilling to anger the dictators. The French and British cabinets hoped that appeasement would satiate the appetites of the Fascists. The United States followed the same course. Warnings of the consequences from Ambassador Claude Bowers in Madrid were unheeded. Roosevelt desired to remain uninvolved and to coordinate policy with France and Britain. He was also unwilling to antagonize American Catholics, who regarded the Spanish republic as antireligious. The neutrality laws were therefore amended (January 1937) to forbid the sale of arms or supplies to combatants in a civil war. The assistance that could legally go to Japan in its undeclared war on China was withheld from the Spanish republic's effort to suppress a Fascist rebellion. On April 1, 1939, Franco completed his victory.

German Aggression The weakness of the European democracies and the isolation of the United States encouraged Hitler to go forward in his program of aggression. The whole pattern had been laid out in advance in his blueprint, *Mein Kampf*, which clearly explained how he would seize and expand power. Yet the delusion persisted that minor concessions might buy him off and lead to peace.

The Nazis took their first step, remilitarization of the Rhineland (March 7, 1936), despite the hesitancy of the German army commanders. Hitler might have drawn back had he met resistance, as he did a year earlier when Mussolini warned him away from Austria, but the French and English irresolutely decided to do nothing to stop him.

The next victim was Austria, which had lost Italian protection. Sentiment in that country for unification with Germany had grown since the French in 1931 had disallowed the proposal for a customs union. What was not conceded to persuasion was now conceded to force. Hitler moved his troops into Vienna in March 1938, while the world simply acquiesced. Meanwhile

a series of agreements in 1936 and 1937 had established the Rome-Berlin-Tokyo Axis uniting the fascists, presumably against communism, but actually to further the aggrandizement of each partner.

A series of flimsy defensive treaties — Franco-Russian, Franco-British, and Franco-Czech — stood in the way of further Nazi aggression. By the terms of these agreements any attack on Czechoslovakia would automatically draw the great powers to its defense. But the British had made it clear in the debates of the Austrian question in the spring of 1938 that they did not consider themselves bound to support the Czechs under all circumstances. That was the signal Hitler needed. He made a series of outrageous demands on behalf of the German minority in the small country, hoping that the Czechs would refuse and thereby provide him with excuse for seizing control. Prague was determined to resist. War threatened.

Munich The French and British sought to mediate, hoping to extort enough concessions from the Czechs to stay Hitler's wrath. But there was no honorable formula for doing so.

In the United States concern mounted. At the height of the crisis, in September 1938, Roosevelt appealed to the powers to save the peace, but he was unable to commit his country to any active role. The French and British interpreted appeasement broadly. At Munich (September 29, 1938) they agreed to let Germany take large sections of Czech territory. In the general dissolution of all sense of morality, the Polish government helped itself to Teschen and the Hungarians put in a claim for part of the dismembered Czech land.

On his return from Munich, Prime Minister Chamberlain announced, "Peace has been achieved in our time." In March 1939, the Nazis undeceived him when they occupied Prague and the Territory of Memel and readied themselves for demands upon Poland. Roosevelt suggested that Hitler and Mussolini give assurances of their peaceful intentions. The dictators did not answer.

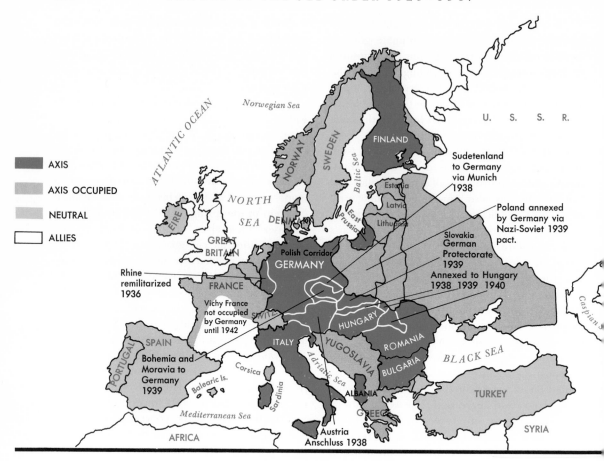

THE SPREAD OF FASCISM IN EUROPE

Responsibility The policy toward refugees illustrated the futility of the American position. The victims of totalitarianism fled for their lives, in relatively small numbers from Russia and Italy, in hundreds of thousands from Germany, Spain, Austria, and Czechoslovakia. Many were Jews, victims of racist laws; others were liberal antifascists.

They had nowhere to go. The United States expressed its sympathy, but the restrictive quota system admitted only a handful of newcomers. International conferences at Evian and Nassau fumbled helplessly with the subject but achieved nothing. No one was his brother's keeper.

▼

The evasion of responsibility was characteristic of the 1930s. Memories of the World War were so fresh that people of good will everywhere were eager to avoid a second disaster. They therefore gave an enormous advantage to men not animated by good will who did not hesitate to use force when it was in their interest to do so. Nonintervention made aggression easy.

In the face of aggression the United States was neutral. The tremendous power it held remained unused, in a massive abdication of responsibility. It did little to halt a world moving toward a cataclysmic war from which it would not, in the end, itself escape.

Paperbacks for Further Reading

Foster R. Dulles, *America's Rise to World Power* (Harper Torchbooks) contains a general survey. Selig Adler, *The Isolationist Impulse* (Free Press Paperbacks) extends into this period. William L. Langer and S. E. Gleason, *The Challenge to Isolation* (Harper Torchbooks) deals with prewar diplomacy in detail. There are also materials in Robert A. Divine, *The Reluctant Belligerent* (John Wiley & Sons, Inc.).

Elting E. Morison, *Turmoil and Tradition* (Atheneum Publishers), a study of Henry L. Stimson, treats the response to the Manchurian incident. Bryce Wood, *The Making of the Good Neighbor Policy* (W. W. Norton & Company, Inc.) deals with Latin America.

On the European aspects of the decade, Hannah Arendt, *Origins of Totalitarianism* (Meridian Books) is a provocative interpretation. Ernest Nolte, *Three Faces of Fascism* (Holt, Rinehart & Winston, Inc.); Alan Bullock, *Hitler* (Harper Torchbooks); and Sir John W. Wheeler-Bennett, *Munich* (Compass Books) are also useful.

THE
GLOBAL WAR

85

For almost six years the business of destruction occupied the attention of most of the world. The confrontation of power exhausted victors and vanquished alike, for technology put at the disposal of the belligerents hitherto unknown methods of killing and burning. Isolation did not protect the United States. It learned painfully that when peace was broken anywhere, the peace of all was in danger.

From beginning to end the statesmen miscalculated. They assumed war would not come and it did. They misjudged its character. And they failed to take account of new social forces that would shape the peace. Nor did the military leaders perceive any better the large outlines of the conflict in which they engaged. They misunderstood the weapons they used. They underestimated the enemy. And they failed to count the costs of destruction. In the end, the survivors were left on a treacherous quicksand, hard put to maintain their balance, much less to carry on the work of reconstruction.

The Road from Munich

The Polish Question   Not even Hitler wanted general war in 1939. The events of the previous three years deluded him into the belief that he could get what he wanted without a conflict. Eastern Europe lived in terror of his power; the Poles, he thought, were no more likely to resist than the Czechs. The men of Munich still ruled Britain and France. After the fall of Prague, they had given broad guarantees to Poland and Romania. But many citizens in the West were then still asking, "Why die for Danzig?" As for the United States, that remote country was confirmed in isolationism.

The Nazis were sure of the benevolent collaboration of the Italians and the Japanese. It remained only to take care of the Soviet Union. Stalin resented his exclusion from the negotiations at Munich, and was suspicious of the intentions of the Western powers. He was ready to come to terms. A sordid deal in August divided Poland between the Reds and the Nazis, and freed the Germans for their next move. On September 1, 1939, without a formal declaration of war, Hitler's troops marched swiftly into Poland. The Russians forthwith launched an invasion from the East, and Poland's ability to resist was shattered.

France and England, hardly better prepared to fight than a year earlier, declared war on Germany on September 3. Although they had been increasing their strength, they had to do without the powerful army that Czechoslovakia would have given them earlier. Yet having rested their faith on Hitler's pledge of good intentions at Munich, they had no alternative but to honor their commitments to the Poles. Furthermore, the Western powers operated under an insane delusion about Hitler's weakness. According to the optimistic theories of 1939, the French fortifications along the Maginot Line were impregnable, and the Nazi army was thought to be

scarcely trained. The Germans lacked oil and rubber and could be easily starved into submission. A firm stand and a blockade would bring them to their knees. These illusions beguiled the Allies in 1939.

The Easy War   There was little fighting in the West while the Nazis completed the subjugation of Poland and Russia moved wantonly into the Baltic states of Estonia, Lithuania, and Latvia. On November 30, the Soviet Union launched an unprovoked attack on Finland, and the French and English seriously considered sending an expeditionary force to fight the Russians. But Swedish and Norwegian neutrality obstructed that action. Belgium and Holland, too, were determined to remain apart from the conflict and resisted any preparation for a united defense against Germany.

American policy labored under serious misapprehensions. There was no doubt now, as there was in 1914, where the sympathies of the country lay, but Roosevelt and his fellow citizens firmly believed that the English and French could easily win once they set themselves to the job. The amended neutrality law (November 4, 1939) permitted belligerents to buy what supplies they wished on a cash-and-carry basis, although American ships were excluded from combat zones. No more was necessary. No torpedoing incidents would embroil the country with the Germans, and still the Allies could get the munitions they needed to win the war themselves.

The Fall of France   In May 1940 these fanciful assumptions collapsed. With the coming of spring, Hitler's legions took to the move. They advanced rapidly through Denmark (April 9) and invaded Norway, while the Swedes stood aside as their Scandinavian neighbors were overwhelmed.

With their northern flank secure, the Germans then turned south. A swift campaign through Holland (May 10), despite that country's professions of neutrality, enabled the Nazis to tumble Belgium's defenses and sweep around the Maginot Line into northern France. On

Winston Churchill Inspects Bomb Damage in Parliament's Debating Chamber, May 1941. (Thomson House)

June 10 Mussolini entered the war and attacked from the south while the Germans moved toward Paris. The remnants of the British forces fled across the Channel from Dunkirk. The French government collapsed, and the next regime under Marshal Pétain in Vichy signed an armistice with Germany (June 22). The Nazis were the unchallenged masters of Europe.

Hitler now considered it necessary only to come to terms with Britain. He had no immediate interest either in conquest of the island or disruption of the empire, but merely sought security in the west while he turned his energies toward his true interest, the east. Though the British feared an invasion, they would not yield. Unaided, they withstood massive air attacks

from August 1940 on through the winter. Winston Churchill, who had become Prime Minister in May, had only one policy — to expend blood, toil, tears, and sweat in resistance to the bitter end.

Away from Isolation The United States now cautiously helped. In September 1940, the President gave the British fifty old destroyers in return for leases on a string of bases in the Western Hemisphere, and the government winked at some evasions of the neutrality laws. But Roosevelt could not decide how far to go. In the election campaign of 1940, he and Wendell L. Willkie, the Republican candidate, while committing themselves to continued support of Britain, promised that they would not send

458

An opponent once described **WENDELL L. WILLKIE** as a simple, barefoot Wall Street lawyer. There was a grain of truth in the jest. Though Willkie moved in a circle of great industrialists, he did not lose the traces of his Hoosier antecedents or shake off the idealistic influences of his grandmother, who was a Presbyterian minister, and of his mother, the first woman admitted to the bar in Indiana.

He was born in Elwood, Indiana, in 1892 into a prosperous family. He attended Culver Military Academy and the University of Indiana, from which he received a law degree in 1916. A campus radical who resisted the fraternity system, he nevertheless moved into a conventional legal career, working first for the Firestone Company and then for the firm of Mather and Newbit.

In 1929, Willkie went to New York to serve as attorney for the Commonwealth and Southern utility empire. Four years later he became president, and soon after was involved in a long conflict with TVA, whose activities threatened Commonwealth and Southern properties. Until then he had been a Democrat, but the unchecked activities of the New Deal now seemed to him to threaten private rights. Ultimately he secured a settlement with TVA. The conflict gained him wide public notice.

Even then, Willkie was not simply a conservative, resistant to everything new. Acquainted with some of the intellectuals in New York, he tried to justify his position in rational terms and sought not merely the preservation of the *status quo*, but limited change that would adapt old institutions to new needs. To the Republican party, divorced from the dominant trends of the 1930s and tired of the negativism of its old leaders, he offered a refreshing opportunity to come abreast of the times. Although he had no political organization or experience, he received the GOP presidential nomination in 1940.

His candidacy kept the election from becoming a test of isolationism. On foreign policy Willkie's position was almost identical with Roosevelt's, and at his defeat he announced that the role of his party would be that of the loyal opposition. Until his death in 1944 he kept that pledge. His *One World* (1943), written after a tour that took him to Asia and Russia, demonstrated the futility of isolation in the twentieth century and sustained Republican support of the bipartisan foreign policy of the years that followed.

American boys to fight overseas. In March 1941, however, Congress made the United States the arsenal of democracy by permitting the President to lend or lease supplies to the British. In the summer American and German ships were trading shots at sea, and in November 1941 the neutrality law was repealed. The change in law owed something to the demonstration that there were no limits to Hitler's ambition. He moved east without having first ended British resistance.

Ellsworth Barnard, *Wendell Willkie* (Marquette, Mich., 1966) is a sympathetic biography.

Hitler underestimated the strength of the Soviet Union. The Red army, crippled by purges, had not performed well in Finland; and its brutality had stirred liberal and socialist opposition in Poland. Within the Soviet Union, the rule of terror cloaked deep popular discontent. Furthermore, the Russian fear of the Nazi army gave the impression that opposition would be no more substantial than in Poland or France.

Hitler gambled. On June 22, 1941, the Germans, despite their treaty, launched a massive attack across the Russian frontier. By the winter they had advanced to a line that ran from the outskirts of Leningrad down beyond Odessa on the Black Sea to Stalingrad. They then ground to a halt, as the problems of governing their conquests and of maintaining communications and supply routes demanded attention. That winter there seemed little prospect that their rule would soon be shaken.

The Far Eastern Crisis

Events in Europe had their effects in the Far East. The Hitler-Stalin pact had shocked the Japanese, still bogged down in war with China. They had joined the Rome-Berlin Axis out of fear of the Soviet Union, which stood across their Manchurian frontier and which had allies among the Chinese Communists, who had just entered a united front with Chiang Kai-shek. At the end of 1939, the Japanese seemed isolated.

The East Indies   The collapse of France and of the Netherlands in the spring of 1940 left their Asian possessions defenseless. French Indochina supplied Japan with a substantial part of its rice, and the Dutch East Indies were an important source of oil and rubber. The Japanese wanted recognition of their special position in the trade of those colonies and began a series of negotiations to assure their supplies. They got encouragement from a tripartite pact with Germany and Italy in September 1940.

The United States, by contrast, encouraged the powerless French and Dutch to resist. Roosevelt had no wish to provoke the Japanese into war, but he insisted on the absolute maintenance of the *status quo* and toward this end forbade export licenses for aviation gasoline, scrap iron, and steel destined for Japan.

Pressure from the United States during the winter of 1940–1941 strengthened the aggressive elements within the Mikado's government. The Japanese civilians were anxious for an accommodation, and naval leaders had healthy respect for Anglo-American sea power. But the Japanese army, with its immense stake in China, pushed for a more forceful policy; and as peaceful negotiations in the spring of 1941 brought no result, expansionist influence mounted steadily. In June the German invasion of the Soviet Union removed any threat of Russian activity in Asia, and the Japanese militarists determined to consolidate their position in the Southeast, whether that brought a war with the United States or not. At the end of July they occupied Indochina.

Pearl Harbor   In response, the Americans froze Japanese assets in the United States, thus stifling Japan's trade. A special Japanese negotiating team sent to Washington in a desperate effort to head off a conflict learned that the Americans would not compromise. The price of a settlement was Japanese withdrawal from Southeast Asia and China.

The United States was unconscious of its vulnerability, for it underestimated Japan's fighting power. Roosevelt had absolute confidence in American might in the Pacific. In the Philippines, General Douglas MacArthur had trained a local army and had at his disposal a heavy complement of American air power. The navy, however, was the mainstay of United States strategy. According to the basic theories developed by Alfred T. Mahan more than a quarter of a century earlier, the decisive element in any future conflict was the size of the battle fleet. The number of capital ships had increased, and they were prepared for the great conflict which, it was assumed, would come somewhere in the mid-Pacific. In the fall of 1941, in preparation for the event, the whole fleet was concentrated at Pearl Harbor, ready to sail forth to engage the smaller Japanese forces.

The naval planners had consistently minimized the potential of air power. They had not been particularly interested in the aircraft carriers that Congress thrust upon them, and they believed firmly in the invulnerability of the battleship against air attack. They were ready, but in terms of their own strategy, not of the strategy under which the enemy would operate.

Basis for Proposed Agreement Between the United States and Japan, 1941

1. The Government of the United States and the Government of Japan will endeavor to conclude a multilateral non-aggression pact among the British Empire, China, Japan, the Netherlands, the Soviet Union, Thailand and the United States.

2. Both Governments will endeavor to conclude among the American, British, Chinese, Japanese, the Netherland and Thai Governments an agreement where-under each of the Governments would pledge itself to respect the territorial integrity of French Indochina and, in the event that there should develop a threat to the territorial integrity of Indochina, to enter into immediate consultation with a view to taking such measures as may be deemed necessary and advisable to meet the threat in question. Such agreement would provide also that each of the Governments party to the agreement would not seek or accept preferential treatment in its trade or economic relations with Indochina and would use its influence to obtain for each of the signatories equality of treatment in trade and commerce with French Indochina.

3. The Government of Japan will withdraw all military, naval, air and police forces from China and from Indochina.

4. The Government of the United States and the Government of Japan will not support—militarily, politically, economically—any government or regime in China other than the National Government of the Republic of China with capital temporarily at Chungking.

5. Both Governments will give up all extraterritorial rights in China, including rights and interests in and with regard to international settlements and concessions, and rights under the Boxer Protocol of 1901.

—Draft Handed by Secretary of State Hull to Ambassador Nomura, November 26. Department of State, *Peace and War. United States Foreign Policy, 1931–1941* (Washington: Government Printing Office, 1943), pp. 810–812.

By the beginning of December 1941, a conflict seemed inevitable. Intercepted messages revealed that the Japanese were moving, but the Americans misjudged the direction. They expected the first drive to be toward Southeast Asia, to pick off the French and Dutch possessions. An attack on the highly guarded bases in Hawaii and the Philippines seemed out of the question.

The miscalculation was tragic. On December 7, 1941, a Japanese carrier force destroyed the fighting capacity of the American fleet. The enemy, swooping down over Pearl Harbor in the quiet of a Sunday morning, disabled 19 vessels and 150 aircraft. More than 2000 soldiers and sailors lost their lives and there were 1200 civilian casualties. Later that day an air armada from Formosa wiped out the American planes exposed on their runways in the Philippines. The United States declared war on Japan on December 8. The Axis partners, Italy and Germany, on December 11, declared war on the United States. The surprise attack shaped the whole character of the war. The United States had expected, if war came, to snap Japan's trade links and then stifle the islands by a relatively

Crewmen on a Japanese Carrier as Aircraft Take off to Attack Pearl Harbor, December 7, 1941. (The Granger Collection)

costless blockade. Instead, it was suddenly fighting on distant battlegrounds across two oceans.

Mobilizing at Home

As in 1917, the United States was unprepared for the kind of war it had to fight. It improvised the means of mobilizing, equipping, supplying, and transporting an army. The crisis made for haste, but it also cut through inefficiencies and obstacles in order to get the job done.

The increase in the size of the army showed the magnitude of the task. In the summer of 1939 the United States Army numbered 174,000 men. Two years later it had expanded to 1,400,-000. At the end of the war it had grown to 8,300,000, with 3,400,000 more in the Navy and 484,000 in the Marines. In all, some 15,-000,000 men and women enrolled in the armed services. A majority of them came by way of the draft. A one-year selective-service law enacted in September 1940 was extended in August 1941 and registered 31,000,000 men, from among whom the draftees were chosen.

The economy mobilized swiftly and efficiently to supply these men and also the English, Russians, and Chinese overseas. Although man power shortages plagued agriculture and manufacturing, output rose, the railroads doubled the ton miles of freight they carried, and convoys shuttled across the oceans. To concentrate the

Donald M. Nelson, *Arsenal of Democracy* (New York, 1946) is an account of wartime industrial mobilization by a participant.

whole economy on war production, a system of rationing, price and wage fixing, and priorities for scarce materials controlled the activity of every American.

The result was a vast output of weapons. The United States had about 2000 aircraft in 1939 and a tiny production capacity. Roosevelt then undertook to create an industry capable of turning out 50,000 planes a year. The primitive airplane manufacturers adopted the techniques of the advanced automobile industry and moved directly into mass production. In 1944 the Air Force had almost 100,000 planes in service. In the five years after the fall of France, the United States built almost 300,000 aircraft, more than 8,000,000 tons of naval and 55,000,000 tons of merchant shipping, more than 85,000 tanks and about 3,000,000 machine guns.

Science played an important part in utilizing the nation's resources for war. The National Defense Research Committee, organized in June 1940, began to enlist the efforts of scholars, and the Office of Scientific Research and Development after May 1941 experimented with rockets, radar, and scores of new weapons. Meanwhile the secret Manhattan Project was at work on the atom bomb, which would change the whole face of war.

The War in Europe

Strategic Considerations Embattled around the world, the United States and its allies had to deploy their limited resources carefully. The initial decision, framed by General George C. Marshall and the Joint Chiefs of Staff, was to hold on everywhere but to pursue the war most actively in Europe. The Germans were considered the most serious opponents; their defeat was the essential first step to victory.

Strategic bombing seemed at first the least costly or at least the readiest offense. American B-17s, in association with the British, launched massive missions against German industry, in the expectation of undermining the capacity to resist. These attacks caused heavy damage to factories, shipyards, and communications, but the result was not enemy capitulation. German plants dispersed or went underground, while the economy proved remarkably resilient. It would not collapse until after an invasion using American man power in a harsh and destructive war.

GEORGE C. MARSHALL was the ideal staff officer. In 1917, when Marshall was a member of the First Division staff in France, Pershing refused his request for a transfer to active duty. Marshall's skills were needed behind the lines. They were even more essential after 1939.

Marshall was a professional soldier but not a West Pointer. Born at Uniontown, Pennsylvania, in 1880, he attended the Virginia Military Institute and entered the regular army in 1902. There followed a dreary period of service in the Philippines and in various unexciting posts. For eighteen years he remained a captain. The prospects for promotion were slight in that period. He distinguished himself during World War I, but did not advance rapidly thereafter. The hostility of Douglas MacArthur, who was chief of staff between 1930 and 1935, may have contributed to the slowness of Marshall's advancement.

Yet even in those years, Marshall's qualities as a leader were apparent. From the time when, as a cadet, he refused to inform on those responsible for a serious bayonet injury during a hazing incident, he adhered to a strict code of honor and duty. He had a knack for integrating de-

(Continued on next page)

Stephane Groueff, *Manhattan Project* (Boston, 1967) is a very readable account of the building of the atom bomb.

Forrest C. Pogue, *George C. Marshall* (New York, 1963–1966) is a biography that extends up to 1942.

(Continued from preceding page)

tails into a large strategic plan. Most important, he was able to keep his temper, an invaluable asset for one who had to work with volatile commanders and politicians, mediate among conflicting interests, and focus his sights on the ultimate objective.

Marshall became deputy chief of staff in 1938 and chief a year later. He remained in over-all charge of the planning for war through the long conflict that followed. His was the painful obligation of deciding on priorities and approving plans the success of which depended upon execution by other men.

At his retirement in 1945, President Truman dispatched him to Chunking in an effort to work out some compromise between the Nationalist and the Communist forces. Although the mission failed, Truman named Marshall Secretary of State, a position from which he commanded the opening stages of the cold war. In 1948 he once more sought retirement, but was called back to service as Secretary of Defense in 1950 and directed the renewed conflict in Korea. It was he who signed the order to relieve MacArthur of his command in 1951. That year Marshall was finally allowed to retire. He died in 1959.

Planning for an assault on the continent of Europe began at once. The alternatives were a direct attack in the west or a sweeping, flanking movement through North Africa and Central and Eastern Europe. The Russians argued strongly for an immediate second front in western Europe, which would divert a substantial number of Germans from the East and permit the Red army to move into the vacated areas without opposition. The American military leaders, reluctant to waste time at the periphery, also wanted to hit the Germans directly through France.

Churchill, however, preferred the flanking operation. German defenses in the west were formidable, and he feared that Allied casualties would be heavy in an immediate attack there. A southerly invasion, through the "soft underbelly" of Europe, would tumble the Vichy regime, exhaust the Nazis in combat far from their bases, and bring the Allies into the heart of the continent, where they would be in a position to influence the peace terms.

Southern Offensives Roosevelt finally acceded to Churchill's view. Feeling unprepared for a head-on assault yet eager for some step in 1942, they fixed upon North Africa as the target. Allied sea power would make a landing there that would be less expensive than one in Europe, and there were hopes of winning over the Vichy authorities, who had nominal control of Morocco and Algeria.

On November 8, 1942, combined English and American forces under General Dwight D. Eisenhower set ashore at Casablanca, Oran, and Algiers. They met light resistance and moved eastward toward Tunisia, where the Germans were entrenched. The fighting then became bitter, but the superior numbers, fire power, and equipment of the Allies forced the Germans in Africa to surrender on May 12, 1943.

The British wanted to make North Africa the staging area for the attack on Central Europe, and the Americans reluctantly agreed. The invasion of Sicily (July 1943) and of Italy (September 1943) went slowly, and in October came to a halt above Naples. By then Mussolini had fallen (July 25) and a new Italian government under Marshal Pietro Badoglio had surrendered (September 8). But the Germans, entrenched along the Volturno line, kept the Allied advance back for months. Rome did not fall until June 1944, and the north at that time was still in enemy hands.

D-Day and After By then a year of preparation had readied almost 3,000,000 men and more than 2,000,000 tons of supplies for the invasion across the English Channel in Operation Overlord. On June 6, 1944, 5000 vessels carried

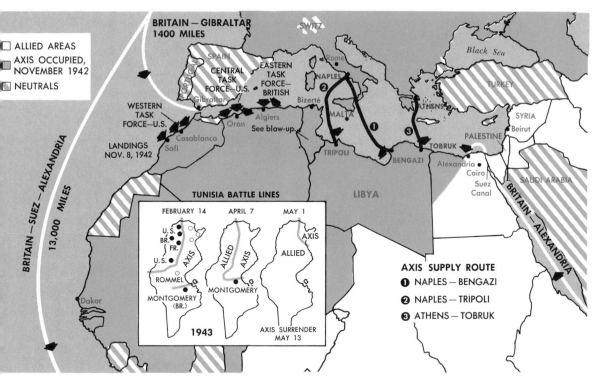

BRITAIN — GIBRALTAR 1400 MILES

SWITZ.

Black Sea

SPAIN

PORTUGAL

CENTRAL TASK FORCE—U.S.

EASTERN TASK FORCE— BRITISH

Rome

NAPLES

TURKEY

Gibraltar

Bizerté

②

WESTERN TASK FORCE—U.S.

Algiers

MALTA

ATHENS

SYRIA

Beirut

Oran

See blow-up

①

③

PALESTINE

LANDINGS NOV. 8, 1942

Casablanca

Safi

TRIPOLI

BENGAZI

TOBRUK

Alexandria

Cairo

Suez Canal

SAUDI ARABIA

BRITAIN — SUEZ — ALEXANDRIA

13,000 MILES

LIBYA

BRITAIN — ALEXANDRIA

TUNISIA BATTLE LINES

FEBRUARY 14   APRIL 7   MAY 1

U.S.
BR.
FR.

AXIS

AXIS

ALLIED

U.S.

ALLIED

AXIS

ROMMEL

MONTGOMERY

ALLIED

Dakar

MONTGOMERY (BR.)

1943

AXIS SURRENDER MAY 13

AXIS SUPPLY ROUTE

❶ NAPLES — BENGAZI

❷ NAPLES — TRIPOLI

❸ ATHENS — TOBRUK

THE NORTH AFRICAN CAMPAIGNS, 1941–1944

An American Landing Craft off the Normandy Beaches, D-Day, June 6, 1944. (The Granger Collection)

465

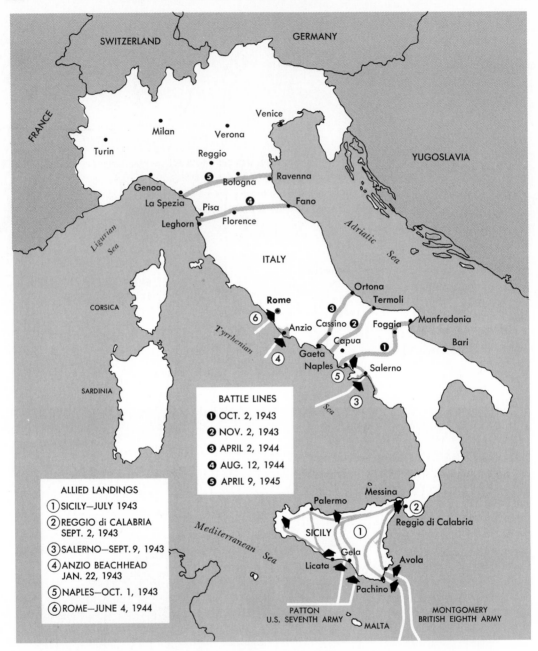

THE ITALIAN CAMPAIGNS, 1943–1945

Invasion of Sicily, 1943

It started getting light in the sea in front of Sicily about 0530. We had pulled in closer to the beach to proceed with landing operations when the shore batteries opened up. We turned, maneuvered, and the whole convoy got out of range while the naval guns roared. It was wonderful how accurate they were. The Navy gave us the go ahead signal and we began the landing operations . . . .

We expected to get hit at any minute. I came in on the first wave of my ship. We sat there, huddled down to protect us from flying metal . . . .

It was very light then, about 0630. The waves were ten feet high near the shore. The boat grounded and we all hopped out . . . .

We were in Comiso, south of Gela, and then we moved toward the Comiso airport. About five minutes later we got shot at by German artillery. We all piled out of the half-tracks and hit the gullies. We were shelled for half an hour and then the infantry finally got the gun. We got back into the vehicle and came within 200 yards of the airport when a jeep dashes up to us and a captain says that the airport is not ours yet and there is going to be a big attack on it in twenty minutes.

We pulled right back quick. We bivouacked right by a gasoline dump. Then I jumped into an unfinished foxhole about two feet deep. One bomb dropped about 120 feet away. You know what that means —the ground shakes and the shrapnel sings and you choke in the dust. This was the worst bombing I have ever been in. I saw myself back in the hospital with nurses running around with giant thermometers.

The bombers missed the dump completely. We took off and came to a group of buildings which had been used by the German cadre. There was the zip zip zip of sniper fire. We pulled out and into the nearest gully. Then in a very academic manner we started cleaning them out with .50-calibre machine gun fire. Tracer fire set the place aflame and rifle grenades finished it off. There were weird howls from the Nazi snipers as they died.

—*The Stars and Stripes*, Algeria, July 10, 1943.

176,000 men to Normandy, where the Allies established a foothold 5 miles deep and 70 miles wide.

Into this pocket they poured 325,000 troops, 50,000 vehicles, and 100,000 tons of supplies. Two American columns along with one British and one Canadian broke out of the peninsula in July, and by the end of August reached Paris and Brussels, where they halted for regrouping.

In December they repulsed a desperate German counterattack, and were ready to resume the advance along a broad front. Meanwhile, the Russians, using American equipment, had begun to thrust the Germans out of Eastern Europe.

In March 1945, the Americans seized the Ludendorff Bridge at Remagen, crossed the Rhine, and in a series of encircling movements captured the Ruhr, center of German heavy

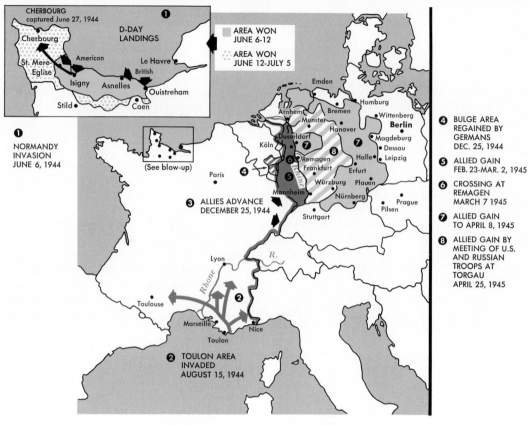

CHERBOURG
captured June 27, 1944

D-DAY LANDINGS

Cherbourg

St. Mere-Eglise

American

Le Havre

British

Isigny Asnelles Ouistreham

Stild Caen

AREA WON
JUNE 6-12

AREA WON
JUNE 12-JULY 5

❶ NORMANDY
INVASION
JUNE 6, 1944

(See blow-up)

Paris

❸ ALLIES ADVANCE
DECEMBER 25, 1944

Lyon

Rhone R.

R.

❷

Toulouse

Marseille

Toulon

Nice

❷ TOULON AREA
INVADED
AUGUST 15, 1944

Emden

Hamburg

Arnhem Bremen Wittenberg

Munster Hanover **Berlin**

Dusseldorf Magdeburg

Köln ❼ Dessau ❼

❻ Remagen ❽ Halle Leipzig

Frankfurt Erfurt

❺ Würzburg Plauen

Mannheim Nürnberg Prague

Stuttgart Pilsen

❶

❹ BULGE AREA
REGAINED BY
GERMANS
DEC. 25, 1944

❺ ALLIED GAIN
FEB. 23-MAR. 2, 1945

❻ CROSSING AT
REMAGEN
MARCH 7 1945

❼ ALLIED GAIN
TO APRIL 8, 1945

❽ ALLIED GAIN BY
MEETING OF U.S.
AND RUSSIAN
TROOPS AT
TORGAU
APRIL 25, 1945

THE CAMPAIGNS IN WESTERN EUROPE, 1943–1945

Front Patrols of the 1st Ukrainian Army and of the United States 1st Army Meet at the Elbe River, East of Torgau, Germany, April 27, 1945. This link-up cut Germany in two and brought Russian and Allied troops together in their campaign against Germany. (U.S. Army Photograph)

Supplies for Overlord, 1944

German strategy . . . was intended to insure that our supplies should never be permitted to begin flowing into the beachheads. The German philosophy was: "Deny the Allies the use of ports and they will be unable to support their armies ashore . . . ." The Germans fully expected us to be able to make a landing at some point on the Channel coast, but they were nevertheless certain that they could dislodge us before supplies could be brought ashore to maintain the troops. They had no knowledge of our artificial harbors, a secret as closely guarded as the time and place of our assault. The impossible was accomplished and supplies came ashore, not afterwards to support a force beleaguered on the beachheads, but actually with the troops as they landed. The Germans were, by virtue of our initial supply, denied the opportunity of dislodging us and were subsequently, throughout the campaign, under sustained attack as the result of the feats of maintenance performed by our administrative organizations . . . .

The comparatively light casualties which we sustained on all the beaches except Omaha were in large measure due to the success of the novel mechanical contrivances which we employed and to the staggering moral and material effect of the mass armor landed in the leading waves of the assault. The use of large numbers of amphibious tanks to afford fire support in the initial stages of the operation had been an essential feature of our plans, and, despite the losses they suffered on account of the heavy seas, on the beaches where they were used they proved conspicuously effective. It is doubtful if the assault forces could have firmly established themselves without the assistance of these weapons.

—Report by the Supreme Commander to the Combined Chiefs of Staff on the Operations in Europe of the Allied Expeditionary Force. June 6, 1944 to May 5, 1945 (Washington: Government Printing Office, 1945), pp. 12, 14.

industry. They then held back to permit the Russians to take Berlin, in accordance with an agreement on the terms of occupation. Toward the end of April, Hitler committed suicide and Italian partisans killed Mussolini. On May 7 (V-E Day), General Eisenhower received the unconditional surrender of the remaining German forces.

The Pacific and the Bomb

The end of the war in Europe did not, however, mean the end of fighting. Another enemy remained. The Japanese had proved far more capable antagonists than the Americans had imagined.

Holding On The enigmatic personality of Douglas MacArthur complicated the war in the Pacific. A succession of defeats in the three months after Pearl Harbor had driven him back to Australia. Yet he retained tremendous prestige and put extraordinary pressure upon the chiefs of staff and the civilian heads of the government. He resented the decision to emphasize Europe and insisted on playing a leading role in carrying forward the war against Japan.

Through most of 1942, the Americans were on the defensive. By April the Japanese had taken Wake Island, the island of Guam, Hong Kong, Singapore, Indonesia, Burma, New Britain, the Solomons, and the Philippines. They intended to fortify a chain of islands from the Aleutians through Midway to Papua which would form a shield behind which to complete the conquest of East Asia.

They overextended themselves in the effort. In the battles of the Coral Sea (May 7–8) and Midway (June 3–6) the Japanese fleet suffered defeats that gave the United States a vital breathing space. The Nipponese plan to develop a base in Guadalcanal in the Solomon Islands from which to block a counterattack out of Australia

Samuel Eliot Morison, *The Two Ocean War* (Boston, 1963) lucidly describes the fighting at sea.

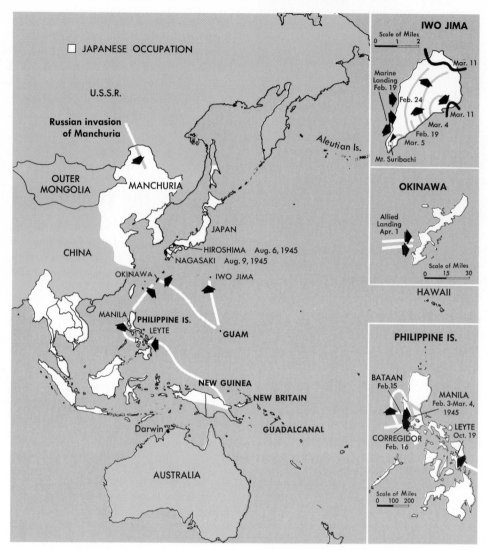

THE WAR IN THE PACIFIC, 1941–1945

Hiroshima After the Atomic Blast. (Brown Brothers)

also collapsed after a bloody six months' battle that began in August 1942.

The Americans meanwhile built up their strength in the Pacific and supported the resistance of the Chinese. Enough supplies got through from Indian bases, either on the Burma Road or by air, to enable Generalissimo Chiang Kai-shek to pin down substantial Japanese forces on the mainland.

Counteroffensive Against the wishes of MacArthur, the navy assumed primary responsibility for carrying the war to Japan. It proved unnecessary to reduce each of the Japanese island strong points. Powerful amphibious American forces in 1943 and 1944 leaped over them while submarines and destroyers wiped out enemy shipping. The drive swept through the Gilbert, Marshall, and Mariana islands and New Guinea. On June 19, 1944, the battle of the Philippine Sea ended the fighting power of the Japanese navy, and in October the battle of Leyte Gulf led to the reconquest of the Philippines. In the next six months, the capture of Iwo Jima and Okinawa gave the United States bases from which to launch an intense air bombardment of the Japanese home islands. In March 1945, American planes spread devastating fires through the crowded cities of Tokyo, Yokohama, and Osaka.

The Bomb When Germany fell, plans were ready for an invasion of Japan. But a new instrument of destruction developed by the scientists made that costly venture unnecessary. The desire to shorten the war dissolved hesitations about use of the new weapon. On August 6, 1945, over Hiroshima and on August 9 over Nagasaki, great mushroom clouds left by the blast of atomic bombs marked the death of thousands and the total destruction of whole cities. This awesome power compelled the Japanese to surrender on August 14, 1945.

▼

The culminating act of destruction over Hiroshima was symbolic of the fury of a war that cost the world uncountable lives and wasted precious resources. There had been no line between soldiers and civilians. The German *Stukas* above Rotterdam, the American flying fortresses over Hamburg, the Soviet secret police who massacred thousands of suspected opponents, respected neither the young nor the aged, neither the women nor the children. The full horror of the Nazi extermination camps was still unknown. Yet much of Europe and Asia was but degrees removed from the devastation left by the atom bomb.

Although hundreds of thousands of American families felt the pain of 962,403 casualties, the soil of the United States was spared the physical destruction visited upon other areas. The shock of war had enlisted the energies of its people in a way that left its economy stronger than ever. The country therefore bore the unique responsibility of using its strength to repair some of the damage war had done the world.

Paperbacks for Further Reading

A. Russell Buchanan, *United States and World War II* (Harper Torchbooks) is a competent two-volume survey stressing military events. There is a brief section on war and diplomacy in Dexter Perkins, *New Age of Franklin Roosevelt* (Chicago History of American Civilization Series). Herbert Feis, *The Road to Pearl Harbor* (Atheneum Publishers) describes developments after 1937. Chester W. Nimitz, ed., in *Triumph in the Atlantic* (Spectrum Books) and *Triumph in the Pacific* (Spectrum Books) treats the naval war, while Dwight D. Eisenhower, *Crusade in Europe* (Dolphin Books and Dolphin Masters) describes the conflict with the Germans. Fletcher Knebel and Charles W. Bailey II, *No High Ground* (Bantam Books, Inc.), is a popular narrative of the atom bomb; and Cornelius Ryan, *The Last Battle* (Crest Books) vividly describes the fall of Germany.

There are collections of primary and secondary material in H. L. Trefousse, ed., *What Happened at Pearl Harbor?* (College and University Press Services); George M. Waller, ed., *Pearl Harbor* (D. C. Heath and Co.); and Clarke A. Chambers, ed., *New Deal at Home and Abroad* (Free Press Paperbacks).

DEMOBILIZATION

86

The troops, weary of fighting, came home in 1945 to a country that was both optimistic and worried. Americans believed that they had avoided the pitfalls which had impeded the restoration of peace after World War I, but they remembered the difficulties of the depression all too well and feared that the cost of the world-wide conflict had added unsupportable burdens to the economy.

Two years were enough to show that the outcome would be quite different from that of the earlier conflict. The victors of World War II did not repeat the errors of Versailles, but new international problems kept them from enjoying the fruits of their sacrifices. Peace was still not secure. The system of production, however, did not collapse. Quite the contrary, the country entered upon a prolonged period of growth. Economic changes scarcely noticed during the war had created conditions favorable to expansion in the decades ahead.

474

Planning for Peace

The Atlantic Charter Roosevelt was determined to think through the shape of a future peace settlement even before the United States openly entered the war. He had no desire to repeat Wilson's errors in this respect. In January 1941, the President justified the lend-lease program as a means of defending the Four Freedoms—freedom of speech, freedom of religion, freedom from want, and freedom from fear. On August 14, 1941, he and Churchill agreed upon a general statement of aims in the Atlantic Charter. Renouncing any territorial gains, they described the objectives of the conflict as resistance to aggression, the guarantee of self-government and self-determination for all peoples, freer trade and international cooperation, and provisions to preserve the peace. On January 1, 1942, a Declaration of the United Nations, signed by the United States and its allies, endorsed the Charter and affirmed that they would make no separate peace with the Fascists.

Agreement in those general terms was easy. But to reduce these to specifics required a succession of conferences which gradually hammered out the terms of the future settlement. In January 1943, after the North African landings, Roosevelt and Churchill met in Casablanca. Victory was still a long way off and the partners were not in complete accord on general strategy. But a statement by Roosevelt then called for the unconditional surrender of Germany. The assertion that there would be no negotiated peace reflected the frustrations of the moment. Designed to appeal to popular sentiment in the United States and to quiet Russian suspicions of the Western allies, the announcement complicated the future conduct of the war and drove the Nazis to last-ditch resistance.

The same two leaders met in Quebec in August 1943 and planned the second front in Europe as well as the campaigns in the Far East. They also took the fateful step of recognizing

The Atlantic Conference, 1941

First, their countries seek no aggrandizement, territorial or other;

Second, they desire to see no territorial changes that do not accord with the freely expressed wishes of the peoples concerned;

Third, they respect the right of all peoples to choose the form of government under which they will live; and they wish to see sovereign rights and self-government restored to those who have been forcibly deprived of them;

Fourth, they will endeavor, with due respect for their existing obligations, to further the enjoyment by all states, great or small, victor or vanquished, of access, on equal terms, to the trade and to the raw materials of the world which are needed for their economic prosperity;

Fifth, they desire to bring about the fullest collaboration between all nations in the economic field with the object of securing, for all, improved labor standards, economic advancement, and social security;

Sixth, after the final destruction of the Nazi tyranny, they hope to see established a peace which will afford to all nations the means of dwelling in safety within their own boundaries, and which will afford assurance that all men in all lands may live out their lives in freedom from fear and want;

Seventh, such a peace should enable all men to traverse the high seas and oceans without hindrance;

Eighth, they believe that all of the nations of the world, for realistic as well as spiritual reasons, must come to the abandonment of the use of force.

—Declaration by President Franklin D. Roosevelt and Prime Minister Winston S. Churchill. *Peace and War. United States Foreign Policy, 1931–1941* (Washington: Government Printing Office, 1943), pp. 718–719.

the French Committee of National Liberation under Charles de Gaulle as the government of the French territories then under their control. Roosevelt was unwilling to go further because he wished the people of occupied France to decide their own future and because he distrusted de Gaulle's dictatorial ideas.

Dealing with the Russians Negotiations with the Soviet Union were more delicate. During the summer of 1943 it became clear that the Russians were supporting the claims of Communists against the exile regimes of Poland, Yugoslavia, and Greece recognized by the United States and Britain. The foreign ministers of the three great powers met in Moscow in October 1943 to adjust this issue. They joined in a declaration in favor of an international organization to maintain peace and announced that Austria would be separated from Germany. But the question of the future of Eastern Europe remained in abeyance.

The meeting of Roosevelt, Churchill, and Stalin in Teheran in December 1943 did not resolve the difference in views about the future of Eastern and Central Europe. In Cairo a month earlier the English and American leaders had agreed with Chiang Kai-shek to strip Japan of its conquests, to assure the territorial integrity of China, including Manchuria and Formosa, and to grant Korea independence. At Teheran, Stalin amiably endorsed these terms and promised some day to enter the war in the Far East. He also learned with pleasure about the impending invasion of France. But he insisted on annexing the eastern provinces of Poland, proposing to compensate Poland with German territory, and he would give no assurances about the fate of Eastern Europe when the Soviet Union would be left the only military power there.

These important questions remained unresolved. While the fighting continued, Roosevelt wished to believe that his allies were all peace-loving, democratic states, united by common goals. The Office of War Information and many respectable commentators as well as outright Communist sympathizers were busy building up the impression that the Soviet Union was very much like the United States. It was tempting, therefore, to gloss over the very real differences between the Communist regime and the democracies.

Yalta As the end of the war approached, however, Roosevelt began to brood about the frightening distance between his views and Stalin's. The climactic confrontation came in February 1945 at Yalta. The Soviet Union revealed that it intended to follow its own line, and the United States and Britain, still engaged in war in Germany and in the Pacific, had to yield on important matters.

The public announcements issued after the Yalta meeting concerned military plans for the defeat of Germany and the liquidation of the Nazi regime. The Reich was to be divided into four zones of military occupation (British, Russian, American, and French) and to be charged an enormous reparations bill. Furthermore, the Communist regimes in Poland and Yugoslavia were recognized. The Russians agreed to broaden those governments to include all democratic elements and to hold free elections as soon as possible. In the other liberated areas of Eastern Europe, the Allies would set up interim governmental authorities broadly representative of all democratic elements of the population and pledged to the earliest possible free elections. But the meanings of democratic and of free elections were left undefined.

Agreements not then made public gave each of the great powers a veto in the new international organization and assured the Soviet Union three votes in the General Assembly (one for the Soviet Union and one each for Byelorussia and the Ukraine). The secret understandings dealt also with the Far East. In return for confirming its promise to enter the war, Russia received substantial concessions in China and was promised the part of Sakhalin and the Kuriles held by Japan.

The bargaining weakness of the British and Americans lay in their weariness of war, in their wishful thinking about Stalin's motives, and in

Winston Churchill (seated left), Franklin D. Roosevelt, and Joseph Stalin at the Yalta Conference, February 1945. (Pix, Inc.)

The Fate of Poland

A new situation has been created in Poland as a result of her complete liberation by the Red Army. This calls for the establishment of a Polish Provisional Government which can be more broadly based than was possible before the recent liberation of the western part of Poland. The Provisional Government which is now functioning in Poland should therefore be reorganized on a broader democratic basis with the inclusion of democratic leaders from Poland itself and from Poles abroad. This new Government should then be called the Polish Provisional Government of National Unity . . . .

This Polish Provisional Government of National Unity shall be pledged to the holding of free and unfettered elections as soon as possible on the basis of universal suffrage and secret ballot. In these elections all democratic and anti-Nazi parties shall have the right to take part and to put forward candidates . . . .

The three Heads of Government consider that the Eastern frontier of Poland should follow the Curzon Line with digressions from it in some regions of five to eight kilometers in favor of Poland. They recognize that Poland must receive substantial accessions of territory in the North and West. They feel that the opinion of the new Polish Provisional Government of National Unity should be sought in due course on the extent of these accessions and that the final delimitation of the Western frontier of Poland should thereafter await the Peace Conference.

—Declaration of the Heads of State at Yalta. *Foreign Relations of the United States, The Conferences at Malta and Yalta, 1945* (Washington: Government Printing Office, 1955), p. 980.

Perspective on Yalta, 1947

One should be fair enough to consider the circumstances under which the promises were made. It was six weeks after the serious German counterattack on the western front. Although progress was being made in both the east and the west, neither the President nor anyone else at that time knew how long the Germans could hold out and how many casualties we would suffer before they surrendered. The President had with him at Yalta the Joint Chiefs of Staff. They knew the situation.

The evidence is clear that the agreement was, in great part, a military decision. The military leaders already had their plans for the invasion of Japan under way. They undoubtedly gave the President their estimate of what such an invasion would cost us in human lives with Russia in the war and what the cost would be if Russia were out of the war. They naturally wanted Russia in the war to engage the Japanese armies in the north. But once Stalin knew our plans for invasion were under way, he knew also that we would want his armies and he could demand more for them. Mr. Stalin is not bashful about making demands.

—James F. Byrnes, *Speaking Frankly* (New York: Harper & Row, Publishers, 1947), p. 43.

Strains Among the United Nations

The United Nations Roosevelt's hopes turned, as Wilson's had, on creation of an international organization that would be able to rectify any errors in the peace settlement. At a meeting in Dumbarton Oaks, attended by Secretary of State Cordell Hull, in August and September 1944, preliminary plans for the charter of the United Nations were drafted, and these were modified in detail at Yalta. The charter, formally adopted at the San Francisco Conference (April–June 1945), provided for a General Assembly in which all member nations had one vote each, except the Soviet Union, which had three; for a Security Council of eleven members (five permanent—the United States, the Soviet Union, Britain, France, and China—and six nonpermanent); and for a Secretariat to handle the business of the organization. In addition, an International Court of Justice, an Economic and Social Council, and a Trusteeship Council received specific tasks. The Conference rejected a proposal for universal membership because the admission of countries which did not subscribe to the goals of the United Nations would impede future action. The success of the organization depended upon the extent to which all those who joined it actually were peace loving.

Postwar Communism It was immediately significant that the Soviet foreign minister, Vyacheslav M. Molotov, did not stay at San Francisco to work out the details of the Charter. His country was busy elsewhere. The Russians were systematically stripping the German, Austrian, and Hungarian areas they occupied of industrial equipment and were installing Communist

the conviction of their military leaders that Russian help against Japan was essential. The strength of the Soviet Union sprang from the actual presence of its troops in Eastern Europe and from its willingness to go as far as necessary to get what it wished. The Russian people, too, were tired of the war, but they had no voice in forming the judgments of their leaders. Roosevelt therefore left Yalta with promises, Stalin with power.

Cordell Hull, *Memoirs* (New York, 1948) is an interesting autobiography.

Leland M. Goodrich, *The United Nations* (New York, 1959) has a good account of its development.

James F. Byrnes, *Speaking Frankly* (New York, 1947) contains interesting reflections on the Potsdam Conference by the Secretary of State.

At Dumbarton Oaks, the aging **CORDELL HULL** saw a dream from the past begin to come true. The old Wilsonian hoped, after almost thirty years, to assist at the rebirth of a true league of nations.

Hull was born in a log cabin in the Tennessee mountains in 1871. With only odds and ends of schooling, he became a lawyer and then entered local politics. Enlisting in the army during the Spanish-American War, he arrived in Cuba too late to do any fighting, but he impressed the regiment with a command of language that was the envy of all the sergeants.

In 1907, Hull was elected to the United States House of Representatives, and he served in Congress for a quarter of a century. His ideas were simple; he fought consistently for a low tariff and for a direct tax on wealth, and he adhered to that program throughout his life. Wilson's New Freedom therefore aroused his enthusiasm, and he guided much of the economic legislation between 1913 and 1917 through the House of Representatives. A confirmed prohibitionist, Hull disliked the growing prominence of city people in the Democratic party. He backed Smith in 1928, but in 1932 Franklin Roosevelt seemed the prefer-able alternative. Support for F. D. R. at the Convention and during the election earned Hull the post of Secretary of State.

Hull's tenure of that office explained some of the anomalies of foreign policy after 1933. Roosevelt allowed him to work for easier trade relations and for the good-neighbor policy in Latin America. But control of most other diplomatic policies remained in the hands of the President, who depended for advice on personal friends like Hopkins. With the outbreak of war in Europe, Hull receded ever further into the background; and after Pearl Harbor he was not even included in the meetings of the War Council. His presence as the head of the Department of State gave Congress and the country a pleasant sense of continuity, but Hull made none of the important decisions of the war.

The proposal to form a new international organization, however, had real meaning to a man who vividly recalled Wilson's struggle and defeat in 1919. Hull led the delegation to Dumbarton Oaks and took an active part in framing the plan for the United Nations. That was his last service to his country. He retired after the election of 1944 and died in 1955.

---

regimes in Romania, Yugoslavia, Bulgaria, Poland, and Albania.

The question of free elections and the future of these territories came up at the meeting of the English, American, Russian, and French heads of state at Potsdam (July 17–August 2, 1945). Franklin D. Roosevelt had died on April 12, 1945, and this was his successor's first venture into diplomacy. Harry S Truman was shocked to learn that the Soviet Union had no intention of interpreting its pledges at Yalta other than as devices for installing a chain of satellites along its frontier. The Conference did arrange the details of the German occupation and the terms of the prospective Japanese surrender, but it arrived at no satisfactory formula for the fate of Central Europe.

The Far East In the next two years one incident after another revealed the extent of the differences between the Western powers and the Soviet Union. The American troops came home, to be speedily demobilized, but in March 1947 the United States was still deeply entangled in the affairs of a disordered world.

It alone occupied Japan. The Russians had taken the northern Kuriles but had gained no foothold to the south, where General MacArthur presided over a revolutionary effort to transform

The Iron Curtain, 1945

I have always worked for friendship with Russia, but like you, I feel deep anxiety because of their misinterpretation of the Yalta decisions, their attitude towards Poland, their overwhelming influence in the Balkans excepting Greece, the difficulties they make about Vienna, the combination of Russian power and the territories under their control or occupied, coupled with the Communist technique in so many other countries, and above all their power to maintain very large armies in the field for a long time. What will be the position in a year or two, when the British and American armies have melted and the French has not yet been formed on any major scale, when we may have a handful of divisions mostly French, and when Russia may choose to keep two or three hundred on active service?

An iron curtain is drawn down upon their front. We do not know what is going on behind. There seems little doubt that the whole of the regions east of the line Lübeck-Trieste-Corfu will soon be completely in their hands. To this must be added the further enormous area conquered by the American armies between Eisenach and [the] Elbe, which will I suppose in a few weeks be occupied, when the Americans retreat, by the Russian power. All kinds of arrangements will have to be made by General Eisenhower to prevent another immense flight of the German population westward as this enormous Muscovite advance into the centre of Europe takes place. And then the curtain will descend again to a very large extent if not entirely. Thus a broad band of many hundreds of miles of Russian-occupied territory will isolate us from Poland.

—Prime Minister Churchill to President Truman, May 12. *Foreign Relations of the United States, Conference of Berlin (Potsdam), 1945* (Washington: Government Printing Office, 1960), vol. I, p. 9.

Japanese society. The United States also occupied the islands in the Pacific once held by the Mikado.

China was divided. The United States, throughout the war, had been anxious to maintain that country's territorial integrity and great-power status as a future counterweight to Japan. The Russians had obligingly promised to recognize only the legitimate Kuomintang government of Chiang Kai-shek. Of course, the Chinese Communists retained their own army but, Stalin assured inquirers, they were like radishes, red on the outside only, white on the inside. The Russians had moved into Manchuria to accept the Japanese surrender and somehow when Chiang Kai-shek's officials arrived they found the Chinese Communists installed in control of the country's most important industrial region. The United States had neither the transport nor the troops to help Chiang get control, but it hoped that a coalition government would soon bring the two parties together.

There were troubles also in Southeast Asia. When the Japanese withdrew, local groups in which Communists and nationalists collaborated challenged the return of the French to Indochina, of the Dutch to Indonesia, and of the British to the Malay States. There were similar difficulties in the Philippines. Burma, Pakistan, and India were gaining their independence, and in the Near East the aspirations of the Jews of Palestine for a state of their own complicated the attempt of the Arabs to develop stable modern governments. In all these areas, the United States urged its allies to liquidate the imperialism of the past and to prepare the subject peoples for self-government.

Europe The situation was gravest in continental Europe, which was shattered by war, its economy disrupted and all controls weak. In France, de Gaulle was deep in his long sulk about the Anglo-Saxons. He resented the fact that the

Milton Viorst, *Hostile Allies* (New York, 1965) is an objective analysis of the relations between Roosevelt and de Gaulle.

DOUGLAS MacARTHUR believed in his destiny. Bred to a military career, he was accustomed to being first in whatever he did and insisted on following his own star, whatever the cost. This determination accounted for both his success and his failure.

His father had remained in the army after the Civil War and ultimately rose to the rank of major general. He was a captain when Douglas was born in 1880 in Fort Dodge, Little Rock, Arkansas. The young man early decided to follow in his father's footsteps; he entered West Point in 1899, made a brilliant record there, and graduated first in his class. He served in the Philippines and in Mexico, everywhere attracting favorable attention.

Although he was a regular army man, habituated to discipline, MacArthur insisted upon using his own judgment even when that meant flouting orders. During World War I, for instance, he took Sedan from the Germans, although the battle plan assigned the task to the French. Yet his ability and the brilliance of his style and personality earned him exemption from the ordinary rules.

In the postwar years MacArthur rose steadily in rank until President Hoover appointed him chief of staff in 1930. Two years later General MacArthur was involved in the disagreeable process of clearing the bonus marchers from Anacostia. There was some criticism of the harshness of the measure, but MacArthur was only obeying the President.

From 1935 to 1941, MacArthur commanded the Philippine army as well as American troops stationed on the islands. Proud of the training he gave these forces, he underestimated the threat from Japan, and his planes, trapped on the runways of Clark Field, met the same fate as the ships at Pearl Harbor. There followed the long disheartening retreat southward to Australia and months of impatient waiting while American energies focused on the war in Europe. But in the end MacArthur did return, as he had promised, not only to the Philippines but also to the deck of the U.S.S. *Missouri*, where he received the Japanese surrender.

MacArthur's greatest success was as peacetime commander of the occupation forces in Japan. His imperious presence, his firmness, his tolerance of the Japanese, and his executive ability furthered the reconstruction of the devastated islands. Japan emerged in the 1950s more prosperous than ever before and with a sound foundation of democratic institutions. The distribution of land to the peasants ended tenancy and also increased the food supply.

The Korean War brought MacArthur back into the field. He led the successful counterattack that advanced almost to the Yalu River, but he misjudged the intentions of the Chinese Communists. His unwillingness to yield to the constitutional authority of the President forced his retirement in 1951. He lived on in bitterness until 1964.

United States had continued diplomatic relations with Vichy in the first years of the war and had dealt with local officials during the North African invasion, and he feared the loss of the French empire. Meanwhile, domestic turmoil persisted, for victory did not heal the basic internal divisions in France. More Frenchmen lost their lives after 1945 for having been Nazi collaborators than fell in battle in 1940. Furthermore, de Gaulle held power by the tolerance of the Communists, who commanded the loyalty of one-third of the voters. The Communists were strong in Italy, too, and both countries suffered serious economic hardships that raised the specter of revolution.

The four powers still occupied Germany. Berlin, deep in the Soviet zone and divided among them, had no free communications with

Harbin, Manchuria, August 1945. Japanese soldiers stack ammunition that is to be turned over to the Red Army. Photograph by A. Novikov. (Sovfoto)

the West. The Russians obstructed every effort at reconstruction or unification, refusing to accept the proposal of a treaty to demilitarize Germany for forty years. It appeared that the occupying American troops would have to remain where they were for years. In the East, moreover, the Russians strengthened their grip on the satellites, the Comintern reappeared after having gone underground during the war, revolution erupted in Greece, and there were menacing gestures toward Turkey and Iran. Even in Latin America, which had proclaimed its solidarity with the United States in the conference at Rio de Janeiro (January 1942) and in the Act of Chapultepec (February 1945), military dictatorships and the threat of revolution gave cause for concern. The fighting was over, but peace was a long time away.

Russian Soldiers in Berlin Pose for Pictures to Send to Their Folks at Home, 1945.
(Robert Capa, Magnum)

A War Economy

In the face of this gloomy outlook, Americans could take unexpected pleasure in the development of their economy since 1939. Military orders had begun to boost output that year. Then the war dramatically revived the whole productive system.

The Changing Economic Outlook Pearl Harbor dissolved opposition to involvement in the conflict. The isolationists could not oppose the struggle thrust upon the United States. The character of the enemy regimes united all liberal opinion behind the war effort. Even the Communists became patriots, once the Soviet Union was on the same side. Above all, the shock of the Japanese attack created a general sense of determination to win which invigorated the society in the years that followed. And the long count of casualties deepened that determination into a willingness to pay the price of victory.

There were now no limits to the power of the government. Whatever was needed to win became possible; no vested rights stood in the way of the war effort. Individuals still sought to further their own interests, but all accepted controls on prices, wages, and profits as a matter of course, and labor and capital understood the necessity for collaboration. The unions gained in membership as the nation recognized their status, and their leaders filled important administrative positions in the government.

A sound fiscal policy financed the war. Heavy sales of bonds, directly to the public and through intermediary bankers, took in substantial amounts and also kept inflation within reasonable limits. The $45,500,000,000 in savings bonds outstanding in 1945 drew out of circulation funds that might otherwise have raised commodity prices. At the same time the bonds created the resources for expenditures deferred until goods were available. Taxes on incomes rose, and were accompanied by new levies on excess and undistributed profits. The result was further restraint on inflation and some redistribution of income, since rising wages were less affected than increased dividends.

Government became the largest single consumer in the economy. Its expenditures, which even in the New Deal days had not gone above $8,000,000,000 annually, zoomed to $100,000,000,000. Every sector of the productive system was geared to the needs of war. Military requirements made the hit-and-miss methods of the past dangerous. Planning and a system of priorities to allocate scarce materials were indispensable. The result was a perceptible rise in efficiency.

The intermingling of military and industrial operations changed the character of business leadership. There was no place for the individualistic entrepreneur of the past. The person who did well was one able to find his way through military and civil government circles and familiar enough with law to deal with complex tax problems. An interchangeable personnel filled the top positions in industry, government, law, and politics. The developing industrial-military-governmental alliance was willing to make a place for labor, and was more concerned with efficient organization than with individual gain.

The Revival of Production All the indices showed a steady rise in output. The gross national product, which had fallen below $100,000,000,000 after 1929, regained that level in 1940 and in 1945 had gone above $213,000,000,000. The labor force rose from 45 million in 1940 to

Federal Finances, 1940–1945

(in billion dollars)

	Total Expenditures	Income and Profit Taxes	Deficit	National Debt
1940	8.9	2.1	3	42
1941	12.7	3.4	5	48
1942	32.3	7.9	19	72
1943	78.1	16.0	55	136
1944	93.7	34.6	49	201
1945	100.4	35.1	53	258

W. S. Woytinsky, et al., *Employment and Wages in the United States* (New York, 1953) is an economic study.

64 million in 1945. Furthermore, American manufacturing inherited from the war a modernized plant and new equipment. Often the government had underwritten the cost in order to procure the desired product. At the end of the war it was the actual owner of more than 50 percent of the capacity for making synthetic rubber, aircraft, aluminum, and machine tools and of more than 3000 miles of oil pipe lines. Alternatively, it had guaranteed loans or made substantial tax adjustments to aid industrial expansion. Even without such aid the security of government contracts sometimes had been sufficient to guarantee the building of new plants.

Businessmen, moreover, regained their assurance. The defensive sense of frustration from which they had suffered in the 1930s gave way to confidence, buttressed by the knowledge that their activity was patriotic as well as profitable. They were aware also of the pent-up spending power of Americans, who had long been postponing purchases. Manufacturers looked forward to a waiting civilian market once military requirements ceased to be pressing. A sudden and not wholly explicable reversal in the trend of the birth rate was also a cause of cautious optimism. The steady decline stopped in 1942. The rise of the next five years was encouraging, whether it reflected a permanent new population trend or was just temporary.

There was no speculative orgy toward the end of this conflict as there had been in 1918 and 1919. Memories of the depression were still fresh, and investors, though optimistic, were wary, particularly since some branches of the economy were vulnerable. The railroads, for example, carried heavy traffic and yielded substantial profits, but their equipment was deteriorating and their efficiency declined.

The improved condition of agriculture paralleled the experience of earlier wars. The loss of man power put renewed emphasis on mechanization, and expanded demand reduced surpluses. Prices and output rose. Yet the question lingered in 1945 whether another farm depression would follow this boom.

International trade revived. The United States had to supply its own forces overseas and also those of its allies throughout the world. In addition, it was obliged through UNRRA, the United Nations Relief and Rehabilitation Administration (1943), to aid the civilian populations of all the war-torn countries. The volume of exports grew steadily, as did the size of the merchant fleet.

The war offered the occasion for reform of the international monetary system, which had been in disorder more than ten years. An international conference at Bretton Woods (1944) laid the foundation for the International Monetary Fund, through which the United States undertook to release international trade from dependence either on specie as before 1932, or on barter as in the 1930s. It would do so by maintaining a constant relationship between gold and the dollar (at $35 an ounce) so that all nations could use their dollar holdings like gold to settle their accounts. But in 1947, with all the world's currency still in disorder, there was no telling how well the system would work.

Conversion to Peace

There was, therefore, cause for trepidation at the end of the war. Americans who remembered the earlier postwar period believed that some readjustment was inevitable, but they wished to limit its repercussions as much as possible. Efforts to devise a plan for demobilization began shortly after the defeat of Germany, in the hope that the American economy would be ready by the time Japan surrendered. The government's program called for the retention of wartime controls until the completion of gradual demobilization. Otherwise, it was feared, the inundation of the labor market by returned veterans would create vast unemployment.

The plan did not work out as expected. Pressure mounted to bring the boys home soon after the war ended. Demobilization was rapid. By the end of 1946 fewer than 2 million men remained in the army, and the other services had shrunk almost proportionately. Nor were production, price, or wage controls long retained. Peace soon justified a return to business as usual. Labor wanted relief from wartime restraints against higher wages, and manufacturers wanted to return promptly to production for the civilian market. Everyone was tired of controls.

Rationing was first to go. Its disappearance immediately threatened the whole pattern of fixed prices. A thriving black market appeared as shortages of consumer goods grew less tolerable. Prices rose, legally or illegally; and a succession of strikes made known labor's demands for pay raises. The system of controls speedily unraveled.

Yet the depression did not come. Instead, the two years after the war were exceedingly prosperous. The mass of consumers eagerly awaiting goods had the means to absorb the rising output of industry. In 1947, the country, far from having entered upon a decline, was actually beginning a boom, with a steady growth in wealth and productive power. That would be a substantial resource for the future.

▼

The complex reasons for the resumption of economic expansion were not fully understood in 1947. Americans ascribed their good fortune of the moment to stored-up demands and to the need for reconstruction. They were cautious rather than speculative in estimates of the future. To that extent it was well that they did not quite comprehend the ultimate economic effects of a rising population and of the increased rational-ization of their productive system. As it was, they demobilized with surprisingly little strain.

On the other hand, the speed with which they did so hampered them in dealing with the rapidly changing world situation. The haste to get out of uniform and to return to peaceful pursuits nurtured the wish-fulfilling belief that reason and persuasion would resolve the remaining problems of Europe and Asia. Only slowly and reluctantly did Americans learn to interpret the disconcerting indications of trouble ahead. Their ability to do so depended on the extent to which they had absorbed the social impact of depression and war.

Paperbacks for Further Reading

Herbert Feis, *Churchill — Roosevelt — Stalin* (Princeton University Press) is a general survey of wartime diplomacy. There is a vivid account of foreign policy in Robert E. Sherwood, *Roosevelt and Hopkins* (Universal Library). William L. Langer, *Our Vichy Gamble* (W. W. Norton & Company, Inc.) takes a sympathetic view of American policy. John L. Snell, *The Meaning of Yalta* (Louisiana State University Press) is a clear analysis, and there is a collection of divergent views in R. F. Fenno, ed., *The Yalta Conference* (D.C. Heath and Co.). Herbert Feis, *Between War and Peace* (Princeton University Press) is a history of the Potsdam Conference. George N. Shuster, *UNESCO* (Harper Torchbooks) is an optimistic treatment of a specialized United Nations agency. Herbert Feis, *The China Tangle* (Atheneum Publishers) covers the years from 1941 to 1945. W. L. Neumann, *America Encounters Japan* (Harper Colophon Books) provides historical background for the occupation. There is material on the whole period in Gaddis Smith, *American Diplomacy During the Second World War* (John Wiley & Sons, Inc.).

COMMUNITIES
UNDER PRESSURE

87

Long depression and bitter warfare seriously weakened institutions that were already in disorder after a half century of change. Few American communities in 1929 were in a position to withstand the dislocations of extended unemployment or of the enlistment of many of their young men and women in the armed forces. The family, the church, and other associations adjusted painfully or not at all to the new circumstances. Peace found these institutions unstable and desperately in need of guidelines. By contrast, the power of government expanded steadily, but the state did not abuse its authority. Its prominent role in the lives of its citizens was, however, a marked departure from the social experience of the past.

Delinquency

THE SMOG THAT SHUT OUT the skies over American cities in the 1930s was symbolic of the deterioration of their society. The factories rarely operated near capacity, yet the stagnant air cast a pall over streets and buildings in want of repair, over men out of work, over communities that had ceased to give their members security.

The Inadequacies of the Family Gloomy complaints about failures of family life had long been familiar in American history. But the 1930s seemed to confirm the forebodings of the pessimists. The depression intensified the earlier sources of tension and sustained the trend of the 1920s.

The roles of all members of the family became ambiguous. Prolonged periods of unemployment deprived the husband of his function as breadwinner and weakened his authority in the home, particularly since his wife and children sometimes found menial jobs more readily than he. Women assumed new responsibilities and the heightened powers that went with them. The difficulty of finding jobs extended the period of adolescence and of expected dependency. Young couples, compelled to live with parents because of their inability to pay the rent for quarters of their own, could not develop the connubial relationship their culture defined as normal. The aged, too, attached themselves to the family unit. The mortality rates continued to decline, as in previous decades, falling from 11.79 per thousand in 1929 to about 10 per thousand in 1947. Advances in medical science increased the number of the elderly people at a time when they were not capable of supporting themselves, and this added further strains.

To escape the weight of these common burdens, individuals often struck out on their own. The high divorce rate was not simply a product of lax legislation. It reflected impatience with

Howard M. Bell, *Youth Tell Their Story* (Washington, 1938) throws light on the effects of depression.

Unemployment and Family Life, 1931

Losing faith and confidence in some one you have leaned upon and trusted is about the worst thing that can come to a human being. When unemployment comes, the husband and wife most often face the situation together. But this unity changes as the wife is harried by debt collectors, the rent man, the insurance man. She sees the children half fed and getting thin, often sick, and needing clothes she can't buy; and then, too, she may be working herself and adding fatigue to worry. In the first days of her husband's job-hunt she is sympathetic and fights to keep his courage up and defends him in the neighborhood. The poignancy of his struggle has not been lost in her own discouragement. I remember when Mrs. White came round to tell of her husband's first pay envelope after nearly a winter's search. "You know," she said, "the look in his face when he give it to me was like a child with a Christmas present." But that was his first winter out. Now, facing the third one, the Whites no longer present a united front. She doesn't believe he tries and is bitter against him, and he no longer cares very much, for he has the gang and is "in on the bottle as it is handed around," and only comes home late to sleep. The strain and disappointment vent themselves in wrangles. As Mrs. White puts it, "There were no ugly words in our house when he was workin', but I'm so tired now I don't know what I'm saying." And to come home from anything as disheartening as "makin' the rounds" only to be accused of not really trying doesn't make for harmony.

—Helen Hall, "Introducing Our Neighbors," as quoted in Clarke A. Chambers, ed., *The New Deal at Home and Abroad, 1929–1945* (New York: The Free Press of Glencoe, 1965), vol. VIII, pp. 43–44.

Riveters, Douglas Aircraft Plant, Santa Monica, California. Women made up 90 percent of the workers in this tail cone assembly department at one period during World
War II. (Brown Brothers)

family obligations or inability to meet them. Moreover, the scant population increase (from 138 million in 1930 to 150 million in 1940) was evidence of postponed marriages and falling birth rates. Improved techniques of contraception permitted families to delay the obligations of rearing children. The result was a loosening of ties that encouraged easy divorce and desertion when the course of marriage ceased to run smoothly.

The relaxation of sexual mores that had begun early in the century accelerated. The traditional beliefs and practices of the past faded and left the individual subject to few restraints other than those he imposed on himself. The war deepened further the problem left by depression. Marriages and divorces were both hastier. Millions of men moved into camps, some far overseas, where there were few guides to proper conduct. They left behind lonely women, many of whom found employment in war plants and learned to get by on their own. The enlistment of thousands of girls in the WAVES, the WACS, and the other branches of the service for women also broke down the concept of a distinctive feminine role.

Crime The slackening of family ties and discipline created forms of delinquency more dangerous to society than those involved in personal morality. The gun and the auto had put power in the hands of potential criminals. The depression made them desperate. Old-

Virgil W. Peterson, *Barbarians in Our Midst* (Boston, 1952) exposes the crime of the period.

Repeal, 1933

SECTION 1. The eighteenth article of amendment to the Constitution of the United States is hereby repealed.

SECTION 2. The transportation or importation into any State, Territory, or possession of the United States for delivery or use therein of intoxicating liquors, in violation of the laws thereof, is hereby prohibited.

SECTION 3. This article shall be inoperative unless it shall have been ratified as an amendment to the Constitution by conventions in the several States, as provided in the Constitution, within seven years from the date of the submission thereof to the States by the Congress.

—Twenty-first Amendment, passed by Congress, February 20, 1933; ratified, December 5, 1933.

fashioned robbers like John Dillinger sporadically shot up banks for whatever loot they needed and drifted violently from crisis to crisis until they themselves met a lethal bullet. The kidnappers and thieves whose misdeeds enlivened the daily press were detached men, guided by no coherent purpose or plan, who vented their fury on the society that failed to reward them.

More calculating personalities systematically organized criminal violence. The end of prohibition did not dissolve the gangs of the 1920s. They found new outlets for their energies—sometimes in legitimate business, but more often in the illicit sale of drugs, controlled prostitution, labor racketeering, and above all gambling, which grew steadily in volume. With Al Capone's imprisonment in 1931, control of his Chicago mob passed to a directorate of which Frank Nitti

and Jake Guzik were leaders. Frank Costello, Charles (Lucky) Luciano, and Dandy Phil Kastel ran a powerful operation out of New York which sometimes cooperated with Louis (Lepke) Buchhalter's Murder Incorporated. The Binaggio crowd tied up Kansas City, and scores of lesser outfits worked other communities.

In the public image, the FBI was engaged in relentless pursuit of these criminals. In fact, although the G-Men occasionally hunted down a notorious public enemy like Dillinger, the main burden of law enforcement fell to ineffective local police authority. While an ambitious prosecutor like Thomas E. Dewey of New York could hunt out the evidence to secure convictions, the usual preference was to let matters alone unless they boiled over scandalously: another set of crooks would only take the place of those jailed. That attitude reflected the apathy of the public, who might be roused to occasional indignation but who had no qualms about patronizing the gangsters. Prohibition, traffic violations, and gambling had already habituated Americans to minor infractions of the law.

Varieties of Failure Many more people were socially delinquent than were ever formally charged with a criminal offense. The depression blocked off the pattern of life considered normal by accepted values—to grow up, get a job, marry, have a home. The boys on the street corners often would not settle for the relief checks that kept their unemployed fathers going. By 1932, hundreds of thousands of youths wandered about the country, hopping rides on freight cars in the company of the hobos, who also had nowhere to go.

But even men who remained where they were, immobilized by resignation or despair, were delinquent insofar as they were unable to perform the first duty of earning a livelihood. The continuing discrepancy between what they could do and what they should do made them conscious of defeat. Until the war gave every man a place in the ranks or the plants, they were at fault in their own eyes if not in those of the law.

Muted Authority

The Churches The absence of authoritative external sanctions deepened the dilemmas of personal behavior. The churches in the 1930s passed into a crisis so deep that few clergymen or laymen were willing to examine it. The end of immigration affected some sects adversely by depriving them of the connection with Europe which had formerly replenished their ranks with devout tradition-oriented communicants. Lutherans, Catholics, and Jews, thrown back on their own resources, then faced the same unsettled future as denominations that had not depended upon additions from abroad.

Most churches had by now adjusted to the intellectual challenge of scientific knowledge. They had surrendered their claim to speak with authority in the areas in which science claimed competence—astronomy, for instance, and sociology, medicine, and politics. That left the rather remote subjects of ethics and metaphysics as the provinces of religion.

Within these spheres, too, modernity exerted great pressure upon orthodoxy. Priests and ministers, challenged to be up to date, tried to answer the political and social questions that troubled their flocks. Father Charles Coughlin and Monsignor John A. Ryan represented quite different Catholic responses to such issues, while some Protestants still heeded the call of the Social Gospel and a few flirted with the socialism and the communism of the radical left. But these clerics delivered the same messages as their secular counterparts. The added creedal elements, practically speaking, made no difference to those addressed. Religion could be accepted or not, at the wish of the individual, as another variety of benevolence.

The Faithful The total rejection of modernity enabled the fundamentalists to hold firm to their faith. Marginal social groups resisted any

crack in the crust of tradition. Negroes, immigrants, and the depressed back-country rural folk clutched fiercely to the gospel of their forefathers. Isolated from the dominant social tendencies of the times, either by their own choice or by segregation, they did not have to test their beliefs in the outer world.

The same groups provided a seed ground for new sects. The membership of the Jehovah's Witnesses increased as their gospel of immediate redemption, first proclaimed in 1872, acquired new relevance. Thousands of Americans sought the consolation of knowing that millions of the living would never die. The assurance of a second coming was explanation enough for all problems.

So too, the movement begun by Father Divine among the depressed Negro population of the eastern seaboard cities acquired white adherents as well. A scheme of cooperation gave it an economic base, and it preached a message of social justice, racial equality, and everlasting life.

Only in these groups did the commitment to faith give churches the vitality to resist erosion by depression and war. The sects sustained values that assisted their own members in dealing with their problems, but such authority satisfied only a minority of Americans.

The Need to Belong

Men in Motion Voluntary associations of almost every sort suffered during the depression and the war. Millions of Americans shifted their residences either because drought or economic change forced them off their farms or because job opportunities drew them elsewhere. Although the tired Okies of the 1930s gave way to the hopeful war-plant workers of the 1940s, the general drift was always northward and westward. The growth of the Negro population in the industrial cities was the most dramatic evi-

Samuel C. Kincheloe, *Research Memorandum on Religion in the Depression* (New York, 1937) is an interesting contemporary analysis.

Sara Harris, *Father Divine, Holy Husband* (New York, 1953) is a well-written account.

Father Divine with a Group of His Followers at the Krum Elbow Estate on the Hudson River, August 9, 1938. (Wide World Photos)

GEORGE BAKER was born in 1877 on Hutchinson Island in the Savannah River. He had no education or profession. Like many other Negroes at the time, he lived by odd jobs, drifting as far north as Pennsylvania, then back to Georgia. Occasionally he preached to congregations of the placeless — people who, like himself, needed faith because they had nothing else. Variously, he was a disciple of Sam Morris (Father Jehovia) and of John Hickerson, who taught "Live ever, die never."

By 1909, Baker had acquired a following of his own in Valdosta, Georgia. He was God and those who believed in him would never die. Five years later he moved to New York; and the word spread through the South that he would find jobs for and protect colored people who joined him in his heaven. His flock grew.

In 1931, the judge who sentenced him to jail as a public nuisance promptly died of a heart attack. "I hated to do it," said Father Divine (as he now called himself). Whether it was because of that demonstration of his godhood or because of the onset of the depression, his Kingdom of Peace flourished. Primitive communism and equality were his basic principles. Father Divine's followers shared their earnings in a primitive cooperation, and they simply denied the reality of color. That some people were dark complected and others not was irrelevant. At the great

(Continued on next page)

(Continued from preceding page)

feasts, there was room for all who greeted each other, "Peace, it's wonderful."

For the Negroes bewildered by the city way of life, Father Divine supplied a redeeming discipline. Those who believed in him abjured sex, tobacco, liquor, and cosmetics; they worked hard and used no obscene language; they attended no movies or plays and accepted no tips. They therefore found jobs even when others were unemployed, and they dutifully handed over their wages to the common fund. If their master rode about in a Rolls Royce and wore $500 silk suits, that was his due. In return he provided them with bread, guidance, and faith.

In time, many whites sought membership in the Kingdom, among them people of means who made their wealth over to "God." The cult operated heavens in New York, New Jersey, Pennsylvania, Illinois, and California. And Father Divine himself lived on a great estate near Philadelphia, where he died in 1965.

Hymn to the Prejudiced, 1930s

If you live on the face of this earth from now on,
You are going to enact the Bill of Rights;
You are going to sit side by side with the one
You spurned in your arrogance and selfish might.

You will see that each has the same hopes and desires,
The same ambitions, the same thoughts—the same prayers as you;
You will see each living soul has a heart just like yours—
That is, if GOD lets you live to see it through.

—Father Divine. As quoted in Sara Harris, *Father Divine, Holy Husband* (New York: Doubleday & Company, Inc., 1953), p. 177.

dence of this migration. But Southern whites, too, participated in the trend, and the states of the Pacific coast drew population from every part of the country.

Unsettlement weakened people's connections with their communities. Transients, not knowing how long they would stay, often did not bother to join social, cultural, and philanthropic organizations. In the hard times of the 1930s, lack of funds reduced the strength of all fraternal societies. The end of immigration deprived ethnic associations of the influx of potential members. Above all, the radical extension of government services pre-empted activities that had formerly fallen to voluntary groups. The relief measures enacted after 1933 soon outdistanced private aid, and in time social security made the insurance and benefit plans of many lodges unnecessary. Even cultural and social activities receded in importance as the Federal government took a role in those areas through the WPA (Works Progress Administration). The result was a sense of drift. The collapse of old organizations created a vacuum and left many individuals with an unsatisfied desire for something to join.

Radicalism satisfied that need for some of the rebellious. The Communist party and its

Marxist rivals offered a cause and a spiritual homeland to intellectuals outraged by the failures of capitalism, to workers confused by the drive for labor organization, and to goodhearted people anxious to protest against war or fascism or racism or such domestic injustices as occurred in the case of the nine Negro Scottsboro boys accused of rape in 1931. But the New Deal enlisted the enthusiasm of most such Americans, and the totals drawn to radicalism remained relatively small.

The Uses of Prejudice People who longed to be part of a group sometimes found no other common bond than the ability to exclude others. The depression heightened the need to belong and also strengthened existing prejudices against racial, religious, and national minorities. With places difficult to secure, discrimination in jobs and in the professions became open and systematic. Quotas limited the entry of Jews and Italians into medical schools. Restrictive covenants kept desirable residential neighborhoods free of outsiders, and clubs, restaurants, hotels, and resorts rigorously excluded guests of presumed inferior stock. Like other minorities, Negroes suffered from the effects, but they endured in addition riots in the North and violence and legal segregation in the South.

Forms of Nationalism In the traditional rural regions of the South, an old-fashioned demagogue like Theodore "The Man" Bilbo played upon the emotions of his audience with meaningless eloquence. But elsewhere orators purveyed a novel gospel based on extreme nationalism. To the displaced millions who longed for solidarity as a means of offsetting their loneliness, the new leaders offered the comradeship, the discipline, and even the uniform of an army and a brotherhood based on national, and often racial, unity. And to those who sought scapegoats for their troubles, the minorities offered convenient victims.

The Silver Shirts, led by William Dudley Pelley, enlisted thousands of members in an openly fascist organization. George Christians' White Shirts were their rivals. Millions of Ameri-

---

The depression hit few places as hard as it hit the state of Mississippi. The lack of industry, low cotton prices, share cropping, tenancy, and racial bitterness brought misery to the land. In 1930 an absolute majority of the population had no gainful employment. This social context explains the Senatorial career of **THEODORE G. BILBO.**

Bilbo was born in 1877 in Juniper Grove, Mississippi. Despite his family's poverty he managed to get some schooling and then tried to work his way ahead. He made a stab at law, got a preacher's license, and ran a girl's boarding school, but the country was just too poor to make any profession but politics profitable.

For Bilbo, the prize of government office, with its access to public funds, justified every tactic. On the stump, he sang hymns, played the melodeon, preached, and attacked the interests. Dressed in a loud, checked suit, he flashed the diamond horseshoe in his red necktie and snapped his red suspenders as he laid into the enemy, with no holds barred. In 1928, he kept Mississippi Democratic with the fanciful charge that Herbert Hoover had once danced with a Negro woman named Mary Booze.

Bilbo was twice governor and had held various other state offices when he was elected to the United States Senate in 1934. He had bankrupted the state and wrecked its educational system. But although he had served only one brief term in jail, he had not done well for himself and he hoped that opportunities would be more promising in Washington. White supremacy and relief for the cotton farmer were the two planks of his platform, and endless empty speech was his weapon. He filibustered to

(Continued on next page)

(Continued from preceding page)

death antilynching and antipoll tax bills, fought much of the New Deal program, talked about sending 12,000,000 Negroes back to Africa, and made a general nuisance of himself. "The Bilbonic Plague" was not the harshest of the epithets applied to him.

During World War II he found his chances and took them. A Senate investigating committee ruled that Bilbo had improperly used his office for personal gain in dealings with war contractors. He died in 1947, still under a cloud but still popular among the voters whose resentments, fears, and hatreds he had expressed.

---

cans joined scores of associations of this sort. Some people no doubt enrolled out of commitment to the particular program the organization espoused. They were fascist or anti-Catholic or anti-Semitic. But many more joined out of the much simpler desire merely to belong to some organized effort that promised to compensate for the frustrations of their own lives.

These groups were never able to coalesce into a single movement, despite General George Van Horn Moseley's efforts to persuade them to do so at a meeting in Philadelphia in 1937. They were too disparate to find a common ground for action although they sometimes pursued common devils. In addition to groups whose membership was native and Protestant in origin, there were similar organizations that attracted minorities. Fritz Kuhn's German-American Bund contained many recent immigrants, and the Christian Front, which enjoyed the support of the Reverend Charles Coughlin after his disillusionment with the New Deal, attracted many Irish-Americans. The inability to draw these diverse elements together prevented the development of a fascist party such as seized power in Germany or Italy.

Bilbo Preaches, 1934

Friends, fellow citizens, brothers and sisters — hallelujah. — My opponent — yea, this opponent of mine who has the dastardly, dew-lapped, brazen, sneering, insulting and sinful effrontery to ask you for your votes without telling you the people of this almighty state of Mississippi what he is a-going to do with them if he gets them — this opponent of mine says he don't need a platform. Why does he ask you for your votes? He asks, my dear brethren and sisters, that you vote for him because he is standing by the President. Standing by the President, folks! So am I. But I'm doing better by you, folks, than that. I'm a-standing right smack on his corns, folks, lest he forget the great sovereign Magnolia state of Ole Miss. . . . I shall be the servant and senator of all the people of Mississippi, brothers and sisters. I shall know no North, no South, no East, no West. The appeal and petition of the humblest citizen, yea, whether he comes from the black prairie lands of the east or the alluvial lands of the fer-tile delta; whether he comes, yea, from the vermillion hills of north Mississippi or the sun-kissed shores of the Gulf of Mexico, yea, he will be heard by my heart and my feet shall be swift. But listen to fair warning, brethren and sisters: Don't you go a-sending me up there to Washington to be anything but your servant, your voice that will never cease to ring down the great, gray marble corridors of our Capitol, your Senator whose thoughts will not wander from the humble, God-fearing cabins of Vinegar Bend . . . —don't go a-sending me to those mighty classic halls of government, if you don't want that kind of a man.

—Quoted in Walter Davenport, "Brethren and Sisters," *Colliers* (March 16, 1935), p. 53.

German Day on Long Island, August 29, 1937. The celebration drew 25,000 persons to Yaphank, New York, for a day of marching, picnicking, and speechmaking. Marchers are shown giving the Nazi salute during part of the program, which was sponsored by the German-American Bund. (Wide World Photos)

Nationalism also took forms less virulent than fascism. The American Legion, along with many patriotic societies, tried to combat subversive ideas and supported activities that expressed the country's unity. But given the actual diversity of the population's origins, nationalism as often drove people apart as it pulled them together. During the Ethiopian War (1935), for example, Mussolini became a hero to Italian-Americans and Emperor Haile Selassie to Negroes. The plight of their coreligionists in Europe drew many Jews to Zionism and led to the adoption in 1943 of a program favoring creation of a Jewish state in Palestine.

The war eased some of the tensions expressed in these movements by giving everyone common foreign enemies and a cause in which all could join. The fact that the foes were fascists discredited the peddlers of similar ideas in the United States, and Roosevelt's articulation of the objectives of the struggle identified Americanism with freedom. Besides, prosperity relieved some of the anxieties that had formerly driven men into the nationalist or fascist ranks.

Social Reconstruction

The forces that counteracted social disorder were slow to assert themselves. The labor movement gradually acquired a communal character; education opened some opportunities to youth; and government began to recognize its responsibilities for social reconstruction.

Labor as a Way of Life Organized labor supplied its members with a satisfying means of fulfilling the desire to belong. The craft unions had inherited fraternal and benevolent features from the nineteenth century. Moreover, they often had an ethnic character, particularly after the depression put a premium on skilled jobs that passed on to sons and relatives. The activities of such groups readily spread from the purely economic to the social.

More impressive was the effort of the new industrial unions to create a sense of community among their diverse members. The sufferings and the bloodshed of costly strikes for recognition imbued the rank and file with the solidarity of crusaders in a righteous cause. Leaders who had themselves been workers sought to give the struggle a noble meaning and to make the outcome a better way of life for the participants.

The International Ladies' Garment Workers Union felt the effects of these convictions. In the 1930s it consisted of people of many ancestries— about 50 percent Italian, about 30 percent Jewish, and the rest a variety of stocks. Yet the Union persistently tried to go beyond bargaining on behalf of its members and sought to supply their cultural and personal needs as well. It published a bimonthly in English, Yiddish, Italian, French, and Spanish editions. An education department conducted courses in many subjects and brought lecturers to its forums. An athletic program served some members, instruction in music and dancing, others. The Union produced plays, arranged picnics, and operated a health service and vacation resort.

The newer organizations in automobiles, steel, and rubber emulated the ILGWU. The right to organize, gained with much difficulty, meant more than a means of getting a little more pay for a little less work. Those who had fought for the union wished it to fill a good part of their lives. In the context of the depression years, the aspiration was realistic.

The Opportunity to Learn   The great expansion of education after 1929 was partly inadvertent and wholly unplanned. The mere fact of the depression made jobs difficult to find and produced a tendency to postpone the school-leaving age. More young people completed their education simply because they had nothing else

Joel I. Seidman, *The Needle Trades* (New York, 1942) touches on the social aspects of unionism.

to do. The percentage who remained through high school and then completed college increased rapidly. Some relief measures helped. The NYA (National Youth Administration), for example, provided part-time jobs which in effect subsidized students without means so that they could complete their training.

The result was a substantial stimulus to social mobility. The depression brought immediate hardships to many, but through education it opened exciting opportunities to those earlier excluded from the possibility of advancement. The war completed the process by its leveling effect on those who passed through the ranks. And after the peace, the G.I. Bill of Rights (1944) permitted numerous veterans to complete their education and to move into the professions.

The Role of Government   Finally, the broadening of the power of government created a basis for dealing with some of the social problems inherited from the past and created by the depression. The repeal of prohibition (1933) was not a withdrawal from social involvement but the liquidation of an unfortunate experiment. The New Deal asserted the competence of the states and the nation to deal with poverty and communal disorder, and fashioned instruments the full use of which would come after 1947.

Some of the developments of the 1930s were tentative and temporary—for instance, the cultural experiments of the WPA writers' and actors' projects. Others had long-range implications. The responsibility for social security and employment forced the government to deal, though very hesitantly, with family disorganization. Officials administering relief learned to cooperate with the voluntary agencies already involved in such problems. By the same token, during the war the government established close connections with the Red Cross and with the private organizations that collaborated in the USO (United Service Organizations). A new pattern developed in which government aided work on important social problems but did not itself pre-empt the field.

The New Deal also edged into an effort to resolve the ethnic causes of conflict. The objective of the Dawes Act (1887) — to dissolve tribal organizations, disperse communal land, and assimilate the Indians in the rest of the population — had not been attained. Between 1887 and 1934 the Indians had deeded away 90,000,000 of their 132,000,000 acres and were no better off than before. Under the Roosevelt Administration, the Department of the Interior shifted to the policy of helping the Indians to retain their traditional tribal forms, and the Wheeler-Howard Act of 1934 enabled them to protect their common landholdings.

The consciousness that distinctive group life was worth preserving animated other aspects of the New Deal also, and was joined to the defense of individual rights. Each man could be what he was, yet deserved equal treatment by society. All the minorities could act together in defense of this principle. Roosevelt's faith in the common man lent it support, and the prominence of the children of immigrants in his entourage gave it political momentum.

The immediate results were slim. Even the protracted effort to enact a Federal antilynching law failed, but the New Dealers hoped to correct social inequities indirectly. Since they believed that economic exploitation was at the root of prejudice, they expected that the abatement of poverty and the elimination of social injustice would cure all other maladjustments. Meanwhile they created an expectation of change and mobilized behind it the support of most of the growing labor movement.

The war accelerated progress toward equality because fascism exemplified the extreme application of racist theories. The United States did not resort to the blatant propaganda of World War I. Nor did it maltreat German and Italian enemy aliens. The Japanese-Americans did suffer a shameful fate. In January 1942, the Pacific coast delegation in Congress pressed for the mass evacuation of 100,000 Japanese, including those who were citizens. The prejudiced military commander in California — pleading

Justice for the Indians, 1934

We can and should, without further delay, extend to the Indian the fundamental rights of political liberty and local self-government and the opportunities of education and economic assistance that they require in order to attain a wholesome American life. This is but the obligation of honor of a powerful Nation toward a people living among us and dependent upon our protection.

Certainly the continuance of autocratic rule, by a Federal Department, over the lives of more than two hundred thousand citizens of this Nation is incompatible with American ideals of liberty. It also is destructive of the character and self-respect of a great race.

The continued application of the allotment laws, under which Indian wards have lost more than two-thirds of their reservation lands, while the costs of Federal administration of these lands have steadily mounted, must be terminated.

Indians throughout the country have been stirred to a new hope. They say they stand at the end of the old trail. Certainly, the figures of impoverishment and disease point to their impending extinction, as a race, unless basic changes in their conditions of life are effected.

— President Franklin D. Roosevelt on the Wheeler-Howard Bill, April 28, in *The Public Papers and Addresses of Franklin D. Roosevelt* (New York: Random House, Inc., 1938), Vol. III, p. 202.

Relocation of the Japanese at the Beginning of World War II. (Library of Congress)

military need which did not exist — recommended that step, and by the summer the victims were confined to relocation camps. The majority of the Supreme Court pusillanimously refused to overrule this invasion of personal rights, maintaining that the war emergency was justification enough.

The revulsion in popular sentiment was prompt, although restoration of the full rights of the Japanese waited until the end of the war. The other minorities made quicker progress. Opportunities in employment opened up as religious and racial prejudice declined. In 1941, after A. Philip Randolph threatened to lead thousands of Negroes in a march on Washington, the President by executive order created a Fair Employment Practices Committee to secure equality of treatment for work in defense plants. Permanent state laws in some places applied the same principle to other jobs and to education, and thus helped all disadvantaged groups. The Negroes also began to attain personal and political rights. Lynchings became less frequent, the number of Negro voters and officeholders increased, and in 1944 the Supreme Court held the white primary unconstitutional.

Social segregation still withstood the pressure for equality; in 1945 Negroes and white men did not yet serve in the same fighting units. Nevertheless, the war had created an impulse that could be delayed but not halted. Those who risked their lives in a common cause would not willingly come home to a society that denied them equal treatment, and the New Deal had armed government with renewed power to advance the social welfare of the people.

▼

Before 1947, the disturbing effects of the depression and of the war were more evident than the means of coping with disorder. Coming when institutions were already disturbed, the shock of these events further unsettled the family, the church, and the community. To the people who suffered from them, the problems were more visible than the cures.

Yet the restoration of economic vitality, the growth of a labor movement, the spread of education, and the increased power of government were potent weapons for dealing with the social difficulties. And new intellectual perspectives gave men the determination to use those weapons.

Paperbacks for Further Reading

Frederick Lewis Allen, *Since Yesterday* (Bantam Books, Inc.) devotes some attention to social development. Oscar Handlin, *American People in the Twentieth Century* (Beacon Press) treats the problems of prejudice, nationalism, and social organization.

Contemporary sociological literature has a considerable amount of information on the developments discussed in this chapter. Gunnar Myrdal, *An American Dilemma* (McGraw-Hill Paperback Series) is a masterly analysis of the Negro; and Horace Cayton and St. Clair Drake, *Black Metropolis* (Harper Torchbooks) describes the ghetto of a Northern city (Chicago). Robert S. and Helen M. Lynd, *Middletown in Transition* (Harvest Books) is a community study of a small city. William F. Whyte, *Street Corner Society* (Phoenix Books) treats the children of Italians in Boston. Other studies include: Edwin H. Sutherland, ed., *The Professional Thief;* Nels Anderson, *The Hobo;* and Charles S. Johnson, *Shadow of the Plantation* (all Phoenix Books). Irving Howe and Lewis Coser, *American Communist Party* (Frederick A. Praeger, Inc.) is a comprehensive history; and William Record, *Race and Radicalism* (Cornell Paperbacks) deals with the Communist efforts to win over the Negroes.

Among the novels that illuminate the social trends of these years are: John Steinbeck, *Grapes of Wrath* (Bantam Books, Inc.); Richard Wright, *Native Son* (Signet Books); Daniel Fuchs, *Homage to Blenholt* (Berkley Publishing Corp.); and James T. Farrell, *Studs Lonigan* (Signet Classics).

INTELLECTUAL
ASSUMPTIONS

88

In his empiricism and his willingness to try anything new, Franklin D. Roosevelt was characteristic of his era. Not himself a systematic thinker, he approached the problems of government with a buoyant optimism that encouraged him to take a chance on the fresh ideas that captured his interest. His fellow citizens, too, were speculative—in both senses of the word. They were willing to take risks and ready to reconsider their basic beliefs.

The disasters of the 1930s and 1940s were intellectually stimulating. The radical changes that disordered social life compelled Americans to rethink their assumptions about man and society. People could not take their understanding of their own situation for granted. The depression and the war forced Americans to explore once more their intellectual heritage of optimism, pragmatic confidence in reason, and faith in the ability of man to shape the future. They learned that the community needed strengthening but that service to the individual was still its purpose.

Progress and the Light of Reason

Optimism The comforting nineteenth-century confidence in the inevitability of progress did not survive the setbacks of two wars and the depression. A society that counted the unemployed and the casualties could not simply affirm that things were getting better year by year. The revelations, at the end of the war, of the atrocities in the Nazi extermination camps and of the holocaust at Hiroshima deepened the doubts already expressed earlier.

Progress was no longer certain. A total cataclysm was possible. The millions of people who panicked in 1938 when they mistook a radio play for a news report of an invasion from Mars expressed the tension under which their countrymen labored as war approached. Actuality would confirm their forebodings, although in the march of Nazi legions rather than the landing of strange beings from outer space.

Yet in the face of these real or imagined disasters, only a few intellectuals suffered a failure of nerve. Most did surrender the illusion of a steady ascent to Utopia. But even those who themselves went hungry nevertheless insisted that improvement and reform were possible through an accurate estimate of the problems and through the correct use of the means for solving them. Neither in practical activities nor in thought did the New Deal generation surrender to despair.

Past failures were not a cause for standing still or going backward, but rather a goad in the search for new discoveries. Only fear need give men concern, for fear limited their willingness to try new paths. The unafraid would keep searching, however frequent the frustrations, until they found the way to the better world they could ultimately bring into being. Progress, although no longer inevitable, and although not to be lightly gained, was still a prize within reach and worth fighting for.

Relativity and Probability Reason was the most dependable guide in the quest for progress, and science furnished the method by which to organize information and solve problems. True, Einstein's universe did not follow the fixed natural laws of Newton's. No relationships were dependably absolute; all were relative. The historian Carl L. Becker had explained in his study of the Enlightenment (1935) that the ideas of reason and progress were themselves a new heavenly city conjured up by people unwilling to face the consequences of the loss of their old faith.

Nevertheless, science, without exaggerating its claims, quieted the doubts about its adequacy. In the perspective of later momentous explorations of the atom, the great achievements of the 1930s seemed to proceed from the discovery of heavy hydrogen, for which Harold C. Urey received the Nobel Prize in chemistry (1934). But in the depression decade scientists of every sort were exploring other, more general, implications of the concept of relativity. Since there were no absolute certainties and men could reckon only on probabilities, it was necessary in genetics and astronomy, as well as in economics and sociology, to learn to combine the skills of measurement and of theoretical inference. Science thus pursued could yield useful tentative conclusions, more reliable than the old formulas because closer to reality.

Social Science The new concepts invigorated American social science. The inability of the economists and sociologists of the past to predict what was happening in the 1930s was not a reason for general condemnation of their disciplines, but a challenge to reconstruct them.

The new approaches increased the importance of testing the learning of the academy in the laboratory of life. More frequently than earlier, professors descended from the ivory tower to take jobs in government offices or to act as consultants to business, increasing the reliability of their knowledge by applying it to

Burleigh T. Wilkins, *Carl Becker* (Cambridge, Mass., 1961) gives the background of Becker's ideas.

practice. Data properly organized could supply the answers to the pressing questions of social reform. *The Encyclopaedia of Social Science*, edited by E. R. A. Seligman (1930–1935), was a monument to that proposition. The New Deal and the war provided ample fields for experiment.

Social science after 1930 emphasized the importance of strengthening its techniques through elaboration of statistical methods and through increased theoretical sophistication. Quantitative data had become central to thinking about the system of production. The Census Bureau and the Departments of Commerce and of Agriculture refined their procedures for assembling such information and the TNEC (Temporary National Economic Committee) and the administrative agencies added to the supply. Furthermore, such private groups as the Brookings Institution (1928) and the National Bureau of Economic Research (1919) under W. C. Mitchell now undertook massive statistical investigations — all this apart from the work that banks and other enterprises carried forward in the course of their own operations.

The effort to sharpen the theoretical questions the data would answer occupied both American and foreign economists. *The General Theory of Employment, Interest, and Money* (1936) by the Englishman John Maynard Keynes, an incisive analysis of modern fiscal policy, was in some respects anticipated by Alvin Hansen in the United States, and both economists drew upon current experience in grappling with the depression. Gottfried Haberler and J. A. Schumpeter, European-born scholars who immigrated to America, contributed to the understanding of international trade and business cycles. Studies by J. R. Hicks and Simon Kuznets laid the basis for the definition of the gross national product as a standard of measurement. Edward H. Chamberlin's analysis of monopolistic competition (1933) provided a more flexible way of understanding the problems of integration than the simpler terms of the past.

Some branches of sociology, too, employed advanced statistical methods. The demographers,

for instance, dealt with questions of sampling and probability, as did the students of attitudes. The polls, popularized by George H. Gallup (1935), drew upon the previous decade's experience of business in market analysis. But most of the work in sociology still consisted of empirical studies of local communities such as R. S. and H. M. Lynd's *Middletown* (1929, 1937) or of specific questions of social policy. The theoretical concepts of Max Weber and Vilfredo Pareto were just becoming known in the United States, and there were as yet only a few efforts to explore the frontier between sociology and social psychology.

The Feasibility of Reform

The Economic Context The depression and the New Deal were not the only influences that led to the preponderant emphasis of the social sciences on economic relationships. It stemmed also from the old progressive assumption that the system of production was basic to all other social institutions. A vague Marxist sentiment, expressed by such popular historians as Matthew Josephson and Charles A. Beard, reinforced the emphasis by placing class interests at the center of all past development.

The primacy of economics was crucial to the social policy of the 1930s. Americans were environmentalists who discounted the importance of genetic factors, but social scientists did not consider the environment fixed by nature. Even those who stressed the significance of regional ecological forces, like the sociologists Rupert B. Vance and Howard W. Odum, pointed to the decisive influence of alterable human factors. The popular impression derived from their work ascribed all deficiencies to faulty institutions. Thus in Sidney Kingsley's *Dead End* (1936) and in the novels of James T. Farrell and Richard Wright the slums were responsible for personal delinquency. Progress depended upon

CHARLES A. BEARD turned to scholarship out of an interest in social reform. He did not wish his learning to remain abstract, but hoped to apply it to the problems of his times. That desire gave him influence among his contemporaries and shaped the character of his writing.

Beard was born in 1874 near Knightstown, Indiana, where his father was a prosperous businessman. Charles interrupted his education with a stint of newspaper work, but graduated from De Pauw University in 1898. He had already spent a summer in Chicago investigating the conditions of labor when he decided to pursue graduate work. He spent several years at Oxford, where he became familiar with the ideas of the Fabian socialists; he then took a Ph.D. in political science at Columbia University, and remained there to teach.

Beard perceived a close relationship between history and social science. The record of the past contained the data from which the scholar could draw generalizations applicable to his own society. As a student of government he wished to understand the forces that made the Constitution, and his research persuaded him that economic self-interest had been basic to the formulation and ratification of that document. These findings aroused widespread public interest and induced Beard to apply the same method to a larger canvas. His *Rise of American Civilization* (1927) inter- preted the whole history of the United States in these terms.

Beard had resigned from Columbia in 1917. A year later, with John Dewey, Thorstein Veblen, and James Harvey Robinson, he founded the New School for Social Research, hoping that it would be a true university dedicated to advanced study. In the 1920s, Beard was a consultant to the Japanese and Yugoslav governments, and in the early days of the New Deal he was close to some of the brain trust.

As foreign policy grew increasingly important, he drew away from Roosevelt, however. In part this reaction was a Hoosier's revulsion against foreign entanglements. Beard came home from Yugoslavia in 1928 convinced that Europe was a big Balkans, a disorder beyond redemption. But isolationism also followed logically from his scholarly premises. Self-interest was the fundamental force in national policy, he believed; all else was hypocrisy. The supreme interest of the United States was to raise the standard of living of its people, and it could do so by emancipating itself from international connections. As events drifted in a direction he considered undesirable, he grew more strident in opposition. By the time he died, in 1948, he had come to a distorted view of the causes of the war, which held Roosevelt responsible for American involvement. Beard's comprehension of the past was not adequate to grasp the noneconomic factors in human affairs.

important reforms that altered the relations of property, labor, and production.

The Law and Social Change Confidence prevailed that peaceful democratic changes would carry forward the reconstruction of society. Only the Fascists and Communists, few in number in the United States, doubted that proposition. Most Americans believed that legislation and persuasion were the proper tactics in their country.

The law was not necessarily an obstacle; it could be an instrument of social change. The decisions of Justices Brandeis and Holmes had already pointed the way. Jerome N. Frank and Thurman Arnold, in influential books, explored the implications. Their arguments broke down faith in an absolute or natural law characterized by principles so eternally valid that the task of judges and Congressmen was merely to discover what was applicable. Rather, the validity of any rule depended upon the function it served. What was right in one place at one time might be wrong in another. The legislator therefore need not feel bound by such immutable rights as contract or property. His duty was to understand the wants of the society and to alter the code as required by circumstances.

The Means of Persuasion Political judgments could rest on reason. Americans were aware of the irrational facets of human behavior, and the growing influence of Freud underlined the importance of subconscious emotional drives. Nevertheless, they believed that men who learned to understand themselves and their society would make rational decisions to further social justice. The attitudes conducive to good citizenship, developed in each child by education, would prepare him to alter and not simply to accept existing institutions. *Dare the Schools Build a New Social Order?* was the title of George S. Counts' influential book. The author, professor at Teachers College, Columbia University, gave an affirmative answer to his question and directed the energies of many educators toward the necessary reconstruction of the curriculum. The lethargy and inertia of most school systems limited the response, but the challenge to apply learning to the social good was widely accepted in theory if not in practice.

The confidence in education, law, science, reason, and progress drew much of its inspiration from such respected philosophers as Morris R. Cohen and John Dewey. These heirs of an earlier pragmatism were still actively involved in a variety of liberal causes. Their evolutionary approach enabled them to absorb new ideas derived from Marx, Freud, and modern physics without doing violence to their own faith in the orderly progress of man's world. Their younger colleagues, more interested in logical positivism and in the technical problems of knowledge, drifted away from the subjects like ethics which had occupied the preceding generation. But Dewey's was still the voice to which the public was most attentive, and it still sounded a call for reform.

Planning for Man

Social Engineering The social sciences in the 1930s directed attention to planning. Undoubtedly the early direction of New Deal efforts at recovery encouraged such speculation. But the tendency had roots within the disciplines themselves and reached back to Lester Ward, Thorstein Veblen, and C. H. Cooley. Even writers who objected to centralized controls nevertheless sought some way to give the small community—regional or local—the means of guiding the lives of its members. The use of some power was essential to the exercise of planned intelligence, whether by a large or a small unit.

The prospect of a single, large, all-encompassing state apparatus frightened those Americans who thought in regional terms. They preferred that national development make allowances for differences among the historical or geographical sections of the country. David E. Lilienthal's *TVA* (1944) took that project as a model which could well be imitated elsewhere. Other writers also argued for the preservation of the distinctive cultural and social features of each area, while aiding the economic advancement of all.

Cultural Pluralism The expansion of government activity emphasized the need for salvaging worthwhile differences among the population. Even in the first two decades of the century, when restrictionist sentiment was rising, many settlement-house workers and thinkers as unlike as Charles W. Eliot, Horace Kallen, and Randolph Bourne had explained that the diversity produced by immigration enriched American culture. Now with the actual inflow of newcomers halted, with some of the strangeness rubbed off, and with the second and third generations rising in prominence, Americans began to recognize the variety of peoples who had built the country. Popular writers like Louis Adamic and histori-

Louis Adamic, *From Many Lands* (New York, 1940) expresses the faith in cultural pluralism.

John Dewey (1859–1952). (Eric Schaal, Pix, Inc.)

JOHN DEWEY was born in 1859 in Burlington, Vermont, where his father kept a general store. John was an undistinguished student, and when he graduated from the University of Vermont in 1879, he drifted into teaching in small-town schools. But his mind was at work, attempting to absorb ideas not conveyed by the traditional curriculum. In college he had read T. H. Huxley and had begun to think through the implications of Darwinism. Correspondence with William T. Harris, who published some of his articles, induced Dewey to think of philosophy as a career. In 1882 he borrowed $500 and entered Johns Hopkins where, two years later, he took the doctorate.

Dewey thereafter was a teacher, at the Universities of Michigan, Minnesota, and Chicago and at Teachers College, Columbia University, but he never accepted the limitations of academic philosophy. His first book was on psychology, because for him the first question seemed to be, as it was for William James, How do we know? The answer, as for James, was that experience was the ultimate authority in knowledge and conduct.

(Continued on next page)

Dewey therefore rejected the dominant tendency of the gilded age toward rigid formalized schooling, and argued in favor of bringing education into a closer relationship with life. His Laboratory School in Chicago and his subsequent writings laid the foundation for progressive education.

Dewey believed, too, that philosophy should be a method of understanding and rectifying social ills. Ideas could be meaningful only in connection with practice. Increasingly, therefore, he took part in liberal causes, and was among the founders of the American Civil Liberties Union. His interest in planning and rationality for a time attracted him to socialism. But underlying his attitudes on specific issues was a basic faith in the value of the individual. He therefore rejected the elitist tendency that swayed some progressives and remained a convinced democrat.

As a result Dewey early recognized the danger from totalitarianism in both its Fascist and Communist forms. He witnessed the onset of World War II with dismay but without confusion, for he understood the stakes involved. He died in 1952.

ans like Marcus Lee Hansen and Carl Wittke detailed the contributions of many groups to national life. Gunnar Myrdal analyzed the situation of the Negro in terms of the dilemma posed by the discrepancy between discrimination and the creed of equality. The calls for 100 percent Americanism subsided, because the preservation of ethnic communities—Negro and immigrant as well as Indian—now seemed a positive good.

Racism lost intellectual respectability. Even before the Nazis demonstrated its horrifying potentialities, the scientists had torn away its scholarly foundation. Franz Boas had shown that physical types were not fixed and unalterable, and other anthropologists pointed out that mankind responded to common urges and needs by developing a variety of cultures under different circumstances. Social psychologists restudied the evidence on the distribution of high and low levels of intelligence and rejected the proposition that some races were superior and others inferior.

While planning served communal needs, the ultimate purpose was, therefore, advancement of the individuals who made up society. John Dewey's important book, *Liberalism and Social Action* (1935), made the point persuasively.

Social action was needed in applying intelligence to the solution of the great problems of the day, but its end was liberation of the individual. Much of the concern with the common man, expressed in the rhetoric of politics and in the scholarship of such works as the "History of American Life Series," reflected the continuing faith that there was worth in each person, whatever his breed or affiliation or status. Communities were important but they existed to serve the people who comprised them.

Americanism and Other Ideologies

Fascism Respect for the individual, in the last analysis, inhibited American attitudes toward totalitarianism. The habit of thinking in progressive terms—that history moved in a straight line upward—evoked a favorable initial reaction to any new regime, particularly if it replaced one that had rested on an old ideology. Italy, it seemed, was a decadent monarchy, its people steeped in superstition; along came the Fascists, who made the trains run on time and professed to serve the common good. With Mussolini's bellicosity, however, his brutal repression of

National Planning, 1934

That statesmanlike national planning will bring us nearer the American goal our experience clearly shows in every range of our life, local, national, public, and private. Statesmanlike planning might prevent the vast losses caused by inattention, as in the case of soil erosion and flood and misuse of national resources. It might prevent the wastes arising from conflicting and clashing policies, as in the case of land reclamation and land retirement, the industrial wastes arising from lack of reasonable coordination, the still more tragic wastage of human material through inattention to the protection and security of productive labor. It might make possible the invention of new technological and managerial devices for increasing the productivity of mankind and social devices for insuring the just participation of our people in their products.

In moments of industrial insecurity and wide-spread and bitter distress, the possibility of a far finer and richer life for the mass of mankind than ever before may seem a mocking unreality. But the sober fact is that in America, with its abundance of natural resources, with its technological and managerial ability, with its energetic and capable blend of peoples, a new world is within our reach if we can organize and act to take possession of it. What stands between us and the realization of the hopes that gleamed before the eyes of our people from the earliest days are only our own attitudes and our social and political management.

—National Planning Board, *Final Report, 1933–1934* (Washington: Government Printing Office, 1934), p. 33.

Cultural Sectionalism, 1935

Each section has a personality of its own, in physiography, industry, psychology. Thinking painters and writers who have passed their formative years in these regions, will, by care-taking analysis, work out and interpret in their productions these varying personalities. When the different regions develop characteristics of their own, they will come into competition with each other; and out of this competition a rich American culture will grow. It was in some such manner that Gothic architecture grew out of competition between different French towns as to which could build the largest and finest cathedrals . . . .

The germ of such a system for the United States is to be found in the art work recently conducted under the PWA [Public Works Administration]. This was set up by geographical divisions, and it produced remarkable results in the brief space of time in which it was in operation. I should like to see such encouragement to art work continued and expanded. The Federal Government should establish regional schools for art instruction to specially gifted students in connection with universities or other centers of culture in the various sections.

In suggesting that these schools should be allied with the universities, I do not mean to commit them to pedantic or even strictly academic requirements. But I do believe that the general liberal arts culture is highly desirable in a painter's training. The artist must know more today than he had to know in former years . . . .

I am willing to go so far as to say that I believe the hope of a native American art lies in the development of regional art centers and the competition between them. It seems the one way to the building up of an honestly art-conscious America.

—Grant Wood, *Revolt Against the City* (Iowa City, Iowa: Clio Press, 1935), pp. 39–43.

opposition, and his disregard for the rights of others opinion gradually shifted. By the time the Nazis seized power in Germany, people in the United States were generally skeptical of the Third Reich. Hitler's anti-Semitism and his aggressions not only aroused hostility toward his movement but also discredited his counterparts in America.

Communism The perspective on communism was different because its totalitarian features did not emerge clearly until the 1930s. The Russian revolution seemed progressive. It toppled an archaic monarchy, and the Bolshevik intellectual lineage went back to the humane socialism of the nineteenth century.

[In an untitled poem, a poet criticizes the Communists, 1935]

kumrads die because they're told)
kumrads die before they're old
(kumrads aren't afraid to die
kumrads don't
and kumrads won't
believe in life) and death knows whie

(all good kumrads you can tell
by their altruistic smell
moscow pipes good kumrads dance)
kumrads enjoy
s.freud knows whoy
the hope that you may mess your pance

every kumrad is a bit
of quite unmitigated hate
(travelling in a futile groove
god knows why)
and so do i
(because they are afraid to love

—Copyright, 1935, by E. E. Cummings; renewed, 1963, by Marion Morehouse Cummings. Reprinted from *Poems 1923–1954* by permission of Harcourt, Brace & World, Inc.

Opinion in the United States therefore polarized. Those who feared the Reds at home regarded the Communists in Russia as godless radicals who threatened orderly society everywhere. Liberals, on the other hand, identified Lenin and even Stalin as modern reformers, situated somewhat to the left of Eugene V. Debs along a progressive spectrum, positions on which depended upon differences in tactics and degrees of haste. In the election of 1932, therefore, Sherwood Anderson, Erskine Caldwell, John Dos Passos, and Theodore Dreiser, among others, supported the American Communist ticket. The struggle against fascism, particularly during the Spanish Civil War, when the Communist party held to the united front line, turned some liberals into fellow travelers willing to work with the Communists toward common ends.

Sensitive party members and intellectual sympathizers were the first to understand the significance of Russian totalitarianism. The small group of Trotskyites quickly perceived the significance of Stalin's seizure of power and of his diplomatic and domestic failures. American socialists, engaged in bitter internecine warfare with the Communists in some sectors of the labor movement, also lost faith in the Soviet experiment. While other writers were still bemused, Edmund Wilson in *Travels in Two Democracies* (1936) explained the effects on his thinking of exposure to the realities of Russian life.

The purges and the great Moscow show trials of 1937 disillusioned still wider circles, as did revelation of the sinister Communist attacks upon their united-front allies during the later phases of the resistance to Franco. The cynical deal with Hitler in 1939, the invasion of Poland, and the war in Finland all exposed the character of the Stalinist regime.

After 1941, the necessities of the American alliance with the Soviet Union obscured the lessons of the 1930s. F. D. R., Ambassador Joseph E. Davies in Moscow, and others learned to call the Communist dictatorship a peace-loving democracy, in part at least to justify a utilitarian partnership. But that illusion was more widespread among politicians than among intellectuals, most of whom by then comprehended the difference between democratic and totalitarian state power. The scope of government had broadened everywhere, but in the totalitarian countries the community grew stronger by dominating the individual; in the United States, it grew stronger in order to liberate him.

Americanism The new ideologies of the 1930s revived interest in exploring the meaning of Americanism. Looking back now beyond the period when nationalism had held racist connotations, Americans rediscovered the meaning that Jefferson and Emerson had attached to the term. Van Wyck Brooks in *The Flowering of New England* (1936) created a nostalgic picture of a Boston and Concord in which liberalism flourished; and New Dealers adopted the Sage of Monticello as their patron saint. Many progressives justified their isolationism by the argument that American institutions were so unique that they were suitable only to their own country. Even revolutionaries for a time found refuge in the slogan that communism was twentieth-century Americanism.

On the other hand, conservative people, too, searched for roots in the past. There was a noticeable increase in interest in national history, in colonial antiques, in folk music, and in square dancing, all demonstrations of a desire, in a rapidly changing world, to retain ties with the past.

"America first," the cry of the isolationists, appealed to the foes of the New Deal who wished to halt the processes that were transforming the country. The Dies Committee of the House of Representatives sometimes interpreted its mandate to investigate un-American activities so broadly as to encompass any objection to existing institutions.

Both the more liberal and the more conservative Americans were eager to find in national character and experience authority for the intellectual positions they took. They fell back upon the past in the search for certainty, conscious as they were of the risks of change.

A Return to Orthodoxy

Doubts about the whole heritage of progressive ideas led an influential minority to return to social and religious orthodoxy. Those affected were not simple people held by an inert tradition, but rather among the most literate and reflective persons in the society. They found orthodoxy attractive not out of habit, but as a conscious, deliberate desire to reject some features of the modern world.

Industrialism, the city, the strange admixture of peoples and cultures, would always lead to personal and social disorder. The remedy was a return to agrarian life, in which fixed social groups knew their places and in which faith, ritual, and accepted truth guided each man in his duties. This was the vision of the Southern writers who contributed to an eloquent volume, *I'll Take My Stand* (1930).

Some expatriates like T. S. Eliot had already escaped from modern America by flight across the ocean. Eliot's poetry in the 1930s celebrated the refuge his Anglo-Catholic orthodoxy offered the weary and confused. Europe, having witnessed at first hand the full damage of World War I as the United States had not, was more ready to look for alternatives to the faith in progress and perfectibility. The speculations of continental religious neo-orthodoxy raised profound questions in the New World. The writings of the Catholic, Jacques Maritain, thus stirred an interest in neo-Thomism, expounded in the United States by Mortimer J. Adler. The work of the Protestant, Karl Barth, influenced Reinhold Niebuhr, whose *Nature and Destiny of Man* (1941–1943) appeared at the depth of the war.

If the sons of Adam were not innately good and not assured of progress, then perhaps faith in the common man was leading the Americans into a blind alley. The Spaniard, José Ortega Y

Donald B. Meyer, *The Protestant Search for Political Realism, 1919–1941* (Berkeley, Calif., 1960) touches on these problems.

Restoring Agrarian Virtues, 1930

Unless steps are taken toward the restoration of the balance of economic forces in America, which was destroyed in 1865, we cannot hope to avoid the unsavory sequel of industrialism outlined above. Industrialism bears its own antidote, but it is a bitter one; the consequences of its course of self-destruction are scarcely justified, even by that foremost American contribution to world-culture, the billionaire. If there exists any effective social and political intelligence in the country it might profitably be mobilized for the conduction of a specific program of rehabilitation of the agrarian economy and the "old individualism" associated with it . . . . The instrumentalities of intelligent political leadership, informed social science, and a definitive social philosophy could have no more important problem than that of trying to effect a synthesis, in some sense, of the unified manner of living inherent in the agrarian family and community with the energy and inventiveness which have been diverted into industrialism.

—Lyle H. Lanier, "A Critique of the Philosophy of Progress," in *I'll Take My Stand* (Gloucester, Mass: Peter Smith, 1951), pp. 153–154.

The Errors of Optimism, 1944

The demonic fury of fascist politics in which a collective will expresses boundless ambitions and imperial desires and in which the instruments of a technical civilization are used to arm this will with a destructive power, previously unknown in history, represents a melancholy historical refutation of the eighteenth- and nineteenth-century conceptions of a harmless and essentially individual human life. Human desires are expressed more collectively, are less under the discipline of prudent calculation, and are more the masters of, and less limited by, natural forces than the democratic creed had understood . . . .

The democratic idealists of practically all schools of thought have managed to remain remarkably oblivious to the obvious facts. Democratic theory therefore has not squared with the facts of history. This grave defect in democratic theory was comparatively innocuous in the heyday of the bourgeois period, when the youth and the power of democratic civilization surmounted all errors of judgment and confusions of mind. But in this latter day, when it has become important to save what is valuable in democratic life from the destruction of what is false in bourgeois civilization, it has also become necessary to distinguish what is false in democratic theory from what is true in democratic life.

The preservation of a democratic civilization requires the wisdom of the serpent and the harmlessness of the dove. The children of light must be armed with the wisdom of the children of darkness but remain free from their malice. They must know the power of self-interest in human society without giving it moral justification. They must have this wisdom in order that they may beguile, deflect, harness and restrain self-interest, individual and collective, for the sake of the community.

—Reinhold Niebuhr, *The Children of Light and the Children of Darkness* (New York: Charles Scribner's Sons, 1944), pp. 30–41.

Gasset, in a book (1932) widely read in the United States, had described the revolt of the masses — the appearance of a mechanized society in which humans without personality stifled all creativity and reduced life to a meaningless routine. The orthodox feared that American culture already suffered from the pressure of the masses.

▼

The orthodox were only a minority in 1947. Most Americans had survived the war and the depression with confidence sharpened by adversity. They had clung to progress, change, and reason not through blind optimism but out of the conviction that these were the best means at their disposal for shaping the world they wished to inhabit. They had fewer illusions about the difficulties before them than earlier generations, but they had nevertheless accepted the challenge of attempting to develop modern communities that would serve rather than master man.

Paperbacks for Further Reading

The best approach to the ideas of this period is through the books of the writers named in this chapter. Among them are: Thurman Arnold, *Symbols of Government* (Harbinger Books) and *Folklore of Capitalism* (Yale University Press); Charles A. Beard, *Idea of National Interest* (Quadrangle Books) and *Economic Basis of Politics* (Vintage Books, Inc.); Carl L. Becker, *The Heavenly City of the Eighteenth-Century Philosophers* (Yale University Press); Morris R. Cohen, *Reason and Nature* (Free Press Paperbacks); and John Dewey, *The Reconstruction of Philosophy* (Beacon Press) and *Liberalism and Social Action* (Capricorn Books).

Daniel Aaron, *Writers on the Left* (Avon Book Div.) discusses their relationship to communism. Hadley Cantril, *The Invasion from Mars* (Harper Torchbooks) deals with the panic after the radio broadcast. Many of the books cited for Chapters 87 and 89 are also relevant here.

CULTURAL
CHANGE

89

Between 1929 and 1947, American culture felt the effects of depression and war, of social dislocation, and of intellectual doubt. All these developments touched people's emotions as well as their ideas. Not only did men and women want to know why the economy failed or aggression occurred; they sought also to respond to crises in ways that would relieve anxiety or stimulate action. They expected their culture to satisfy the need for explanation and emotional outlet.

The rapid transformation of all media of communication during these decades limited their ability to provide that satisfaction. The movies and radio continued to attract massive audiences, but those media, by their nature, left important subjects of personal and social concern unexpressed. However, the development of new cultural forms liberated the creative energies of many artists who captured in words and sounds and shapes the significance of their disorderly and fluid society.

The Impact of the Mass Media

THE DEPRESSION KILLED the moribund official culture inherited from the past. The artificial support for that culture vanished with the paper wealth of its patrons. The museums and some symphony orchestras in the major cities survived, but were forced to retrench and their influence diminished.

Audiences The old culture of the common people also disintegrated, for it was incapable of withstanding the impact of new media. The movies and the radio commanded immensely powerful resources and attracted the talent of the ablest performers and the attention of the largest audiences. The popular press and stage therefore steadily lost ground. With the end of immigration and increased mobility, the specialized foreign-language and rural audiences became smaller, thereby reducing the patronage of the ethnic newspapers and theaters and of the itinerant circuses.

The disappearance of vaudeville was symptomatic of the trend. The comedians, acrobats, singers, and dancers had worked in close rapport with the spectators. The most skillful personalities kept their popularity by acute sensitivity to the responses of the onlookers. Still struggling for existence in 1930, vaudeville had vanished by the end of the decade, rendered obsolete by the talking motion picture and the radio.

The new media were mechanical and they separated performers from audiences. The man at the microphone had no way of knowing his listeners, nor could he adjust to their distinctive qualities. He spoke to a vast undifferentiated mass and could deliver only a general message they could all understand.

By Film and by Air The silent movies of the 1920s had supplemented vaudeville rather than competed with it, but invention of the technique for recording sound on film altered the situation. Detailed scripts with the dialogue precisely timed

to the action deprived the directors of the freedom to improvise. The last elements of spontaneity disappeared. Productions were expensive, required heavy financing, and depended upon an elaborate star system. The formidable risks of departing from tried and true formulas were therefore rarely taken. The bulk of the output was routine, and occasional attempts to depart from convention, like John Ford's *The Informer* (1935), proved that box office success and critical esteem did not go together. Charlie Chaplin was the sole exception. His universal popularity and his autonomy as producer, director, and writer as well as actor freed him to shape his art as he wished.

Radio had been in its infancy in the 1920s, its potentialities hardly perceived. In 1929 fewer than 40 percent of American families had receivers. Despite the depression, the percentage rose steadily thereafter and radio came into its own.

The willingness of advertisers to buy segments of time in return for absolute freedom to sell their wares created an unexpected and abundant source of income. Furthermore, the development of long-distance transmission lines permitted a multitude of different stations to broadcast a single program simultaneously. The networks, already in existence but losing money before 1929, now began to increase their sales and their profits. National advertisers, able to command the attention of millions, paid handsomely for time, and the enormous incentives thus created empowered the radio to draw talent from any source.

Broadcasting was a limited monopoly, since access to the air depended upon a license from the Federal government. Yet no national policy guided the grant of the wave lengths. Nor was there a serious effort to influence the character of the programs. For want of a policy, the United States simply handed the air waves to a small number of entrepreneurs, who were free to use them as they wished.

Radio was unrivaled as a speedy transmitter of news, and the voices of Lowell Thomas,

Gabriel Heatter, H. V. Kaltenborn, and Walter Winchell were soon heard in households across the country. Speed and immediacy created interest in reports of sporting events. Most other programs were entirely unimaginative. A good deal of time went to aimless music which created an undemanding background noise for the housewife at her chores or the adolescent at his studies. Light comedy, much of it with vaudeville antecedents, along with the voices of the crooners, filled out the evening programs.

The Question of Control Technical innovations enabled newspapers and magazines to expand their circulations with analogous results. The number of publications dropped, so fewer different points of view and interests were represented. *The Saturday Evening Post* and *Colliers,* the high circulation magazines that survived from an earlier era, lost some of their individuality as they struggled for subscribers. *Readers Digest, Time,* and *Life* — brisk, casual, and undemanding — soon outdistanced the older journals. The prominence of book clubs had the somewhat similar effect of concentrating attention on a few highly publicized volumes to the neglect of the rest.

In radio and the periodicals — with the notable exception of *Readers Digest* — advertising was a prominent source of revenue. Even publications with substantial circulations could not survive without income from that source. Editorial content was therefore of minor significance. An inoffensive tone was usual, one attractive by virtue of its neutrality rather than for any distinctive message it conveyed.

Critics of American culture who sometimes complained that advertisers controlled the press, or bankers the movies, were inaccurate. No one controlled the new media. The Legion of Decency, municipal censors, and any one of scores of pressure groups could veto the contents of a movie or broadcast. The overriding desire of the producers was to antagonize no one. These powerful instruments therefore lacked relevance to the issues and played a limited part in the life of their audience. They were incap-able, for instance, of influencing politics. Almost all the newspapers opposed the New Deal in vain. Powerful personalities like Father Coughlin or F. D. R. in his fireside chats could use the radio; the station owners could not.

Experiments in Expression

The Taste for the Modern Dissatisfaction with the mass media and a sense of the inadequacy of the old forms drew many Americans on in a search for novelty and innovation. The latest fashion, whether in clothes, in dance steps, or in furniture, acquired an inherent attractiveness — as if what was new might supply the satisfaction that the familiar lacked. The resulting permissiveness toward experiment released a good deal of creative energy. Furthermore, the influence of government, of migration from Europe, and of fresh sources of patronage stimulated a variety of departures in the forms of expression.

Under the New Deal, the government acquired a substantial role as artistic impresario. The Rural Resettlement Administration thus commissioned Pare Lorentz's notable documentary films, "*The Plow That Broke the Plains*" (1936) and "*The River*" (1937). The WPA sponsored creative activities in the theater, the fine arts, and literature, ostensibly at least to aid the unemployed. The help was indiscriminate and undoubtedly perpetrated a good deal that was mediocre and sleazy. But it also permitted such painters as Ben Shahn and Peter Blume to find themselves, and it gave incomes to a poet like Conrad Aiken and a novelist like Richard Wright. In a related development, some universities began to support writers, artists, and playwrights in residence; and the Guggenheim and other foundations provided them with grants.

Selden Rodman, *Portrait of the Artist as an American* (New York, 1951) is a biography of Ben Shahn.

A Still from *The Plow That Broke the Plains* (1936), a Documentary Film by Pare Lorentz. (The Museum of Modern Art)

BENJAMIN SHAHN was born in Russia in 1893. His father, a carpenter and wood carver, earned but a meager livelihood and the family suffered all the disabilities to which the Tzarist regime subjected Jews. When Ben was eight years old, the Shahns made the long migration to the United States and settled in a cold-water flat in Brooklyn, New York.

Shahn was fortunate. At the age of fifteen he was apprenticed to a lithographer, thus acquiring a skill allied to art. In the evenings he studied at The City College and at the National Academy of Design. Through the 1920s he struggled, unrecognized, to develop a style adequate to put onto canvas the world around him. He sought the visual significance of the workers in factories, of the shapes and tones of city life, of the contrasts between men and their surroundings.

In 1922 and 1929 Shahn traveled in Europe and noted with interest the work of Rouault and other painters. But he contin-ued to search for a technique of his own. During the depression, he tried his hand at satire, doing paintings inspired by the Sacco-Vanzetti and Mooney cases. He also worked with Diego Rivera on the frescoes for Rockefeller Center. But the active patronage of the arts by government under the New Deal gave Shahn the opportunity he needed. He executed commissions for the Farm Security Administration and for the Federal Relief Administration and in both capacities was able to treat the subjects that concerned him.

In the 1940s Shahn worked first for the Office of War Information and then for the CIO Political Action Committee, still using his palette to convey his sympathy for mankind. His reputation grew in that decade to the point at which he was self-sufficient and able to be selective about what he painted. Thereafter his style mellowed. Yet he continued to express a humane understanding of the complex world about him.

Europe, too, contributed to the modern influence. Disillusion with the Old World and a need for native roots induced some expatriates to return to the United States, where they strengthened the avant-garde communities in New York, Boston, and San Francisco. Fascism and war drove other talented people to America, where they contributed to the vigor of its culture. The architects Walter Gropius, Richard Neutra, and Ludwig Miës van der Rohe; the musicians Paul Hindemith, Igor Stravinsky, and Kurt Weill; the writers Aldous Huxley, Thomas Mann, and Franz Werfel; and the film director Fritz Lang were among the immigrants.

Patronage for Experiment Finally, there was enough patronage to sustain the creative efforts that originated in the avant-garde. The vogue for the modern among educated people of wealth supported experiments in literature and music and new institutions like the Museum of Modern Art. Financial aid came to the rescue of the little magazines, which made no effort to attract a large general audience and depended upon subsidies to stay alive. The State of Louisiana indirectly supported *The Southern Review* (1935–1942); and Yale, Kenyon, Antioch, and North Carolina were among the colleges that maintained similar publications. *Partisan Review* (1934) also had support in its attempt to combine Marxist social criticism with a responsible aesthetic.

The little reviews had few readers, just as modern music had few listeners. But linkages with the mass media diffused the reputations of the creative personalities throughout the society. The purchasers of records learned to value serious music, even though their choices were less often contemporary than conventional classics. The readers of the press learned that T. S. Eliot was a great poet and Igor Stravinsky a great composer, even though they did not themselves expect to understand a line or a measure. Some of the most prominent artists,

Frederick J. Hoffman, *The Little Magazine* (Princeton, N. J., 1946) is a brief history.

> ## *Revolutionary Literature, 1934*
>
> We propose to concentrate on creative and critical literature, but we shall maintain a definite viewpoint—that of the revolutionary working class. Through our specific literary medium we shall participate in the struggle of the workers and sincere intellectuals against imperialist war, fascism, national and racial oppression, and for the abolition of the system which breeds these evils. The defense of the Soviet Union is one of our principal tasks.
>
> We shall combat not only the decadent culture of the exploiting classes but also the debilitating liberalism which at times seeps into our writers through the pressure of class-alien forces. Nor shall we forget to keep our own house in order. We shall resist every attempt to cripple our literature by narrow-minded, sectarian theories and practices.
>
> —Editorial Statement, *Partisan Review*, I (February–March, 1934), p. 2.

as a result, gained substantial rewards from their activity; all of them enjoyed a freedom that stimulated self-expression.

Artistic Freedom

Creativity The environment of the two decades after 1929 encouraged experimentation and gave broad scope to the creative personality. Liberated from the necessities of either satisfying the artificial standards of an official culture or of supporting himself by appeals to the popular audience, the artist could develop interior standards of performance and, on some occasions, reach satisfying levels of creativity.

The developing forms of expression followed no simple pattern. The effects of govern-

The Golden Gate Bridge, San Francisco. (Werner Bischof, Magnum)

ment involvement on architecture were dreary, whether seen in the blank white buildings that spread across Washington, D.C., or in the monotonous Georgian post offices that the New Deal built across the nation. On the other hand, the clean beauty of the George Washington (1931) and Golden Gate (1937) bridges reflected their engineered simplicity. Meanwhile in various parts of the country and in different ways, Gropius, Miës van der Rohe, and Frank Lloyd Wright were laying the groundwork for the international style that would dominate the second half of the century.

Strong modern currents brought new vigor to American music, as Aaron Copland and Virgil Thomson cut loose from academic limitations. Among the painters, Charles Burchfield, Edward Hopper, and Jack Levine and among the sculptors, William Zorach and Alexander Calder displayed both a command of their crafts and sharp perceptions of the world around them. There had been no earlier American tradition of the dance, except for the rather eccentric efforts of Isadora Duncan. Martha Graham now worked out ballet forms that drew on folk themes yet in their angular composition bore an unmistakably modern aspect.

Literary Currents A good deal of the best writing of the time took the form of criticism. Meanings in modern literature, art, and architecture were not close to the surface and required interpreters such as Lewis Mumford and Edmund Wilson. Moreover, through criticism the writers often addressed each other rather than the general public, feeling that a broad audience was unnecessary and that communica-

Sherman Paul, *Edmund Wilson* (Urbana, Ill., 1965) deals with literary criticism in this period.

A Scene from *The Adding Machine* (1923), a Play by Elmer Rice. (New York Public Library)

tion could remain fixed within a rather narrow circle.

Poetry remained experimental. The veterans —Frost, Pound, Eliot, and Cummings—continued their work and also inspired younger men like Robert Lowell, Delmore Schwartz, and Karl Shapiro, who explored still newer styles. Though the difficulty and obscurity of their language limited the number of their readers, they had shaken off popularity as a criterion in favor of rigid standards of their own.

The drama was much less selective than poetry and therefore had a wider appeal. The Theatre Guild increasingly catered to a commercial Broadway following, but Orson Welles's Mercury, the Group, and the WPA theaters continued to experiment. They offered established dramatists, notably Eugene O'Neill, Maxwell Anderson, and Elmer Rice, stages for treating radical social themes. Younger writers, like Clifford Odets and Tennessee Williams, felt

no restraint in their attacks upon the economic and social system. The fact that the theater audience was much smaller than that of the movies permitted greater flexibility and variety. Yet there was also an overlap. The gay comedies of George S. Kaufman and the elaborately staged musicals of Richard Rodgers and Lorenz Hart, and of Oscar Hammerstein 2d took shape on the stage and then were translated to the screen.

Variety was characteristic also of the novel. There were few bold new stylistic departures, such as had marked the previous two decades, and more interest in social content. In the work of Ernest Hemingway and John Dos Passos, the shift in emphasis was not damaging. But it inflated the reputations of Thomas Wolfe and James T. Farrell, who were undisciplined social

Hallie Flanagan, *Arena* (New York, 1940) is a history of the federal theater project by its former director.

Philip Young, *Ernest Hemingway* (New York, 1952) treats the start of the writer's career.

ERNEST HEMINGWAY wanted to be where the action was. There was a war in Europe. He wangled his way to Italy and drove an ambulance, although he never actually saw the rout at Caporetto he later described. He did catch a fragment of a mortar shell, which earned him a medal. He was then nineteen years old.

He was born in 1899 in Oak Park, Illinois, where his father was a physician. The young Hemingway made it through high school but had no patience for further formal education. He had owned a shotgun from the age of ten, and, like his father, was fond of hunting and fishing.

In Chicago after the war, he was restless. Insomnia bothered him. Working for newspapers, he learned to get a story down in clipped comprehensible sentences. He learned also to size people up, to catch the pattern of their speech, to guess at their feelings.

Then the desire to write took him to Paris, where he fell in with the crowd that gathered at Sylvia Beach's bookshop. Gertrude Stein, André Gide, and James Joyce of an older generation, Scott Fitzgerald of his own, talked to him; he lived on little and wrote furiously in a carpenter's loft.

In 1926, *The Sun Also Rises* made him famous. There followed two other novels, like the first, about the lost generation adrift after the war. Then he had money,

could move back and forth across the Atlantic, hunt. The Spanish Civil War altered his perspective. He went to cover the story as a journalist and became involved in the great drama of a people divided against itself, plunged in bloody combat. His sympathies were with the Republic but he was an honest reporter and described men and women as they were, with all the blemishes of character mingled with the heroism. Out of that experience came *For Whom the Bell Tolls* (1940).

By then the greater war was spreading across Europe. Hemingway understood the significance of the conflict against fascism, and he left his pleasant home in Cuba to see what the fighting was like. But he refused to yield to illusion or to make myths for the future. He tried to puzzle out the meaning. But there were no easy answers. In the fifteen years after the war, a search for meaning infused his writing. For a while there was still an escape in action, hunting in Africa, fishing from Cuba. But then he felt age weakening his power, as did the protagonist in *Across the River and into the Trees*. Perhaps he thought about his father who had shot himself to death in 1928. More than anything he feared illness and the dependency that would make him less than himself. In 1961, at his home in Ketchum, Idaho, he put a bullet through his head.

---

chroniclers, and it led Sinclair Lewis into sterile repetitions of familiar formulas. The test of social significance also exaggerated the value of works of little merit which took a correct political or social position. The same criterion, by contrast, obscured the value of books that did not conform to conventional expectations. Some of the best writing of the period, in the novels of Henry Roth, Daniel Fuchs, and Nathanael West, went unnoticed.

The Modes of Escape

Whatever their range of choice among forms, artists and audiences after 1929 wished their culture to express the meanings of depression, fascism, and war. These overwhelming external events intruded into the subject matter of every artistic form. The response varied according to the group addressed and according to the limitations of the medium.

Dreams For many people, the problems were simply too great. There were no evident solutions to the dilemmas raised by joblessness or divorce or the failures in personal obligations. Furthermore, there were not even convincing explanations of these immense difficulties. Whose was the fault and where the remedy? Many Americans wished to escape even the need for facing these questions.

To such men and women, the culture offered daydreams. In the arenas, the best men won. In the movie houses, a happy ending concluded every story. Romantics swayed to the beat of the swing from the bands of Benny Goodman or Glenn Miller. Across the afternoon air waves came the pulsating soap operas, realistic in their description of problems which never ended but, as in real life, followed one another in ceaseless complication so that the sighing listener's emotions found release in the awareness that others suffered too.

Some daydreams conjured up heroic images — the Lone Ranger or Superman for the young, the private eye for their elders. In one way or another the magic of a special integrity or virtue imparted the power that enabled a man alone to triumph over seemingly superior hostile forces.

Images of violence and erotic sexual fantasies offered avenues of escape. Brutal shootings and assaults punctuated the novels of Dashiell Hammett and James M. Cain and the tough movies of James Cagney and Edward G. Robinson. Liberal reinterpretations of the law permitted open expression of sexual stimuli, theretofore taboo. The all but nude figures peeped at their audiences from the slick pages of *Esquire* and from the bare boards of the burlesque stage. Despite censorship, the movies were often suggestive, and there were few restrictions on the written word. The novels of John O'Hara and the plays of Erskine Caldwell and Tennessee Williams treated sexual encounters openly, diverting attention, for the moment, from a world of other problems.

Laughter Comedy offered a means not only of forgetting the terrible problems of the day but

The End of Rico, 1930

Brakes scream as the car comes to a sudden stop; Flaherty and others quickly get out. Then Rico comes into view. He stands near the billboard; and we see the police car and three detectives behind him. They are advancing toward him with drawn guns.

FLAHERTY (seen in a close-up, advancing with his gun drawn). Stick 'em up, boy. And keep 'em up.

A close-up shows an enigmatic grin playing around the corners of Rico's mouth. He shrugs his shoulders, and starts to reach toward the inside of his coat. And a close-up of Flaherty shows him firing three or four shots.

Rico is then seen falling — and his hand clutches a comb! The view then expanding, Flaherty and the others run into sight as Rico lies half-sprawled, half-propped up against a corner of the billboard.

RICO. Hello, Flaherty — you buzzard. I told you you'd never put no cuffs on me!
FLAHERTY (seeing the man is dying). You should have stuck 'em up when I asked you to.

Rico defiantly grins up at him and feebly tries to get his hand up high enough to comb his hair. A spasm of pain racks his whole body. Then a close-up makes it apparent that Rico is dying.

RICO (gasping). Mother of Mercy — is this the end of Rico?

Rico's hand comes into close view: The nerveless fingers slowly relax their grip on the comb. Rico is dead.

The scene fades out.

—*Little Caesar*, a screenplay by Francis Edward Faragoh based on W. R. Burnatt, *Little Caesar*. Copyright 1943 by Warner Brothers Pictures, Inc.

Senator Claghorn on Politics, ca. 1946

CLAGHORN The Army and the Navy is wastin' money. The Army's throwin' money around like the taxpayer was the enemy. Ah found one item: the Army spent two billion dollars for fly swatters to send to Alaska. When the fly swatters got up there they found there wasn't no flies in Alaska.

ALLEN They sent the fly swatters back?

CLAGHORN Not the Army, son! The Army spent four billion dollars more to raise flies to ship to Alaska so's they could use them fly swatters. That's how the Army works, son!

— Allen's Alley. Fred Allen, *Treadmill to Oblivion* (Boston: Atlantic–Little, Brown, 1954), pp. 203–204.

also of striking back subtly at those responsible for them. W. C. Fields was a total nihilist. Boozy, belligerent, and unwilling to work, he hated all the sacred institutions — bank presidents, motherhood, children, dogs, and order. The Marx brothers turned all logic on its head, as they careened destructively through college or store. In *My Man Godfrey*, the idle upper class was helpless; only the butler could take care of himself and of them. Often in the movies, the tycoon and the politician were figures of fun, pompous, bumbling windbags, useless in an emergency. For months on the Broadway stage, *Of Thee I Sing* (1931) mocked the presidency and patriotism.

The radio was a less tolerant medium. The most popular comedians, Edgar Bergen's Charlie McCarthy, Jack Benny, and Eddie Cantor, for instance, stayed away from satire. The immense and prolonged vogue of Amos 'n' Andy rested on little more than familiar darky stereotypes, though performed with appreciative

fondness. Still, the wry commentaries of Fred Allen and of the Easy Aces mixed little barbs among the quips.

The Search for Social Significance

The novel, the short story, and the drama seldom were vehicles for humor. The serious writers and readers of this generation did not wish to escape. Imbued with earnestness and impressed with the crisis about them, they strove to give their work social significance. Injustice, poverty, and war were causes not for laughter but for revolution or change. The function of the artist was to heighten awareness of the need for action by laying bare the ills of the society.

Perhaps the most effective depictions were those of the painters — not the exaggerated blasts from George Grosz or William Gropper cartoons, but the bleak buildings and the desolate urban scenes of Edward Hopper and the rigid lines of Grant Wood's country people, who formed a striking contrast with the sensuous countryside. These canvases, without preaching, conveyed a sense of modern isolation not merely in their subject matter but also in their tight draftsmanship and their manipulation of light and color.

The writers tended to idealize the lower classes. By contrast with the idle rich and the frivolous aristocracy, men who worked in the factories or on the soil were purified by poverty and had a true vision of life. Their struggles were therefore genuine and their responses human rather than conventional. The Spanish peasants in Hemingway's *For Whom the Bell Tolls* and the American Okies in John Steinbeck's *Grapes of Wrath* knew reality as hollow well-to-do people did not. The heroic workingman made an appearance in many proletarian novels although he was a less common figure than the tiller of the soil.

The tendency to exaggerate the virtues of the poor redeemed by their suffering owed

"Nighthawks." A painting, 1942, by Edward Hopper. (The Art Institute of Chicago)

something to the older romantic notions of the innocence of nature. Writers like William Faulkner and Robinson Jeffers took a harsher view of nature and of man's passions. But the dominant tone of the 1930s was that set in Marc Connelly's *Green Pastures* (1929) in which humble Negroes were symbols of truth, dignity, and beauty. The idealization of workers and peasants was in accord with the desire to locate in these groups the potential for reforming the whole society. Since they were the least powerful and thus least to blame for existing problems, the increase in their strength might improve the lot of all. So too, the labor movement's heroic struggle for organization against powerful odds seemed worthy of celebration, as in *Black Fury* (1935), an exceptional movie set in the coal mines.

War and fascism were condemned. *The Green Table*, a modern satire of war and diplo-macy presented by the Jooss Ballet, received an enthusiastic reception in the United States (1933); and *Johnny Johnson* (1936), a lyrical musical, voiced a poignant protest against the senseless destructiveness of combat. In *The Great Dictator* (1940), Chaplin subjected Hitler to merciless satire, and in *It Can't Happen Here* (1935) Sinclair Lewis described a coming American fascism. Yet these were tricky themes, the complexity of which appeared after 1939 when war became the means of fighting fascism. Robert E. Sherwood, whose pacifist play *Idiot's Delight* appeared in 1936, a few years later was praising the resistance of the gallant Finns against the Russian invaders in *There Shall Be No Night* (1940).

In the end the search for social significance returned to the individual. Writers without illusions, yet nevertheless firm in their own convic-

Things Important to Me, 1936

The law doesn't know that a lot of things that were very important to me—silly things like a belief in justice, and an idea that men were civilized, and a feeling of pride that this country of mine was different from all others—the law doesn't know that those things were burned to death within me that night. So it would be silly for me to stand here and say I'll forgive and forget. . . . I came here today for my own sake. I came here because I couldn't stand being alone. Maybe what I'm saying doesn't make sense to you, but my thoughts are all jumbled up, and I've got to tell them as they come to me. . . . I still don't know whether I was right or wrong. . . . I don't know. All I know is that the only way I could go on living was to come here today.

—Joe Wheeler (Spencer Tracy) in *Fury*, a screenplay by Bartlett Cormack and Fritz Lang, produced by Metro Goldwyn Mayer, based on a story by Norman Krasna.

A Still from the Film *Black Fury* (1935). (The Museum of Modern Art)

tions, stated clearly the objectives of their society. In Hemingway's widely read novel *For Whom the Bell Tolls,* the hero Robert Jordan continued to fight, knowing that he would probably fail and that even if he won his ideals would be corrupted. In a world only slightly responsive to his wishes, the individual could do no more than struggle to fulfill his personality as best he could. A novel which began by asserting that no man was an island unto himself concluded that in the end each man had to light his own way in the darkness.

▼

Reaffirmation of the worth of the individual was as far as the intellectual resources of American society could carry creative artists. After 1929, they stood in a favorable position. The most important restraints on their freedom had dissolved, and a large though conglomerate audience awaited their insights. The issues of social justice and war provided themes worthy of their best efforts and elicited creditable achievements. Furthermore, the nation's capacity to convey communications through a variety of media and across all social levels provided the means for unifying it during the trial of war and the complexities of peace.

Paperbacks for Further Reading

There are essays on this period in Edmund Wilson, *American Earthquake* (Anchor Books) and *Shores of Light* (Vintage Books, Inc.). Hortense Powdermaker, *Hollywood the Dream Factory* (Universal Library) is a contemporary analysis of the movies. Robert Lewis Taylor, *W. C. Fields* (Signet Books) places that entertainer in his social setting. There is a good selection in William Faulkner, *Portable Faulkner* (Viking Paperbound Portables), and most of the other writers mentioned in the text are also available in paperback.

THE POLITICS OF
REFORM

90

The two-party system survived the Depression, the New Deal, and the war. In 1947, the voter in his booth looked at a ballot on which the Republicans and Democrats confronted each other as they had in 1929. Moreover, the intervening decades had witnessed relatively few structural alterations in government. Congress and the cabinet, the municipalities and the state legislatures, functioned as they had earlier despite the great social and economic changes of the 1930s.

Yet beneath the surface continuity of the politics of the period, important realignments affected the relative strength of the two parties and their capacity to act. Shifts in the location of power explained not only Roosevelt's long tenure of office but also his ability to thread a course that effected reforms without losing the confidence of the nation.

The Roosevelt Majorities, 1932–1944

Party	1932 Electoral	1932 Popular (millions)	1936 Electoral	1936 Popular (millions)	1940 Electoral	1940 Popular (millions)	1944 Electoral	1944 Popular (millions)
Democratic	472	22.8	523	27.7	449	27.3	432	25.6
Republican	59	15.7	8	16.6	82	22.3	99	22.0
Socialist	–	0.8	–	0.1	–	–	–	–
Union	–	–	–	0.8	–	–	–	–

The Reform Coalition

THE OVERWHELMING MAJORITY with which Roosevelt won the election in 1932 gave him tremendous leverage for the enactment of any program he wished. The crisis that gripped the country in March 1933 and his success in restoring confidence consolidated his support. Although he had to keep in mind the dissenting views of Congressmen and local leaders, he was himself never thereafter in danger of defeat at the ballot box.

The Composition of the Democratic Party The army of voters which followed his lead consisted in the beginning of the most heterogeneous elements. But the test of the first term brought to the fore those who were loyal, leaving aside those who had joined as a result of mistaken estimates of the man and his policies.

Substantial New Deal support always came from tried and true Democrats. No one who had voted for Smith in 1928 was likely to desert Roosevelt in 1932, and most Southerners who had drifted to Hoover in the earlier year came back in 1932. Party solidarity and the eagerness for patronage were strong after the long period of deprivation and remained important.

But Roosevelt also drew the votes of people who were not simply partisan Democrats. Out of the ranks of the progressive Republicans and out of the smaller splinter parties came sizable groups that favored the New Deal program as it evolved. It took shrewd maneuvering to manage these blocs and to weld them into a dependable coalition.

Secretary of Agriculture Henry A. Wallace was representative of an important phalanx of midwestern agrarians. Many, like Wallace himself, were Republicans alienated by the Coolidge and Hoover administrations. Others had been in quest of an affiliation since the failure of the Bull Moose and the La Follette campaigns of 1912 and 1924. Still others were formally enrolled in the Farmer-Labor party, which had gained strength in the 1920s among the wheat farmers and which controlled some offices in Minnesota and the Dakotas.

The Urban Vote Urban progressives were a more conglomerate group. Among them were independents and Republicans like Secretary of the Interior Harold L. Ickes of Chicago and Mayor Fiorello H. La Guardia of New York who had long records of battle with the local Democratic machines. To retain the support of such individuals without alienating the Tammany and other bosses was delicate work.

Common dependence on a pool of voters loyal to Roosevelt for ethnic and economic reasons held the reformers and the machines together. In the big city wards the Irish, the Jews, the Italians, and the Negroes, among others, had identified themselves with the Democratic party since 1928. The President took pains to cultivate their loyalty. The same people were also workingmen, hard hit by the depression. To them the New Deal was not only the source of relief and

Samuel Irving Rosenman, *Working with Roosevelt* (New York, 1952); and Alfred B. Rollins, Jr., *Roosevelt and Howe* (New York, 1962) have useful information on Roosevelt's political methods.

Fiorello H. La Guardia (1882–1947). (U.P.I.)

FIORELLO H. LA GUARDIA was born in New York City in 1882. His father had come to the United States as accompanist to the singer Adelina Patti and he stayed on as an army bandmaster. The family traveled to various army posts and Fiorello spent most of his youth in Prescott, Arizona.

When his father died in 1898—a victim of putrefied army beef—Fiorello went with his mother to Europe and in time held posts as American consular agent in Trieste and Fiume. In 1906 he returned to New York and, while supporting himself as an interpreter on Ellis Island, studied law at night. He knew the immigrants; his father was Italian, his mother Jewish, and he had seen thousands pass through the gates to the New World. Once admitted to the bar, he began to practice among them.

La Guardia became a progressive Republican, partly through the influence of T. R.'s 1912 campaign, partly because the Irish had just about taken over the Democratic party. In 1914 he made an impressive showing in a race for the United States House of Representatives and two years later was elected. With the exception of two brief interludes, while he was in the United States air service during World War I and while he served as president of the Board of Aldermen of New York, he remained in the House of Representatives until 1932.

La Guardia was not much help to the Republicans. He represented a district in East Harlem the population of which consisted of Italian and Jewish working people. His own convictions and political strategy both dictated a course that antagonized the party leaders. He fought furiously for laws against labor injunctions and against the poll tax, and for unemployment insurance and old-age pensions. Ironically, the New Deal landslide in 1932 swept him from office.

The scandals exposed by the Seabury Committee investigation of the government of New York City offered La Guardia a greater opportunity, however. The "Little Flower" maneuvered reformers and Republicans into supporting him on a fusion ticket in the mayoralty campaign of 1933. He was elected and held command of City Hall until 1945. He proved an efficient as well as popular and liberal executive; he balanced the budget, yet built hospitals, parks, and highways, and he kept the morale of the people high during the dark days of depression and war. Although he remained nominally a Republican, he managed to collaborate with the New Deal. When he left the service of the city, he acted briefly as director of the United Nations Relief and Rehabilitation Administration (UNRRA). He died in 1947.

the hope of recovery but also the shield behind which they had been able to organize. As the unions gained strength, they ventured into politics and effectively mobilized mass support for Roosevelt. Labor's Nonpartisan Political League (1936), formed by the AF of L but dominated by John L. Lewis, was never neutral on the New Deal issues and provided important reserve strength. The CIO Political Action Committee (1943) would later prove an even more reliable ally.

The bosses and reformers struggled to enlist labor support, but however bitterly they fought on the local level, they could not turn against F. D. R. without risking the loss of their own popular support. La Guardia—a shrewd manipulator in his own right—met the needs of the situation in New York by forming the American Labor party (1936) with some trade union and Socialist support. Reform-minded individuals could thereafter vote for him, a Republican, and for F. D. R., a Democrat, on the same ticket. And the President, without any breach of party regularity, increased his independence of the bosses.

The Demagogues   La Guardia could not hope to use the American Labor party against the President and therefore was no threat. But Roosevelt had a more difficult time with men who did not follow the rules of the political game and who used popular discontent to build rival movements. Huey P. Long had served three years as governor of Louisiana when he went to the United States Senate in 1931. Ambitious, ruthless, and able, the Kingfish had built roads, schools, and a powerful machine. He expected that the demagogic skill which had brought him thus far would carry him still further. From the Senate he aimed to move to the White House by way of a national campaign to "share-our-wealth." When he was assassinated in 1935, he had split with Roosevelt and then been reconciled but he was undoubtedly planning some independent move. His state machine survived and his admirers throughout the country were receptive to the blandishments of new messiahs.

Political Tactics, 1933

In the last days before the election he told me that I was to function as a Deputy Attorney General of New York. Each side was allowed a few to patrol the Election. I went downtown and was sworn in. The night before election I will never forget. Fiorello sent for me and we went off by ourselves behind a big screen. His powerful jaw was set. He said, "Ernest, what are you going to do if they try to steal the election tomorrow?" His eyes glittered with a thousand lights, like the hard, cold glitter in the eyes of a poised black panther. I was almost hypnotized; I know I had difficulty swallowing before I could speak.

"Listen, Major," I said. "I took an oath and I'll live up to it. I know a crime when I see one. Nobody has to tell me what to do!"

"What will you do?" he persisted.

"I'll arrest them," I said angrily, "or get killed trying to."

He put his hand on my arm. "No," he said, "we don't want arrests; we want votes. If they rush the machine, knock them away from it. Then cast as many votes for me as they stole. You hear? Vote until they knock you out!"

—Ernest Cuneo, *Life with Fiorello* (New York: Crowell, Collier and Macmillan, Inc., 1955), pp. 171–172.

Father Charles E. Coughlin, whose radio talks reached a national audience from his parish near Detroit, was also once a New Deal supporter. He, too, found the pace of change too slow and demanded social justice by way of inflation. His calls for a living annual wage and for the nationalization of natural resources and banking, as well as his criticism of the President, threatened to cut into the reform following. In 1936, he campaigned against Roosevelt.

Arthur Mann, *La Guardia* (Philadelphia, 1959) is a lively account of a political career.

Allan P. Sindler, *Huey Long's Louisiana* (Baltimore, 1956) is a good analysis of state politics.

Share the Wealth, 1935

We are calling upon people whose souls cannot be cankered by the lure of wealth and corruption. We are calling upon people who have at heart, above their own nefarious possessions, the welfare of this country and of its humanity. We are calling upon them, we are calling upon you, we are calling upon the people of America, upon the men and women who love this country, and who would save their children and their neighbors from calamity and distress, to call in the people whom they know, to acquaint them with the purposes of this society and secure organization and co-operation among everyone willing to lend his hand to this worthy work . . . .

Here is the whole sum and substance of the share-our-wealth movement:

Every family to be furnished by the Government a homestead allowance, free of debt, of not less than one-third the average family wealth of the country, which means, at the lowest, that every family shall have the reasonable comforts of life up to a value of from $5,000 to $6,000. No person to have a fortune of more than 100 to 300 times the average family fortune, which means that the limit to fortunes is between $1,500,000 and $5,000,000, with annual capital levy taxes imposed on all above $1,000,000.

— Huey P. Long, Letter to Club Members. *Congressional Record,* 74th Cong., 1st sess., vol. LXXIX, p. 8042.

California was a case unto itself. In January 1934, Dr. Francis E. Townsend of Long Beach proposed a plan for paying every citizen of 60 or more $200 a month in scrip that had to be spent within a month. The resulting expenditures, Townsend claimed, would not only make it easy to finance the scheme by a sales tax but would also restore demand and cure the depression. In 1935, about 3 million members had joined Townsend Clubs, and there were many more sympathizers.

Also in California, Upton Sinclair, the socialist novelist, ran for governor in 1934 on the Democratic ticket. He proposed to End Poverty in California (EPIC) by an antique barter scheme, yet lost only by a narrow margin in a contest in which his opponents unscrupulously misrepresented him.

All such movements put pressure on Roosevelt. He could not let himself be outflanked lest he lose important segments of his strength. His course had to be far enough left to prevent significant defections in response to calls for action such as these, which were still powerful in 1937.

The Liberal Offensive

Conservatism Reminders were not lacking that there was a right wing also to the President's following. Roosevelt's strongest backing in the contest for nomination had come from the South. In 1931, in a move to block Al Smith, he had helped put through the Democratic National Committee a resolution which provided that between conventions the party spokesmen on policy matters were primarily the Democratic members of Congress. After 1933, Southern Senators and Representatives dominated the key committees of both chambers by virtue of seniority. F. D. R. was often impatient with the Congressional leaders, yet was unable to push the New Deal beyond the limits they set. His personal popularity was not an adequate counterweight against their control of the machinery of the House and Senate.

Furthermore, some wealthy Northern Democrats, who had accepted Roosevelt reluctantly, viewed his unpredictable political course with dismay. John J. Raskob, Jouett Shouse, and others had formed the American Liberty League (1934) to oppose excessive government tampering with the economy. They, too, were a threat.

Between 1935 and 1938, F. D. R. decided that the weight of political pressure came from the left, and that he needed its support for enactment of his program. He counted on holding the South and discounted Liberty League

The Supreme Court, Washington, June 1932. Justice Roberts (left), Justice Butler, Justice Brandeis, Justice Van Devanter, Chief Justice Charles Evans Hughes, Justice Sutherland, Justice Stone, and Justice Cardozo. Not present, Justice McReynolds. (Erich Salomon, Magnum)

resistance. In the election of 1936, the Republicans nominated Governor Alfred M. Landon of Kansas, a progressive who had the endorsement of William Randolph Hearst. The new Union party with the approval of Father Coughlin ran Representative William Lemke of North Dakota on a radical antibanker platform. Although Al Smith and some of his followers defected, Roosevelt won by a larger majority than in 1932, carrying every state but Maine and Vermont.

The Court Plan Emboldened by success, Roosevelt determined, in his second administration, to remove the obstacles that blocked the path to reform. His attention focused on the Supreme Court. The nine old men on the bench, a majority of them his resolute opponents, had declared measure after measure unconstitutional. Without regard for the needs of the situation they had invariably placed property rights before human rights. Six of them were aged seventy or more and yet they showed no disposition to move on. In his first four years in office, the President had not had the opportunity to make a single new appointment.

On February 5, 1937, Roosevelt introduced a plan to reorganize the Supreme Court. The plan made judges who reached the age of seventy eligible for voluntary retirement. In the event that they did not choose to retire the President was empowered to appoint additional members for each one who remained on the bench, bringing the Court up to a maximum of fifteen. Had the proposed law been enacted, Roosevelt could at once have added six justices and assured a more favorable attitude toward New Deal legislation.

The Court Plan, 1937

I share your disappointment that many important measures have been declared unconstitutional by a narrow and unconvincing vote of the Supreme Court. Unfortunately, however, I feel that the end which you desire to attain does not justify the means which you recommend. I do not believe that your plan will permanently correct the situation with which you have been confronted since a mere enlargement of the Court will not remove the possibility of narrow decisions in the future. I feel, too, that nothing should be done which is merely an attempt to meet an immediate situation at the expense of orderly and deliberate processes of government. From a governmental standpoint, whatever gain might be achieved through liberalizing the decisions of the Court would be far more than balanced by the loss of confidence which would result from the enactment of your proposals.

— Governor Lehman to President Roosevelt, February 26, as quoted in Allan Nevins, *Herbert H. Lehman and His Era* (New York: Charles Scribner's Sons, 1963), p. 190.

However, the proposal aroused a storm of controversy. The President was accused of intending to pack the court. Despite his immense popularity, a group formed in Congress to block the measure. Conservatives used the issue of usurpation of power as a convenient stick with which to beat the New Deal. But staunch liberals like Senator Burton K. Wheeler of Montana and followers of the President like Governor Herbert H. Lehman of New York also joined the opposition. Public opinion was hostile, roused no doubt by the press and the legal profession. Every indication revealed lack of support for the plan. The President nevertheless did not drop the bill until the death in July of Senator Joseph T. Robinson of Arkansas, who was managing it.

The failure was not complete. The justices had read the meaning of the warning and had already shown new moderation. In March and April 1937 they had upheld a minimum wage law and the Wagner act. Furthermore, the retirement of Willis Van Devanter enabled the President to appoint the first in a series of men in whom he had confidence. The Court ceased to be a major obstacle.

The Purge The incident revealed the extent to which conservative members of Congress could block Roosevelt's program. He determined to intervene in the election of 1938 to aid his friends and to defeat those who had frustrated him. He may already have had in mind a scheme for party reorganization that would draw together Farmer-Laborites, American-Laborites, and New Dealers into a liberal Democratic party and drive the conservatives into the arms of the Republicans.

His campaign had two aspects; he sought first to secure the nomination of his allies in the primary and then to win a Democratic victory in the mid-term election. During a transcontinental tour in the summer and by way of the radio, he made his preferences known.

Roosevelt failed. The primary purge met with some success in New York, Kentucky, and Oklahoma. But in the crucial tests, the doughty Senate conservatives, Walter George of Georgia, Cotton Ed Smith of South Carolina, and Millard Tydings of Maryland defeated the President's allies. In the election, the Republicans made substantial gains in Congress and took control of several states away from the Democrats.

The causes of the defeat were complex. Probably the recession of 1937 disheartened some and the court-packing plan alarmed others, and in any event mid-term elections normally saw a decline in the strength of the party in power. More important, Roosevelt's offensive bogged down in the decentralized American political system. Unlike its parliamentary counterparts in Europe, the party in the United States

The patrician bearing of **WALTER F. GEORGE** never quite concealed his plebeian antecedents. He was born on a tenant farm near Preston, Georgia, in 1878 and received such schooling as he could. The boy had oratorical ability; at fifteen he addressed a Masonic convention, and five years later, while a student at Mercer University, he won an intercollegiate contest with a speech on the Constitution. Clearly he had a political future.

After taking his law degree in 1901, George practiced in Vienna, Georgia, and then entered the state judicial system. In 1917, he was at the top, in the Georgia Supreme Court. His sights now shifted to the national scene. When a seat in the United States Senate became vacant at the death of Tom Watson in 1922, George put in a claim for it. In his campaign he denounced the League of Nations along with all other foreign alliances, opposed immigration, labor legislation, and antilynching proposals, and demanded stricter enforcement of the prohibition law. Elected in a landslide, he held the seat until his death in 1957.

George was an old-fashioned, regular Democrat who believed in states' rights, low taxes, and a tariff for revenue only. He was against any step that projected government into the private lives and affairs of the people. He was therefore in an anomalous position when the election of 1932 put Franklin D. Roosevelt in the White House. Party loyalty induced George to support some New Deal measures, including NRA, TVA, and AAA, but he was restive at the necessity of voting for laws about which he had doubts. When the Northern liberals began to attack Southern institutions, he decided to go his own way.

The Costigan-Wagner antilynching bill of 1935 was the turning point. George rebelled and thereafter opposed the New Deal coal, housing, holding company, and wage-and-hour bills. He also led the fight against the proposal to reorganize the Supreme Court in 1937. He was therefore a prime target during Roosevelt's purge a year later.

George's victory in 1938 left him at odds with the Administration, yet the Senate seniority system steadily increased his power. His positions on the Foreign Affairs and the Finance committees made him a formidable antagonist of the President. George fought the third term in 1940 and assembled around him a clique of antiadministration Democrats. Although the hostility subsided under the pressure of the war, it lingered beneath the surface and would emerge once more after 1945 in running conflicts between the President and the Senate leadership dominated by Southerners.

was truly national only during a presidential election. At other times, the state and local organizations could resist coercion. Roosevelt's friends controlled the local machinery in New York and he therefore succeeded in ousting Congressman John J. O'Connor there, but he could not touch the entrenched Southern Senators who had their own sources of power.

Roosevelt did not cease to consider party reorganization desirable, yet he read the lesson of his defeat correctly. Conservative Democrats and Republicans could combine in Congress to defeat any New Deal measure. It was therefore necessary to mediate with them, to shift somewhat to the right. Meanwhile the approach of war raised other questions on which cooperation was important. The reform coalition still existed but its power, for the time being, was curtailed.

Foreign Policy and Politics

The Third Term By 1940, the pivotal issue had become foreign policy. Roosevelt's decision to seek a third term prevented a Democratic split on the issue. He made the choice he did, apart from reluctance to drop the reins of power, because he believed that only thus could he keep party control from falling to conservatives or isolationists. His prestige was great enough to secure the nomination without difficulty and also to drop Garner as his running mate in favor of the more liberal Henry A. Wallace.

The Republicans, on the other hand, divided sharply and the split in their ranks endured. The Western isolationists backed either Senators Robert A. Taft of Ohio or Arthur H. Vandenberg of Michigan; the Eastern internationalists supported Thomas E. Dewey of New York. On the sixth ballot an overwhelming demonstration in the convention hall gave the nomination to Wendell Willkie, a progressive public utilities executive with no previous government experience. F. D. R. won handily.

Bipartisanship In the next five years, foreign affairs dominated politics. Roosevelt refrained from pushing divisive domestic issues and he avoided Wilson's mistake of antagonizing the Republicans. When the danger of war grew imminent, he consulted with prominent members of the opposition in the effort to make foreign policy bipartisan. In 1940, he brought two distinguished Republicans into his cabinet — Henry L. Stimson in the Department of War and Frank Knox in the Department of the Navy. Roosevelt also pacified Vandeberg and included Republicans in important delegations.

As a result foreign policy did not become a party issue. The Western isolationists remained impotent. Their contest with the Eastern Republicans had by no means come to an end, but the war prevented the GOP from opposing Roosevelt squarely on foreign policy.

In 1944, military success was close enough and the disappointments of peace still remote enough so that the familiar and popular wartime leader had no difficulty in gaining re-election. The Republican Convention was more concerned with future control of the party machinery than with the nebulous prospect of capturing the White House. Dewey's nomination over Taft on the first ballot showed that the Easterners were still in command.

By then Roosevelt had shifted a little more to the center. He did not respond to the liberal demand that he keep Vice-President Wallace on the ticket and instead let the nomination go to the more moderate Senator from Missouri, Harry S. Truman, who had gained attention as chairman of a Congressional committee to investigate war contracts.

There were no surprises in the election. Roosevelt's strength was so well distributed that he was able to gain almost as large a vote in the electoral college as he had in his previous campaigns. His mandate for leadership was undiminished.

The shock of Roosevelt's death in the first year of his term made a deep impression, but it did not fundamentally alter the structure of politics as the New Deal revolutions had left it. Truman lacked his predecessor's political style and the ability to charm millions by a fireside chat, but there was no break either in the governmental or the party chain of command.

The Postwar Situation

The Majority Party The Democratic party emerged from the war the majority party in the nation. Its strength rested on its popular support, its leadership, and its long control of the Federal government. By contrast, the divisions among Republicans were strong.

The Democrats retained the loyalty of groups traditionally affiliated with the party. The South was changing, but it was still firm in its support. The urban machines competed with reformers, yet had nowhere else to go in national politics. Furthermore, organized labor and the ethnic minority groups had established the firm habit of voting Democratic. The combination of the large city and the Southern votes, frequently with Midwestern agrarian support, stabilized the party position.

Furthermore, Democratic leadership was strong, long identified as it was with power.

Control over the state governments produced powerful executives with good reputations and command of adequate patronage. Herbert H. Lehman of New York, Frank Murphy of Michigan, Culbert L. Olson of California, J. H. McGrath of Rhode Island, and Charles Edison of New Jersey provided useful backing to the national party.

Long tenure of Congressional power had taught the Democrats how to avoid schisms. The attempted purge of 1938 was not repeated. The liberal Northern and the conservative Southern wings cooperated on the war and on some, though not all, economic issues. Seniority gave the smaller Southern group control of the committees, and the Senate filibuster left them a veto power over legislation to which they objected. In a showdown, too, they could often count upon Republican support. The more numerous Northern Democratic liberals had the weight of numbers behind them and usually the support of the President. Moreover, they inherited the mantle of the New Deal and the potential popular following left by the reform coalition of the 1930s.

The Minority By contrast, the Republicans were not only a minority but deeply split. Dewey and the Easterners controlled the national party, but its greatest strength lay in the West, where Robert A. Taft was a hero. Dewey's followers were internationalists and were, as well, willing to accept the changes of the 1930s. Taft's were inclined toward isolation and dreamed of undoing the New Deal legislation. In 1947 the two forces approached a test of strength, for the mid-term election of 1946 gave the Republicans command of Congress. High prices, the fear of a recession, and grievances accumulated during the war convinced many voters everywhere that it was time for a change. The GOP would have to use its power responsibly.

The Structure of Government The New Deal and the war produced surprisingly few changes in the structure of government. The Twentieth,

or Lame Duck, Amendment (1933) shortened the time between elections and the change of administrations to avoid the embarrassing interregnum of 1933. The Democrats eliminated the two-thirds rule that had long complicated the process of making a nomination in their conventions. Otherwise, the executive, legislative, and judicial departments remained in 1947 much as they had been in 1929. The same was true of state and municipal government.

Yet as the Federal government assumed new functions, the size of the bureaucracy multiplied. The number of civilian employees rose from 588,000 in 1931 to 1,370,000 in 1941. At the same time, new agencies, unrelated to one another, piled up in a loose and sprawling administrative tangle. Roosevelt in 1937 had suggested extensive reorganizations, but the Congress, fearing unrestrained presidential power, would go no further in the next year than to consolidate a number of boards into the Federal Security, the Federal Works, and the Federal Loan agencies. Perhaps the very magnitude of the social and economic changes taking place made Americans reluctant to embark upon any radical tinkering with their political system.

▼

Though the structure of government remained largely unchanged, the political system did feel the effects of depression and war. Under the pressure of an unsettled economy, Americans demanded positive action by the state, which established a new relation to the productive system. Furthermore, requirements of a long expensive global war compelled government to take on unprecedented functions.

The power of decision in these matters rested in the hands of an administration animated by the intellectual and cultural values of the New Deal. Its basic strength lay in the popular support of a reform coalition, but it operated within a party system that limited its freedom of action.

Allan Nevins, *Herbert H. Lehman and His Era* (New York, 1963) includes a good treatment of the governorship.

The Twentieth Amendment

SECTION 1. The terms of the President and Vice-President shall end at noon on the twentieth day of January, and the terms of Senators and Representatives at noon on the third day of January, of the years in which such terms would have ended if this article had not been ratified; and the terms of their successors shall then begin.

SECTION 2. The Congress shall assemble at least once in every year, and such meeting shall begin at noon on the third day of January, unless they shall by law appoint a different day.

SECTION 3. If, at the time fixed for the beginning of the term of the President, the President-elect shall have died, the Vice-President-elect shall become President. If a President shall not have been chosen before the time fixed for the beginning of his term, or if the President-elect shall have failed to qualify, then the Vice-President-elect shall act as President until a President shall have qualified; and the Congress may by law provide for the case wherein neither a President-elect nor a Vice-President-elect shall have qualified, declaring who shall then act as President, or the manner in which one who is to act shall be selected, and such person shall act accordingly until a President or Vice-President shall have qualified.

SECTION 4. The Congress may by law provide for the case of the death of any of the persons from whom the House of Representatives may choose a President whenever the right of choice shall have devolved upon them, and for the case of the death of any of the persons from whom the Senate may choose a Vice-President whenever the right of choice shall have devolved upon them.

SECTION 5. SECTIONS 1 and 2 shall take effect on the 15th day of October following the ratification of this article.

SECTION 6. This article shall be inoperative unless it shall have been ratified as an amendment to the Constitution by the legislatures of three-fourths of the several States within seven years from the date of its submission.

—Passed by Congress, March 3, 1932; ratified February 6, 1933.

The country emerged from the double crises of depression and war with undiminished strength, but its political system then had to meet the problems of still more rapid change in a still disordered world.

Paperbacks for Further Reading

Samuel Lubell, *Future of American Politics* (Harper Colophon Books) and Harold F. Gosnell, *Negro Politicians* (Phoenix Books) deal with aspects of ethnic politics. Among the useful biographical studies are: Edward J. Flynn, *You're the Boss* (Collier Books); Oscar Handlin, *Al Smith and His America* (Little, Brown & Co.); and Arthur Mann, *LaGuardia Comes to Power* (J. B. Lippincott Co.). There is a chapter on Huey Long in T. Harry Williams, *Romance and Realism in Southern Politics* (Louisiana State University Press).

The role of the courts is treated in: Carl Brent Swisher, *The Supreme Court* (New York University Press); Fred Rodell, *Nine Men* (Vintage Books, Inc.); A. T. Mason, *Supreme Court from Taft to Warren* (W. W. Norton & Company, Inc.); Allison Dunham and P. R. Kurland, eds., *Mr. Justice* (Phoenix Books); and Walter F. Murphy, *Congress and the Court* (Phoenix Books). William N. Chambers, *Democrats* (Anvil Books) has a brief account of this period. Ernest S. Griffith, *Congress: Its Contemporary Role* (New York University Press) also has some material on these years.

PEACE IN A WORLD

OF CONFLICT

1945–1966

X

THE FAIR DEAL

91

The war bequeathed a burdensome heritage to Americans of the decades after 1947. A good part of the world beyond their borders was in disorder, shaken by the effects of the conflict and by the aspirations of social groups previously submerged. The United States bore unprecedented responsibilities in furthering stability for it was one of the two great powers that commanded sufficient force to make itself felt anywhere. Furthermore, because its wealth and resources were intact, it felt the obligation to aid those who had suffered more.

The four Presidents who made the major decisions in this period had to deal also with a confusing internal situation. Rapid social change transformed the country and called for radical adjustments in modes of thought and action. Yet the old political machinery remained virtually unchanged. The nation's great asset was a surprisingly resilient economy. With recovery from the effects of the war, a period of economic development began that was quite different from that which had followed the peace of 1918. Enough controls over the economy survived to prevent a repetition of the experience of the 1920s and 1930s. Growth altered political thought and action and provided the means of sustaining a vigorous foreign policy. Tensions nevertheless remained, as Americans groped for a way to deal with the armed peace that kept them constantly on the alert.

Politics, But Not as Usual

The Truman Administration Truman did not bring into office a general program. He had been an admirer of F. D. R., and his experience on a wartime Congressional investigating committee had taught him the importance of stressing the interests of the whole society rather than of special interests within it. Shortly after the Japanese surrender he had set the goals of his administration in liberal terms: full employment, higher minimum wages and social security payments, more public housing, and a fair employment practices act. In addition Truman suggested entirely novel measures of long-range planning, Federal aid to science and education, medical insurance, and the nationalization of atomic energy.

But it was hard for any Vice-President without a popular mandate to take command of the government and it was particularly difficult for a relative newcomer to succeed F. D. R., who had occupied the White House for fourteen critical years. Some old New Dealers like Leon H. Keyserling stayed on, hoping to bring to fruition reforms postponed from the 1930s. Frances Perkins, Harold L. Ickes, and Henry A. Wallace left after disagreements with the new leader. Truman gave prominent cabinet posts to more conservative men like Secretary of the Treasury John W. Snyder and Secretary of Agriculture Clinton Anderson, and he leaned heavily on the advice of Clark Clifford, a St. Louis lawyer and a moderate. Since foreign affairs usually occupied the President's attention and since it took time to master the intricacies of administration, he left many decisions to the Department heads.

Truman's inability to control Congress further limited his capacity for action. The President was sensitive to the needs of the whole country. The legislators were not, for their interests were local and sectional. The structure of the Senate gave a disproportionate number of seats to the small rural states, and the failure to adjust electoral districts to shifts in population often had the same effect in the House of Representatives. As in the past, the seniority system usually kept power in the hands of conservatives elected again and again with little opposition. Truman therefore met formidable resistance to the measures he proposed.

After the election of 1946, the Republican majority that ruled both houses of the Eightieth Congress compounded Truman's problems. Speaker Joseph W. Martin and Senate majority leader Robert A. Taft were eager to undo the work of the New Deal or at least to prevent its extension. These GOP leaders had the cooperation of some Southerners in a conservative alliance hostile to the President.

Prices and Wages In the first years of peace, the primary domestic problem was the inflation that resulted from the precipitate removal of wartime rationing against the advice of Chester Bowles, head of the Office of Price Administration. The process had actually begun in 1944 as the administration yielded to pressure from the producers of agricultural and industrial goods. The hope that price controls alone would prevent rises when one commodity after another was freed of rationing restrictions proved vain.

Consumers with aggregate savings of billions rushed into the market to make the purchases they had previously postponed. They discovered frustrating shortages. The returned veterans could find no housing, for the country suffered from a backlog in building almost twenty years old. Many foods were also in short supply, as were some manufactured goods.

The black market had flourished even during the war; its activity increased with the peace, when patriotic scruples no longer kept people in line. While the price level established by law remained relatively stable, the actual costs paid by consumers soared in the two years after May 1944. In June 1946, the President and Congress were unable to agree on the terms for renewal of the OPA and price controls expired. Thereafter the legal prices rose to black-market levels. In

Luck was not with **HARRY S. TRUMAN** through most of his life. He was born in 1884 in a small town in Barton County, Missouri, and grew up in nearby Independence. When he graduated from high school, he secured an appointment to West Point but his eyes were bad and he was rejected. He drifted from one job to another as a clerk and bookkeeper until 1904, when a bachelor uncle left him a farm. For the next twelve years, Truman was a farmer.

His father had been active in politics, helping out the local Pendergast machine. Harry followed in his footsteps. He also joined the National Guard with which he drilled for six years. He enlisted during World War I, served with the field artillery in France, and rose to the reserve rank of major.

When he returned home, he decided to settle down and advance himself. He married at the age of thirty-three. But his venture into business proved unsuccessful. He lost all his savings and spent fifteen years paying off his debts. Pendergast then came to the rescue, securing for Truman the election as one of the judges of the County Court, an administrative agency of local government. Truman served for two years and studied law at night. In the next ten years he held various other political posts, but when he secured the nomination and election as United States Senator in 1934, it was essentially as a reward for party loyalty and regularity.

In 1940 he managed to be re-elected only because two rival reform candidates killed each other off. During the war he attracted some attention by his conscientious leadership of the Special Committee to Investigate Contracts under the National Defense Program (1941). But he was far from being one of the stars of the Senate when he was chosen to run for the vice-presidency after Roosevelt decided to get rid of Wallace. It was to Truman, however, that the burden of the greatest decisions of the war and of the postwar period fell. Scarcely prepared for office, he nevertheless acquitted himself well.

Under Truman's leadership the United States gradually shifted its sights from the goals of the 1930s to those of the 1950s. In domestic policy Truman saw the need for going beyond the New Deal to positive action by government to further the social welfare of the people. In foreign policy, he realized that no return to isolation would be possible; the nation would have to bear the responsibilities of a world power. The little man from Missouri courageously faced up to decisions momentous in their implications for the future.

---

the first two weeks of July 1946, the prices of basic commodities went up 25 percent. Meat cost the housewife 20 cents a pound more than a few days earlier.

Businessmen had little difficulty, because they generally could pass the increases on to the helpless consumers. Laborers, by contrast, felt the pinch of higher living costs even in 1945. Yet their demand for higher wages met the determined resistance of employers, who feared that a depression was on the way, as after World War I. Since inflation was considered an imminent danger, the workers' demands attracted more notice than the price increases achieved by farmers and entrepreneurs.

The year of strikes—1946—placed Truman in an awkward position. Walkouts by the auto and steel workers had already won gains in earnings of about 18 percent, which the corporations recouped by lifting their prices. The President feared that inflation would spiral out of control. Although he was a friend of labor, he nevertheless acted against the unions in the great coal strike of April of that year and in the threatened railroad stoppage a month later. He forced labor to back down by seizing the mines and threaten-

Miners at the New Orient Mine, West Frankfort, Illinois, Walk off the Job, November 19, 1946. (UPI)

ing to draft the railway men into the army to keep the trains running. The infuriated CIO leaders announced that they were through with Truman for he had undermined their right to strike, the ultimate resource in collective bargaining. The conservative Republican senator Robert A. Taft of Ohio had also denounced the President's actions as steps toward Hitlerism, Stalinism, and totalitarianism.

The GOP unwittingly pulled the President's chestnuts out of the fire. Secure in its rural constituencies, it made the strikes of 1946 the excuse for passing the Taft-Hartley law (1947) over Truman's veto. That measure authorized state right-to-work laws which forbade the closed shop by permitting employers to hire whomever they wished. The Taft-Hartley law also recognized the union shop by providing that those hired could be required to join the union if the majority of workers desired. Labor organizations were

not allowed to make political contributions and were required to publish financial statements and to exclude Communists from leadership. In addition, the law established a cooling-off period for strikes that involved the national health and safety.

The Taft-Hartley law confirmed the belief of organized labor that the Republicans were basically inimical to it. While many workers resented Truman's actions during the strikes, they ultimately conceded that the right to bargain collectively was more secure under the Democrats than it would be under the GOP.

The Election of 1948   Nevertheless, Truman's prospects for re-election seemed gloomy in the spring and summer of 1948. He had not distinguished himself in political battle. The success of the Republicans in 1946, when they gained control of both houses of Congress and twenty-five governorships, added to the dissatisfaction

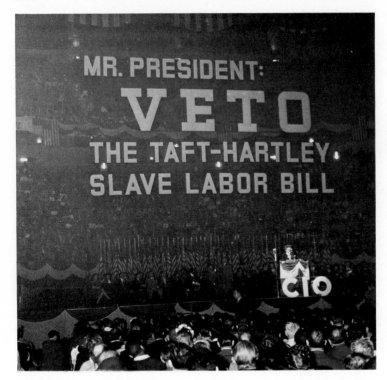

The CIO Protests Passage of the Taft-Hartley Bill, Madison Square Garden, New York, June 10, 1947. (UPI)

in the President's party. Senator J. William Fulbright of Arkansas then suggested that Truman resign, and liberal Democrats had hoped to persuade General Eisenhower to accept the nomination. The President's popularity declined steadily. The public-opinion polls pointed to his defeat down to the day of the election.

The Republican ticket, led by Governors Thomas E. Dewey of New York and Earl Warren of California, was young, aggressive, and popular. The candidates had demonstrated their attractiveness in the two most populous states of the Union, and they promised to preserve the gains of the past twenty years but to govern with greater efficiency and vigor.

By contrast, Truman chose as his running mate an elderly Senator, Alben W. Barkley, like himself the representative of a border state. Moreover, the Democrats ran the risk of losing votes to bolters on both the right and the left. In the Convention, the liberals put through a strong civil rights plank calling for Federal legislation to prevent lynching, the poll tax, and discrimination in employment. The die-hard Southerners thereupon placed their own Dixiecrat ticket in the field and threatened to pull away some of the segregationist states. Meanwhile Henry A. Wallace, running as a Progressive, called for the votes of labor and of some liberals who disagreed with the President's foreign policy.

The inability of the Republicans to square the statements of their candidates with the record of the Eightieth Congress gave Truman the victory. Dewey understood, from his New York gubernatorial race, that the Negro vote was growing and that the immigrant ethnic stocks were significant political factors. Success depended on winning over the loyalty of some of these people.

Yet the Eightieth Congress undermined popular confidence in any promises the Republican candidates might make. Under the leadership of Speaker Joseph W. Martin of Massachusetts

The Twenty-second Amendment

SECTION 1. No person shall be elected to the office of the President more than twice, and no person who has held the office of President, or acted as President, for more than two years of a term to which some other person was elected President shall be elected to the office of the President more than once. But this Article shall not apply to any person holding the office of President when this Article was proposed by Congress, and shall not prevent any person who may be holding the office of President, or acting as President, during the term within which this Article becomes operative from holding the office of President or acting as President during the remainder of such term.

SECTION 2. The article shall be inoperative unless it shall have been ratified as an amendment to the Constitution by the legislatures of three-fourths of the several States within seven years from the date of its submission to the States by the Congress.

—Passed by Congress, March 24, 1947; ratified, March 1, 1951.

A Challenge to the Republicans, 1948

There is a long list of these promises in that Republican platform. If it weren't so late, I would tell you all about them. I have discussed a number of these failures of the Republican 80th Congress. Every one of them is important. Two of them are of major concern to nearly every American family. They failed to do anything about high prices, they failed to do anything about housing.

My duty as President requires that I use every means within my power to get the laws the people need on matters of such importance and urgency.

I am therefore calling this Congress back into session July 26th.

On the 26th day of July, which out in Missouri we call "Turnip Day," I am going to call Congress back and ask them to pass laws to halt rising prices, to meet the housing crisis—which they are saying they are for in their platform.

At the same time I shall ask them to act upon other vitally needed measures such as aid to education, which they say they are for; a national health program; civil rights legislation, which they say they are for; an increase in the minimum wage, which I doubt very much they are for; extension of the social security coverage and increased benefits, which they say they are for; funds for projects needed in our program to provide public power and cheap electricity. By indirection, this 80th Congress has tried to sabotage the power policies the United States pursued for 14 years. That power lobby is as bad as the real estate lobby, which is sitting on the housing bill.

—President Harry S. Truman, on Accepting the Democratic Nomination, July 15. *Public Papers of the Presidents, Harry S. Truman, 1948* (Washington: Government Printing Office, 1964), pp. 409–410.

and Senator John W. Bricker of Ohio it had rejected Truman's proposals for liberalizing social security and minimum-wage standards and had cut the funds for reclamation, conservation, and crop storage. The Twenty-second (two-term) Amendment was a slap at Franklin D. Roosevelt. The Displaced Persons Act (1948), Truman pointed out, discriminated against Jews and Catholics; and there was no action at all on his request for a civil-rights act or for aid to education.

By calling a special session of Congress, Truman threw down a challenge to the Republicans to make good the promises of their platform. The assembled legislators did nothing but provide him with additional material. Republican efforts to shift ground to criticism of Roosevelt's

544 PEACE IN A WORLD OF CONFLICT 1945-1966

softness at Yalta failed. Nor did GOP appeals to the patriotism of the veterans evoke much response. The returned veterans did not form a powerful lobby, as they had in the 1920s. The very size and disparity of the group prevented its mobilization on behalf of any specific interest.

Determined to "give them hell," Truman made 356 speeches in a 31,700-mile swing through the country attacking the do-nothing, good-for-nothing Eightieth Congress. Saying little about his opponents, he kept coming back to the record and persuaded a plurality of the voters that they would do better with him. Truman got 24 million votes, Dewey about 22 million, and Wallace and the Dixiecrat candidate, J. Strom Thurmond, each a little more than a million. The electoral margin was substantial, 303 for the President as against 189 for Dewey and 39 for Thurmond and none for Wallace. Truman lost Alabama, Louisiana, Mississippi, and South Carolina in the once Solid South and also the Northern industrial states of Connecticut, Michigan, New Jersey, New York, and Pennsylvania. Yet firm backing in the West carried him into office and, along with him, Democratic majorities in both houses of Congress.

The Fair Deal
in Action

The Politics of Inflation The effects of inflation contributed to the surprising outcome of the election. Everyone agreed in the abstract that some control over spiraling prices and wages was desirable. A Gallup poll in August 1948 showed that many Americans desired some restraint by law. Nevertheless, inflation in practice favored some groups. Businessmen gained as profit margins held up, and labor enjoyed a second round of increases in 1947 and a third in 1948. Inflation also eased, if it did not cure, the farmers' plight. With the return of peace, surpluses once more became a problem and they remained so in the decade that followed. But the situation was tolerable as long as government support kept

prices rising. When the Republicans in the Eightieth Congress cut that support, they earned votes for Truman.

Inflation did not prove disastrous because the economy expanded at the same time. The level of production rose steadily and with it the level of employment. Furthermore, an increasing share in the rewards of growth spread among the whole population.

Changes within the system of production contributed to the reversal of the trend of the 1930s,* but industrial growth also owed something to the favorable political environment. The Federal government did not abandon the principles of the New Deal but gradually refined and advanced them. The program which Truman sketched before 1948 and which he would begin to implement after that date gave most Americans a stake in society and thus improved their positions as producers and consumers. Yet it assured entrepreneurs a return for their efforts and ingenuity and encouraged them to resume the habit of taking risks.

The Second Term Victory was heady medicine to the man from Missouri, particularly because it came in the face of so many predictions of defeat. Truman entered upon his second term renewed in confidence and determined to carry through his full program, which he labeled the Fair Deal in his address to Congress in January 1949. He still faced serious opposition from the Southern-Republican coalition, but he now had a popular mandate.

In 1949 Truman persuaded Congress to provide for low-income public housing and urban renewal and to raise social security payments and minimum wages. He also obtained extension of the programs for conservation, flood control, public power, and rural electrification, all of which enlarged the range of government expenditure. Although the Congress rejected his appeal for a fair employment practices act, he was able to end segregation in government agencies and in the armed forces

---

* These are discussed in Chapter 96.

Truman to Congress, the Fair Deal, 1949

In this society, we are conservative about the values and principles which we cherish; but we are forward-looking in protecting those values and principles and in extending their benefits. We have rejected the discredited theory that the fortunes of the Nation should be in the hands of a privileged few. We have abandoned the "trickle-down" concept of national prosperity. Instead, we believe that our economic system should rest on a democratic foundation and that wealth should be created for the benefit of all . . . .

The American people have decided that poverty is just as wasteful and just as unnecessary as preventable disease. We have pledged our common resources to help one another in the hazards and struggles of individual life. We believe that no unfair prejudice or artificial distinction should bar any citizen of the United States of America from an education, or from good health, or from a job that he is capable of performing.

The attainment of this kind of society demands the best efforts of every citizen in every walk of life, and it imposes increasing responsibilities on the Government.

— President Harry S. Truman, January 5. *Public Papers of the Presidents, Harry S. Truman, 1949* (Washington: Government Printing Office, 1964), pp. 1, 2.

Declaration of Economic Policy, 1946

The Congress hereby declares that it is the continuing policy and responsibility of the Federal Government to use all practicable means consistent with its needs and obligations and other essential considerations of national policy, with the assistance and cooperation of industry, agriculture, labor, and State and local governments, to coordinate and utilize all its plans, functions, and resources for the purpose of creating and maintaining, in a manner calculated to foster and promote free competitive enterprise and the general welfare, conditions under which there will be afforded useful employment opportunities, including self-employment, for those able, willing, and seeking to work, and to promote maximum employment, production, and purchasing power.

— The Employment Act of February 20, 1946. *United States Statutes at Large* (1946), vol. LX, part I, p. 23.

by executive action. Despite the failure of his efforts to develop a more rational farm program, to secure repeal of the Taft-Hartley law, or to get some provision for medical insurance, for aid to education, and for middle-income housing, he could justifiably view the record of the Eighty-first Congress with satisfaction.

From the New Deal experiments, from the ideas of John Maynard Keynes, and from the experience of the war, Truman was learning to manipulate fiscal policy to control the development of the economy. Conversion to the new economics was by no means complete. The financial interests, well represented in the Federal Reserve Board, consistently sought to apply a more traditional approach. But the President had at his disposal the immense spending and borrowing powers of the Treasury, which could offset the Board's control over credit.

Like everyone else, Truman regarded inflation as undesirable. But he was committed to preventing a reversion to the past in which a large labor force had been perennially the victims of fluctuations in the number of jobs. The Employment Act (1946) had set up a Council of Economic Advisers authorized to recommend action and thereby had enunciated as a valid governmental objective the maintenance of a

A. E. Holmans, *United States Fiscal Policy* (New York, 1961) treats developments between 1945 and 1959.

productive system that would provide work for all who wished it.

The decisive tests of the full employment policy came in the recessions of 1949 and 1951. Each resulted when the bankers, fearful of inflation, raised the interest rate in order to slow down economic growth. Truman could not persuade them of the desirability of keeping the rate down to maintain full employment. The Federal Reserve Board retained its power over the availability of credit. But a budget deficit attained by lowering taxes and increasing Federal expenditures stimulated business. This experience showed that government action could counterbalance tendencies toward recession. Shifts in fiscal policy could adjust the rate of economic growth and the levels of employment. The bankers could keep inflation under control; the Treasury, deflation. It was only necessary to know how to use these instruments and to wish to do so.

Equality   The ability of the government to act also directed attention to other long-hidden issues in American life, among them the need for extending complete equality to the minorities. In the 1930s, the pattern of racist thought that had supported prejudice had dissolved, although the depression limited the practical effects. During the war, universal service by men of all races, creeds, and national origins made anachronistic the residual discriminations of the past. The conflict fought in terms of the Four Freedoms created a momentum toward change. The members of the minority groups came back from the battlefields determined to gain the equal place in society they deserved.

Although differences existed among these groups, a common underprivileged situation united them in this period. Their initial objective was the elimination of all patterns of governmental discrimination and the full realization of the concept of equality before the law. Many municipalities and some states enacted laws that forbade discrimination in private employment and education. Furthermore, the National Association for the Advancement of Colored People

and allied organizations representing other groups vigorously pressed the courts to hold discrimination unconstitutional because of its denial of the equal rights guaranteed by the Fourteenth Amendment. In *Shelley* v. *Kraemer* (1948), the Supreme Court ruled unenforceable restrictive covenants by which the owners of desirable housing agreed not to sell to minorities. In *Sweatt* v. *Painter* (1950), the Court struck down some forms of educational segregation.

Yet such progress was painfully slow, for it depended on a case by case battle through the courts. In 1947, a presidential commission on civil rights pointed to the need for legislation, but the combination of Southern and Midwestern conservatives in Congress blocked a proposal for a permanent, national fair employment practices act.

Nor did President Truman succeed in altering the country's immigration policy. Successive efforts to open the gates of the United States for some of the millions of persons displaced by the war resulted only in increasing the number of admissions from 205,000 to 415,000 (1950). Calls for an end to the national origins quota system had no greater effect. The McCarran-Walter Act passed over Truman's veto in 1952 actually consolidated and strengthened the provisions that favored applicants from northern Europe and discriminated against those from the Mediterranean, although it did abolish the absolute bar against Asians. There was still a long way to go to realize the objectives of the Fair Deal.

The Subversives

National Security   The failure to liberalize the immigration laws or to deal more speedily with the plight of the minorities revealed the extent to which fear of strangers endured after 1948. The disappointments of the peace settlement and the frustrations that beset foreign policy nevertheless did not produce an upsurge of isolationism or an inclination to shirk the responsibilities of world power. But anxieties about national security drove Congress to excessively repressive measures.

The confusion about communism as an issue within the United States revealed the distortions in postwar American politics. Frightened conservatives conjured up the vision of a vast Red network that had seized control of the government under the New Deal and that was responsible for handing Europe over to the Russians and Asia to the Chinese. Irresponsible charges damaged many individuals guilty of no more than dissent from accepted views and a flurry of state loyalty and sedition laws burdened the statute books with measures that were potentially dangerous to conscientious innocents and yet would not trouble the truly seditious or treacherous.

On the other hand, too many liberals reacted by denying that there was any problem at all. Even those who mistrusted Stalin and Mao were inclined to regard all domestic charges of communism as a red herring that masked reactionary intentions. The resulting turmoil offered a demagogue the opportunity further to confuse the situation.

There had been a Communist danger—not from the goodhearted supporters of plausible causes, nor from the sympathizers with the Spanish republic, nor even from most of the open party members. The threat came from underground agents of the Soviet secret police or army and from dupes induced to spy for Moscow. To deal with this problem, President Roosevelt had authorized loyalty checks of government employees after 1942.

The discovery in 1945 of classified documents in the office of *Amerasia*, a Communist-front magazine, and the exposure a year later of a spy ring operating from Canada led Truman to broaden the investigations of security risks. By 1951, 3,000,000 officials had been cleared, 2000 had resigned, and 212 had been dismissed. Ample legislative authority to deal with subversion existed, not only in the laws against espionage but also in the Smith Act of 1940, which prohibited conspiracies to teach the violent overthrow of government by force. In the Dennis case (1951) the Supreme Court upheld the conviction in 1949 of eleven Communist leaders under the terms of the last-named measure. Nevertheless, concern persisted, stimulated by the inability to differentiate among various types of radicals and dissenters.

The Hiss Case The House Un-American Activities Committee contributed to the confusion. It heard a train of repentant Communists reveal their past activities. The witnesses often implicated others without discriminating among those who were party members, fellow travelers, or independent foes of fascism. Public uncertainty about the ramifications of the Red network mounted.

The testimony in 1948 of Whittaker Chambers, once member of a Soviet espionage ring, led to a denouement. Chambers referred mostly to events in the 1930s, and some of the people he named candidly admitted their past errors. But he also mentioned Alger Hiss, a former official in the Department of State, who had been present at the Yalta and San Francisco conferences. Hiss, then president of the Carnegie Endowment for International Peace, had impeccable connections and charged Chambers with perjury. In a reflex reaction liberals rushed to defend Hiss. Chambers thereupon produced documentary evidence to corroborate his story, and Hiss, brought to trial for perjury, was convicted in 1950.

McCarthyism The Hiss case undermined the credibility of the liberals and laid the groundwork for the rise to prominence of Joseph R. McCarthy. A few weeks after the Hiss trial, the junior Republican Senator from Wisconsin announced that he had a list of known Communists in the State Department. On the very next day a

Earl Latham, *The Communist Controversy in Washington* (Cambridge, Mass., 1966) is a good analysis.

Whittaker Chambers, *Witness* (New York, 1956), the autobiography of Alger Hiss's accuser, contains interesting material on the context of American communism. The best treatment of the case is Alistair Cooke, *A Generation on Trial* (New York, 1950).

Whittaker Chambers After Testifying Before the Federal Grand Jury, New York, December 7, 1948. (Brown Brothers)

Disloyalty, 1950

No sensible man could any longer maintain that there was no threat to his country. The problem . . . was how to protect the innocent citizen from getting pinched between the reality of the threat and the epidemic fear of it . . . . For the principals in this case were idealists at a time when idealism, and the nature of loyalty, were undergoing an historic test. If Hiss had said he had done all this, that he had passed papers proudly to confound the Nazis, to quicken the day of deliverance of enslaved popula-

tions, he could have been a greater Wadleigh. But because he had not stolen them, or could not or would not say he had, the defense had to argue from the impossible position that such gentle, trusted types are incapable of disloyalty. After Fuchs, we knew better. And what we were left with was not the tragic hero of a whole generation that had misjudged the endurance of national pride or the resilience of the Western tradition. What we were left with was a tragedy *manqué*.

—Alistair Cooke, *A Generation on Trial* (New York: Alfred A. Knopf, Inc., 1950), pp. 340–341.

The La Follettes had been prominent in Wisconsin politics so long that young Bob hardly thought it necessary to campaign for his Senate seat in 1946. He spent about two weeks back home before the Republican primary and then, in an upset, lost to **JOSEPH R. McCARTHY**, a virtually unknown judge of the state circuit court.

McCarthy was born in Grand Chute, Wisconsin, in 1908. His youth was hard. He worked in grocery stores, gas stations, and restaurants and ushered in a theater while he got himself through high school and law school. He became tough, a fighter determined to get ahead. In 1936, at the depth of the depression, he was a small-town lawyer with few prospects. Three years later, when he was elected judge, his future was still uncertain.

During the war he served in the Pacific as a ground officer in the Marine Air Force Intelligence. He came back ready for action and the place in the Senate offered him an appropriate forum.

McCarthy's initial years in Washington were uneventful, but a speech in Wheeling, West Virginia, on February 9, 1950, claimed the whole nation's attention. He then professed he held in his hand a list of fifty-seven card-carrying Communists and fellow travelers who, he said, still shaped American foreign policy in the State Department. A few months later a Senate subcommittee concluded that the charge was a fraud and a hoax, but McCarthy was launched on his career.

McCarthy's speech came a few weeks after Hiss's conviction and while the trial of Judith Coplon for espionage was still in progress. A day after the Senator spoke, the scientist Klaus Fuchs was arrested in England and confessed to having passed atomic secrets to the Russians. Millions of Americans, confused by the turn of postwar events, suddenly found an explanation—a Red conspiracy had subverted the nation's security.

McCarthy played his luck to the utmost. He intervened in the elections of 1950 in Maryland and Connecticut to secure the defeat of opponents in the Senate, and took charge of a subcommittee with a vague mandate to hunt Communists in any government department. Nor did his zeal abate when the Republicans took office in 1953. The efforts of President Eisenhower and Secretary of State Dulles to appease him wrecked the foreign and the information services but only spurred the Senator on to wilder accusations.

His downfall came when an attack on the army led to Senate hearings that were televised and exposed his buffoonery to the scrutiny of the public (April–July 1954). A vote of censure by the Senate in December 1954 drained away his power. He died in 1957, with the confusion caused by his irresponsibility still not cleared.

plot to transfer atomic secrets to the Reds was uncovered in London. McCarthy's fraudulent charges became credible. If respectable scientists like Fuchs and well-known statesmen like Hiss were working for the Soviet Union, then anyone might be.

In the years that followed, the uninhibited use of wild accusations of communism brought McCarthy notoriety and actual power. He diverted the energies of government officials from their proper tasks and shattered the morale of the State Department. Success inflated his ego and egged him on to further efforts. His strength derived from genuine popular confusion about the relationship of communism to disloyalty and also from the willingness of the Senate conservatives to use him to knock the President and the liberals off balance.

The political implications of the hunt for subversives became clear when the conservatives used the issue to make some gains in the Congressional elections of 1950. During that campaign, the McCarran Internal Security Act, which passed over Truman's veto, compelled Communist and Communist-front organizations to register, forbade the employment of their members in defense plants, and excluded anyone ever affiliated with a totalitarian movement from admission to the United States.

▼

The fear of subversives deepened as a result of developments in foreign policy after 1947. The end of the war had not led to peace but to a series of frustrating conflicts with a dangerous and unpredictable enemy. Uncertainty about the outcome produced the tensions at home on which McCarthy capitalized.

Yet the internal development of the United States had provided the resources for dealing with the emergencies abroad. Economic recovery and growth armed the country for the long cold war ahead, and the promise of the Fair Deal gave the people a sense of what they were fighting for. An anachronistic structure left Congress in the control of a conservative alliance that temporarily blocked the complete fulfillment of that promise. But the forces were ready to carry the effort on, once the problems in the outer world were resolved.

Paperbacks for Further Reading

Eric F. Goldman, *Crucial Decade* (Vintage Books, Inc.) and Herbert Agar, *Price of Power* (Chicago History of American Civilization Series) are general surveys of the postwar decade. Clinton Rossiter, *The American Presidency* (Mentor Books) and Walter Johnson, *1600 Pennsylvania Avenue* (Little, Brown & Co.) include material on the Truman administration. Stephen K. Bailey, *Congress Makes a Law* (Vintage Books, Inc.) is an illuminating study of the Employment Act of 1946. Bernard R. Berelson *et al., Voting* (Phoenix Books) is a study of the formation of opinion during the election of 1948. Irving Howe and Lewis Coser, *The American Communist Party* (Frederick A. Praeger, Inc.) includes a section on the repression of the party.

THE COLD WAR

92

Domestic politics in the United States after the war evolved against a background of increasing international tension. Americans now confronted a resolute antagonist with a view of the postwar settlement radically different from theirs. Dispute after dispute sharpened the issue. The occupation of Germany, Austria, and Korea, intended to be temporary, stretched out indefinitely. The free elections in Eastern Europe never took place, and although the wartime agreements assured the security of all democratic elements, the Soviet Union liquidated any that were not Communist fronts.

Behind the Iron Curtain a revolutionary movement prepared to assault the established institutions of the free world. The determination of the United States to resist opened a cold war in which the participants faced each other armed but withheld the shots that would bring the conflict to a head. Latin America was secure, for the time being, but doubts about the durability of the peace in Europe and in Asia explained the anxieties of the citizens who worried about McCarthy and Hiss. The fate of freedom, in America and elsewhere, still hung in the balance.

Latin America

THE WAR HAD CEMENTED the close ties among the independent nations of the Western Hemisphere. All of them had severed relations with the Axis powers—even, in the end, fascist Argentina, which had long hung back. Some countries had sent detachments to take part in the fighting; others had collaborated in the war at sea. In 1945, all of them had become members of the United Nations. In reciprocation, $500,000,000 in lend-lease aid had flowed south from the United States.

Peace brought an awareness of the desirability of strengthening the machinery of mutual aid and cooperation. In the Pact of Rio (1947) the Latin American countries and the United States agreed to consider an attack on any one as an attack on all. They arranged to consult in the event of danger and agreed to act by a two-thirds rather than unanimous vote. A year later the Charter for the Organization of American States provided the permanent institutions for implementing the Rio understandings. In the interests of collective security, a Council and its auxiliary bodies were to coordinate activities in order to preserve the peace and to further economic development and cultural understanding. All these actions came within the framework of the United Nations Charter, which recognized the validity of such regional understandings.

Blueprint for Revolution

Postwar Communism A dynamic revolutionary movement kept other parts of the world unstable. After the withdrawal of the Allied troops, the Russian army, entrenched in a line that ran from the Baltic to the Mediterranean, was the strongest power on the Continent. Behind it lay a country in turmoil. During the war the Russians had suffered more than any other people—from battle casualties, from Nazi

Charter of the Organization of American States, 1948

Convinced that the historic mission of America is to offer to man a land of liberty, and a favorable environment for the development of his personality and the realization of his just aspirations; . . .

Confident that the true significance of American solidarity and good neighborliness can only mean the consolidation on this continent, within the framework of democratic institutions, of a system of individual liberty and social justice based on respect for the essential rights of man;

Persuaded that their welfare and their contribution to the progress and the civilization of the world will increasingly require intensive continental cooperation; . . . [and]

Resolved to persevere in the noble undertaking that humanity has conferred upon the United Nations, whose principles and purposes they solemnly reaffirm; . . .

The American States establish by this Charter the international organization that they have developed to achieve an order of peace and justice, to promote their solidarity, to strengthen their collaboration, and to defend their sovereignty, their territorial integrity and their independence. Within the United Nations, the Organization of American States is a regional agency.

—Signed at Bogotá, March 30–May 2, 1948, in O. C. Stoetzer, *The Organization of American States* (New York: Frederick A. Praeger, 1965), pp. 116–117.

brutality, and from the discipline of their own masters. The Communist party apparatus and the ruthless secret police maintained Stalin firmly in command. Not until after his death in 1953 would the West learn the details of the permanent terror by which he kept control. But in 1947 his expansionist and antidemocratic intentions were clear to all but the most gullible.

The Stalinist leaders understood events in terms of a dogmatic history of the past and blueprint of the future. The war had been the cataclysm predicted by Marxist theorists as the start of the dissolution of capitalist society. The Soviet Union had to strengthen itself for the crisis, both by enforcing obedience to the party and by developing the heavy industry essential to carry forward the next stage of the struggle. Millions suffered in the process, but it was not possible to make an omelet without breaking eggs. "Stalin ordered me to dance, so I danced"—thus Khrushchev later apologized for the death of millions.

The conflict was international. Since 1917, dogged Marxists everywhere had fanatically been building an organization, sometimes openly, sometimes under cover, and sometimes from bases in Moscow. There were shades of difference among these people, but loyalty—to an idea and to the party—held them together even in the absence of formal communication with one another. The Cominform supplied a network for intelligence and for the coordination of activity.

The world outside the Soviet Union, in the Communist view, fell into three parts. The first part, the area within the periphery of the Red Army occupation, was ripe for plucking. For the time being, the wartime agreements and the inhibiting presence of Western forces prevented the Soviet Union from absorbing Poland, Czechoslovakia, and their neighbors, as it had the Baltic nations which simply became constituent republics within the Soviet Union. The Russians had to treat the countries they occupied as independent governments capable of making their own decisions. The Communist parties of each were represented in the Cominform, established in 1947, which was to coordinate the decisions of all until the transitional regimes transferred power to the dictatorship of the proletariat.

Forming the second part were Western Europe and the United States, which Communists believed were approaching the final stage at which internal contradictions would produce the collapse of capitalism. Where parliamentary systems permitted them to do so, party members were to try peacefully to win over the working class in preparation for revolution. Elsewhere they were to labor underground toward the same end. Imperialist exploitation had provided capitalists with the means for holding control. Once its overseas possessions slipped away, the power of the ruling class would crumble.

In colonial areas, the third part of the world as Communists saw it, foreigners had prevented the indigenous development of capitalism, and the inert peasants were the most numerous part of the population. Here, therefore, the revolutionaries were to ally themselves with the local intellectuals and bourgeoisie in movements of national liberation, in the hope of directing anti-imperialist sentiments into more general social upheavals. Communists confidently faced the world in 1947 armed with this explanation of history and forecast of the future.

The Satellites Foretastes of what was to come had appeared before 1945 in the annexation of the Baltic states and the murder of Polish officers and socialists. Yalta provided a grimmer indication. At the Potsdam Conference, the Russians revealed the strength of their hand. Their armies occupied Eastern Europe, and they insisted that the future regimes there remain Soviet satellites. The prospect of free elections vanished.

One by one in the next few years, Poland, Czechoslovakia, Hungary, Romania, Bulgaria, Yugoslavia, and Albania, against the wishes of their people, fell under the sway of Communist

There are sensitive observations of postwar Europe in Edmund Wilson, *Europe Without Baedeker* (Garden City, N. Y., 1947).

Soviet Troops Enter Bucharest, 1944. (Sovfoto)

rulers. The Russians revealed their hard line in the negotiation of treaties (1946) with Bulgaria, Finland, Hungary, Italy, and Romania—the former German allies. The Soviet Union insisted on heavy reparations, the military occupation of Trieste, substantial transfers of territory, and Communist control over navigation of the Danube. The result left the Communists dominant in southeast Europe.

Nuclear Weapons Most disconcerting was the issue raised by efforts to control the atom bomb, of which the United States still had a monopoly. Accounts published shortly after Hiroshima explained the basic process. No one could guess how soon another power would enter the race, but the danger of multiplying the store of nuclear weapons was evident. The United States proposed to outlaw the bomb, subject to the previous creation of a system of international inspection. The Soviet Union re-

quested instead that existing American stocks first be destroyed, after which it would be willing to discuss the method of future control. Inspection it rejected under any circumstances. The reasons for its stubborn refusal to let outsiders investigate Russian industry did not become apparent until later revelations of the disorder in the interior of the country. Whatever the cause, Soviet intransigence rendered negotiations fruitless.

The American Response

Peace and Defense Americans at first assumed that peace by negotiations was somehow within reach. The United States wished not simply to halt the spread of communism but also to reconstruct European society so that the people of the Continent could shape their own destiny. The role of the United States was to be that of collaboration and support.

That was the spirit of the first postwar measures, governmental and private. The Fulbright Act (1946, extended by the Smith-Mundt law of 1948) thus set up a program to advance cultural understanding by international exchange of students, scholars, and teachers, and the Rockefeller Foundation undertook to help restore European universities. Associations of all sorts reached across the ocean to assist. The AF of L–CIO, the American Association of University Women, and many religious and philanthropic organizations allocated some of their resources for aid. Americans also participated in such international efforts as UNNRA (the United Nations Relief and Rehabilitation Agency), CARE, and various medical and children's funds.

Such activities continued to receive support in the United States in the 1950s and 1960s, but faith in peaceful persuasion waned after 1947. That year the United States recast its policy and its system of defense. The belief in an early return to prewar normality vanished, and the country prepared for a long hard contest. Although it continued to hope that the cold war would not heat up, it readied itself for any contingency. The National Security Act set up the National Security Council, consisting of the President, Vice-President, the secretaries of State and Defense, and the director of the Office of Emergency Planning to coordinate all foreign policy. The Central Intelligence Agency, operating under the direction of the Council, was to gather information by any means, including espionage. And the armed services were unified in the National Military Establishment (name changed to Department of Defense, 1949).

The Truman Doctrine The modernized organization was needed because the United States was already resisting the further extension of Soviet influence. Greece was the most vulnerable area. Since the war, a liberation movement, dominated by Communists, had kept the country in disorder. Supplied from the neighboring

A Guerrilla Sniper Captured by Greek Army Troops in Northern Greece near the Albanian Frontier, January 26, 1948. (UPI)

satellites — Albania, Yugoslavia, and Bulgaria — 20,000 guerrillas controlled much of the countryside by terror. The British, who had helped to police Greece since 1944, were exhausted and announced that they could no longer carry the burden. Turkey, too, felt threatened by the Soviet Union along an extended frontier.

On March 12, 1947, the President appeared before Congress with a request for $400,000,000 for economic and military aid to Greece and Turkey. He explained in a statement which became known as the Truman Doctrine that the United States would assume the task of defending these countries against internal subversion or external aggression. The legislation promptly enacted permitted the dispatch of military advisers under General James A. Van Fleet. The Greek army, with this help, suppressed the rebellion in the next two years, and the government

Dimitrios George Kousoulas, *Revolution and Defeat* (New York, 1965) describes events in Greece.

The Truman Doctrine, 1947

The peoples of a number of countries of the world have recently had totalitarian regimes forced upon them against their will. The Government of the United States has made frequent protests against coercion and intimidation, in violation of the Yalta agreement, in Poland, Rumania, and Bulgaria. I must also state that in a number of other countries there have been similar developments . . . .

I believe that it must be the policy of the United States to support free peoples who are resisting attempted subjugation by armed minorities or by outside pressures.

I believe that we must assist free peoples to work out their own destinies in their own way.

I believe that our help should be primarily through economic and financial aid which is essential to economic stability and orderly political processes.

The world is not static, and the *status quo* is not sacred. But we cannot allow changes in the *status quo* in violation of the Charter of the United Nations by such methods as coercion, or by such subterfuges as political infiltration. In helping free and independent nations to maintain their freedom, the United States will be giving effect to the principles of the Charter of the United Nations . . . .

The seeds of totalitarian regimes are nurtured by misery and want. They spread and grow in the evil soil of poverty and strife. They reach their full growth when the hope of a people for a better life has died.

We must keep that hope alive.

The free peoples of the world look to us for support in maintaining their freedoms.

If we falter in our leadership, we may endanger the peace of the world — and we shall surely endanger the welfare of this Nation.

— President Harry S. Truman, Address to Congress, March 12. *Public Papers of the Presidents, Harry S. Truman, 1947* (Washington: Government Printing Office, 1963), pp. 178–180.

stabilized its situation. The Turks were also able to maintain their security.

The Marshall Plan To halt the spread of communism, it was necessary also to remove the economic causes of discontent throughout Europe. The United States had taken the first step in this direction in 1946 when it made a loan of $3,750,000,000 to Great Britain. In June 1947, Secretary of State George C. Marshall announced a plan to assist all the nations of the Continent, including Russia, in a form effective enough to rebuild and reform their economies.

The scheme worked out in the next year used a regional approach to promote cooperation and to increase efficiency by enlarging the markets within which producers operated. The participating countries formed an organization for European Economic Cooperation. That body allocated to various national projects about $12,000,000,000, drawn from the United States, with an eye to the maximum benefit of all. Mean-

Marshall Plan Aid to Europe, 1948–1952

(in million dollars)

Country	Amount
Great Britain	3,176
France	2,706
Italy	1,474
Germany	1,389
Netherlands	1,079
Greece	694
Austria	677
Belgium-Luxembourg	556
Denmark	271
Norway	254
Turkey	221
Ireland	146
Yugoslavia	109
Sweden	107
Portugal	50
Trieste	32
Iceland	29

Harry B. Price, *The Marshall Plan and Its Meaning* (Ithaca, N.Y., 1955) is a full analysis.

Purpose of the Marshall Plan, 1947

The truth of the matter is that Europe's requirements for the next three or four years of foreign food and other essential products—principally from America—are so much greater than her present ability to pay that she must have substantial additional help, or face economic, social, and political deterioration of a very grave character.

The remedy lies in breaking the vicious circle and restoring the confidence of the European people in the economic future of their own countries and of Europe as a whole. The manufacturer and the farmer throughout wide areas must be able and willing to exchange their products for currencies, the continuing value of which is not open to question.

Aside from the demoralizing effect on the world at large and the possibilities of disturbances arising as a result of the desperation of the people concerned, the consequences to the economy of the United States should be apparent to all. It is logical that the United States should do whatever it is able to do to assist in the return of normal economic health in the world, without which there can be no political stability and no assured peace.

Our policy is directed not against any country or doctrine but against hunger, poverty, desperation and chaos. Its purpose should be the revival of a working economy in the world so as to permit the emergence of political and social conditions in which free institutions can exist. Such assistance, I am convinced, must not be on a piecemeal basis as various crises develop. Any assistance that this Government may render in the future should provide a cure rather than a mere palliative.

Any government that is willing to assist in the task of recovery will find full cooperation, I am sure, on the part of the United States Government. Any government which maneuvers to block the recovery of other countries cannot expect help from us. Furthermore, governments, political parties or groups which seek to perpetuate human misery in order to profit therefrom politically or otherwise will encounter the opposition of the United States.

—Secretary of State George C. Marshall, Address at Harvard University, June 5. *New York Times*, June 6, 1947, p. 2.

---

while the European Payments Union was set up as a sort of clearing house to facilitate trade.

The logical next step toward a common market came in 1950 when the European Coal and Steel Community began to pool the resources of the Continent according to a plan proposed by Robert Schuman, the French foreign minister. Meanwhile, Point 4 of President Truman's inaugural address of 1949 proposed to extend aid to the underdeveloped countries of the world.

Defensive Alliance The Marshall Plan stabilized society throughout free Europe, and thus frustrated the Communist expectation of an imminent collapse. Economic recovery, however, depended upon sufficient security against attack to sustain confidence. As long as Russian power remained a potential danger, doubts about the future undermined planning and weakened efforts at reconstruction. In July 1947, just after the Marshall Plan was made public, the journal *Foreign Affairs* published an anonymous article

European Recovery Plan Machinery Arrives in Liverpool, February 25, 1949. Mechanical excavating equipment supplied by the United States is being unloaded. (UPI)

entitled, "Sources of Soviet Conduct" (the author of which was later identified as George Kennan, a foreign service officer). His analysis, which remained basic to American policy, recommended patient containment of the Communist danger. Kennan hoped to persuade the Communists of the futility of aggression by consistently resisting any moves they might make. At the same time he sought to avoid any threat to the Soviet system at home that might trigger a defensive response.

The policy of containment required a military organization in Europe capable of warning the Russians off or of stifling little incidents before they flared up into all-out war. The British and French had already taken the first step toward alliance in the Treaty of Dunkirk (1947). In March 1948, Belgium, the Netherlands, and Luxembourg joined them. Finally, the United States, Canada, and most of the free European countries entered the North Atlantic Treaty Organization. Signed in April 1949 and ratified by the United States Senate in July, the NATO agreement involved a far-ranging commitment to common planning and defense, including provision for integrating the armed forces of the participating countries. The proposal in 1952 for a European Defense Com-

munity would have gone even further, but the French later vetoed it. Nonetheless, NATO placed a shield across Europe behind which the tasks of economic development could go forward in security.

Containment, 1947

The Soviet pressure against the free institutions of the western world . . . can be contained by the adroit and vigilant application of counter-force at a series of constantly shifting geographical and political points, corresponding to the shifts and manoeuvres of Soviet policy, but . . . cannot be charmed or talked out of existence. The Russians look forward to a duel of infinite duration, and they see that already they have scored great successes. It must be borne in mind that there was a time when the Communist Party represented far more of a minority in the sphere of Russian national life than Soviet power today represents in the world community.

—George Kennan, "The Sources of Soviet Conduct," *Foreign Affairs*, XXV (July, 1947), p. 576.

558

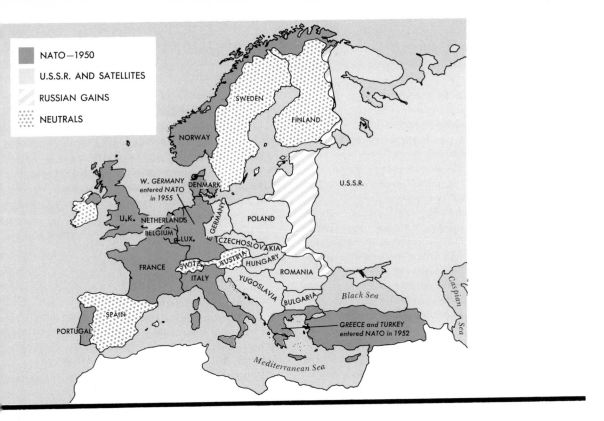

NATO—1950

U.S.S.R. AND SATELLITES

RUSSIAN GAINS

NEUTRALS

SWEDEN

FINLAND

NORWAY

DENMARK

W. GERMANY entered NATO in 1955

U.K.

NETHERLANDS

BELGIUM

B-LUX.

E. GERMANY

POLAND

U.S.S.R.

CZECHOSLOVAKIA

FRANCE

SWITZ.

AUSTRIA

HUNGARY

ITALY

YUGOSLAVIA

ROMANIA

BULGARIA

Black Sea

Caspian Sea

SPAIN

PORTUGAL

GREECE and TURKEY entered NATO in 1952

Mediterranean Sea

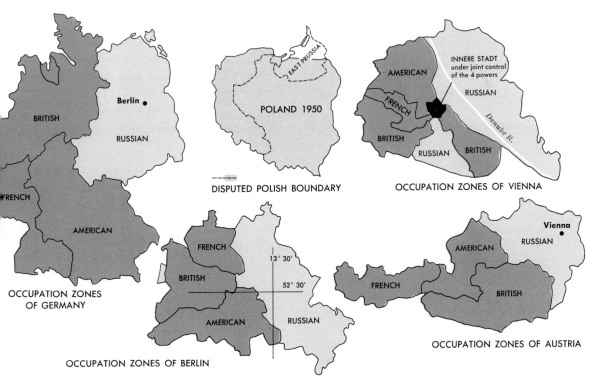

BRITISH

Berlin

RUSSIAN

FRENCH

AMERICAN

OCCUPATION ZONES
OF GERMANY

EAST PRUSSIA

POLAND 1950

– – – – DISPUTED POLISH BOUNDARY

AMERICAN

FRENCH

BRITISH

RUSSIAN

INNERE STADT
under joint control
of the 4 powers

RUSSIAN

Danube R.

BRITISH

OCCUPATION ZONES OF VIENNA

FRENCH

BRITISH

AMERICAN

RUSSIAN

13° 30'

52° 30'

OCCUPATION ZONES OF BERLIN

AMERICAN

Vienna

RUSSIAN

FRENCH

BRITISH

OCCUPATION ZONES OF AUSTRIA

ARTHUR H. VANDENBERG's lifelong role was in the middle of the road, trying to resolve opposing extremes. He played an important part in the development of bipartisanship and in the break with isolationism. He swayed enough Republicans to stifle the political maneuvers that had complicated peacemaking in 1919.

Vandenberg was born in 1884 in Grand Rapids, Michigan. His father's harness business failed in the depression of 1893, and Arthur had to work as a boy, yet he still managed to head his high school class. He got a job on the local newspaper and in time became editor. His early literary ambitions faded and his interests turned to politics. He was a good Republican, amiable and a florid orator.

In 1928, he was appointed to a vacant seat in the United States Senate, where he served the rest of his life. Before 1941, foreign involvements made no sense to him. He had opposed the League of Nations, and no doubt reflected the wish of his constituents as well as his own convictions when he fought for the neutrality laws of the 1930s. Distrust of Roosevelt strengthened his hostility to any form of intervention.

After Pearl Harbor, Vandenberg loyally supported the war effort, and F. D. R., determined to avoid Wilson's mistakes, made special efforts to win over this influential Republican. As the conflict proceeded, Vandenberg became aware that it would never be possible to return to the old aloofness from world affairs. In January 1945, in a Senate speech, he renounced his former isolationism, in a signal that his party would not obstruct an international settlement. He served as a delegate to the San Francisco Conference that adopted the Charter of the United Nations, and he helped secure ratification.

Republican gains in the Congressional elections of 1946 made Vandenberg chairman of the Senate Foreign Relations Committee. He therefore occupied a key role in implementing the Truman and the Marshall plans. He also helped to save the reciprocal trade agreements in 1948. That year he no doubt hoped that he might be rewarded for his statesmanship with the presidential nomination, if the Dewey and Taft wings were divided enough to need a dark horse, but he was disappointed. He died in 1951.

Between 1947 and 1949 the United States assumed obligations that dramatically altered its historical foreign policy. The Truman Doctrine, the Marshall Plan, and the NATO alliance were expressions of a total involvement in the future of Europe. The oceans no longer guaranteed American security. Whatever threatened the peace of the Old World threatened the New; and safety called not only for the defense of distant frontiers but also for the strengthening of all countries to the point at which they could protect themselves. The bipartisan support of these commitments, signaled by the conversion from isolationism of Senator Arthur H. Vandenberg, reflected the revision in national attitudes toward the outer world.

Stalemate in Europe

The Display of Red Power The vigorous American reaction unsettled the Communists. The countries of Eastern Europe, including the Soviet Union, were invited to join the Marshall Plan. Czechoslovakia and Finland were interested and even the Russians, at first, were tempted. Stalin, however, had no wish to take part, no matter how badly the Russian economy needed help. He was unwilling either to recognize the durability of the existing regimes in Western Europe or to open the Soviet Union to inspection by outsiders. He therefore recalled his envoy V. M. Molotov from the planning conference and frightened the Czechs and Finns away. He also tightened the screws on the satellites. In February 1948 the Communists dropped their mask and seized control of Czechoslovakia. Foreign Minister Jan Masaryk, a democrat and liberal, had attempted in good faith to make the United Front work. Now, despondent at the betrayal, he committed suicide on discovering the hopelessness of coalition with the Communists.

The Russians met a serious reverse in Yugoslavia, however. A conflict over economic policy led to an open break between the two Communist states during May and June 1948. Marshal Tito's organization had stronger local roots than did the Communist parties in the other satellites. He was therefore able to resist pressure from Moscow. Moreover, there were no Soviet troops in his country and the presence of American forces in neighboring Greece made the Russians wary of intervention. Economic aid under the Marshall Plan stiffened the Yugoslavs' will to go their own way. In the next decade Tito oscillated between the Soviets and the West. He thereby showed that a Communist nation need not be part of a homogeneous power bloc but could follow an independent policy if it wished.

The German Problem Stalin's greatest fear was a revived Germany. Although partition of that country was originally regarded as temporary, he realized by 1948 that any scheme for unification would leave Germany in the Western camp and threaten the still unsettled Polish-German boundary. The Russians therefore obstructed any move to alter the four-power occupation status and carefully protected the puppet regime in their own zone when the Americans, French, and British permitted the creation of a democratically elected West German government. In 1948, when a currency reform stabilized that regime, the Soviets in retaliation attempted to cut off Berlin, access to which was possible only through their zone. A complete halt to all rail, canal, and road traffic threatened to starve the city out.

The American reaction was decisive. In June 1948 an airlift mounted with British aid brought relief to the beleaguered city. The planes shuttled back and forth until May 1949, when the Russians withdrew the blockade and reopened the normal supply routes. The demonstration of firmness forced Stalin to recognize that he could not have Berlin without a fight, and at that prospect he drew back. When John J. McCloy arrived as High Commissioner in 1949, West Germany, reassured, began staggering to its feet, and by 1952 it was well on the way to recovery. In a treaty in May of that year the United States, Britain, and France recognized its independence and its equality as a sovereign state.

The Terms of Truce An uneasy truce thereupon settled over Europe. Neither side was content, but neither wished to take the risk of any disruptive action. In September 1949 the Soviet Union exploded its own atom bomb and raised the stakes of any future conflict. The United Nations Atomic Energy Commission, which had wrestled unsuccessfully with the problem of disarmament, dissolved. Thereafter, a race for ever more powerful weapons was on. The United States and the Soviet Union both felt the necessity of developing still greater bombs and their related delivery systems.

Never before had Americans been compelled to consider strategic problems seriously. Their normal state had been peace, and when they had gone to war, they had mobilized their full power to win as quickly as possible. Now

Lucius DuBignon Clay, *Decision in Germany* (New York, 1950) is written by the American commander in Germany between 1947 and 1949.

W. P. Davison, *The Berlin Blockade* (Princeton, N.J., 1958) deals with the significance of the relief of the city during the blockade.

When President Truman named **JOHN J. McCLOY** High Commissioner for Germany in 1949, he sent to that troubled area a man of great ability with intimate links to American legal, banking, and military circles. The mission was an indication of Germany's importance in the postwar world.

McCloy was born in Philadelphia in 1895. His father s death six years later left the family dependent upon the mother s earnings, and John had to work his way through high school and Amherst College. After graduation he moved on to the Harvard Law School, but the war intervened. He enlisted and served in France and Germany until 1919. He then returned to take his degree in 1921, attracting the favorable attention of such professors as Felix Frankfurter.

In the next two decades, McCloy found a place among the great New York international lawyers, first with Cadwalader, Wickersham & Taft and then with the Cravath firm. For a time he lived in Paris, and he became familiar with Germany from work on the complex problems growing out of espionage during World War I.

In 1940 Secretary of War Stimson appointed him special assistant on counter-espionage. McCloy remained in the government service through the war. He formed the intelligence unit that broke the Japanese codes, encouraged the creation of the French Committee of National Liberation in 1943, planned the Nuremberg war-crime trials, and was privy to the secret of the atom bomb.

He returned briefly to the law in 1945, but remained a consultant to the State Department and in 1947 became president of the World Bank. Two years later he went to Germany, where he remained for three years, his chief task being restoration of economic stability. When he left, the task was well under way. From 1953 to 1960, McCloy was chairman of the board of the Chase National Bank, but his usefulness to the government continued and was independent of politics. McCloy was an intimate adviser of both Presidents Eisenhower and Kennedy, and helped preserve the continuity of postwar foreign policy.

they accepted a permanent condition — half war, half peace. As a result they had to devise means of resisting aggression short of an all-out conflict. Furthermore, they had to engage in activities that democratic regimes in the past had considered outside their province, among them the espionage of the Central Intelligence Agency and the propaganda of the information service. Refugee groups and extreme nationalists continued to talk about the liberation of Eastern Europe, but the policy of the United States government was to halt subversion or invasion rather than to oust the Communists where they already held power.

The United Nations failed to provide an effective instrument of mediation or negotiation. Events had not confirmed its fundamental premise, that all its members were peace-loving. It was unable to act because the Security Council could not usually reach agreement. In the first six years the Soviet Union used the veto more than forty times, the United States not once. The General Assembly remained largely a debating chamber, and the hope of developing an international rule of law to displace armed force faded. By 1952 the prospects for concord between the East and West in Europe were slimmer than at any time since the end of the war.

▼

Postwar conditions of Europe frustrated the hopes for peace in this generation. On that devastated continent, economic reconstruction was possible only in the West, which enjoyed American assistance. East of the Iron Curtain a repressive regime, intent upon expanding, remained unstable and a standing threat to its neighbors.

In 1947, the United States intended to aid the recovery of the war-torn countries, hoping thus to restore stability. But the Communists rejected this help, so only the West profited from it. The division between East and West turned Europe into an armed camp. While Americans succeeded in defending the threatened nations, it was at the cost of maintaining a standing condition of cold war. Even that, however, was preferable to the situation in the Far East, where the war became hot.

Paperbacks for Further Reading

John W. Spanier, *American Foreign Policy since World War II* (Frederick A. Praeger, Inc.) is a short general survey. Edwin Lieuwen, *U.S. Policy in Latin America* (Frederick A. Praeger, Inc.) briefly reviews the period since 1945. Most of the space in O. C. Stoetzer, *The Organization of American States* (Frederick A. Praeger, Inc.) is devoted to documents.

Hugh Seton-Watson, *From Lenin to Khrushchev* (Frederick A. Praeger, Inc.) is a good history of world communism; and the same author's *Neither War Nor Peace* (Frederick A. Praeger, Inc.) deals with the cold war. Joseph M. Jones, *The Fifteen Weeks* (Harbinger Books) describes the origins of the Marshall Plan. Max Beloff, *The United States and the Unity of Europe* (Vintage Books, Inc.) is a broad analysis.

KOREA

93

In the Far East even more than in Europe, communism was a threat to the free world. Entrenched in China, the Communists commanded vast man power resources, and revolutionary fervor pressed them into action to prevent any non-Communist society from achieving stability.

Resistance was more difficult than in Europe. Asia was unfamiliar to the Americans who had to make decisions about it. Despite its long interest in the Orient, the United States misjudged the social forces at work and was unable to apply across the Pacific techniques of containment that were effective across the Atlantic. Miscalculations led to the bitter conflict in Korea, and the great expense and heavy casualties of that war failed to eradicate the seeds of future difficulties.

American Objectives

THE UNITED STATES, which had borne the brunt of the conflict against Japan, had not expected the relatively swift surrender that came after Hiroshima and Nagasaki. Military needs that seemed to make Russian aid desirable had influenced the agreements at Yalta and Potsdam, and gave the Soviet Union a strategic vantage point not only in Europe but also in east Asia.

Japan and China An inaccurate assessment of the situation governed American assumptions about the postwar future of the Far East. The most serious problem seemed that of preventing future Nipponese threats to peace. In the half century before Pearl Harbor, the Mikado's obedient subjects had expanded their empire down to the South Pacific and deep into China. The United States believed, first, that a long and thorough occupation of Japan would be required to obliterate militarism completely and to end all future danger to neighboring countries.

A second objective of American policy was also important but seemed to pose fewer difficulties. Since early in the twentieth century, the United States had sought to strengthen China by maintaining its territorial integrity so that it could play the role of a great power and offset Russian and Japanese influence in Asia. Franklin D. Roosevelt had made every effort to protect China's interests during the wartime negotiations and had promised to restore to it the islands seized by Japan in 1895, including Taiwan. Yet after V-J Day many Americans doubted that Chiang Kai-shek's dictatorial Kuomintang regime could unify and stabilize a country torn by revolution and dissension since 1910, exhausted by a long war, and plunged in economic and social chaos.

Imperialism The United States expected that its third objective, the liquidation of imperialism in Asia, would cause the least trouble. Recognizing the strength of nationalist emotions, Americans looked forward to a gradual withdrawal by the European colonial powers as indigenous democratic governments took form. There was general pleasure at the decision of the English to emancipate India and Pakistan (1947). The United States persuaded the Dutch to relinquish their hold on Indonesia (1949) and unsuccessfully urged the French to grant independence to Indochina. It was a delicate matter to put pressure on allies who were at the same time receiving aid in Europe. But Americans wished, without weakening the regimes at home, to convince them peacefully to give up their aspirations for empire.

The hopes attached to national liberation failed to take account of grim social realities, however. Nationalism was a powerful force in Asia but one that moved relatively small groups of middle-class professional and intellectual people. The peasants were inert, bound to their villages and innocent of all political experience. The ruling elements — whether they collaborated with or fought the imperialists — relied on violence to retain power, had no feeling for the mass of the population, were often corrupt, and usually thought only of their own interests. These were not the most promising materials for a democratic society.

Some well-intentioned Americans, shocked by glimpses of Oriental poverty, corruption, and misrule, all too easily concluded that a total revolution was necessary, without reckoning that its most likely leaders would be the small Communist cells entrenched in the nationalist movements. This miscalculation further bedeviled the effort to chart a course toward democracy in the postwar years.

Reform by Power By 1952, the United States had succeeded phenomenally well where it least expected to and elsewhere had encountered disheartening difficulties it had not anticipated. The difficulties arose out of the disparate social situations it encountered and the degree of control it was able to exercise.

Lucien Bodard, *The Quicksand War* (Boston, 1967) is a brilliant history of the war in Indochina to 1950.

The occupation of Japan proved peaceful. Though ravaged by war, the country had a modern economic structure. The Emperor cooperated, as did the people. Weary of fighting and of the oppressive government under which they had lived for decades, they welcomed the American presence and quickly adapted to the requirements of the victor. A new democratic constitution (1946) limited the size of the armed forces, forbade future wars, and installed free institutions. Trade unions appeared, and land reform gave holdings to the peasants and made the nation agriculturally self-sufficient. Trade and industry developed and the standard of living gradually rose.

After some years of obstruction by Russia, a peace conference in San Francisco in 1951 negotiated a settlement with Japan and the occupation ended. A separate Japanese-American Security Treaty signed at the same time permitted United States forces to remain in the islands and effected an enduring working alliance.

Relations with the Philippines, too, followed a satisfactory course, although the native government there struggled until 1954 to suppress the Communist (Hukbalahap) guerrillas. Still, land reform and modernization brought the islands rising income and internal stability. A treaty with the United States, signed on August 30, 1951, provided for mutual defense against armed attack.

Japan and the Philippines were islands under complete American control and guarded against external attack by the unchallenged sea power of the United States. Much could be done there that was difficult to achieve elsewhere.

Red China

On the mainland of Asia, the advantage lay with the superior man power of the antagonist. The limits of American action were therefore narrower, especially in the first critical postwar

years when the United States hastened to demobilize. The results were failure in China and war in Korea.

The Communists Take Over The conflict between the Kuomintang government of Chiang Kai-shek and the Communists had ravaged China since the 1930s, even during the Japanese invasion. Until 1945, Stalin had accepted Chiang as an ally and had professed contempt for the Chinese Communists, to whom he had nevertheless handed the highly developed industrial areas the Russians had occupied at the surrender. From there Mao Tse-tung launched a massive campaign to demolish the Kuomintang and take the whole of China.

Tired of fighting, Americans were reluctant even to consider intervention. They put their faith instead in the effort to maintain a cease fire and to effect a coalition between the Communists and the Nationalist government. Fearful lest Chiang become intransigent in the negotiations, the United States gave him little military equipment and only a small part of the aid authorized by Congress. Meanwhile the Communists took advantage of the truce to consolidate and regroup their forces.

The failure of General Marshall's mission to work out a compromise between the Communists and the Nationalists (December 1945–January 1947) left the United States without an alternative policy. Occasional speculations about the possibility of forming a liberal Third Force led to nothing. And there seemed little to choose from as between the Communists and the Kuomintang. Despite the efforts of a China Lobby, Chiang's reputation in the United States sank, as superficial or cynical journalists spread Stalin's myth: Mao and his followers were not really Communists but moderate agrarian reformers fighting for liberty against the landlords. Meanwhile a few State Department officials, persuaded by their study of geopolitics that China lacked the resources to become a great power, wished to write that country off entirely from calcula-

Walt Sheldon, *The Honorable Conquerors* (New York, 1965) is a lively account of the occupation of Japan.

Tang Tsou, *America's Failure in China 1941 to 1950* (Chicago, 1963) is a sober analysis.

The People's Liberation Army Enters Canton, 1950. (Sovfoto)

tions of the future security and interests of the United States.

The lack of vigorous American support demoralized the Nationalist government, which was in any case weak, corrupt, and ineffective. After 1947, Chiang concentrated on holding the cities, while the Communists spread through the countryside. Some peasants took flight. Others, who knew the nature of their past oppression but could not imagine the deeper tyranny of which they were about to become victims, welcomed the Communists, who were lavish in promises. Once the Communists gained control, they exterminated all potential opponents and tightened their grip on province after province. In 1949, the isolated cities fell—Tientsin and Peking in January, Nanking in April, Shanghai in May, Canton in October. In December, Chiang fled to Taiwan.

Thereafter he launched occasional raids against the mainland but the Communists proceeded to consolidate their power. In October 1949, a new constitution had organized China on a Communist basis and shortly thereafter a military alliance tightened the links to the Soviet

American Estimates of the Chinese Communists, 1949

We Americans mainly saw the good things about the Chinese Communists, while not noticing carefully the intolerance, bigotry, deception, disregard for human life and other evils which seem to be inherent in any totalitarian system. We kept Communist meanings for such objectives as progressive, democratic, liberal, also bourgeois, reactionary, imperialist, as they intended we should do. We failed to realize fully the achievements to date and the potentialities of Chinese democracy. Therefore, we cannot escape a part of the responsibility of the great catastrophe—not only for China but also for America and the free world—the loss of the Chinese mainland.

—Ambassador John L. Stuart, *Fifty Years in China* (New York: Random House, Inc., 1954), pp. 237–238.

DEAN G. ACHESON was born in Middletown, Connecticut, in 1893. His father was Episcopal bishop of Connecticut and the family was well connected. Acheson went to Groton and to Yale, made the crew and the good clubs, and earned a Phi Beta Kappa key. In World War I he was an ensign in the navy.

The unexpected element in his career came when he fell under the influence of Felix Frankfurter at the Harvard Law School and then spent two years as clerk for Justice Brandeis. Although Acheson entered the private practice of law in 1921, he retained a commitment to public service. F. D. R. appointed him Under Secretary of the Treasury in 1933, but the two men had an abrupt falling out later the same year when the President sought to raise prices by tinkering with the gold rate—a step Acheson considered illegal. He resigned and returned to the practice of law.

Roosevelt called him back to Washington as Assistant Secretary of State early in 1941. Acheson became Under Secretary in 1945 and Secretary in 1949, a position he held to the close of the Truman administration. He thus participated in shaping the important wartime and postwar policies.

Like Roosevelt, Acheson saw no essential clash between the Soviet and American interests and hoped that peace would usher in a period of collaboration between the two great powers. He also wished to defend the State Department against irresponsible accusations of Communist infiltration.

When the harsh Russian intentions became clear, Acheson attempted to adjust the nation's policy so that it would be able to resist aggression and yet avoid the danger of a renewed total war. He helped formulate the Truman Doctrine and worked out the essential elements of the Marshall Plan in 1947. The prospects for building strong indigenous societies capable of defending themselves against communism did not seem as hopeful in Asia. He therefore suggested a perimeter beyond which American commitments would not extend, but the Korean War showed that such a line could not be maintained.

Although Acheson left office in 1953 to return to his law practice, Presidents Kennedy and Johnson continued to seek his advice on foreign policy.

Union. The Russians forthwith demanded recognition of their protégé as the sole legal government of China, along with a seat for Communist China in the Security Council.

American Policy The United States hesitated. In the United Nations it argued that the Communists had not yet qualified for membership. On the other hand, few Americans thought seriously of coming to Chiang's rescue. On January 5, 1950, President Truman clearly stated the American position. The United States understood that Taiwan was part of China; it had no intention of interfering in the civil conflict then in progress; and it would not provide military aid or advice to Chiang's forces.

The implication that the Americans would not resist the spread of Communist power to Taiwan was not enough for the Russians. They wanted immediate recognition of the Chinese Communists, and on January 11, when the Security Council refused to expel the Nationalists, the Soviet delegates walked out of the meeting. A day later, Secretary of State Dean Acheson reiterated his country's policy. The American defensive perimeter in the western Pacific ran south from the Aleutians through Japan and the Ryukyu Islands to the Philippines. China, Taiwan, Indochina, and Korea were presumably beyond the line at which the United States would protect its interests. But Acheson also stated that the entire civilized world under the Charter of the United Nations would be committed to defend the people beyond the perimeter against attack.

The defeat and the disarmament of Japan has placed upon the United States the necessity of assuming the military defense of Japan so long as that is required, both in the interest of our security and in the interests of the security of the entire Pacific area and in all honor in the interest of Japanese security. We have American troops in Japan . . . . I can assure you that there is no intention of any sort of abandoning or weakening the defenses of Japan and that whatever arrangements are to be made, either through permanent settlement or otherwise, that defense must, and shall be, maintained.

This defensive perimeter runs along the Aleutians to Japan and then goes to the Ryukyus. We hold important defense positions in the Ryukyu Islands and those we will continue to hold. In the interest of the population of the Ryukyu Islands, we will at an appropriate time offer to hold these islands under trusteeship of the United Nations. But they are essential parts of the defensive perimeter of the Pacific and they must, and will be, held.

The defensive perimeter runs from the Ryukyus to the Philippine Islands. Our relations, our defensive relations with the Philippines, are contained in agreements between us. Those agreements are being loyally carried out and will be loyally carried out. Both peoples have learned by bitter experience the vital connections between our mutual defense requirements. We are in no doubt about that and it is hardly necessary for me to say an attack on the Philippines could not and would not be tolerated by the United States. But I hasten to add that no one perceives the imminence of any such attack.

So far as the military security of other areas in the Pacific is concerned, it must be clear that no person can guarantee these areas against military attack. But it must also be clear that such a guarantee is hardly sensible or necessary within the realm of practical relationship. Should such an attack occur — one hesitates to say where such an armed attack could come from — the initial reliance must be on the people attacked to resist it and then upon the commitments of the entire civilized world under the Charter of the United Nations which so far has not proved a weak reed to lean on by any people who are determined to protect their independence against outside aggression.

—Secretary of State Dean Acheson, January 12. *Congressional Record*, 81st Cong., 2d sess., vol. XCVI, p. 674.

The Korean Invasion

A statesman's line could not, however, contain the dynamism of a revolution that pressed outward against contiguous territory. Aid from China transformed the situation in Indochina, where the French, determined to retain their empire, had begun to reassert their power. Now fraternal help from the north enabled the Communist Ho Chi Minh and his nationalist allies to regroup and strike back.

Communist Aggression The consequences in Korea were graver. To facilitate the surrender of the Japanese, the Russians had agreed to occupy Korea north of the 38th parallel, while the United States moved into the south. The arrangement was temporary, intended soon to give way to a united country. In 1949, both the Soviet Union and the United States withdrew their troops.

As in the other occupied territories, partition had by then led to the appearance of two

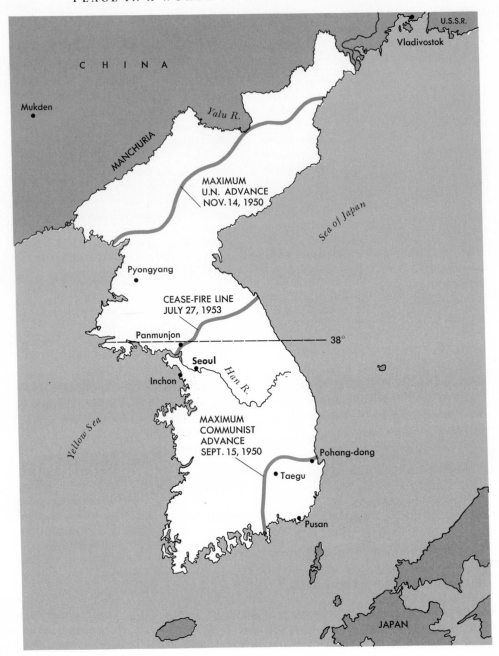

THE WAR IN KOREA, 1950–1953

separate regimes. In North Korea a puppet government controlled by the Communists held power. Although it ruled the richer part of the country, it encountered economic difficulties and became increasingly oppressive. It therefore looked jealously at the remainder of the peninsula, which laboriously attempted to organize a representative system. Under Syngman Rhee, South Korea took the first steps toward constitutional government and slowly began to recover its independence after the long Japanese occupation.

The Communists therefore were unwilling to observe the forms of international law while waiting for the Americans gradually to withdraw to the perimeter. In the early morning of Sunday, June 25, 1950 (June 24 in Washington), the North Koreans sent their massed armies across the border. A force of 100,000 men led by Russian-built tanks swiftly overcame the disorganized defenders and headed toward the capital, Seoul.

The UN Acts Word of the invasion invoked an immediate and forceful reaction. It was apparent that the Communists would exercise none of the restraint needed to work out a pattern of peaceful coexistence and would take what they could without regard for legality. Despite the reluctance to be involved in a land war and despite the earlier talk of an outer defense perimeter, the United States responded without hesitation, and international support was prompt. The Security Council met the day after the attack and by a vote of 9 to 1 (with the Soviet Union absent and Yugoslavia abstaining) declared that a breach of the peace had occurred, asked the North Koreans to pull back, and requested all UN members to aid the South. President Truman immediately ordered American forces into action.

The Russians, then boycotting the Security Council in protest against continued recognition of Nationalist China, were unable to block action. Although the United States and South Koreans would do most of the fighting, fifteen other nations made contributions and the war was

The Security Council on Korea, 1950

The Security Council, . . .

Welcomes the prompt and vigorous support which governments and peoples of the United Nations have given to its resolutions of 25 and 27 June 1950 to assist the Republic of Korea in defending itself against armed attack and thus to restore international peace and security in the area;

Notes that Members of the United Nations have transmitted to the United Nations offers of assistance for the Republic of Korea;

Recommends that all Members providing military forces and other assistance pursuant to the aforesaid Security Council resolutions make such forces and other assistance available to a unified command under the United States;

Requests the United States to designate the commander of such forces;

Authorizes the unified command at its discretion to use the United Nations flag in the course of operations against North Korean forces concurrently with the flags of the various nations participating.

— Resolution of July 7. "Review of United Nations Charter. A Collection of Documents," 83d Cong., 2d sess., Sen. Doc. 87 (1954), p. 594.

conducted on behalf of the United Nations. Feverish activity in the next two weeks prepared the resistance to the Communists. The UN reaffirmed its stand and authorized the use of its flag. Consultation with the Organization of American States mobilized support in the Western Hemisphere. A statement by Truman revised his policy with reference to Chiang. He would now consider the occupation of Taiwan by the Communists a direct threat to the security of the United States. The Seventh Fleet was accordingly ordered to prevent any attack from the mainland, while Chiang was requested to refrain

General MacArthur (left) and President Truman Speaking, with Major General Courtney Whitney, Wake Island, April 1951. (UPI)

Korean Refugees, South of Seoul, Korea, January 5, 1951. With the roads packed for miles with Koreans fleeing the advancing Chinese Communists, the UN Forces frequently had to make their way by slowly pushing refugees out of the way. (Pictorial Parade)

from all aggressive measures that might extend the war.

Summoned from Japan to take command, General Douglas MacArthur found that the South Korean defenses had been shattered. Lacking armor or heavy weapons, the poorly equipped UN troops fell back. The precipitate retreat did not halt until September 1950 when only the southeast tip of the peninsula remained under their control. By the time any significant number of Americans arrived at the port of Pusan, the North Koreans had overrun most of the country and it was difficult to launch a frontal counterattack.

MacArthur's bold counteroffensive strategy used command of the sea to good advantage. A powerful flanking movement led to a landing at Inchon near the 38th parallel and well behind the North Korean line (September 15, 1950). Other American troops moved north from Pusan and shattered the North Korean army, which was cut off from its base.

The issue then was whether to halt at the 38th parallel or pursue the fleeing Communists beyond that line. A halt would give the aggressors the opportunity to regroup and perhaps strike back. A further advance might bring in the Chinese. Toward the end of September the Joint Chiefs decided to go forward to the destruction of the North Korean armed forces. Discounting warnings from Peking, the UN on October 7, 1950, voted to take all appropriate steps to restore order throughout Korea. At a conference on Wake Island on October 15, President Truman communicated these decisions to MacArthur, whose troops thereafter raced north of the old frontier. In November they neared the Yalu River and the Chinese boundary.

At Wake Island, MacArthur had discounted the possibility that the Communist Chinese would intervene. The prediction proved wrong. Before the end of October, Peking had begun to

Roy E. Appleman, *United States Army in the Korean War* (Washington, 1961) is a detailed history of the first months of the war.

send its forces in. Regular army divisions disguised as volunteers and supported by Russian planes poured across the frontier. The UN troops, caught off balance, retreated south of the 38th parallel. Between November 1950 and March 1951, the line of battle shifted back and forth, as the allies held, counterattacked, and were held.

The Communists displayed the dogged intransigeance basic to their strategy. They believed that the United States was a paper tiger, a decadent democracy incapable of standing up to determined revolutionaries. Just as in China they had fought rear-guard actions for twenty years before finally winning, so in any future confrontation it was only necessary never to recognize defeat in order to win.

MacArthur clung to the American military tradition of mobilizing the maximum force to compel the antagonist to surrender. He wished to strike at the privileged sanctuaries in China from which supplies flowed into Korea and from which the Communist air force operated; and he contemplated a summons to Chiang's troops, which might have opened out a general Asian war.

His superiors were not willing to take that risk. Now that they knew the Chinese were in, the President, the Joint Chiefs of Staff, and the allies preferred to avoid a full confrontation with the limitless hordes Peking commanded. They feared also that the Russians might ultimately take a hand, so that the fighting would spread to Europe and lead to the use of atomic weapons. The decision was for limited war, painful and frustrating as that was.

MacArthur chafed under the restraints placed upon him. Informed on March 20, 1951, that efforts toward a diplomatic settlement should be made before any advance north of the 38th parallel, MacArthur issued a public statement that looked forward to an early Chinese defeat. He did so despite a previous warning from the President against such pronouncements. Shortly thereafter an open letter from MacArthur to Republican Speaker Joseph

W. Martin also called for victory over the Communists. The General's criticism of the President's conduct of the war—in violation of the Constitutional principle of subordination of the military to the civil authority—led to his removal in April 1951.

Stalemate

The war dragged on inconclusively. In June 1951, the Russians made known the desire of the Chinese for a truce. Negotiations looking toward an armistice began the next month, but there was to be no agreement for almost two years, and in the interim the fighting went on intermittently but fiercely.

Meanwhile the United States strengthened its diplomatic position by treaties with Japan and the Philippines, and the ANZUS pact with Australia and New Zealand (1951) aligned those countries for mutual defense against armed attack. At the same time, the Declaration of Washington (1951) sustained the solidarity of the American states against communism. An end to the conflict was not yet in sight, as the thoughts of Americans turned to the presidential election of 1952.

Impatience with the interminable conflict was a factor in the electoral campaign. Republican isolationists like Senator Taft attacked Truman's unnecessary war, and ex-President Hoover called for a withdrawal to the Western Hemisphere, the Gibraltar of civilization. The Republican candidate, Eisenhower, did not agree with them but during the campaign he promised to do something about Korea.

Once the votes were counted, the President-elect's first obligation was to redeem his pledge. In December 1952, Eisenhower visited the battlefields, and after he took office he pressed for conclusion of the negotiations. The death of Stalin in March 1953 probably softened the

No Substitute for Victory, 1951

I am most grateful for your note of the 8th forwarding me a copy of your address of February 12. The latter I have read with much interest, and find that with the passage of years you have certainly lost none of your old-time punch.

My views and recommendations with respect to the situation created by Red China's entry into war against us in Korea have been submitted to Washington in most complete detail. Generally these views are well known and clearly understood, as they follow the conventional pattern of meeting force with maximum counter-force as we have never failed to do in the past. Your view with respect to the utilization of the Chinese forces on Formosa is in conflict with neither logic nor this tradition.

It seems strangely difficult for some to realize that here in Asia is where the Communist conspirators have elected to make their play for global conquest, and that we have joined the issue thus raised on the battlefield; that here we fight Europe's war with arms while the diplomats there still fight it with words; that if we lose the war to communism in Asia the fall of Europe is inevitable, win it and Europe most probably would avoid war and yet preserve freedom. As you pointed out, we must win. There is no substitute for victory.

—General MacArthur to Congressman Joseph W. Martin, March 20. Senate Foreign Relations and Armed Services Committees, *Hearings, Military Situation in the Far East,* 82d Cong., 1st sess., pp. 3543–3544.

ROBERT A. TAFT was long known as Mr. Republican, yet he never gained the presidential nomination he eagerly sought. Despite his great ability and his familiarity with the problems of government, important elements in the party could not accept his leadership in foreign policy.

He was born in Cincinnati, Ohio, in 1889, educated in good schools, and graduated from Yale in 1910, while his father was President of the United States. A degree from the Harvard Law School in 1913 enabled Taft to enter practice in Cincinnati. Poor eyesight kept him from serving in the army during World War I; instead he worked with Hoover in the Food Administration. In the 1920s, Taft combined law practice with service in the Ohio legislature, and in 1938 he was elected to the United States Senate seat he held for the rest of his life.

He arrived in Washington as the war approached and almost at once found himself in opposition to Roosevelt. Taft was an isolationist by conviction. He felt that the United States should remain strong and apart, setting an example of the good life that other nations would emulate. He therefore voted against selective service, lend-lease, and revision of the Neutrality Act. He was a conservative on most domestic issues.

With the coming of peace, Taft hoped for a loosening instead of a strengthening of foreign ties. He was suspicious of such international agencies as the UN and the World Bank and had doubts about the wisdom of the Truman policies. Paradoxically, he favored a stronger line in Asia, although he attacked Truman's conduct of the Korean War.

In the Senate and in the country, Taft became the spokesman of a substantial group of Republicans who wished to stem the tide toward internationalism and toward the growth of the power of the Federal government. The main strength of this element was in the Midwest and its chief opposition was Eastern. From 1940 on, the battleground was the National Convention and the prize, the presidential nomination. Each time, Taft failed. His last chance passed in 1952 when Dwight D. Eisenhower was the party's choice. Taft supported Ike loyally in the election but died soon after, in July 1953.

Communist stand, and the American threat to use atomic weapons finally produced a compromise settlement along a line near the 38th parallel (July 27, 1953). The sixteen allied nations issued a pious but meaningless promise that they would return to help if the Communists violated the truce. But in 1957 the burden fell to the United States when open disregard of the agreement brought American troops armed with atomic weapons back to Korea.

Nevertheless, Americans in 1953 greeted the end of the fighting in Korea with relief. They had lost 33,629 lives in battle, and while the Communist casualties were far higher, the enemy's supply of men seemed limitless. There was a good deal of impatience with President Rhee when he endangered the armistice by refusing to force North Korean prisoners to return home against their will. Those who wanted the war over were grateful for peace, despite its slight gains.

The Communists learned that aggression did not always pay, but they also learned that the risk in such incidents was limited. When they met resistance, they could always pull back to the previous position. The United States, by

There is an account of the armistice negotiations in Carl Berger, *The Korea Knot* (Philadelphia, 1964).

contrast, had to meet Communist probes anywhere around the world, never certain which would build up into full-scale conflicts, never itself able to take the military initiative.

▼

The Korean War was one aspect of the confused problem of the Far East. In Asia, communism was a dynamic force that could ally itself with nationalism in ancient societies just entering upon modernization. Few Westerners were willing to face the consequences of the revolution then transforming that vast continent or to devote to it the energy necessary to bring freedom to the area.

Abstractly, the United States recognized that it had a stake in Asia, but it could not decide whether to devote to the Orient the same effort it did to Europe. The overt attack on Korea elicited an instinctive response, but the war showed the difficulties of arriving at a long-term solution. Haunted by the specter of an exhausting conflict with the Chinese masses and by the possibility of an atomic holocaust, Americans preferred the way out the Eisenhower administration offered them. But the underlying problem of the Far East remained and would yet return to unsettle the peace.

Paperbacks for Further Reading

Herbert Feis, *The China Tangle* (Atheneum Publishers) is a good survey. John W. Spanier, *The Truman-MacArthur Controversy* (W. W. Norton & Company, Inc.); and Richard H. Rovere and Arthur Schlesinger, Jr., *The MacArthur Controversy* (The Noonday Press) treat the central issue in the Korean question.

THE EISENHOWER ERA

94

The eight years of the Eisenhower administration differed markedly from the previous two decades when the Democrats had held power. The Republicans in the 1950s were still a minority in the country, and they lacked experience in managing the Federal government. The President was cautious, a congenital middle of the road man, and he depended for political support on a divided party. He was not likely to embark upon bold new ventures in foreign or domestic policy.

Nevertheless, the country resisted the temptation to revert to isolationism or to cast aside the heritage of the New Deal and the Fair Deal. Eisenhower's insistence on Modern Republicanism moderated the pressure from the extreme right wing of the party and prevented a damaging split in the nation. If he failed to take advantage of some of the opportunities of these years, he also avoided the most dangerous pitfalls.

The Return of the Republicans

Democratic Failings In 1952 even independent voters believed that the Democrats had been in office too long. The party in power had accumulated so many liabilities that people thought more of its failures than of its achievements. Commentators frequently argued that a Republican victory would preserve the two-party system. The GOP, reinvigorated by responsibility, would drive out its extremists and bring new life to American politics. This prediction confirmed an underlying hankering for new leadership.

There was also much talk in 1952 about inflation and about corruption close to the White House. Congressional committees exposed the "Five percenters," the influence peddlers who maneuvered government contracts through the bureaucracy. The wife of a Reconstruction Finance Commission official had received a $9,000 mink coat. Harry H. Vaughan, the President's military aide, was accused of accepting a $500 deep freeze. This seemed all of a piece with Senator Estes Kefauver's revelations of a national crime syndicate and with the scandals that rocked the athletic world. So much dishonesty, people thought, showed that there was something wrong in the country; and in a vague way those moral failings seemed also connected with the inflation, which had destroyed the purchasing power of the dollar. By 1952, a hundred cents could buy less than sixty had in 1939.

These doubts added to the concern that the Democrats had not been sufficiently vigilant in fighting subversion. Truman's unwillingness to take the initial accusations seriously now cost him dear. The suspicion persisted that perhaps all that was rotten in the nation was due to still undetected Communists, as Senator McCarthy's sweeping accusations claimed. Respectable politicians hesitated to disavow McCarthy's outrageous calumnies and most of them were perfectly willing to accept his support. The effect was further to undermine confidence in the Truman administration.

In the background of all these anxieties and grievances was the war in Korea, with its heavy costs in lives and dollars. Americans could not understand why the world's most powerful nation was bogged down in a remote conflict with no clear end in sight. Could MacArthur have been right after all?

The Candidates As people cast about for a strong leader who would put Washington to rights, attention focused on Dwight D. Eisenhower. Ike had enjoyed more than a decade of favorable attention as commander of the Allied forces in the war and as organizer of the NATO defenses since 1950. An amiable man who made friends easily, he inspired confidence in the liberals, who had thought of using him to displace Truman in 1948. Four years later, he was the natural champion to head off the traditional Midwestern isolationists whose favorite was Senator Taft. A well-organized movement led by Wayne Morse, Henry Cabot Lodge, and Thomas E. Dewey brought Eisenhower the nomination.

His running mate satisfied the right wing of the party and was in a position to exploit popular fears. The exposure of Alger Hiss had gained Richard M. Nixon a national reputation. The young Senator from California was a reliable party member in the eyes of the professionals. During the campaign he clattered noisily about, firing accusations of communism and corruption against the Democrats. Then the need to justify a special fund put at his disposal by businessmen brought him before a nationwide radio and television audience of 55 million (September 23, 1952). Out poured the familiar soap opera—the story of a common man worrying about common problems and all questions dissolved in sentimental slush. Thereafter he was "my boy" to the fatherly Eisenhower.

Dwight D. Eisenhower, *The White House Years* (New York, 1963–1965) is the President's own account.

DWIGHT D. EISENHOWER was born in 1890 in Denison, Texas, but his family moved shortly thereafter to Abilene, Kansas. Dwight went through high school and graduated in 1915 from the United States Military Academy at West Point in the top third of his class. He served in various military posts in the next ten years and in 1925 attended the Command and General Staff School at Fort Leavenworth, where he was first in his class.

Between 1929 and 1933 he was an assistant in the office of the Secretary of War and there became acquainted with General Douglas MacArthur. He served under MacArthur in the Philippines and in 1939 became chief of staff for the Third Army. In that capacity he attracted the attention of General Marshall, who brought him into the War Department general staff. His demonstrated ability to master complex operations and to get along with people earned him the post as Commanding General of the European Theater of Operations in June 1942.

Later that year, Ike organized and led the Allied forces that invaded North Africa. The success of that effort put him in charge first of the expeditions to Sicily and Italy and then of the drive across the Channel into the heart of Germany. He inspired affection among the enlisted men, proved capable of rising above the quarrels among his subordinates, and showed diplomatic skill in dealing with his British and Russian allies.

After the peace he served as chief of staff and then as president of Columbia University. In December 1950 Truman called him out of retirement to organize the NATO armed forces. Ike returned from Europe in the summer of 1952 to campaign for the first of his two terms in the White House. The eight years in office were not happy for him, punctuated as they were with two serious illnesses. His personal popularity remained high, but his chosen successor was defeated at the polls in 1960, and in 1964 his party fell into the hands of men who repudiated Modern Republicanism.

The Republican ticket attracted many different kinds of voters. Eisenhower refused to quarrel with McCarthy, patched matters up with Taft, and launched a partisan attack upon the Democrats. He denounced bungling in high places and promised to bring the war in Korea to an early and honorable end. He also implied that he would unleash Chiang Kai-shek for an attack on the mainland and would liberate Eastern Europe. Ike gave the impression of being a kindly wise leader who was also a strong military commander able to restore American power.

Against him the Democrats pitted Adlai Stevenson, a moderate whose position was not far from that of the Eastern Republicans. To appease the Southern wing of the party, he accepted John J. Sparkman of Alabama as vice-presidential candidate and refrained from stressing civil rights. The Democrats appealed to labor by asking for repeal of the Taft-Hartley law. But Stevenson's comments on foreign policy were defensive. Introspective and witty, he failed to inspire in most Americans the impression of solidity appropriate to the office he sought.

Eisenhower won a sweeping victory, to be repeated in 1956. In both cases success was a tribute to his personality. In 1952, he carried enough Republicans into office to give him a narrow majority in the House of Representatives and a tie in the Senate (which Nixon's vote could break). But the GOP lost control of Congress in 1954 and never regained it. Through most of his two terms, therefore, Ike had to deal with a Senate and House controlled by the opposition. An alliance of the conservatives in both parties generally supported his policies but rarely left him freedom of action in domestic affairs.

Eisenhower organized the Administration by drawing upon the Dewey wing of the Republican party for top personnel. The dominant figures were Secretary of State John Foster Dulles, who took command of diplomacy, and Secretary of the Treasury George M. Humphrey, who set fiscal policies. Ike was content to let these men run their own departments. His task

JOHN FOSTER DULLES was born in Washington, D.C., in 1888 but spent much of his early life in Watertown, New York, where his father was a Presbyterian minister. Dulles graduated from Princeton in 1908 and later earned a law degree at George Washington Law School.

Diplomacy was always close to his interests. While he was a junior at college he accompanied his grandfather, former Secretary of State John W. Foster, to the Hague Conference, and the same connection secured him a place with the international law firm of Sullivan & Cromwell. An uncle, Secretary of State Robert Lansing, found Dulles a place in the general staff when defective eyesight barred him from active service during World War I. He also accompanied the American delegation to the Paris Peace Conference.

In the interwar years, Sullivan & Cromwell was actively engaged in resolving some of the international financial problems left by the war, and Dulles got a close view of European economic difficulties. As a participant in the meetings of the World Council of Churches, he faced some of the spiritual dilemmas of the times. From these experiences came the conclusion that the Versailles settlement had failed because it left no room for peaceful change and a determination that the mistakes of 1919 would not be repeated a quarter century later.

In the 1940s Dulles worked closely with Governor Dewey, and he served on numerous diplomatic delegations, including those that framed the UN Charter and the Japanese peace treaty. He was therefore well qualified to take the post of Secretary of State to which Eisenhower appointed him in 1953 and which he held until his death in 1959. Since he commanded the President's confidence throughout, Dulles was in a position to dominate foreign policy. Yet he proved more capable of formulating abstract principles than of applying them to practice. The phrases he coined—massive retaliation, liberation, moral offensive—sometimes confused the effort to attain immediate goals and were not very helpful in crises. He was therefore a less reliable guide to the problems of the 1950s than Eisenhower expected.

---

he conceived to be that of persuasion and conciliation. Routine matters he left to his chief assistant, Sherman Adams.

The New Look in Foreign Policy

Above all, Eisenhower wished to crown his success as a general by the statesmanship that would earn a lasting peace. He hoped that a dynamic foreign policy would stabilize the situation in Asia and Europe. Yet good intentions counted for little during his first term. He could not match the vigor of his Secretary of State's rhetoric with action and met a series of frustrations.

Indochina Peace in Korea created a danger that Ike foresaw but could not avoid. Eisenhower knew that relief from pressure at one end of the Chinese border would create new pressures at the other. Events in Indochina soon proved him correct. Among Frenchmen, the war against the Viet Minh was unpopular, fought by volunteers and mercenaries, and financed by American aid. The French army lacked resources, committed serious tactical blunders, and in 1953 approached the limit of its endurance.

Secretary of State Dulles favored intervention, for he believed that the loss of Indochina to the Communists would cost the free world all of Southeast Asia and thrust the American defensive perimeter back to Australia. But he could find no international support; the French

The Threat of Assault, 1953

This war is, for Americans, the most painful phase of Communist aggression throughout the world. It is clearly a part of the same calculated assault that the aggressor is simultaneously pressing in Indochina and in Malaya, and of the strategic situation that manifestly embraces the island of Formosa and the Chinese Nationalist forces there. The working out of any military solution to the Korean War will inevitably affect all these areas.

—President Dwight D. Eisenhower, State of the Union Message, February 2. *Public Papers of the Presidents, Dwight D. Eisenhower, 1953* (Washington: Government Printing Office, 1960), p. 6.

were exhausted and the British had no taste for the adventure. Eisenhower therefore faced a dismal prospect. He did not want a Communist victory. Yet having just extricated the United States from a land war in Korea, he was unwilling to send American forces to fight alone for a territory that the French were not themselves defending. Nor was he ready to use atomic arms. The fall of Dien Bien Phu on May 7, 1954, destroyed French power, yet found the Americans standing helplessly by.

France thereupon agreed to a peace settlement. At a conference of the interested parties in Geneva, Indochina was divided into three parts. Three separate agreements (July 1954) established the independence of Laos, Cambodia, and Vietnam, although the last-named was to remain divided at the 17th parallel until elections after two years determined its future. The United States did not become a signatory to the pacts but agreed not to impede their implementation. Two states therefore existed in Vietnam just as in Korea and Germany. In the next six years South Vietnam and North Vietnam struggled to achieve stable and durable regimes, the former with American aid, the latter with help from the Russians and Chinese.

Meanwhile the United States hoped to limit the repercussions from the collapse in Indochina by a mutual defense treaty with Korea and by a counterpart of NATO in the South Pacific. In September 1954 it joined with Great Britain, France, Australia, New Zealand, Pakistan, Thailand, and the Philippines in the Southeast Asia Collective Defense Treaty (SEATO) calling for mutual economic cooperation and protection against subversion or aggression. A special protocol shielded South Vietnam, Laos, and Cambodia.

Taiwan The next challenge in Asia, however, came in Taiwan, where the fate of the Nationalist regime hung in the balance. After the Japanese surrender the Kuomintang government had established control by severely repressive measures. But once Chiang Kai-shek himself was installed (1949), he began to pacify the indigenous population. Land reform and economic development sustained a rising level of productivity and local political institutions took form. Stability nevertheless still depended upon recognition of the regime as the legitimate government of China and upon the hope of an eventual return to the mainland.

Eisenhower, however, was in no position to unleash Chiang and risk an Asian war. It was not even clear whether the United States would help protect the offshore islands of Quemoy and Matsu, which were subject to Communist bombardment. A Congressional resolution authorized the President to do so (1955) but only if a Communist attack threatened Taiwan. In 1958, when trouble flared up once more, Chiang was persuaded to renounce the use of force as a means of returning to the mainland. The crisis passed when the failure of their extravagant economic and social experiments distracted the Chinese Communists, but in 1960, uncertainty still clouded the Far East.

The Crisis of 1956

Central Europe Eisenhower's diplomacy met its critical test in 1956 in Europe and the Near East. The Soviet Union, shaken by the revelation of Stalin's crimes and by economic setbacks, passed under the leadership of several successors and alternatively used pleas for peaceful coexistence and threats of force to consolidate its position. Yet Eisenhower was unable to capitalize on the opportunities of these years of transition and, indeed, antagonized the closest friends of the United States.

Tolerable compromises ended the Austrian occupation in 1955 and adjusted the status of Trieste. But Germany remained divided. The line between East and West, regarded as temporary in 1945, grew increasingly rigid with the divergence in the political and social institutions of the two sections. Berlin remained a source of irritation to both parties—to the West because it was exposed and vulnerable; to the East because through it a constant stream of refugees passed to the West, weakening the East German state.

The French rejection of the scheme for a European Defense Community in 1954 and the subsequent admission of West Germany to NATO frightened the Russians, who dreaded above all a revived and rearmed Germany. A Russian, British, French, and American summit meeting at Geneva in July 1955 accomplished nothing and tension remained high.

Then came an immediate threat to the Soviet position in Eastern Europe. In the satellites, stripped of resources by the Russians and hampered by restrictive controls, the Red purges had left a deep undercurrent of unrest. The death of Stalin, the maneuvers among his successors, and the revelation of his terrorism touched off riots in East Germany and Poland. In Hungary, in October 1956, a mass revolution overturned the Communist party leadership and Soviet troops moved in. The Hungarian government then appealed to the United Nations for

The German Crisis, 1953

The continued partition of Germany is a scandal. It is more than that. It is a crime. Originally, there were four zones of occupation, one each for Britain, France, the United States, and the Soviet Union. This was designed as a convenient way for the Allies to administer the first phases of the surrender terms. It was never intended that Germany should be indefinitely partitioned. Britain, France, and the United States over 4 years ago put their zones together. The Soviet Union has stubbornly held on to the part of Germany it occupies.

This is not only wrong to the Germans; it is a menace to the peace. The Germans in the Soviet zone, now cut off from their fellows for over 8 years and subjected to the despotic rule of Soviet puppets, are becoming increasingly restless. Their pathetic economic plight is shown by the eagerness with which they seek the food packages made available to them in West Berlin. They have sought these by the millions, even at great personal risk. Their growing resentment at their rulers is shown by the riots and strikes which led even unarmed Germans with stones to seek to resist the Red Army tanks which were sent to subdue them . . . .

It is the view of Great Britain, France, and the United States that the first step for the solution of the problem of Germany is to have all-German free elections to bring about unification. When that has happened, then there will be a truly representative German government and then the Allies can make a peace treaty which, if accepted by the all-German Government, will have a true endorsement on the part of the German people which they can be expected to honor.

—Secretary of State Dulles, Statement to the Press, September 3. *American Foreign Policy, 1950–1955* (Washington: Government Printing Office, 1957), vol. II, pp. 1843–1844.

Liberty in the Satellites, 1955

While we maintain our vigilance at home and abroad, we must help intensify the will for freedom in the satellite countries behind the Iron Curtain. These countries are in the Soviet backyard, and only so long as their people are reminded that the outside world has not forgotten them — only that long do they remain as potential deterrents to Soviet aggression.

The great majority of the 70 million captives in these satellite countries have known liberty in the past. They now need our constant friendship and help if they are to believe in their future . . . .

I know that our country and our friends behind the Iron Curtain can count on you for active participation and leadership in this most critical of all battles — the winning of men's minds. Without this victory, we can have no other victories. By your efforts, backed up by America, we can achieve our great goal — that of enabling us and all the peoples of the world to enjoy in peace the blessings of freedom.

— President Dwight D. Eisenhower, February 8. *American Foreign Policy, 1950–1955* (Washington: Government Printing Office, 1957), vol. II, p. 2069.

assistance. For more than a decade, Radio Free Europe and other Western voices had called for precisely such an uprising. Now was the time for the liberation of enslaved populations to which Dulles had referred in the election campaign of 1952.

Suez Almost simultaneously the UN faced a crisis in the Near East. Rival nationalisms had kept that area in a turmoil for more than a decade. Roosevelt had attempted to arrive at an understanding with the Arabs because he foresaw the end of imperialism and wished to protect vital American oil interests. But recognition of the state of Israel in 1948 by the United States

and the United Nations antagonized the Arabs, who were further embittered by their failure to crush the new nation by force of arms. King Farouk of Egypt fell as a result, and the military leaders in 1954 installed Gamal Abdel Nasser as president. A commitment to nationalism and socialism persuaded him to seek the immediate departure of the British and to launch a campaign of harassment against Israel.

No doubt with Russian encouragement, the Czechs in 1955 began to supply arms to the Egyptians. Nasser, who already had great influence in Syria, stirred up a revolution in Jordan and recognized Communist China. The United States underestimated the gravity of the situation. Secretary of State Dulles, who thought that economic pressure would compel Nasser to yield, broke off negotiations for American aid in building the Aswan Dam. But Nasser already had a Russian offer to do the job and had no need of the West. He struck back by nationalizing the Suez Canal Company in which France and England were the dominant participants. In the complicated discussions that followed Dulles failed to support his European allies.

In the fall of 1956, Israel, Britain, and France concerted their actions. Having lost hope of redress through peaceful channels, they determined to use force. On October 29, just after the Hungarian uprising, the Israelis attacked the Isthmus of Suez, and when Nasser's army melted away, the French and British intervened to protect the canal.

These measures encountered the unexpected opposition of the United States. The issue came before the United Nations at the same time as the Hungarian problem, and it demonstrated the weakness of the world organization. With American help, the UN compelled the democracies to withdraw from Suez. But the Soviet Union simply defied world opinion by brutally crushing the Hungarian government. Instead of developing a rule of law applicable to

Herman Finer, *Dulles Over Suez* (Chicago, 1964) contains a sharp criticism of American policy.

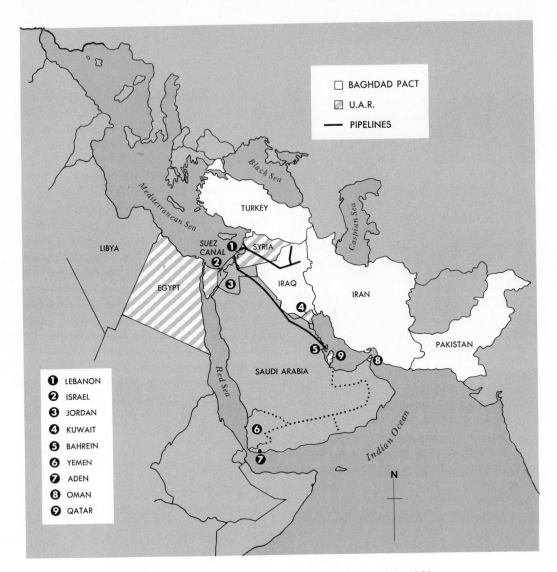

BAGHDAD PACT

U.A.R.

PIPELINES

Black Sea

Mediterranean Sea

TURKEY

Caspian Sea

LIBYA

SUEZ
CANAL

SYRIA

EGYPT

IRAQ

IRAN

PAKISTAN

Red Sea

SAUDI ARABIA

Indian Ocean

N

❶ LEBANON
❷ ISRAEL
❸ JORDAN
❹ KUWAIT
❺ BAHREIN
❻ YEMEN
❼ ADEN
❽ OMAN
❾ QATAR

THE UNITED STATES IN THE NEAR EAST, 1950–1960

all, the UN had become an instrument for repressing those willing to abide by its recommendations.

Meanwhile, the Communists had acquired a foothold in the Near East which they vigorously expanded. In the next decade, revolutionary disorder swept through Iraq and Syria and almost penetrated to Lebanon, where the United States briefly landed troops (1958). Eisenhower had pleased neither the Israelis nor the Arabs. He had wounded the British. And the French,

already resentful at the loss of their empire and suspicious of American closeness to Germany, felt a resurgence of nationalism.

Strategic Obligations

During most of his second term, Eisenhower's foreign policy remained frozen. He made fewer rhetorical statements, but neither

John C. Campbell, *Defense of the Middle East* (New York, 1960) is a balanced study of American objectives.

584

Surrounded by Heavily Armed "Barbudos" (the Bearded Ones), Castro Enters Havana in Triumph. His revolution, begun in 1956 with a handful of guerrillas, succeeded in ousting Batista by January 1, 1959. (UPI)

did he take the initiative to ease the deadlock on any of the world's problems.

Latin America Military dictators, heedless of the popular welfare, ruled most Latin American countries. Adhering to the doctrine of nonintervention, the United States refused to meddle in their affairs, although its military aid indirectly strengthened the regimes in power. Yet social discontent kept the region on edge.

American policy wavered between fear of possible Communist subversion and a desire to encourage the modernization of its neighbors. In 1954, aid from the United States helped a conservative revolution oust a Communist regime in Guatemala, just at about the same time that the British intervened to cut off a possible Communist take-over in their colony in Guiana. But these negative measures were not adequate to develop stable societies.

The fall of the Perón dictatorship in Argentina (1955) started a revolutionary process throughout Latin America. The hostile reception accorded Vice-President Nixon during his tour in the spring of 1958 showed that the United States was usually identified as the colonialist supporter of the old regimes. Eisenhower had already begun to shift emphasis from military to economic aid through the Export-Import Bank, and the Inter-American Development Bank (1959) was designed to accelerate that tendency.

Cuba showed how late the shift was. Impatience with the cruel Batista dictatorship finally induced the United States to cut off aid, and that enabled Fidel Castro to take power, in January 1959, professing a liberal, middle-class program. But Castro immediately betrayed his promise to hold free elections and ruthlessly

President Eisenhower (left) with Premier Khrushchev, September 1959. They are seen during the Russian Premier's visit to the United States, when he agreed to negotiate further on Berlin. (UPI)

used terror against any dissenters. The liberals fled into exile, many of them to the United States, and Castro became ever more extreme, moving toward communism as his scatterbrained schemes ran into trouble. By 1960, Eisenhower faced the dilemma, whether to intervene or to tolerate an infection that might spread to the whole continent.

Peace at the Summit   Until May 1960, the President still clung to the hope that he could crown his administration with a decisive act to restore world peace. He believed that once he reached an accommodation with the Soviet Union other problems would fall into place. Stalin's successors also desired peace but without

yielding on their ultimate objectives. Conferences on disarmament, on a nuclear test ban, and on Berlin continued intermittently, the tone growing friendlier when the Russians' hopes were down, more belligerent when they thought they could have their way.

Khrushchev's visit to the United States and his meeting with Ike at Camp David in 1959 raised expectations that another encounter between the two men might improve relations. But the shooting down of an American U-2 reconnaissance plane over their territory in May 1960 gave the Russians an excuse to end any further possibility of *rapprochement*. In the next month Eisenhower suffered the additional humiliation of the withdrawal of an invitation to visit Japan and found, in the turbulence of the Congo, cause for concern about the future of Africa.

Armed Vigilance   The indefinite continuation of the cold war compelled Americans to consider the problems of strategic policy which in the past had occupied only a few isolated thinkers like Captain Mahan. Peace and war overlapped and there was no time for improvisation. Strategy and weapons had to be ready at once for there were not likely to be second chances. Furthermore, the new arms were so complex that they required a long planning and production process. It took six years to bring the B-52 from the drawing boards to the airfields.

The determination never again to slip into a Korean type of war and the desire for economy shaped the strategy of the Eisenhower administration. During the Korean War military expenditures had risen from about 6 percent of the gross national product to above 14 percent. After 1953 the Department of Defense cut spending back to about 9 percent through reductions in conventional forces.

Secretary of State Dulles argued that the savings did not diminish American strength. The nation's atomic power was so great as to deter any aggression against it or its allies by the threat of massive retaliation. The hydrogen bomb (March 1954) and the expanded Strategic

The Russian Earth Satellite "Sputnik." It is shown mounted on a stand prior to the launching on October 4, 1957. (UPI)

Air Command added to the armory that would keep the peace.

Yet the Indochinese crisis and the deadlock elsewhere showed the inadequacy of that doctrine. The Russians also had the hydrogen bomb and the United States would not risk a total nuclear holocaust to win local conflicts. Yet without conventional troops for such engagements, it was impotent either for liberation or containment. In October 1957, Dulles pointed out that tactical nuclear weapons could serve as substitutes in minor engagements, but neither his countrymen nor his potential enemies found the argument convincing. That very year the Sputnik showed the Russian superiority in rocketry. The ominous Soviet lead in intercontinental ballistic missiles lay in the background of Eisenhower's frantic pursuit of peace in his second term.

Constant research and the development of new weapons were essential to make the American threat credible. In 1950, the Federal government directly or indirectly spent about $1,000,000,000 for these purposes. By the end of the decade annual expenditures had risen to above $7,000,000,000. The Massachusetts Institute of Technology, Stanford, the California Institute of Technology, and other universities received substantial proportions of their budgets from government sources, as did special operations research organizations like the Rand Corporation.

Domestic Issues

As a Modern Republican, Eisenhower had no desire to turn the clock back to 1932, but the lack of boldness and the desire for economy kept

Modern Republicanism, 1956

Modern Republicanism . . . is a type of political philosophy that recognizes clearly the responsibility of the Federal Government to take the lead in making certain that the productivity of our great economic machine is distributed so that no one will suffer disaster, privation, through no fault of his own. Now, this covers the wide field of education and health, and so on.

We believe likewise in the free enterprise system. We believe that it is free enterprise that has brought these blessings to America.

Therefore, we are going to try our best to preserve that free enterprise, and put all of these problems in the hands of localities and the private enterprise of States wherever we can. It happens that the great difference, as I see it, between myself and people of a philosophy that believes in centralized government, is that I believe to have this free enterprise healthy, you must have, first, integrity in your fiscal operations of the Government; second, you must preserve a sound dollar or all of our plans for social security and pensions for the aged fall by the wayside, they are no good; and thirdly, in this dispersion of power.

— President Dwight D. Eisenhower, Press Conference, November 14. *Public Papers of the Presidents, Dwight D. Eisenhower, 1956* (Washington: Government Printing Office, 1958), p. 1103.

him from dealing adequately with the great issues of the 1950s.

The Politics of Conservatism Caution was the keynote of a domestic policy shaped in collaboration with the conservative Congressional coalition. The President did nothing to restrain Senator McCarthy, even when the Army became the target of attack. It finally took action by a group of courageous Senators to bring McCarthy to heel by a vote of censure (1954).

The fiscal program of the Administration aimed at a balanced budget that would permit the reduction of taxes and prevent inflation. When interest rates rose and production slackened, the government was reluctant to act despite growing unemployment. As a result, the rate of growth declined and there were serious recessions in 1953, 1957, and 1960.

In most matters, the President preferred to withhold government initiative and to allow private interests to act. Thus it seemed plausible to let the Dixon-Yates combine rather than TVA build a plant to supply power to Memphis, or to transfer offshore oil lands to the states. Nor did Ike object to a bill to end the right of the Federal Power Commission to set the price of natural gas at the wellhead. His appointees on the Federal Communications Commission passed out television licenses without much regard to the public stake in the matter. That there were occasional hints of scandal in some of these transactions was less important than the general contraction of the government's role.

Eisenhower did press for the organization of the Department of Health, Education, and Welfare (1953), for aid to scientific research, and for the admission of Alaska and Hawaii as states (1959). The Twenty-third Amendment gave residents of the District of Columbia the right to vote in presidential elections. Ike also approved four increases in social security payments and he expressed genuine sympathy for laborers and farmers. But the Landrum-Griffin Act which restricted union powers (1959) antag-

The Twenty-third Amendment

SECTION 1. The District constituting the seat of Government of the United States shall appoint in such manner as the Congress may direct:

A number of electors of President and Vice-President equal to the whole number of Senators and Representatives in Congress to which the District would be entitled if it were a State, but in no event more than the least populous State; they shall be in addition to those appointed by the States, but they shall be considered, for the purposes of the election of President and Vice President, to be electors appointed by a State; and they shall meet in the District and perform such duties as provided by the twelfth article of amendment.

SECTION 2. The Congress shall have power to enforce this article by appropriate legislation.

—Passed by Congress, June 16, 1960; ratified April 3, 1961.

The Unconstitutionality of Segregation, 1954

We conclude that in the field of public education the doctrine of "separate but equal" has no place. Separate educational facilities are inherently unequal. Therefore, we hold that the plaintiffs and others similarly situated for whom the actions have been brought are, by reason of the segregation complained of, deprived of the equal protection of the laws guaranteed by the Fourteenth Amendment. This disposition makes unnecessary any discussion whether such segregation also violates the Due Process Clause of the Fourteenth Amendment.

Because these are class actions, because of the wide applicability of this decision, and because of the great variety of local conditions, the formulation of decrees in these cases presents problems of considerable complexity. On reargument, the consideration of appropriate relief was necessarily subordinated to the primary question — the constitutionality of segregation in public education. We have now announced that such segregation is a denial of the equal protection of the laws.

—*Brown et al.* v. *The Board of Education of Topeka et al.* 347 United States, p. 495.

onized the former and declining farm incomes, the latter.

Civil Rights With the President and Congress both conservative, the judiciary emerged as the chief liberal force in the 1950s. The Supreme Court carefully scrutinized the legislation that infringed upon individual rights and it faced up to the issue of civil rights, but it got little cooperation from the other two branches of government.

In the case of *Brown* v. *The Board of Education* (1954) the Court at last held unconstitutional the doctrine of separate but equal enunciated in *Plessy* v. *Ferguson*. It therefore ordered the desegregation of schools everywhere with all deliberate speed.

The President and other political leaders, however, took no steps to implement this decision and thereby freed hostile local authorities to work out ways of evasion. In the election of 1956, neither candidate expressed himself very strongly on the matter and the Southern states set about circumventing the law. White citizens' councils appeared throughout the South, bent on maintaining segregation.

In 1957, the Administration collaborated with the moderates in Congress to secure passage of the first civil rights law since Reconstruction. The measure was less important for its details, which were much watered down in the

Negro Students Attend School in Little Rock, Arkansas, Escorted by the National Guard, October 14, 1957. (Bern Keating, Black Star)

course of enactment, than for the demonstration that a determined majority could overcome resistance. But the same year the President vacillated when Governor Orval E. Faubus of Arkansas called out that state's units of the National Guard to block a court order admitting nine Negro children to a white school. Ike finally sent Federal forces into Little Rock to secure obedience to the law, but he did so hesitantly and without any commitment to equality. Progress toward that goal in the remainder of his term was slight. In the school year that began in September 1960, only about 11 percent of the Southern districts had made even a gesture toward desegregation.

The Eisenhower administration did not drag the United States back into the past. There was no escape from the difficult problems of the twentieth century, uncomfortable as they were. The cold war deprived Americans of the luxury of a return to isolationism. In Asia, in Europe, and at home the Republicans continued the policies of their predecessors in most matters, once the campaign rhetoric of 1952 subsided. But Eisenhower was not capable of moving the country ahead to adjust to new situations as they unfolded. A new generation of political leaders would do so.

Paperbacks for Further Reading

Dwight D. Eisenhower, *The White House Years: Mandate for Change* (Signet Books) deals with the first term. Sherman Adams, *Firsthand Report* (Popular Library, Inc.) is by the President's close assistant. Emmet J. Hughes, *The Ordeal of Power* (Dell Publishing Co., Inc.) is a revealing account by a disillusioned Modern Republican.

There are a good many detailed analyses of foreign policy in the 1950s. Don K. Price, ed., *The Secretary of State* (Spectrum Books) discusses the organization of diplomacy. Sydney D. Bailey, *The United Nations* (Frederick A. Praeger, Inc.) is a brief guide. Hedley Bull, *The Control of the Arms Race* (Frederick A. Praeger, Inc.) and Bernard Brodie, *Strategy in the Missile Age* (Princeton University Press) deal with armaments. Eugene Staley, *The Future of Underdeveloped Countries* (Frederick A. Praeger, Inc.); and Max F. Millikan, *et al., The Emerging Nations* (Little, Brown & Co.) treat the problem of economic development. Cecil V. Crabb, Jr., *The Elephants and the Grass* (Frederick A. Praeger, Inc.) examines the neutrals. A. Doak Barnett, *Communist China in Perspective* (Frederick A. Praeger, Inc.) deals with the 1950s. Theodore Draper, *Castro's Revolution* (Frederick A. Praeger, Inc.) contains an incisive discussion of Cuba.

Albert P. Blaustein and Clarence C. Ferguson, Jr., *Desegregation and the Law* (Vintage Books, Inc.) treats the Brown case; and the civil rights movement is described in Martin L. King, *Stride Toward Freedom* (Perennial Library). James Q. Wilson, *The Amateur Democrat* (Phoenix Books) is good on local politics.

THE NEW
FRONTIERS

95

The Americans of the 1960s began to explore new frontiers. The political leaders who had guided the nation through war and depression were replaced by the next generation. Young men, moving to take command, tried to formulate questions relevant to the second half of the century. Some of the old issues had faded in importance. Others, like civil rights at home and security abroad, had been so long postponed that they now neared a crisis. Still others, like medical care and pollution, attracted widespread attention for the first time.

In the face of these problems, there were frequent calls for a reassessment of the national purpose. The goals of the past were no longer adequate to a future in which man would hold in his hands the power either to perfect or to destroy all forms of human life. That awareness subtly altered the emphasis in American politics after 1960 and also influenced economic and social development.

The Election of 1960

A New Generation There was a perceptible shift in political leadership after 1960. The New Dealers and their opponents of the 1930s, the interventionists and the isolationists of the 1940s, no longer dominated the scene. Although the committee structure of the House and the Senate still unduly emphasized seniority, new voices were heard in both chambers, and youthful governors took command of many states.

Young men in both parties played central roles in the presidential campaign of 1960. Richard M. Nixon of California was the chosen Republican heir. Still less than fifty that year, he had earned Eisenhower's full confidence during eight years as Vice-President, and the White House prestige was sufficient to pass the mantle on. Henry Cabot Lodge of Massachusetts provided the Eastern balance to the ticket.

The Democratic nomination was in greater doubt. Adlai Stevenson had twice been a loser and few party chieftains were willing to risk supporting him again. He retained the enthusiastic allegiance of a devoted group of followers but, plagued by self-doubt and pride, he refused to declare himself an open candidate and preferred to wait in the wings for a call that never came.

The candidates preferred by the old Senatorial leadership were Lyndon B. Johnson and Hubert H. Humphrey, both of whom had served expertly in the upper chamber. As majority leader Johnson had exercised masterly control of the party since 1954, and he held the loyalty of Southern Democrats whose mediator he had been in the 1950s. The seat of Humphrey's strength was the Middle West, where he drew upon somewhat the same liberal supporters as Stevenson. To some extent Johnson and Humphrey offset each other. The former was too moderate, the latter too liberal, the one antagonized Northern, the other Southern, voters.

The nomination went to forty-three year old John F. Kennedy, who had masterfully steered himself into a strategic position. Kennedy was younger than his rivals and did not match them in experience. From his safe sanctuary in Massachusetts he had played a cautious role in the House and the Senate, refusing to take an exposed stand on controversial issues, making few friends and few enemies. In 1956 he had grasped boldly but unsuccessfully for the vice-presidential nomination. He knew that the prize was worth little but used the opportunity to project his name into national prominence. In the next four years he campaigned quietly but vigorously in every part of the country.

With the aid of a competent staff and of a superb sense of public relations, Kennedy turned his liabilities into assets. As a Catholic in the West Virginia primary, he converted the taboo that had contributed to Al Smith's defeat in 1928 into a test of tolerance and won handsomely. His inexperience became the challenge of youth promising to introduce new vigor into a tired government. He came into the Convention with a substantial lead that his opponents were unable to overcome. Having secured the nomination, he realistically patched matters up with Johnson, whose position on the ticket won essential support in the South.

The Kennedy Victory The campaign itself was uneventful. The necessity for defending the Eisenhower record was a burden to Nixon. In the face of a dismal diplomatic performance, he had to argue that American prestige was at an all-time high, and he had to maintain that the economy of the United States was thriving while a recession still dragged on. Kennedy's was the more strategic role of critic, warning against the deterioration of American strength abroad, complaining about the lowness of the growth rate. In the television debates that brought these arguments before 70,000,000 viewers, Kennedy was the abler and more attractive performer.

The vote, which followed predictable lines, elected Kennedy by a margin so slight as to leave the outcome in doubt through election night.

Aida Di Pace Donald, ed., *John F. Kennedy and the New Frontier* (New York, 1966) contains an interesting selection of views about Kennedy.

JOHN FITZGERALD KENNEDY was born in 1917 in Brookline, a suburb of Boston, Massachusetts. His father was by then a well-to-do investor and speculator whose wealth would continue to grow. Three generations of residence in America had not effaced the family's Irish antecedents. Rebuffs from the Brahmins induced him to move to a New York suburb where the social environment was less rigid.

Jack was then nine years old. He grew up a rich kid; private schools, summers in Hyannis Port, travel, and Harvard were part of his life. In 1938 he spent six months in London while his father was United States ambassador and there gathered the material for his first book, *While England Slept* (1940), a study of appeasement. He enlisted when the war came, commanded a motor torpedo boat, and behaved heroically in the crisis of its sinking. After the war he worked as a correspondent for the Hearst newspapers.

By then, however, he felt another obligation. His brother Joe, who in family thinking had been destined for a political career, had been killed in the service in the summer of 1944. Jack felt the duty to carry on. A realistic appraisal showed that Boston was the most advantageous base. His grandfather had been a congressman and mayor, the clan was well known there, and a Kennedy could count on the loyalty of the dominant Irish political groups.

In 1946, John F. Kennedy was elected to the United States House of Representatives for the first of his three terms. In 1952, he moved to the Senate, defeating Henry Cabot Lodge despite the Eisenhower landslide. There followed an easy re-election in 1958.

Family background and experience in Congress endowed Kennedy with political shrewdness but also with a sense of quality. He appreciated excellence and was eager to draw upon the services of first-rate people. He worked hard, traveled widely, and became familiar with the most important domestic and foreign problems of the nation. These attributes stood him in good stead when he entered the White House in 1961.

His first two years in office were uncertain. He hesitated in the face of grave decisions in Europe, Asia, and the Caribbean, and he was unable to command the wholehearted support of Congress. Yet even in those years, his youth, determination, and style captured the imagination of the country.

In 1963 he was more sure of himself, able to act courageously in foreign affairs, and willing to follow through on the implications of the New Frontier at home. In that year, too, he prepared to make the election of 1964 a decisive test of policy. He was engaged in that task when he was assassinated.

Presidential Elections, 1960, 1964

	1960	1964
Popular Vote (thousands)		
Democrats	34,227	43,126
Republicans	34,109	27,174
Electoral Vote		
Democrats	303	486
Republicans	219	52

Republicans actually gained 21 seats in the House and 2 in the Senate, and they increased their popular support in the South, where Ike had made the first inroads eight years earlier.

The Kennedy Administration

The Limits of Power Kennedy's determination to distinguish himself pressed him into bold

John F. Kennedy and Richard M. Nixon During Television Debates, 1960. (CBS)

A Trumpet Call, 1961

In your hands, my fellow citizens, more than mine, will rest the final success or failure of our course. Since this country was founded, each generation of Americans has been summoned to give testimony to its national loyalty. The graves of young Americans who answered the call to service surround the globe.

Now the trumpet summons us again — not as a call to bear arms, though arms we need — not as a call to battle, though embattled we are — but a call to bear the burden of a long twilight struggle, year in and year out, "rejoicing in hope, patient in tribulation" — a struggle against the common enemies of man: tyranny, poverty, disease and war itself.

Can we forge against these enemies a grand and global alliance, North and South, East and West, that can assure a more fruitful life for all mankind? Will you join in that historic effort?

In the long history of the world, only a few generations have been granted the role of defending freedom in its hour of maximum danger. I do not shrink from this responsibility — I welcome it. I do not believe that any of us would exchange places with any other people or any other generation. The energy, the faith, the devotion which we bring to this endeavor will light our country and all who serve it — and the glow from that fire can truly light the world.

And so, my fellow Americans: ask not what your country can do for you — ask what you can do for your country.

My fellow citizens of the world: ask not what America will do for you, but what together we can do for the freedom of man.

Finally, whether you are citizens of America or citizens of the world, ask of us here the same high standards of strength and sacrifice which we ask of you. With a good conscience our only sure reward, with history the final judge of our deeds, let us go forth to lead the land we love, asking His blessing and His help, but knowing that here on earth God's work must truly be our own.

— President John F. Kennedy, Inaugural Address, January 20. *Public Papers of the Presidents, John F. Kennedy, 1961* (Washington: Government Printing Office, 1962), pp. 2–3.

Construction of a School in Souk el Arba, Tunisia. Lowell W. Sykes, a Peace Corps volunteer, supervises the work. (Paul Conklin, Peace Corps Photograph)

utterances, but the narrowness of his victory also made him extremely cautious. On the one hand, he summoned the country to a New Frontier and called for innovations in government. On the other, he assured conservatives that he would be prudent. The one impulse led him to bring into the administration young intellectuals; the other led him to designate a Republican banker, Douglas Dillon, as Secretary of the Treasury. Kennedy consulted frequently with ex-President Eisenhower and announced at once the reappointment of J. Edgar Hoover to the FBI and Allen Dulles to the CIA.

A profound ambiguity thus ran through the first two years of the Kennedy administration. At times, the President was courageous and firm. He recognized more clearly than any of his predecessors the need for using fiscal policy to guide the economy, and he announced himself an adherent of the theories of compensatory spending. Although he did not bait business, he

spoke out forcefully and secured a retraction when the refusal of the United States Steel Corporation to hold the line on prices threatened the stability of the economy (1962). He also took an imaginative view of the role of education and of science and significantly expanded the scope of the space program. Likewise, the Peace Corps was a novel step toward utilizing the idealism of American young people in foreign affairs.

But the President knew from the start that he depended for support on a Congress dominated by the same conservative coalition which had held power for more than two decades. During the first session he fired off twenty-five messages and was rewarded with some improvements in the social security and minimum wage systems. He also managed to get a housing act through that authorized grants or loans for middle-income buildings and for park and transit development. With the cooperation of Speaker Sam Rayburn he secured an enlargement of the

Protests Against Segregation, Birmingham, Alabama, April 1963. Police use fire hoses to disperse the demonstrators. (F. H. Rockstroh, Pix, Inc.)

House Rules Committee that made room for some liberals. That body nevertheless remained a formidable hurdle. Most of the New Frontier program failed to pass despite Kennedy's efforts to win his opponents over by cajolery and by the use of patronage. The President grew testy as criticism mounted; he gave up his brief experiment with live television press conferences and found it difficult to put his ideas before the people. The most substantial achievement of his second year in office was a trade bill that gave him authority to adjust the tariff for cooperation with the European Common Market.

The Congressional elections of 1962 were encouraging. Instead of the normal mid-term decline, the Democrats increased their majority in the Senate and lost only two seats in the House. Reassured, Kennedy in 1963 began to press for action on his programs, particularly since the lagging growth rate convinced him of the need for some stimulus to the economy. Yet Congressional obstruction still limited his ability to act. His request for a reduction in the income tax, even if it meant a budget deficit, went unheeded. Nor did the legislators respond to the scheme he outlined for medical care for the aged and for Federal aid to education.

Civil Rights Above all, the civil rights issue plagued the President. In October 1960, at the height of the campaign, he had telephoned Mrs. Martin Luther King while her husband was in an Atlanta jail. The widespread attention that gesture gained helped keep the Negro vote Democratic. But in the next two years, while the demands for desegregation grew more pressing, hard-core Southern opposition stiffened. Direct action on both sides grew more important than court proceedings. The passive resistance advocated by King since 1955 and the sit-ins carried out by young people after 1960 pressed the demand for speedy equality. The segregationists used the state and local governments to impede progress and increasingly resorted to violence.

The cross fire trapped Kennedy. His sympathies lay with equality and he knew the importance of the Northern liberals in his following, but he could not totally alienate the Southerners, whose support he needed in Congress. As the Negro sit-ins met violent retaliation, the President spoke out in favor of law and order, but satisfied neither side. When Governor Ross R. Barnett of Mississippi flouted a court order to admit James Meredith, a Negro student, to the state university in October 1962, Kennedy had to act. Yet the violence that followed dispatch of an army of Federal marshals left liberals indignant and segregationists furious.

In April 1963, King led a series of protests in Birmingham, Alabama. The police used dogs and fire hose to break up the demonstrations, making more than a thousand arrests. A Federal emissary finally arranged a truce; outbreaks soon erupted elsewhere, in the North as well as in the South; and stubborn segregationists struck back with bombings and shootings.

Kennedy determined to go beyond calls for law and order to take a vigorous stand in favor of equality. In June, he proposed a sweeping civil rights bill and began to mobilize pressure for its enactment. He requested guarantees of equal access to hotels, restaurants, and other public accommodations and authority for the Attorney General to help speed school desegregation. In August, a great march on Washington, originally launched by Negro radicals, turned into a demonstration on behalf of the President's program. Congress was still recalcitrant but Kennedy's stand was clear.

The issue was still in doubt on November 22, 1963. On the day before, the President had come to Texas to mend political fences. From Fort Worth he had gone to Dallas where assassination ended his hopes and his promise.

Johnson in Power

The Succession Lyndon B. Johnson took office at once and moved into the White House a few days later. The Texan was a professional. Few understood the mechanism of government or its relationship to political reality more clearly than he. He realized at once that he faced two related assignments. As a President by accident, he had to maintain continuity with the Administration of his predecessor and demonstrate the ability to complete its program successfully. He made his intentions clear in an address to a joint session of Congress on November 27, which stressed the special importance of the civil rights bill.

Johnson also had to prepare for the election of 1964, less than a year away. His chances of winning a term of his own depended on the ability to persuade suspicious Northern liberals that they could trust a Southerner to act in the common interest. He intended to do so.

Johnson's performance was masterly. Most of the Kennedy appointees remained in office, although few found the new President personally congenial. The smoothness of the succession reassured the country. Furthermore, Johnson pushed through the programs for which Kennedy had labored in vain.

The new President's first year in office was an unbroken succession of triumphs. Respect for the memory of the dead young leader undoubtedly supplied some psychological support to the effort. In addition, Johnson's tactical skill guided the desired measures around all obstacles, for years of service in Congress had taught him every trick of the political game. Retaining the votes of the loyal, persuading the doubtful, and winning over the hostile, he sought a broad consensus to end obstruction and paralysis and liberate the energies of the nation.

The Program Fulfilled Early in 1964 Johnson gained the tax cut Kennedy had requested a year earlier. Renewed confidence immediately invigorated the economy. In the months that followed Johnson put through a revised agricultural program for the farmers and a mass transportation act for the city dwellers. Social security benefits rose once more, and Congress finally moved to expand provisions for wilderness conservation, space exploration, and higher education. The budget deficit declined but Federal employees got pay increases. There was something for everyone!

To those suspicious of the sincerity of his change of heart, Johnson presented a civil rights bill that included provisions he had stricken out as Senate leader seven years earlier. Moreover, he helped get it over the longest filibuster in Senate history (June 1964). The new law forbade discrimination in any public facilities, in places of accommodation and amusement, in any program receiving Federal aid, in employment, and in union membership. The literacy test could no longer serve as a cover to exclude Negro voters. The Attorney General and the Civil Rights Commission received added enforcement powers, and a community relations service was created

LYNDON BAINES JOHNSON entered politics through the New Deal. He was born in 1908 near Stonewall, Texas, grew up in a family with few material resources, and graduated from a nearby teachers' college in 1930 as the depression set in. He taught school for a while, then got a job as secretary to Congressman Richard M. Kleberg. In 1935 Johnson became state director of the National Youth Administration. Two years later, he won his first election to the United States House of Representatives, a post he retained until 1948 when he advanced to the Senate.

This long experience gave him an intimate understanding of the operations of Congress. His friendship with Speaker Sam Rayburn was helpful, as was his ability to get along with the Southern leaders. Yet Johnson also commanded the respect of the liberals in both houses. He was able, worked hard, and was a shrewd dealer who proved invaluable in working out the compromises essential in the legislative process. Meanwhile a good marriage had brought him some capital, and sound investments built a comfortable fortune.

In the 1950s, Johnson was the dominant figure in the Senate, responsible for the liaison between the Democrats and the Republican President. The important task then was to arrive at a consensus that would get some action but would be moderate enough to antagonize no one. His skill won him considerable support, especially in the South, when he reached for the presidential nomination in 1960.

Kennedy offered him the vice-presidency in order to mobilize that support behind the ticket, but he made relatively little use of Johnson's services after the election. The transition after Kennedy's death was therefore painful, although the new President tried to preserve administrative continuity.

Once in the White House, Johnson used his mastery of Congressional tactics to get enactment of many of the measures that had languished in committees since 1961. Moreover, the dignity of the office brought him a clearer sense of purpose than before. Remembering the poverty-stricken farms of his youth, the hardships of the depression, and his own labors on a road gang, he created a vision of the Great Society, free of want. Recalling his naval service in the Pacific, he determined to conduct a vigorous foreign policy with peace through international law as its objective. Although he lacked the smoothness of style and the quality of evoking affection of Kennedy or F. D. R., his resounding victory in 1964 showed that he had framed a program of which the country approved.

to help in the voluntary settlement of racial disputes.

That same year Johnson launched the war on poverty, aiming at nothing less than the complete abolition of dependency. In August, Congress authorized a $200,000,000 program, of which Sargent Shriver became head, to start the work of expanding incomes, job retraining, and community development.

To cap it all, 1964 was a good year for American space efforts. The Saturn rocket and the Ranger craft succeeded and work started on the supersonic transport airliner.

The Election of 1964 These undeniable achievements put Johnson in an excellent position for the campaign of 1964. He shrewdly chose as his running mate Hubert H. Humphrey who had been his co-worker in the Senate and whose liberal reputation supplemented the President's strength in areas where support was most needed.

The Republicans collaborated by handing over their nomination to Senator Barry M. Goldwater of Arizona. This was an act of desperation. The liberal wing of the party was in disarray. Divorce and remarriage damaged the prospects of Governor Nelson A. Rockefeller of New York and Governors William W. Scranton of Pennsylvania and George W. Romney of Michigan were indecisive. By contrast, the extreme conservatives knew what they wanted and united behind Goldwater. They had been excluded from positions of control for more than thirty years and now demanded a chance to give the voters a genuine choice, not an echo. By the time the Convention met in July 1964, only the influence of Eisenhower could have prevented a Goldwater nomination and he refused to intervene.

As a result, the campaign, more than any other in recent history, followed ideological lines. Johnson stood squarely by the program of the preceding four years, claiming credit for prosperity at home and peace abroad and promising to expand the welfare activities of the government in the future. Goldwater was saddled with positions he could not compromise or explain away—against the civil rights bill, for cuts in social security, for states' rights, and for the use of tactical nuclear arms in Vietnam.

The outcome was not unexpected, but the magnitude of the Democratic victory was surprising. Goldwater got the votes of five Southern states. On the other hand, he lost the support of many people who were normally Republican. Johnson gained a larger percentage of the popular vote (61 percent) than any other recent contender, and his electoral majority was second only to that of Franklin D. Roosevelt in 1936.

The Great Society

With this mandate, Johnson hastened into action. In a speech in May 1964 he had expressed the aspiration for a Great Society that would use the country's wealth to enrich and elevate national life. He wished in 1965 to devote his efforts to the elimination of poverty, to the improvement of the quality of urban life, to beautification and the control of pollution, and to advances in education. The President hoped to achieve the transformation without

sharp internal divisions, by the consensus at which men arrived when they reasoned together for the common good.

Equality and Security Johnson made substantial headway with the aid of the increased Congressional majority he carried with him in the election. The first session of the Eighty-ninth Congress enacted eighty-six substantial administration measures. Some carried forward the earlier programs. The Voting Rights Act, for example, authorized Federal registrars in some cases to enroll Negroes barred from the suffrage. A new immigration law at last abolished the national origins quota system.

The problems of the farmers and of the poor also received attention. The Food and Agriculture Act laid out a fresh omnibus program for modified price supports and accelerated cropland retirement along earlier lines. The war on poverty was extended and expanded. New laws provided for the development of Appalachia and other depressed regions, and a Department of Housing and Urban Development was created, with the injunction to devote special attention to the needs of low-income groups. Federal contributions to welfare programs rose. The desire to expand the opportunities of the children of the poor shaped two laws for the support of education. Public and private elementary schools received aid in proportion to the number of their pupils from low-income families, and college scholarships and work programs provided for the needy. The Federal government supported libraries, the construction of college facilities, and the purchase of educational equipment. A National Teachers Corps set about recruiting instructors for depressed areas.

Medicare extended the social security system in a totally new direction. The inability of the aged to pay the cost of proper medical services had long called for remedial action. The Kerr-Mills Act of 1960 had been inadequate because it depended upon a means test, yet Kennedy's suggestions for reform (1962) had met no response from Congress. Johnson now

The Right to Vote, 1965

My first job after college was as a teacher in Cotulla, Tex., in a small Mexican-American school. Few of them could speak English and I couldn't speak much Spanish. My students were poor and they often came to class without breakfast, hungry. They knew even in their youth the pain of prejudice. They never seemed to know why people disliked them. But they knew it was so, because I saw it in their eyes. I often walked home late in the afternoon, after the classes were finished, wishing there was more that I could do. But all I knew was to teach them the little that I knew, hoping that it might help them against the hardships that lay ahead.

Somehow you never forget what poverty and hatred can do when you see its scars on the hopeful face of a young child.

I never thought then, in 1928, that I would be standing here in 1965. It never even occurred to me in my fondest dreams that I might have the chance to help the sons and daughters of those students and to help people like them all over this country.

But now I do have that chance—and I'll let you in on a secret—I mean to use it. And I hope that you will use it with me.

This is the richest and most powerful country which ever occupied the globe. The might of past empires is little compared to ours. But I do not want to be the President who built empires, or sought grandeur, or extended dominion.

I want to be the President who educated young children to the wonders of their world. I want to be the President who helped to feed the hungry and to prepare them to be taxpayers instead of taxeaters. I want to be the President who helped the poor to find their own way and who protected the right of every citizen to vote in every election.

I want to be the President who helped to end hatred among his fellow men and who prompted love among the people of all races and all regions and all parties.

I want to be the President who helped to end war among the brothers of this earth.

—President Lyndon B. Johnson to Congress, March 15. *Public Papers of the Presidents, Lyndon B. Johnson, 1965* (Washington: Government Printing Office, 1966), pp. 286–287.

---

succeeded. The new law provided health insurance for people over the age of sixty-five, with supplementary benefits to cover charges at hospitals and nursing homes.

The Quality of Life For the first time, it seemed a proper concern of government to control the environment in order to make life safe and pleasant for the people. The Department of Housing and Urban Development was not only to help provide more quarters but also to remove urban blight. In addition, the President called for and got laws to restrict advertising along highways, to screen junkyards, and to control pollution and plan the proper use of water resources. Finally, a National Foundation provided for the arts and the humanities the same type of support the government already gave to science. The vision of the Great Society was still a long way from becoming a reality, but substantial progress had been made toward the goal since 1961.

New Political Forces Subtle shifts in power after 1960 explained part of Johnson's success. In 1962, the Supreme Court ordered Tennessee to correct by reapportionment the system of representation that gave a rural county almost sixty times the weight of an urban one. Two years later the Court applied the same ruling to Congressional districts. The principle of one man, one vote, alerted state and Federal legis-

The Twenty-fourth Amendment

SECTION 1. The right of citizens of the United States to vote in any primary or other election for President or Vice President, for electors for President or Vice President, or for Senator or Representative in Congress, shall not be denied or abridged by the United States or any State by reason of failure to pay any poll tax or other tax.

SECTION 2. The Congress shall have power to enforce this article by appropriate legislation.

—Passed by Congress, August 27, 1963; ratified, January 23, 1964.

Federal Aid to Local Government, 1953–1967

(in million dollars)

Purpose	1953	1959	1962	1964	19
Agriculture	97	322	524	656	
Natural Resources	23	34	35	45	
Commerce and Transportation	528	2,671	2,842	3,979	4
Housing	68	207	354	452	
Health and Welfare	1,810	2,800	3,554	4,259	6
Education	231	281	405	479	2
Others	82	465	455	492	
Total	2,857	6,813	8,190	10,314	14

*Budgeted

The Twenty-fifth Amendment

SECTION 1. In case of the removal of the President from office or his death or resignation, the Vice President shall become President.

SECTION 2. Whenever there is a vacancy in the office of the Vice President, the President shall nominate a Vice President who shall take the office upon confirmation by a majority vote of both houses of Congress.

SECTION 3. Whenever the President transmits to the President pro tempore of the Senate and the Speaker of the House of Representatives his written declaration that he is unable to discharge the powers and duties of his office, and until he transmits to them a written declaration to the contrary, such powers and duties shall be discharged by the Vice President as Acting President.

SECTION 4. Whenever the Vice President and a majority of either the principal officers of the executive departments or of such other body as Congress may by law provide, transmit to the President pro tempore of the Senate and the Speaker of the House of Representatives their written declaration that the President is unable to discharge the powers and duties of his office, the Vice President shall immediately assume the powers and duties of the office as Acting President.

Thereafter, when the President transmits to the President pro tempore of the Senate and the Speaker of the House of Representatives his written declaration that no disability exists, he shall resume the powers and duties of his office unless the Vice President and a majority of either the principal officers of the executive department or of any such body as Congress may by law provide, transmit within four days to the President pro tempore of the Senate and the Speaker of the House of Representatives their written declaration that the President is unable to discharge the powers and duties of his office. Thereupon Congress shall decide the issue, assembling within 48 hours for that purpose if not in session. If the Congress, within 21 days after receipt of the latter written declaration, or, if Congress is not in session, within 21 days after Congress is required to assemble, determines by two-thirds vote of both houses that the President is unable to discharge the powers and duties of his office, the Vice President shall continue to discharge the same as Acting President; otherwise, the President shall resume the powers and duties of his office.

—Passed by Congress, July 6, 1965; ratified February 11, 1967.

lators to their obligations to the city dwellers who formed an increasingly large part of the population. The entry of the Negroes into the Southern electorate created a similar sense of responsibility to them among Southern office-holders except in Alabama and Mississippi.

A new relationship also began to emerge between Washington on the one hand and the states and municipalities on the other. The vast programs for urban renewal, road building, education, welfare, and medical care depended upon collaboration rather than rivalry. By the end of 1966, there were some two hundred kinds of Federal authorization for financial payments to local government. The need for working together created pressure for modernizing the archaic systems of state and county administration, and in time it would alter the political power that had long rested on a local base.

The ultimate effects still remained to be seen. They would very likely be more important than the Twenty-fourth Amendment, which abolished the poll tax as a requirement for voting in Federal elections, or the Twenty-fifth, which regulated the presidential succession.

Change created anxiety. Americans who felt that the pace was too fast went to one extreme; those who wanted more speed, to another. But despite signs that resentment about Negro demands produced a white backlash in some states and despite the election of conservative Republican governors in California and Florida in 1966, indications were that most citizens preferred a gradual adjustment to the new conditions underwritten by the economic strength of the nation.

During the interlude of the 1950s, the country had absorbed the reforms of the preceding quarter century. In 1960, it was prepared to advance toward new frontiers beyond which lay a society in process of change. John F. Kennedy and Lyndon B. Johnson explored the edges of the territory ahead, mapping out new modes of government action on behalf of the people they led. Their dreams were not unrealistic, because the productive system, since 1947, had expanded at an unprecedented rate. The economy was capable of turning out goods. The polity had to determine what use would be made of them.

Paperbacks for Further Reading

Theodore C. Sorensen, *Kennedy* (Bantam Books, Inc.) and Arthur M. Schlesinger, Jr., *A Thousand Days* (Crest Books) are interesting accounts by men close to the President. William S. White, *The Professional* (Crest Books) is a sympathetic biography of President Johnson to 1964. Theodore H. White, *The Making of the President* (Pocket Books, Inc.) and *The Making of the President 1964* (Signet Books) treat the elections of 1960 and 1964 but touch also on the general political situation. James W. Silver, *Mississippi: the Closed Society* (Harvest Books) discusses the problem of integration in that state. Leo Fishman, ed., *Poverty Amid Affluence* (Yale University Press) gives the background of the war on poverty. Oscar and Mary Handlin, *The Dimensions of Liberty* (Atheneum Publishers) treats the general concept as it appeared in the 1960s.

Donald R. Matthews and James W. Prothro, *Negroes and the New Southern Politics* (New York, 1966) is a perceptive analysis in depth.

THE NEW ECONOMY

96

Because Americans after the war so often had to think in terms of defending inherited values, they tended to overlook the radical internal changes through which their society passed. They were aware that they no longer suffered from the economic weakness of the 1930s. Industrial growth and agricultural prosperity brought many problems theretofore regarded as insoluble close to solution. Yet few people understood the peaceful revolution that made growth possible.

The productive system that had developed in the late nineteenth and early twentieth centuries disappeared some time in the 1930s. Large-scale manufacturing remained central to the economy, but the individual entrepreneur and the corporation ceased to operate in a self-regulating market. During the depression and the war the outlines of a new industrial organization had taken form. In the two decades after 1947 it acquired the stability and power that enabled it to bear the heavy burdens imposed upon it.

Economic Growth

AMERICANS WHO RECALLED the discouraging experience of the 1930s could hardly credit the evidence of renewed vigor in the economy after 1945. All the indices spiraled upward. The gross national product increased steadily with only occasional years of faltering. Industrial production, having risen markedly between 1947 and 1955, remained on a plateau until 1959 and then leaped upward. Using the level of 1957–1959 as 100, the index reached 160 in 1966. The measurements of employment and productivity also went up and incomes mounted at an unprecedented rate.

Associated with this growth was a rapid increase in population. The expectation that the American population would level off at about 140 million gave way to a realization that some time in the 1960s it would reach the 200 million mark. Most of the increase was internally generated. Immigration — largely of refugees — was at a higher level than in the quarter century after 1925, but far below that of the years before that date. The rising birth rate was the more important factor in the population increase of the 1950s. The upward trend that had begun during the war continued without interruption until 1957 and thereafter remained well above the level of the 1930s.

Corporate Enterprise

Economic growth owed a good deal to basic transformations in the organization of American enterprise. The roots of the changes extended back into the 1920s. They developed fully after 1947.

The Modern Corporation The classical capitalist, the self-made individual entrepreneur, practically ceased to exist. In a few interstices, notably in the services and retail trades, there was still room for the small businessman, but in the most significant sectors of industry and commerce, the large corporation absorbed all but a tiny fraction of productive activity.

United States Gross National Product Selected Years, 1947–1966

(in billion dollars; current prices)

1947	234.3
1950	284.6
1952	347.0
1956	419.2
1960	500.0
1966	740.0

The corporations of the 1960s were far removed in size, form, and spirit from their predecessors. The United States Steel Corporation in 1900 had been a phenomenon because its capitalization ran to a billion dollars. In 1965, the invested capital of each of twenty-five corporations ran above that figure and fully sixty companies registered annual sales of a billion dollars or more.

Immense resources gave these institutions tremendous power and responsibility. In law the stockholders were the owners. But the hundreds of thousands of transient investors rarely influenced the course of business. The corporations enjoyed considerable independence also in dealings with the banking system and the market place. They usually had a good deal of choice in the methods of arranging their financing, and they could absorb fluctuations in the rate of profit with little difficulty.

Control actually rested in the hands of a managerial bureaucracy. The highly developed skills embraced in the engineering, production, sales, and legal departments of these enterprises replaced the improvisation of the earlier period. Admission to the managerial force came after advanced education in schools of engineering, business, or law; promotion followed rigidly set paths, based largely although not entirely on merit. Free-wheeling individuals still found opportunities to exercise their skill. But men like Robert R. Young in railroads or Meshulim Riklis in merchandising generally confined their

The Industrial Giants of 1965

Company	Sales (billion dollars)	Assets (billion dollars)	Invested Capital (billion dollars)	Employees (thousands)
Automobiles				
General Motors	20.7	12.5	8.2	734
Ford	11.5	7.5	4.9	364
Chrysler Corporation	5.2	2.9	1.5	166
Oil				
Standard Oil of New Jersey	11.4	13.0	8.6	148
Texaco	3.7	5.3	4.0	56
Socony Vacuum	4.9	5.2	3.4	80
Gulf Oil	3.3	5.2	3.8	55
Others				
General Electric	6.2	4.3	2.1	300
United States Steel	4.3	5.4	3.6	208
International Business Machines	3.5	3.7	2.5	172

The Responsibilities of Corporate Planning, 1954

Production in large units . . . set up a grouping within many industries. These groups, although . . . they disposed of great powers in their own organizations, in time were oftener than not compelled to attempt or join in planning operations. . . . In greater or less degree, the practice of national industrial planning is now familiar throughout great areas of the twentieth-century corporate capitalist system. Participation in it is frequently a function, and in any case an occupational hazard, of the managements of large corporations. . . .

The really great corporation managements have reached a position for the first time in their history in which they . . . must consider the kind of a community in which they have faith, and which they will serve, and which they intend to help to construct and maintain. In a word, they must consider at least in its more elementary phases the ancient problem of the "good life," and how their operations in the community can be adapted to affording or fostering it.

—A. A. Berle, Jr., *The 20th Century Capitalist Revolution* (New York: Harcourt, Brace & World, Inc., 1954), pp. 165–167.

attention to over-all financial problems and left the detailed conduct of the enterprise in the hands of the bureaucracy.

The Dynamics of Size Diversification increasingly became the general pattern of the strong corporations. The tendency was no longer simply an extension of the process of integration but rather reflected the desire to end dependence upon a single field. The enterprise spread its skills and capital. General Motors had early explored the advantages of a transfer of engineering techniques from one product to another when it moved outside the production of automobiles. Similarly, oil companies invaded the realm of chemicals; cigarette manufacturers used their salesmanship to market razors and foods; and electric shavers, office machines, and the equipment for aircraft carriers were among the products of a single firm.

The large corporations became international in scope. The auto makers had shown the way in the 1920s by building plants abroad. After 1945, the need for the reconstruction of European industry and the desire of the underdeveloped countries for industrialization offered Americans new opportunities. An unfavorable balance of payments limited the export of capital after 1964, but not enough to halt the trend.

A variety of factors increased the size and complexity of the corporate units. Undoubtedly economies of scale often diminished expenses and raised output. Yet such potential advantages were not always decisive. Indeed, many corporations found it desirable, in the interests of flexibility and lower costs, to disperse their plants and to subcontract for supplies among hundreds of small producers.

Other factors favored large size. The magnitude of corporate enterprises permitted sophisticated centralized planning, with its attendant efficiencies. Ample resources also absorbed the consequences of mistakes; only companies as large as Ford or General Dynamics could survive the losses of hundreds of millions of dollars caused by miscalculations as on the Edsel automobile and the Convair airplane.

Great size generated the resources for a rational organization of research and development efforts not feasible within smaller entities. In effect, some corporations became management teams loosely allied with experimental laboratories, which applied discoveries wherever they were appropriate, rather than focusing investigation on a single product. Thus Eastman Kodak branched out from cameras and film to synthetic fibers. The emphasis was on growth rather than immediate direct returns.

Organized Labor In the light of this shift in objectives, many corporations recognized that unions were not necessarily enemies but could actually collaborate in organizing and disciplining the labor force. Membership in these organi-

ROBERT R. YOUNG was known as the daring young man of Wall Street, willing to take a chance, ambitious to make it big. Yet he saw more clearly than his conservative peers some of the trends of the postwar economy.

Young was born in Canadian, a town in the Texas panhandle, in 1897. A skinny little boy, he went to local schools and then was sent off to a military academy and to the University of Virginia. He abruptly ended his education in his sophomore year and went to work for Du Pont as a clerk. He shifted from one job to another until 1922, when he found a place in General Motors and he advanced steadily in the bureaucracy.

All along he had a zest for speculation. He had invested and promptly lost a small inheritance in 1920, but he was not discouraged and bode his time. In 1932, he bought a seat on the New York Stock Exchange and started to purchase securities at cut-rate depression prices. A year later he began to acquire shares in the Allegheny Corporation, a railroad holding company, and by 1942 was in control.

The railroads did well during the war but Young perceived trouble ahead unless they altered their anachronistic methods. He broke the dependence of his Chesapeake & Ohio on the New York investment bankers by finding alternative means to float its bonds, and after 1946 he began to battle the entrenched and apathetic lines. His advertisement, "A hog can cross the country without changing trains, but you can't," finally led to the establishment of through transcontinental service. He also tried to stir up the Association of American Railroads and to develop means of cooperation with the cities the lines served.

In 1947, the Allegheny Corporation gained control of the New York Central, and Young then assumed oversight of that powerful corporation, acting as chairman of the board from 1954 till his death, in 1958. But his flamboyant methods were not enough to achieve modernization. Inertia was a powerful force; labor resisted some aspects of mechanization; and the government tended to obstruct mergers and innovations. Despite Young's efforts, the railroads drifted to their crisis of the 1960s.

Pickets in Front of the New York *Times* Building, September 16, 1965, After the American Newspaper Guild Struck the Newspaper. The walkout, caused by a desire for job security in the face of automation, lasted twenty-five days, during which six other major metropolitan papers suspended publication because of a publishers' pledge to stand united against the union. (UPI)

zations had risen from 8 million at the beginning of the war to 14 million at the end and then climbed steadily to 17 million in 1954, at which point it leveled off. With most of the industrial labor force enrolled, the AF of L and the CIO joined forces in 1955. Conflict subsided as laborers and employers became aware of their common interest in productivity and efficiency. The unions, which themselves controlled the investment of mammoth pension funds, understood the problems of capital, and the corpora-

tions no longer aimed to beat wage costs down as far as possible. Moreover, with increasing prosperity the workers themselves discovered their middle-class aspirations. Their class consciousness waned as rising wages gave reality to dreams of cars and suburban cottages.

The reconciliation of John L. Lewis and the United Mine Workers' Union with the mine companies was typical. After decades of conflict, the union collaborated in modernizing the whole industry. The longshoremen and other formerly militant workers now also proved cooperative.

Craft unions in printing, building, railroads, and other laggard branches of the economy still struggled to preserve featherbedding and similarly privileged practices, but patterns of mutual accommodation emerged in most forms of manufacturing. Periodic negotiations to revise the terms of contracts governing wages and conditions of work were often bitter and occasionally led to strikes, but these disturbances came within a framework of mutual interdependence. To some extent, the struggles bore a token quality because the corporations generally passed the cost on to consumers.

Industrial organization thus moved into a new phase. The managers of the great corporations were intermediaries who balanced a variety of forces emanating from investors, consumers, suppliers, and labor. The organization itself set the ultimate objectives. Generally the goal was power and growth, rather than immediate profit. The whole economy felt the impact of that shift in orientation.

The Role of Government

Planning and Taxing   The state participated in the development of a more rational economic order, but not in the way anticipated by the

Seymour E. Harris, *Economics of the Kennedy Years* (New York, 1964) treats the role of government.

JOHN L. LEWIS inherited his loyalty to the union. His father, who had come from Wales to dig coal in the New World, was repeatedly blacklisted for activity in the Knights of Labor. John was born in 1880 near Lucas, Iowa, and after having reached the seventh grade he went to work in the mines. In 1901, he cut loose. A hard-drinking, tough, poker-playing type, he wandered in the West for five years, doing odd jobs, looking for a break.

In 1906, he was back in Lucas and soon thereafter became deeply involved in the affairs of the United Mine Workers. From 1908 on he held various jobs in the union and in the AF of L, and after 1919 he was president of the UMW. Fiercely loyal to the men, he was ready to use any tactics to improve their lot. He led numerous great strikes between 1919 and 1950. In the 1920s he fought the Communists who were trying to filter into his organization; in the next decade he cooperated with them.

His crucial decisions came over the questions of industrial unionism, politics, and mechanization. In the 1920s he learned that as long as the great mass of workers was unorganized, labor would not achieve its goals. He was therefore the driving force in the formation of the CIO and in the unionization of steel, autos, and the other heavy industries.

From the time he served on the National Defense Council in 1917, he was aware of the importance of government. He took an active part in politics, supported the New Deal in 1936, broke with the Democrats in 1940 over the war, and helped mold labor into a potent force on election day.

Above all, he was aware that the coal industry would have to modernize if it was to thrive and afford a decent wage for its employees. In 1924 he approved a plan for a minimum wage even though that would force out marginal producers and reduce the number of jobs. For the same reason he favored some national control either through the NRA or through direct regulation.

In the 1950s he realized that automation was the only way out and encouraged the introduction of labor- and cost-saving devices. In that decade the number of workers in the soft-coal fields fell from 500,000 to 180,000 but the efficiency of the mines increased so that production and wages just about doubled. Meanwhile the size of the union remained stable because the catch-all District 50 Lewis formed took in all sorts of workers who were not miners. And after 1946 a royalty on every ton of coal mined went into a welfare fund, which was able to pay out about $150,000,000 a year in benefits to miners and their families.

technocrats and by some New Dealers. It did not lay out an over-all plan. Suggestions for such an effort had produced no useful results before 1947, and were not seriously revived thereafter. Indeed, the failure of comprehensive planning in the Soviet Union and some other socialist countries put an end to these speculations.

The government subsidized shipping directly and commercial aviation indirectly. But it abstained from making decisions about the communication system as a whole until 1966, when a new Department of Transportation gave it an instrument for doing so. Although competition from motor cars and trucks caused a marked decline in the situation of the railroads, the reluctance to extend political control kept the level of planning to a minimum.

Government, however, remained important as a consumer not subject to the usual rules of the market place. Armament expenditures sloped off after the war, then rose during the Korean crisis and again when the fighting became active in Vietnam. But after 1953, the government also launched vast nonmilitary programs in space exploration, road building, urban renewal, and education, the pace of which significantly influenced economic activity. Spending was a stimulus, cutbacks a deterrent.

The power to tax was as important as the power to buy. Indirectly and unintentionally, government policy contributed to the development of the great corporations. Although persistent antitrust attitudes restrained tendencies toward monopoly, the tax system encouraged expansion. The high levies on incomes as compared with those on capital gains created an incentive to hold earnings within the firm, particularly after the abolition of the wartime undistributed profits tax. Corporate profits after taxes rose from $26 billion in 1960 to $48 billion in 1966, while cash dividends went up from only $13 billion to $21 billion. The widening margin was available for diversification or could be held as reserves. Furthermore, losses could be written off by tax savings or carried forward to offset future gains. The ability to shift the penalties of risk and to make constructive use of rewards was indicative of the growing orderliness of the economy.

Fiscal Policy However, the fiscal policy was the decisive means for influencing the productive system. The compromise of 1951 endured. The Federal Reserve Board controlled the interest rate and therefore the availability of credit; the Treasury managed the debt and therefore the flow of currency. The Board, responsive to bankers' views, was more likely to apply the brake than the Treasury, but the two generally offset one another. In the Eisenhower years, efforts to balance the budget and a high interest rate tended to slow down the pace of expansion in order to prevent inflation. After the return of the Democrats to power in 1961, the trend shifted. Tax cuts and lower interest rates stimulated the economy until the boom threatened to get out of hand in 1966, when a moderating influence was applied. Fiscal policy thus proved a serviceable means of regulating fluctuations and maintaining growth.

Robert Lekachman, *The Age of Keynes* (New York, 1966) contains a clear discussion of fiscal policy.

As a result these decades escaped the alternations of boom and depression that had characterized the nineteenth and the early twentieth centuries. Brief recessions in 1953, 1957, and 1960 punctuated the periods of accelerated growth, but these setbacks were kept within bounds. The rate of unemployment could be contained quite consistently at a manageable 4 percent or less. American economic policy, in its own way, effectively followed the precepts of Keynesian economics.

The moderate inflation characteristic of the postwar decades did little more than keep pace with the growth of the population and of the economy. Kept within control, it stimulated growth by encouraging the productive sectors of the population and by preventing vested interest from becoming an economic drag. Those who lived on fixed incomes were at a disadvantage while the venturesome gained. Banks accordingly reduced their holdings of government bonds in favor of business paper, and pension plans raised the proportion of their investments in common stocks from 20 percent in 1955 to 40 percent in 1965.

The stock markets had their ups and downs but governmental restraints kept speculation within bounds. The power of the Securities and Exchange Commission to fix margin requirements and of the Federal Reserve Board to set interest rates prevented values from rising excessively. Moreover, the assets of institutional investors—foundations, pension and mutual funds, and universities—rose to the point at which they exercised a stabilizing influence on the investment market.

Spending and Inventing

Purchasing Power Economic growth, guided by government policy, rested upon a firm basis of expanding demand and improved technology. Federal spending for defense, space, roads, education, and urban renewal continued to

The Effects of Social Security and Retirement, 1960

Not working is the fastest growing of all major "occupations" in the U.S. today. The number of nonworkers has roughly doubled in the past decade, and might well double again by 1970. In the process, the U.S. is forming a new kind of rentier class . . . .

The significant fact about these newer kinds of income is that they are growing much more rapidly than personal income as a whole, while dividends, interest, and rent have been declining as a share of all personal income — from 12 per cent in 1940 to 8 per cent in 1959. The newer kinds of rentier income are already close to 8 per cent — i.e., they add up to about $28 billion of the total $375 billion in personal income. Something like 15 per cent of all personal income, then, is already paid out for non-work — which is getting to be an extremely attractive occupation.

— The Editors of Fortune, *Markets of the Sixties* (New York: Harper & Row, Publishers, 1960), pp. 94–95.

stimulate production. The capacity for private expenditure also grew with the rise in incomes and in population. The increase in the size of the young and the old age groups expanded the ranks of the users of goods relative to those of the producers and thus boosted demand. Moreover, people had the means with which to buy. The consumer-oriented industries flourished with the aid of a tremendous burst of installment credit, which rose from under $10,000,000,000 in 1947 to more than $50,000,000,000 in 1966, at which point about 25 percent of disposable incomes went into repayments.

Purchasing power held up at all levels of the population. Effective labor organization sustained the wages of the workers. Unemployment insurance provided an effective cushion against fluctuations in hiring rates. By 1966, social security and private retirement plans covered almost all employees. The poor were a significant social problem, but broad welfare coverage kept even the dependent elements of the population among the consumers. Since the personal incomes of the more prosperous were also rising, the internal markets for the products of industry kept expanding.

The continued growth of foreign markets added to the demand. Trade with Japan and Western Europe grew steadily once their economies regained their vigor. Furthermore, government aid to the underdeveloped countries, beginning with Truman's Point 4 program and extending through the Agency for International Development and the Alliance for Progress, made dollars available to overseas purchasers of American goods. The negative balance of payments that persisted in 1966 was due not to a deficiency of exports but to heavy military commitments overseas.

The New Technology Inventions and new processes raised productivity to meet growing demand. An airline network reached across the nation. Some innovations known earlier but inhibited by the depression now developed rapidly — plastics and petrochemicals, for example. Wartime research subsidized the electronics industry, which expanded rapidly after the war. The support of research by government and private industry sustained the process of discovery. Vast armies of engineers and scientists working on atomic, missile, and space projects found improvements transferable to a variety of uses. Some developments led directly to new consumer products such as television. Others, like the laser, opened up possibilities it would take years to explore. Still others were hidden in processes that resuscitated old industries. A change-over from the open-hearth to the basic oxygen process thus enabled Bethlehem Steel's Lackawanna plant to reduce the number of its furnaces from 14 to 2, yet raised capacity from 1,900,000 to 2,200,000 tons. The ailing

to Nome and JAPAN
to Fairbanks
to Anchorage

global route to EUROPE

to EUROPE

Vancouver

Seattle   Spokane

Portland

Billings

Minneapolis   Detroit

Pittsburgh   Boston

Chicago   New York

San Francisco   Salt Lake City   Denver   Washington

Kansas City

to Honolulu

Los Angeles   Atlanta

Phoenix   Dallas

El Paso   Jacksonville

Houston

to Mexico City   New Orleans

Miami

Monterrey

SCHEDULED FLIGHTS (WEEK)   to Rio de Janeiro
PASSENGER AND CARGO   Tampico   Buenós Aires

1-6   Mexico City
7-25
OVER 25

THE TRUNKLINE AIRLINES, 1950

coal mines, whose output had declined from 688,000,000 to 420,000,000 tons between 1947 and 1961, revived enough under the stimulus of new methods to get production back to 550,000,000 tons in 1966.

A complex of refined techniques of automation did more than extend the earlier phases of mechanization. The advanced instruments of the 1950s and 1960s replaced not only unskilled but also skilled labor. Harnessed to computers that stored information, the machines performed delicate functions, responded to feedback from results, and adjusted without human intervention to a variety of situations with great savings in the handling of materials and in the operation of complicated production lines.

The ability to process goods efficiently cost some types of workers their jobs. Some new chemical plants needed no operating hands at all, only maintenance engineers to check against breakdowns. When the Chrysler Building in New York automated its elevators, it reduced the number of operators from 74 to 38. Multiplied many times across the country the result was to contract opportunities for those new to the labor market and without special skills. The number of unemployed between the ages of nineteen and twenty-four doubled in the ten years after 1953, and Negroes who arrived in the cities in the same years had great difficulties in finding jobs.

But the over-all effects of automation did not lead either to a decline in the labor force

Seattle
Tacoma
Portland
Minneapolis-St. Paul
Flint
Detroit
Buffalo
Boston
Lansing
Erie
New York
Salt Lake City
Chicago
Toledo
Cleveland
Philadelphia
Pittsburgh
Baltimore
San Francisco
Denver
Kansas City
St. Louis
Los Angeles
Dallas
Birmingham
Atlanta
Fort Worth
• CENTERS OF
MAIN ECONOMIC ACTIVITY
Baton Rouge
Mobile
Pensacola
Beaumont
New Orleans
Galveston
Port
Arthur
Corpus Christi

AL FIELDS
ranium deposits

CORN AREAS
■ corn belt

COTTON

N ORE

MAJOR
OIL FIELDS

WHEAT AREAS

THE NEW ECONOMY, 1950–1966

or to a reduction in its income. The factors that sustained demand permitted instead more efficient utilization of man power within a shorter working week.

Computer-guided operations also stimulated the consolidation of large producing and distributing areas within which goods and information flowed speedily and smoothly. One such megalopolis stretched some 500 miles from Boston to Washington. Another reached out from Chicago around Lake Michigan. Others conformed to the metropolitan areas described by the census. These were the massive units of the new economy.

613

Corn Harvest, Iowa, 1959. The International Harvester McCormick Ear Corn Harvester in operation at Garst Farms, near Coon Rapids. (Joe Munroe, Photo Researchers)

Agriculture

Changes in agriculture were fully as dramatic as those in industry. The level of production remained high, yet suddenly the surpluses and debt vanished. Government policy and technology solved those ancient problems.

In the first decade after the war, the old difficulties of inadequate prices and surpluses returned. Under the Truman and Eisenhower administrations the remedies of crop control, subsidy, and credit proved ineffective. The one hopeful element was the Food for Peace and similar programs which provided subsidized export markets for American agriculture.

Government policy, however, had an unanticipated and at first unnoticed effect. The subsidies began to liquidate the old family farm. Such payments rose from $500,000,000 in 1947 to $3,400,000,000 in 1965, while the number of farms declined from 6 to 3.25 million. The government thus indirectly supplied the larger, more efficient producers with the means of buying out the marginal farmers on advantageous terms. The average size of holdings increased as the number declined, and the large units absorbed an ever greater share of the market. The result was concentration of production equivalent to that in industry.

Farm technology improved radically and with it output per man hour. Modern machines performed a multitude of tasks efficiently. The cotton picker, the cherry-tree shaker, and numerous other devices joined the old harvester. A tractor-drawn corn drill planted the seed and at the same time laid down chemicals to kill insects and weeds. A self-propelled combine harvested six rows at a time, removed the husks, shelled the corn, and threw out the waste. Sales of such units, which cost $15,000 to $18,000 each, rose from 12,000 in 1955 to 50,000 in 1966. The saving in human energy meant a sharp reduction in the amount of migratory labor used in agriculture.

Continuing changes in location removed many of the old trouble spots. Cotton growing thus shifted away from the South Central states, where it had been plagued by inefficient share-cropping labor, to Texas, Arizona, and California, where it used heavy machinery. Meanwhile, the abandoned lands in states like Louisiana, Arkansas, and Mississippi were given over to cattle grazing.

As a result of the more efficient use of land and machines and of improved fertilizers and management the net yield per acre in American farming rose about 4 percent annually. At the same time improvements in processing—including the deep freezing and dehydration of meat, grains, and dairy products—reduced the spread between consumers' costs and farmers' receipts.

An era thus came unnoticed to an end. The free farmer of tradition was no longer an important factor in American life. The number of persons employed in agriculture declined absolutely; and the flow to the cities carried along most of the former residents of the farms and their children.

▼

The postwar decades witnessed a profound transformation of the American economy. The independent individual farmer, like the independent individual entrepreneur, became a figure of the past. In agriculture, as in industry, the large organization became the dominant factor in production. The result was an ability to organize and plan production rationally. The concomitant danger was a loss in spontaneity and in flexibility. The American economy shed its disorderly features—boom and bust, extremes of irresponsible wealth and desperate poverty, chaotic success and miserable failure. The question was whether with them would go the old concepts of freedom and individual rights. The same decades were occupied with the social adjustments that tested the capacity of Americans to live under the new terms and yet to save something of the old values.

Paperbacks for Further Reading

Among the useful studies of the American economy are: Adolf A. Berle, *American Economic Republic* (Harvest Books) and his *20th Century Capitalist Revolution* (Harvest Books); Peter F. Drucker, *The Concept of the Corporation* (Mentor Books) and his *The Future of the Industrial Man* (Mentor Books); J. K. Galbraith, *American Capitalism* (Sentry Editions) and his *The Affluent Society* (Mentor Books); and S. E. Harris *et al.,* *American Business Creed* (Schocken Books, Inc.). Eugene V. Rostow, *Planning for Freedom* (Yale University Press) discusses the relationship to public law. There is an interesting collection of essays in S. H. Slichter, *Economic Growth in the United States* (Collier Books). Peter d'A. Jones, *The Consumer Society* (Penguin Books, Inc.) has a useful historical perspective, while The Editors of Fortune, *America in the Sixties* (Harper Torchbooks) contains projections into the future. Arthur J. Goldberg, *AFL-CIO* (McGraw-Hill Paperback Series); Joel Seidman, *The Brotherhood of Railroad Trainmen* (John Wiley & Sons, Inc.); and Ely Chinoy, *Automobile Workers and the American Dream* (Beacon Press) treat various aspects of the position of labor.

THE QUEST FOR SECURITY

97

In a world charged with uncertainty security bore a high value. The generation that had matured during the war had learned how prevalent were risks, how rare was the opportunity for predictable choice. Since peace was never fully restored, Americans after 1947 never could be sure that the world which revolved in the shadow of the bomb would remain firm beneath their feet. Furthermore, the great economic and social organizations that pre-empted their lives narrowed the possibility of personal control.

The result thrust the Americans who moved into middle age in the 1950s back upon themselves. By a variety of expedients, they sought to create islands of security within which they could maintain some degree of detachment from external events. In turn, they left their sheltered children, who knew nothing of war or of depression, with an unfulfilled yearning for experience. Meanwhile many people who lacked the means to lead the lives their society considered normal remained restless and discontent.

The Problems
of a Large Society

Impersonality The organizational development connected with economic growth in the postwar years was part of a profound change in the structure of American life. The individual entrepreneurs and farmers gave way to massive enterprises staffed by bureaucracies. Government, universities, and all other institutions expanded and in the process lost the personal intimacy that could take account of individuals. Everyone was a serial number on a payroll or a social security card.

Voluntary associations fell in with the trend. Labor unions, for instance, acquired the massive characteristics of the corporations with which they negotiated — rigid rules, substantial financial resources, and an apparatus that separated the member from the officers. Even medicine with its close relationship to health and personality was more likely to fall within the province of a large group practice than of the familiar family doctor. Whether a person wore a white or a blue collar, he was part of an organization that set the rules by which he lived and worked. The range of his own choices shrank alarmingly.

The decay of the old ethnic, social, and cultural associations had already left a vacuum in the lives of many Americans. Those who were lonely, though they lived in crowds, felt disoriented and helpless. The world spread its dangers everywhere before them. An outburst of anxiety about automobile safety in 1966, although the accident rate was lower than in any other modern country, expressed the underlying concern of the insecure.

Back to the Family There was therefore a continuing quest in these years for the security that some smaller unit might provide. The anonymous people governed by abstract rules that disregarded their individual identity were like soldiers. Society was an army powerful in the mass but heedless of personal desires. Americans sought eagerly for a way to retain control of that part of their lives which remained their own.

The family became the goal of that quest after the war. In the 1920s and 1930s, that institution had suffered from the debilitating strains of a rising divorce rate and a shrinking birth rate. The family then seemed a burden, heavy with residual obligations and restrictions that often prevented the individual from expressing himself fully.

The growing attractiveness of the family in the 1940s was not simply a temporary effect of the war. The trend persisted after 1945 and became more pronounced in the 1950s. It revealed a genuine alteration in the habits and practices of the society. The increase in the number of births continued after 1945 although the techniques for contraception were readily available. Family size was no longer, as in the past, a factor of farm residence, foreign birth, or poverty. Well-to-do urban parents considered a home with children normal. That attitude and the stabilization of the divorce rate reflected a new view of the family and of the relationship of the individual to it.

The family of these decades was neither the traditional household nor the means of fulfillment of a conjugal couple. Rather it was the core around which a cluster of individuals organized their social experience. Family life gave coherence and unity to its participants. Early marriages and the prompt appearance of children were the means of achieving personal stability and order. Furthermore, where possible there was an effort to eliminate differentiations based on age, sex, and role. Husbands and wives, parents and children were pals. Common involvement in all activities was a means of attaining the togetherness toward which all aspired.

Suburbia The renewed importance of the family in the postwar decades explained the desertion of the central city and the development of the suburbs. The centrifugal movement had long been a feature of American urban life. But the automobile and the radial road networks

The Family and Society, 1947

People of all ages are asking today what is the relationship between their personal lives and their personal choices, and between the personal lives and personal choices of their neighbors, their clients, their patients, their students, and the great crisis that faces the human race. For this is the greatest crisis, perhaps, since a small group of prehistoric men wandered north with fire that they knew how to keep but knew not how to make. The relationship between family structure and coherent personality and citizenship, and faith in the continuance of the human race, is something which we can stress for the very young and for those who are beginning family life at a period which is fearfully unrewarding in its prospects for stability and for continuance. But if we recognize the extent to which the present situation is partly temporary and partly a function of the whole world crisis, if we tie in personal choices to the possibility of people feeling strong enough and optimistic enough to go on, and if we recognize the extent to which the family has changed, and the sort of support it needs, we may be able to develop an ethic appropriate to the new and fragile family forms that we have in this country today.

— Margaret Mead, "What Is Happening to the American Family?" *Proceedings of the National Conference of Social Work* (New York: Columbia University Press, 1947), p. 74.

the city deteriorated, the urgency to escape increased. The census of 1960 revealed the same characteristics in almost every urban area, a thinning out of population in the interior, growth around the periphery.

Los Angeles was the characteristic metropolis of the 1960s, as New York had been of the 1890s. The prominence of speculators in its early history had started Los Angeles on its sprawling development even before World War I. A real estate boom in the 1920s furthered the process, and the motor car, the industrial development of the 1940s, and the rapid population growth of the 1950s completed it.

The city was a vast political and administrative entity, but it lacked a center and therefore had no unified coherent social life. Los Angeles was all suburb. Individuals shuttled on their private errands among scores of small communities, but nothing held the people together except the payment of certain common taxes and the use of a few common services. The public transportation system remained primitive, while the automobile flourished, because the flow of traffic followed no regular pattern. Los Angeles in this respect was the extreme manifestation of a tendency other metropolitan areas also displayed in these years.

Throughout the United States after 1950, the suburbs changed their nature as they grew. They ceased to be merely bedrooms of the core city. Many attracted light industry, for the truck and the automobile carried freight and laborers more easily to the outlying districts than rails could to the center. Great clusters of shops where every type of merchandise was available, along with parking space, movies, and restaurants, also reduced dependence upon the old downtown. In the 1960s, furthermore, the single-family house standing in its own plot shared the space of the suburbs with multiple-family dwellings and high-rise apartments. Here the intimacy and neighborliness presumed to be characteristic of the small community faded and life was as impersonal as in the heart of the city.

now made the drift outward easier, and the preoccupation of the child-centered family with an appropriate setting for its existence hastened the tendency.

With the continued northward migration of Negroes, dense in-town districts came to be associated with racial problems and added intensity to the move to the suburbs. Precisely to the degree that conditions in the central parts of

Levittown, New York, 1949. This mass-produced residential development of more than 17,000 moderately priced homes, built by the firm Levitt and Sons, Inc., is one of the nations largest post–World War II suburban communities. (Litton Industries– Aero Service Division)

The American Way of Life

Values Nevertheless, even after its transformation, the suburb remained attractive to many Americans. Economic growth had put the means to live there in the hands of a large part of the population. In the 1960s, more than 60 percent of all families in the United States had annual incomes of $5,000 or more, and the proportion in the metropolitan areas was higher than the national average. A wide range of businessmen, managers, and white collar workers as well as technicians, engineers, and skilled craftsmen sought here to lead lives by middle-class standards.

Despite immense variations according to region, income level, and ethnic antecedents, there were significant uniformities in tastes and values among these groups. The influence of the mass media generated a demand for material possessions that justified high expenditures and indebtedness for home ownership, household equipment, automobiles, and television. These objects were important not merely for the pleasure and convenience of their use but also because they were symbols of the status of their possessors.

Considerable amounts of leisure permitted indulgence in a good deal of recreation—boating in New England or on the Pacific Coast, hunting and fishing in the South and Midwest, and vacation travel everywhere. Distractions in a multi-

619

Distribution of Families by Total Income, 1962

Total Money Income	Percent of Families
Under $3,000	19.9
$3,000–$4,999	19.1
$5,000–$6,999	22.4
$7,000–$9,999	20.9
$10,000 and over	17.7

tude of forms occupied people's attention — a craze for bowling among some groups, spectator sports and gambling among others, some idle viewing of television among almost all. These ways of passing time, which earlier generations of Americans would have considered idle, now absorbed many for whom work was a routine that ended when they left the shop or office.

The declining rates of mortality and disease did not diminish the worrying about health. Life expectancy at birth had risen to about seventy years, and heart disease and cancer — failings of old age — were the leading causes of death. Yet heavy spending for medical care and also for patented drugs showed widespread concern with physical well-being. Graphic warnings in TV ads about the frailty of the flesh beat upon the consciousness. Counseled constantly to be vigilant against the enemy within, Americans were readily susceptible to dietary fads and stylish nostrums.

Education   Above all, people who lived by middle-class values felt intense anxiety about their children. Families devoted much thought to the upbringing of the young. Books and magazines that offered practical advice on these problems enjoyed an ample and expanding market. Parents, as a matter of course, lavished immense care on the health, emotional security, and proper education of their offspring.

One of the great attractions of the suburb was the satisfactory schooling it provided. The economy emphasized trained personnel and devalued the work of the unskilled. Although many kinds of man power were in short supply, there was little demand for the services of uneducated hands. The proper start along the established sequence of schools was essential to access to the professions or to other desirable types of employment. The growing impersonality of the economy made it difficult simply to inherit positions or to move into good places without the proper credentials.

As a result, the average school-leaving age advanced steadily, as did the proportion of each age group being educated. Completion of high school became the norm; and an increasing number of students enrolled in college and professional courses. These were the steppingstones to worthy places in society.

The schools in the United States had always been avenues of social mobility, but they now encompassed the whole spectrum of opportunities and their importance rose correspondingly. Furthermore, their function as the means of selecting who would get ahead and who would not overshadowed all other aspects of their operations. The task of evaluating those who sought promotion to the next rung of the ladder became as important as that of teaching, and students regarded themselves as competitors in a race in which all the rewards went to the winners.

The resulting tension affected all family life. James B. Conant and others pointed out that the children of low-income families had to find a place through the school or else drift into the ranks of superfluous man power. At the middle and upper levels of society, the pressure toward achievement placed a heavy burden on each individual, for the penalty of failure was a loss of status. Thus even people who took refuge in their suburban families found their islands of security vulnerable; no matter how favored, they could not altogether escape the problems of the society in which they lived. After midcentury, the men and women troubled about the external world had to worry increasingly also about their own place within it.

Aspirations, 1960

He looked at the teacher earnestly. "I want Marjie to go to college and be a doctor—she's interested in nature things and animals. I buy her all the chemistry sets I see and we keep plenty of pets. We have a parakeet and two cats and a dog home right now—I try my best to ready her to be a doctor. But my kid brother—he had more schooling than me and he says her lessons are all moron stuff. She wouldn't be able to go to college with that kind of learning."

Ruby hated this part of her job. "Please sit down, Mr. Paul, and I'll try to explain." She pushed a chair close to her desk. She wouldn't be able to explain—how could she tactfully make this sober, devoted father . . . [understand] that his child was so slow she would never read beyond the third grade? Gently, with great care, like a sculptor tracing on precious stone, she outlined his daughter's limited capacities . . . .

"So you see," she told the troubled father, who was sitting tensely, his hands holding his knees, listening to her every word, "they don't have departmental because they're not as quick as the others. People are good in different ways. I read and write well but I can't sew. Your Marjorie is already a competent dressmaker and designer. Did you see the white nylon dress she just finished?"

"I don't want her to be a dressmaker," he said. "I don't want her to work with her hands. I want her to have a brain job. Her mother was a seamstress and her eyes were strained all the time. I don't want that for Marjie." He looked at Ruby, his face twisted with unhappiness. "I want her to be a doctor. I'll work hard and send her to school. I haven't got a son but I always said Marjie was just as good—she could be a doctor."

—Reprinted from *Come Back on Monday* by Sheila Solomon Klass. By permission of Abelard-Schuman, Ltd. All Rights Reserved. Copyright © 1960 by Sheila Solomon Klass.

JAMES BRYANT CONANT arrived indirectly at the understanding that education was a national asset. Born in Boston in 1893, he was a precocious student who gained his first degree at Harvard in 1913 and his doctorate in chemistry three years later. After a brief try at manufacturing and duty in the Chemical Warfare Service, he settled down to an academic career at his alma mater.

In 1933, having advanced up the professorial ranks, he became president of the university. His chief attention in the years that followed went to making the institution national in scope, reorganizing the tenure system for the faculty, and encouraging a program of general education.

The threat of war forced him to shift his attention outside the university. In 1940 he became a consultant to the government on defense research, and a year later he was named chairman of the Office of Scientific Research and Development. He took a prominent part in the Manhattan Project that built the atom bomb and remained an adviser on the problems of atomic energy after the war.

This experience persuaded him that education was vital to the security and the progress of the country. In 1947 he urged the creation of a national professional school and of a science foundation to support research. The latter proposal was implemented in 1950.

In 1953 he resigned his position at Harvard to become first high commissioner and then ambassador to Germany. On his return to the United States in 1957, his attention reverted to the problems of education, which he now believed were most critical at the secondary level. A thorough-going reconstruction of the high school was essential to develop talent and prepare it for more advanced training. A series of incisive reports called attention to the problems of the urban, suburban, and slum schools and laid the groundwork for expanded educational efforts in the 1960s.

The Poor

Middle-class life and its values, moreover, remained out of reach for substantial numbers. About 20 percent of American families in the 1960s earned less than $3,000 a year and about 20 percent more, less than $5,000. Somewhere between those two lines—the precise place depended upon a combination of circumstances—people lacked the means to maintain themselves in the way their society considered normal.

Sources of Dependency In the 1960s, when poverty became a political issue, it was common to refer to all such men and women as the poor. That designation no doubt reflected the belief that money could cure all ills. Yet the term covered a variety of human types. For some people, insufficient income was unquestionably the whole cause of difficulty, but for others, the lack of funds was only one feature of more complex problems that caused dependency.

During that decade, there were about 35,000,000 poor in the country. For the poverty of more than 5,000,000 of these people there was a short and simple explanation—old age. One-third of the men and women who reached the age of sixty-five were incapable of supporting themselves; they had lost their earning power and their pensions or social security and welfare payments were too small. In addition, considerable numbers in this age group eked out a grim existence by labor. The prolongation of life and the inability to find places in the homes of children created the problem. The humiliation of failure added bitterness to the sense of helplessness and loneliness that beset the elderly.

A still larger group among the poor consisted of 15,000,000 persons under the age of eighteen. About 3,000,000 of them lived in fatherless families either because they were illegitimate or because their mothers were deserted. In either case, such children grew up in an abnormal environment which limited their

Floyd A. Bond *et al., Our Needy Aged* (New York, 1954) treats the problems of old age.

In a Fatherless Family, ca. 1960

But we never took from Welfare. We felt kind of—you know—with pride. We were like alone. And while my mother was looking for work I was doing some shoe shining on the side and my sister and little brother were going to school. I think I was about eight then. I was going to school too, but I would play hooky most of the time. I was surprised when I found out I was passing in all my grades anyhow.

I was making enough money then to provide sort of like what we couldn't do without. You know, when my mother didn't have enough or she needed a couple of dollars, I would have it. And usually I would take care of my little brother and my sister by this shoe shining thing. I mean, if my mother's working and there's no money for something, I would have the money to go down the stairs and buy them something to eat.

Boy! I know what it feels like to be hungry. You watch somebody eat downstairs or you see him walk by with ice cream and it drops on the floor or something. You feel like killing the person, you know, letting all that food go to waste.

And the neighbors, they couldn't help. They were worse off than we were. Their kids were out for themselves. Whenever they'd get food, they ate it up like as if it was no end to it and whatever was left they would throw away. They wouldn't bother to take it home. They were like savages. I agree that we were on the same level as they were at the time. But when you are hungry, I mean, what can you do?

—Juan Gonzales, as quoted in Charlotte L. Mayerson, ed., *Two Blocks Apart* (New York: Holt, Rinehart and Winston, Inc., 1965), p. 21.

chances from the day of their birth. There was a high probability that their poverty would perpetuate itself in the next generation. The other minors—in families deprived of adequate incomes by unemployment, illness, or lack of skill—were better off, although to what extent depended upon the circumstances of the particular locality and upon the length of dependency.

Many of the poor were rural by residence or origin. In the 1950s, about 2,000,000 migratory laborers picked the fruit and vegetables of American farms, in addition to some 500,000 Mexicans who came legally by contract or illegally by wandering over the border. Such hands rarely earned more than $700 a year and, drifting about, never gave their children a chance to strike roots. Mechanization in the next decade began to thin out this tattered army, but remnants were still on the move in 1966.

Stagnant pockets of poverty existed also in the hill country of the South and of Appalachia, an area that runs north to New York State and south through West Virginia, Kentucky, and Tennessee. The times had passed these farmers by. They might cling to their tiny holdings, making out with jobs in mills or mines, but their incomes remained low until they summoned up the energy and initiative to move on.

Migration The large numbers who did desert the countryside for the promises of city life encountered extraordinary difficulties. Few could extricate themselves from poverty in their new homes. The greatest shift of population in the two decades after 1947 took millions of Negroes and whites from the South to the North and the West. A smaller movement carried thousands of Puerto Ricans to New York, Philadelphia, and Chicago.

The newcomers and the communities to which they came were unprepared for each other. Unskilled, uneducated, and unfamiliar with urban life, the migrants entered cities where the opportunities for untrained labor were shrinking, where housing was in short supply, and where prices were rising. They found poorly paid jobs in the service trades and in the backward branches of manufacturing. Life in the crowded slums weakened their families, and their children grew up without discipline or a sense of orientation to the society of which they were expected to be a part. All too often such people were incapable of managing their meager incomes and plunged into a poverty that extinguished all hope.

In addition, the Negroes and Puerto Ricans were the victims of prejudice and discrimination, which compounded the effect of their low economic status. Life in the ghettos restricted the educational opportunities of their children, and lack of training led to inferior jobs, in a vicious cycle that tended to perpetuate itself. The gains other minorities had made since the 1930s did not extend to these groups.

The Complications of Race

The End of the Minority Alliance In 1947 an effective alliance existed among all the underprivileged ethnic groups, religious and national as well as racial. Their growing political power and their acculturation made them unwilling to postpone fulfillment of their demands for equality, and together they possessed the means of making their wills felt.

The first stage of the struggle, which lasted down through the 1950s, sought abolition of prejudice and discrimination. The rejection of racism and the emphasis on the obligations of equality led to considerable success. From government, in this period, the minorities asked neutrality. The state was to refrain from recognition of group differences and was to treat all individuals alike. The desegregation decision of 1954 and the Civil Rights Act of 1957 were the high points of this effort.

The gradual lowering of barriers opened opportunities that brought swift advance to most of these people. Religious groups, like the Jews and Catholics, national groups like the

A Back Yard in Harlem, 1966. (Bruce Davidson, Magnum Photos)

Italians and Greeks, and even racial groups like the Japanese and Chinese, no longer felt themselves victims of injustice. But the Negro 10 percent of the population and, to a lesser extent, the Puerto Ricans and Mexican-Americans lagged behind.

Two factors complicated the problem and isolated the Negro. The South remained intransigent. Six years after the Supreme Court's desegregation decision, most states had made only token progress and some none at all. Restiveness with the inaction grew steadily as it

became clear that most of the South would fight implementation every inch of the way.

Furthermore, the continued northward migration created conditions that equal treatment alone would not solve. The Southern forms of discrimination did not exist above the Mason-Dixon line. But other handicaps held the Negroes down. The most recent arrivals in the city, least prepared for its life and recipients of the lowest incomes, they crowded into slum ghettos, where the character of the neighborhood was enough to segregate the schools. Race compounded all the disorders of urban life. In the Watts district of Los Angeles, for instance, 56 percent of the children under eighteen in 1965 lived in broken families. While other groups moved ahead, the Negroes' chances in life remained narrow. The result of the divergence in experience was the dissolution after 1960 of the old minority coalition.

New Aspirations Increasingly, Negroes demanded that the government be not color blind but conscious of their special problems. Their goal was not merely desegregation but positive political action to improve their plight – preferential hiring to give them representation in desirable positions, quotas to assure mixed residences, and racial balance in the schools. The lack of competent leaders and the weakness of communal institutions enabled the Black Muslims and other extremists to exaggerate these calls for action and often led to internal conflicts and misunderstandings with other groups.

Fear of where these tendencies might lead evoked a reaction among whites. People who had struggled hard for the security of stable family and community life did not wish to see their gains dissipated in hazardous social experiments. There was no revival of the old racist prejudice, nor was there any effort to defend segregation by law, but the election of 1966 showed a determination to draw the line. White Americans were willing to concede to all complete equality in treatment before the law, in the rights of citizenship, and in opportunities

MARTIN LUTHER KING was born in 1929 in a middle class family in Atlanta, Georgia. His father and grandfather had both been college graduates and had in turn occupied the pulpit of the Ebenezer Baptist Church. King's circumstances were thus comfortable insofar as segregation made that possible for a Negro.

At Morehouse College from which King graduated in 1948, he determined to become a minister, and he was ordained even before he took his degree. He studied theology at Crozer Theological Seminary and at Boston University and in 1954 became pastor of the Dexter Avenue Baptist Church in Montgomery, Alabama.

That was the year of the Supreme Court's decision in the Brown case, when Negroes throughout the country began to take new strides toward freedom. King had long been a member of the National Association for the Advancement of Colored People. His Christian training drew him to the ideal of equality and human brotherhood, and from Mohandas K. Gandhi he learned to have faith in the techniques of nonviolence. In the next decade he labored to keep the struggle for equality on a nonviolent basis.

A casual incident in December 1955 led to a spontaneous boycott of the Jim Crow buses by the Negroes of Montgomery. King became the leader of the movement and gained national attention by his eloquent statements and because of the violence the segregationists directed against him. In 1957 he helped form the Southern Christian Leadership Conference and became its president. As the civil rights movement gained force, King became its voice, appealing to the conscience of Americans. He supported the sit-ins and the freedom rides and appealed to the Federal government for corrective action. In 1963 he led the mass protest in Birmingham and participated in the march on Washington. The Civil Rights Act of 1964 owed much to his agitation, and the voting rights law of 1965 was passed in the wake of the indignation aroused by the clash with authorities in Selma, Alabama. The Nobel Peace Prize he received in 1964 recognized these services.

King was a prophet, and effective when he called attention to the injustices of segregation. However, he lacked a clear program to deal with the problems of community organization the Negroes faced after the legal barriers of discrimination were removed. His efforts at action in Northern cities after 1965 were not successful, and demagogues and radicals competed with him for leadership. Still vigorous in his mystical pursuit of brotherhood, he was left in 1966 seeking a definable cause for which to do battle.

---

to compete for the prizes of life, but they were not ready for forcible measures in housing and education that would endanger existing communities.

By then, many Negroes, too, had begun in practice to perceive better the means by which progress would come. In the South desegregation, which was a product of law, remained a clear objective, and they had taken the decisive steps toward attaining it through the sit-ins, the nonviolent campaigns of Martin Luther King, and the voter registration drive in Mississippi and Alabama. By 1966 the weight of that protest, supplemented by the activity of the Federal government, made itself felt, except in the smallest rural communities. As important, the struggle gave the Negroes a distinctive focal point for social reconstruction. They gradually assumed control of the various organizations in the civil rights movement, which became the rallying ground for the whole group.

Meanwhile there were slow and tentative efforts to stimulate the development of local community organization. Tenants' councils and

Dr. Martin Luther King (second from left) and Followers Assembled for a March from Selma to Montgomery, Alabama, March 9, 1965. A Federal marshal reads the text of a Federal court injunction prohibiting the march. (UPI)

Civil Rights Volunteers in Mississippi, 1964

It's night. It's hot. No lights because there aren't any curtains—meaning they can see you and you can't see them. *They*, the word *they*, takes on its full meaning here. You slap at a dozen or so mosquitoes that are buzzing in. You doze off and the phone rings again, about the fifth time, and the other end stays mum. By now you know that somebody, someone on the other side, knows where you are. They know who you're staying with . . . .

Violence hangs overhead like dead air —it hangs there and maybe it'll fall and maybe it won't. Sometimes it's directed at people in the movement, sometimes it's indiscriminate. Cars have been roaming around; seven or eight vigilante trucks with their gun racks and no license plates have been seen meeting at the city dump. What will they do? When? Something is in the air, something is going to happen, somewhere, sometime, to someone . . . . A few nights ago cars roamed the streets, empty bottles flew from their hands, striking cars and homes. They were empty that night—the next night the bottles were loaded—exploding as they hit the church and setting it afire.

—Letter from Ruleville, as quoted in Elizabeth Sutherland, ed., *Letters from Mississippi* (New York: McGraw-Hill Publishing Company, 1965), pp. 149–150.

experimental associations in Chicago and New York taught people how to get together to act for common ends. The greatest spur to these efforts came through the Community Action phases of the war on poverty, under which some seven hundred programs were launched.

In 1966, it was too early to tell what the fate of these projects would be. Set up by intellectuals and bureaucrats, they had yet to take root among the people. Moreover, there was a deep ambiguity in the whole process of their formation. The bulk of participants in many places were Negroes, yet the programs encompassed all the poor. Were the new communities to preserve Negro identity as the advocates of black power wished, or were they to seek integration in some larger units? That question remained unanswered.

▼

The quest for security in the postwar decades led Americans into an effort to build communities. They were slow to recognize the problem. They had inherited an earlier individualistic tradition, and their first response to the uncertainties of the time was a yearning for stable family life. But as the years passed, the middle-class majority and the deprived minority alike discovered that they could achieve personal and family security only within the context of some coherent community.

They did not, however, understand what kind of community they sought. In the fluid conditions of a rapidly changing society, institutional forms and habits of action could not descend intact from the past. Nor could people in need of guidance, discipline, and direction wait for communities to develop slowly over time. In the suburbs or the slums, they had to act as best they could, within the framework of whatever common values they could define. The effort led them into probing examination of their own beliefs as they weighed the alternative goals before them.

Paperbacks for Further Reading

Frederick Lewis Allen, *The Big Change* (Bantam Books) has general observations on society at mid-century. There is interesting material in David Riesman, *The Lonely Crowd* (Yale University Press) and in his *Faces in the Crowd* (Yale University Press). J. B. Conant's ideas on schools are expressed in his *The American High School Today* (McGraw-Hill Paperback Series) and in his *Slums and Suburbs* (Signet Books). The problem is also treated in Martin Mayer, *The Schools* (Anchor Books). Edgar May, *The Wasted Americans* (Signet Books); Michael Harrington, *The Other America* (Penguin Books, Inc.); and Leo Fishman, *Poverty Amid Affluence* (Yale University Press) treat aspects of dependency. Martin Luther King, *Stride Toward Freedom* (Perennial Library) and his *Why We Can't Wait* (Signet Books) express his ideas. Oscar Handlin, *Fire-Bell in the Night* (Beacon Press) and C. Eric Lincoln, *The Black Muslims in America* (Beacon Press) treat aspects of civil rights. Ernest R. May, *Anxiety and Affluence* (McGraw-Hill Paperback Series) is a documentary collection.

THE MEANINGS
OF FAITH

98

In the quarter century after the end of the war prolonged conflict abroad and rapid social changes at home left Americans in need of intellectual and emotional support. The familiar ideology of progress could not answer their questions about the past and the future. Events did not fall neatly into the pattern optimistic humanitarians had once taken for granted. Domestic prosperity did not make people happier; victory did not bring peace; and the spread of independence around the world did not lead to freedom. The men and women who tried to order their own lives and shape new communities in these years were eager for faith to justify their actions. Many turned to the churches to fill the need.

The revival of religious interest reversed a downward trend almost a century in duration, but it did not take Americans back to the faiths of their fathers. The return to the churches was a complex phenomenon consisting of a number of distinct intellectual and social efforts by postwar men to explain the situations that troubled them.

The Return to Religion

UNTIL PEARL HARBOR, the churches seemed gripped in an irreversible decline. Since the challenge of science to the accepted religious doctrines in the 1870s, secularism had spread widely and many people ceased to consider traditional views authoritative. The status of the minister had also fallen. He was the poorest paid of the professionals and the least influential of the intellectuals. Mobility and urbanization had lowered church membership, and the end of immigration had cut off the European sources of regeneration. The institution that had occupied a central place in American life in the 1930s became a peripheral concern of much of the population.

Interest revived during the war. The crisis elicited a great deal of religious rhetoric; "Praise the Lord and pass the ammunition," went the line of a popular song. Individuals and families who suffered turned to worship for consolation. Furthermore, the government recognized the churches by the appointment of chaplains and by asking each man in the armed services to designate himself as the adherent of some faith.

The trend persisted unexpectedly into the postwar decades. All the indices of affiliation moved in the same upward direction. Church membership rose, as did attendance. Religious institutions grew in strength, and their publications achieved wide circulation. Secular marriage almost disappeared, and the place of the ministers in the society improved noticeably. Despite continued mobility and the instability of many aspects of American life, the churches in the 1960s were probably stronger than at any time in the past century. Intellectual and social forces of great intensity had combined to produce the change.

The Limits of Science

The Popular Understanding The inadequacy of science to answer all the questions of life persuaded many people of the need for another kind of knowledge. Certainly there was no decline in the respect accorded the laboratory. Its prestige was measurable in the funds and energies devoted to research by government and business. But the best brains in the world, working together, had produced the fruit of the mushroom cloud over Hiroshima; and however much information the men of learning accumulated, they seemed incapable of providing guidance about how to use the multitude of gadgets they so easily devised.

Popular discontent stemmed in part from tendencies within science. As each discipline developed, it placed greater emphasis upon the elaboration of its specialized techniques. Many became increasingly mathematical and quantitative and often were dependent upon machine computation. The results, stated in a language foreign to the layman, were usually comprehensible only to experts. Few intermediaries were capable of making the rapidly changing conclusions available in a literary form that would be widely assimilated. No philosopher of this generation took the place of John Dewey in bringing knowledge to bear on problems of morals, politics, and esthetics. Instead, the philosophers themselves became specialists in logical techniques and theories of knowledge, writing in terms incommunicable to the uninitiate.

The physical sciences seemed both remote and engaged in activities the purpose of which was not altogether clear. Americans took pride in the number of their Nobel laureates, but few could understand the achievements for which

William Gilman, *Science: USA* (New York, 1965) is a readable survey.

J. ROBERT OPPENHEIMER learned painfully and slowly the dilemmas created by the interrelation of science and politics. For the first thirty years of his life he thought only of learning; then the confusion of world affairs swept him into actions the consequences of which were not predictable.

He was born in New York City in 1904, educated in private schools and at Harvard, and early demonstrated his scientific ability. He went on to study in laboratories in England, Germany, Holland, and Switzerland for there were no national boundaries to the problems of mathematics and physics that occupied him. From 1929 on he taught at the University of California and at the California Institute of Technology. He was a man of broad culture, familiar with the classics, but he had no telephone, read no newspapers, and saw no reason to vote. His was the world of quantum theory and cosmic rays.

He cast a vote for the first time in 1936, for by then external events were intruding. The depression, the rise of the Nazis to power, and the Spanish revolution excited him as they did other men of conscience. He discussed these issues with a circle of leftists and liberals in Berkeley—some of them Communists—although he was himself never a member of the party. For the first time he felt that he was coming to be part of the life of his time and his country.

In 1941 he was one of the scientists consulted on the possibility of manufacturing an atom bomb. The next year he directed some preliminary experiments, and in 1943 he became head of the laboratory at Los Alamos, New Mexico, where his leadership and inspiration carried the group through the essential steps to the momentous explosion.

After the war, he became director of the Institute for Advanced Study at Princeton, New Jersey, and consultant to the atomic energy commission. In the latter capacity he advised against the effort to build a hydrogen bomb, perhaps because of scientific doubts about the feasibility of the project, perhaps for humanitarian reasons.

His motives became an issue in 1953 when his security clearance was revoked. At that time his association with Communists more than a decade earlier created suspicion about his good judgment and candor, although not about his loyalty. The painful raking over of past events, in an atmosphere inflamed by McCarthyism, left his position ambiguous until President Kennedy resolved it in 1962 by inviting him to dinner at the White House. A year later Oppenheimer received the Atomic Energy Commission's Fermi Prize. He died in 1967.

---

the prize was awarded. Nor could many respond to the intellectual challenges raised by the discoveries of these years. Astronomers, now looking beyond the galaxies to the quasars, revised their whole conception of the universe, just as biochemists investigating the DNA molecule began to speculate about the concept of life itself. Yet these potentially exciting theories created little wonder or doubt. They were part of a massive flow of miscellaneous data, noted by some part of the public but without speculation about the intellectual consequences. There was no re-examination of men's view of the universe and of their own place in it such as Darwinism had occasioned a century earlier. Americans no longer held a coherent view of the world which science could shake.

The Purposes of Knowledge Science was also suspect because it was so pliant a tool that it seemed devoid of all moral purpose. J. Robert Oppenheimer, for instance, out of the desire to serve mankind, helped build man's most terrible instrument of destruction. There was no way of knowing whom the experimenter served.

He produced antibiotics and the hydrogen bomb; he worked for a hospital or a business corporation or the army; and his efforts bore little correlation to the human needs of the world about him.

Doubts about the uses of knowledge applied to the social as well as to the physical sciences. Economics by the 1960s had developed the most precise methods among the disciplines of the former category. Its models rested upon sophisticated mathematical methods joined in an elaborate theoretical framework. Every businessman and politician depended to some extent upon the reading of its charts. Yet much of the work in this field seemed directed merely at finding techniques to implement the decisions of those who sponsored its work. The whole subject of the economics of development, for instance, arose in response to the problems created by the Marshall Plan, the Agency for International Development (AID), and similar programs.

The scientists themselves felt the lack of understanding and purpose and reached out for external props to validate their activities. The designation scientist in the 1960s covered a variety of thinkers, experimenters, engineers, and technicians. The more sensitive of them were aware of the extent to which the increase of information revealed the greater areas of their ignorance. The *Bulletin of the Atomic Scientists* (1945) expressed the puzzlement of some about the moral consequences of their achievements. Others were content to separate their activities in the laboratory from their lives and thoughts outside it. Still others reached for reassurance to politics or to some sort of mystical faith, as the vogue for Arnold J. Toynbee and Pierre Teilhard de Chardin showed.

Crisis or Adjustment

The Goad of Theology   The intellectual context of the day explained the variety of routes by which Americans traveled back to faith after 1947. During the war and shortly thereafter religious thinkers in the United States discovered

The Prospects for Progress, 1964

It is an error to think that the progress of mankind would be safe and irresistible if only natural selection were permitted to operate unobstructed by civilization. Natural selection does not guarantee even the survival of the species, let alone its improvement. Dinosaurs became extinct despite their evolution having been piloted by natural selection quite unhampered by culture. Natural selection is automatic, mechanical, blind. It brings about genetic changes that often, though not always, appear to be purposeful, furthering the survival and opposing the extinction of the species. And yet, natural selection has no purpose. Only man can have purposes . . . .

Human evolution has forced mankind to a crossroad from which there is no turning back and no escape. Our animal past is irretrievably lost—we could not go back to it even if we wished to. The choice is between a twilight, cultural as well as biological, or a progressive adaptation of man's genes to his culture, and of man's culture to his genes . . . . I am an optimist because I know that mankind, the living world, and the whole universe have evolved and are evolving . . . . Whether one feels that beauty and good or that ugliness and evil predominate in the world, one knows that this world was not created all at once, fixed and unchangeable forever. Creation is not an event, but a process, not complete but continuing. Progress and betterment are by no means guaranteed or vouchsafed in evolution. However, man may strive to bring them about, and this striving is what gives meaning and dignity to human life, individually and collectively.

—Theodosius Dobzhansky, *Heredity and the Nature of Man* (New York: Harcourt, Brace & World, Inc., 1964), pp. 163–165.

the crisis theology that had developed in Central Europe in the previous decade. The new ideas arose from a tradition that had not earlier been widely held in the United States. A line of writings reaching back to Sören Kierkegaard and down to Karl Barth had argued that rational means were not adequate to comprehend the universe, that evil was an inescapable reality, and that man could apprehend the nature of his own existence only through a mystical confrontation with God's will.

These convictions were particularly attractive to Protestants with a Lutheran background. Reinhold Niebuhr's successive books had considerable impact, as did those of Paul Tillich, who came to the United States from Germany in 1933. An analogous influence, derived from Central European sources, played upon American Judaism. Martin Buber's studies of traditional mystical sects were widely read in the United States, although he himself migrated from Germany to Jerusalem. Abraham J. Heschel did come to New York where he helped train a new generation of rabbis and labored to make Orthodoxy relevant to modern man's condition.

The issue was somewhat more complex among Catholics, who recognized the authority of the Pope in matters of faith and who accepted the discipline of a world-wide hierarchy. Nevertheless, they too felt the forces that affected other religious groups. The call to a contemplative life sounded by the Trappist monk Thomas Merton was an effort to impart intellectual relevance to his faith, as was the insistence of the Jesuits, Gustave Weigel and John Courtney Murray, that the Church engage itself in confrontation with modern thought.

These ideas commanded respect, even of the secular-minded, to an extent greater than in many decades. They fitted the impressions derived from German and French existential philosophy, which had a great vogue in literary circles in the decade after the war. The demand for faith expressed by the theologians was both tough and subtle and its full meaning escaped

most Americans. For most of the population its chief function was to validate a return to the churches which had quite different causes.

Assurance By and large, the people who craved belief in these years had no wish to wrestle in anxiety with the spirit of God. They sought rather a faith that would aid their adjustment and ease their doubts. To the adherents of almost every denomination, popular writers were ready to promise a healing certainty as a reward for the suspension of questioning. Rabbi Joshua Loth Liebman, Monsignor Fulton J. Sheen, and the Reverend Norman Vincent Peale articulated in the titles of their widely read books the goals their readers sought—*Peace of Mind* (1946), *Peace of Soul* (1949), and *The Power of Positive Thinking* (1952). In this view, the function of faith was largely sedative. Belief made few demands of the individual but rather quieted his anxieties. Church attendance was a kind of therapeutic distraction from the tensions of middle-class life.

A somewhat different outlet was available to the more traditional believers. The evangelical element in American religion had never died out, particularly in rural regions and in the Negro churches. Revivalists, who had had a hard time of it in the 1920s and 1930s, came back after the war. The most popular of them, Billy Graham, drew audiences in the cities as well as in the countryside, abroad as well as at home. His message was simple and undemanding for it offered a single all-encompassing answer to the questions that troubled twentieth-century man. Faith, which came to any believer who sought it, would solve all problems.

The return to religion thus had several totally different meanings. A variety of intellectual paths led men back to the church.

William G. McLoughlin, *Billy Graham* (New York, 1960) sets Graham within the revivalist tradition.

THE MEANINGS OF FAITH

Faith for Dreaming, 1955

I tried to pin her down on what she really believed (we'd had enough to drink by then so that such a discussion wasn't embarrassing). She was curiously evasive. She said that the professors of comparative religion were like bright kids with clocks. They could take a religion apart and show how it ticked, but they couldn't put it back together so it would work for anybody. I mildly suggested that the day was past, maybe, when religion could work for any educated person. She flared a bit; said religion still worked for a hell of a lot of people. She said her parents would never have survived the death of Seth without it, and that she didn't know whether she and Milton could have stayed in one piece after the baby died if they hadn't had their religion. At this point I was probing, perhaps cruelly, to strike bottom. I said, "Well, Margie, maybe that only proves the power of a dream." Like a flash she answered—and her voice sounded just as it did in the old days, full of life and sparkle, "Who isn't dreaming . . . ?"

—Herman Wouk, *Marjorie Morningstar* (Garden City, N.Y.: Doubleday & Company, Inc., 1955), p. 562.

The Church and the Community

The Family Context The mass of men and women who returned to the churches in these decades did so for social rather than for doctrinal or theological reasons. Affiliation supplied the rites for recognizing the important incidents and emotional crises of life—birth, marriage, and death. Often people let years go by without

Releasing Inner Powers, 1952

Believe in yourself! Have faith in your abilities! Without a humble but reasonable confidence in your own powers you cannot be successful or happy. But with sound self-confidence you can succeed. A sense of inferiority and inadequacy interferes with the attainment of your hopes, but self-confidence leads to self-realization and successful achievement. Because of the importance of this mental attitude, this book will help you believe in yourself and release your inner powers.

—Norman V. Peale, *The Power of Positive Thinking* (Englewood Cliffs, N.J.: Prentice-Hall, Inc., 1955), p. 1.

Repentance, 1965

Repentance is the launching pad where the soul is sent on its eternal orbit with God at the center of the arc. When our hearts are bowed as low as they can get and we truly acknowledge and forsake our sins, then God takes over and like the second stage of a rocket, He lifts us toward His Kingdom. The way up is down. Man got into difficulty when he lifted his will against God's. He gets out of trouble when he bows to the divine superiority, when he repents and says humbly: "God be merciful to me a sinner." Man's extremity then becomes God's opportunity.

—Billy Graham, *World Aflame* (Garden City, N.Y.: Doubleday & Company, Inc., 1965), p. 151.

Billy Graham, Baptist Preacher, Delivers a Sermon at Soldier Field, Chicago, 1960s. (Black Star)

WILLIAM F. GRAHAM was born in 1918 on a farm near Charlotte, North Carolina. His boyhood was uneventful. It was long his ambition to be first baseman for the Philadelphia Athletics, but in his senior year in high school he attended a revival meeting and was converted. Although his parents were Presbyterians, he went to Bob Jones University, a fundamentalist Baptist College in Tennessee, and after further training at the Florida Bible Institute he was ordained a Baptist minister in 1939.

Billy briefly occupied a pulpit in Illinois but soon turned to evangelism. He was tall, blond, and attractive and his persuasive baritone voice called his listeners back to the old-time religion. He did not use the antics of an earlier generation of revivalists, but the essential message was the same: the nation had departed from the fundamentals of faith stated in the Ten Commandments; it had yielded to wickedness and sin so that destruction at the hands of the Communists was possible; but repentance and a return to Christ could stay God's judgment.

Between 1945 and 1949 Graham slowly developed a following and an organization, aided by his association with Youth for Christ, an aggressive neofundamentalist group. In the fall of 1949, he attracted national attention in a nine-week revival in Los Angeles. In the restless atmosphere of Southern California, Graham and his "All Star Supporting Party" drew hundreds of thousands of men and women to his canvas cathedral. Among those converted were Stuart Hamblen, a former rodeo champion, who sold his string of race horses; Louis Zamperini, an Olympic track star, who gave up liquor; and J. Arthur Vaus, a well-known gambler. Fully as important was a telegram from William Randolph Hearst to all his newspapers: "Puff Graham."

In the 1950s, Graham traveled millions of miles around the world, his appearances managed by a staff of four hundred and publicized by all the techniques of modern advertising. A magazine *Decision* and a radio program "Hour of Decision" brought his word also to millions in their homes. His message was simple: faith, for which so many people yearned, would solve their problems. Gradually he acquired the co-operation of many churches although the core of his support remained in those affiliated with the National Association of Evangelicals. Graham's tone gradually changed. He subdued the message of imminent doom and began to reflect upon the problems of the world. He integrated his own staff, for instance, and refused to preach to segregated audiences. But how far his sensitivity to current issues would alter his position remained to be seen.

feeling the need for association and worship, but generally, the establishment of a family and a household made them wish to belong. The problems of raising children in a turbulent modern environment underlined the desirability of an external source of discipline and also of a social grouping in which youngsters could associate with others like themselves. The church thus became a means of stabilizing the family in an era in which its values bore a heavy strain.

To some Americans, religion also was a means of preserving ethnic ties. Awareness of European origins no longer satisfied the nostalgic longing—expressed by such novelists as Herman Wouk, Bernard Malamud, Edwin O'Connor, and Nick Petrakis—for a cross-generational identity with roots in the past. With the end of immigration old connections were severed; and communism made such countries of origin as Poland and Romania increasingly alien to those who were in any case now third- and fourth-generation Americans. It was, however, possible to preserve ethnicity in the one difference that American society recognized and indeed enshrined in the Constitution, religion. If it was less meaningful than before to be a Polish-American, being a Catholic could satisfy some of the desire for identity.

Increasingly, Americans considered themselves divided among three religious affiliations —Protestant, Catholic, Jewish. Each category in actuality covered very considerable doctrinal differences. The beliefs of Unitarians and Quakers were, for instance, closer to those of Reform Jews than to those of Baptists or Lutherans. But the tripartite division was less creedal than social. In a rough way it outlined the groupings, based largely on ethnic antecedents, within which families preferred to make marriages and maintain associations. The distinction recognized the extent to which the church was a social institution that supplied a setting for some communal activities.

Tolerance and Unity Regarded in its social context, religious affiliation was a matter of personal preference. Each man could go to the church of his choice—which he chose was a secondary matter. Efforts at proselytization came to an end and with them much of the old sectarian bitterness. With the subsidence of theological differences, a broad degree of tolerance developed which assumed that any faith was compatible with good citizenship. The condemnation by his superiors of Father Leonard Feeney (1949), who insisted that no salvation was possible outside the Catholic Church, was indicative of the open attitude toward men of all creeds.

The diminishing emphasis on doctrinal differences led to a movement for unity, at least among Protestant sects. Various mergers before the war had already brought together a number of Methodist, Lutheran, and Presbyterian bodies. The United Church of Christ (1957) joined two Congregational groups, and there was a proposal in 1962 to fuse the Episcopalians, Presbyterians, and Methodists. The National Council of Churches (1950) provided a means of coordination short of union for a variety of specialized agencies in which various Protestant denominations joined. Meanwhile, the National Conference of Christians and Jews (formed 1928) proved increasingly effective in promoting interfaith understanding.

Such modes of common action were useful because of the rapid intrusion of government into education and social welfare, areas in which religious groups had formerly worked. The effort by Catholics to secure a share of public funds for the support of parochial schools led at first to acrimonious controversy, as in the exchange of angry statements between Mrs. Franklin D. Roosevelt and Francis Cardinal Spellman of New York (1949). Fear of stirring up the issue probably postponed a Federal education bill for several years. But in the 1960s shared time and the provision of supplementary services to parochial school students provided a basis for compromise. It was not altogether clear whether these devices con-

Robert Lee, *The Social Sources of Church Unity* (New York, 1960) is a thoughtful analysis.

formed to the Constitutional principle of separation of church and state which the Supreme
Court upheld with increasing consistency in such
other contexts as school prayers. For the majority
of Americans, nevertheless, these were no longer
causes for conflict. The tolerance which took for
granted common goals in all the churches permitted an accommodation that recognized a
parity among them.

As the churches broadened their social
activities, they became more alike in all but the
essentials of rite and worship. The points of
similarity ranged from modern architecture to
an increased role for the laity, from a concern
with mental health to attention to public relations.

Significant modifications of the position of
the Papacy in its relationship to other faiths
aided the Catholic adjustment. Among Protestants, the ecumenical movement had culminated
in the establishment of the World Council of
Churches in 1948. In the next year the Sacred
Congregation of the Holy Office in Rome permitted qualified priests informally to participate
in interchurch discussions. After a decade of
contact, John XXIII in the Second Vatican
Council (1962) encouraged a modernization of
Catholic attitudes and a renewed openness
toward the world. His successor Paul VI defined
a cooperative relationship with other Christian
churches and with the non-Christian religions
as well.

The shift in Catholic attitude derived partly
from years of scholarly study and partly from the
defensive posture forced on Christians who
faced on the one hand an aggressive communism
and on the other, nationalist movements by
people of other religions in Africa and Asia.
But pressure from Americans of all faiths was
also a factor in the change in emphasis from
differences in doctrines to the concordance of
ethical goals.

The Goals of Faith

Within the United States, the most influential churches devoted increasing energy to
defining the goals of faith. As the ministers
became less active as expounders of doctrine,
they assumed the role of interpreters of the
moral imperative they read into their faith.
Often their difficulty lay in discovering the
appropriate problem. The evils against which
the earlier social gospel had directed its shafts
were either under control or the subjects of
widespread consensus. There was no challenge
in pleading the causes of labor or reform.

The civil rights movement, on the other
hand, supplied a basis for an appeal to conscience that underscored the ideals of equality
and human brotherhood. In the 1965 demonstration in Selma, Alabama, garbed nuns, priests,
ministers, and rabbis marched together in a
manifestation of unity. Martin Luther King
acquired spiritual stature in the eyes of many,
not through his ability to organize a coherent
movement or to formulate specific goals, but
through the challenge he posed to the conscience
of men.

In 1965 and 1966, attention shifted to the
war in Vietnam. The civil rights movement had
passed the point beyond which affirmations of
principle were less useful than the detailed work
of implementing them, and the mounting intensity of the conflict in Southeast Asia seemed more
important. Peace, like equality, could be stated
as an absolute imperative, without concern for
the political or diplomatic issues involved. Protest
in this case also was a means of bearing witness
to faith.

Paradoxically, the religious leaders shared
the impulse to protest with the small minority of
Americans who professed no faith at all and saw
no need for any. Some disillusioned intellectuals and impatient young people drifted toward
a nihilism that rejected all ideals, and valued
only the action of the sit-in or the demonstration.
In a confused way those who longed to believe

Freedom Marchers on the Way to Montgomery Pause for a Lunch Break near Selma, Alabama. (UPI)

A Meaning for the Twentieth Century, 1963

There was a time when the Church was very powerful. It was during that period when the early Christians rejoiced when they were deemed worthy to suffer for what they believed. In those days the Church was not merely a thermometer that recorded the ideas and principles of popular opinion; it was a thermostat that transformed the mores of society. Wherever the early Christians entered a town the power structure got disturbed and immediately sought to convict them for being "disturbers of the peace" and "outside agitators." But they went on with the conviction that they were a "colony of heaven" and had to obey God rather than man . . . .

Things are different now. The contemporary Church is so often a weak, ineffectual voice with an uncertain sound. It is so often the arch-supporter of the *status quo.* Far from being disturbed by the presence of the Church, the power structure of the average community is consoled by the Church's silent and vocal sanction of things as they are.

But the judgment of God is upon the Church as never before. If the Church of today does not recapture the sacrificial spirit of the early Church, it will lose its authentic ring, forfeit the loyalty of millions, and be dismissed as an irrelevant social club with no meaning for the 20th century.

—Martin Luther King, "Letter from the Birmingham City Jail," April 16, as quoted in *New Leader* (June 24, 1963), p. 10.

and those who did not occupied a common ground of protest from which they cried out the wrongs of the world. They thus bore prophetic witness against evil without recognizing the obligation to present realistic alternatives that would right it.

Faith in the postwar decades lacked the simple meaning it had presented to men in earlier periods. It conveyed no orderly vision of human destiny or of divine intentions. For the majority of Americans, it created an acceptable framework for a stable personal and family life, supplying continuity across the generations and discipline within the home. For people who did not ask the big questions, faith supplied the answers to the small ones.

But for those who sought an intellectual content as well, who searched for understanding of the problems of a disorderly world, faith brought anguish as often as consolation. The mysterious earth of God's creation was laden with the potential for evil. The wonders of nature included the explosive force of the atom. And progress might as well lead to man's utter destruction as to his redemption. In a situation in which all choices were ambiguous, protest was the only clear form of affirmation. "Stop the

World, I Want to Get Off," was the title of a popular play in 1965.

Faith bore still another meaning for those who wanted to stay on, who accepted the necessity for decisions and choices and who believed that small steps away from the greater evils might approach the relatively good. Those who bore the responsibility for the conduct of American diplomacy after 1960 rarely could take refuge in sweeping affirmations of principle such as had buoyed up Woodrow Wilson or Franklin D. Roosevelt. They could only deal with each crisis as it arose, knowing as they did that on their decisions rested the fate of much of mankind.

Paperbacks for Further Reading

Will Herberg, *Protestant Catholic Jew* (Anchor Books) is an influential interpretation. William Barrett, *Irrational Man* (Anchor Books) treats the underlying philosophical trends. There is an account of the Vatican councils in Xavier Rynne, *Letters from Vatican City* (Doubleday Image Books). Among the works of the authors mentioned in the text are: Thomas Merton, *The Seven Story Mountain* (Signet Books); John Courtney Murray, *We Hold These Truths* (Doubleday Image Books); Abraham J. Heschel, *God in Search of Man* (Harper Torchbooks); Billy Graham, *Peace with God* (Pocket Books, Inc.); and Paul Tillich, *Dynamics of Faith* (Harper Torchbooks).

THE CHALLENGE
OF ATOMIC
DESTRUCTION

99

Over all domestic concerns — personal as well as social — hung the shadow of the atomic weapons with which the great powers had armed themselves. No American could escape the consciousness that a mistake or a miscalculation might unleash destruction unparalleled in man's history. Peace was the universal desire.

Yet there was no peace. For more than a decade, disruptive new forces touched off a succession of incidents that kept the world on the verge of war. Latin America, Asia, and Africa seethed with unrest. In those vast areas, nationalism and social revolution kept disturbing existing conditions and readily spread across established boundary lines. Through the difficult years after 1960, the United States pursued a tortuous course, struggling to avoid war yet determined to honor its commitments to freedom. The strain tried the patience of the citizens and exacted a heavy cost of the economy.

May Day Parade Through Moscow, 1961. The Russian antiaircraft missile "Guild" shown here has an estimated slant range of over 30 miles and an effective ceiling of about 100,000 ft. (Camera Press/Pix)

Combat-ready Titan. This Titan II intercontinental-range missile, ten stories tall, is shown on its 150-foot-deep underground pad, or silo, ready for launching. (U.S. Air Force Photo)

Nuclear Strategy

The Weapons The conditions of prolonged atomic stalemate produced a steady increase in the size and power of weapons and their delivery systems. The antagonist's capacities were unknown and were therefore subject to exaggeration. But no officeholder responsible for the defense of the nation could fail to take account of the danger of falling behind. The presidential campaign of 1960 heard charges that a missile gap had appeared between the capabilities of the United States and those of the Soviet Union. The Kennedy administration, once in power, hastened to close that alleged gap. A rapid building pro-

gram set up a system of impregnable, deep silos and also equipped a fleet of nuclear submarines able to make extended cruises and armed with Polaris missiles. These weapons were designed to prolong the stalemate by using the threat of inevitable retaliation to deter aggression.

But the experience of the 1950s had revealed the inadequacy of massive retaliation as the sole instrument of foreign policy. That strategy left the United States without the power to deal with small brush-fire incidents not worth the risk of atomic holocaust. The Russians and Chinese, by contrast, were willing to draw upon their limitless man power in hit-and-run adventures which sometimes paid off. The Kennedy administra-

The task of recasting the American defense system fell in 1961 to a new type of military planner, one whose nearsightedness barred him from active duty in World War II, but who rose to the rank of colonel through his powers of analysis which mastered the details of complicated problems.

ROBERT S. McNAMARA was born on June 9, 1916, in a middle-class California family. He did well in high school, studied economics and philosophy at Berkeley, from which he graduated in 1937, and attended the Harvard Graduate School of Business Administration, where he became an assistant professor.

The outbreak of war in 1941 altered the pattern of his career. The Army Air Force, overwhelmed by the problems of controlling the vast flow of matériel, money, and personnel through its bases around the world, called on McNamara for aid in setting up a statistical system that would inform it what and who was where and when. The art of supply in this conflict proved as important as the ability to handle weapons. McNamara served with distinction in England, India, China, and the Pacific.

His talents were as useful to the peacetime needs of industry as they had been to the military needs of war. In 1946 he joined the Ford Motor Company, which was still in transition from a family firm to a modern corporation. His skill in planning and financial analysis brought him steadily through the bureaucracy to the rank of president in 1960.

Although McNamara was nominally a Republican, he was the choice for Secretary of Defense because Kennedy was aware of the importance of fresh insights in the military establishment, upon which the safety of the country rested and which absorbed a substantial part of the Federal budget. In his first five years in office, McNamara streamlined operations, recast important branches of the services, and held costs within controlled limits. In the process, he sometimes antagonized important interests both in Congress and in the armed services. But he contributed substantially to the redefinition of American strategy. Then the problems of Vietnam increasingly occupied his attention, as they did that of other Americans.

---

tion under Secretary of Defense McNamara therefore made an effort to develop new tactical weapons, including some that used atomic power, which would supply highly mobile forces armed with intense fire power for limited engagements.

Paradoxically, Americans shied away from speculation about and experimentation with antimissile missiles. Their hesitation was due not only to the cost of an effective program but also to their desire for peace. While maintaining its own strength, the United States had to reassure the Soviets that its intentions were pacific. The ability to strike down or blunt a Russian attack would upset the nuclear balance and might frighten the enemy into precipitate action.

Graduated Deterrence Calculations of how to preserve the balance arose out of new strategic concepts developed since 1945. The American objective was no longer, as it had been in 1941 or 1917 or 1861, to develop the maximum power in order to compel the foe to surrender. Such a conflict would destroy both the victor and the vanquished. Rather, the objective was to accumulate enough force to deter aggression. If fighting broke out, the modulated use of power was to repel the enemy but not frighten him into total war. The country was to prepare to take gradu-

Urs Schwarz, *American Strategy* (Garden City, N.Y., 1966) is a lucid account of the development of military thought in the United States.

ated steps of escalation, but at the same time to keep open the possibility of de-escalation. The game theorists worked out abstract formulas to solve the problem. But to apply these formulas in practice was another matter.

The concept of graduated deterrence rested on a willingness to believe that, for unexplained reasons, there had been a fundamental shift in Soviet policy some time around 1956. While resisting any overt aggression, the United States had to leave open the possibility that the Russians were sincere in their talk about peaceful coexistence. It was necessary to hold a stick to beat back the enemy if he became violent, but also a carrot to win him over if he wished to be friendly.

The Balance of World Power

Peaceful Coexistence   More than a decade later, the reasons for the thaw in Soviet attitudes were still not altogether clear. The stabilization of the regime under Nikita S. Khrushchev and the weariness of the people and their desire for an improved standard of living contributed. But the fundamental factor seemed to be the recognition within the Soviet Union of the failure of Stalinist communism.

Immediately after the war, Communist party leaders had nurtured high expectations of revolution in Western Europe and in the underdeveloped countries. In Italy and France, powerful Red organizations challenged a weak and disorderly capitalist society. Ten years later, Western Europe had fully recovered from the war and its institutions were firm. Nor had success in the underdeveloped countries been commensurate with the Kremlin's hopes. The end of imperialism made the new nations independent but not Communist. Above all, the Russian people lagged behind those west of the iron curtain, both in the material and the spiritual conditions of life.

Khrushchev desired therefore to focus his country's energies on internal development. The Soviet Union did not cease to be interested in the spread of communism and sometimes even took reckless gambles to further that aim. But it was willing for the time being to set aside the goal of revolution elsewhere while it provided food and housing for its people, in the expectation that successful development ultimately would attract imitators throughout the world.

The Communist Split   Their shift in policy drew the Russians into a bitter conflict with their Chinese allies, who gave a narrower reading to Marxist doctrines. Peking insisted that all efforts, including support of national liberation movements in Asia, Africa, and Latin America, be directed immediately to complete the Revolution. Isolated and ignorant of conditions in the West, Mao Tse-tung did not fear the costs of war as Khrushchev did, and was willing to make any sacrifices to win at once. The divergence in viewpoint led to the withdrawal of Soviet aid and technicians from China in 1960 and split the Communist world. Though both sides insisted that the ultimate victory over capitalism was inevitable, the United States could draw some comfort from the division in the enemy camp.

Neutralism   The realignment of the great powers encouraged an increasing number of countries to refuse to commit themselves definitely to one side or the other. Small states such as Sweden and Switzerland had long traditions of noninvolvement, and refused to participate in any form of alliance. By contrast the neutralism of the 1950s and 1960s aimed not at withdrawal but rather at the creation of an intermediary bloc able to play the United States and the Soviet Union off against each other.

This course had special attractions for the newly independent nations. Their leaders were usually intellectuals predisposed to socialism, yet suspicious of Communist intentions. They resented the former imperialist powers yet had absorbed much of the culture of their colonial rulers. These countries were internally weak yet given to expansionist dreams. Furthermore, they believed that economic development would cure

Peking Railway Station, November 4, 1966. Revolutionary masses and Red Guards welcome back 65 Chinese students whose studies in the Soviet Union were suspended by the Soviet Government. (Eastfoto)

all their problems, and they sought what aid they could get from whoever would offer it.

The neutralists assumed a parity of motives and interests between the United States and the Soviet Union. But, like mediators in every situation, the neutralists drifted toward the position of the intransigeant party to any conflict and therefore often ended on the anti-American side. In any case, their effort to organize a substantial force proved futile. The Bandung Conference (1955), which included China, produced only a windy statement; and while separate organizations of Arabs and Africans endured, they were incapable of acting on any important issue. Neutralist sentiment grew as the number of independent states increased. But in 1966, it had still not generated an autonomous force in world politics.

The vortex of neutralism in Europe whirled about Charles de Gaulle, who had assumed power in France in 1958. A nineteenth-century nationalist who mistrusted the Anglo-Saxon nations and harbored Napoleonic illusions of French glory, he set himself the task of extricating his country from the commitments of the NATO alliance and of minimizing the role of all supranational organizations. He dreamed instead of a Europe of sovereign states within which France would play the dominant role. To that end, he sought a *rapprochement* with both the Soviet Union and China. By 1966 he had succeeded in only two aspects of his policy: he had thrown the plans for European integration into disarray and he had developed a nuclear weapon.

Atomic Proliferation   China by then had also shown the ability to build the bomb. Although

Selected Members of the United Nations, 1964*

Country	Estimated Population (in millions)	Contribution to UN Budget (percent of total)
China†	656.22	4.57
India	471.62	2.03
USSR	226.25	14.97
United States	195.50	32.02
Japan	97.36	2.27
United Kingdom	54.21	7.58
Italy	50.95	2.24
France	48.41	5.94
Canada	19.23	3.12
Trinidad and Tobago	.92	.04
Congo (Brazzaville)	.84	.04
Mauritania	.78	.04
Cyprus	.58	.04
Gabon	.45	.04
Kuwait	.38	.04
Luxembourg	.33	.05
Malta	.32	–
Iceland	.18	.04

* Total membership in 1965 was 117.

† Population given is for all of China, although membership was held by the regime in Taiwan.

neither it nor France as yet appeared to possess adequate delivery systems, the proliferation, which threatened also to spread to other nations, was ominous. The elaborate stalemate between the United States and the Soviet Union depended upon calculations feasible when the ultimate weapon rested in the hands of two countries only. The increase in the number of players in the game multiplied the variables to be taken into account and made controls difficult. Perhaps that was why the Russians in 1966 began to deploy an elaborate antimissile system.

The United Nations The UN was able to make no useful contribution toward resolving the extended and deepening crisis of the 1960s. The liberal use of the Russian veto still immobilized the Security Council. The General Assembly had grown to unmanageable size, and most of its members, new to world politics, acted solely out of concern for their own interests. Among the specialized agencies, the World Health Organization and the Food and Agricultural Organization played a useful technical role. But the UN, by and large, had surrendered the pretense that it might develop a pattern of international law and government, and served primarily as a forum within which the contending nations confronted one another. The hope for peace rested not there but in the careful use of power by the Soviet Union and the United States.

The Definition of American Policy

The New Administration John F. Kennedy and Lyndon B. Johnson, the Presidents whose decisions were critical in the 1960s, had become familiar with the problems of foreign policy through experience in the Senate. Although they brought new advisers into the White House and new administrators under Dean Rusk into the State Department, they knew the gravity of the issues and the seriousness of the risks involved and were cautious about upsetting existing arrangements. The Department of State and the United States Information Agency remained largely the shambles the McCarthy era had left them. Despite the campaign talk about a vigorous new approach to diplomacy, Kennedy in his first two years in office was hesitant and indecisive, unwilling to gamble with the heavy stakes in his charge. The results became evident in tactical losses in Latin America, in the Far East, and in Europe.

The Bay of Pigs and Its Results Kennedy had inherited a difficult situation in Latin America, as elsewhere, and wished to chart a new course. But good intentions were difficult to implement.

Cuba was the most serious problem, for Fidel Castro had moved definitely in a Communist direction. In the closing months of the Eisen-

DAVID DEAN RUSK understood that it was the responsibility of the President to make foreign policy, which it was the duty of the Secretary of State to implement. Rusk was therefore not an innovator; he devoted his energies largely to carrying through the decisions Kennedy and Johnson made. He contributed to American diplomacy genuine skill as a negotiator, a realistic understanding of the world, and a humane commitment to freedom.

Rusk's great opportunity came when he went as a Rhodes Scholar to St. John's College, Oxford. He was born in Cherokee County, Georgia, the son of a poor Presbyterian minister who eked out a living by teaching school, carrying the mail, and farming. After graduating from high school in Atlanta, Rusk took a job and then managed to work his way through Davidson College, North Carolina. The world now opened before him, but he never forgot his roots in the poor white society of the South or lost sight of the meaning of freedom for his country.

In 1934 Rusk returned to the United States from Europe to teach at Mills College, where he remained until he entered the army in 1940. A variety of posts in intelligence brought him to the China-Burma-India theater under General Joseph Stilwell. After the peace he moved into the State Department. Rusk became Assistant Secretary for Far Eastern Affairs in 1950, and suffered through the problems of conducting the Korean War, managing MacArthur, and defining a China policy. With the change of administration in 1952, he left government service for the presidency of the Rockefeller Foundation.

Kennedy, seeking a man of experience familiar with the Far East, brought him back. In the troubled years that followed, Rusk loyally carried through the President's intentions, adjusting where necessary to a variety of pressures from Kennedy's advisers in the White House. Vivid memories of the problems of Chinese Communism made Rusk conscious of the vital American stake in Asia. For him, too, Vietnam became the ultimate test of the feasibility of the deterrence strategy.

---

hower administration Cuban exiles had prepared an invasion of Cuba from a base in Guatemala, where the CIA was supervising their training. President Kennedy was unwilling either to give the project the full support originally planned or to take the responsibility for canceling it. Inaccurate information and assurances from the experts that the anti-Castro Cubans could supply their own air cover fed the wishful thinking that the attack might succeed without American intervention. On April 17, 1961, some 1500 exiles landed at the Bay of Pigs and, after an initial success, exhausted their ammunition and succumbed to the 20,000-man army that confronted them. The ships that bore needed supplies were sunk by Castro's jets, which commanded the skies unopposed. The calamity was a prelude to the total extermination of anti-Castro resistance within the island.

The disaster cast a somber shadow over Kennedy's proposal, during his first month in office, that the nations of the Western Hemisphere unite in an alliance for progress. A conference at Punta del Este, Uruguay, in August 1961, however, developed plans for coordinated aid to Latin American economic development. The appearance of liberal regimes in Peru and in the Dominican Republic was also encouraging; but by the summer of 1963, despite open support from the United States, both had toppled before new military dictatorships.

Laos Trouble broke out in Southeast Asia soon after Kennedy's inauguration. In 1961, with North Vietnamese support and Russian

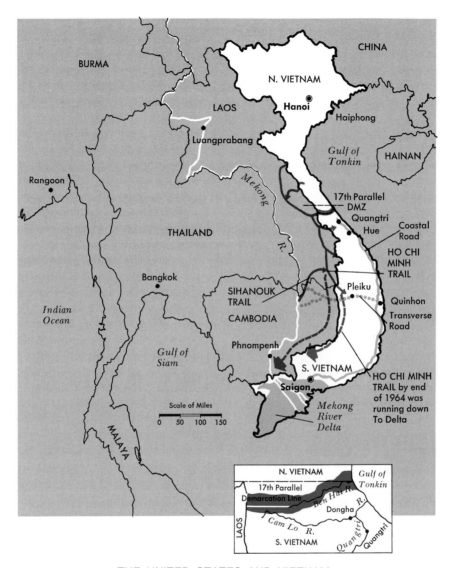

THE UNITED STATES AND VIETNAM

supplies, the Communist Pathet Lao party rebelled in Laos, through which ran the supply route from Hanoi into the Mekong Delta. At about the same time guerrillas across the border in North Vietnam organized the National Front for the Liberation of South Vietnam, dominated by the Lao Dong (Communist) party in Hanoi, and stepped up the terrorist campaign against the Diem government.

President Kennedy recognized the importance of these attacks for the stability of the whole peninsula, and in a forceful statement (March 23, 1961) warned that unless armed attacks by externally supported Communists ceased, the United States would reconsider its position. But the Bay of Pigs disaster had made Kennedy and his advisers unwilling to risk direct intervention. After months of maneuver, a con-

National Liberation, 1961

These problems . . . all pose for us the test of learning to deal with what is called, in the inverted language of communism, "wars of national liberation." Behind this concept is the notion that the safest way to extend Communist power and influence in the contemporary world is to exploit the inevitable turbulence which accompanies the revolutionary movement toward modernization, by building a political base rooted in local frustrations, painful memories and unfulfilled aspirations, and by mounting, on that base, insurrectional activity aided from outside the country. The objective is, of course, not national liberation but entrapment within the Communist bloc. This method, from the Communist point of view, is designed to bypass American nuclear strength, to bypass the conventional strength that we have helped build with our allies, and to tear down institutions not under their own control.

—Dean Rusk, *The Winds of Freedom* (Boston: The Beacon Press, 1963), p. 31.

ference in Geneva finally produced an agreement to neutralize Laos (July 1962). The pact, however, was never effective. The North Vietnamese refused to withdraw and retained control of the Ho Chi Minh Trail.

By the time the discussions ended, the events in Laos had already increased terrorism in South Vietnam and hastened infiltration from the North. A special report of the International Control Commission on June 2, 1962, found evidence beyond a reasonable doubt of North Vietnamese aggression in violation of the 1954 Geneva agreements.

Meanwhile the efforts of President Diem to strengthen his authority intensified dissent, which in turn led to further repression and the loss of American support. In 1963, the suspension of aid from the United States touched off a military coup during which Diem and his brother were murdered. A succession of generals took charge, the country fell into disorder, and the capacity to resist was weakened. A Communist take-over seemed imminent. The whole region felt the repercussions. Cambodia and Burma backed away from the United States and prepared for *rapprochement* with China, and Indonesia withdrew entirely from Western contact.

Berlin The unsolved problem of Europe was still Germany. Fifteen years after the war, the situation of that country was still anomalous, divided by the Iron Curtain and with its chief city occupied by conquerors. Berlin was the one gap in the stockade within which the Soviet Union and its satellites imprisoned their populations. Here Germans from the East Zone could see the contrast between the Communist and the Western regimes—the desolate rubble-lined streets on one side, the booming prosperity on the other. Here, too, was an escape route taken by some three and a half million people by the summer of 1961. Freedom was but a subway ride away for the thousands who daily passed to the West.

In that year the Soviet Union would no longer tolerate the enfeeblement of East Germany and demanded a settlement of the problem. A confrontation between Kennedy and Khrushchev in Vienna in June 1961 dealt with this question along with the still open issue of Laos. The Russians were adamant. Two months later the East German government proceeded illegally to seal off its section of the city by a wall. Thereafter only a handful of refugees were smuggled out through tunnels or scrambled over the wall in a hail of gunshot. Few as they were, they revealed the continuing discontent in the other city.

The Wall was not worth a war. President Kennedy made the gesture of sending additional American troops into Berlin, but he avoided an all-out conflict. Gradually he was defining a position. The cost of nuclear war was so awesome that it could not be risked even to extend

Site of Cuban Missile Base, October 29, 1962. Soviet activity is seen in the construction of this MRBM launch facility in the San Cristobal area of Cuba. (UPI)

the area of freedom—in Cuba or Laos or Berlin. But neither could the United States withdraw indefinitely under the threat of nuclear blackmail. It would draw the line—refrain from efforts to spread its own system but resist attempts of others forcefully to impose communism upon nations to whose defense it had committed itself. The strategy of graduated deterrence, which was the instrument of doing so, would shortly be tested first by Kennedy and then by Johnson, in the Caribbean and in Asia.

Exercises in Deterrence

The Missile Crisis   American weakness at the Bay of Pigs emboldened the Russians in the summer of 1962 to locate missile sites in Cuba from which the eastern cities of the United States were within reach. Here there was no possibility of American retreat. The missiles threatened to neutralize the whole American nuclear arma-

The World's Watchman, 1963

In this Administration also it has been necessary at times to issue specific warnings—warnings that we could not stand by and watch the Communists conquer Laos by force, or intervene in the Congo, or swallow West Berlin, or maintain offensive missiles in Cuba. But while our goals were at least temporarily obtained in these and other instances, our successful defense of freedom was due not to the words we used but to the strength we stood ready to use on behalf of the principles we stand ready to defend.

This strength is composed of many different elements, ranging from the most massive deterrents to the most subtle influences . . . .

First, . . . the strategic nuclear power of the United States has been so greatly modernized and expanded in the last thousand days, by the rapid production and deployment of the most modern missile systems, that any and all potential aggressors are clearly confronted now with the impossibility of strategic victory—and the certainty of total destruction—if by reckless attack they should ever force upon us the necessity of a strategic reply. . . .

But the lessons of the last decade have taught us that freedom cannot be defended by strategic nuclear power alone. We have,

therefore, in the last three years accelerated the development and deployment of tactical nuclear weapons—and increased by 60 per cent the tactical nuclear forces deployed in Western Europe.

Nor can Europe or any other continent rely on nuclear forces alone, whether they are strategic or tactical. We have radically improved the readiness of our conventional forces. . . . Finally, moving beyond the traditional roles of our military forces, we have achieved an increase of nearly 600 per cent in our special forces—those forces that are prepared to work with our Allies and friends against the guerrillas, saboteurs, insurgents and assassins who threaten freedom in a less direct but equally dangerous manner. . . .

We in this country, in this generation, are, by destiny rather than choice, the watchmen on the walls of world freedom. We ask, therefore, that we may be worthy of our power and responsibility, that we may exercise our strength with wisdom and restraint, and that we may achieve in our time and for all time the ancient vision of "peace on earth, good will toward men."

—John F. Kennedy, undelivered speech to the Dallas Citizens Council, released to the press noon, November 22, 1963, as quoted in *John F. Kennedy, The Burden and the Glory,* Allan Nevins, ed. (New York: Harper & Row, Publishers, 1964), pp. 273–277.

---

ment so that the Soviet Union would be free to have its way throughout the world.

In the face of the most serious threat of total war since 1941, Kennedy combined firmness with flexibility. He insisted that the missiles had to go and ordered a partial blockade of Cuba, together with a state of readiness for the armed services. At the same time he explained his actions openly before the United Nations and refrained from steps that might humiliate or permanently anger the Russians. The crisis subsided with the withdrawal of the missiles

and a tacit understanding on Cuba. The Soviet Union would not give Castro offensive weapons; the United States would not attack him.

The Dominican Crisis President Johnson demonstrated the same firmness when a revolution in the Dominican Republic left open the possibility of a Communist take-over there. Juan Bosch, the exiled constitutional President in whose name the uprising took place, was unable

Elie Abel, *The Missile Crisis* (Philadelphia, 1966) is a straightforward narrative.

to provide firm leadership, a reactionary military clique threatened a blood bath, and the indiscriminate distribution of arms to the populace created a situation ripe for a Castro-type revolution.

The prompt landing of Marines contained the fighting within a small area of the capital city, and troops of the Organization of American States restored stability and permitted an election in which the people made a free choice of their President. In 1966, the troops were withdrawn and some degree of order returned to the unhappy republic.

Vietnam The climactic test of American policy came in Southeast Asia. The weakness of the successive military governments that had attempted to establish their legitimacy after the death of Diem encouraged the National Liberation Front to step up its guerrilla campaign. Disorder forced Saigon into greater expenditures and more extensive recruitment of troops, which compounded its difficulties. Toward the end of 1963, the assassination of President Kennedy and the mistaken assumption that the change of administration would confuse American policy encouraged the Vietcong in the belief that victory was near. Regular troops from North Vietnam moved south to give the *coup de grâce* to the tottering regime in the South.

An attack on United States ships in the Gulf of Tonkin in 1964 was the occasion for the decision to honor American commitments even though that might involve a large-scale land war in Asia. A resolution of Congress gave the President authority to resist aggression in Southeast Asia. The number of military personnel increased and the conflict deepened.

Hanoi, deceived by the belief that weariness over a remote conflict would compel the Americans to yield as the French had, refused to back

John Bartlow Martin, *Overtaken by Events* (Garden City, N.Y., 1966) is a convincing account of Dominican affairs by the former American ambassador to the republic. Juan Bosch, *The Unfinished Experiment* (New York, 1965) is worth reading for the insight it offers into the views of a key figure in the crisis.

down. There followed the game of escalation that the strategists had predicted. The United States bombed naval installations to retaliate against the incident in the Gulf. Air attacks upon North Vietnam and the full-scale use of American troops followed a Vietcong assault on the American camp at Pleiku in February 1965. The failure of the enemy to respond to the 37-day suspension of air strikes beginning on December 24, 1965, led in June 1966 to the bombing of oil depots near Hanoi and Haiphong. Meanwhile American troops, supplied with helicopters and heavy armaments, broke up the Vietcong main forces and began to strike at the guerrilla strongholds in the Mekong Delta.

The objective of the United States was to make its power credible. It did not seek to destroy the Hanoi regime; rather, it used only as much force as would persuade the Communists that they had no hope of victory and had better negotiate peace.

The North Vietnamese counted on the inability of the Americans to sustain a prolonged war, exaggerating the influence of opposition which they expected would ultimately force the United States to withdraw. Having already spent a quarter of a century in the struggle, Ho Chi Minh was reckless about the cost in lives and was willing to accept the prospect of a long war. In 1966, peace still seemed remote in Vietnam and the fighting that had never really stopped in Laos had spread to Thailand.

American policy, however, had already gained for the South Vietnamese a breathing spell during which to begin to shape their own fate. The election of a constituent assembly in September was the first step toward a popular government that could command the spontaneous support of the people. Meanwhile, the neutral states of Burma and Indonesia and the friendly ones of Thailand, the Philippines, Taiwan, and Korea, assured of the capacity of the United States to resist aggression, saw the prospects of building a society free from Communist hegemony.

Leap from a Helicopter near Cu Chi, Vietnam, January 20, 1967. These members of a long-range reconnaissance patrol were on a fact-finding mission for the 25th Infantry Division. (U.S. Army Photograph)

American Objectives in Vietnam, 1966

It is, first of all, a war of limited objectives.

It is a war fought, not to gain territory or dominion, but to prove that despots cannot work their will by spreading the fires of violence.

In this war, the battlelines are not clear. But our goals are very clear.

We intend to prevent the success of aggression.

We intend to make it possible for a young nation to begin its experiment with democracy — without staring down the barrel of an aggressor's gun.

Such a war . . . demands, of all of us, a new kind of courage: the fortitude to endure a long and bitter and sometimes confusing struggle; it requires the patient courage to seek something more than a swift and terrible military triumph.

There are those who ask if such a struggle is worth the lives of our young men. To them, I say: study the answer which this man gave. Study the answer which other Americans are giving.

These men are fighting with one hand — and they are building with the other.

They are building schools and hospitals. They are building bridges and dams. They are building dikes and roads.

They are caring for the sick and injured.

That is the kind of victory we seek.

We do not know when that victory will come.

But surely the first long mile was reached on Sunday when 4,200,000 South Vietnamese citizens — more than 80 percent of that little country's registered voters — marched to the polls without fear to elect members of the constituent assembly. They gave us a lasting lesson in democracy.

— Lyndon B. Johnson, at Marvin Shield's award ceremony, September 13, 1966. *Weekly Compilation of Presidential Documents,* September 19, 1966, vol. II, no. 37, p. 1285.

Americans carried the struggle almost alone. South Korea, Australia, and New Zealand sent small contingents to share the fighting. But the neutrals were unwilling to help and the United Nations was incapable of acting. The European allies of the United States preferred to rest complacently behind the shield of American defense.

▼

In the 1960s, the United States bore a heavy responsibility for preserving the peace It was the world's most powerful state. Yet power brought responsibility. It alone could preserve freedom and stability in the great part of the world not dominated by communism. Hence, it shouldered the burden of economic and military aid in many corners of the earth. And it watched anxiously the efforts of new nations in Africa and the Near East to use their independence creatively.

But part of the responsibility connected with the possession of power was knowledge of the limitations on its use. The primary objective of American policy was to avoid the necessity for ever unlocking the great silos or letting the Polaris missile fly. In the 1960s, the experience of Cuba, Berlin, and Southeast Asia revealed the cost of preserving the stalemate in which safety lay.

Paperbacks for Further Reading

Dumas Malone and Basil Rauch, *America and World Leadership, 1940–1965* (Appleton-Century-Crofts); John W. Spanier, *American Foreign Policy Since World War II* (Frederick A. Praeger); and Temple Wanamaker, *American Foreign Policy Today* (Bantam Books) contain the material for a general view of the diplomacy of the 1960s. H. L. Trefousse, ed., *The Cold War* (Capricorn Books) contains a collection of basic documents. Dean Rusk, ed., *The Winds of Freedom* (Beacon Press) includes selections from the speeches and statements of the Secretary of State.

On more specific questions, there are useful discussions by journalists and analysts and helpful collections of sources. Arthur I. Waskow, ed., *The Debate over Thermonuclear Strategy* (D. C. Heath and Co.) presents contrasting positions; and Hedley Bull, *The Control of the Arms Race* (Frederick A. Praeger) deals with disarmament. A. Doak Barnett, *Communist China and Asia* (Vintage Books) and Alice L. Hsieh, *Communist China's Strategy in the Nuclear Era* (Spectrum Books) deal with the Red Chinese. And *Mao Tse-Tung* (Mentor Books) is an enlightening anthology of the writings of the leader of Asian Communism edited by Anne Fremantle. Peter Paret and John Shy, *Guerrillas in the 1960s* (Frederick A. Praeger) describes the warfare basic to national liberation movements. Edgar S. Furniss, Jr., *France, Troubled Ally* (Frederick A. Praeger) focuses on de Gaulle. Henry M. Pachter, *Collision Course: The Cuban Missile Crisis and Coexistence* (Frederick A. Praeger) treats the confrontation; and Tad Szulc, *Winds of Revolution* (Frederick A. Praeger) is a general survey of Latin America. Robert Shaplen, *Lost Revolution* (Harper Colophon Books) is an adequate factual account of the Vietnam problem between 1946 and 1966, but it is naïve and unsympathetic to the American position.

THE BURDENS OF
MATURITY

100

Americans rarely paused to take stock of their situation or to speculate abstractly about the goals or purposes of their society. Most of them dealt with each problem as it arose, pragmatically without introspection or deep concern about abstract principles.

Yet deeply rooted assumptions about their own character influenced their judgments and guided their actions. Those assumptions grew out of their history and sometimes were not in accord with the conditions of the 1960s. A people accustomed to taking risks in an expansive environment now had to learn to restrain the power maturity brought them.

Restraints on Power

OFTEN AMERICANS confronted the outer world with petulance. They were not understood. They were not loved. The fact that more than a touch of envy affected the emotions of foreigners about them did not mitigate the resentment at the injustice. In the face of the clear record to the contrary, the United States was regarded as belligerent and selfish. Enemies, neutrals, and, indeed, even friends almost instinctively judged it harshly and took sides against it.

Since 1947 it had fought its great wars practically alone. Despite the UN sponsorship, it bore almost the whole cost in lives and dollars of support for the South Koreans. In Vietnam it received little aid even from its allies. In the free world, it was almost the only nation to conscript young men.

The United States was also isolated in administering aid to the underdeveloped world. Western Europe was prosperous, but once it cut away from its colonies it felt only a slight sense of obligation to them. When the Russians and the Chinese, for reasons of their own, extended help to other countries, they did so in precisely measured quantities.

By the 1960s the American burdens of war and aid were costly. Despite the continued growth of exports from the United States the outward flow of funds to support American troops abroad and to help other peoples' development created an adverse balance of payments. To meet the deficit, gold was sent abroad, thus diminishing the American stock of bullion. Yet Europeans felt little urgency to cooperate by holding dollars. The withdrawal of gold began almost as soon as the economic recovery of Europe was complete and continued with few pauses. France, driven by the extreme ambitions of de Gaulle, was chiefly but not solely responsible.

In the face of these provocations, the American response was measured and deliberate. The United States could no more use its full economic strength in peace than it could use its atomic weapons in battle. It did not wish by retaliation to weaken France or to hamper the development of Ghana or allow India to suffer from starvation. Power had brought with it responsibilities that severely limited freedom of action and made endless demands on the patience of the people. By the same token, Americans had to allow the Russians to be first in pushing the armaments race to a new level by an antiballistic missile program.

The unique position of the United States was the penalty of its success. History had given it a stake in peace and freedom everywhere and the power to protect them. But it could attain its objectives only by restrained and circumspect action.

The Issues at Home   The burdens of maturity also pressed heavily upon life within the United States. Americans discovered that power and liberty created more problems than they solved, both for the individual and for society. They could act with greater effectiveness than ever in their past and they had abundant time at their disposal. But now that they could do what they willed, they had to discover what it was they willed.

In earlier periods, such ideals as equality and justice were remote. People could adhere to them in the abstract because the means were inadequate to attain them immediately. Now the means were available. Despite the demands of commitments overseas, an abundant economy was capable of producing immense stores of goods and tremendous energy. As a result unprecedented questions arose to which no clear answers were ready.

There had never, for instance, been any challenge to the legal right of eminent domain. The government had the power to take land for a fair compensation to build a courthouse, and it could transfer that power to a railroad that needed a right of way. In the 1950s and 1960s the government used the same authority to clear whole neighborhoods for urban renewal,

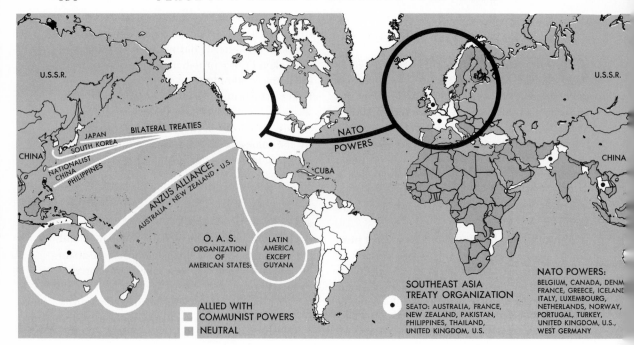

THE WORLD IN 1966

ousting the former residents in the process. The objective of razing the slums was desirable, but was it proper to dislocate the lives of thousands to attain that goal? In city after city, bitter protesters asked that question and a mere restatement of the law was not an adequate answer.

In some places, although not in all, that question overlapped issues raised by the changing definition of civil rights. Often the displaced slum residents were Negroes, to whose difficulties there was still no solution in the 1960s, despite the advances that had been made since 1947. The problem had been simpler when it focused upon the inequities produced as a result of discrimination by law. In 1966, the Jim Crow pattern was everywhere shattered, yet the Negro still had not attained equality. His disabilities now sprang from low incomes, from the inability to find housing in desirable neighborhoods, and from inferior education without family discipline in poor schools. How far was the government justified in acting to compensate

for these disadvantages, if in the process it intruded upon the rights of others to privacy and the freedom of choice?

In the 1930s a simple formula had governed the relief of the poor. Society was obliged to provide those incapable of supporting themselves with the means of subsistence. That meant, with enough to keep them from starving. Twenty years later, the formula no longer sufficed. The commentators who wished to guarantee each family a minimum annual income argued that an affluent society could afford to provide each of its members with some degree of comfort, whether he contributed to its welfare or not. Yet many Americans refused to contemplate a future in which part of the population would live in perpetual functionless idleness. Again there was no answer to numerous questions. Did the welfare client's right to privacy preclude surveillance of his personal life? Were there no limits to the number of children for whose support an unmarried woman could turn to the community? Ought the well-to-do impose their own values on the poor whom their taxes sustained?

Conversely, did suburban commuters deserve a public subsidy in the form of expensive thruways for their cars or below-cost railway service? Was an outlying district justified in maintaining a separate and superior school system while education in the central city lacked support?

In the past, the need for developing the country's resources had overriden every other consideration. The pioneer ruthlessly felled the forest. The dam builder chose the most economical site. Tillable land and power were the supreme goods. In the 1960s, however, Americans also were trying to reckon the value of beauty. How much was the Grand Canyon worth, as against the more efficient utilization of the waters that flowed through it? No count of votes or weighing of the relative strength of contending interests would answer questions such as these. It would take a patient search for understanding and restraint on all sides in pressing their own opinions to work toward acceptable solutions.

Communications

The inability of large parts of the population to hear one another's views impeded the effort at understanding. In the 1950s and 1960s Americans had available at the flick of a switch means of communication of unparalleled efficiency. But the likelihood that they would say or hear something meaningful was no greater than before. In fact, the overwhelming flow of words and images helped only slightly to clarify the issues of the postwar era.

The New Media Television after the war speedily spread its messages into every American home. In 1965, the average set was in operation four hours a day. A satellite tossed into space transmitted images from far off in Europe.

Gary A. Steiner, *The People Look at Television* (New York, 1963) is a study of audience attitudes.

Enormous audiences in their living rooms could watch the exploding shells of remote wars and catch the words and see the faces of distant statesmen.

There was some effort at first to experiment with imaginative uses of the new medium, in the variety offerings of *Omnibus* or in the dramas of Paddy Chayefsky, for instance. But the impulse quickly flickered out. Control rested in the same hands that ruled the radio, and the overriding interest was that of the advertisers. The bulk of the programs by the 1960s consisted of routines warmed over from radio, supplemented by old movies and a large quotient of sports. The impressive technical expertise the industry commanded was more often devoted to the commercials than to the intervening presentations. One chairman of the Federal Communications Commission in 1961 characterized television as a wasteland but did nothing to fertilize it. Its situation was symptomatic of the dilemma of all the mass media: there was enormous power to communicate, but nothing to say.

The Dilemma of Art The minority of creative artists met the greatest difficulties in this respect. The consumer had choices; public libraries, hi-fi records, paperbacks, and cheap prints brought him a phenomenal array of the world's music, literature, and art. He had only to know what he wished to hear or see to have it. But there was no prospect of creation without something to say.

Expenditures Under the Library Services and Construction Act, 1957–1966

(in thousand dollars)

1957	5,678
1958	15,290
1959	16,782
1960	19,757
1961	22,266
1962	26,418
1963	26,779
1964	27,587
1965	113,167
1966	131,244

Television Taboos, 1956

One of the edicts that comes down from the Mount Sinai of Advertisers Row is that at no time in a political drama must a speech or character be equated with an existing political party or current political problems. Some of these problems, however, are now so hoary with age and so meaningless in modern context that they are stamped as acceptable. Slavery, for example, can now be talked about without blushing. Suffrage is another issue that need make no one wince. The treatment of the lunatic in chains and dungeons can no longer be considered controversial. But *The Arena* took place in 1956, and no juggling of events can alter this fact. So, on the floor of the United States Senate (at least on *Studio One*), I was not permitted to have my Senators discuss any current or pressing problem. To talk of tariff was to align oneself with the Republicans; to talk of labor was to suggest control by the Democrats. To say a single thing germane to the current political scene was absolutely prohibited. So, on television in April of 1956, several million viewers got a definitive picture of television's concept of politics and the way the government is run. They were treated to an incredible display on the floor of the United States Senate of groups of Senators shouting, gesticulating and talking in hieroglyphics about make-believe issues, using invented terminology, in a kind of prolonged, unbelievable double-talk.

—Rod Serling, "About Writing for Television," from Rod Serling, *Patterns* (New York: Simon and Schuster, Inc., 1957), pp. 24–25.

The architects were exceptional. They still operated under the restraints of the uses to which space would be put and of the engineering required to hold their buildings up. Furthermore, the vast amounts of institutional construction and the desire of many corporations for prestige headquarters made ample funds available. The international style, already pioneered before 1947, had substantial achievements to its credit in the next two decades.

Other artists were utterly free to depart from convention and therefore more confused. In an earlier generation, a creative tension between the desire for self-expression and the limits of the form forced the writer or painter to put what he had to say in a framework that would convey a meaning to the audience. Now the artist, liberated from the requirement of plot or subject, poured out his impressions without regard to their impact upon the viewer or reader. In the novels of William S. Burroughs the words spilled out in chaotic globs from which emerged only a kaleidoscopic succession of sensations. Painting moved from Jackson Pollock's splashes of color to the complete improvisation of Andy Warhol. Music, whether in the compositions of pure chance by John Cage or in the electronic computations of Milton Babbitt, detached itself from the obligation to communicate to responsive listeners. The vogue for formless happenings in all these media was the result of the surrender of any expectation of coherence in art as in life and the acceptance instead of detached sensual impressions.

The Will to Will Despite the striving for spontaneity, the works of these artists often seemed contrived and synthetic, as if their creators were trying to express emotions they did not really feel but thought they ought to. Therein they shared in an acute form a compulsion that influenced many other Americans as well. Millions of people, having secured a competence that relieved them of the anxieties of struggling for existence, felt their lives slip into a placid pattern inadequately filled with routine tasks, and they looked eagerly for ex-

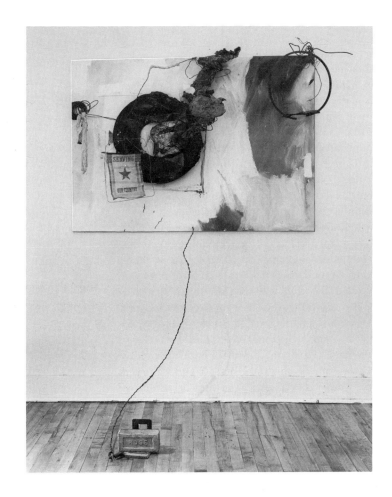

"Magician II." A Combine Painting, 1961, by Robert Rauschenberg. (Leo Castelli Gallery)

ternal stimuli that would make them will more, feel more.

Ironically, such well-off people shared their apathetic condition with many of the poor, whom some of them envied and others resented. Thousands of men and women, having lost all hope of advancement, relaxed in dependency. Some were born in poverty, others slipped into it; and as the distance from self-support widened with increased mechanization, they grew accustomed to life on welfare payments.

Poor and rich alike had abundant leisure but did not know what to do with it. Living in crowded cities, they felt alone. Able to make many choices and express any emotions, they had no will and no feelings to guide them. The rising count of the mentally ill and neurotic and the spreading dependence upon psychoanalysis in some sectors of society showed the toll of the strains that came with freedom.

Forms of Escape and Rebellion

Those impatient of all restraints found a variety of forms of escape. The law was increasingly solicitous of individual freedom, especially after the subsidence of wartime fears. Invasions of privacy and abusive police methods did not come immediately to an end, but legislation and judicial rulings steadily expanded the protection of personal rights. Censorship and all other efforts to control behavior narrowed in scope, and informal communal sanctions lost their effectiveness.

Anti-Americanism A dogged anti-Americanism expressed the frustration of some intellectuals. The critical sense that had exposed many social shortcomings in the past was still capable of making valuable contributions when it brought to light instances of corruption or of failures in public policy. But for some people, muckraking hardened into a total negativism about their country so that they instinctively assumed it was always in the wrong. As time revealed their own errors, these critics grew more passionate and more dogmatic. *The Nation,* for instance, long refused to believe in Stalin's crimes and blamed the cold war on the United States. It hailed Mao Tse-tung as a progressive and perceived fascism creeping across the United States in the 1950s. For some, opposition to the war in Vietnam rested on the assumption that peace would come if only the United States wanted it.

Youth The desire to escape or revolt was particularly strong among youth. In 1966, about half the total population was under the age of twenty-five, that is, too young to have had any experience of depression or war. The rise in the birth rate produced a bulge in the age distribution, while prolonged schooling delayed employment, and early marriage gave the young a sense of identity and of peculiar problems unknown to the rest of society.

In the decade after 1945 young people, who had passed their childhood in depression and wartime, yearned mostly for security and framed their ideals in terms of stable family life and orderly communities. But the emphasis changed as the decade of the 1950s drew to a close. Most born after 1940 spent their childhood under relatively comfortable circumstances and were therefore subject to quite different influences. Indulgent middle-class parents, who projected their need for love upon their children, emphasized adjustment and were slack in discipline. Life in the child-centered suburb was undemanding and defined the important goals in terms of good performance in the schools. The

Finding Love, 1957

We are a gutted generation, born in the depression and obsessed with prosperity. Well, we got prosperity, and what have we got? A hysterical woman upstairs who needs barbiturates to put her to sleep, Dexedrine Spansules to wake her up, and tranquilizers to keep her numb, who has a nervous breakdown once a year and has tried to kill herself at least four times that the public knows. I don't want my daughter to grow up like that. Or like me. A twisted, loveless man, patched together by psychoanalysis. My daughter was a very strange little girl for a long time, well on her way to continuing the desolate pattern of her parents, her grandparents, and all the generations before her, the long parade of history that has brought us to this year of suicide and insanity . . . .

Life is unbearable, if you don't love something. . . . People like us can never love anything but our children. But that's something. She's given me moments of great pleasure — moments when I can see that life is fine.

—Paddy Chayefsky, *The Goddess* (New York: Simon and Schuster, Inc., 1958), pp. 156, 163–164.

young people who had spent their adolescence in the remorseless testing that marked success in moving from one grade to another empathized with Holden Caulfield in J. D. Salinger's *Catcher in the Rye* (1951). The prospect of the inadequate and unworthy challenges of the life ahead was distasteful to boys and girls starved for affection, who felt themselves lone wolves remote from everyone else.

Some among them were as discontent as the youth of the poor who left school without skills or the prospect of desirable jobs. Childhood in the slums, and particularly in the Negro ghettos, lacked the ease and comfort of the suburbs and

The life of **MALCOLM LITTLE** was brief and violent. Through most of it he raised an incoherent cry of outrage at a world that refused him justice. He was born in 1925 in Omaha, Nebraska, but spent a good part of his youth in Lansing, Michigan. When he was six years old his father was run over by a streetcar and his mother soon after was committed to a mental asylum. Malcolm lived with relatives and left school after the eighth grade.

He was utterly disorganized. His father had been a Black Nationalist, a follower of Marcus Garvey. But Malcolm felt that it was some kind of status symbol to be light-complexioned; he straightened his hair with lye and drifted into underworld circles in Boston and New York where color did not count against him. He pimped, peddled dope, and lived by his wits. He was a victim not of segregation but of his own lack of purpose and identity.

In 1946 he was sentenced to ten years in jail and served six years of his term. Behind bars, he encountered the doctrines of the Black Muslims, which explained that his difficulties were all the product of the white man's Christian world. He came to hate the white blood in his veins, dropped the name the blue-eyed devils had imposed upon his forebears, and was thereafter known as Malcolm X.

After his parole Malcolm rose steadily in the Black Muslim ranks, and was regarded by many as presumptive successor to the prophet Elijah Muhammad. Malcolm became increasingly violent in his rhetoric. Ballots would not work but bullets would, he explained, as he called for the creation of an armed American Mau Mau. When President Kennedy was assassinated in 1963, Malcolm crowed that it was a case of chickens coming home to roost.

Elijah Muhammad thereupon suspended his follower, and Malcolm, believing himself betrayed, broke away. In 1964 he made a pilgrimage to Mecca, took the name of Al Hajj Malik Shabazz, and came back to New York to start a new movement among the Negroes. He had by then qualified his Black racism, but that same year, before he could formulate a program, he was gunned down in the Audubon Ballroom in Harlem.

---

often lacked also the guidance of close family life and the discipline of the father. An upbringing like that of Malcolm X in such an environment quickly generated hostility to society, and the furious aggressions of adolescence found few legitimate channels of expression.

Rebellion also took the form of a conscious rejection of the accepted norms of society and a deliberate defiance of its conventions. The variations in modes of escape were numerous and shifting. From time to time cults appeared among the young, centering upon some symbol that indicated repudiation of authority—James Dean in the movies, Mickey Spillane in the pulps, or the Beatles on records—saying no to the solemn nonsense of the rulers of the world. Eccentric styles of behavior or dress flouted convention so widely in the 1960s that they themselves became conventional, and the uniform of the Beatnik was everywhere recognizable.

The Thrill of Violence Young people were prominent among the Americans of all ages who sought some excitement through external stimuli—alcohol, drugs, sex, or violence. The general permissiveness of society made all these means of heightening consciousness available and weakened external restraints on their use. Respectable suburbs were rocked by scandal often enough to show that such problems occurred not in the slums alone.

JAMES DEAN once explained why he liked to race sports cars, "What better way to die? It's fast and clean and you go out in a blaze of glory." He kept a noose hanging in his living room and played at sticking his head into it. At the age of twenty-four he was killed in the wreck of his Porsche.

Dean was born in Indiana in 1931, the son of a Quaker dentist. He grew up during the war, in which he was too young to fight, and after completing high school studied for two years at the University of California. He then interrupted his education to go to New York where he hoped to make a career on the stage. Although he was short and nearsighted, he aspired to act and picked up small parts on television while he studied at the Actors' Studio.

He was restless and after a while tried Hollywood where he made three movies. He was very competent but did not have to be, for he played himself. In *Rebel Without a Cause*, he was a juvenile delinquent, expressing the discontent of a whole generation—the climax in the movie came, as in his life, in a sequence in which he and his rivals raced their cars over the edge of a cliff.

Three thousand fans attended his funeral and heard the eulogist conclude, "The career of James Dean has not ended, it has just begun. And remember, God Himself is directing the production." His fans insisted that Dean could not be dead. They developed the belief, on no evidence whatever, that he had been disfigured and was recuperating in a sanitarium. Young people wrote to him as if he were still alive. A year after his death, an average of five thousand letters a month were still coming in to the studio and fifty active fan clubs were in existence. The myth spread. A flood of books, records, and magazines were devoted to him, and the faithful could buy casts of his head, for $3 in stone, for $5 in plastic that felt like human flesh, or for $150 in bronze.

Long after his death his black leather jacket, blue jeans, and riding boots remained the characteristic uniform of the generation for which he was a symbol. They too were rebels without a cause.

The frustrations of unchallenging lives often erupted in violence. The great riots in Harlem in 1964 and in Los Angeles in 1965 involved large numbers of Negroes and were touched off by conflicts with the police. But they were not race riots in the sense that the disturbances earlier in the century had been; that is, they were not conflicts between two different groups in the population. Rather, the outbreaks of the 1960s were indiscriminate orgies of looting and burning that expressed a desperate sense of outrage at a world that failed to fulfill expectations. The same wild anger exploded pathologically when one young man in Texas assassinated President Kennedy and when another, from a tower, haphazardly pumped bullets into a dozen strangers. The inclination toward violence appeared also in less overt ways, in the destructive racing of automobiles in the suburbs and the intermittent gang wars of the slums. Meanwhile rates of criminality and juvenile delinquency showed a persistent upward trend.

Activism Protest drove some young people to activism. The satisfaction of doing something concretely good drew many to enlist enthusiastically in the Peace Corps or to volunteer for service to the underprivileged at home. But there was an added satisfaction in doing something that showed independence of authority, even if only in holding a banner during a demonstration or sitting down to defy the police. The civil rights movement with its emphasis on equality enlisted the idealism of the young. Their involvement reached a peak in the summer of 1963, then subsided. The peace movement thereafter was more attractive, and some energy went also into demonstrations of student concern with the conduct of their colleges.

However expressed, activism reflected the reluctance to settle down in some large organization. Youth for many was the season in which to achieve something personal before donning the

Jerry Cohen and William S. Murphy, *Burn, Baby, Burn!* (New York, 1966) is a journalistic account of the riot in the Watts district of Los Angles.

A National Guard Jeep Patrols a Street in the Watts District of Los Angeles, August 14, 1965. The riot was finally brought under control by 2000 National Guardsmen carrying rifles and police armed with shotguns. (UPI)

grey flannel suit of a career. For others, it was a period for fad and experimentation before becoming reconciled to the inevitable dullness of life.

Reaction Resentment about the shape of the present also led to protest by Americans unwilling to accept the newness of society. Dismayed by the drift away from the norms of the past, they consoled themselves with the insistence that the old verities were still unchanged.

The elderly were most likely to hold these sentiments. They had yearned for security, but now found it a not altogether satisfying goal. As inflation eroded fixed incomes, those who had worked years for retirement watched in dismay while heedless younger generations mocked by their disorder the values of a lifetime. For the more affluent, able to resettle in one of the com-

munities of senior citizens that shared the sun in Florida or Southern California, time passed effortlessly so long as they cut themselves off from the untoward events of the outside world, but anxieties about the future of the country intruded to dispel the hard-won peace of mind. Similar concerns agitated the rural membership of the fundamentalist sects, which had joined in 1941 to form the American Council of Christian Churches. Under the vigorous leadership of Carl McIntire, they denounced the soul-destroying modernist whom they linked with the Communist tendencies of the times.

In 1950, it was still possible to argue that the new direction was a temporary aberration only and to seek a scapegoat for the undesirable developments. The primacy of foreign affairs focused attention on the Communists and fed

Notes Before Committing a Murder, 1966

My life will probably end with a whimper — a depressed whimper. Possibly with a bang. Since I cannot live like a man, I hope to die like one. I am entering the final state of unreality . . . . You say that I am sick — you are right. You dismiss me because I am sick — in that you are wrong . . . . The dark side of creativity is sickness . . . . Anyway, in our society to be normal is to be sick, to be hung up on loneliness, insecure about one's stature, uncertain about one's self, overly concerned about pleasing every-body, being 'nice' all the time — damn nice-ness! . . . not offending anyone, so that one winds up pleasing no one and, to boot, not knowing who or why one is. . . .

My distorted, disoriented voice, either barely uttered or tremendously violent, gives you a slight horrifying glimpse into the dehumanized future that awaits you and your unfortunate children, who will be healthy, comfortable and secure beyond your fondest dreams and just as diseased. Since I feel that I am no longer able to make any significant creative contributions I shall make a destructive one. . . . Suffer in your frozen hells of apathy, boil in the self-hate of outraged impotence. Listen to my voice, you deaf ones. Listen to how sick, sad, lonely and forlorn it is.

— Richard Wishnetsky, as quoted in T. V. Lo Cicero, "The Murder of Rabbi Adler," *Commentary* (June, 1966), pp. 51, 53.

---

suspicions of a Red conspiracy that had sub-verted the Republic. This was the soil within which McCarthyism had briefly flourished. Later in the decade, the wish to halt subversion gave birth to the John Birch Society and helped gain followers for Barry Goldwater in 1960 and 1964.

Reconstruction

Both extremes — radical and conservative — were a minority in the country as a whole. Most Americans, no matter how uncomfortable they felt in their new situation, recognized the chal-lenge before them and were willing to face rather than evade it.

The postwar period had substantially altered the basic institutions of society. A mature econo-my, orderly yet capable of expansion, organized in large, complex units, afforded the population a rising level of well-being. But by breaking down familiar community ties, it also forced people into an unprecedented involvement with strangers at home and abroad.

The new circumstances demanded an ad-justment in values. Many more men and women now than formerly escaped the hardships and tragedies of the pioneers who entered the wilder-ness or of the immigrants who crossed the ocean. But many fewer, too, achieved the satisfaction of turning the forests into farms or of attaining the dignity of independence by the sweat of their brows. It was necessary now to measure achieve-ment in terms of a common purpose. The fron-tiersman had relied on his own ax to clear a way over the mountain; the astronaut knew that the fate of his voyage depended upon the coopera-tion of thousands in the laboratories and the command center.

The efforts at reconstruction, confused and uncertain as they were, showed a desire to ex-plore the means of maintaining the freedom of the individual while preserving the security of

Young People Attending a Peace Rally Protesting the War in Vietnam, Central Park, New York, April 15, 1967. (Photograph by Ken Heyman)

the group. Coming while the nation repeatedly faced the danger of atomic war and carried the burdens of world-wide responsibilities, they called for the full energies, the restraint, and the tolerance of the people.

▼

The burdens Americans bore in the 1960s were the product of two decades of world-wide effort to restore the economic strength and internal freedom of Western society. After 1947 the United States struggled to apply the wealth its system of production yielded to the solution of grave social and cultural problems. At the same time, the nation carried heavy responsibilities abroad. It could neglect neither the domestic nor the foreign difficulties. At home, the grievances of a large part of the population sprang from the awareness that society lacked places that would reward all with an adequate sense of life's purpose. Elsewhere, economic retardation, nationalism, and communism produced the costly conflicts that disturbed a world in which most people sincerely desired peace.

There was no escape from either set of problems. A nation conceived in liberty could not put off the challenge of opening equal opportunities and extending social justice to all its people. Nor could it dream of isolating itself from the rest of the earth while a dynamic technology compressed all distances and confirmed the interconnectedness of peoples everywhere.

With the twentieth century two-thirds over, Americans could look back upon a long past in the course of which they had expanded into the interior of an unknown continent, had developed autonomous institutions, and had created a sense of national identity bound up with a commitment to the concepts of natural rights and the consent of the governed. The citizens of the United States had come a long way by the 1960s from those first tight communities in which habit and discipline were central to all existence. Yet their experience had been continuous.

The strands of development were connected in a firm web that linked the past and the present. Three hundred and sixty years after the first permanent settlements, Americans still bore the marks of their antecedents. In a new and unique environment they had attempted to create a distinctive civilization, not out of a desire to cut themselves off from the rest of the world, but with the intention of helping to redeem it. In many ways, the recollection of that mission still moved them centuries later.

Paperbacks for Further Study

Richard N. Gardner, *In Pursuit of World Order* (Frederick A. Praeger, Inc.) and Herbert Feis, *Foreign Aid and Foreign Policy* (Delta Books) touch on international responsibilities. Chester E. Eisinger, *Fiction of the Forties* (Phoenix Books) and Patrick D. Hazard, ed., *TV as Art* (National Council of Teachers of English) treat some cultural trends. William Burroughs, *The Nova Express* (Evergreen Black Cat Series); Paddy Chayevsky, *Television Plays* (Simon & Schuster, Inc.); Joseph Heller, *Catch–22* (Delta Books); and Rod Serling, *Requiem for a Heavyweight* (Bantam Books, Inc.) are among the works of the authors mentioned in the text.

Index of Sources

INDEX

Boldface numbers indicate biographical sketches.